MOBILIZING THE PAST
FOR A
DIGITAL FUTURE

MOBILIZING *the* PAST *for a* DIGITAL FUTURE

The Potential of Digital Archaeology

Edited by
Erin Walcek Averett
Jody Michael Gordon
Derek B. Counts

The Digital Press @
The University of North Dakota
Grand Forks

Book Design: Daniel Coslett and William Caraher
Cover Design: Daniel Coslett

Library of Congress Control Number: 2016917316
The Digital Press at the University of North Dakota, Grand Forks, North Dakota

ISBN-13: 978-062790137
ISBN-10: 062790136

Version 1.1 (updated November 5, 2016)

Table of Contents

Part 2: From Dirt to Drones

Part 3: From Stratigraphy to Systems

Part 4: From a Paper-based Past to a Paperless Future?

Part 5: From Critique to Manifesto

Preface & Acknowledgments

This volume stems from the workshop, "Mobilizing the Past for a Digital Future: the Future of Digital Archaeology," funded by a National Endowment for the Humanities Digital Humanities Start-Up grant (#HD-51851-14), which took place 27-28 February 2015 at Wentworth Institute of Technology in Boston (http://uwm.edu/mobilizing-the-past/). The workshop, organized by this volume's editors, was largely spurred by our own attempts with developing a digital archaeological workflow using mobile tablet computers on the Athienou Archaeological Project (http://aap.toumazou.org; Gordon *et al.*, Ch. 1.4) and our concern for what the future of a mobile and digital archaeology might be. Our initial experiments were exciting, challenging, and rewarding; yet, we were also frustrated by the lack of intra-disciplinary discourse between projects utilizing digital approaches to facilitate archaeological data recording and processing.

Based on our experiences, we decided to initiate a dialogue that could inform our own work and be of use to other projects struggling with similar challenges. Hence, the "Mobilizing the Past" workshop concept was born and a range of digital archaeologists, working in private and academic settings in both Old World and New World archaeology, were invited to participate. In addition, a livestream of the workshop allowed the active participation on Twitter from over 21 countires, including 31 US states (@MobileArc15, #MobileArc).[1]

---

[1] For commentary produced by the social media followers for this event, see: https://twitter.com/electricarchaeo/status/571866193667047424, http://shawngraham.github.io/exercise/mobilearcday1wordcloud.html, https://twitter.com/electricarchaeo/status/571867092091338752, http://www.diachronicdesign.com/blog/2015/02/28/15-mobilizing-the-past-for-the-digital-future-conference-day-1-roundup/.

Although the workshop was initially aimed at processes of archaeological data recording in the field, it soon became clear that these practices were entangled with larger digital archaeological systems and even socio-economic and ethical concerns. Thus, the final workshop's discursive purview expanded beyond the use of mobile devices in the field to embrace a range of issues currently affecting digital archaeology, which we define as the use of computerized, and especially internet-compatible and portable, tools and systems aimed at facilitating the documentation and interpretation of material culture as well as its publication and dissemination. In total, the workshop included 21 presentations organized into five sessions (see program, http://mobilizingthepast.mukurtu.net/digital-heritage/mobilizing-past-conference-program), including a keynote lecture by John Wallrodt on the state of the field, "Why paperless?: Digital Technology and Archaeology," and a plenary lecture by Bernard Frischer, "The Ara Pacis and Montecitorio Obelisk of Augustus: A Simpirical Investigation," which explored how digital data can be transformed into virtual archaeological landscapes.

The session themes were specifically devised to explore how archaeological data was digitally collected, processed, and analyzed as it moved from the trench to the lab to the digital repository. The first session, "App/Database Development and Use for Mobile Computing in Archaeology," included papers primarily focused on software for field recording and spatial visualization. The second session, "Mobile Computing in the Field," assembled a range of presenters whose projects had actively utilized mobile computing devices (such as Apple iPads) for archaeological data recording and was concerned with shedding light on their utility within a range of fieldwork situations. The third session, "Systems for Archaeological Data Management," offered presentations on several types of archaeological workflows that marshal born-digital data from the field to publication, including fully bespoken paperless systems, do-it-yourself ("DIY") paperless systems, and hybrid digital-paper systems. The fourth and final session, "Pedagogy, Data Curation, and Reflection," mainly dealt with teaching digital methodologies and the use of digital repositories and linked open data to enhance field research. This session's final paper, William Caraher's "Toward a Slow Archaeology," however, noted digital archaeology's successes in terms of time and money saved and the collection of more data, but also called for a more measured consideration of the significant changes that these technologies are having on how archaeologists engage with and interpret archaeological materials.

The workshop's overarching goal was to bring together leading practitioners of digital archaeology in order to discuss the use, creation, and implementation of mobile and digital, or so-called "paperless," archaeological data recording systems. Originally, we hoped to come up with a range of best practices for mobile computing in the field – a manual of sorts – that could be used by newer projects interested in experimenting with digital methods, or even by established projects hoping to revise their digital workflows in order to increase their efficiency or, alternatively, reflect on their utility and ethical implications. Yet, what the workshop ultimately proved is that there are many ways to "do" digital archaeology, and that archaeology as a discipline is engaged in a process of discovering what digital archaeology should (and, perhaps, should not) be as we progress towards a future where all archaeologists, whether they like it or not, must engage with what Steven Ellis has called the "digital filter."

So, (un)fortunately, this volume is not a "how-to" manual. In the end, there seems to be no uniform way to "mobilize the past." Instead, this volume reprises the workshop's presentations—now revised and enriched based on the meeting's debates as well as the editorial and peer review processes—in order to provide archaeologists with an extremely rich, diverse, and reflexive overview of the process of defining what digital archaeology is and what it can and should perhaps be. It also provides two erudite response papers that together form a didactic manifesto aimed at outlining a possible future for digital archaeology that is critical, diverse, data-rich, efficient, open, and most importantly, ethical. If this volume, which we offer both expeditiously and freely, helps make this ethos a reality, we foresee a bright future for mobilizing the past.

* * *

No multifaceted academic endeavor like *Mobilizing the Past* can be realized without the support of a range of institutions and individuals who believe in the organizers' plans and goals. Thus, we would like to thank the following institutions and individuals for their logistical, financial, and academic support in making both the workshop and this volume a reality. First and foremost, we extend our gratitude toward The National Endowment for the Humanities (NEH) for providing us with a Digital Humanities Start-Up Grant (#HD-51851-14), and especially to Jennifer Serventi and Perry Collins for their invaluable assistance through the application process and beyond. Without the financial support from this grant the workshop and this publication would not have been possible. We would also like to thank Susan Alcock (Special Counsel for Institutional Outreach and Engagement, University of Michigan) for supporting our grant application and workshop.

The workshop was graciously hosted by Wentworth Institute of Technology (Boston, MA). For help with hosting we would like to thank in particular Zorica Pantić (President), Russell Pinizzotto (Provost), Charlene Roy (Director of Business Services), Patrick Hafford (Dean, College of Arts and Sciences), Ronald Bernier (Chair, Humanities and Social Sciences), Charles Wiseman (Chair, Computer Science and Networking), Tristan Cary (Manager of User Services, Media Services), and Claudio Santiago (Utility Coordinator, Physical Plant).

Invaluable financial and logistical support was also generously provided by the Department of Fine and Performing Arts and Sponsored Programs Administration at Creighton University (Omaha, NE). In particular, we are grateful to Fred Hanna (Chair, Fine and Performing Arts) and J. Buresh (Program Manager, Fine and Performing Arts), and to Beth Herr (Director, Sponsored Programs Administration) and Barbara Bittner (Senior Communications Management, Sponsored Programs Administration) for assistance managing the NEH grant and more. Additional support was provided by The University of Wisconsin-Milwaukee; in particular, David Clark (Associate Dean, College of Letters and Science), and Kate Negri (Academic Department Assistant, Department of Art History). Further support was provided by Davidson College and, most importantly, we express our gratitude to Michael K. Toumazou (Director, Athienou Archaeological Project) for believing in and supporting our research and for allowing us to integrate mobile devices and digital workflows in the field.

The workshop itself benefitted from the help of Kathryn Grossman (Massachusetts Institute of Technology) and Tate Paulette (Brown University) for on-site registration and much more. Special thanks goes to Daniel Coslett (University of Washington) for graphic design work for both the workshop materials and this volume. We would also like to thank Scott Moore (Indiana University of Pennsylvania) for managing our workshop social media presence and his support throughout this project from workshop to publication.

This publication was a pleasure to edit, thanks in no small part to Bill Caraher (Director and Publisher, The Digital Press at the University of North Dakota), who provided us with an outstanding collaborative publishing experience. We would also like to thank Jennifer Sacher (Managing Editor, INSTAP Academic Press) for her conscientious copyediting and Brandon Olson for his careful reading of the final proofs. Moreover, we sincerely appreciate the efforts of this volume's anonymous reviewers, who provided detailed, thought-provoking, and timely feedback on the papers; their insights greatly improved this publication. We are also grateful to Michael Ashley and his team at the Center for Digital Archaeology for their help setting up the accompanying Mobilizing the Past Mukurtu site and Kristin M. Woodward of the University of Wisconsin-Milwaukee Libraries for assistance with publishing and archiving this project through UWM Digital Commons. In addition, we are grateful to the volume's two respondents, Morag Kersel (DePaul University) and Adam Rabinowitz (University of Texas at Austin), who generated erudite responses to the chapters in the volume. Last but not least, we owe our gratitude to all of the presenters who attended the workshop in Boston, our audience from the Boston area, and our colleagues on Twitter (and most notably, Shawn Graham of Carlton University for his word clouds) who keenly "tuned in" via the workshop's livestream. Finally, we extend our warmest thanks to the contributors of this volume for their excellent and timely chapters. This volume, of course, would not have been possible without such excellent papers.

As this list of collaborators demonstrates, the discipline of archaeology and its digital future remains a vital area of interest for people who value the past's ability to inform the present, and who recognize our ethical responsibility to consider technology's role in contemporary society. For our part, we hope that the experiences and issues presented in this volume help to shape new intra-disciplinary and critical ways of mobilizing the past so that human knowledge can continue to develop ethically at the intersection of archaeology and technology.

Erin Walcek Averett (Department of Fine and Performing Arts and Classical and Near Eastern Studies, Creighton University)

Jody Michael Gordon (Department of Humanities and Social Sciences, Wentworth Institute of Technology)

Derek B. Counts (Department of Art History, University of Wisconsin-Milwaukee)

October 1, 2016

How To Use This Book

The Digital Press at the University of North Dakota is a collaborative press and *Mobilizing the Past for a Digital Future* is an open, collaborative project. The synergistic nature of this project manifests itself in the two links that appear in a box at the end of every chapter.

The first link directs the reader to a site dedicated to the book, which is powered and hosted by the Center for Digital Archaeology's (CoDA) Mukurtu.net. The Murkutu application was designed to help indigenous communities share and manage their cultural heritage, but we have adapted it to share the digital heritage produced at the "Mobilizing the Past" workshop and during the course of making this book. Michael Ashley, the Director of Technology at CoDA, participated in the "Mobilizing the Past" workshop and facilitated our collaboration. The Mukurtu.net site (https://mobilizingthepast.mukurtu.net) has space dedicated to every chapter that includes a PDF of the chapter, a video of the paper presented at the workshop, and any supplemental material supplied by the authors. The QR code in the box directs readers to the same space and is designed to streamline the digital integration of the paper book.

The second link in the box provides open access to the individual chapter archived within University of Wisconsin-Milwaukee's installation of Digital Commons, where the entire volume can also be downloaded. Kristin M. Woodward (UWM Libraries) facilitated the creation of these pages and ensured that the book and individual chapters included proper metadata.

Our hope is that these collaborations, in addition to the open license under which this book is published, expose the book to a wider audience and provide a platform that ensures the continued availability of the digital complements and supplements to the text. Partnerships with CoDA and the University of Wisconsin-Milwaukee reflect the collaborative spirit of The Digital Press, this project, and digital archaeology in general.

Abbreviations

AAI	Alexandria Archive Institute
AAP	Athienou Archaeological Project
ABS	acrylonitrile butadiene styrene (plastic)
ADS	Archaeological Data Service
Alt-Acs	Alternative Academics
API	application programming interface
ARA	archaeological resource assessment
ARC	Australian Research Council
ARIS	adaptive resolution imaging sonar
ASV	autonomous surface vehicle
BLM	Bureau of Land Management
BLOB	Binary Large Object
BOR	Bureau of Reclamation
BYOD	bring your own device
CAD	computer-aided design
CDL	California Digital Library
CHDK	Canon Hack Development Kit
cm	centimeter/s
CMOS	complementary metal-oxide semiconductor
CoDA	Center for Digital Archaeology
COLLADA	COLLAborative Design Activity
CRM	cultural resource management
CSS	Cascading Style Sheet
CSV	comma separated values
DBMS	desktop database management system
DEM	digital elevation model
DINAA	Digital Index of North American Archaeology
DIY	do-it-yourself
DoD	Department of Defense
DVL	doppler velocity log
EAV	entity-attribute-value
EDM	electronic distance measurement
EU	excavation unit/s
FAIMS	Federated Archaeological Information Management System
fMRI	functional magnetic resonance imaging
GIS	geographical information system
GCP	ground control point
GNSS	global navigation satellite system
GPR	ground-penetrating radar

GUI	graphic user interface
ha	hectare/s
hr	hour/s
Hz	Hertz
HDSM	high-density survey and measurement
ICE	Image Composite Editor (Microsoft)
iOS	iPhone operating system
INS	inertial motion sensor
IPinCH	Intellectual Property in Cultural Heritage
IT	information technology
KAP	Kaymakçı Archaeological Project
KARS	Keos Archaeological Regional Survey
km	kilometer/s
LABUST	Laboratory for Underwater Systems and Technologies (University of Zagreb)
LAN	local area network
LIEF	Linkage Infrastructure Equipment and Facilities
LOD	linked open data
LTE	Long-Term Evolution
m	meter/s
masl	meters above sea level
MEMSAP	Malawi Earlier-Middle Stone Age Project
MOA	memoranda of agreement
MOOC	Massive Online Open Course
NGWSP	Navajo-Gallup Water Supply Project
NeCTAR	National eResearch Collaboration Tools and Resources
NEH	National Endowment for the Humanities
NHPA	National Historic Preservation Act
NPS	National Park Service
NRHP	National Register of Historic Places
NSF	National Science Foundation
OCR	optical character reader
OS	operating system
PA	programmatic agreement
PAP	pole aerial photography
PARP:PS	Pompeii Archaeological Research Project: Porta Stabia
PATA	Proyecto Arqueológico Tuti Antiguo
PBMP	Pompeii Bibliography and Mapping Project
PDA	personal digital assistant

PIARA	Proyecto de Investigación Arqueológico Regional Ancash
PKAP	Pyla-Koutsopetra Archaeological Project
Pladypos	PLAtform for DYnamic POSitioning
PLoS	Public Library of Science
PQP	Pompeii Quadriporticus Project
PAZC	Proyecto Arqueológico Zaña Colonial
QA	quality assurance
QC	quality control
QR	quick response
REVEAL	Reconstruction and Exploratory Visualization: Engineering meets ArchaeoLogy
ROS	robot operating system
ROV	remotely operated vehicle
RRN	Reciprocal Research Network
RSS	Rich Site Summary
RTK	real-time kinetic global navigation satellite system
SfM	structure from motion
SHPO	State Historic Preservation Office
SKAP	Say Kah Archaeological Project
SLAM	simultaneous localization and mapping
SMU	square meter unit/s
SU	stratigraphic unit/s
SVP	Sangro Valley Project
TCP	traditional cultural properties
tDAR	the Digital Archaeological Record
UAV	unmanned aerial vehicle
UNASAM	National University of Ancash, Santiago Antúnez de Mayolo
UQ	University of Queensland
USACE	U.S. Army Corp of Engineers
USBL	ultra-short baseline
USFS	U.S. Forest Service
USV	unmanned surface vehicle
UTM	universal transverse mercator
XML	Extensible Markup Language

Introduction

Mobile Computing in Archaeology: Exploring and Interpreting Current Practices

Jody Michael Gordon, Erin Walcek Averett, and Derek B. Counts

So 2024 Won't Be Like "1984": Mobilizing the Past at a Critical Time

On January 22, 1984, during the third quarter of Super Bowl XVIII, one of the most famous advertisements in television history was aired: a commercial that heralded the advent of the Apple Macintosh computer (Raw 2009: 21). The advertisement was called "1984," and it was directed by Ridley Scott, who was coming off the success of his human-versus-robot drama, *Bladerunner* (1982). "1984" alluded both to the current year as well as George Orwell's dystopian novel of the same name, *Nineteen Eighty-Four* (1949), which explored the elimination of individual thought and innovation by a totalitarian-inspired government surveillance system known as "Big Brother." The commercial depicts hundreds of vapid human subjects listening to a filmed address focused on a speaker celebrating the triumph of the "unification of thoughts." This terrifying future is disrupted by a free-thinking woman, depicted like an Olympic athlete, who hurls a sledgehammer into the movie screen and destroys the speaker's ideological power. The commercial ends with a voiceover reciting a scrolling black text: "On January 24th, Apple Computer will introduce Macintosh. And you'll see why 1984 won't be like "1984."

The commercial announced Apple's arrival into the PC market that was controlled by IBM, depicted in the ad as "Big Brother." It drew upon dystopian cyber-punk imagery, the counter-cultural bent of the punk rock movement, and the propagandistic conformity of the Cold

War communist world. It also foregrounded a battle of innovation against conformity, and the power of technology to liberate or disrupt the status quo, leading to new ideas, liberalization, and a vision of a future unfettered by traditional, restrictive, and top-down ways of doing things. "1984" was a disruptive commercial designed to challenge the soul-crushing, streamlined, and regimented life of industrial capitalism by insisting that another company offered a liberating alternative: the way to prevent the IBM-dominated dystopia of 1984 was to buy a different, and seemingly more innovative and creative, product. The commercial also caused a generation of computer users to begin thinking about how technology might shape their future.

The commercial aired nationally only once, but it coincided with the increased visibility and popularity of Apple's Macintosh computer, which would lay the corporate, financial, and technological foundations for the smart phones and tablets that have recently transformed archaeological practice. Indeed, Apple's interest in archaeological data collection (and archaeologists/academics as consumers) began soon after in 1985, when the famous "While studying prehistoric Greece, Dr. John Cherry discovered the computer" ad was released (Wallrodt 2011). Since then, mobile devices produced by companies using both Apple (e.g., iPad) and Google Android-based (e.g., Samsung Note) platforms have enhanced the mobility, speed, and efficiency of archaeological methods while revolutionizing the way people live their lives more generally.

Despite Apple's self-fashioned role as liberator in 1984, the company's success has transformed it into that of its original nemesis, "Big Brother." This metamorphosis has had implications for current archaeological practice since Apple products have become increasingly ubiquitous on archaeological projects. In addition, Apple is a company that strongly protects its lucrative patents and ideas, and collects more data about its product users (Neal 2013) than any other company besides, perhaps, Google (Rosenfeld 2014). Perhaps ironically, the perceptions surrounding Apple's new "Big Brother" status have not been lost on Google with its recently released "be together. not the same" Android marketing campaign. In one example, Apple's single-version IOS universe is mocked as a piano that only plays one note, Middle C ("Monotune": https://www.youtube.com/watch?v=xLhJIFC8xkY). As Rabinowitz (Ch. 5.2: 495) notes: "the paper, writing instruments, cameras and film of the analog era were not as closely coupled as our digital tools are to the agendas of corporate entities." Indeed, our mobile devices have become extensions of ourselves; they are so deeply entrenched in our society that it has become easier to be distracted by the devices' "bells and whistles" and to embrace the moment's conformity than to engage in productive and reflexive critiques that might prevent 2024 from becoming like "1984."

This volume explores the changing nature of 21st-century personal computing in archaeology and celebrates its positive influences on methods and practices. However, the book also cautions that we may be entering the "1984" phase of our discipline. We have embraced for our purview a range of innovative digital approaches and techniques that have been recently referred to as "digital or cyber archaeology" (see Levy 2014b). We define "digital archaeology" here as the use of computerized—especially internet connected and portable—tools and systems aimed at facilitating the documentation, interpretation, and publication of material culture. The volume approaches archaeological fieldwork technologies with both a practical and critical eye. Indeed, digital or "paperless" tools, systems, and publishing platforms have been integrated into archaeological projects for several years now with no signs of abating.

Thus, we are at a critical time for digital archaeology as it moves from its initial experiments to more established and widely adopted practices. The time is ripe to reflect. After decades of nearly frenetic technological innovation, it is time to slow down, step back, and think reflexively about how new technologies can alter – or have altered – archaeological practices, interpretation, and ethics. Based on the opinions of our workshop participants and the views of our respondents and reviewers, it seems clear that a deliberate, measured, and critical approach to digital archaeology represents the most effective and responsible way forward.

The idea for the "Mobilizing the Past" workshop was a direct result of our own attempts to integrate new mobile technologies using portable tablet computers on Davidson College's Athienou Archaeological Project (AAP), which has been excavating in Cyprus since 1990 (Toumazou et al. 2011; Toumazou et al. 2015). Our excavation is in many ways a typical, medium-sized academic project with a tuition- and grant-based funding scheme that precludes a large and permanent paid staff and dedicated digital technologists. Like many projects, we have relied on the dedication of students and academic staff to integrate technology into our project workflows. Through AAP's early adoption of relational databases, laptops, and digital photography, as well as more recent born-digital data recording and 3D-modeling techniques, we have stayed on top of technological advances in the discipline (Counts *et al.* 2016; Gordon *et al.*, Ch. 1.4). Yet, we have also been reluctant to adopt technology in an experimental way, preferring instead to integrate with care new technologies that advance our project mission in terms of undergraduate education and archaeological data collection, synthesis, and dissemination.

The AAP experience is consistent with trends in archaeology over the last five years—a time during which archaeological projects have had to contemplate how to integrate emergent digital technologies into their workflows. AAP's experience, then, has not been unique. Currently, several forces seem to be spurring the adoption of digital archaeological techniques in the 21st century. First, there is growing pressure on archaeologists to collect and publish more data, more quickly, and more efficiently. This phenomenon is perhaps created by academic pressure to produce "tech-savvy," "wow factor," or "data-driven" results that can attract university and governmental grants, which are now more often oriented toward the STEM disciplines (Science, Technology, Engineering, and Math) rather than fields in the humanities and social sciences. Within the discipline of archaeology itself, these institutional pressures coincide with the growing impact of development, salvage archaeology, permit limitations, and political instability in archaeologically-important regions to address the "need for speed" that many digital devices can provide. Indeed, these pressures along with rapid technological changes have fueled a wave of technological solutionism that views the use of digital tools as offering significant benefits in terms of archaeological data collection, manipulation, and interpretation (for the idea of technological solutionism, see Morozov 2014; Kansa, Ch. 4.2). More immediately, the release of a variety of multitasking and rugged, mobile, and Wi-Fi-equipped tablet computers has spurred the speedy adoption of devices that can manipulate archaeological field data in different, and *sometimes* more effective ways than traditional tools. In short, digital tools offer us new ways of exploring past human action that coincide with changes in contemporary archaeological and academic culture. Yet, the question remains: how will adopting these digital tools and systems change the way we do archaeology both now and in the future? This question lies at the heart of this volume.

WHERE ARE WE NOW: PARADIGM SHIFT OR PROCESS?

Over the last five years an undeniable shift has occurred in archaeological field practice with a movement toward portable, fully digital, data recording systems. This change has brought with it a "new language" with a new technical vocabulary that saturates this volume's chapters and represents a harbinger of change (Kersel, Ch. 5.1; Rabinowitz, Ch. 5.2). Although the adoption of mobile technology by a range of projects may seem incredibly rapid, digital developments are not exactly new. Archaeology has been digital since the late 19th century, at least in the limited or discrete values sense of exacting recording (Watrall 2011: 171; Caraher, Ch. 4.1). By the 1960s, further digitization occurred when processualist scholars emphasized the rigorous collection of comparative datasets, some of which began to be analyzed on computers (Dibble and McPherron 1988; Wallrodt 2011; Renfrew and Bahn 2012: 33–43). However, with the postprocessualist recognition that limited values objectivism in archaeology is difficult (Hodder 1985: 1–3), some archaeologists have begun to balance the inherent limitations of streamlined computer-generated data with reflexive methodologies that permit the collection of more diverse data types by a wider range of subjective interpretive voices (Daly and Evans 2006: 3–5; Zubrow 2006: 17–18; Morgan and Eve 2012; Caraher 2013; Roosevelt 2015: 325, 329). Indeed, with the creation of a host of robust and powerful mobile devices since 2010, many archaeologists have been forced to reconsider how digital innovations can affect archaeological practices.

Maurizio Forte and Thomas Levy have referred to the recent intensification of digital methods in archaeological research as "cyber archaeology" (Forte 2010, 2015; Levy 2014b), and they divide its practical features into four interrelated components associated with data: acquisition, curation, analysis, and dissemination. More recently, Christopher Roosevelt and his team at the Kaymakçı Archaeological Project (KAP) have suggested that the integration of new digital tools across the spectrum of archaeological work represents "a shift to a digital paradigm" (Roosevelt *et al.* 2015: 339). The KAP team supports this perspective mainly based on their own experience developing an accurate, efficient, and immersive born-digital data recording system that offers a "high-quality recording of an excavator's interactions" with archaeological materials, even if a "pristine, objective archaeological record" remains admittedly unattainable (Roosevelt *et al.* 2015: 325). Roosevelt and his colleagues emphasize that the enhanced speed, accuracy, and reproducibility of digital methods (e.g., volumetric 3D trench models) produce more robust, standardized, and multidimensional archaeological data that support more sophisticated and sensitive engagements with the "total archaeological record" (Roosevelt *et al.* 2015: 326, 339). Additionally, they suggest that the skills and reflexivity associated with conventional (e.g., paper- and tape measure-based) recording systems are not lost with digital modes, but are merely "shifted from analog to digital" (Roosevelt *et al.* 2015: 339). From this perspective, digital archaeology does not fundamentally change accepted archaeological practices, such as how to interpret stratigraphy. Instead, it provides an enhanced toolset that permits more rapid, and presumably more accurate and informed, archaeological decision-making, especially at the trowel's edge. Thus, Roosevelt and colleagues' thought-provoking article has challenged archaeologists utilizing digital methods to consider which techniques are improving workflows and interpretations and which are not.

Digital recording systems have become progressively entangled with archaeological practice, even though a complete "shift to a digital paradigm" is hard to support. Indeed, scholars have increasingly experimented with digital platforms not only because they might provide more data, but also because they ideally provide different or novel kinds of data (e.g., volumetric measurement or limited value data entry), offer new analytical techniques (e.g., 3D visualizations, GIS modeling, or RTI computational photography), and result in potentially more integrative, democratic, ethical, and pluralistic methodologies (e.g., archaeological methods that enhance cognition, team communication, methodological reflexivity, and data sharing). The KAP team has itself developed an innovative and largely do-it-yourself (DIY) system of paperless workflows that has improved the quality of "recording an excavator's interactions" with material culture (e.g., making them more mindful of the inherent volumetric nature of archaeological work; Roosevelt *et al.* 2015: 325). According to Roosevelt and colleagues, this enhanced ability to engage with reconstructing the "total archaeological record" has led excavators to "(re)frame excavation strategies" in ways that increase "engagement with the material archaeology at hand" (Roosevelt *et al.* 2015: 326, 340).

For KAP, the end goal of adopting such digital strategies seems to be the achievement of "meaningful analysis across contexts, excavation areas, and even sites and regions" (Roosevelt *et al.* 2015: 342). In short, these digital methods provide better archaeological interpretations of past human actions.

Several chapters in this volume likewise claim that digital archaeological methods are beginning to provide novel datasets that potentially offer more exacting archaeological interpretations than those collected through conventional paper-based methods. Yet, at the same time, there remains room for debate about the paradigm-shattering nature of digital archaeology's enhanced explanatory power. A key critique that can be made of KAP's article is that, despite their claims to the contrary, the authors do not convincingly illustrate how digital archaeology's current epistemic development fully equates with Thomas Kuhn's standard of a paradigm shift, which encompasses a fundamental change in a discipline's key explanatory concepts and analytical methods to the point that previous methods and concepts are no longer considered valid (Kuhn 1996: 66–76; see also Richter *et al.* 2013; Perry 2015). For example, although paper-based data recording may be in decline among archaeological projects, it has not been completely abandoned by those practitioners who feel that it provides interpretive results that remain different and equally valid (or even complementary) to those produced by digital methods. As a result, such overwrought claims about digital archaeology's superiority and the current shift to a digital paradigm as a *fait accompli* have led Sarah Perry (2015) to note how within digital archaeological discourse "the language used is obfuscating—deploying the wow-factor to draw people into what I would argue is an unproductive, and in many cases fallacious, conversation about the revolutionary nature of the methodologies." As Perry points out, there is a tension between the perceived potential of digital archaeology and the language and definitions used to describe what it actually does. The result of this tension is that incremental processes of change are often equated with paradigm shifts and revolutions in disciplinary thought. Based on such observations, it seems hard to argue for a full paradigm shift to digital archaeology at present because the types of data collected are largely the same as those traditionally collected, and because the explanatory theories that govern their interpretation remain largely unchanged (see also Rabinowitz, Ch. 5.2; cf. the potential of virtual reality archaeology in Castro López *et al.*, Ch. 3.1).

For the KAP project, the insertion of the "digital filter" at the trowel's edge through 3D photogrammetry and rapid access to a suite of digital files permitted the excavators to think volumetrically about stratigraphic relationships. In this scenario, stratigraphic levels are transformed from the uniform boxes in a Harris Matrix to shapes that reflect context formation processes as well as chronological, spatial, and by extension, ancient social, relationships. These 3D objects reflect wholly new ways of presenting the artifacts of excavation, as well as traditional archaeological practices and knowledge; yet many projects that have used these techniques have stopped short at explaining *how* these new types of data have impacted short term archaeological analyses and our understanding of the ancient past. A case in point might be KAP's detailed description of how they used photogrammetry to document an ancient granary. Did their new digital excavation strategies and volumetric thinking result in new ways of understanding granary construction and social function in the Bronze Age (Roosevelt *et al.* 2015: 337-339)? If so, this information is only hinted at within their article; although the digital results' enhanced explanatory power will perhaps emerge within the final publication. Indeed, many of the advantages accrued from their digital system are discussed in terms of "long-term" benefits (Roosevelt *et al.* 2015: 339; see also Nakassis 2015). Thus, the use of innovative digital techniques can sometimes overstate the explanatory power of digital data. Digital systems tend to thrive at the intersection of new techniques and traditional practices and epistemologies. As a result, it is often difficult to establish whether novel methods of collecting data, improving organization, curation, and publication have actually changed the fundamental character of archaeological knowledge production.

From our perspective, archaeology has yet to undergo a complete Kuhnian paradigm shift to a new digital era. In fact, it remains possible to practice archaeology using pre-digital tools (e.g., paper notebooks and trench drawings) or hybrid practices (i.e., adopting some digital technology alongside traditional practices) while still contributing to how we understand the past. Although the ability of digital tools to produce more robust datasets certainly strengthens archaeologists' capacity to measure changes in material culture, current digital field practices are more symptomatic of a continuous process of adapting new tools and practices to centuries-old fieldwork techniques than to changing—fundamentally—the ways that archaeologists explain past human actions. As a result, it is perhaps less useful to talk about paradigm shifts and revolutions and more constructive to discuss what is occurring in archaeology today as part of a wider *process* of academic and social change that is manifested through the integration of digital technologies into archaeological workflows. Indeed, if we want to explore and critique the current nature of digital archaeology, it seems best to view it as a mode of archaeological practice that is still engaged in a process of development, but that has the potential to produce different datasets that may one day engender wholly innovative views on the past than those provided by paper-based methods.

One of the reasons that digital tools and methods have not yet realized their full potential in terms of contributing to new ways of understanding the past could be because they have been "black boxed." Mary Leighton (2015: 68) drew upon Bruno Latour's concept of black boxing to look at the diversity of field practices understood as too basic to discuss in archaeological publication. According to Latour (Latour and Woolgar 1979: 51; see also Caraher, Ch. 4.1), black boxing is a social process referring to the way in which the details of scientific and technical work, once successful and common, become obfuscated. Leighton's study revealed that the details of archaeological work, despite being treated as "common sense," were in fact directly linked to the production and nature of archaeological knowledge. In short, the archaeological interpretations that publications provided were the direct result of commonplace field methods that were practiced in uncritical and unreflexive ways—an issue that may have potentially hindered their explanatory power. We argue that archaeological methods employing digital tools should be critiqued in the same vein, both in a practical sense, as well as in terms of their influence on how we produce data and understand the past. Thus, this volume is a call for more discussion, debate, and critique aimed at not only looking at digital archaeology as a process, but also as a mode of knowledge creation whose black-boxed practices may require some "opening up."

This volume underscores the need for a more reflexive analysis of what digital archaeology does and how its tools, systems, and practices are shaping the discipline (Huggett 2004, 2015a and b; Berggren *et al.* 2015; see also Caraher, Ch. 4.1; Kansa, Ch. 4.2; Kersel, Ch. 5.1; Rabinowitz, Ch. 5.2). We must move beyond viewing digital technologies as merely tools in the hands of technicians and consider how they can inform new approaches to archaeology and aid in the production of new archaeological knowledge and interpretation (as observed by Schollar 1999; Llobera 2011). Making explicit how new digital tools produce new forms of knowledge might also mitigate the dubious "wow factor" impression that digital archaeology creates when the digital supersedes the archaeological. As Jeremy Huggett (2015a: 80) notes, "archaeological computing has been a follower rather than an innovator," and most computer-based tools used by archaeologists are borrowed from other sectors. However, some papers in this volume indicate that this trend may be changing with several projects developing bespoke digital systems that could have broader applications (e.g., Dufton, Ch. 3.3; Fee, Ch. 2.1; Sobotkova et al., Ch. 3.2). Huggett (2015a: 83–84) has issued a "grand challenge" for digital archaeology to become more ambitious and innovative in ways that will transform not only our own discipline, but extend across other academic fields. We hope that this volume responds, at least partially, to Huggett's call and that it can contribute to wider debates concerning the influence of technology on a range of Digital Humanities disciplines (Allington et al. 2016).

Whether one believes in digital archaeology's promise or not, most scholars recognize that in the Information Age we are all digital archaeologists—at least to some extent (Morgan and Eve 2012: 523). Ellis (Ch. 1.2), for example, argues that all projects are digital, and today it is only a question of when, where, and how a project applies its "digital filter" that determines whether the filter's application enhances archaeological interpretations or simply replicates paper-based data in digital form in order to produce novel or compelling results. Although some replicable practices in digital archaeology are emerging that save time and money and produce higher quantities and more detailed and consistent data, there still does not seem to be a single system that fits the goals and logistical challenges of every project (Caraher 2014; see also the various chapters in Levy 2014a).

Instead, digital archaeology's utility might stem from its new approach to both data collection and dissemination grounded in a range of project-specific approaches. Thus, as with pre-digital recording methods (despite calls for their standardization, see Pavel 2010), digital archaeologies seem to offer a range of innovative and creative approaches to data recording. For example, some approaches seem capable of focusing on both specific projects' goals and recording data in formats that can be widely shared (e.g., via online repositories or open linked data systems) and that may even offer a degree of objectivity. Digital archaeology's innovative and experimental DIY spirit supports scholars' efforts to grapple with the inescapable digital filter found in 21st-century archaeology. These efforts are enhanced by the continued reflexive and pluralistic analysis of how scholars are attempting to solve archaeological questions with digital means. By examining a range of digital archaeologies (such as those presented in this volume), scholars can begin to discern which practical methodological advancements are producing valuable new ways of interpreting the past and which have been less successful. In some ways, digital archaeology shares its ethos with what Caraher (2014) calls "punk archaeology." For Caraher, a punk archaeology is one that embraces the punk notions of performance, an openness to challenging long-held ideas, and spontaneity in an effort to forge new solutions to old practical and interpretive problems. It is these types of experiments and attitudes that mark the *process* of creating a critical digital archaeology informed by comparative exempla that reveal what is working and what is not. Indeed, such an endeavor is part of this volume's wider mission (see Rabinowitz, Ch. 5.2).

It is vital, of course, that digital archaeology embraces continuous experimentation, as well as a more mature critique. Thus, after the first initial and enthusiastic years of experimentation and adoption of mobile computing devices in the field, we have entered a reflexive phase based on these early trials. The papers collected here include calls for critical, thoughtful, and ethical uses of digital technologies as well as best practices. The "digital filter" is likely here to stay, or, as Morgan and Eve state: "We are all digital archaeologists" (Morgan and Eve 2012: 523; see also Roosevelt et al. 2015: 325). These sophisticated and nuanced discussions of the broader impact of digital technologies in our discipline represent an important part of the critical process of engaging with digital tools and methods in order to achieve more efficient, insightful, and data-rich archaeological interpretations.

CURRENT TRENDS IN MOBILE DIGITAL ARCHAEOLOGY

Mobile digital practices cut across a number of vital domains in archaeology. Because archaeological fieldwork and analysis tends to marshal tools, systems, practices, and publication methods into a disciplinary whole, many of the papers in this volume consider several of these key workflow elements.

Tools

At a basic, granular, and practical level, most of the papers in this volume emphasize digital tools. The emergence of robust and portable devices with significant computing power and internet connectivity has marked a divide between pre-tablet digital archaeology and the mobile-based systems that characterize many of today's archaeological processes. From apps and programs (e.g., tablet-based databases, see Ellis, Ch. 1.2, Motz, Ch. 1.3, Wallrodt, Ch. 1.1, and others) to 3D-modeling software (see Olson, Ch. 2.2) to new hardware (e.g., iPads, see Gordon *et al.*, Ch. 1.4) to drones (see Wernke *et al.*, Ch. 2.3), most of the adoption of new technologies stems from the need to solve practical problems in archaeological field recording that pertain to efficiency, accuracy, scale, and scope.

The success of these technologies is typically measured against practical needs relating to whether the digital methods improved data collection accuracy, speed, or quantity; saved money; led to quicker and wider publication; or other common archaeological goals. It often remains difficult, however, to evaluate whether projects were successful at harnessing these presumed benefits partly because archaeologists have not developed or considered methods for measuring such improvements (cf. Berggren *et al.* 2015; Gordon *et al.*, Ch. 1.4). This issue has led some scholars to question the benefits of many of these tools to archaeological practice and interpretation. For example, Kersel (Ch. 5.1) questions whether the famous Tel Dan inscription would have ever been found without the "hands-on" tactile and human intervention of the "paper-based" architect Gila Cook.

Nevertheless, most authors aver that their experiments with new digital tools were beneficial at least when compared to their previous use of non-digital tools. Such benefits can be as simple as the time saved in recopying paper-based field notes by utilizing tablet computers to record excavators' insights in a born-digital, and hence searchable and reproducible, format. Yet, the benefits of digital tools seem even more convincing in chapters like that of Wernke and colleagues (Ch. 2.3) where drone-based technologies have, for the first time, revealed entire archaeological landscapes, such as the Inkan imperial road system. Mapping such monuments using conventional, paper-based methods have been previously prohibitive given the temporal and financial restrictions placed on most academic archaeological projects, and so the use of such digital tools is truly a game changer.

For many, digital devices provide more efficient, and sometimes more data-rich, ways to do old, often paper-based, things. Simply put, these technologies save time. This "saved" time can be put toward increased analysis (Poehler, Ch. 1.7) and field school student education (Bria and DeTore, Ch. 1.5; Gordon *et al.*, Ch. 1.4). Technologies, however, can also go beyond basic archaeological efficiency and allow for archaeological work that scale or environments would render impossible using traditional methods. Again, Wernke and colleagues' mapping of extensive road networks (Ch. 2.3) or Buxton and associates' use of digital tools to streamline underwater survey (Ch. 2.4) are cases in point. Yet, scholars have also questioned whether efficiency "for the sake of efficiency" is reason enough to adopt a new tool (Nakassis 2015; see also Caraher, Ch. 4.1; Kersel, Ch. 5.1). For example, Caraher (Ch. 4.1) suggests that in industrial practice, Taylorist approaches to managing workflows (i.e., workflows developed specifically with an eye toward efficiency and productivity) have led to a "de-skilling," or the loss of skills related to traditional, haptic, work practices (e.g., in archaeology, the move from paper-based illustration to 3D modeling). However, virtually every attempt to economize process—digital or not—presents certain challenges to interpretation and knowledge production, and thus all attempts should be analyzed critically in terms of their methodological or interpretive efficacy. Digital archaeological techniques, then, like all archaeological methods, must be carefully considered before implementation to determine how they might impede or improve data collection and interpretation.

Rabinowitz (Ch. 5.2) further asserts that digital archaeology's reconfiguration of time in relation to the logistical and procedural elements of practice has a pivotal influence on how and why we mobilize the past. Moreover, he suggests that time's intersection with cost has emerged as another key consideration in the adoption of digital tools. The purchase of technology is often the main expense incurred in digital archaeology, even though relatively large-scale government and university grants can offset such costs (see Castro López *et al.*, Ch. 3.1; Ellis, Ch. 1.2; Gordon *et al.*, Ch. 1.4; Sobotkova *et al.*, Ch. 3.2). In the private sector, the cost of adopting digital technology is especially important (Spigelman *et al.*, Ch. 3.4) because the decision about how to go digital or whether to do it at all is often dependent on the company's bottom-line financial and operational logistics, as well as on the desires of clients to whom such costs are often passed along. On the other hand, the relatively low cost of some devices (such as mobile tablets, smart phones, or similar products) and software programs (many, such as Agisoft Photoscan, provide educational discounts or free trial versions) have encouraged experimentation and the widespread adoption of these tools. Some projects even adopt a BYOD (bring-your-own-device) policy (Wallrodt, Ch. 1.1), which, although useful, can complicate recording methods through the introduction of multiple devices and platforms and can feed the perception that archaeology is reserved for those who can afford it (Opitz 2015; Kersel, Ch. 5.1). As Sayre has illustrated (Ch. 1.6), a project's engagements with technology can be interpreted as a display of privilege.

At the same time, however, digital tools and born-digital archaeological data also have the potential to expand the impact of archaeological projects into local communities (Kersel, Ch. 5.1). For example, the Proyecto Qhapaq Ñan's (Wernke *et al.*, Ch. 2.3) mapping of endangered Peruvian sites and the public outreach initiatives of the Forum MMX Project in Spain (Castro López *et al.*, Ch. 3.1) focused on virtual reality reconstructions are both designed to engage local communities through digital methods. Sayre's chapter on digital archaeology in Peru (Ch. 1.6) further describes how digital tools have allowed archaeological projects to collaborate in new ways, particularly with the indigenous communities whose past they interpret, while also acknowledging that digital tools can serve to exacerbate the privilege that foreign archaeological projects often hold over host communities. Such studies illustrate that a self-aware digital archaeology can present opportunities for both outreach and critical views of the growing impact of technology on contemporary culture.

Despite digital archaeology's potential to make research processes more participatory, many digital tools remain expensive and only accessible to projects with large budgets and technology specialists (see Buxton *et al.*, Ch. 2.4; Castro López *et al.*, Ch. 3.1; Ellis, Ch. 1.2; Sobotkova et al., Ch. 3.2; Wernke et al., Ch. 2.3). A long-term issue is that with more software moving to subscription-based fees, the need to migrate data to updated media and the newest versions of software and hardware, and the persistent costs of long-term digital storage schemes, projects not only need start-up grants for the purchase of technology, but they also require funding for the continuous support of existing digital infrastructure. Thus, projects are increasingly required to plan for long-term finances to keep up with technological change. Moreover, for those projects seeking funding from institutional agencies, there continues to be some danger of privileging technical innovation over archaeological research questions. For example, the use of digital tools to produce "wow factor" or "tech-savvy" academic products (e.g., 3D-printed artifacts or the construction of virtual environments) might seem impressive to institutional funders, but their use may not actually succeed in answering pressing archaeological questions (Allington et al. 2016; Kansa, Ch. 4.2).

Systems

The next domain to consider is that of the integrated project workflow systems within which digital tools are manipulated. At this level, archaeologists' concerns are related to the ways in which tools function within technological and human ecosystems and how people, machines, and data input, sharing, and output interact to produce meaningful results. For example, how does one integrate 3D structure-from-motion (SfM) imagery into traditional recording and publication practices? How does one manage the flow of wireless data between an archaeological site and a lab-based server? Or, how do various personnel (e.g., producer/consumer; teacher/student; director/digger; data collector/computer specialist) work together to marshal, manipulate, and interpret data in effective ways? In order to elucidate such questions, several chapters in this volume deal with the technical structure of digital systems including issues of data management, the movement of data between connected devices, the convergence of digital technologies and functions, and the social organization of digital practices (Castro López et al., Ch. 3.1; Dufton, Ch. 3.3; Fee, Ch. 2.1; Motz, Ch. 1.3; Sobotkova et al., Ch. 3.2; Wallrodt, Ch. 1.1). While the main thrust of this scholarship is practical, several chapters also reflect on the disciplinary impact of such approaches. Overall, we must view digital archaeologies not as a congeries of tools, but rather as functional systems so that we can better understand how these methods affect our recording and interpretation of archaeological data.

One of the primary issues currently associated with digital systems in archaeology concerns the relationship between collecting, interpreting, disseminating, and preserving accurate data. At trench-side, excavators using digital tools now collect a much wider range of data types than ever before (e.g., photogrammetry or video files in addition to traditional data types such as context forms or diary entries). The results can lead to "data deluge" (Bevan 2015) or "avalanche" (Levy 2014b), that is, the production of a massive and unwieldy dataset that is too larger to analyze, interpret, and publish effectively and expeditiously. In fact, these archaeological data floods are often collected in highly fragmented ways that require significant post-processing to reassemble the parts into an integrated, holistic, and ultimately manageable and interpretable representation of material and space (Caraher 2015; cf. Wallrodt, Ch. 1.1). As a result, archaeological systems designers and managers now need to pay close attention to how the data being collected relates to research goals, how it can be organized and integrated coherently, and how it can be published and curated properly. Access and management of data, thus, continues to be a topic of concern as does sustainability, archiving, curation, and publication standards (Elliot *et al.* 2012). Yet, when digital systems are thoughtfully and critically managed, they can often provide quicker and more effective ways to collect, preserve, and disseminate data and, in doing so, offer new ways to facilitate archaeological interpretations.

Many papers highlight a tension between custom-designed, integrated systems and those created from off-the-shelf apps. Developers have crafted integrated digital systems such as the Federated Acquired Information Management System (FAIMS; see Sobotkova *et al.*, Ch. 3.2), the Archaeological Recording Kit (ARK; see Dufton, Ch. 3.3), and TooWaste (Serrano Araque and Martínez Carillo 2014; and others, e.g., Codifi Pro, not discussed in this volume) to fit a specific project's in-field logistics, workflow goals, and even publication and preservation aims. FAIMS, for example, offers the complete package from the trench to the final phase of publication and archiving. In addition, some of the programs, most notably FAIMS and ARK, have adopted open-source standards so that they can be modified to suit a project's particular needs. Another, perhaps equally common, approach to the development of digital systems, is the DIY model. These are systems that utilize off-the-shelf apps and devices according to a range of configurations and protocols in order to improve project workflows in terms of time, money, and, ideally, archaeological interpretation. Even off-the-shelf, proprietary apps like FileMaker Go offer a degree of customizability in terms of color schemes and scripts that can effectively facilitate and streamline the recording process (Motz, Ch. 1.3). Furthermore, sometimes a single bespoke app, such as Fee's PKapp (Ch. 2.1), can be combined with other off-the-shelf apps to create an integrated DIY system. Overall, the chapters by Wallrodt (Ch. 1.1), Ellis (Ch. 1.2), Motz (Ch. 1.3), Gordon *et al.* (Ch. 1.4), Bria and DeTore (Ch. 1.5), Sayre (Ch. 1.6), and Fee (Ch. 2.1) illustrate the wide variety of ways that archaeological projects work to shepherd information from the trench to the lab and to publication.

The development of a coherent system is more than just a technical concern; indeed, the issues of who controls digital recording systems and how the disparate voices within the archaeological process are integrated should also be discussed. Projects are composed of a range of individuals (including directors, excavators, artifact specialists, architects, illustrators, registrars, conservators, and online archivists or publishers), who collaborate to produce archaeological knowledge. Many digital systems allow each project member to participate explicitly in the archaeological process (Berggren 2015; see also Ellis, Ch. 1.2; Wallrodt, Ch. 1.1). In many ways, this collaborative knowledge building makes visible a plurality of voices, beyond the names that grace the covers of final publications. Digital archaeology, when practiced in this way, can thus have a positive, pluralistic, and democratic influence on how archaeological knowledge is formed and disseminated.

When uncritically adopted, however, digital systems can also put limits on the democratic nature of archaeological practice. For example, some mobile databases record all users' file changes and limit the values that can be entered in the name of data clarity and efficiency. This "Big Brother" monitoring of user actions and the delimiting of a user's interpretive and expressive vocabulary can thus be undemocratic if these functions are deployed in an uncritical and top-down fashion. Nevertheless, if they are critically deployed, they can also make visible who is involved in knowledge production and who controls and limits the process (Caraher, Ch. 4.1; Rabinowitz, Ch. 5.2); they can also help to safeguard more participatory and open forms of archaeology. In sum, understanding the impact of these practices is vital for the future of digital archaeology since it can help to define which emergent practices will be more democratic, participatory, and bottom-up and which will be simply more streamlined, narrow, and top-down. As they have done in traditional archaeological settings, power relations continue to play a role in how digital archaeologies are created and practiced.

Interpretation

Despite the increased prevalence of digital tools and integrated systems, it is also becoming clear that there are a variety of ways that digital technologies impact archaeological practices. For example, technological changes in recent years seem to most often occur on projects that are well funded because they can afford to hire the requisite technological personnel. On the other hand, the decreasing costs of mobile devices and the emergence of open-access sharing of protocols has allowed smaller, less well-heeled projects to integrate DIY digital workflows (for DIY archaeology more generally, see Morgan and Eve 2012; Caraher 2014; Morgan 2015).

Caraher (2015; Ch. 4.1) has issued a clarion call for a more reflexive set of digital practices, especially in the field, through his espousal of what he has coined "slow archaeology." This concept arose from his recognition that there was a growing celebratory (and often self-congratulatory) chorus of archaeologists who touted the improvements brought by digital tools, without adequately assessing how such tools impact archaeological practice. Thus, drawing on the popular slow food movement and more sophisticated philosophical critiques of speed, Caraher views this development as a problem that stems from the uncritical adoption of various digital tools and methods. In short, he states (Caraher, Ch. 4.1: 437): "[s]low archaeology challenges any claim that gains in efficiency through the use of digital tools is sufficient reason alone to incorporate them into the archaeological workflow."

Caraher scaffolds his critique of digital practices by illustrating that archaeology as a modern discipline has always faced tensions related to data fragmentation and uncontextualized analysis. He suggests that these issues have stemmed from the need to process material culture remains in an efficient manner that has often embraced

Taylorist principles and eschewed more descriptive techniques. Such trends have tended to separate "data collection" from archaeological interpretation. New Archaeology reinforced such systematic practices to the extent that certain activities, such as the creation of Harris matrices, systematized the divergent practices and ambiguities that actually occur in field archaeology (see also Pavel 2010: 145). The result of these divides and the matter-of-fact acceptance (or black boxing) of certain archaeological practices is that archaeologists often accelerate crucial steps in the interpretative process that previously provided a deep familiarity with material, practices, and embodied processes. In particular, Caraher has cautioned that the uncritical use of technology can potentially privilege processes and uniform types of data collection, which can fragment and narrow archaeologists' perspectives (cf. Wallrodt, Ch. 1.1, on the fragmentation of data). Digital archaeological methods can allow *more* data to be collected faster, but the results do not necessarily yield *better* data that promote more insightful interpretations.

Rabinowitz (Ch. 5.2: 503) also critiques digital archaeology's ability to aid in the interpretation of the past by stating, "[m]achines can collect data and they can begin to integrate them into the contextual systems that we think of as information, but they cannot perform the leap of informed imagination." Similarly, Caraher advocates for a slow archaeology that thoughtfully considers *why* digital tools are integrated into workflows and *how* they might affect archaeologists' "informed imaginations." Such an informed archaeology does not require the abandonment of digital tools and methods, but rather it emphasizes that one should take the time to engage critically with the potential risks of black boxing and not simply adopt methods for the sake of efficiency alone. Instead, archaeologists should carefully consider which digital tools might best be employed without denigrating (or eroding) human practitioners' interpretive powers and skills.

Publication

From the outset, the goal of this volume was to focus on how mobile computing technologies, such as tablets, smart phones, and the on-site systems that support them, have changed the way we are practicing archaeology and interpreting the past through material remains. For the "Mobilizing the Past" workshop, however, we also included voices concerned with what happens to the archaeological data once they leave the lab. Kersel (Ch. 5.1) laments the lack of space many chapters devote to how and when they intend to publish the results of their digital projects. This lack of focus on publication and its attendant issues of long-term data accessibility and preservation, which has been a central concern of the discipline since its inception, is indeed a notable omission in the digital archaeological process at present.

Eric Kansa's Open Context (http://opencontext.org) is one of several online data-publishing platforms that have emerged in recent years along with the Digital Archaeological Record (tDAR), the Digital Index of North American Archaeology (DINAA), the Online Cultural and Historical Research Environment (OCHRE), Heurist, and Mukurtu. Each platform has grappled with issues related to the publication and preservation of the digital archive; Kansa has written extensively about the possibilities for an open and accessible digital space(s) for archaeological data (see http://opencontext.org/about/bibliography). He has also raised ethical concerns about the creation and preservation of such places in the face of a range of pressures stemming from the socio-economic conditions affecting the so-called alt-ac (alternative-academic) liminal academic spaces where digital data repository projects currently reside. Kansa's contribution to this volume foregrounds several important issues about where the archaeological data are going, how they are curated, and who will have access to them.

Kansa offers a new approach to these issues in his concept of "slow data," a concept modeled on Caraher's slow archaeology. He calls for a critical approach to access that considers the need to protect provisional and sometimes sensitive data while also offering a framework for linked and machine readable data sets. For Kansa, a slow data approach to digital archaeology should involve a thoughtful process of data management and dissemination that strives for excellence in data quality and takes the time to consider the communities that should have access to the data and for what reason from the perspective of professional anthropological ethics. Perhaps Caraher (Ch. 4.1) has phrased this best as a process of imbuing archaeological datasets with a "human character." By mitigating the "publish or perish" academic reward system with a new "slow" model, the commercialization of alt-ac digital tool development and the monopolistic practices that attend this process can be avoided to allow for new, more critical, open and ethical ways of publishing, disseminating, and preserving the increasingly large datasets created by digital archaeologists.

An Ethical Digital Archaeology

Current trends in digital archaeology have demonstrated that practitioners are doing more than simply adopting tools, systems, and practices best suited for streamlining collection, interpretation, and publication of archaeological knowledge. Archaeologists are now actively debating the ethical and methodological character of technological change in the discipline. The final four papers in this volume—by Caraher, Kansa, Kersel, and Rabinowitz—bring together a cross-section of ethical and methodological critiques of digital practices in archaeology. These papers, as well as the general spirit of critique throughout, make clear that the tools and techniques we use shape the kind of knowledge we produce.

Kersel's response, "Living a Semi-digital Kinda Life," draws upon on her wide-ranging experience as a field archaeologist and cultural heritage expert and focuses on the ethical implications of archaeologists' "semi-digital" lives (Ch. 5.1). Like Caraher and Kansa, she questions the "need for speed" in archaeology and its results. Kersel (Ch. 5.1: 478) cuts to the heart of any arguments for efficiency when she asks, "are we publishing more? . . . Are we thinking more?" Archaeologists have always considered how they are going to publish the massive amounts of data they gather; yet, data collection in a born-digital age has perhaps compounded such concerns. Kersel (Ch. 5.1: 481) argues that academic digital archaeology must consider the publication of results as one of the discipline's key ethical responsibilities: "whether we are 'born-digital,' semi-digital, or paper-based, our ethical obligations to the people, places, and objects with which we work remain the same." The first obligation she highlights is that digital archaeologies need to be inclusive in terms of who can use them and who can participate in shaping local pasts. She pointedly notes that digital technologies have great potential to increase efficiency, accuracy, and data collection; yet, if they are uncritically implemented, they also have a more disturbing power to accentuate disciplinary problems already present in our field, such as gender imbalances, socio-economic inequality, the use of the past for political gain, and divides between practice and theory.

Time for a Manifesto

Rabinowitz's response, "Mobilizing (Ourselves) for a Critical Digital Archaeology," recognizes the importance of time's intersection with money within the context of capitalism (Ch. 5.2). In recent years, neoliberal philosophies focused on speed and efficiency have caused practitioners to redesign archaeological systems in ways that leverage digital tools to achieve enhanced data collection, accuracy, and quantity. Rabinowitz advocates for the creation of a manifesto for a "Critical Digital Archaeology," which he outlines via three intersecting mini-manifestos, each of which is flavored with a different attitude: celebratory, reflexive, and cautionary. It is easy enough to celebrate the potential of our ever-expanding digital tool kit, but for Rabinowitz, a digital archaeology must be both critical and cautionary in its ethos. Following Huggett's (2015b) "introspective and open" manifesto, Rabinowitz calls for a more reflexive digital archaeology among practitioners. In particular, he suggests that archaeologists need to be aware of how digital tools can distance users from their objects of inquiry and how their interactions with different types of tools (e.g., pen and paper versus a digital tablet) can lead to different haptic experiences and, consequently, different effects on people's cognitive processes of understanding and re-imagining the past. Rabinowitz's most significant critique, however, takes aim at the current economic model that sustains many digital projects. Money (along with time), as it is procured and used within the context of current socio-economic structures, in many ways dictates how digital archaeology is practiced, what it produces, and how such "deliverables" are disseminated and shared in society. Although archaeologists will likely be forced to work under such structural conditions for the foreseeable future, Rabinowitz cautions that a critical (and ethical) digital approach to archaeological practice must recognize the economic forces that shape it.

Kansa's ironic title, "Click Here to Save the Past," (Ch. 4.2) critiques the spirit of technological solutionism by emphasizing that digital archaeology remains entangled with commercial and semi-commercial interests that both shape and reflect wide ranging social pressures (Morozov 2014). He argues that our critical appreciation of technological change involves more than just selecting the best digital tool for the job; instead, it requires archaeologists to engage critically with the economic, cultural, social, and political trends playing out in both academia and contemporary society. Indeed, such analyses of the social contexts wherein digital tools are used and how the data they produce are curated sit at the heart of Kansa's slow data concept. Thus, by incorporating slow data into this manifesto, perhaps digital archaeology can make its most meaningful contribution to the increasingly contentious debates about the role of neoliberal ideologies in the digital humanities and academia in general (most recently, see Allington *et al.* 2016; *contra* Greenspan 2016).

FROM THE TABLET'S EDGE TO THE DIGITAL ARCHIVE AND BEYOND

This volume's themes move from the practice of archaeology in the trench and the collection of information to the curation and dissemination of data via the digital archive. It concludes with two broader reflective responses.

Part I, *From Trowel to Tablet* (Wallrodt, Ch. 1.1, Ellis, Ch. 1.2, Motz, Ch. 1.3, Gordon *et al.*, Ch. 1.4, Bria and DeTore, Ch. 1.5, Sayre, Ch. 1.6, and Poehler, Ch. 1.7), provides testimonies from a range of field projects working in both the New and Old World that have attempted to implement born-digital workflows via mobile computer data acquisition and manipulation. In particular, this section offers myriad perspectives on digital archaeology that occur on-site at a level barely removed from the archaeological remains themselves and the modern peoples that identify with them. It reveals an emergent discourse on how hardware devices and software apps intersect—often via DIY systems—within the context of on-site workflows to provide new modes of data collection, curation, and analysis that have changed the way archaeologists both practice and learn their discipline. Moreover, the diverse experiences of projects working in different cultural and economic contexts reveals that there are larger social forces at play in terms of social class or pedagogical concerns and that these practical issues can affect how digital devices and skills are used and taught on-site.

Part II, *From Dirt to Drones* (Fee, Ch. 2.1, Olson, Ch. 2.2, Wernke *et al.*, Ch. 2.3, Buxton *et al.*, Ch. 2.4), presents studies dealing with the development of tools beyond the trench, from data recording apps to the manipulation of various 3D imaging and mapping technologies in both terrestrial and marine archaeological landscapes. Because these tools are still used to record archaeological artifacts in situ, these chapters also complement the workflow analyses covered in Part I. At the same time, they shed light on the slow mechanization of archaeological practices. From apps that correct practitioners' errors, to cameras that document artifacts and architecture in granular detail, to aerial drones and marine remotely operated vehicles (ROVs), these devices replace some tasks previously performed by human archaeologists (see also Rabinowitz on "transhuman archaeology," Ch. 5.2). Part II illustrates both how new apps and devices are transforming archaeological practices—and especially analyses—and how these changes might significantly alter how future archaeology is practiced for better or for worse.

Part III, *From Stratigraphy to Systems* (Castro López *et al.*, Ch. 3.1, Sobotkova *et al.*, Ch. 3.2, Dufton, Ch. 3.3, Spigelman *et al.*, Ch. 3.4), reviews the development of more-or-less complete digital systems and workflows from the perspectives of both academic and cultural research management (CRM) projects. In particular, this section presents a forum for archaeologists—several of whom double as digital technologists—to discuss how and why they developed bespoke archaeological systems that can shepherd data from the tablet in the field to a final online repository. In addition, these papers further address the economic and technical debates about whether to create bespoke fully digital recording systems or use the DIY approach highlighted in Part I with off-the-shelf apps and hybrid paperless/paper-based systems and protocols. Lastly, this section offers testimony from Paleowest, a CRM company that explores how the use of new archaeological devices, workflows, and systems are revolutionizing the way private-sector firms practice archaeology in relation to legal strictures, tight budgets, and fixed deadlines.

Part IV, *From a Paper-based Past to a Paperless Future?* (Caraher, Ch. 4.1, Kansa, Ch. 4.2), provides two critical views of the current state of digital archaeology and thoughts on its future. These chapters offer reflexive and cautionary perspectives on how current social and structural pressures affecting 21st-century politics, economics, and institutions of higher learning are contributing to the at times unreflexive and rapid adoption of born-digital fieldwork with questionable results for archaeology. They also touch on the contentious issues of technology's effect on human haptics and the risk of "de-skilling" through increased tool use, as well as on the need for open and accessible modes of online data publication and preservation that are both sustainable and ethical even as neoliberalist social pressures are transforming how such projects are developed.

Finally, Part V, *From Critique to Manifesto* (Kersel, Ch. 5.1, Rabinowitz, Ch. 5.2), provides two invited responses from established archaeologists not directly involved with our workshop. Our first respondent, Morag Kersel, is a field archaeologist who has experimented with some digital technologies, but is not a digital expert (in her own words, she is a self-professed "Luddite outsider" facing a "digital life"). Our second respondent, Adam Rabinowitz, is an engaged digital archaeologist with experience in developing digital workflows at a range of sites. We selected these two archaeologists purposely because they have experienced the rapid transition from paper-based to increasingly paperless workflows over the last five years, and we felt that that they could provide some historical and disciplinary context for what a mobilized and digitized archaeology is doing right and what it could do better or avoid. In prompting their response, we provided few guidelines other than that they engage with the chapters from their own viewpoints. Both respondents have provided erudite and vital observations about how we can and should be mobilizing the past.

Mobilizing the Past

We initially envisioned the "Mobilizing the Past" workshop as a forum for developing a set of best practices and protocols—a manual of sorts—for archaeological projects to use in the adoption of mobile tablets in the field. In retrospect, this proposed outcome was naïve and overly simplistic. In truth, there is a staggering array of practical and theoretical considerations at stake in adopting mobile computing for archaeological data recording. A one-size-fits-all solution for implementing such schemes proved not only impossible, but also undesirable. Instead, the workshop reinforced the close ties between the deployment of mobile computing tools and systems in archaeology and the methods, research goals, and pedagogical priorities of individual projects. Given the many ways that projects are beginning to integrate digital tools, we structured the workshop and its subsequent publication as an opportunity for projects to share their ongoing successes and failures, methods, and practices.

At the same time, workshop participants recognized that we are at a critical time for digital archaeology as it moves from its initial experiments to more established and widely adopted practices. Indeed, given the stimulating ideas and debates raised during "Mobilizing the Past," it seems that the discipline will benefit from continuing such discussions at academic annual meetings and at fora such as Michigan State University's Institute on Digital Archaeology Method & Practice's summer institutes (http://digitalarchaeology. msu.edu) and the Digital Archaeology Commons (http://commons. digitalarchaeology.msu.edu), an online forum, which they describe as "dedicated to supporting work and community building around digital methods and practice in archaeology and closely related fields." Hopefully, such new online spaces will offer digital archaeology practitioners a democratic and open locus to continue this dialogue. For now, however, our hope is that this volume can contribute to such scholarly discourse and perhaps formalize, for a brief moment, conversations that are often informal. As Kersel proclaims (Ch. 5.1), a mantra for all field archaeologists with regard to their data should be "we publish them!" We agree, and thus we offer these fresh and vital dialogues about archaeology freely, digitally, and in a timely fashion via this open-access volume.

ACKNOWLEDGMENTS

We would like to thank the presenters at the "Mobilizing the Past" workshop and the contributors to this volume for coming together in person and in print to engage in lively and insightful discussion on this timely topic. The ideas and perspectives in this introduction could not have been generated without our contributors' revelatory experiments with digital archaeology. We would also like to thank Bill Caraher for his insight and help with this introduction, which, like the volume itself, required a steady editorial hand and a deep understanding of both digital archaeology's successes as well as its challenges. All errors remain our own.

https://mobilizingthepast.mukurtu.net/ collection/00-mobile-computing-archaeology-exploring-and-interpreting-current-practices

http://dc.uwm.edu/arthist_mobilizingthepast/2

REFERENCES

Allington, D., Brouillette, S., and D. Golumbia. 2016. "Neoliberal Tools (and Archives): A Political History of Digital Humanities." *Los Angeles Review of Books*, https://lareviewofbooks.org/article/neoliberal-tools-archives-political-history-digital-humanities/

Berggren, A., N. Deel-Unto, M. Forte, S. Haddow, I. Hodder, J. Issavi, N. Lercari, C. Mazzucato, A. Mickel, and J. S. Taylor. 2015. "Revisiting Reflexive Archaeology at Çatalhöyük: Integrating Digital and 3D Technologies at the Trowel's Edge," *Antiquity* 89: 433–448.

Bevan, A. 2015. "The Data Deluge," *Antiquity* 89: 1473–1484.

Caraher, W. 2013. "Slow Archaeology," *North Dakota Quarterly* 80: 43-52

Caraher, W. 2014. "Toward a Definition of Punk Archaeology," in W. Caraher, K. Kourelis, and A. Reinhard, eds., *Punk Archaeology*. Grand Forks: The Digital Press at the University of North Dakota, 99–103.

Caraher, W. 2015. "Understanding Digital Archaeology." *Archaeology of the Mediterranean World*, https://mediterraneanworld.wordpress.com/2015/07/17/understanding-digital-archaeology/

Counts, D. B., E. W. Averett, and K. Garstki. 2016. "A Fragmented Past: (Re)constructing Antiquity through 3D Artefact Modeling and Customised Structured Light Scanning at Athienou-*Malloura*, Cyprus," *Antiquity* 90: 206–218.

Daly, P., and T. Evans. 2006. "Introduction: Archaeological Theory and Digital Pasts," in T. L. Evans, ed., *Digital Archaeology: Bridging Method and Theory*. New York: Routledge, 3–9.

Dibble, H. L. and S. P. McPherron. 1988. "On the Computerization of Archaeological Projects," *Journal of Field Archaeology* 15: 431–440.

Elliot, T., S. Heath, and J. Muccigrosso. 2012. "Report on the Linked Ancient World Data Institute," *Information Standards Quarterly* 24(2/3): 43–5.

Forte, M. 2010. "Introduction to Cyber-Archaeology," in M. Forte, ed., *Cyber-Archaeology. British Archaeological Reports International Series* 2177. Oxford: Archaeopress, 9–14.

Forte, M. 2015. "Cyber Archaeology: A Post-virtual Perspective," in P. Svensson and D. T. Goldberg, *Between Humanities and the Digital*. Cambridge, MA: The MIT Press, 295–309.

Greenspan, B. 2016. "The Scandal of Digital Humanities." *Hyperbolic*, http://thehyperlab.ca/the-scandal-of-digital-humanities/

Hodder, I. 1985. "Postprocessual Archaeology," in M. B. Schiffer, ed., *Advances in Archaeological Method and Theory* 8. Orlando: Academic Press, 1–26.

Huggett, J. 2004. "Archaeology and the New Technological Fetishism," *Archeologia e Calcolatori* 15: 81–92.

Huggett, J. 2015a. "Challenging Digital Archaeology," *Open Archaeology* 1: 79–85.

Huggett, J. 2015b. "A Manifesto for an Introspective Digital Archaeology," *Open Archaeology* 1: 86–95.

Kuhn, T. S. 1996. *The Structure of Scientific Revolutions*. 3rd edn. Chicago: University of Chicago Press.

Latour, B. 1993. *We Have Never Been Modern*. Trans. C. Porter. Cambridge, MA: Harvard University Press.

Latour, B. and S. Woolgar. 1979. *Laboratory Life. The Social Construction of Scientific Facts*. Sage Library of Social Research 80. Beverly Hills, CA: Sage.

Leighton, M. 2015. "Excavating Methodologies and Labour as Epistemic Concerns in the Practice of Archaeology. Comparing Examples from Britain and Andean Archaeology," *Archaeological Dialogues* 22(1): 65-88.

Levy, T., ed. 2014a. "Cyber-Archaeology." Special issue, *Near Eastern Archaeology* 77(3).

Levy, T. 2014b. "From the Guest Editor," *Near Eastern Archaeology* 77(3): inside cover.

Llobera, M. 2011. "Archaeological Visualization: Towards an Archaeological Information Science (AISc)," *Journal of Archaeological Method and Theory* 18: 193–223.

Morgan, C. 2015. "Punk, DIY, and Anarchy in Archaeological Thought and Practice," *AP: Online Journal in Public Archaeology* 5: 123–46.

Morgan, C., and S. Eve. 2012. "DIY and Digital Archaeology: What Are You Doing to Participate?" *World Archaeology* 44: 521–537.

Morozov, E. 2014. *To Save Everything, Click Here: The Folly of Technological Solutionism*. New York: PublicAffairs.

Nakassis, D. 2013. "Linear B in 3D." *Archaeology of the Mediterranean World*, https://mediterraneanworld.wordpress.com/2013/09/26/linear-b-in-3d/

Nakassis, D. 2015. "Thinking Digital Archaeology." *Aegean Prehistory*, https://englianos.wordpress.com/2015/08/10/thinking-digital-archaeology/

Neal, M. 2013. "Apple Says It Isn't Interested in Your Data: Here's What Apple Does and Doesn't Know about You." *Motherboard*, http://motherboard.vice.com/blog/what-apple-does-and-doesnt-know-about-you

Opitz, R. 2015. "Teaching Practice while Developing Practice: Mobile Computing at the Gabii Project Field School." Paper read at the Mobilizing the Past for a Digital Future: The Potential of Digital Archaeology Workshop, 28 February 2015, Boston.

Pavel, C. 2010. *Describing and Interpreting the Past: European and American Approaches to the Written Record of the Excavation.* Bucharest: University of Bucharest Press.

Perry, S. 2015. "Why Are Heritage Interpreters Voiceless at the Trowel's Edge: A Plea for Reframing the Archaeological Workflow." *Sara Perry: The Archaeological Eye*, https://saraperry.wordpress.com/2015/04/02/why-are-heritage-interpreters-voiceless-at-the-trowels-edge-a-plea-for-reframing-the-archaeological-workflow/

Raw, L. 2009. *The Ridley Scott Encyclopedia.* Lanham: Scarecrow Press.

Renfrew, C., and P. Bahn. 2012. *Archaeology: Theories, Methods, and Practice.* 6th edn. New York: Thames & Hudson.

Richter, A., D. Vanoni, V. Petrovic, S. M. Parish, and F. Kuester. 2013. "Digital Archaeological Landscapes and Replicated Artifacts: Questions of Analytical Phenomenological Authenticity and Ethical Policies in CyberArchaeology," in C. Jianping, Z. Ying, and W. Juan, eds., *Proceedings of the Digital Heritage International Congress (DigitalHeritage) 2: Federating the 19th International VSMM, 10th Eurographics GCH, and 2nd UNESCO Memory of the World Conferences, 28 Oct–1 Nov 2013, Marseille, France.* Piscataway: Institute of Electrical and Electronics Engineers, 569–572.

Roosevelt, C., P. Cobb, E. Moss, B. Olson, and S. Ünlüsoy. 2015. "Excavation is ~~Destruction~~ Digitization: Advances in Archaeological Practice," *Journal of Field Archaeology* 40: 325–346.

Rosenfeld, S. 2014. "4 Ways Google Is Destroying Your Privacy and Collecting Your Data." *Salon*, http://www.salon.com/2014/02/05/4_ways_google_is_destroying_privacy_and_collecting_your_data_partner/

Schollar, L. 1999. "25 Years of Computer Applications in Archaeology," in L. Dingwall, S. Exon, V. Gaffney, S. Laflin, and M.
van Leusen, eds., *Archaeology in the Age of the Internet: CAA 97.
Computer Applications and Quantitative Methods in Archaeology:
Proceedings of the 25th Anniversary Conference, University of Bir-
mingham, April 1997. British Archaeological Reports International
Series 750.* Oxford: Archaeopress, 5–10.

Serrano Araque, M., and A. L. Martínez Carillo. 2014. "El sistema
TooWaste, ver. 0:Tecnologías para la traslación arqueológica de
las historias en la tierra," *Siete Esquinas* 6: 15–16.

Trigger, B. 1989. *A History of Archaeological Thought.* Cambridge:
Cambridge University Press.

Toumazou, M. K., P. N. Kardulias, and D. B. Counts, eds., 2011. *Cross-
roads and Boundaries: The Archaeology of Past and Present in the
Malloura Valley, Cyprus. Annual of the American Schools of Oriental
Research 65.* Boston: American Schools of Oriental Research.

Toumazou, M. K., D. B. Counts, E. W. Averett, J. M. Gordon, and P. N.
Kardulias. 2015. "Shedding Light on the Cypriot Rural Countryside: Investigations of the Athienou Archaeological Project in the
Malloura Valley, Cyprus, 2011–2013," *Journal of Field Archaeology*
40: 204–220.

Wallrodt, J. 2011. "Apples in Archaeology." *Paperless Archaeology,* https://paperlessarchaeology.com/2011/10/08/
apples-in-archaeology/

Watrall, E. 2011. "iAKS: A Web 2.0 Archaeological Knowledge Management System," in E. Kansa, S. Witcher Kansa, and E. Watrall
eds., *Archaeology 2.0: New Approaches to Communication and
Collaboration.* Cotsen Digital Archaeology 1. Los Angeles: Cotsen
Institute of Archaeology, 171–183.

Zubrow, E. B. W. 2006. "Digital Archaeology: A Historical Context,"
in T.L. Evans, ed., *Digital Archaeology: Bridging Method and Theory.*
New York: Routledge, 10–32.

Part 1: From Trowel to Tablet

1.1.
Why Paperless: Technology and Changes in Archaeological Practice, 1996–2016

John Wallrodt

The documentation process for academic field projects is constantly changing. Academics are not bound by the same strict documentation practices of cultural resource management (CRM) firms. The requirements of the host countries in which we work allow a great deal of flexibility. Academic archaeologists (as opposed to CRM archaeologists) are also in a near constant state of experimentation. The various principal investigators (PI) have their own research interests that might propel them to push the envelope in terms of remote sensing, excavation technique, and environmental survey, to offer some examples. Even a single PI can run two consecutive projects of the same type, temporal focus, and geographic region, and adjust their research design, sometimes drastically, between projects.

As an archaeologist who has managed datasets for many short- and long-term field survey and excavation projects in the Mediterranean conducted by the Department of Classics at the University of Cincinnati and other institutions over the last two decades, my task is to take into account the PI's research design and expectations for data recording, the project's resources, the team members' collective technological comfort levels, and the overall project culture, to develop the best documentation methodology possible for the project. There is no single *industrial* approach to academic archaeological documentation processes. Instead, each project has a unique combination of constraints and opportunities tied to research design and resources, such that the documentation process is *crafted* to each individual project.

Over the past two decades I have helped to effect the progress from analog to digital field recording for academic projects. Almost all of these projects have been conducted in locations where there is no electricity on the site, and often without the benefit of even a good cellular connection that would allow data transfer over a network. With the exception of 1.5 days in Pompeii, all of the solutions I have developed have been for offline, battery-only field projects. What follows is a narrative concerning how we went from analog pieces of data to a more integrated digital data model that many field projects—including several discussed in this volume—are pursuing. This is not a review of the *introduction* of new technology into field archaeology, but a review of how field archaeologists have *used* technology. Notably, introduction is not the same as adoption. While my overall approach to archaeological documentation is comprehensive (i.e., each step has a purpose that leads toward better analysis, publication, and archiving), the focus of this review is the use of digital recording by the people actually standing in the dirt.

I focus particularly on the examples of Troy (1988–2002), the Pompeii Archaeological Research Project: Porta Stabia (PARP:PS, 2008–), and the Keos Archaeological Regional Survey (KARS, 2012–). The examination of the use of technology in archaeological fieldwork from multiple perspectives (that of specialists, excavators, and data managers) reveals four stages of adoption: (1) the commoditization of hardware, (2) the early adoption of this hardware by specialists, especially as personal equipment, (3) the increased mass of field data that required purely digital workflows, and then, finally, (4) learning from that experience and applying it to direct digital entry inside the trench during excavation and out in the landscape during survey.

PIECES OF DATA

Archaeologists adopt technology piecemeal. Although early photography was a difficult and costly process, it was adopted almost immediately, long before it became convenient (Harp 1975). The benefits were incalculable, but the resulting photographs were kept in sleeves, albums, or shoeboxes separate from other records. Similarly, although various forms of electronic distance measurements (EDMs) were used early on, the resulting spatial data gathered by surveyors and architects, and the plans that they produced, were separate from the scaled drawings produced in the field. Forms were introduced in the 1970s as a way to standardize the data traditionally recorded in narrative form in notebooks and they quickly increased in number (Pavel 2010: 35). As such, this proliferation of forms—long before the ubiquity of desktop computers—predated their maximum potential. Examining the records of a particular context on paper required an entire table to display the various notebooks, forms, finds analysis pages, plans, contact sheets, photographs, and specialist reports.

In the past decade, the most exciting advances in field recording have mostly to do with these various pieces of technology coming together *to talk to each other*. This shift has been facilitated primarily because all of the information is now in the same state: digital. There are a great number of things that you can do with data once it can talk to other data. Photographs, for instance, can be recorded into a database in such a way that every subject in the photograph can be linked to its associated data, even that of different types. A single image can include objects linked to a finds table, people linked to a people table, and geography tied to stratigraphic units. Moreover, everything we know about a photograph can be exported from that database and installed into the metadata area inside the photograph itself, making the image file a stand-alone document with everything we know about it embedded in the image, and independently searchable (Wall-rodt 2011).

EARLY PAPERLESS SOLUTION AT TROY (1996)

An example of the adoption of digital-born technology can be seen in the Troy excavations, conducted from 1988 to 2002, a critical period for born-digital data as it saw the introduction of portable networks and digital photography. Computing at Troy focused on the metadata from the excavation. Excavators used paper forms in the field, and rather than entering the contents of those forms into a database, they were scanned and distributed as PDF documents (the workflows for each of these is documented on Paperless Archaeology, http://paperlessarchaeology.com). The Troy database recorded only data about the finds, their associated metadata (drawings and photography), and field photography. Those finds, however, required a lot of tracking from place to place and that required many paper forms. The Troy project was chronologically divided into two teams: the Bronze Age (BA) team and the Post Bronze Age (PBA) team.

The workflow for an artifact was as follows: (a) the item was given a field serial number by the excavator; (b) went to the BA registrar for entry into a master database table named "Master Behälter"; (c) was given to the PBA registrar; (d) was sent to conservation; (e) was given a second inventory number and full description by the registrar; (f) was sent to photography; (g) was sent to the government representative; and (h) was then sent either to storage in the on-site depot or in the Çanakkale Museum.

In order to track the artifacts through these eight steps the team used 10 separate forms (picking up at c above):

1 (c): "UC Fundheft Form." Form used to record the existence and the context of an item.

2 (c, h): "Small Finds Tracking Form." A second list for the same finds, but this one is meant to track the item through the conservation, registration, photography, government review, and storage phases.

3 (d): Conservation Logs. A basic logbook for tracking items in and out of conservation.

4 (e): "Inventory Form." A form recording standard inventory information for most small finds in two pages.

5 (e): "Inventoried Lamps Form." (4 pages) A form created to records information for this specific artifact type to prepare for publication.

6 (e): The Green Book. A hard-bound green ledger book with pre-written inventory numbers.

7 (f): "Photoliste." Form used to record black and white negative photos and color slides.

8 (g): "Final Tracking List."9. "Container Tracking Form." Form used for recording post-inventory movement of items.

10. "Inventory Addendum Form." Form used for edits to the existing record.

Most of these forms were handwritten, un-sortable lists of numbers, and each of these lists had to be consulted in order to locate an artifact (see the set of PDF forms titled "Troy PBA Finds Forms 1989–1996," doi:10.7945/C2F30F).

In 1996, when I joined the Troy project eight years after it began, I developed the first paperless workflow for the project, focusing on the small finds. In this new system, when artifacts came to the registrar, the first step was to create a new record in the database. The object's movement through the registration process was then tracked by a series of date stamps in the database, with a paper inventory form printed for inclusion in the files. Changes to the record were entered into the database, but not transferred to the paper forms. By my second season at the site, the entire workflow for the small finds registration was paperless, with the exception of the conservation logs, bringing the forms down from 10 to one.

At the end of the 1996 season, I wrote a lengthy report on my digital work for the project. At the end of the document I wrote a section with the header "Science Fiction":

> As computers become more useful for archaeologists, there will be more ways to use them. With the existing technology, the notebooks in the field can be replaced with hand-held Newton devices with database software. Upon entering the compound, this data can be directly imported into FileMaker Pro and the Tagebücher (including the hand-made drawings and scanned negatives) can be produced 100% electronically. Within a small period of time, and a digitized plan of the site, these finds can be mapped immediately and plans could be automatically updated throughout the season.
>
> Just something to think about.

BETTER WORKFLOWS DERIVED FROM NEW HARDWARE (1996–2000)

The paperless workflow described above was not possible in 1988 when the project started (Dibble and McPherron 1988). The key was the development of an inexpensive portable network, which only became available in the mid-1990s. Although Apple had developed a proprietary network protocol named AppleTalk by 1985, it did not have regular TCP/IP networking support until System 7 Pro (v.7.1.1) in 1993. Similarly, Windows 3.1 did not have TCP/IP networking until 1994 (this was initially available only for Windows for Workgroups; Young 2009; see also Gilbert 1995). Once better networking hardware became affordable, the software had to follow. While FileMaker Pro v.2 had networking in 1994, it was not until 1995 with version 3 that it got both TCP/IP network support and a relational database model. Since the new finds workflows relied upon multiple people accessing the database at the same time, networking was essential to the paperless process.

Beyond inexpensive networking, the first decade of the 21st century brought hardware advances that proved irresistible to field archaeologists: more powerful laptops, wireless networks, and digital cameras. Although laptops of the early 1990s were vastly underpowered compared to their desktop counterparts, they were absolutely necessary. This was especially true for American projects in locations abroad where power was unreliable and the data had to be brought home at the end of each season. By 2000, however, performance and price had improved enough that many academic archaeologists used laptops as their sole computer.

At the same time that laptop adoption became the norm, wireless networks also came into use. Because wired networks required a router that had a limited number of ports, access to the database was limited to computers connected to those ports. Significantly, wireless networking opened up access to databases to anybody on the project with a wireless capable laptop and the database software.

Similarly, many field projects in the 1990s experimented with digital cameras, even though their image quality was not yet good enough to replace film. The use of digital cameras was particularly vital to those working abroad. Film either had to be locally developed or transported back to home for development, and either method increased the chance of data loss. Digital photography was the only way to securely check the quality of the image before resuming fieldwork. Improved digital cameras appeared around 2000, and by 2005 digital photography had become the norm for field projects.

Specialist Uses of Tech

There are three factors that led specialists to increasingly rely on technology for digital documentation and to bring their own equipment with them to field projects: large datasets, early adoption of statistical methods to deal with those datasets, and their itinerant nature.

True to the pattern of the adoption of experimental technology, archaeologists have used computers since the punch card days of the

1960s (Lock 2003: 9). Early uses were highly specialized and were used for discreet data sets rather than for overall project recording (for a good example, see Matheson and Koheler 1989). During the intervening decades, with the rise of processualism, characterized by empirical approaches focused on spatial analysis and environmental archaeology (e.g., Binford and Binford 1968; Clarke 1968), several specialists such as zooarchaeologists, lithic analysts, and ceramics experts adopted data collection standards tied to statistical methodologies developed for their own subjects. For example, the "Knocod" system for animal bone analysis developed by Hans-Peter Uerpmann was used at Troy during the duration of the project (Uerpmann 1978). Similarly, the BA ceramics team used coded forms for collection of statistically useful data from their ceramics (Pernicka *et al.* 2014: 565–573).

Other systems were also being developed. Clive Orton developed his "Pie-slice" analytical software for use with ceramics (Orton and Tyers 1990), but others found it useful for other materials, such as faunal remains (Moreno-Garcia *et al.* 1996). WinBASP started in the 1970s as a statistical package, and it was expanded to meet additional uses including the creation of Harris matrices (Anon. 1977). Although specialists in the 1990s increasingly looked to these digital solutions to handle what could be very large data sets, digitally-recorded data remained highly specialized and were collected in a piecemeal fashion, rather than integrated into larger databases. Moreover, many specialists actively resisted the incorporation of their data into the master data set, for fear that project directors and other archaeologists would misinterpret and misuse the results. Instead, specialists typically submitted season-end reports with summary data.

Similarly, post-excavation specialists also dealt with a different dataset than excavators. Because excavators typically focus on single-site analysis, usually concerning the description of the single unit (trench) in front of them, their data is completed on-site and stays at the site when they leave. Specialists require detailed data from multiple sites and regions in order to assess patterning in their data sets; therefore, they wanted all of their data with them all the time.

Materials specialists' appetites for digital data grew even further during the first decade of the 21st century. It was not until 2009 that Intel coined the term BYOD (bring your own device), but that is exactly the principle that was a catalyst for the acceptance of digital data to the field (Lai 2010). For example, while directors initially resisted digital photography, and therefore used digital cameras in tandem with standard film photography, sometimes for several years, this bias was largely overcome by the project specialists who incorporated digital-born data into their own personal datasets. Ceramicists did not have to wait for official project photography anymore and could take study photos of all of their objects (to their satisfaction) in a single afternoon. Digital cameras were in use at Troy as early as 2000 by ceramicists, and the project started using them for publishable finds photography in the following year. By the middle of the decade the hardware had been so commoditized that most of the specialists would arrive at Troy with their own laptops and digital cameras. They would take study photos of their objects with their cameras and create datasets directly on their computers. When they left the project for the season, they asked for information in digital format: PDFs of things that could be scanned, and read-only copies of the database that they could reference offline. They did not want photocopies of notebooks.

Field projects, in turn, benefitted from this increase in digital creation in concert with their own focus on making the core archaeological data available in database form. As project databases became more common, and the specialists saw a greater return on the integration of their data sets, specialist data started to be incorporated into the master data, and by the end of the decade, it became more common for specialists to surrender their data sets for incorporation into the whole. Not only were the data sets talking to the master field data, they were talking to each other: the data created by the finds specialists and environmental specialists could reference each other directly.

Uses of Tech in the Trench

While post-excavation specialists had been providing digital data for years, this type of born-digital data entry rarely made it into the trench. There was certainly *some* technology in the trench: point and shoot digital cameras had been adopted after specialists began using them (most by 2005), and electronic distance measurement (EDM) machines had been used for decades in the field, often by the excavators themselves (as opposed to a separate team). But the base recording methods had not evolved since the widespread use of forms instead of narrative journal entries in the 1970s. While digital technology became ubiquitous on field projects, excavators in the trenches were still using paper and pen to record their initial observations of finds and stratigraphy.

Paper to digital has been the normal workflow for almost as long as there have been forms. There are many problems with this approach, but the single fatal flaw that affects all paper to digital workflows is the revision process. Data that had been written, then typed, cannot be adequately tracked when revisions are made in either direction. This was evident even in fully paper-based projects, and predates the ubiquitous use of databases for field data. The field forms for Troy, for example, were photocopied and kept in three separate places: Tübingen, Cincinnati, and Troy. If somebody wanted to change an earlier notebook, they had to fill out a piece of paper called the "Change to Tagebücher" form. That form was photocopied and a copy kept in all three places with the original notebook. Each project had their own workaround for this problem, but none was satisfactory.

Paper to digital is also the least efficient use of the trench supervisor's time. The trench supervisor maintains the notebooks, supervises the excavation, directs people where to dig, keeps track of the many numbers created during the project, tracks the number of buckets removed, and decides when to photograph, when to draw, and when to stop digging. The trench supervisor makes the initial stratigraphic interpretation. They write the first story of the trench. This is an often overwhelming amount of work to ask of one person, and it is most often done in the least efficient manner possible: by writing everything down on paper during the day and typing it up during the evening or weekends, thereby doubling their work.

The worst part of the paper to digital workflow is that the trench data took so long to be digitized, often months after the season ended, that errors and emendations crept into the data set. For example: initial descriptive observations can become interpretations, so "chunky, dark, loose fill" can become "interior of drain" when the form is typed into the database. Forms might be typed in but sketches were most often not digitized in any meaningful way in the field, and there was no mechanism for the field drawings to be incorporated into the data set either. The data were not speaking to each other.

Mobile Devices (2010–2015)

Mobile devices were the next big hardware leap that allowed tech to get inside the trench, but mobile devices were problematic. Some field projects had experimented with them, notably Palm devices and field based laptops. The Landscape Research Centre (UK) has been publishing work concerning their digital experiments since 1984, but even in their data flow diagram from 2010 (Powlesland and May 2010: fig. 45) there were lots of devices used: total station, personal digital assistant (PDA), flatbed scanner, digitizing tablet, and laptop. The Athenian Agora excavations also used the Palm platform to talk directly to their total stations. But as Palm changed their hardware and operating system (OS) it became difficult for them to find the hardware that was compatible with their systems (Hartzler 2009: 129) shows screenshots from their Palm Pilot use in 2005, right around the time that Palm stopped making those devices; mention of their difficulties finding hardware is from personal communication). The Agora workflow described in 2009 also required that the information in the Palm be transcribed to the notebook by hand (Hartzler 2009: 132).

Troy Excavations

I mentioned the Newton above, but it was specifically the Newton OS that I wanted to use at Troy. That would have come in the form of the eMate, a device originally marketed toward elementary schools. In 1995, Claris, the parent company that owned FileMaker Pro, announced a version of FileMaker for the Newton OS (for original press release see: http://www.ebyss.net/pages/FMCpr.html). That software already had record-level syncing, and in some ways was more useful than the solution we used in 2010 at Pompeii. Since it was designed for schools, the eMate had the ability to act as a teacher/student system. The teacher would beam (via infrared) the assignment to the students, and they would beam their answers back. In our case we wanted to collect the field data from spreadsheets on the devices and import them into the master database. But the Newton OS and the eMate were both discontinued in 1998.

The Palm OS had better developer support and more software, and while some projects used it to great effect, it suffered from a fatal flaw: all data deleted when the device ran short of power. The only intervening device worth considering was the Microsoft Tablet PC, a full-sized laptop with a touch screen that required a stylus. They were heavy, their batteries lasted only a few hours, and they were incredibly expensive.

While all of these devices were being used on some field projects, their use did not become the norm for any significant segment of archaeological fieldwork. These were devices that projects purchased for use for the duration of the fieldwork, they were not devices that scholars wanted to purchase for themselves and use in their own work.

Pompeii Archaeological Research Project: Porta Stabia

The iPhone was released in 2007, and in 2008 third-party programs were able to run on the device. In 2009 the PARP:PS team experimented with databases running on the iPhone. In 2010, with the introduction of the larger iPad, and Android-based tablets soon after, archaeologists finally had a device that worked all day, had no moving parts to break, did not require a network (although having one would be nice), and had a screen size significant enough to allow direct digital entry for any field-related task. These were the devices that scholars brought into the field themselves in true BYOD fashion. In the first nine months of sale, Apple sold 15 million iPads; more, they claimed, than every Tablet PC ever sold (from 2000–2011; see https://www.youtube.com/watch?v=TGxEQhdi1AQ at the 5:30 mark).

In 2010–2012 at PARP:PS we used iPads to enter and edit records in the database (first FM Touch and then FileMaker Go), draw scaled plans and profiles (with iDraw, then TouchDraw), keep a free-form notebook (Pages), and keep Harris matrices (OmniGraffle) up to date (the workflows for each of these is documented on *Paperless Archaeology*, http://paperlessarchaeology.com). As a result, we had our first fully digital archive of the project.

At first the data were still in pieces. They were in proxy apps: digital equivalent of their paper counterparts. There is value in the ease of use and accuracy of the proxy apps over paper, but they were still in digital pieces. The database recorded that there was a plan, but didn't actually link to it. The Harris matrices were portable, but they did not communicate with the database.

In subsequent years we learned to make the field drawings talk to the larger computer-aided design (CAD) workflow. By using CAD output as the background for all field drawings, and keeping the scale of the drawings at 1:1 (the software TouchDraw allowed infinite zoom, which meant that we could draw at full scale, which removed an entire mental process from the activity: no more mentally scaling all measurements), we were able to feed the field drawings directly back to the CAD operator, sometimes on the same day, so that we could address any areas of the drawings that were difficult to interpret (Tucker and Wallrodt 2013).

What was important is that there was finally a way to get direct observation from the trench in a digital format. The traditional workflow of paper to digital no longer applied and we opened up the field data to immediate review by the rest of the team. With immediate access to the form data, the data managers and other members of the project became immediate editors. The spatial team caught errors or inconsistencies in drawings that were immediately fed back to the field team and created a process for revisions. Similarly, the ceramics team received daily matrix information that helped them to better understand the stratigraphy and therefore better process the ceramics. More importantly, units could be tagged as "high priority," thereby allowing the post-excavation specialists to readjust their priorities.

There is no standard metric for the success of a new recording process for an archaeological project. Clearly the most important is that it satisfies the research design and can answer the questions that the PI puts to the data. As mentioned above, that is a different requirement for different projects. PARP:PS is a complex project with many voices contributing to the story of the site. Key to getting that story is the timeliness of data retrieval: What volume of dirt was brought out of these units? Which units were "sealed" contexts? How large is this feature? Is this type of feature related to these kinds of charcoal, fauna, pottery? Where is everything from this context stored? In previous years at PARP:PS these questions were time consuming to answer. In later years, there were very quickly determined. More dirt may have been moved during the paperless years at PARP:PS (see Ellis, Ch. 1.2), but that was an unexpected benefit. The main benefit is the speed at which anybody could receive answers from the data set (Wallrodt et al. 2015).

Keos Archaeological Regional Survey Project

This improvement in the efficiency of data retrieval was also obvious to the Project Directors at the Keos Archaeological Regional Survey (KARS) project on the island of Keos, which began in 2012. Survey teams carried iPads pre-loaded with georeferenced satellite photography (the imagery was from 2005) in a geographical information system (GIS) application. Since the iPads had GPS built in, the team leader knew their exact position and drew the tract polygon directly on the GIS (there have been several web articles written about the accuracy of consumer level GPS devices, including the iPad, and most sources have put the accuracy at within 2 m; see Hodel 2013). In previous paper-based survey projects there was often some indecision concerning the exact location of the team in relation to rough paths, temporary waterways, and electrical lines that seemed to change with surprising rapidity. Measurements and angles of movement were often inconsistently applied. Many pencil lines were erased and redrawn. The tablet technique at KARS not only allowed the teams place themselves on the correct side of these cartographical features, but they could verify their location by counting the rows of olive trees. With a swipe to their database app, they immediately added the same data that they would normally put into their notebooks. Photographs taken by the iPads were automatically geotagged. The rough GIS plans were downloaded daily, were properly snapped in the master GIS documents, and were then re-loaded into the tablets before the next day's fieldwork. The database entries were synced to the master database each day, and any records concerning the finds that were brought back to the dig house could be attached to those records immediately.

Conclusions

When archaeological data are unbound from their analog predecessors, they no longer exist as discrete pieces. In digital form, through data connections and transfers, we move away from multiple pieces of disconnected individual observations and toward a singular dataset. Although form data are held in databases, they can be exported for visualization in spreadsheets or other specialized software. Both CAD and GIS are separate applications for similar data, and the data is easily shared between the two. With the exception of 3D data, which is beyond the scope of this essay, any data can be printed.

Techniques of paperless data collection are still very new, and they are constantly evolving. Recalling the early adopters of field computer use, we might look to what specialists are doing. For example, voice data entry and skip logic on touch screens shows great promise for those who have to enter coded data for large data sets (Austin 2014). While custom software has been in use within archaeology for as long as there have been computers, complete desktop archaeological programs such as Intrasis are not the norm (http://www.intrasis.com/index.htm). For the majority of academic field projects, desktop and laptop computer use focuses on customized uses of commercially available software, rather than custom-developed software. The two largest database programs, Microsoft Access (Windows only) and FileMaker Pro (Windows and Mac) are middleware development platforms that allow custom solutions to be built. This is the closest that many projects come to custom software. Using off-the-shelf software solutions is the lowest barrier for entry for a new field project.

Similarly, the best archaeological uses of mobile platforms that I have seen follow this same pattern, relying primarily on off-the-shelf software, although the names of these programs might be less familiar (TouchDraw, iGIS). As a rule, they are intentionally chosen based on their ability to output data in the format needed to connect to other platforms. For example, at PARP:PS, we used TouchDraw, which can output to SVG, as an intermediary step for integration of field drawings into the CAD environment. TouchDraw can also output to PDF format for long-term archival storage. Another example comes from the KARS survey, for which iGIS was selected for use because it writes to what has become a standard spatial file format, .shp.

From the beginning of mobile field recording at PARP:PS, we focused on making sure the output of the software was usable. Although some newer notebook applications with more features than a straight word processor were available, we did not use these because they could not output the file in a reusable format. Similarly, the vector drawing applications we selected had to be able to export cleanly to other file formats while preserving their layer structure. Rather than using a standard Harris matrix program at PARP:PS, we relied on OmniGraffle because it allows export as a vector-editable PDF, even though it stores items in its own file format.

While custom-developed software is likely to increase, these solutions are not without obstacles. The two biggest roadblocks we face in the application of custom-made desktop or mobile software are (1) operating platform differences, and (2) software maintenance needs, both of which are tied to constantly evolving hardware. While it is conceivably easy to target a single platform for data collection for a single field season, one must also consider not only the diversity of devices used by various team members—such as specialists, who want to be able to work with data on their own platforms and take it with them—but also challenges of multi-year projects and long-term project needs. With the rapidly changing pace of advances in hardware and operating system in the mobile space, it is not possible to be certain that specific software will be able to function in even three years. In the past decade, we have already confronted this problem with the change from 32 to 64 bit architecture in desktops and the difficulty of Android devices to upgrade to later operating systems. For example, because WinBASP did not make the change to 64 bit architecture, it was abandoned. Hardware component makers will not stop innovating, and this necessitates changes in operating systems and changes to the application programming interfaces (APIs) that software relies upon.

All of these considerations—custom designed versus commercially available software, cross-platform capability, usability, output, and data integration—are all carefully considered parts of the overall data collection and retention scheme developed by the projects's data architect. Because the data management scheme is tailored to the research design and the technical acumen of the team members, the use of mobile devices to create digital born data is a decision that each project should make for themselves. It is the newest tool in the archaeologists' kit and one of the most exciting new tools introduced in the past two decades that has allowed us to rethink the best practices that we use to record and interpret the past.

Acknowledgments

This essay should be seen as a companion to my 2015 keynote talk of a similar name at the "Mobilizing the Past" workshop held in Boston in February 2015. I would like to thank the organizers of the workshop for inviting me to participate, and especially Jody Gordon for talking through ideas for this paper. I would also like to thank the reviewers for their comments.

https://mobilizingthepast.mukurtu.net/collection/11-why-paperless-technology-and-changes-archaeological-practice-1996-2016

http://dc.uwm.edu/arthist_mobilizingthepast/3

References

Anon. 1977. "History of BASP." http://www.uni-koeln.de/~al001/basp5.html.

Austin, A. 2014. "Mobilizing Archaeologists: Increasing the Quantity and Quality of Data Collected in the Field with Mobile Technology," *Advances in Archaeological Practice: A Journal of the Society for American Archaeology* 2, 13–23. doi:10.7183/2326–3768.2.1.13

Binford S. R. and L. R. Binford. 1968. *New Perspectives in Archeology.* Chicago: Aldine Publishing Company.

Clarke, D. L. 1968. *Analytical Archaeology.* London: Methuen.

Dibble, H., and S. P. McPherron. 1988. "The Use of Computers in Archaeological Projects," *Journal of Field Archaeology* 15: 431–440.

Gilbert, H. 1995. "Adding MS TCP/IP to Windows for Workgroups 3.11." http://www.yale.edu/pclt/WINWORLD/WFWG311.HTM

Harp, E., ed. 1975. *Photography in Archaeological Research. School of American Research Advanced Seminar Series.* Albuquerque: University of New Mexico Press.

Hartzler, B. 2009. "Applying New Technologies," in J. M. Camp and C. A. Mauzy, eds., *The Athenian Agora: New Perspectives on an Ancient Site.* Mainz am Rhein: Verlag Philipp von Zabern, 128–137.

Hodel, J. 2013. "So What's My Accuracy??? Mobile Device GPS with iPad, iPhone, & Android." http://www.cloudpointgeo.com/blog/blog/2013/4/26/so-whats-my-accuracy-mobile-device-gps-with-ipad-iphone-android

Lai, E. 2010. "The Year of 'Bring Your Own Computer' to Work." *ZDNet*, http://www.zdnet.com/article/the-year-of-bring-your-own-computer-to-work/

Lock, G. R. 2003. *Using Computers in Archaeology: Towards Virtual Pasts*. New York: Routledge.

Matheson, P. M. W., and C. G. Koehler. 1989. "AMPHORAS: A Database on Ancient Wine Jars." http://projects.chass.utoronto.ca/amphoras/allc89.htm

Moreno-Garcia, M., C. Orton, and J. Rackham. 1996. "A New Statistical Tool for Comparing Animal Bone Assemblages," *Journal of Archaeological Science* 23: 437–453. doi:10.1006/jasc.1996.0039

Orton, C., and P. A. Tyers. 1990. "Statistical Analysis of Ceramic Assemblages," *Archaeologia e Calcolatori* 1: 81–110.

Pavel, C. 2010. *Describing and Interpreting the Past: European and American Approaches to the Written Record of the Excavation*. Bucharest: Editura Universitatii din Bucuresti.

Pernicka, E., C. B. Rose, and P. Jablonka, eds. 2014. *Troia 1987–2012: Grabungen und Forschungen. Studia Troica Monographien 5*. Bonn: Habelt.

Powlesland, D., and K. May. 2010. "DigIT: Archaeological Summary Report and Experiments in Digital Recording in the Field." *Internet Archaeology* 27, http://dx.doi.org/10.11141/ia.27.2

Tucker, G., and J. Wallrodt. 2013. "CSA Newsletter: Rethinking CAD Data Structures—Pompeii Archaeological Research Project: Porta Stabia." *The CSA Newsletter: Published by the Center for the Study of Architecture*, http://csanet.org/newsletter/spring13/nls1302.html

Uerpmann, H. P. 1978. "The 'Knocod' System for Processing Data on Animal Bones from Archaeological Sites," *Bulletin of the Peabody Museum of Archaeology and Ethnology* 2: 149–167.

Wallrodt, J. 2011. "Image Handling at PARP:PS." *Paperless Archaeology*, https://paperlessarchaeology.com/2011/02/22/image-handling-at-parpps/

Wallrodt, J., K. Dicus, L. Lieberman, and G. Tucker. 2015. "Beyond Tablet Computers as a Tool for Data Collection: Three Seasons of Processing and Curating Digital Data in a Paperless World," in A.

Traviglia, ed., *Across Space and Time: Papers from the 41st Conference on Computer Applications and Quantitative Methods in Archaeology, Perth, 25–28 March 2013*. Amsterdam: Amsterdam University Press.

Young, W. 2009. "Winsock Programmer's FAQ: The History of Winsock." http://tangentsoft.net/wskfaq/articles/history.html

1.2.
Are We Ready for New (Digital) Ways to Record Archaeological Fieldwork? A Case Study from Pompeii

Steven J. R. Ellis

One of the more fundamental developments in archaeological field-work in recent years, and arguably much longer still, has been the introduction of the tablet computer. No other fieldwork tool, or even methodological approach, can be shown to have as many uses, with so much impact, across so many of our current fieldwork recording practices. Yet while I initially described the impact of the tablet as "revolutionizing" archaeological fieldwork, now six summers worth of fieldwork experience has given me some cause to question the impact of tablet computing across the broader discipline (see, esp., Apple Inc. 2010 for the coverage of our research that was profiled on the Apple.com website for much of 2010). To be clear, I stand by the claim that tablets like the iPad will ultimately be seen as having *eventually* revolutionized the ways we record our archaeological fieldwork. The question is, however: why is it taking so long? Systemic revolutions are normally known for their rapidity as much as for their ubiquity.

If tablet computing can be seen as transforming the ways we record archaeological fieldwork, then its impact will have to be measured through the lens of hindsight by those in a generation or two or more. One aim of this chapter is to provide the future student, inter-ested in (the history of) archaeological methodologies, a sense of the disciplinary reception of tablet computers in the recording of archae-ological fieldwork (said student would do well to read the thoughts on this "paradigm shift" in Roosevelt *et al.* 2015, esp. 339–340; see also Biddle's observations of systemic change, of almost half a century ago, in Biddle and Kjolbye-Biddle 1969). For while there may be an inevitable sense that computers should be used in undertaking and

Figure 1: Plan of the PARP:PS excavation site with locations of trenches.

Figure 2: General view of the PARP:PS excavation site.

advancing archaeological research, there is still considerable consternation for change in the way we do our fieldwork.

My experience over the *longue durée* (of barely six field seasons . . .) of using the iPad to record archaeological fieldwork is fairly extensive, covering a handful of projects under my direction and co-direction that can be summarized as follows:

1. *Archaeological excavations*. A large ("big dig") excavation of two Pompeian insulae and their surrounds (FIGS. 1, 2) as part of the Pompeii Archaeological Research Project: Porta Stabia (PARP:PS), which is based at the University of Cincinnati and the American Academy in Rome (for select publications, see Ellis 2011; Ellis *et al.* 2011, 2012, 2015; Ellis in press a; for a more complete bibliography, see http://classics.uc.edu/pompeii/). The comprehensiveness of the PARP:PS team's approach to urban excavations, as well as the scale of the site itself—some 600 years of the social and (infra-) structural making of an urban neighborhood covering around 4,500m², including 10 building plots with 20 shop-fronts, as well as infrastructure from fountains to fortifications and from main streets to one of the city's busiest gates—amounted to a massive and complicated digital recording strategy and dataset. Our use of the iPad covered excavation and post-excavation seasons; the project's earliest years pre-dated the iPad.

2. *Architectural surveys*. A survey of the standing remains of one of the largest structures in Pompeii, the Quadriporticus. The Pompeii Quadriporticus Project (PQP), which I co-direct with Eric Poehler, is based at University of Massachusetts Amherst and the University of Cincinnati (see Poehler and Ellis 2011, 2012, 2013, 2014; Poehler, Ch. 1.7). Our four fieldwork seasons were all undertaken with the iPad.

3. *Archival and legacy data studies*. A legacy data project, including architectural survey, of the Panhellenic sanctuary at Isthmia, Greece (see Ellis *et al.* 2008; Ellis and Poehler 2015).

4. *Urban field surveys*. A study of the retail landscapes of more than 100 Roman cities throughout the Mediterranean (Ellis in press b).

Pompeii and the iPad

Before offering something of a very brief overview of my experience with tablets in archaeological field recording, some points of clarification are necessary. The first is that the remainder of this chapter will draw mostly from my experience of using iPads at our Pompeii excavations. The second clarification is that our team's use of these tablets was as a *field device*. This may seem obvious, but it is a point that I have often had to clarify to (conference) rooms full of archaeologists, some of whom have wondered, and often-enough assumed, that we had used the iPad to replace all forms of digital technology from site cameras to office computers. Rather, we use them *mostly* in the field to replace paper notebooks, paper forms, and mylar paper; only rarely did they supplement computers in the field office or library. A third and broader point of clarification—one that is lost to many of the current debates about "going digital"—is the fact that *all* archaeological "projects" are essentially digital projects; I think it is necessary here to define an archaeological "project" *only* as research that is being systematically published. Unless we are to submit photo- or carbonized-copies of our paper-based records (numbering as they are in the hundreds and thousands) to archival holdings and university libraries or elsewhere, taking all of those data and observations or ideas from the trench, site, or field to publication requires passing it through some kind of digital filter. As blindingly obvious as that point may be, it has some resonance for some of the following discussions. To my mind, that digital filter works best—not just for efficiency of data recording, but for the quality and quantity of information that comes from the essentially close relationship between digital recording and engagement with the material—when it is fitted to the site itself.

The final point of clarification is that the overview that follows is aimed at (or perhaps limited to) what are, to me, the more interesting and deeply entrenched aspects of the use of tablets in archaeological fieldwork. It is thus not about the types of apps we have used or an assessment of how we used them. Besides, for the past three seasons we have conducted so-called study seasons with no excavations, and thus—for the most part—have had a somewhat limited need for tablets as field devices. During this time, which is about half the life of the iPad itself, practically every app we had ever used during the excavations has since been significantly updated, while countless others have appeared that we have yet to use. Even the hardware of the iPad has changed significantly enough from the versions we used for the first three fieldwork seasons; it is now possible to use them to take (at least) decent photos, for example, and to do respectable photogrammetry. Even with these issues aside, much better articles than the one I could write—or rather, could want to write—have focused on the more detailed utility of apps, iPad hardware, and, more interestingly, on calculating the ways in which tablets have improved the efficiency, clarity, volume, and value of field data (from among several, see Fee, Ch. 2.1; Motz, Ch. 1.3; Poehler, Ch. 1.7; Wallrodt, Ch. 1.1; see also, esp., Berggren *et al.* 2015; Roosevelt *et al.* 2015, as well as Poehler and Ellis 2012, 2013, 2014; Fee *et al.* 2013; Austin 2014).

What is worthwhile to point out is that our results and experiences are rather similar, or at least familiar, to those who have actually used tablets in recording field research. The impact of our use of the iPad on our project can be (overly-)summarized as having brought:

1. Faster and more efficient data capture. This data was also cleaner and more accurate than we had ever collected on paper. For example, of the hundreds of thousands of words and numbers recorded on the iPad, not a single one proved illegible. The simplest measure of a spellcheck, for example, ensured that most words were correct, and the occasional process of respelling a word often prompted some necessary review of the syntax of the sentence just written. Data and word searches were especially helpful for recalling various details. More information was recorded for every structure, trench, and context, whether in tabular form or as written descriptions, than had been achieved with pen and paper. Moreover, that (extra) information, from simple descriptions to more thoughtful observations and analyses, was typically of a richer quality (some thoughts on gauging "quality" in field recording are given below).
2. More dynamic data. The entering of more types of data improved our engagement with the material during the recording process, as well as (immediately) fueling a series of otherwise less obvious questions of the metadata behind the more overt datasets and questions.
3. More secure data. All of our field data was regularly backed up through the course of a day, and in multiple places. Whereas our earlier paper-based systems saw our documents and forms

being backed up by scans and photocopies, the more immediate system of backing up our digital data to several devices and servers provided an arguably more stable system of data storage and security. Certainly the newfound simplicity and speed with which our data could be backed up meant that it was done more often than could ever have been feasible in our earlier paper-based system.

4. Better on-site access to the data, and to so much more information besides. Even without access to the Internet, there is an extraordinary amount of data that can be pulled up to benefit the field observations and analyses (see, esp., Poehler and Ellis 2014). The ability to draw on such a wealth of data while still in the field is of enormous analytical benefit to the ongoing research and recording.

The iPad thus radically transformed the ways in which we recorded, and engaged with, the excavation of a large urban site. Many of these improvements from using tablet computers instead of pieces of paper were to be expected, but other advantages were not as readily anticipated. For example, the ability to access live data—whether from trench to trench, or between the various teams of excavators or bio-archaeologists or conservators—caused a heightened engagement between the different cogs of the team network, creating something of an "interdisciplinary" communication that was more active and fruitful than our experience from the pre-iPad years of the project (on the approaches to improving the communication of various subgroups across large fieldwork teams, see Berggren *et al.* 2015: 436, 446). Another striking advantage relates to the non-technical and simple (but not *simplified*) utility of so many of the apps. Almost all of the apps we used had familiar interfaces: for example, we used File-Maker for our databases, Pages for our word-processing, and iDraw and TouchDraw for our vector-based drawing. With genuine respect to those who have spent some years toward developing custom-built, stand-alone apps that can handle a host of archaeological field recording practices, our experience has been one of contentment with the range of commercial apps chosen. This was in part a product of necessity. Given our adoption of the iPad immediately upon its release in 2010, our fleet of apps were those "off-the-shelf" and immediately available (credit here should be given to John Wallrodt of the University of Cincinnati, who tirelessly tested and developed our paperless system so that we were in the field with a fully-operational paperless system just two months after the release of the iPad; see Wallrodt, Ch. 1.1). But with the proven effectiveness of those apps, their minimal cost (constituting a tiny fraction of 1% of the project budget), stability and available technical support (and ongoing updates), and not least the fact that the vast majority of field data for all archaeological projects is really rather simple and easily handled by such apps, what was once a necessity—the off-the-shelf app—has since become something of a philosophy.

Naturally, some more difficult aspects were encountered along the way to recording digitally in the field, even if their currency or impact on the project has been close to minuscule by comparison to the number and scale of the benefits of going digital. The most significant of these has been the integration of all parts—or rather, people—of the project; it is one thing to convert a paper-based project to a paperless system, but it is another to convert *all* of the project's team members to that system (for some of the challenges of integrating digital systems into established fieldwork projects, but from a pre-iPad perspective, see Fisher *et al.* 2010). It is a common practice for "specialists" on archaeological projects, for example, to bring with them their own rather idiosyncratic systems, honed over decades and on multiple types of projects, to record their data. A good many of the specialists on the Pompeii excavations maintained these time-honored, paper-based recording systems. Naturally that data made its way into our system using more traditional, and achingly time-consuming, methods of data-entry, and the time spent doing that was a reminder of how such resources of a project can be better spent. The integration of paper-based records into a digital system also exposed just how limited the range and potential utility of "traditional" data can be. In part, this experience also served as a reminder that the use of tablets leads toward, and promotes, more of a centralized and integrated system for data structure that is beneficial for everything from data-security to site-wide and multivariate analyses to the management of productivity and publication goals.

DIGITAL RECORDING IN ARCHAEOLOGICAL FIELDWORK

Our experience in converting a paper-based project to a paperless one has thus been overwhelmingly positive. As much seems true for the several other archaeological projects that have since adopted tablets in their field recording strategies (see, e.g., Austin 2014; Roosevelt *et al.* 2015). But for all the ways in which tablet computers have revolutionized the recording process of so many archaeological projects, the reception of tablets in field archaeology has been strikingly pessimistic and polarizing. It is especially the sharply negative reception of the tablet that I currently find to be of more interest than the continued detailing and explication of their value and utility, especially as much of the reaction speaks to a romanticization of 20th-century fieldwork methodologies married to a broader disciplinary consternation for change in the way we do things. So while an integrated digital data system—from site to analysis to publication and archive—can be described as the "Holy Grail" (May and Crossby 2010: 49), it still is questioned whether it could—or rather, *should*—be possible to convert the "complexities" of the archaeological recording process from tried and tested blank pieces of paper and forms to a computerized system. To be clear, the remainder of what I have to say about the negative, or at least pessimistic, reactions to tablets in archaeology is drawn more from "front-line" experience than from what I can learn via peer-reviewed publications. And this scenario can only in part be pinned on the fact that the topic—if for tablets more so than digital devices per se—is still relatively new; even so, Christopher Roosevelt and his colleagues have now shown us that a comprehensive treatment of the topic can be made in a relatively brief period (Roosevelt *et al.* 2015).

Part of the aim of my contribution to this volume is to gauge something of the disciplinary-wide reception to tablets in the recording of archaeological fieldwork. Many will agree that this is a watershed moment in our approach to archaeological fieldwork. And many will also agree that much valuable information about the immediate reception of such paradigm shifts can be too easily lost, forgotten over time unless accounts like (but also against) this one are presented; similarly, it was through people like Martin Biddle and Birthe Kjolbye-Biddle that we now have, for just one example, a contemporary voice on the rapid and fundamental reorganization of archaeological fieldwork under the metric system (Biddle and Kjolbye-Biddle 1969; for related developments under the Winchester Research Unit, see most recently Leighton 2015: 74). To wait for a more steady stream of (potentially revisionist?) publications on our matter at hand is to risk losing the sense of how these digital developments were played out at precisely the time of their advent. Especially important is the fact that the lack of peer-reviewed publications on the reception of tablets in archaeology currently belies the views of a rather sizable demographic in field archaeology who are otherwise considerably vocal—whether in classrooms or conference halls, on-site or online—about their distrust of digital devices in the recording of archaeological fieldwork, and (so) of the data and knowledge these approaches produce.

To return to those arguments for the continued use of paper over computer, a good number of them have explored the limits of logic, with complaints that range from the naive to the more measured and constructive. Those at the former end hardly warrant reaction. A strange but common question, for example, is how a tablet could possibly operate in the rain—a question as easily applicable to a piece of paper as a tablet—to how secure the digital data might be should a giant magnet fall from the sky. This represents something similar of the concerns for how digital tools might—or rather, will not—stand up to the rigors of archaeological fieldwork that were encountered in the responses of archaeologists to digital pens (collected in Fisher *et al.* 2010, esp. 5–6). That loose-leaf paper and pencil may be the preferred medium for recording in the midst of a rainstorm, or during some apocalyptic magnet attack, demonstrates just how far we can often be from a reasoned discussion of emerging field methodologies. Even so, no small amount of time has been lost in allaying these concerns, whether in the field, at archaeological conferences, or, perhaps ironically, through debates conducted in (no-longer-live) online blog entries.

Especially common are the concerns for the (immediate and ongoing) security of digital data; this is of course a concern that is as valid for digital data as it should be for paper-based data. Given our collective experience, this is of little wonder: it might be impossible to find a practicing archaeologist of any generation who has not experienced some traumatic loss of digital data, particularly prior to the most recent advances in cloud-based server technologies. From an inability to open, or even find, old digital files, to the misplacing or physical breakage of floppy disks, Zip disks, and thumb-drives, the threat of losing digital data challenges our confidence in converting to a fully digital system. And while it has been pointed out to me that a paper notepad might survive the fall from a 4th-story window better than an iPad (for which I have some personal experience), it remains harder to scrunch up or tear apart a tablet like it is a piece of paper. But our collective experiences of data loss are for the most part generational, and arguably amateur. More than tablets, it is the related advent of cloud-based storage that should remind us of the anachronistic nature of our memory for lost data. While an iPad can be misplaced or break (not quite) as easily as a paper notepad or floppy disk, the fact that its data can have already, and immediately, been synchronized to any number of devices and servers should drastically minimize most fears of data loss. Of course our (inevitable) inability to lose digital data does not solve what should be the principal, omni-present concern: data curation. Just as it is not enough to simply *have* hard-copy datasets—they require ongoing organization and physical maintenance—so too are digital datasets demanding of constant curatorial care. This is an important topic for which more discussion, and a different and more developed paper than this one, is essential (see Eiteljorg 2011).

SLOW ARCHAEOLOGY:
DE-SKILLING AND (OR IN?) THE "GOLDEN AGE"

From among the range of concerns for digital field recording are a number of more thought-provoking issues that are worthy, and sometimes demanding, of response. Several of these fall under the notion that field recording with tablets threatens the once careful and considered field methodologies of the past (see, e.g., Caraher, Ch. 4.1; see also Caraher 2013; and, in support, Nakassis 2015). The most convincing among the proponents of this threat is Bill Caraher, who has championed the intellectual value of a "slow archaeology," a kind of archaeological philosophy that urges more caution about the speed and growing industrialization of our fieldwork processes, a good many of which are (in)arguably associated with the shift from analog to digital recording tools (Caraher 2013; Ch. 4.1). More specifically, these concerns for digital field recording are about a "de-skilling" (after Caraher) of archaeological method, as well as a worry that the efficiency brought about by digital field recording leads mostly—or rather, merely—to the collection/creation of more and more data. Especially interesting is the idea that the use of a tablet to complete forms, construct narratives, and draw archaeological objects and their stratified relationships leads to a lack of engagement with the subject matter and thus ultimately risks a de-skilling of our otherwise craft-like archaeological fieldwork methodologies. To the (well-intentioned) provocation that those of us using technology to record our fieldwork are becoming "de-skilled," at least by comparison to those who record on paper, I might, in keeping with the spirit of Caraher, tease with another: if it is not simply an assumption, where is the weight of evidence that our broader discipline was ever very *skilled* at field recording in the first place?

As hubristic as it may seem to some archaeological circles to question our broader disciplinary skill set, the reality is that for the vast majority of data that survive from (too few) academic archaeological projects over the past century or so, the bulk of it was not skillfully crafted by the deft hands of the archaeological doyens who led these projects, but was cobbled together by their inexperienced students or (rarely much better) their apprenticing supervisors (see Leighton 2015 on how the structure of archaeological teams can vary so markedly across contemporary cultures and the impact this has on the methodologies and outcomes). The evidence lays in the legacy data, which too often constitutes the *only*—skilled or otherwise—record of field research and the corresponding intellectual understanding of a site. And it is here that any challenging of the archaeological skill sets of those who record with iPads, or of those who generated the legacy datasets from paper, requires some necessary clarification. Are we targeting the quality of the fieldwork and its "knowledge production," and thus, unfortunately, the archaeological acumen of the individual or of the team? Or are our critiques directed at *only* the quality of the recording? There is, of course, a complex interconnection between doing archaeological fieldwork and recording archaeological fieldwork. It is often the same thing, and yet sometimes not. But for as long as the data and archives and (more rarely the) publications are all that survive of the fieldwork and ideas and (more commonly the) destruction, then these datasets represent the skilled and unskilled fieldwork methodologies and results in their *entirety*.

To stage our understanding of recorded fieldwork, therefore, on the notebooks of named scholars—whether Carl Blegen, Frank Brown, Flinders Petrie, or Alfred Morley—is to deny that the vast majority of fieldwork data survives instead from the hands of relatively inexperienced students (on the history of diary entries in archaeology, see Mickel 2015, 301–302; see also Kidder 1959; Hodder 1989; Pavel 2010; on inexperience in archaeological teams, see Leighton 2015).

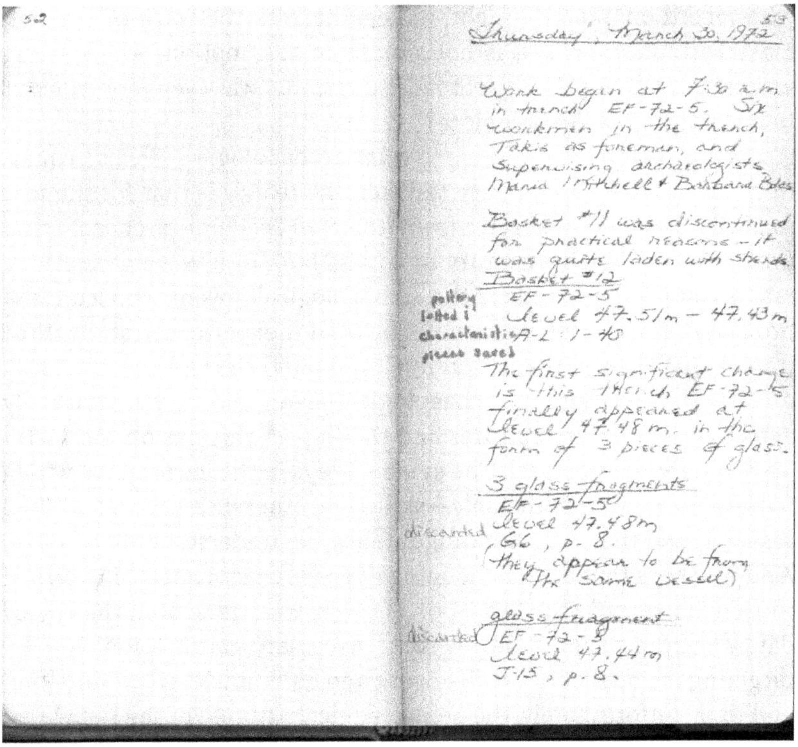
52

53
Thursday, March 30, 1972

Work begun at 7:30 a.m. in trench EF-72-5. Six workmen in the trench, Takis as foreman, and supervising archaeologists Maria Mitchell + Barbara Boles

Basket #11 was discontinued for practical reasons – it was quite laden with sherds.

Basket #12
EF-72-5
Level 47.51m – 47.43m
A-L: 1-48
pottery sorted; characteristic pieces saved

The first significant change in this trench EF-72-5 finally appeared at level 47.48 m. in the form of 3 pieces of glass.

3 glass fragments
EF-72-5
Level 47.48m
G6, p. 8.
discarded
(they appear to be from the same vessel)

glass fragment
EF-72-5
Level 47.44m
J-15, p. 8.
discarded

Figure 3: A fairly typical daily entry from the Isthmia excavation notebooks; here we learn that a context was closed because it contained so many artifacts, while another context is identified by a "significant change" because it contained three pieces of glass (Pages 52–53 of Isthmia Notebook 1972-MM-BB-I).

Almost all of the recorded fieldwork for the American excavations at the Panhellenic sanctuary at Isthmia, for example, was not crafted by Oscar Broneer or Paul Clement, but scribbled down by well-intentioned novices (FIG. 3; see Ellis *et al.* 2008; Ellis and Poehler 2015; on the question of "trust" in the production of field records, see Leighton 2015: esp. 75–77). For my own legacy data project at that site, barely 10% of the recorded, stratified contexts from the 1970s excavations can be reassembled to form an approximated matrix; these records, however, come from a period in our discipline that should otherwise (or arguably) be seen as foundational to our understanding of taphonomy, site formation processes, and the recording of stratified sequences (Schiffer 1972, 1987; Harris 1975; see also Biddle and Kjolbye-Biddle 1969). Even the briefest of surveys of legacy data for so many 20th-century excavations, even if too rarely available, shows that our experience at Isthmia is hardly unique (see, e.g., Bibby 1993: 110; see also Mickel 2015: 301). It is rare to happen upon a legacy data project that reports skillfully crafted, paper-based datasets (Allison 2008). I want to be careful here to avoid the slippery slope toward unfairly deriding the archaeological acumen of past generations (see, e.g., Matskevich's 2011 review of Pavel 2010). Exceptions exist, albeit arguably, for expertly excavated sites with *all* attendant parts: accompanying and suitably skilled notebooks, datasets, and, by definition, resultant publications and well-maintained archives. But these are surely too few to reconcile any such notion that dependable skill sets once defined the paper-based recording of archaeological fieldwork, or that we should endeavor to maintain those standards.

REVISIONISM AND THE INFALLIBILITY OF PAPER

A related socio-academic development connected with the consternation for tablets in fieldwork is the coincidental revisionism of traditional paper recording methods. Opponents to paperless methods now speak to an infallibility of paper, where the horrors of the past (but also present)—be they easily lost or damaged forms, limited and physically located copies, faded and illegible information—are now either forgotten or cast in a more positive and forgiving light. Set against the fragility of a tablet, paper records are (re)imagined as dependable and indestructible, or "real" and "secure" (May and Crossby 2010: 49), robust characters in a halcyonic vision of when archaeology was done right (see, e.g., some of the collected opinions on analog and digital methods in Warwick *et al.* 2009). As much as I do not want to present digital data as perfect in every way, neither can I accept the same fantasy for paper-based records. Paper, moreover, is presented as a superior medium for the many associated tasks of field recording, from the jotting down of the simplest notes and records, to the nuanced and crafted care of site illustration, or the transcribing of complex and intellectual thought. In this context, the cognitive freedom of a blank page of a paper notebook is presented in opposition to the rigidly organized database fields that atomize the bits of data that are thought to be more typically collected in an iPad (for more on these debates on the use of structured forms or diary-style entries, see Latour 1987; Bibby 1993: 110; Pavel 2010: 142–146; Matskevich 2011).

That there is some reflexive value in recording data and thoughts onto a blank page is undeniable, even if such a method, when performed exclusively, is less effective (Mickel 2015 demonstrates how each form of recording, albeit redundant, is essential; on studies for and against the metacognitive value of digital and paper-based note-taking methods, see: (those for) Driver 2002; Bebell and Kay 2010; (those against) Awwad *et al.* 2013; Sana *et al.* 2013). But the unstructured diary entry onto a blank page is not an exclusive privilege of the paper notebook, and nor is the intellectual value of that kind of recording method necessarily jeopardized by the use of an iPad. The unstructured blank page, being the best-equipped feature of a piece of paper's arsenal, is, after all, but one of the hundreds of utilities enjoyed on a tablet. For our recording of the Pompeii excavations, open-page diary-style entries were effectively produced in concert with the forms and database recording. Whether reflexive or redundant, recording in this way produced a richer body of data; each data structure, after all, whether in the form of drop-down lists and check-boxes, or free-form textual descriptions and sketches, has (potential) value and (some) limitations. And in reality, our post-excavation processing of the data has drawn immeasurably more valuable information from the structured data. Still it is necessary to recognize the related role of diary-style entries in the formation of those datasets, difficult though it may be to qualify or quantify. So while it is true that field data is becoming more and more atomized—a scenario that is promoted or exacerbated, depending on one's view—by the bringing of databases into the trench via tablets, I would argue that both structured and unstructured recording should, and can, be performed regardless of the medium.

Digital Illustration is Illustration

Some confusion and misunderstanding similarly circulates about the use of a tablet to draw archaeological objects and their stratified relationships and contexts. There is some irony here, given that in our experience it was digital illustration where we made some of the most significant improvements to the quality, not just quantity, of information we could gather while in the field; this is similarly the case for the use of tablets for illustration at Çatalhöyük in Turkey (Berggren *et al.* 2015: 443). Streamlined though the illustration process may now be, particularly given the utility of templates in vector-based drawing environments, still—and critically—the drawing process is not entirely automated. So while there is an appearance that digital illustration with a tablet is somewhat akin to the automated process of taking a 3D laser scan or a digital photograph, in reality the process retains the essential, or "traditional" skills and values of illustration; the objects and their stratified relationships are individually drawn by hand on-site and not (just) laser-scanned. Digital illustration is still illustration. There is no less engagement with the trench or architecture; rather, it could be argued that there is a heightened commitment to the material given that the ability to draw directly into a vector-based layering system allows for a more dynamic, yet cleaner, drawing process (on the knowledge-making of visual recording, see Perry 2014, esp. 194–198; on improved engagement between excavation and recording with tablets at Çatalhöyük, see Berggren *et al.* 2015: 443). Both accuracy and precision are thus improved, not least because drawings can now be easily achieved at any scale, including 1:1. On the one hand, the scale and precision of digital illustration allows for more detail as necessary; on the other hand, the utility of the medium allows for simple but accurate sketches that combine photographs and other datasets. Whether through technical illustration or more free-form sketches, the value of engaging, even slowly, with every last object and relationship is not lost to digital illustration.

A Question(ing) of Efficiency

Odd though it may seem to any archaeologist who has tried to balance the research goals of a team of scholars with the many financial, administrative, and peer/academic pressures, some of the benefits or outcomes from the increased levels of efficiency in fieldwork brought about by tablet computers have been called to question (Caraher 2015; Ch. 4.1; Nakassis 2015). Beyond the concerns that efficiency amounts to less engagement with the trench or site, doubts have been cast as to whether the improved efficiency corresponds with a greater understanding of the subject matter (e.g., Hopkins (2010) has questioned whether the efficiency associated with these new methods represents any kind of advance in knowledge over the way sites were investigated some 150 years ago; see also Nakassis (2015), who in response to Roosevelt *et al.* (2015), questions whether their ultimate contributions are in any way better because of the efficiency of their fieldwork). That line of enquiry is at once reasonable, even if any proposed answer— one way or the other—will prove subjective and difficult to attest; surely any such demonstration of an improved understanding of a site that is based on a recording system, whether digital or paper-based, is endlessly debatable (see, again the example of Nakassis (2015), noting the efficiency and impressive documentation of the fieldwork [on a granary] as outlined in Roosevelt *et al.* 2015, questions if their efforts "get us something important. . . does it help us interpret the granary any better? It hasn't seemed to thus far."). How does one, for example, demonstrate that the ideas and analyses of a team of scholars are now stronger under a newer recording system? Or that the intellectual value of a more traditional project, if eventually published, is that much stronger than that of a paperless project? The measure of sound fieldwork and recording methods must surely and always be relative to a healthy and respectable publication record.

In any case, it is hard to imagine that many archaeologists would— indeed *should*, as a matter of best practices—argue against a more efficient and productive fieldwork system. Not only are most archaeological projects obliged to publish as much high-quality research as is (un)reasonably possible, but the best of these projects of course *want* to be active and productive. Efficiency in the way we do things is for the vast majority of projects, paperless or otherwise, more of an aspiration than a distraction. It is a goal that does not come at the cost of intellectual engagement, but in my experience is paid for by the time once spent performing some of the most time-consuming and menial but necessary duties: typically data-entry and scanning, but the list of tedious tasks is a long one. None of this need necessarily threaten the core values that are being attributed to a slow archaeology. That there is some value in the brand(ing) of slow archaeology is, of course, inarguable: more time spent in the field giving thought and discussion to the archaeology, rather than merely to recording it, is crucial to our understating of the site. In this we should remain grateful to Caraher for (re)raising these issues, or aspirations, at a time of great change in the way we collect data for the production of knowledge. And it should follow that just as much be true for our published records, which should provide analysis, context, and interpretation of the material, not just a record of it; can I therefore call for a "Slow Publication" movement? In the meantime, to stick with the recording processes, I simply do not see that digital recording methodologies, by definition, should pose such a grave threat to knowledge production. For in spite of the efficiency of tablets, and true though it may be that more and more data can be collected with them (as if an abundance of data were a problem for a discipline that has been plagued by unpublished research projects with nonexistent datasets), it is by far the greater engagement with the archaeology, while still in the trench or the field, that characterizes my own experience of paperless archaeology. For the Pompeii excavations, and I suspect as much is true for other paperless projects, the emphasis has never shifted from in-trench engagement and analysis to some kind of robotic, single-minded (or mindless, as is the inference) hunger for more and more data.

OUR DISCIPLINARY CONSTERNATION FOR CHANGE

Should we be surprised by the opposition to paperless archaeology? For all the new developments that ameliorate each generation of archaeological research, we continue to be a discipline that more often prides itself on our traditional ways of doing things (e.g., the long-held recording systems, whose increasingly inveterate nature lends some kind of earnest but imagined authority and quality). In some ways this is not unlike the "blackboxing" of older methods, whether weak or strong, from necessary and ongoing scrutiny (Leighton 2015: 68–69;

Figure 4: The little grey notebook so familiar to any Greek archaeologist of the past century (Photo courtesy of Jack Davis).

for the term "blackbox," see Latour and Woolgar 1979: 51). Some of these systemic routines are manifest in the little gray notebooks used almost universally, and for close to a century, in Greek archaeology (FIG. 4). It is their heredity that transcends their practical qualities as sturdy, conveniently-sized books to write things in; as much seems true of the olive-oil, motor-oil, and feta tins that have been (re)used as artifact storage containers by the Athenian Agora excavations from the 1930s until the present (they are now lined, not replaced, to minimize corrosion of artifacts). These objects, and the systems they maintain, are continually used—indeed, celebrated—because they have always been used. While I share the same fond nostalgia for objects of heritage in our field, I am as much intrigued as I am concerned by the opposition we create between tradition and innovation in the ways which we record our fieldwork. Venerated notions of experience are ceremonially draped over the more traditional systems so as to explain, maintain, and not least ritualize the status quo (for the broader setting, see Morris 1994). The wider socio-academic implications of what is a willful rejection of change, however, are troubling: can we really imagine that there is some intellectual value in continuing to record data in the same ways as was done generations ago?

As convinced as I am of the values of going digital in archaeological fieldwork, I believe it all the more important that regardless of the paper-based or paperless medium, we should recognize the intellectual value in developing and testing new ideas in methodology rather than maintaining and championing old ones. And while this may require a more realistic than romantic retrospection of our discipline's past, it also demands the kinds of debates that have been rightly provoked by the call for (a return to) slow archaeology. Here we should remind ourselves that the values associated with a slow archaeology are the same as those for a "Good Archaeology," and that none of these need necessarily be the exclusive purview of a paper-based recording system, past or present. But the methodological introspection prompted by these debates—even if it has been aimed more squarely at paperless archaeology—is in any case critical for a period that will inevitably be seen as the transition from paper to digital recording. How long this transitional period lasts—one generation, or two, or more(?)—is difficult to answer. The more important measure should be of the products of paperless (and any surviving paper-based) archaeological projects: the quality and quantity of their data, the maintenance of their archives, and the overall contribution of their publications and broader outreach.

ACKNOWLEDGMENTS

My first round of appreciation must go to the organizers of the workshop—Erin Averett, Derek Counts, and Jody Gordon—not just for their invitation to present at the workshop of this published proceedings, but for putting together such an extraordinary group of scholars from whom I learnt so much. The collection of thoughts in this paper have benefitted immeasurably from the discussions at that event. More generally my ideas on digital recording have been shaped in all sorts of ways by my interactions with Eric Poehler, Chris Motz, John Wallrodt, Rachel Opitz, Bill Caraher, Sebastian Heath, Allison Emmerson, Kevin Dicus, Leigh Lieberman, and Gregory Tucker: I thank them very gratefully, while also admitting there are many others besides. I take much pride in thanking the late Steve Jobs, and the team at Apple, for his initial—and their ongoing—interest in, and support of, our archaeological research.

None of this paperless fieldwork could have been carried out without the generous assistance and support of the Soprintendenza Archeologica di Pompei and the Beni Culturali; thanks are due to so many in the SAP, but not least to Massimo Osanna for his continued support of our fieldwork. This research has been very generously funded by the Semple Fund of the Department of Classics at the University of Cincinnati, where the project is based, with additional and extraordinary support from the Loeb Classical Library Foundation, the National Geographic Society, the National Endowment for the Humanities, the American Council of Learned Societies, and not least the American Academy in Rome which serves as our Italian base. This paper was written at the American Academy in Rome while I was an ACLS residential Fellow; my immeasurable thanks to everyone at the Academy and the ACLS for providing such an unparalleled environment in which to work.

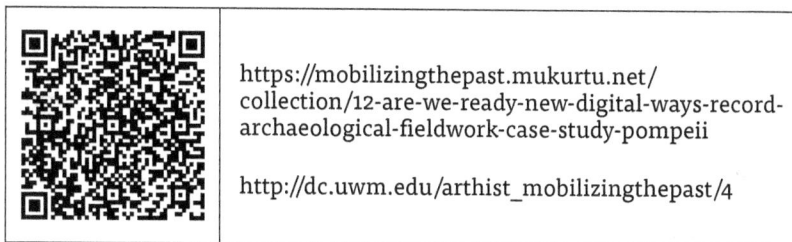

https://mobilizingthepast.mukurtu.net/
collection/12-are-we-ready-new-digital-ways-record-
archaeological-fieldwork-case-study-pompeii

http://dc.uwm.edu/arthist_mobilizingthepast/4

REFERENCES

Allison, P. M. 2008. "Dealing with Legacy Data—An Introduction,"
Internet Archaeology 24, http://intarch.ac.uk/journal/issue24/
introduction.html

Apple Inc. 2010. "Discovering Ancient Pompeii with iPad." http://
www.apple.com/ipad/pompeii. Archived at https://classics.
uc.edu/pompeii/images/stories/ipad/Apple%20-%20Discov-
ering%20ancient%20Pompeii%20with%20iPad.pdf

Austin, A. 2014. "Mobilizing Archaeologists: Increasing the Quantity
and Quality of Data Collected in the Field with Mobile Technology," *Advances in Archaeological Practice* 1: 13–23.

Awwad, F., A. Ayesh, and S. Awwad. 2013, "Are Laptops Distracting
Educational Tools in Classrooms," *Procedia—Social and Behavioral
Sciences* 103: 154–160.

Bebell, D., and R. Kay. 2010. "One to One Computing: A Summary of
the Quantitative Results from the Berkshire Wireless Learning
Initiative," *Journal of Technology, Learning, and Assessment* 9(2):
5–59.

Berggren, Å., N. Dell'Unto, M. Forte, S. Haddow, I. Hodder, J. Issavi, N.
Lercari, C. Mazzuccato, A. Mickel, and J. Taylor. 2015. "Revisiting
Reflexive Archaeology at Çatalhöyük: Integrating Digital and 3D
Technologies at the Trowel's Edge," *Antiquity* 89: 433–448.

Bibby, D. I. 1993. "Building Stratigraphic Sequences on Excavations:
An Example from Konstanz, Germany," in E. D. Harris, M. R.
Brown III, and G. J. Brown, eds., *Practices of Archaeological Stratig-
raphy*. London: Academic Press, 104–121.

Biddle, M., and B. Kjolbye-Biddle. 1969. "Metres, Areas and Robbing,"
World Archaeology 1: 208–219.

Caraher, W. 2013. "Slow Archaeology," *North Dakota Quarterly* 80:
43–52.

Caraher, W. 2015. "Understanding Digital Archaeology." *Mediterranean Archaeology*, https://mediterraneanworld.wordpress.com/2015/07/17/understanding-digital-archaeology/

Driver, M. 2002. "Exploring Student Perceptions of Group Interaction and Class Satisfaction in the Web-Enhanced Classroom," *The Internet and Higher Education* 5(1): 35–45.

Eiteljorg, H. 2011. "What Are Our Critical Data-Preservation Needs?" in E. C. Kansa, S. W. Kansa, and E. Watrall, eds., *Archaeology 2.0: New Approaches to Communication and Collaboration. Cotsen Digital Archaeology Series 1*. Los Angeles: Cotsen Institute of Archaeology Press, 250–264. http://escholarship.org/uc/item/1r6137tb

Ellis, S. J. R.. 2011. "The Rise and Re-Organization of the Pompeian Salted Fish Industry," in S. J. R. Ellis, ed., *The Making of Pompeii: Studies in the History and Urban Development of an Ancient Town. Journal of Roman Archaeology Supplementary Series 85*. Portsmouth, R.I.: Journal of Roman Archaeology, 59–88.

Ellis, S. J. R. in press a. "Reevaluating Pompeii's Coin-Finds: Monetary Transactions and Urban Rubbish in the Retail Economy of an Ancient City," in M. Flohr, and A. Wilson, eds., *The Economy of Pompeii*. Oxford: Oxford University Press.

Ellis, S. J. R. in press b. *Roman Retail Revolutions*. Oxford: Oxford University Press.

Ellis, S. J. R., and E. E. Poehler. 2015. "The Roman Buildings East of the Temple of Poseidon on the Isthmus," in E. Gebhard and T. E. Gregory, eds., *Bridge of the Untiring Sea: The Corinthian Isthmus from Prehistory to Late Antiquity. Hesperia Supplement 48*. Princeton: American School of Classical Studies, 271–287.

Ellis, S. J. R., A. L. C. Emmerson, A. K. Pavlick, and K. Dicus. 2011. "The 2010 Field Season at I.1.1-10, Pompeii: Preliminary Report on the Excavations." *The Journal of Fasti Online* 220, http://www.fastionline.org/docs/FOLDER-it-2011-220.pdf

Ellis, S. J. R., A. L. C. Emmerson, K. Dicus, G. Tibbott, and A. K. Pavlick. 2015. "The 2012 Field Season at I.1.1-10, Pompeii: Preliminary Report on the Excavations." *The Journal of Fasti Online* 328, http://www.fastionline.org/docs/FOLDER-it-2015-328.pdf

Ellis, S. J. R., A. L. C. Emmerson, A. K. Pavlick, K. Dicus, and G. Tibbott. 2012. "The 2011 Field Season at I.1.1-10, Pompeii: Preliminary Report on the Excavations." *The Journal of Fasti Online* 262, http://www.fastionline.org/docs/FOLDER-it-2012-262.pdf

Ellis, S. J. R., T. E. Gregory, E. Poehler, and K. Cole. 2008. "Integrating Legacy Data into a New Method for Studying Architecture: A Case Study from Isthmia, Greece." *Internet Archaeology* 24, http://dx.doi.org/10.11141.ia.24.3

Fee, S. B., D. K. Pettegrew, and W. R. Caraher. 2013. "Taking Mobile Computing to the Field," *Near Eastern Archaeology* 76: 50–55.

Fisher, C. R., M. Terras, and C. Warwick. 2010. "Integrating New Technologies into Established Systems: A Case Study from Roman Silchester," in B. Frischer, J. W. Crawford, and D. Koller, eds., *Proceedings of the 37th Annual Computer Applications and Quantitative Methods in Archaeology Conference, March 22–26, Williamsburg, Virginia, USA, 2009*. Oxford, http://discovery.ucl.ac.uk/1324501/1324501/1324501.pdf

Harris, E. C. 1975. "The Stratigraphic Sequence: A Question of Time," *World Archaeology* 7: 109–121.

Hodder, I. 1989. "Writing Archaeology: Site Reports in Context," *Antiquity* 63: 268–274.

Hopkins, C. 2010. "iPad at Pompeii: Does Tech Really Revolutionize How We Seek the Past? [Update]." *New York Times Technology Blog*, http://www.nytimes.com/external/readwriteweb/2010/10/11/11readwriteweb-ipad-at-pompeii-does-tech-really-revolution-31382.html?scp=1&sq=pompeii&st=cse

Kidder, A. V. 1959 "The Diary of Sylvanus G. Morley," *Proceedings of the American Philosophical Society* 103: 778–782.

Latour, B. 1987. *Science in Action: How to Follow Scientists and Engineers through Society.* Cambridge, Mass.: Harvard University Press.

Latour, B., and S. Woolgar. 1979. *Laboratory Life: The Social Construction of Scientific Facts.* Beverly Hills: Sage Publications.

Leighton, M. 2015. "Excavation Methodologies and Labour as Epistemic Concerns in the Practiceof Archaeology: Comparing Examples from British and Andean Archaeology," *Archaeological Dialogues* 22: 65–88.

Matskevich, S. 2011. Review of C. Pavel, *Describing and Interpreting the Past: European and American Approaches to the Written Record of the Excavation. Bryn Mawr Classical Review* 2011.08.19, http://bmcr.brynmawr.edu/2011/2011-08-19.html

May, S. C., and V. Crosby. 2010. "Holy Grail or Poison Chalice? Challenges in Implementing Digital Excavation Recording," in F. Nicolucci and S. Hermon, eds., *Beyond the Artifact: Digital*

Interpretation of the Past. Proceedings of CAA2004, Prato 13–17 April 2004. Budapest: Archeolingua, 49–54.

Mickel, A. 2015. "Reasons for Redundancy in Reflexivity: The Role of Diaries in Archaeological Epistemology," *Journal of Field Archaeology* 40: 300–309.

Morris, I. 1994. "Archaeologies of Greece," in I. Morris, ed., *Classical Greece: Ancient Histories and Modern Archaeologies.* Cambridge: Cambridge University Press, 8–47.

Mueller, P. A., and D. M. Oppenheimer. 2014. "The Pen Is Mightier Than the Keyboard: Advantages of Longhand over Laptop Note Taking," *Psychological Science* 25: 1159–1168.

Nakassis, D. 2015. "Thinking Digital Archaeology." *Aegean Prehistory*, https://englianos.wordpress.com/2015/08/10/thinking-digital-archaeology/

Pavel, C. 2010. *Describing and Interpreting the Past: European and American Approaches to the Written Record of the Excavation.* Bucharest: Editura Universitătatii din Bucuresti.

Perry, S. 2014. "Crafting Knowledge with (Digital) Visual Media in Archaeology," in R. Chapman and A. Wylie, eds., *Material Evidence: Learning from Archaeological Practice.* London: Routledge, 189–210.

Poehler, E. E., and S. J. R. Ellis. 2011. "The 2010 Season of the Pompeii *Quadriporticus* Project: The Western Side." *The Journal of Fasti Online* 218, http://www.fastionline.org/docs/FOLDER-it-2011-218.pdf

Poehler, E. E., and S. J. R. Ellis. 2012. "The 2011 Season of the Pompeii *Quadriporticus* Project: The Southern and Northern Sides." *The Journal of Fasti Online* 249, http://www.fastionline.org/docs/FOLDER-it-2012-249.pdf

Poehler, E. E., and S. J. R. Ellis. 2013. "The Pompeii *Quadriporticus* Project: The Eastern Side and Colonnade." *The Journal of Fasti Online* 284, http://www.fastionline.org/docs/FOLDER-it-2013-284.pdf

Poehler, E. E., and S. J. R. Ellis. 2014. "The 2013 Season of the Pompeii *Quadriporticus* Project: Final Fieldwork and Preliminary Results." *The Journal of Fasti Online* 321, http://www.fastionline.org/docs/FOLDER-it-2014-321.pdf

Roosevelt, C. H., P. Cobb, E. Moss, B. R. Olson, and S. Ünlüsoy. 2015. "Excavation is ~~Destruction~~ Digitization: Advances in Archaeological Practice," *Journal of Field Archaeology* 40: 325–346.

Sana, F., T. Weston, and N. J. Cepeda. 2013. "Laptop Multitasking Hinders Classroom Learning for Both Users and Nearby Peers," *Computers and Education* 62: 24–31.

Schiffer, M. B. 1972. "Archaeological Context and Systemic Context," *American Antiquity* 37: 156–165.

Schiffer, M. B. 1987. *Formation Processes of the Archaeological Record.* Albuquerque: University of New Mexico Press.

Warwick, C., C. R. Fisher, M. Terras, M. Baker, A. Clarke, M. Fulford, M. Grove, E. O'Riordan, and M. Rains. 2009. "iTrench: A Study of User Reactions to the Use of Information Technology in Field Archaeology," *Literary & Linguistic Computing* 24: 211–223.

1.3.
Sangro Valley and the Five (Paperless) Seasons: Lessons on Building Effective Digital Recording Workflows for Archaeological Fieldwork

Christopher F. Motz

On March 8, 2011, I sent a foolish email. Earlier, during the winter, I had played around with creating a basic FileMaker Pro database for my iPhone that could be used in the field. I thought it had potential for field use, and I had read about iPads being used at Pompeii by the Pompeii Archaeological Research Project: Porta Stabia (PARP:PS) team the previous summer (Apple Inc. 2010; Ellis and Wallrodt 2011), so I sent a few screenshots to my excavation director and asked if she would be interested in using such a system during the coming excavation season of the Sangro Valley Project (SVP). At most I thought she might agree to test its use with one or two iPads, and maybe switch over fully the following year. Instead, after a brief email exchange she told me she wanted the project to go entirely paperless in the coming summer.

My first reaction was surprise. My second was fear. What had I gotten myself into? I had four months to develop a full excavation database, complete with syncing and new image handling procedures. I had limited experience with FileMaker, was a full-time, first-year graduate student, and had a part-time job. Compounding all of this was a lack of resources that could help one build this kind of system. Excavation databases were not new, but this particular combination of hardware and software had never before been available. Furthermore, a research database and a recording system are two different beasts. Even proper iOS app developers were still figuring out how to design effective interfaces for tablets. Our experiment easily could have failed.

Through a combination of long hours, help and advice from John Wallrodt (including his blog posts on http://paperlessrchaeology.com, which have been a valuable resource for many other projects and remain the best starting point for those interested in building a paperless recording system; see Butina 2014; see also Bria and DeTore, Ch. 1.5; Gordon *et al.*, Ch. 1.4) and Google, I managed to build a functional but unfinished system. It worked, but it was a beta-quality solution that required constant maintenance and bug fixes. All of the critical parts worked at the beginning of the season, but I continued to add and change many elements throughout the summer. Our field staff's patience and their willingness to cooperate in this experiment played a large part in its success.

Since 2011 I have continued working on the system for the Sangro Valley Project (directed by Susan Kane; see http://www.sangro.org). I have also developed a paperless recording system for the Say Kah Archaeological Project in Belize (SKAP, directed by Sarah Jackson and Linda Brown), which was deployed for the first time in the summer of 2015, and since 2013 I have managed and continued the development of the paperless system that John Wallrodt built (Ellis and Wallrodt 2011; Wallrodt *et al.* 2015; Wallrodt, Ch. 1.1) for PARP:PS (directed by Steven Ellis; Ellis *et al.* 2015; for a full bibliography, see http://classics. uc.edu/pompeii/; see also Ellis, Ch. 1.2). During this time, my skills as a FileMaker developer have grown considerably, but far more valuable are the lessons I have learned from our successes and failures, from watching people use paperless systems, and from the feedback they have provided.

In the first part of this chapter I will summarize the paperless system at SVP and how it has evolved from the initial creation and deployment in 2011, to the redesigned interface in 2012, and to a focus on documentation in 2013. I will then present some lessons learned during five seasons of paperless recording at SVP (2011–2015), supplemented by observations I made during my work with SKAP (2015) and PARP:PS (2013–2015). I will identify some of the most common problems that I have encountered during the design and use of paperless recording systems, and I will offer some recommendations for avoiding or fixing them. Many of these problems are not unique to projects with digital recording systems, and most of the difficulties were not technical in nature. Rather, many of the most significant problems arose from integrating workflows: not only digital and physical workflows, but also the workflows of different actors in the project. Finally, I will engage with recent critiques of paperless field recording, in particular Bill Caraher's provocative philosophy of "Slow Archaeology," which cautions against the (over)eager pursuit of efficiency and promotes methods that nurture interpretative insight (Caraher 2013; 2015b; Ch. 4.1). I will offer SKAP as a case study of how digital recording practices can help to further our understanding of the ancient world in qualitative ways, not merely quantitative ones.

SANGRO VALLEY PROJECT: 1994-2010

The Sangro Valley Project was founded in 1994, and it is now managed by Oberlin College in collaboration with the Soprintendenza per i Beni Archeologici dell'Abruzzo and the University of Oxford. The project operates a summer field school in Italy for students from Oberlin, Oxford, and other institutions. The goal of the project is to characterize and investigate the nature, pattern, and dynamics of human habitation and land use in the *longue durée* within the context of a Mediterranean river valley system—the Sangro River valley of the Abruzzo region of Italy, which was the territory of the ancient Samnites.

As a regional project, SVP does not excavate at a single site. Instead, excavators move from site to site; the duration of study at each site depends on the amount of time required for a proper investigation, and in some seasons the project has been active at multiple sites. The project also employs pedestrian survey and other methods of data collection; therefore, the project's infrastructure needs to be mobile and flexible, and researchers cannot count on having access to anything other than what they bring into the field. Although SVP does have a well-equipped computer lab with an Internet connection in the dig house (generously provided by the town of Tornareccio), there is no Internet and no power in the field. These constraints did not pose much of a problem for paper-based recording, but they were to have a significant impact on the coming digital system.

Over its first 16 years, SVP employed various formats to record, store, manage, and analyze its data, as was common among archaeological projects active in the 1990s and 2000s (Ellis and Wallrodt 2011; Betts 2012; Houk 2012; Fee *et al.* 2013; Vincent *et al.* 2014; see Gordon *et al.*, Ch. 1.4; Sayre, Ch. 1.6; Wallrodt, Ch. 1.1). Excavation, survey, finds, and sample data were recorded on an array of paper forms in the field and in the lab, and the same information often needed to be recorded on more than one form. At the end of each season, these forms were scanned and transcribed into one of a number of digital formats that varied throughout the years (Microsoft Access, Excel spreadsheets, and fillable PDFs). Supervisors kept notebooks that were scanned at the end of each season but were never transcribed. Spatial data were gathered with a total station (for excavation) and handheld GPS units (for survey). These files were incorporated into a geographic information system (GIS) for spatial analysis, of which SVP was an early adopter (Lock et al. 1999; Bell et al. 2002). Drawings were done on Mylar sheets, which were eventually scanned and turned into digital vector drawings. Photographs were taken with digital cameras; despite being "born digital," they still required secondary processing. Supervisors were supposed to upload and caption their digital photos at the end of the day, but the process frequently was deferred for a day or two, and this delay of labelling the photos several hours or days after they were taken often led to errors. The dispersion and disconnection of our data made it very difficult to get a complete picture of all the information that existed for any given area or object; it promoted the introduction of errors in cross-referencing and labeling, and left the recognition of these errors to chance; and it caused supervisors to spend much of their time managing data rather than thinking critically about their trench, the site, or the region as a whole.

SVP 2011 Season

The opening of a new site in 2011 provided an opportunity to rethink how the project would collect and manage data for all future work. For years, the directors and staff of SVP had bemoaned the inefficiencies and mistakes that accompanied paper-based recording, of which we all had been both victims and perpetrators at various times. The obvious solution was always some sort of digital system, but nothing existed that met our needs until the iPad was introduced in 2010 (see Wallrodt, Ch. 1.1, who also makes clear that similar discussions had been taking place at other projects). The email exchange mentioned at the start, from March of 2011, was the culmination of a long search for a solution to what was, for us, a very real problem.

The paperless system that we employed in 2011 took an eclectic and somewhat fragmented approach, necessitated by the limitations of the software that was available in those early years of mobile app development (Motz and Carrier 2013). Rather than using one multi-functional app, we employed multiple pieces of off-the-shelf software (for off-the-shelf vs "bespoke" software, see Roosevelt *et al.* 2015; see also: Ellis, Ch. 1.2; Gordon *et al.*, Ch. 1.4; Sobotkova *et al.*, Ch. 3.2; Spigelman *et al.*, Ch. 3.4).

The heart of the system was a custom FileMaker database. The FileMaker platform combines moderate customization with high reliability and commercial support, making it one of the most popular choices among archaeologists (e.g., Jennings 2011; Houk 2012; Prins *et al.* 2014; see also: Bria and DeTore, Ch. 1.5; Ellis, Ch. 1.2; Spigelman *et al.*, Ch. 3.4; Wallrodt, Ch. 1.1; see below for many more options). All excavation data were captured in the field using FileMaker Go on iPads. In keeping with SVP's educational mission as a field school, students have always participated in the recording process—including photography, drawing, writing notebook entries, and filling out context, find, and sample forms—under the guidance of the trench supervisors, who were ultimately responsible for all field recording and still performed the majority of it. None of this changed with the adoption of iPads. Each trench was allocated only one iPad in order to avoid numbering conflicts and duplicate records. Due to the infrastructural constraints described above, data were stored locally on the individual iPads in the field rather than communicated directly to a central server.

The iPads were synchronized twice per day with a main database hosted on the project's local Mac mini server. This occurred when the teams returned to the dig house at lunch and at the end of the day, the same times when new finds and samples were brought in from the field. After the field data were synced with the server, specialists in the labs could then enter detailed information about the new small finds, pottery, and environmental samples, and this information would be available on the iPads after the next sync. The synchronization process that I used is not time-consuming (Wallrodt 2011a, 2011b), but it is complex and involves a series of steps that must be performed in a particular order by the database administrator (see below on the importance of documentation).

I also updated the project's field photography workflow, moving the captioning process out into the field in order to avoid the errors

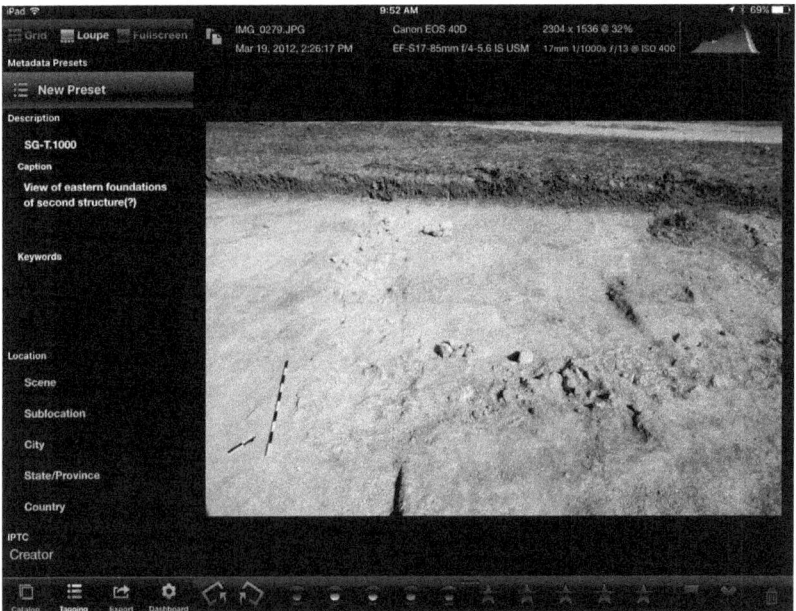

Figure 1: Photosmith iPad app.

from previous years. Excavators and surveyors used Eye-Fi cards, which are camera memory cards with built-in Wi-Fi. These cards were able to create their own ad-hoc networks, allowing them to send photos directly to an iPad—no wireless router or Internet needed. Field personnel then added captions and labels to the images' metadata using the Photosmith app on the iPad (FIG. 1). We used the "title" field for a structured subject code, while the "caption" field was for standard, plain-text descriptions. When the iPads returned to the lab, the labeled photos were uploaded to the server and imported into the database, where a set of scripts parsed the subject code to automatically link each photo with its subject record.

In addition to FileMaker and Photosmith, SVP used a handful of other iPad apps to assist with field recording. Several compass, calculator, and ruler apps were used in place of their more traditional counterparts, and a clinometer app proved particularly useful to the terrace survey team in measuring the approximate angles of slopes. Field notebooks were written with Apple's Pages program, which allowed excavators to integrate both drawings and photos into their accounts (FIG. 2). The project also used several drawing apps, but not in a systematic way. Supervisors were encouraged to experiment with different apps to find what worked best for them. We found that the vector drawing app TouchDraw was used most effectively for annotating and highlighting contexts in photos (FIG. 3) and for keeping running schematic plans that could easily be added to as the season progressed (FIG. 4); some supervisors used the program to draw measured sections and plans (FIG. 5). Simpler brush- or pencil-based apps were used frequently for quick sketches.

We identified numerous benefits to the paperless recording system used in the 2011 season: there was much quicker exchange of information between the field personnel and specialists; a significant decrease in human error through automation and controlled data entry; improved consistency of terminology through the use of pull-down menus and other structured fields; increased efficiency and time savings by eliminating the need to scan and digitize paper records; improved security of field data due to twice-daily syncing and backup; and an increase in the accessibility of information to all staff members, due largely to the fact that records could be accessed in both the field and the lab, whereas a paper record could be in only one place.

worked stones.

Sarah made another slot this afternoon, against the 2010 wall and 2022 red context. It appears to be made of some sort of degraded sandstone. We have taken a sample and left this since it appeared to be natural.

Southern Area:

This morning Jordan removed contexts 2021 and 2020. This revealed that both contexts sat on top of a rocky layer which I designated 2026. This appears to be a continuation of the foundation for the wall 2005 and/or the cocciopesto 2004. The cut visible between 2014 and 2020 continues down into 2026, suggesting that 2020 and 2026 are at least part of the same construction and may actually be different manifestations of the same original layer.

Contexts 2021 and 2020 before excavation.   Context 2026 after excavation of 2021 and 2020.

24-Jul-12

Discussions with B:

Whilst discussing the function of the basin we started thinking about access. There is no clear break in the wall of ctx.2010 that would provide a point of entry or exit. We will have to think again about how people used the room, perhaps there was a lower section of wall somewhere/ wooden ladders of some kind etc.

She suggested that the structure of the basin and the drain at an angle are more reminiscent of later basins, but the pottery and glass fragments from within 2003 and 2017/2019 are of early imperial date.
Her identification wavered towards the more functional working surface interpretation. She suggested that the alignment with the other building and very close proximity might suggest that they were not contemporary with one another.
She had a look at the vitrified material that had come out of 2003 and identified it as iron slag, and possible a very brunt piece of crucible. She suggested it seemed more like smithing slag than smelting slag. As a result, we might have some kind of small scale metal working on the site or nearby.

She identified the glass from 2003 and 2017/2019 as being early imperial date and probably all parts of vessels. This ties in with our pottery dates spanning a similar period in these contexts.

S. Graham

26-Jul-2012

Southern area:
This morning only Jordan and I are working around the drainage feature. We began by designating the darker area in between the cocciopesto (2004), pipes (2006), and white deposit (2020) as a new context numbered 2021. It appears similar to the fills above

South of T.2000 at 11:00 am on 26-Jul-2012, showing new context 2021 and location of new cuts

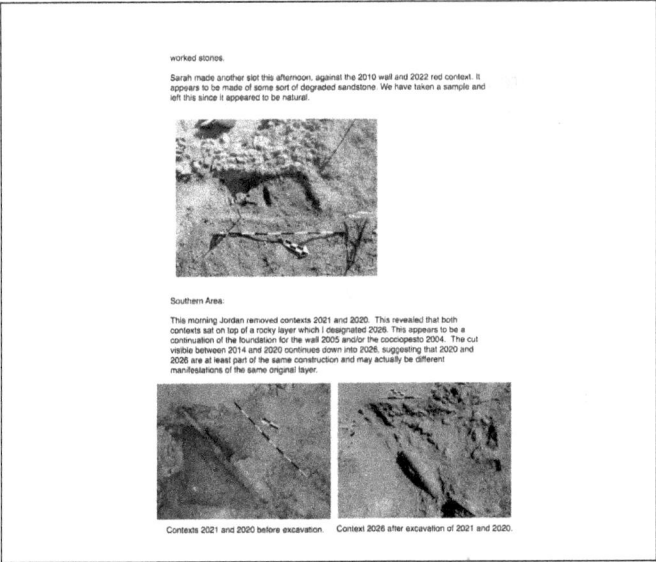

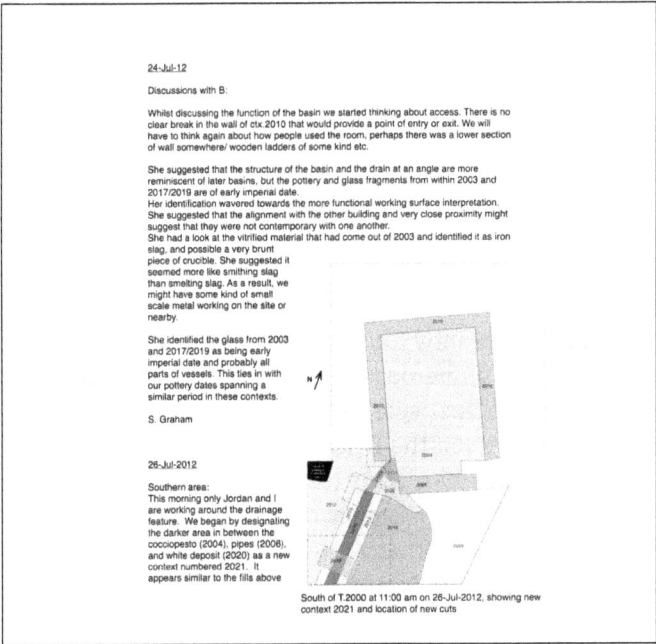

Figure 2: Portions of field notebooks written in Apple's Pages.

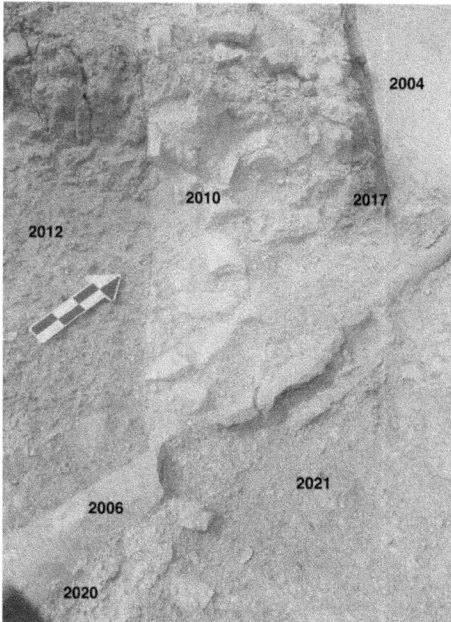

Figure 3: Example of a photo annotated with TouchDraw: original photo (top); annotated photo (bottom).

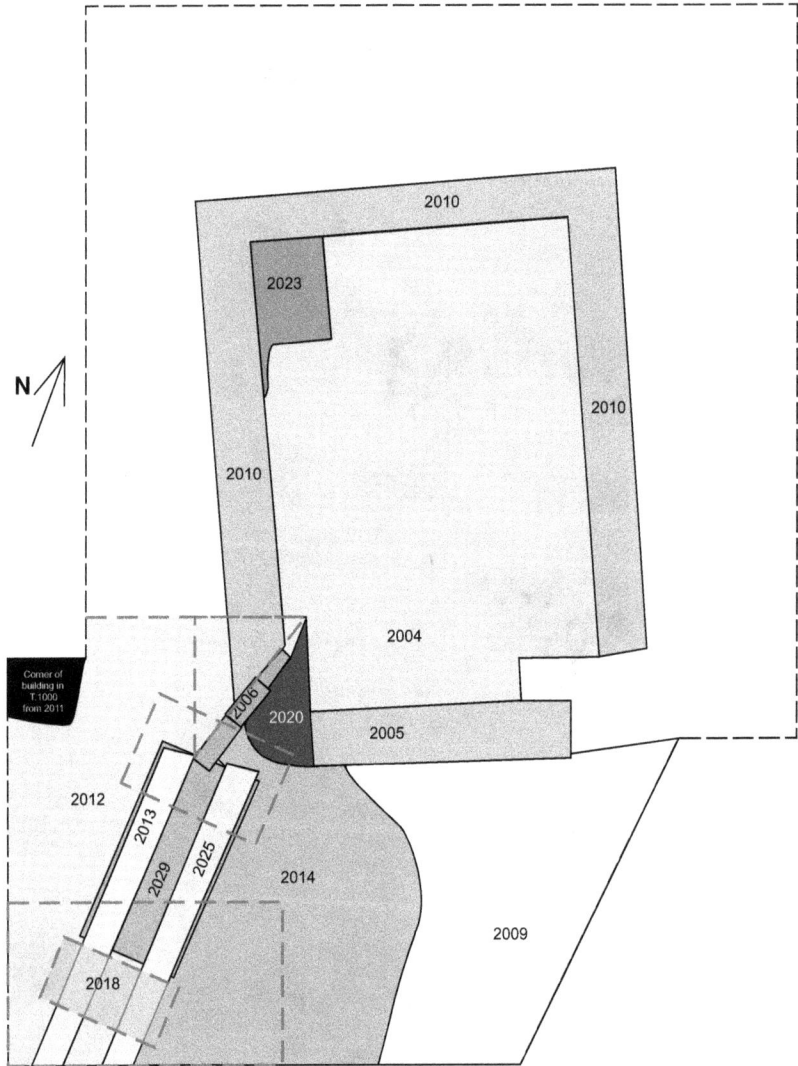

Figure 4: Schematic trench plan created with TouchDraw.

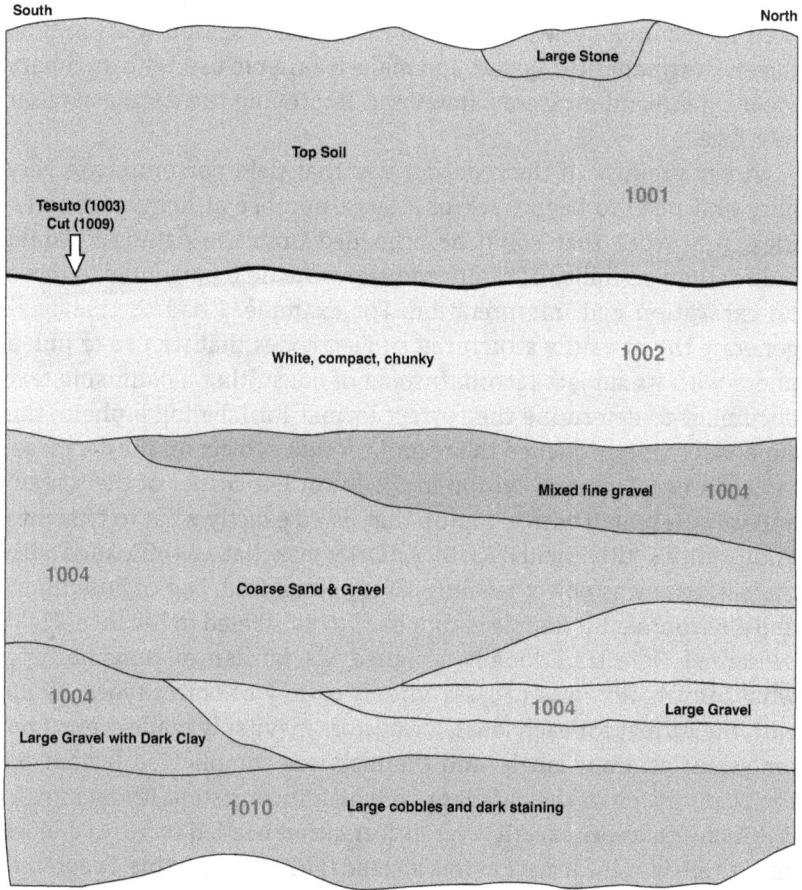

OPI T.1000
West section
Scale 1:10
E.Sanford
27 Jul 2012

South   North

Large Stone

Top Soil

Tesuto (1003)
Cut (1009)   1001

White, compact, chunky   1002

Mixed fine gravel   1004

1004   Coarse Sand & Gravel

1004   1004   Large Gravel

Large Gravel with Dark Clay

1010   Large cobbles and dark staining

Figure 5: Measured section drawing created in TouchDraw.

SVP 2012 SEASON

I asked the staff for feedback after the 2011 season. Much to my relief, everyone felt that the hardware and software themselves worked well. Most of the problems the staff noted were related to how the project used its technology. My main goal for the 2012 season was to refine the existing paperless system and make it easier to use, with a primary focus on streamlining workflows and improving the database's user interface.

A key premise of the redesign was that field personnel are very busy and need to keep track of a large number of items and activities. Any work that could be offloaded onto the database would reduce the possibility of errors and allow the field personnel to focus on excavation and interpretation. For example, I had the database generate the carefully structured subject codes that we use to link a photo with its subject record. Instead of consulting a confusing text document to determine the correct format for labeling a photo, the supervisor simply opened the record for that subject on the database, tapped a new "camera" button in the lower left corner of the screen, and was presented with a pop-up that listed exactly what to type into Photosmith's "title" field (FIG. 6). Another task that was offloaded onto the database was object labeling. Every small find, bag of bulk finds, and environmental sample is supposed to be labeled in the field. Field personnel were traditionally assigned the burden of remembering what information was necessary for a variety of object types, along with the format for each label. Excavators inevitably made errors and omissions on their labels, and the task was complicated further by the 2011 version of the database, in which inconsistent layouts made it difficult to know exactly what information needed to go on a label and where that information was located (FIG. 7). To fix this, I centered the redesign around new "digital labels," which are directly analogous to the physical labels and which gathered all of the basic identifying information into the same place for each record type (FIG. 8). As was done in 2011, the excavator would create a record on an iPad when an object was found or a soil sample was taken, and they would then label the object by either writing on the bag or putting a piece of tape on a sample bucket (FIG. 9). But unlike before, all they needed to do now was look at the digital record they had just created and write exactly what they saw on the digital label. Because the find or sample was brought back to the lab at the same time as the iPads were synced, the project's specialists could immediately look up the new items and identify any errors or missing materials. And since the labels were written in a consistent way, it was much easier for the specialists to match the physical labels with the digital record. After adopting this method, the project has had far fewer mislabeled bags and orphaned objects. These changes to both photo and object labeling gave the excavators fewer things to worry about. The risk of "deskilling" here is minimal, since these are skills that few supervisors were able to master reliably (cf. Ellis, Ch. 1.2).

As these examples show, the design of a user interface can directly impact the effectiveness and efficiency of associated workflows. User-interface design and layout were considerations in the first version of the database, but my priority had been building a functional system. The result was aesthetically lackluster. Interface elements were scattered, and there was some organization, but the design was not consistent or intuitive, which made it harder to use. I felt that a better user interface would offer more than just aesthetic benefits, so I undertook a complete redesign for the 2012 season. A comparison of the original and redesigned versions of several screens illustrates the changes (FIGS. 10–12).

In order to produce more cohesive and intuitive user interfaces for SVP's 2012 season and for subsequent databases, I have routinely employed several design principles, of which I will highlight four. The first is to develop a consistent visual language. This can take many forms. For example, I used color coding to help differentiate between various data and interface elements. Each record type has its own color and these colors are consistent throughout the database. This means that when a user taps on the orange "Contexts" button in the top right of the home screen, the orange color persists throughout all Contexts screens, just as blue designates a Small Find and green designates an Environmental Sample (Supplementary Material 1).

The second principle is to utilize a clear organizational system. The more complex the database, the more important it is to have a simple and consistent layout and a clear navigational structure. I have dealt with this in two very different ways. When I began building SVP's system in early 2011, I simply copied the old paper system of

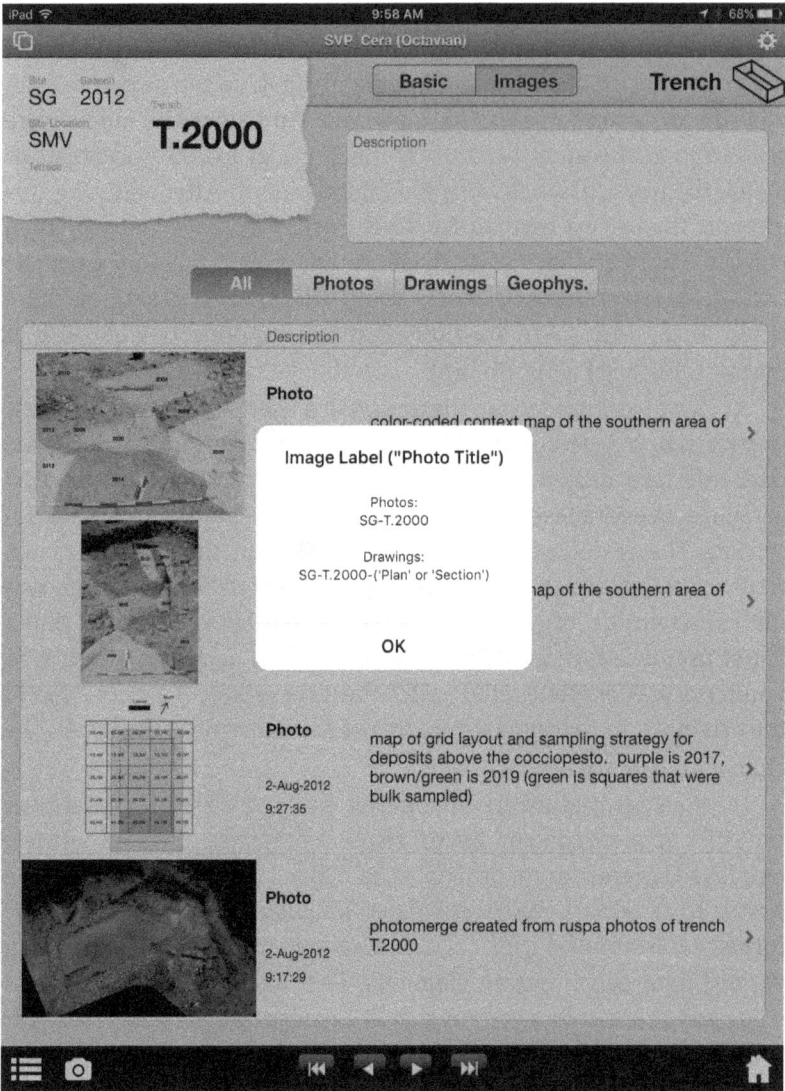

Figure 6: Image label pop-up.

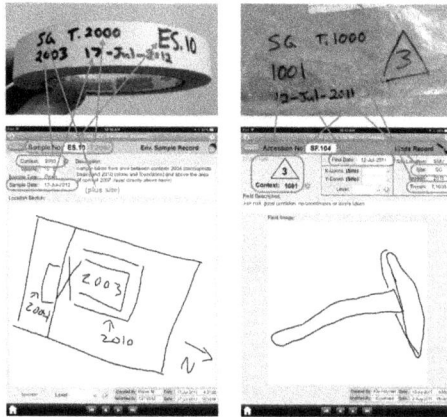

Figure 7: The original screens for environmental samples (left) and small finds (right), with arrows showing where information needed to go on the physical labels.

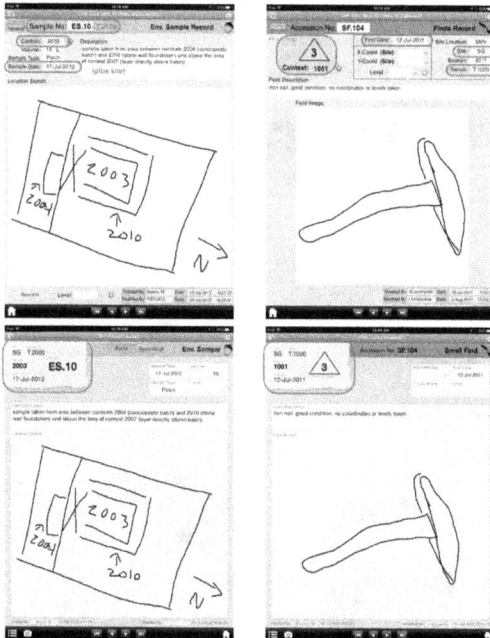

Figure 8: The original and revised screens for environmental samples (left) and small finds (right), with label information highlighted.

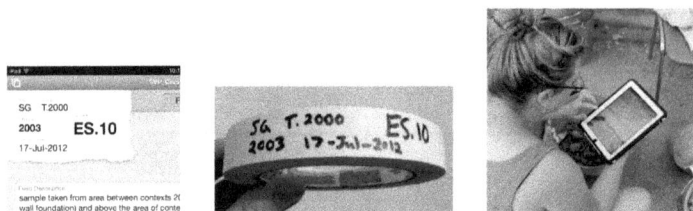

Figure 9: Examples of labeling workflows for an environmental sample (top row) and small find (bottom row): left) An excavator creates a record on an iPad; center) The excavator labels the object; right) Specialists view new items.

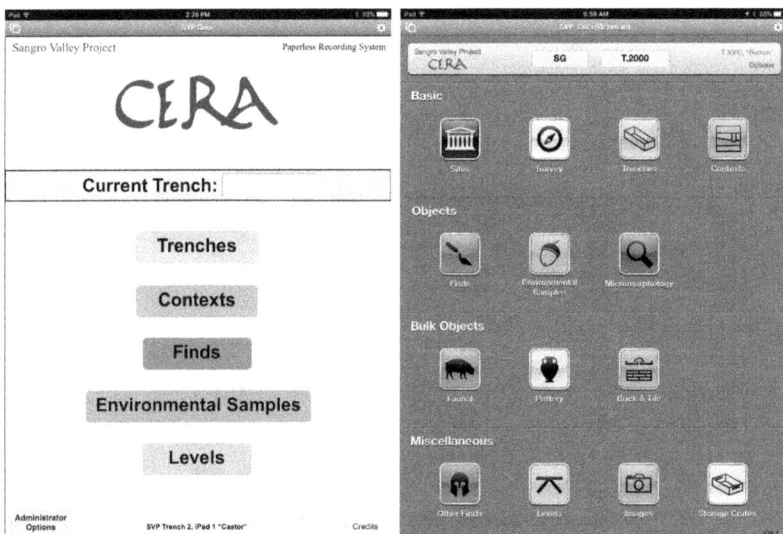

Figure 10: Examples of revised user interface, home screen: original (left); Revised (right).

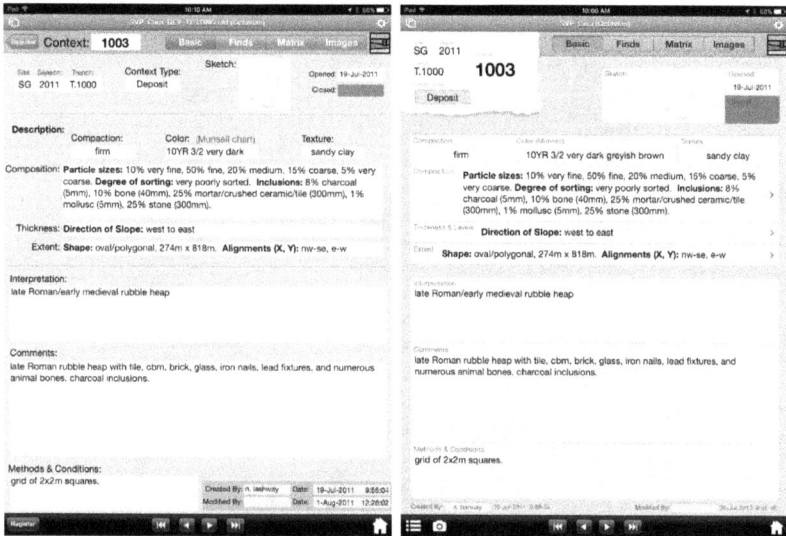

Figure 11: Examples of revised user interface, context screen: original (left); revised (right).

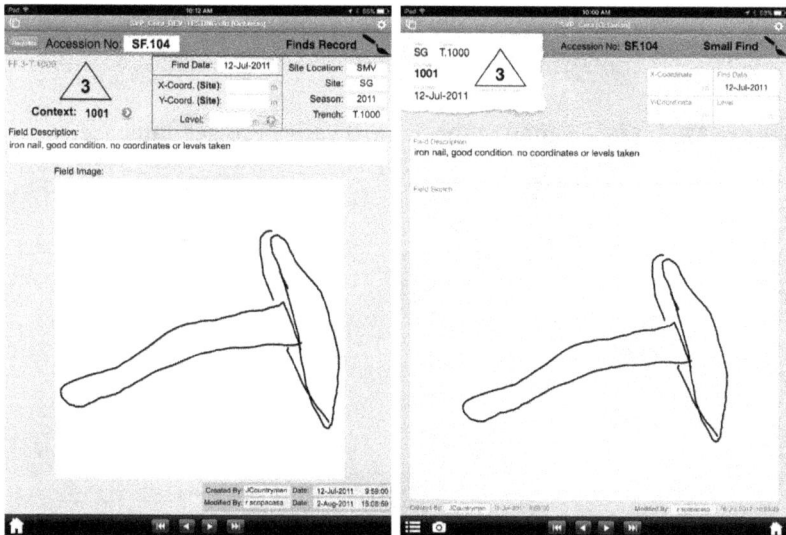

Figure 12: Examples of revised user interface, small find screen: original (left); revised (right).

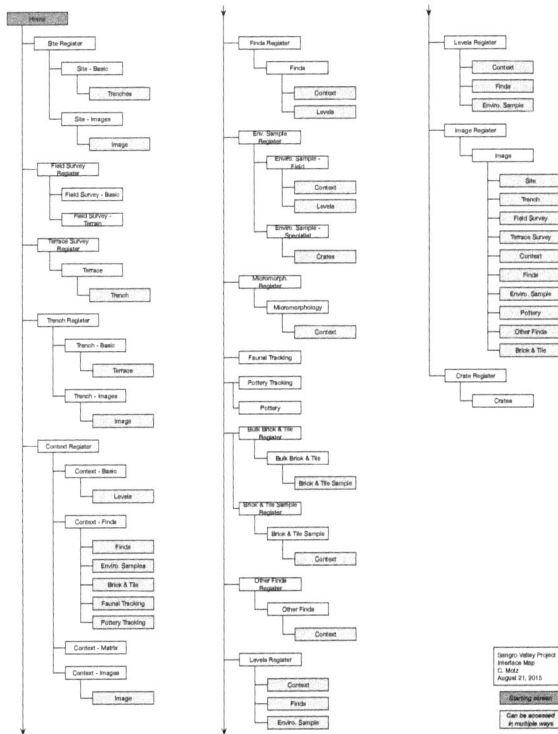

Figure 13: Interface map of the Sangro Valley Project database.

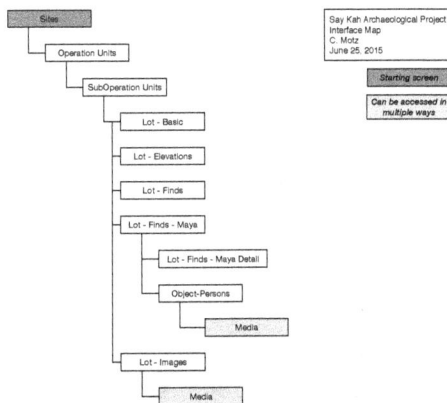

Figure 14: Interface map of the Say Kah Archaeological Project database.

registers and records that I was familiar with from previous seasons (cf. Wallrodt, Ch. 1.1), which resulted in a compartmentalized navigational structure that does not reflect how sites, trenches, contexts, and finds are related to each other (FIG. 13). When I started working on the SKAP database in 2014, I wanted to try something different. For SKAP I adopted a linear navigational structure that mirrored "real" data hierarchy and relationships (FIG. 14). In this model, the user navigates back and forth along a single "line" of data, drilling down into smaller analytical units or pulling back out to see larger ones. Both approaches have their pros and cons, but I think that the latter is better overall, helping to keep clear the relationships between different elements in the data structure, as well as the relationship between the data structure and the physical world.

The third design principle is simplification. Different actors in the research process often need to see different information about the same items. When an excavator enters a new small find, all they need to record is a brief description, a sketch, the object's location, and their name (FIG. 15A). The finds officer needs both to see all of the data recorded by the excavators and enter much more detailed information, but I keep the field and specialist data visually separated (FIG. 15B). Rather than showing everything to everybody and falling prey to the ever-increasing "data avalanche" (Kansa 2011: 1–2; Levy 2014; Huggett 2015b), I show each person only what they need and make clear the respective origins of the different pieces of data.

The fourth and final user interface element that I have found helpful is automation. As I mentioned above, having the database automatically enter information and perform certain tasks frees staff to focus on excavation and analysis. In addition to directly entering data (tasks like numbering new records, linking them to the correct trench or context, or entering the date), I would include under this heading those automated tasks that do not *directly* enter data but do make life easier in other ways, such as the generation of image codes that I discussed earlier. Another example of this comes from SKAP. When a SKAP supervisor enters or changes an excavation unit's datum and trench orientation, she or he is provided with a visual representation of the trench's position (Supplementary Material 2). This information is also displayed on the context screen in order to help excavators orient themselves when recording the thickness at various points in the context. This automated and responsive interface element helps to ensure that elevations are recorded in the correct location.

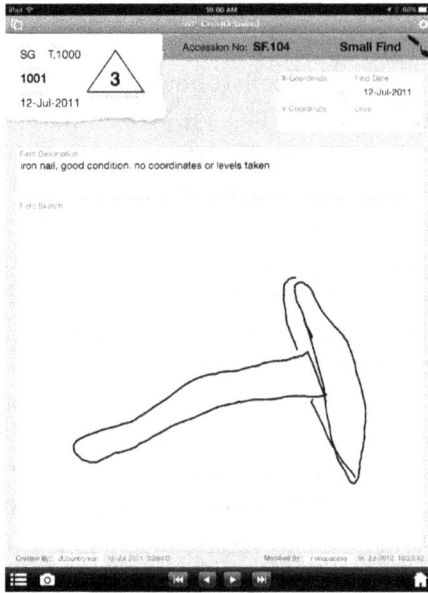

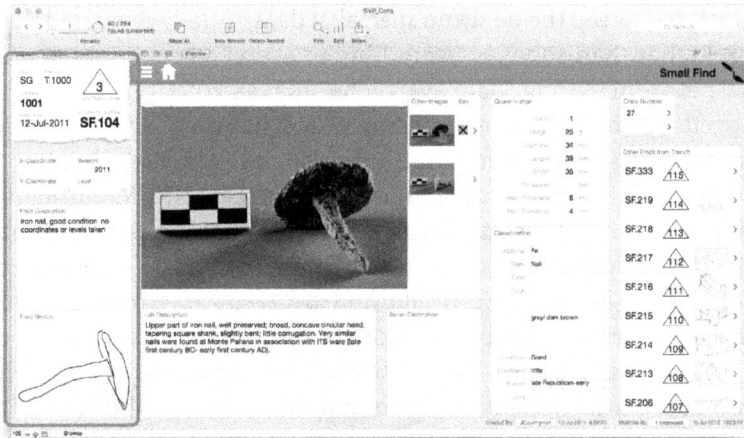

Figure 15: Different views of small find data: iPad layout for excavators (top); computer layout for specialists, with the field data circled in red (bottom).

SVP 2013 Season

Due to the success of the redesign, the SVP database has remained largely static since 2012 except for occasional bug fixes. In 2013, however, I began working with the Pompeii Archaeological Research Project: Porta Stabia, whose seasons always coincided with those of SVP. This meant that I would no longer be able to run SVP's system during the field season. Therefore, we needed to find and train my replacement. We were fortunate enough to be contacted by a Master's student from Lund University, Luke Aspland, and we enlisted a SVP alumna, Miriam Rothenberg, now a Ph.D. student at Brown University. I began training Miriam and Luke by email and Skype during the winter and spring of 2013, and we met for a week of intensive training in Oberlin, Ohio, in early May.

The three of us quickly discovered that much of the understanding of how to run the paperless system existed only in my head, so I decided to create a set of documentation. As I outlined at the beginning of this paper, the database was in a state of semi-completion when SVP's 2011 season began. The project had decided to go paperless only in March 2011, and the dig season began in early July, so the development and testing process was rather rushed. When excavation began in early July, all of the most critical elements were mostly functional and mostly stable, but I continued to refine, fix, and add numerous elements throughout the season. Due to the incomplete nature of the system, as well as my inexperience in running anything like it, producing documentation was a much lower priority than producing a fully featured and stable recording system. The highly fluid and evolving nature of our procedures and of the database itself added further barriers to generating documentation. It was not until the middle of the second season, when the system had reached a point of stability, that writing a user guide appeared on our radar screens.

In hindsight I wish that I had produced such documentation earlier, because it would have made the job of running the paperless system much less stressful for the first two seasons. The more elements you add to something—the syncing, the image handling, the various pieces of hardware and software—the more difficult it becomes to keep it all straight in your head, let alone to hand off the system to someone else. In addition to a user guide, we created several types of documents

Database Syncing Procedures

1	Make sure no devices are connected to Parent DB (Server) and that they remain disconnected until entire syncing process is completed
2	Close Parent DB (Server)
3	Make backup copy of Parent DB (Public / Database / Backups / SVP Cera Backups)
4	Reopen Parent DB

5	Close Child DB (iPads)
6	Copy Child DB from iPad to server (Desktop / Incoming Databases)
7	Sync Child DB with Parent DB (0_0_2 Run All Sync Scripts)
8	Rename Child DB and move to backups folder (Public / Database / Backups / SVP Cera field Backups)
9	Repeat for all database iPads

10	Close Parent DB
11	Copy DB onto iPads (from Public / Database)
12	Charge iPads

13	Reopen Parent DB
14	Tell specialists they can connect again

Notebook Syncing Procedures

1	Open Pages, make sure notebooks have all synced via iCloud

Sangro Valley Project 2013:
Syncing Workflows

Figure 16: Checklist of syncing procedures.

Event	Result	Solution
New on child	Import into parent	
New on parent	Stays in parent	
New on both (same number)	KEEPS BOTH	Manually resolve the conflict AFTER sync

Event	Result	Solution
Changed on child	Updates in parent	
Changed on parent	Stays in parent	
Changed on both	Dialogue box, conflict resolution screens	Manually resolve the conflict DURING sync

Event	Result	Solution
Delete existing on child	Stays on parent	Manually delete from parent
Delete existing on parent	Remains deleted from parent	
Delete existing on both	Remains deleted from parent	

Sangro Valley Project 2013:
Syncing Event Matrix

Figure 17: Chart of events that can occur during syncing.

that have proven particularly useful. The first of these were files documenting the syncing process, which always has been complex. One file was a checklist of all of the steps involved in syncing the database and notebooks (FIG. 16); the other file was a chart covering everything that can occur while syncing the database, along with what the result is and what action needs to be taken, if any (FIG. 17). Another set of documents were workflow diagrams. One workflow presents all the steps for image processing, which was used mainly by the database administrator and the photographer (FIG. 18). Another diagram charts the steps involved in recording and processing various object types and samples recovered during excavation (FIG. 19). We found that by creating these workflow diagrams we were better able to communicate to various staff members how their physical tasks integrated with their database tasks and how their role—be it field or lab—fit into the workflow as a whole. I made a point of generating similar documents during the development of the SKAP database, and, as a result, the system has been much more manageable in its first season (2015) than the SVP database was in either its first or second seasons.

PROBLEMS AND RECOMMENDATIONS

In addition to the discussion above, I would like to offer three recommendations for improvements to workflows based on observations I have made while working with these three projects. First, proactive communication with all staff members and users of the system is critical, especially in the first season or two and especially with users who are new to the system. Many people do not realize that the system can be changed to fit how they work, and they often do not bring up problems that arise because they do not realize that they can be fixed. Several times users have assumed that they had to change how they worked to fit the database, which often results in ad hoc, improper, and inadequate solutions to easily solvable problems. For example, if a field did not already exist, very often users would type descriptions or additional information into whatever field they thought was appropriate, rather than asking for a new field. Another example of an easily solvable problem is the tab order, or the order by which the cursor moves through fields when the user presses the "Tab" key; several times I have discovered that an unexpected tab order—which

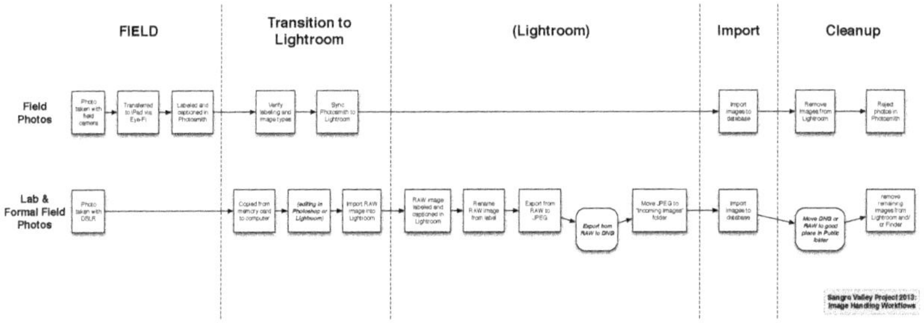

Figure 18: Image handling workflows.

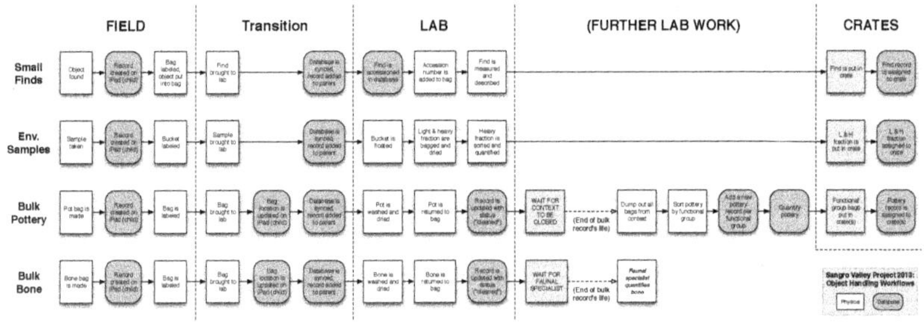

Figure 19: Object and sample handling workflows.

can be fixed in about 30 seconds—had been slowing down users for days or weeks before it came to my attention. This was especially troublesome during the study seasons at PARP:PS (2013–2015), when team members were engaged in the industrialized task (Caraher 2013; Ch. 4.1) of processing large volumes of materials. I suspect that this common user behavior—or more accurately, lack of behavior—is a symptom of most people's experiences with computers and software being a passive one. For example, users do not get to change how Microsoft Excel works. Fortunately, this function is easy for a developer to remedy by actively seeking feedback from users. In my experience, users quickly learn that the system can be changed, and before long they will offer suggestions and ask for changes without prompting.

Second, everyone must remember that the database administrator and/or developer is a member of the excavation team and a partner. It is important that the developer understand how each person works and how that fits into the database and the entire recording process, and it is important that each project member understand how they fit into the process so that tasks or objects do not fall through the cracks (see Holtorf (2002) and Yarrow (2008) on some interpretive implications of archaeological workflows). Diagrams and flowcharts are helpful in this but there are a range of ways to accomplish this goal, including building progress bars and trackers. For example, I have built for SKAP some digital flags that get raised depending on certain actions: an excavator can check a box if a find needs to be photographed or examined more closely, which triggers a visible flag in that find's parent records (Supplementary Material 3). These flags help both excavators and specialists keep track of what objects need further attention.

Third, there are things that the administrator or developer can do to ensure that the system will run smoothly no matter who is in charge. As I mentioned above, a user guide is useful for training field staff, and documentation of the inner workings of the system is useful for both current and future administrators. While paperless systems are effective, they are not yet simple to run. Furthermore, a description of the recording system's technical details should be included with other metadata in any final repository or publication to aid in the contextualization of the data that it helped to produce (Atici *et al.*

2013; Kansa and Kansa 2013). Documentation is essential at all stages of the research process.

I will return for a moment to my first two recommendations, which highlight what I see as the central place of the database administrator or data manager within a web of team members. Other contributors to this volume (Caraher, Ch. 4.1; Ellis, Ch. 1.2; Wallrodt, Ch. 1.1) touch on the role of digital technologies within the structures of archaeological projects, but the digital technologists themselves have been considered only tangentially. We would be wise to confront more directly and comprehensively how databases and data managers should fit into the broader communication and social networks of a project (Berggren and Hodder 2003; Frankland and Earl 2014; see also: Roosevelt *et al.* 2015 on using technology to facilitate intra-team communication), but this issue deserves a fuller exploration than can be contained in this chapter.

Many of the problems that I have presented are not unique to paperless projects, but digital recording systems make you aware of them and force you to confront them much earlier (for a debate on the perpetual fallibility of archaeologists regardless of recording media, see Caraher 2013; Ch. 4.1; Ellis, Ch. 1.2). When designing paper forms, for example, you do not have to be explicit in how the different parts relate to each other. When you design a relational database, you do have to be explicit in this (see Wallrodt, Ch. 1.1, on joining the "pieces" of data). The same underlying problems and needs still exist in both cases. However, with traditional methods you may not realize that you have a deep problem with your data structure or procedures until it comes time to analyze the data.

The technological landscape has changed in the last five years, yet the early lessons retain their value as a second generation of paperless projects is born. Early adopters like PARP:PS, SVP, the E'se'get Archaeology Project (Betts 2012), the Chan Chich Archaeological Project (Houk 2012), and the Pyla-Koutsopetria Archaeological Project (Fee *et al.* 2013; Fee, Ch. 2.1) were converts from paper, and their use of digital recording relied on incremental translations of existing practices in order to maintain internal consistency. Now, new projects like SKAP and the Kaymakçı Archaeological Project (Roosevelt *et al.* 2015) are being conceived as paperless from the start. This freedom from existing legacy data and procedures has allowed scholars the flexibility to redesign completely their archaeological workflows and data structures, with exciting results (Roosevelt *et al.* 2015; Jackson *et al.* 2016). At the same time, the development of commercial or open-source archaeological software, which previously had focused on data analysis and dissemination, has turned increasingly toward field recording on mobile devices (e.g., ARK (Dufton, Ch. 3.3), Codifi (Prins *et al.* 2014), FAIMS (Sobotkova *et al.*, Ch. 3.2), iDig (Hartzler 2015), OpenDig (Vincent *et al.* 2014), and TooWaste (Castro López *et al.*, Ch. 3.1)). Archaeologists now have a higher number and higher quality of digital tools to choose from, and I am excited to see what comes next. Amid the often dizzying pace of technological innovation, I urge that we maintain a goal of creating digital solutions that play nicely with human team members and with the physical aspects of fieldwork.

Efficiently Slow Archaeology

Paperless systems are becoming more widespread and they are already revolutionizing the way archaeological data are collected, managed, and analyzed. However, these developments have not gone unquestioned (Huggett 2015a; Nakassis 2015). Many of the critiques—in particular the recent push for "Slow Archaeology" (Caraher 2013; Ch. 4.1)—force us to consider our reasons for adopting new technology and the benefits that we gain from employing it, and they thus serve a useful role in checking the blind adoption of technology for its own sake (Ellis, Ch. 1.2).

I agree with many of the arguments extolling the virtues of careful, thoughtful practice, and I believe that digital recording can promote such practice. I suggest that while some aspects of field recording do require careful thought and attention, not every recording task is equally deserving. The focus of Slow Archaeology on drawings and notebooks, two distinctly non-repetitive activities, supports this implicitly (Caraher 2015b). Much of the time savings found in paperless systems are gained by eliminating the repetitive tasks inherent in the form-based recording of a modern "industrialized" (after Caraher) archaeological project, and by centralizing tasks that otherwise would be spread across multiple sheets of paper and notebooks. Supervisors can spend a surprising amount of time manually numbering stratigraphic units and small finds, tracking bags of materials from the field to the lab, adding up sherd counts, and ensuring that any changes to recorded data are updated in all the relevant forms and notebooks. A computer is able to perform these jobs more quickly and (perhaps more importantly) more reliably than a human. Forcing a supervisor to expend considerable energy on these repetitive tasks can promote their perception of the archaeological remains as a fragmented data set that consists only of identification codes and quantifications. By shifting much of this burden, the efficiency of digital recording can help to achieve some of the goals of Slow Archaeology while still meeting the expectations of modern archaeological practices (cf. Caraher 2015b).

At the end of the day, paperless recording is merely a tool, and it is up to us to decide how to use it. The time that excavators save with an efficient paperless system can be used in a myriad of ways: they can put more time into drawings or produce more of them; they can spend more time teaching field school students, something that digital systems can both facilitate and complicate (Opitz 2015; see also Bria and DeTore, Ch. 1.5); they can excavate with their own hands, which many supervisors yearn to do more and which can improve their understanding of a site; and yes, they can simply gather more data (Caraher 2015a; 2015b; Ch. 4.1; Nakassis 2015; Roosevelt et al. 2015; Ellis, Ch. 1.2). But these digital systems also open up exciting possibilities for new interpretive approaches (e.g., Roosevelt et al. 2015).

For example, during the 2015 season of the Say Kah Archaeological Project, we used our paperless system to include different world views in the recording process (Jackson et al. 2016). One of the goals of SKAP is to recognize and decenter the dominance of modern, Western archaeological visions of the material record, in order to make space for Classic Maya understandings of the material world. A digital recording system can seamlessly switch between different ways of viewing data. This flexibility enabled us to integrate emic views in the recording process, and to give equal footing both to Western, dualist ways of reading the archaeological record and to indigenous Maya understandings of this material. Our excavation permit from the Belize Institute of Archaeology and the umbrella project under which we work, the Programme for Belize Archaeological Project, mandated the submission of particular forms with the final report. Similar reporting requirements often are cited as a barrier to the full adoption of digital archaeology in some sectors, but in many cases these can be overcome easily by creating layouts that replicate the required forms for printing, or saving PDFs, as we did (see Spigelman *et al.* (Ch. 3.4) for an example of success within cultural resource management, but cf. Dufton (Ch. 3.3) on operating within the constraints set by the City of London). Using a digital recording system allowed us to meet these recording requirements while also collecting additional types of data, but without the increased workload and conceptual divide of two physically separate forms. The efficiency we gained by transitioning to digital recording freed both time and space for excavators to turn their attention to the additional types of data that we are collecting; the increased efficiency directly facilitated the addition of these new elements. Our experience indicates that paperless systems allow for nimble movement between multiple ways of seeing and recording, a capability that can radically shift our understanding of archaeological sites and materials even while in the field, allowing interpretive insight to occur simultaneously with the excavation process and in-field planning and execution.

CONCLUSION

The community of paperless projects has grown quite a bit since 2010, as has the community of people developing paperless recording systems. This volume is evidence of that growth. There are now many more resources available to those who are developing apps and databases for tablets: Apple provides excellent documents like the "iOS Human Interface Guidelines," FileMaker has posted videos and a variety of guides, and countless websites offer resources both for general mobile development and that specific to FileMaker. The lessons that we learned in those first few years, however, are still valuable, and it is from that perspective that I have tried to offer some insight into building an effective paperless archaeological recording system.

We as archaeologists should no longer be satisfied with just getting a paperless system to function successfully—although that is certainly no small feat. We need to continue experimenting and thinking about how to make these systems work as an integral part of the research process. It is not enough for developers or administrators to possess technical skills; they need to have visual design skills and to be able to communicate effectively through the system. They need to work *with* specialists and excavators, not be tyrants. Digital recording systems can streamline fieldwork, improve the quality and quantity of data collected in the field, significantly reduce errors and misunderstandings, and facilitate new interpretive approaches, but they do require careful and thoughtful preparation and implementation. I hope our experiences will help others to implement paperless recording systems successfully within their own projects.

ACKNOWLEDGEMENTS

I would like to thank Susan Kane (SVP), Steven Ellis (PARP:PS), Sarah Jackson (SKAP), and Linda Brown (SKAP), as well as all members of these projects for their support. None of this work would have been possible without them. The opinions and conclusions expressed here are my own and do not necessarily reflect the opinions of the research projects or their directors. My final thanks go to the editors of this volume and the anonymous reviewer for their helpful comments.

https://mobilizingthepast.mukurtu.net/collection/13-sangro-valley-and-five-paperless-seasons-lessons-building-effective-digital-recording

http://dc.uwm.edu/arthist_mobilizingthepast/5

REFERENCES

Apple Inc. 2010. "Discovering Ancient Pompeii with iPad." http://www.apple.com/ipad/pompeii. Archived at https://classics.uc.edu/pompeii/images/stories/ipad/Apple%20-%20Discovering%20ancient%20Pompeii%20with%20iPad.pdf

Atici, L., S. W. Kansa, J. Lev-Tov, and E. C. Kansa. 2013. "Other People's Data: A Demonstration of the Imperative of Publishing Primary Data," *Journal of Archaeological Method and Theory* 20: 663–681.

Bell, T., A. Wilson, and A. Wickham. 2002. "Tracking the Samnites: Landscape and Communications Routes in the Sangro Valley, Italy," *American Journal of Archaeology* 106: 169–186.

Berggren, Å., and I. Hodder. 2003. "Social Practice, Method, and Some Problems of Field Archaeology," *American Antiquity* 68: 421–434.

Betts, M. 2012. "Going Paperless." *E'se'get Archaeology Project*, https://coastalarchaeology.wordpress.com/2012/07/07/going-paperless/

Butina, E. 2014. "The Use of iPad as a Documenting Tool on an Archaeological Excavation on Govce 2011 Project in North-Eastern Slovenia," in G. Earl, T. Sly, A. Chrysanthi, P. Murrieta-Flores, C. Papadopoulos, I. Romanowska, and D. Wheatley, eds., *Archaeology in the Digital Era 2: E-Papers from the 40th Annual Conference on Computer Applications and Quantitative Methods in Archaeology (CAA), Southampton, 26–29 March 2012.* Amsterdam: Amsterdam University Press, 48–56.

Caraher, W. R. 2013. "Slow Archaeology," *North Dakota Quarterly* 80(2): 43–52.

———. 2015a. "Understanding Digital Archaeology." *The Archaeology of the Mediterranean World*, https://mediterraneanworld.wordpress.com/2015/07/17/understanding-digital-archaeology/

———. 2015b. "Revisions of Slow Archaeology." *The Archaeology of the Mediterranean World*, https://mediterraneanworld.wordpress.com/2015/11/16/revisions-of-slow-archaeology/

Ellis, S. J. R., and J. Wallrodt. 2011. "iPads at Pompeii." *Pompeii Archaeological Research Project: Porta Stabia*, http://classics.uc.edu/pompeii/index.php/news/1-latest/142-ipads2010.html

Ellis, S. J. R., A. L. C. Emmerson, K. Dicus, G. Tibbott, and A. K. Pavlick. 2015. "The 2012 Field Season at I.1.1–10, Pompeii: Preliminary Report on the Excavations." *The Journal of Fasti Online* 328, http://www.fastionline.org/docs/FOLDER-it-2015-328.pdf

Fee, S. B, D. K. Pettegrew, and W. R. Caraher. 2013. "Taking Mobile Computing to the Field," *Near Eastern Archaeology* 76: 50–55.

Frankland, T., and G. Earl. 2014. "Implications for the Design of Novel Technologies for Archaeological Fieldwork," in G. Earl, T. Sly, A. Chrysanthi, P. Murrieta-Flores, C. Papadopoulos, I. Romanowska, and D. Wheatley, eds., *Archaeology in the Digital Era 2: E-Papers from the 40th Annual Conference on Computer Applications and Quantitative Methods in Archaeology (CAA), Southampton, 26–29 March 2012.* Amsterdam: Amsterdam University Press, 30–36.

Hartzler, B. 2015. "iDig—Recording Archaeology." *iTunes Preview*, https://itunes.apple.com/us/app/id953353960

Holtorf, C. 2002. "Notes on the Life History of a Pot Sherd," *Journal of Material Culture* 7: 49–71.

Houk, B. A. 2012. "The Chan Chich Archaeological Project's Digital Data Collection System," in *The 2012 Season of the Chan Chich Archaeological Project. Papers of the Chan Chich Archaeological Project 6.* Lubbock: Texas Tech University Department of Sociology, Anthropology, and Social Work, 73–82.

Huggett, J. 2015a. "Challenging Digital Archaeology," *Open Archaeology* 1: 79–85.

———. 2015b. "A Manifesto for an Introspective Digital Archaeology," *Open Archaeology* 1: 86–95.

Jackson, S. E., C. F. Motz, and L. A. Brown. 2016. "Pushing the Paperless Envelope: Digital Recording and Innovative Ways of Seeing at a Classic Maya Site," *Advances in Archaeological Practice* 4: 176–191.

Jennings, M. 2011. "Guest Post: Michael Jennings at Jericho Mafjar Project." *Paperless Archaeology,* http://paperlessarchaeology.com/2011/02/10/guest-post-michael-jennings-at-jericho-mafjar-project/

Kansa, E. 2011. "New Directions for the Digital Past," in E. Kansa, S. W. Kansa, and E. Watrall, eds., *Archaeology 2.0: New Approaches to Communication and Collaboration.* Los Angeles: Cotsen Institute of Archaeology, 1–26.

Kansa, E., and S. W. Kansa. 2013. "We All Know That a 14 Is a Sheep: Data Publication and Professionalism in Archaeological Communication," *Journal of Eastern Mediterranean Archaeology and Heritage Studies* 1: 88–97.

Levy, T. E. 2014. "From the Guest Editor," *Near Eastern Archaeology* 77(3): inside cover.

Lock, G., T. Bell, and J. Lloyd. 1999. "Towards a Methodology for Modeling Surface Survey Data: The Sangro Valley Project," in M. Gillings, D. J. Mattingly, and J. van Dalen, eds., *Geographical Information Systems and Landscape Archaeology. Archaeology of Mediterranean Landscapes* 3. Oxford: Oxbow Books, 55–63.

Motz, C. F, and S. Carrier. 2013. "Paperless Recording at the Sangro Valley Project," in G. Earl, T. Sly, A. Chrysanthi, P. Murrieta-Flores, C. Papadopoulos, I. Romanowska, and D. Wheatley, eds., *Archaeology in the Digital Era: Papers from the 40th Annual Conference of Computer Applications and Quantitative Methods in Archaeology*

(CAA), *Southampton, 26–29 March 2012.* Amsterdam: Amsterdam University Press, 25–30.

Nakassis, D. 2015. "Thinking Digital Archaeology." *Aegean Prehistory*, https://englianos.wordpress.com/2015/08/10/thinking-digital-archaeology/

Opitz, R. 2015. "Teaching Practice while Developing Practice: Mobile Computing at the Gabii Project Field School." Paper read at the Mobilizing the Past for a Digital Future: The Potential of Digital Archaeology Workshop, 28 February 2015, Boston.

Prins, A. B., M. J. Adams, R. S. Homsher, and M. Ashley. 2014. "Digital Archaeological Fieldwork and the Jezreel Valley Regional Project, Israel," *Near Eastern Archaeology* 77: 192–197.

Roosevelt, C. H., P. Cobb, E. Moss, B. R. Olson, and S. Ünlüsoy. 2015. "Excavation is ~~Destruction~~ Digitization: Advances in Archaeological Practice," *Journal of Field Archaeology* 40: 325–346.

Vincent, M. L., F. Kuester, and T. E Levy. 2014. "OpenDig: Digital Field Archeology, Curation, Publication, and Dissemination," *Near Eastern Archaeology* 77: 204–208.

Wallrodt, J. 2011a. "Let's Call This a Beta [updated]." *Paperless Archaeology*, http://paperlessarchaeology.com/2011/06/07/lets-call-this-a-beta/

———. 2011b. "That's Why It's Called a Beta." *Paperless Archaeology*, http://paperlessarchaeology.com/2011/08/20/thats-why-its-called-a-beta/

Wallrodt, J., K. Dicus, L. Lieberman, and G. Tucker. 2015. "Beyond Tablet Computers as a Tool for Data Collection: Three Seasons of Processing and Curating Digital Data in a Paperless World," in A. Traviglia, ed., *Across Space and Time: Papers from the 41st Annual Conference of Computer Applications and Quantitative Methods in Archaeology, Perth, 25–28 March 2013.* Amsterdam: Amsterdam University Press, 97–103.

Yarrow, T. 2008. "In Context: Meaning, Materiality and Agency in the Process of Archaeological Recording," in C. Knappett and L. Malafouris, eds., *Material Agency: Towards a Non-Anthropocentric Approach.* Berlin: Springer, 121–137.

1.4.
DIY Digital Workflows on the Athienou Archaeological Project, Cyprus

Jody Michael Gordon, Erin Walcek Averett, Derek B. Counts, Kyosung Koo, and Michael K. Toumazou

LESSONS FROM A QUARTER CENTURY OF DATA RECORDING IN THE MALLOURA VALLEY

During its first two decades, the Athienou Archaeological Project (AAP; established 1990) developed a robust excavation recording system that closely documented stratigraphic and artifactual data via integrated paper and paper-to-digital methods. From the onset, paper forms and notebooks were used to record field notes, which became digital immediately afterward in the lab by re-entering the information into databases and word processing files. This two-step system served AAP's pedagogical and research goals because it employed a meticulous recording system and archaeological workflow that were user-friendly for both staff and field-school students. It provided both quantitative and qualitative information in written, drawn, and photographic form for all contexts, architecture, samples, and finds. The manual, secondary input of paper-based data into digital formats further provided the project with a large, queryable, and complementary (and duplicate) digital dataset.

Today, however, AAP has moved toward a more paperless system—a hybrid system that employs the same meticulous data recording protocols, while using some born-digital data in place of secondary data entry. In some ways, little has changed. AAP's long-standing recording system and workflows remain, yet, the project's DIY (do-it-yourself) movement into digital workflows at the advent of mobile computing devices via the adoption of Apple iPads for field

Figure 1: The Malloura Valley, Cyprus.

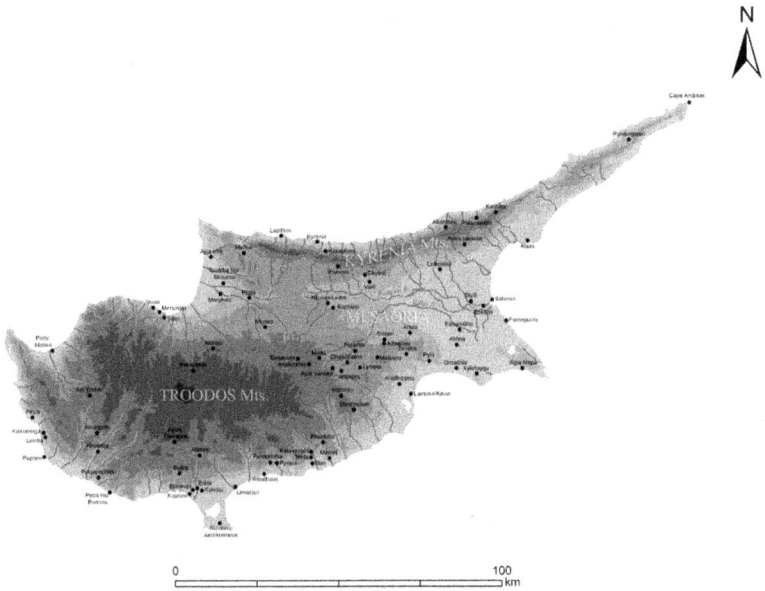

Figure 2: Map of Cyprus showing the location of the Malloura Valley in rectangle. Map by D. Massey.

recording reveals quantitative and qualitative changes to the ways that AAP staff members *do* archaeology at the trowel's edge.

This chapter explores the contexts, motivations, and decisions that influenced the shift to on-site mobile computing at AAP so that other field school projects grappling with the questions of whether and when to "go digital" might learn from our experiences. Since many scholars would now claim that "we are *all* digital archaeologists" or "excavation is digitization," this seems a particularly pressing methodological transition to examine (Morgan and Eve 2012: 523; Roosevelt *et al.* 2015: 325). We discuss how even a modest-sized project without full-time digital technologists can transition to a tablet-based recording system that employs a hybrid digital/paper-based workflow, and how our experiment impacted both our research and pedagogical goals. Although our discussions of interpretive improvements mainly derive from the authors' own reflections, our pedagogical successes are supported by user surveys and recorded team conversations focused on trench supervisor experiences.

METHODOLOGY, DATA RECORDING, AND THE ROLE OF TECHNOLOGY AT AAP IN THE PRE-TABLET ERA

Since 1990, AAP has been investigating long-term culture change in the Malloura Valley of central Cyprus's Mesaoria plain through a multidisciplinary project for undergraduate students that combines field (excavation and survey) and laboratory training in archaeological methods with research analyses. The valley served as a locus for activity for nearly 3,000 years, a period that begins in the early first millennium B.C. and continues to the modern era. This long occupation, coupled with the diversity of archaeological remains encountered (domestic, religious, industrial, and funerary), makes the valley an ideal training ground in archaeological methodology (FIGS. 1, 2; see also Toumazou *et al.* 2011, 2015b).

More recently, the project has focused on the excavation of a Cypro-Geometric through Roman-period sanctuary at the site of Malloura (FIG. 3), and our excavations have shed new light on first-millennium B.C. Cyprus, especially regarding the nature of votive religion in the hinterlands of the island. Yet, Malloura has also proven to be a stratigraphically complex site because it was frequently looted

Figure 3: Aerial view of the sanctuary of Athienou-*Malloura* in 2005.

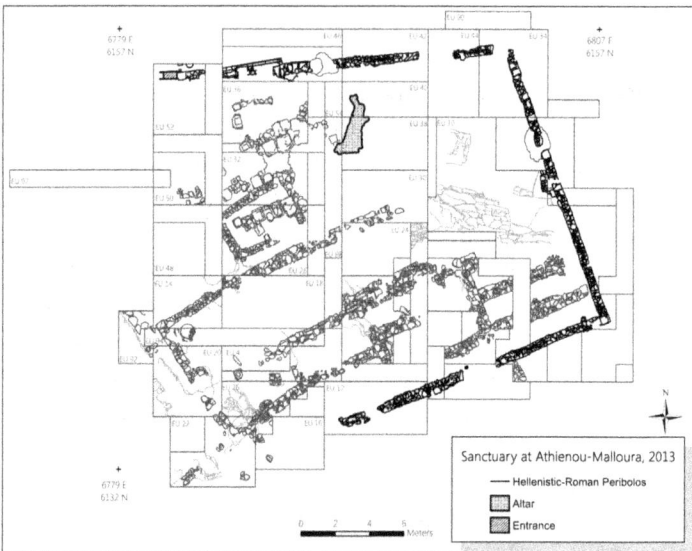

Figure 4: Site plan of Malloura showing excavation units (EUs). Drawing by Remko Breuker; updated by Kevin Garstki.

in the recent past. Hence, considering the site's archaeological importance and complexity, an exacting system of on-site data recording has always been a key part of AAP's modus operandi. Furthermore, throughout the project's history, AAP has also prioritized the archaeological training of undergraduate and graduate students, which includes instruction in excavation and survey methodologies and recording systems as well as the processing of finds and data in the lab and museum. Thus, a significant portion of the staff's time is devoted to on-site or classroom instruction, and the majority of funds (raised both via tuition and National Science Foundation Research Experiences for Undergraduates [NSF-REU] grants) are dedicated to student travel, room and board, and educational expenses. AAP's complementary goals of understanding the long-term history of the Malloura Valley and providing rigorous training of students in archaeological field techniques has led to a deliberate process of excavation, and these factors explain our cautious incorporation of technology.

Like many projects excavating in the 1990s and early 2000s (see e.g., Dibble and McPherron 1988; Ancona *et al.* 1999; see also Motz, Ch. 1.3), AAP embraced "digital" elements in its workflows from an early date in an effort to improve data quality and manipulation. Yet, in the absence of any durable and portable computing devices, these digital methods were lab-based and mainly focused on data duplication, preservation, and analysis (or querying). In terms of its more general data recording process, AAP developed a data workflow from the field to the lab that was primarily paper-based and tailored to the Malloura site, and this workflow has since permitted interpretation from the macro to micro levels as outlined in AAP's "Handbook of Excavations" (for an overview excavation methods, see Toumazou and Counts 2011: 71–75).

AAP's on-site data recording workflow primarily involves the following process. Excavation Unit (EU; i.e., trench) supervisors record stratigraphy and finds in an exacting manner using a variety of paper-based forms, hand-drawn sketches, photographs, and notebooks. Stratigraphic Unit (SU; similar to a "layer" or "stratum") forms record key data pertaining to the unit's location, stratigraphic position/nature (e.g., looters' pit/stratified or disturbed), features (e.g., walls, hearths), soils, organic and inorganic remains, ceramics, and objects, as well as references to associated photos and drawings (FIG. 5); a grid permits easy drawing of the SU's horizontal limits and any features. Square

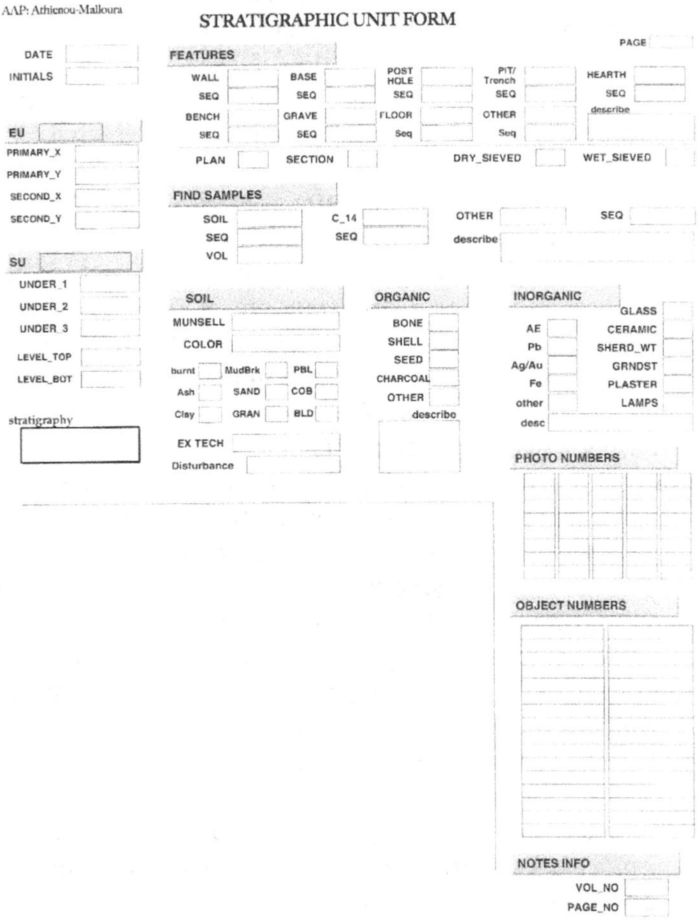

AAP: Athienou-Malloura

STRATIGRAPHIC UNIT FORM

PAGE

DATE
INITIALS

EU
PRIMARY_X
PRIMARY_Y
SECOND_X
SECOND_Y

SU
UNDER_1
UNDER_2
UNDER_3
LEVEL_TOP
LEVEL_BOT

stratigraphy

FEATURES
WALL SEQ
BASE SEQ
POST HOLE SEQ
PIT/ Trench SEQ
HEARTH SEQ
BENCH SEQ
GRAVE SEQ
FLOOR Seq
OTHER Seq
describe
PLAN
SECTION
DRY_SIEVED
WET_SIEVED

FIND SAMPLES
SOIL SEQ VOL
C_14 SEQ
OTHER describe
SEQ

SOIL
MUNSELL
COLOR
burnt MudBrk PBL
Ash SAND COB
Clay GRAN BLD
EX TECH
Disturbance

ORGANIC
BONE
SHELL
SEED
CHARCOAL
OTHER
describe

INORGANIC
AE
Pb
Ag/Au
Fe
other
desc
GLASS
CERAMIC
SHERD_WT
GRNDST
PLASTER
LAMPS

PHOTO NUMBERS

OBJECT NUMBERS

NOTES INFO
VOL_NO
PAGE_NO

Figure 5: A paper stratigraphic unit (SU) form used at Athienou-*Malloura*.

Meter Unit (SMU) forms provide further resolution and also include a gridded drawing that records the SMU's architectural features and in situ artifacts. Other forms (Object, Photography, Elevation) connect the field's data to the lab in a systematic way. Finally, EU supervisors maintain field notebooks (once paper-based, now entered digitally on mobile tablet computers) that provide them with a non-delimited writing space to record their excavation decisions and observations about the trench in narrative form.

The paper-based system was relatively simple to learn, implement, and archive. As with all paper archives, however, there were some logistical difficulties in terms of storage and collating that made long-term access and rapid synthesis for on-site and off-site decision making and interpretation slow and limited. For example, the database could not be accessed on-site. In addition, in the lab, the time required for the digitizing and trascribing of paper-based data was slow and increased the potential for human error with data entry.

During AAP's first 20 years, the project sought to create archaeological workflows that accurately recorded Malloura's ancient past, to help students engage with "hands-on" archaeological research, and to integrate computing tools aimed at strengthening data collating, integration, and analysis. The project was thus always "tech-friendly" and willing to entertain changes to its workflow when the technology was affordable and could enhance project goals. Although various computing tools were employed since its inception, AAP did not progress to a more digital stage in the pre-tablet era partly because of the harsh working conditions at Malloura. The site is extremely dry, dusty, and hot in the summer, and there is no available power source or Internet connection. Such conditions presented problems in the early 2000s because laptops were not robust enough in terms of battery power and design to endure an eight-hour workday in the site's torrid environment. Moreover, the project's FileMaker database would be of little use remotely without a Web-based interface and Internet access. As a result, there was a digital divide between the site (entirely paper-based) and the lab (a hybrid between paper and digital).

AAP and the Advent of Paperless Workflows

The decision to adopt born-digital field recording methods was based on AAP's research goals and openness to experimenting with new technology, as well as on the revolutionary changes that had begun to occur in archaeological computing (see also Levy 2014; Roosevelt *et al.* 2015: 326; Gordon *et al.*, Introduction). By the late 2000s, in tandem with the information technology revolution, progress in lowering the cost of nanotechnology led to the development of relatively cheap, light-weight, touch screen–enabled, Internet-ready, and camera-equipped mobile computing devices with long battery lives (e.g., iPhones). These devices were soon followed by the first tablet computers with the launch of the Apple iPad in April 2010. Because tablets were portable, user-friendly, and could be synched to existing databases via Web-based apps, archaeologists started to recognize their ability to integrate tasks into fieldwork that had once only taken place in the lab (Fee *et al.* 2013: 50). Within a year, Apple iPads had begun to be used by archaeologists needing durable, portable computing devices that could be used effectively in the field to record excavation data and function as "digital notebooks." It was this development that spurred the first attempts at so-called "paperless" excavation recording workflows (see Wallrodt, Ch. 1.1). These methods are now becoming more common on archaeological sites and—according to some scholars—are indicative of a significant shift in archaeological practice (Roosevelt *et al.* 2015: 339–340; Gordon *et al.*, Introduction).

The first major Mediterranean archaeological project to experiment with iPads as portable digital recording devices in the field was the Pompeii Archaeological Research Project: Porta Stabia (PARP:PS) where Steven Ellis and John Wallrodt devised a DIY mobile data-recording system. Trench supervisors were issued iPads equipped with "off-the-shelf" apps that could record, integrate, and analyze excavated field data and upload it to servers for long-term digital storage (Ellis and Wallrodt 2011; see Ellis, Ch. 1.2; Wallrodt, Ch. 1.1). Besides Apple's built-in iOS applications (e.g., iBooks and Camera), their original workflow included a database application (FM Touch), a digital drawing app (iDraw), a word processor app (Pages), and a flowchart app (OmniGraffle) used for creating Harris matrices. In the spirit of Web 2.0 data sharing and hacks, Wallrodt reflexively discussed the

PARP:PS system on his weblog, *Paperless Archaeology* (http://paperlessarchaeology.com). In addition to general observations about the tablets' user-friendly nature, their durability in the field, and how much written and photographic data they could record, Wallrodt also provided instructions as to how to develop a DIY digital workflow that would require little technical know-how, be cost effective, and would teach novice archaeologists digital skills and new ways of manipulating stratigraphic data.

The pioneering work done by PARP:PS is important to acknowledge here because Wallrodt's blog allowed AAP, under the supervision of assistant director Jody Gordon, to "go digital." This process of knowledge sharing and easy adoption/adaption is significant since it underscores the influence of new technological developments on archaeology in the Web 2.0 age (Morgan and Eve 2012; Caraher 2014b; Morgan 2015). Archaeological methods and practices can now be shaped by open-access digital means, and devices' and programs' utility and interoperability open the door to myriad ways to address archaeological goals and problems. For most projects, as Ellis has argued, a "digital filter" is inserted at some stage (Ellis, 1.2). Thus, archaeology's very transformation into a "digital" discipline that permits the enhancement of research goals, even within existing logistical limitations, influenced AAP's decision to move toward digital workflows and provided a kickstart to our thinking about the benefits of digital archaeology.

The next step for AAP was to establish whether the perceived benefits of converting to digital data recording—most significantly, the collection of born-digital data captured on-site via tablet computers without paper complements/duplicates—were compatible with the project's dual goals of understanding the Cypriot past and training students. Wallrodt highlighted many of the benefits of mobile data recording in *Paperless Archaeology*, and since 2011 many more scholars have argued that utilizing tablets and creating born-digital files has many advantages (e.g., Motz and Carrier 2013; Wallrodt *et al.* 2013; Prins *et al.* 2014; Roosevelt *et al.* 2015). Mobile recording arguably produces "more and better" data with less human error, preserves it in more places, easily integrates it, permits immediate intra-site and eventual inter-site analyses via relational databases, and democratizes data by streamlining it so that it can be easily shared between team members or even the public through published digital archives affiliated with linked open data or blogs (Kansa *et al.* 2007: 193–194; Kansa and Kansa 2011:57–59; Morgan and Eve 2012: 526; Prins *et al.* 2014: 196; Roosevelt *et al.* 2015: 342). These digital advantages promised improvements over AAP's existing paper-based field recording system that might offer enhanced interpretations of Malloura's archaeology.

In recent years, scholars have also stressed that paperless archaeology is practical from a logistical standpoint, and these factors further influenced AAP's decision to "go digital" (Motz and Carrier 2013: 29; Wallrodt, Ch. 1.1; Ellis, Ch. 1.3; Fee, Ch. 2.1; Sobotkova *et al.*, Ch. 3.2; Dufton, Ch. 3.3; Roosevelt *et al.* 2015: 339, 341). By eliminating the recopying of paper forms and notes, some scholars have argued that valuable time required for site analysis and object processing is saved (e.g., see Motz, Ch. 1.3; Poehler, Ch. 1.7), while the outfitting of a project with the basic components of tablets, a desktop computer with a relational database, a high-end digital camera, and a series of off-the-shelf—or even open-source—apps is relatively inexpensive (Roosevelt *et al.* 2015: 341). Internet connectivity further enhances the digital process, but it is not always required or available. Another logistical benefit is that the technology is often user-friendly in that it can be easily taught and implemented by field supervisors without programming skills (Bria and DeTore, Ch. 1.5). Likewise, the device's usability encourages projects to attract students who have grown up using mobile devices and who are interested in learning about their applied use, with the result that over time, the project's technological knowledge base may be enhanced.

According to recent studies, the interpretive and pedagogical benefits of paperless archaeology are not uniform and seem to vary according to a project's implementation scheme and goals (Opitz 2015; Bria and DeTore, Ch. 1.5). Nevertheless, when first considering adoption in 2011, AAP identified several benefits based on the experience of PARP:PS, which have since been supported by other projects. For example, the time saved from digitizing paper records permits other research activities, like object drawing and student training, while the rapid accessibility and searchability of the data beyond the lab—especially *on-site*—promotes its sharing and interpretive power (cf. Morgan and Eve 2012: 525). In terms of pedagogy, the on-site entry of field data and the immediate accessibility of existing project files (which can easily be preloaded onto tablets) and online databases (when Internet access is available), provides excavators with new transferable skills, including the ability to use mobile devices and apps (Opitz 2015; Bria and DeTore, Ch. 1.5) to multitask with several programs to solve stratigraphic questions, and to think volumetrically or in terms of wider project workflows (Wallrodt *et al.* 2013; Roosevelt *et al.* 2015: 339). Hence, traditional post-excavation activities, such as intra-site comparisons of materials, can now take place on-site *during* excavation (Opitz 2015). Digital workflows with real-time updateable databases also contribute to novel forms of group-think integration between excavators, artifact specialists, and IT professionals, allowing for multiple team members to offer rapid insights on excavations (Morgan and Eve 2012: 524; Wallrodt *et al.* 2013). These interactions also contribute to reflexive re-evaluations of the interpretive value of the workflows as they develop (Berggren *et al.* 2015). Together, these perceived pedagogical benefits initially pioneered by PARP:PS promised to enhance the AAP's goal of preparing college students for archaeological careers, which by the 2010s, would require some literacy in on-site mobile computing, in addition to traditional excavation and survey training.

More recently, however, some scholars have suggested that the complete abandonment of paper-based excavation recording or the uncritical adoption of new technologies to streamline workflows could be detrimental to some aspects of archaeological practice. William Caraher (2015; Ch. 4.1), for example, has proposed that digitization can result in de-skilling, or the loss of traditional archaeological skills like trench illustration, while other scholars, like Dimitri Nakassis (2015), have questioned whether the time saved by digital data entry truly results in better stratigraphic interpretations or engagements with other archaeological tasks (e.g., lab-based object analysis). In 2011, however, the perceived benefits of experimenting with paperless archaeology were great enough that AAP decided to follow the PARP:PS model and experiment with a DIY digital workflow using Apple iPads.

Toward Digital Data Recording at the Trowel's Edge at Athienou-Malloura

The following section describes how the implementation of a DIY, near-paperless archaeological workflow successfully enhanced our project's goals. At present, there are three main ways to implement digital archaeology: (1) the use of fully digital, customized devices, apps, and systems (e.g., Federated Archaeological Information Management Systems (FAIMS); see Sobotkova *et al.*, Ch. 3.2), (2) the use of fully digital DIY workflow solutions that leverage proprietary and existing systems and devices (e.g., Archaeological Recording Kit (ARK); see Dufton, Ch. 3.3), and (3) the use of a combination of the two previously listed approaches that also involves some paper (e.g., like that used at the Proyecto de Investigación Arqueológico Regional Ancash (PIARA); see Bria and DeTore, Ch. 1.5). With limited IT personnel and funding for technology, AAP opted to follow the third route and develop a DIY approach using off-the-shelf apps along with paper-based legacy forms.

In an ideal world with unlimited funding and access to technical equipment and trained support personnel, bespoken digital archaeology systems with custom-built apps (like FAIMS) might represent the best way to turn paper-based archaeology into paperless. In reality, however, low-cost DIY digital workflows that utilize off-the-shelf apps, like those of PARP:PS, play a key role in democratizing the use of digital archaeologies (Daly and Evans 2006: 5; Morgan and Eve 2012: 527). Recently, William Caraher has written about the importance of an "archaeology DIY" approach that has "its roots in the improvised and ad hoc approach to challenges in the field, limited resources, and difficulties accessing tools designed for every circumstance from remote locations" (Caraher 2014a). Overcoming these challenges with DIY solutions is important because it can assist the further implementation of digital methodologies that can improve data capture and analysis for a range of project types (see Watrall 2011: 171–172). For AAP in particular, the DIY approach enabled us to assemble a series of devices and apps that would fit our time restraints and budget, while simultaneously enhancing our research and teaching goals.

In the 2011 season, AAP decided to beta test a single 16 GB iPad 2 for in-field, born-digital data recording. The field testing was undertaken by Gordon, who had followed PARP:PS' experiment online (FIG. 6). Since PARP:PS's system was only a year old and untested elsewhere, AAP decided to progress cautiously and not abandon its well-tested paper-based methods until Gordon had tested the technology and developed a protocol that would function on-site and integrate with the project's legacy data. Thus, our paper-based system was retained in 2011, while Gordon—who was *not* an IT specialist—experimented with the single iPad 2 to test its on-site usability. The iPad was not used for full-time excavation recording during this trial season; instead, it was used periodically to test its functionality vis-à-vis data recording needs and Malloura's harsh conditions.

Gordon equipped the iPad 2 with many of the same off-the-shelf apps used by PARP:PS. He took field notes in Pages (made easy with a Bluetooth keyboard); tested digital drawings using iDraw (particularly EU plans and vector tracing of objects); drew flowcharts with Omni-Graffle; and utilized Numbers for basic elevation calculations. He also tested the quality of the still and video digital cameras, as well as the feasibility of annotating digital imagery in iDraw. The iBooks app proved to be a useful repository for reference PDFs including the "AAP Handbook of Excavations," previous trench reports, balk and artifact drawings, and scanned images. These formerly paper-based resources, stored in the lab, were now immediately accessible on-site. A database program was not initially tested, however, because our FileMaker database was not yet Web accessible (there was no on-site Internet) and we did not have the IT personnel to monitor daily synching of the database records via USB to the master lab database. Nevertheless, in terms of the other more standard files generated on-site (e.g., PDFs of the daily notes), synching the iPad to both the lab registrar's desktop and a field-based laptop via USB was straightforward, and cloud-based data transfers in the Wi-Fi-enabled lab (using Google Gmail) were also successful.

These on-site experiments demonstrated the iPad's overall ability to contribute to project goals. In terms of positive results, the iPad withstood Malloura's heat and dust, and it maintained its power supply for an entire workday as long as it was charged fully the night before. Apps like Pages and OmniGraffle were user-friendly and permitted the incorporation of text and images, while iBooks allowed for the accessing of reference images and files in a manner that facilitated intra-site decision making. The iPad's video camera could record site tours, which provided a completely new and highly descriptive source of field data, and the tablet's photographic and written data could be regularly backed up to a laptop in the field or in the lab. In terms of shortcomings, some recording elements were more elusive or ineffectual. Digital drawing was a complicated matter. For example, iDraw was useful for drawing trench outlines, but sketching finds with shading was more difficult. Photos taken by the iPad were of a

Figure 6: AAP assistant director Jody Gordon testing an iPad in the field.

Figure 7: AAP trench supervisor Kevin Garstki using a Bluetooth keyboard to write in the "digital notebook."

Thursday, June 25, 2015
Field Supervisor - Kevin Garstki
Students - Ariel Ehrman (University of Houston)
Caity Ewers (Creighton University)
Nina Raby (University of New Mexico)
Will Pedrick (University of Virginia)
Written by Kevin Garstki

Daily notes:
We began work today at 6:30. WP will not be in the field today. Our objectives for today will be to complete **SU 5601**, down the ~15 cm level, and to begin identifying and articulate the pits present in this EU. Once these pits are identified we will work to remove all of the pitted soil so as to leave only the stratified deposits. AE, CE, and NR worked together using trowels and crock picks to remove the **SU 5601** soil in the northwest 1/2meter of the EU. The pitting may be more extensive than KJG originally thought. A wallstone at ~N6156.60 E6783.9 had old looters pick marks on it, and stones at ~N6155.8, E 6781.8 with similar marks.

This 1/2meter area of the SU was a much more compact, silty clay soil in the previous SU (**5600**). However, CE and NR are finding a much looser soil. This does not appear to be an extension of the pitting, though this cannot fully be determined at the moment. Just a few pieces of pottery, bone, and shell were recovered from the remaining **SU 5601**. **SU 5601** was completed just after 9:30am and a photo was taken of the closing photos (IMG_4388.tif). A plan map was also completed for this SU, and elevations were taken (see table 1).

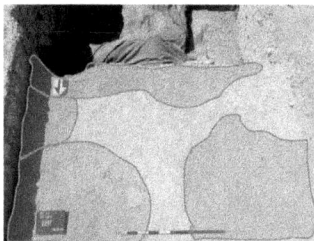

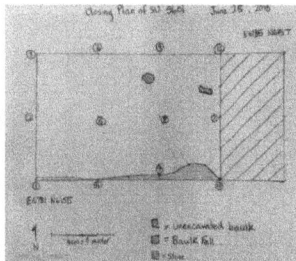

Following lunch, it was decided by MKT to begin a new arbitrary SU (**SU 5602**). This will be a single ~15cm pass down across the 3x2meter area of EU 56 we are currently digging (E6781 N6155). This SU will match with the SU 5203 closing from the EU 52 to the south. AE, CE, and NR began **SU 5602** by taking 15cm pass across the EU from the south baulk. This was decided because large areas of the SU are pits; at least 4 different pits and perhaps as many as 6 (see image below). By removing this level we hope to make the pitting more clear and begin to remove each on its own, leaving only the stratified deposits. **SU 5602** was removed approximately 15cm to the north of the south baulk with crock picks and trowels. The soil in the

Figure 8: A sample page from the "digital notebook" written by AAP trench supervisor Kevin Garstki in 2015.

Figure 9: A queried SU form as it appears in the AAP's Web-based FileMaker database.

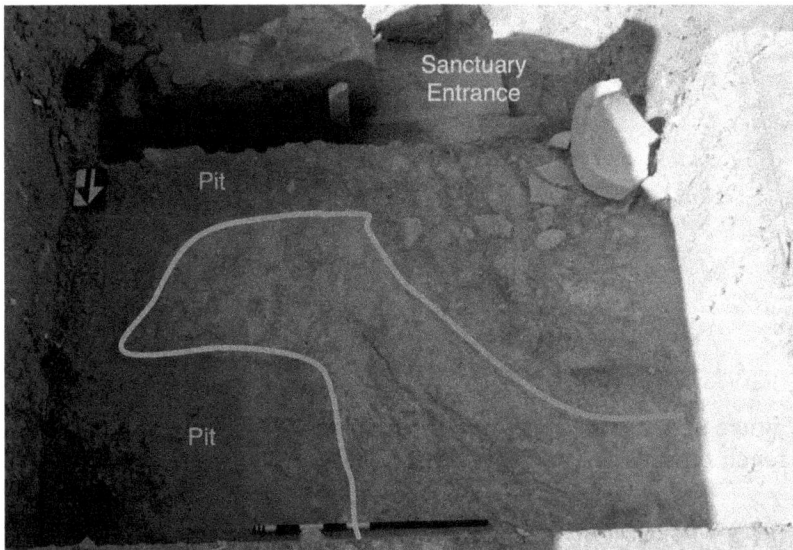

Figure 10: An iPad photo with annotations produced in iDraw.

good enough quality to be used for daily notes and annotations, but they were not archival quality, and a high pixel-rate digital camera was still required. Finally, typing on a reflective screen under direct Mediterranean sunlight proved difficult (cf. Fee *et al.* 2013: 53), and thus recording under a sunshade using a Bluetooth keyboard became a preferred method (FIG. 7).

This combination of programs, accessories, and workflow hacks ultimately proved that a user-friendly mode of digital archaeological recording using iPad tablets could provide AAP with born-digital data, save time, and teach students the basic rudiments of on-site archaeological computing in addition to traditional archaeological methods. From this experimental process, AAP's version of a "digital notebook" emerged, consisting of notes, photos, and drawings combined within the Pages app, and replaced AAP's paper-based EU notebook (FIG. 8). At the same time, Kyosung Koo, an academic technologist, was recruited to make the AAP database Web-accessible so that it could be accessed in the lab—and ideally on-site—by utilizing a Wi-Fi equipped mobile device. Koo migrated the database to a Web server and developed a Web application through which our staff could access the database via Web browsers on mobile devices (FIG. 9; Koo *et al.* 2013).

In 2012, based on our successful 2011 beta test, AAP implemented digital data recording in the field using iPads as part of its standard procedure (Toumazou *et al.* 2015a). Newly released and relatively affordable (under $600 US each), 32 GB iPad 3s, with improved processors and cameras, were issued to each of the four trench supervisors, who would use the devices along with the traditional database forms (e.g., SU, SMU, Object) that could not be digitized due to lack of database access on-site. Our immediate goals consisted of introducing supervisors to iPad use, standardizing our digital workflows via the creation of a protocol and, most importantly, not losing any data (cf. Berggren *et al.* 2015: 443). We also recognized that conversion to digital workflows would be a gradual process that would involve some paper, at least until additional full-time IT staff and funding could be integrated into project logistics. The resulting recording system might be best described as "hybrid-paperless" because it combined both digital and paper-based recording methods.

Gordon wrote a supervisor/lab protocol (see Supplement Material 1) with an introduction to the iPad and a discussion of how different apps incorporated much of our paper-based recording procedures (for written protocols, see also Motz 2015; Motz, Ch. 1.3). The protocol described operating system basics as well as how to multitask between apps, and it outlined a workflow for the hybrid-paperless recording system built within AAP's existing excavation process. Apart from the paper-based forms and a paper sketchbook used for artifact and EU drawings, the EU notebook would be born-digital, recorded directly into a flexible Pages template that would also provide writing space for supervisors' analyses and observations. This narrative would also incorporate elevations from Numbers as well as annotated photos (of trench features or artifact sketches) and hand drawings, scaled and digitized SU top plans (imported from iDraw), and Harris matrices outlined in OmniGraffle. At the end of a workday, the "digital notebook" was saved as an archival PDF and stored in multiple places: on the supervisor's iPad, on the registrar computer's hard drive, and in the cloud on AAP's Gmail account (which has now been upgraded to Google Drive).

The AAP workflow provided immediate benefits. First, for our budget, the iPads were a relatively inexpensive purchase at around $2,500 US for four units—they have been continuously used for field seasons through 2015. Second, they were user-friendly. No supervisor complained about using the tablet's apps (aside from iDraw), and all were able to master the workflow. As one supervisor remarked in a user survey focused on AAP's digital turn, "the transition [to digital recording] was fairly easy, and the device is user-friendly, with some idiosyncrasies that need to be learned." In addition, the entire workflow was DIY and therefore straightforward enough to be set up by a non-IT specialist. Third, since supervisors were accustomed to typing and using tablets/phones in their daily life, detailed descriptions of on-site work were created that were now enhanced by photos, photographed sketches, iDraw drawings, and elevations based on formulas. Annotated digital images (shaded with different colors and with text and arrows) particularly elaborated on the written narrative and enriched its explanatory power (FIG. 10). Fourth, several supervisors felt that they had learned new, more integrated, ways of recording using the iPad's camera and apps, and that they could work and make decisions faster based on the ability to reference and search previous days' PDFs as well as images and final reports from previous years. Responding to the user survey mentioned above, one supervisor provided the following testimony:

Looking back, I would say it caused me to document the excavation more closely, particularly through photography. It also made me more confident in my decisions about stratigraphy. Having daily overhead images of the trench gave me time to analyze what was going on in the trench after the day's excavation was done, which allowed for further analysis that I would not have had without an iPad.

Fifth, time was used more efficiently since born-digital note-taking now allowed the time previously devoted to retyping paper-based notes in the lab to be used for other tasks, such as object sketching or analysis. When asked whether time was saved, one of our supervisors in the user survey stated, "YES! It saved so much time because I didn't have to be redundant by copying notes. The app for elevations also saved time by having the machine do the math." Sixth, data were preserved in multiple, more shareable ways beyond paper, thus moving AAP data closer to their eventual reposition in a permanent digital repository. Our new digital workflows, therefore, enhanced AAP's dual goals: (1) more descriptive and visual data were collected that could be studied in depth by more people, and (2) students learned new ways to record, visualize, and understand site stratigraphy.

The 2012 season was a success in terms of hardware/software utility, student supervisor learning curve, and data collection and archiving. Therefore, during the 2013 excavation season we attempted to further enhance our digital recording system by establishing an Internet connection at Malloura in order to search and upload data on-site. Our part-time academic technologist enhanced the FileMaker app for uploading notes and images so that we could try to use a battery-powered, 3G, unlocked SIM card–based wireless router (We3G brand) with an Internet "hotspot" that could be accessed by the iPads. Unfortunately, it soon became clear that only a 2G wireless signal was available at the rural site of Malloura, which was too slow for efficient data recording (cf. Motz and Carrier 2013: 25–26). Thus, SU, SMU, and Object forms continued to be recorded on paper in the field and subsequently typed digitally in the lab. Paper also continued to be used for object drawings, although supervisors did improve their skills at image annotation in iDraw. For video recording, we solved an earlier problem of weak iPad microphone receptivity by utilizing a Panasonic

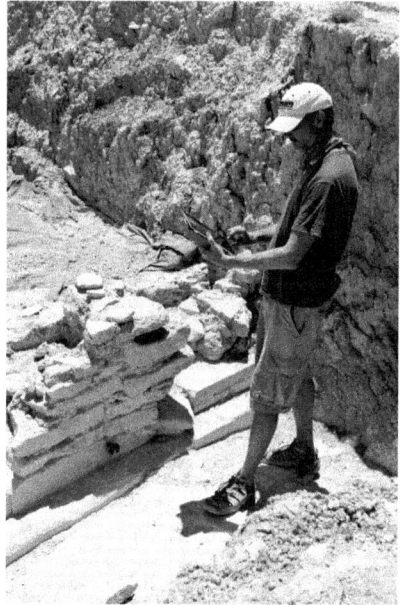

Figure 11: Using iDraw: annotated digital photo created to document the reuse of statuary in the sanctuary wall in 2011 (left); assistant director Jody Gordon documenting wall stones in 2015 (right).

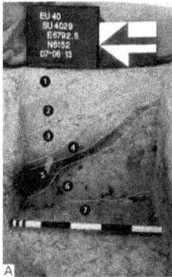

Figure 12: Using iDraw: Annotated digital image of the central altar in the Malloura sanctuary produced in iDraw showing stratigraphic layers (left); unannotated cross-section of the central altar (right).

Bluetooth microphone that allowed the speaker to stand 20 m away from the videographer and still render clear sound. Following a 2014 study season, we continued to use our existing "hybrid-paperless" workflow during the 2015 excavation season with continued success.

Mobilizing the Cypriot Past: Advancing Archaeological Interpretation and Education at Athienou-Malloura through Mobile Computing

Based on the first several years of "hybrid-paperless" data recording at AAP, our experiences have reinforced many of the perceived benefits of digital or "paperless" archaeology recognized by other projects, while also providing specific insights unique to AAP's workflows and goals. To begin with, a primary argument for engaging in digital archaeology is the enhanced preservation of data (Faniel *et al.* 2013: 3; Berggren *et al.* 2015: 443; Roosevelt *et al.* 2015: 325–326). If data will be lost, then paper, which is relatively more durable, should not be abandoned. In over four years of tablet-based data recording at AAP, no files have been lost, all are backed up to multiple hard-drives and the cloud (Gmail and Google Drive), and no iPads have been damaged. Our data is now backed up in more formats and places than ever before.

AAP's experience, like that of PARP:PS (Wallrodt *et al.* 2013), Gabii (Opitz 2015), and the Pyla-Koutsopetra Archaeological Project (PKAP; Fee *et al.* 2013; Fee, Ch. 2.1), has shown that tablet computers are user-friendly and their apps are easy to learn. Student supervisors are quickly able to use the devices to capture more information about a trench than was previously possible. More information is recorded because students can often type faster than they can write, and the visual data (e.g., annotated photos) can be inserted easily into the notebook narrative, a process that enriches supervisor descriptions. For example, with regard to the transition from paper to digital recording, one of our student supervisors remarked that:

> The transition was very easy and the device very much user-friendly. The majority of functions were easy to pick-up, especially after having used a smart phone. The apps, especially [P]ages and [N]umbers, were fairly intuitive. iDraw was the only app slightly more difficult to use.

The ability to integrate imagery with interpretative note-taking has helped our supervisors document and better understand Malloura's complex site formation processes and architectural remains (as has been noted on other projects, e.g., Berggren *et al.* 2015: 437–438; Bria and DeTore, Ch. 1.5). In particular, iDraw's photo annotation capabilities are a valuable tool for stratigraphic recording. By allowing supervisors to mark up trench photographs with visual layers that can be annotated with writing, polygons, and drawings, iDraw has added a digital visual dimension to describing excavation processes. For example, in a unique instance, a small, upper portion of a wall was briefly disassembled to retrieve an exposed limestone statue in danger of being looted; each stone was photographed and then easily annotated in situ using iDraw on the iPad, so that this part of the wall could be reconstituted afterward (FIG. 11). Another example would be the annotation of artifact find-spots within a trench or the complex stratigraphic layers of Malloura's main mudbrick altar (FIG. 12). Such a visual narrative enriches a supervisor's ability to document the excavation process and interpret its results.

Moreover, the iPad's ability to store archival images and reports has put years of legacy data at the supervisors' fingertips. This immediate access to information has enhanced AAP excavators' ability to access existing project data, such as the locations of artifacts (e.g., fragments of limestone sculpture discovered in multiple trenches) or architecture (e.g., spatial data on the likely position of the sanctuary's boundary wall; see also Berggren *et al.* 2015: 443). For example, several looters' pits at Malloura are quite large, and the same pit can be found in EUs that do not share balks. Using the archival data on the iPad, a supervisor can easily compare images of pits discovered in nearby areas, even those from previous seasons that may also extend into their own trench. The ability to make such stratigraphic realizations rapidly on-site can quickly enhance decision-making with regard to how to excavate a SU. Such comparative references were previously more tedious when paper reports were stored in the lab.

On the broader site level, having such information in a digital, searchable format has helped the directors rapidly synthesize information about an array of archaeological issues including: where and when the site has been affected by looting, the design of the Hellenistic-Roman *peribolos* wall, the form and use of the central altar, or the location and nature of Roman era activity. In this way, crossing the "digital Rubicon" has helped with the swift production of synthetic site reports, conference papers, and recent journal articles (e.g., Toumazou *et al.* 2015b).

It is clear that even AAP's hybrid-paperless workflow has led to progress in our ability to record, access, and archive data. Yet, this experience has also highlighted some common problems with digital archaeology at the trowel's edge. The most obvious issue is that going completely paperless is difficult and the process must be handled gradually, especially on projects with legacy data and pre-existing effective workflows. At AAP, for example, the difficulty of mastering digital drawing (at least on iPads) and maintaining Internet connectivity (as well as the costs associated with full-time IT personnel; Roosevelt *et al.* 2015: 341) has forced us to retain paper-based drawing and paper forms, at least until more effective mobile drawing or modeling programs appear and Internet connectivity becomes reliable onsite (for advances in modeling, see Olson and Placchetti 2015).

Other problems have been related to the hardware, and such issues have resulted in logistical complexities. A major problem with iPads at Malloura has been the reflective sun glare, which makes typing in the trench extremely difficult (FIG. 13; cf. Fee *et al.* 2013: 53; Roosevelt *et al.* 2015: 334). Moreover, our supervisors (in recorded team discussions) complained that the iPads frequently overheat, rendering them unusable for approximately 20% of a typical workweek. Both of these hardware issues have affected the devices' usability and have often forced supervisors to leave their trenches to work under a sunshade. Despite these complications, our supervisors unanimously argued that the tablets' benefits—especially image annotation and the ability to multitask and create an illustrated daily narrative—outweighed hardware issues, allowing them to craft descriptively richer trench interpretations.

Conversely, one of the main benefits of adopting hybrid-paperless workflows has been the enhancement of AAP's goal of training undergraduate students in archaeological methods. Yet, unlike projects like Gabii (Opitz 2015), our students (as opposed to graduate trench supervisors) do not employ digital workflows in their own recording. This was a deliberate decision since we felt strongly that students need to learn the traditional methods of field recording before being confronted with digital ones. As stated by Caraher (2015),

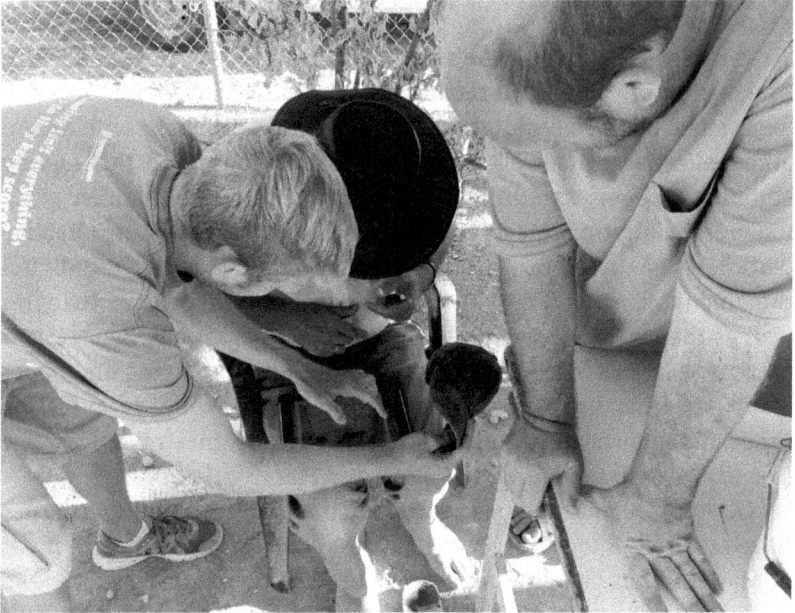

Figure 13: AAP trench supervisor Kevin Garstki (left), director Michael Toumazou (center), and associate director Derek Counts (right), examine an image on an iPad.

"archaeological skills are grounded in archaeology, not the attendant technologies relevant (or even vital) to the field" (see also Bria and DeTore, Ch. 1.5). Although our field school undergraduates often do data entry on their supervisors' tablets, our methods still concentrate on providing undergraduates with a thorough training in excavation techniques, which involve recording daily notes in paper-based journals and drawing sketches of objects and trench plans.

For our graduate student supervisors, however, gaining competence in technological tools that improve on-site data collection and analysis are now key parts of their archaeological training. Given the increasing ubiquity of paperless workflows in archaeology, such experiences prepare students for future projects where mobile devices will be standard tools. Utilizing digital devices helps students to "think digitally." By becoming proficient with apps, databases, and devices, our graduate students, like the students at PIARA (Bria and DeTore, Ch. 1.5) or Gabii (Opitz 2015), gain transferable, technical, and critical thinking skills (see also Burdick *et al.* 2012: 132–134) that can be used for intra-site archaeological analyses and that are widely used in careers outside archaeology. Although most AAP supervisors were literate with mobile devices *before* they used them on-site, one of our supervisors stated that she "learned about how multiple apps can be successfully utilized to solve problems." Overall, such competencies are valuable in the Information Age where archaeological careers are in short supply and nearly every profession requires some ability to organize, analyze, and visualize data within a digital framework.

Lastly, despite the project's educational successes, this case study of AAP's experiment with paperless archaeology also reveals some pedagogical issues. First, some aspects of a born-digital process take more time for training than a six-week field season allows. As discussed, digital drawing, relational database creation and management, and data storage maintenance are three areas that are too difficult to teach supervisors rapidly (although cf. Wallrodt's creation of "homework" exercises for supervisors learning app-specific skills on his *Paperless Archaeology* blog). Another issue is that some students do not immediately grasp how digital recording improves traditional paper-based tasks. As many projects have argued about communication (Motz 2015; Opitz 2015), students need to be informed of the entire digital workflow—either through protocols, meetings, or classes—so that they understand how the digital process enhances archaeological work. A related issue is that some staff members—especially from the pre-mobile computing generation—resist using the technology, even as younger students are urged to adopt it (Zubrow 2006: 13; Caraher 2015). Although such resistance to technological change is common throughout history (for resistance to digital humanities, see Greetham 2012), such disunity can have an effect on team-based learning goals as students question the validity of technology adoption and use.

MAKING HASTE SLOWLY WITH PAPERLESS ARCHAEOLOGY AT AAP

The adoption of a hybrid-paperless, on-site workflow at AAP can be deemed a success because it has enhanced our project goals of understanding the Cypriot past and educating students in archaeology. In addition, it has underscored the efficacy of DIY digital archaeology. Like other projects, AAP operates within specific logistical parameters with regard to funding, staffing, and research—parameters developed over 25 years of experience. Our experience has shown that based on a careful decision making process, certain technologies and workflows can be employed that are both cheap and user-friendly, and they may provide better ways of understanding Malloura's complex stratigraphy.

When compared with the experiences of other archaeological projects engaged in implementing born-digital workflows, AAP has encountered similar benefits and problems. One observation is that there are many ways to engage in digital archaeology: from complete bespoken systems like TooWaste (Serrano and Martinez 2014) and FAIMS, to fully digital DIY systems like those employed at Kaymakçı Archaeological Project (KAP; Roosevelt et al. 2015) and PARP:PS, to mixed DIY systems like those used at PIARA, PKAP, or AAP. It is also apparent that all methodologies seem to have their pros (e.g., providing students with new digital skills and potentially collecting more and better data), as well as their cons (e.g., possibly de-skilling archaeological practitioners and creating a data "deluge" that still has to be studied by subjective human interpreters; see Bevan 2015). Yet, one thing that is becoming increasingly clear is that a shift is occurring in archaeology as the portability, durability, and utility of mobile devices affect archaeological practices (Gordon et al., Introduction). Projects can choose to engage with this shift or not. As the chapters in this volume illustrate, however, change is in the air, and it will arguably affect the way students learn and researchers *do* archaeology for many years to come.

Given this fluid atmosphere of change, it is important for projects like AAP to share their experiences while learning from others so that best practices can be developed that enhance paperless archaeology's power to interpret humanity's past and guide its future. Furthermore, by comparing its methods to those of other projects, AAP can continue to improve its engagement with paperless archaeology. For example, inexpensive improvements, such as the adoption of bluetooth/or Wi-Fi–enabled digital cameras capable of geo-tagging (like the Samsung Galaxy cameras used by KAP; Roosevelt *et al.* 2015: 334), might improve the quality of image annotation in iDraw. In addition, creating bespoke forms in FileMaker (e.g., Motz and Carrier 2013: 26–27), using customized apps like PKAP's PKapp (Fee *et al.* 2013: 51–53) or Codifi (created by the Center for Digital Archaeology in partnership with the Jezreel Valley Regional Project; see Prins *et al.* 2014: 195–197), or testing an online app like Evernote (Fee *et al.* 2013: 53; Roosevelt *et al.* 2015: 335) for recording excavation narratives might improve the organization and quality of the digital notebook. Alternatively, future project grant proposals could center on procuring funds for enhancing AAP's digital workflow through the creation of a local area (or even relayed) network at Malloura (cf. Roosevelt *et al.* 2015: 332–333), the further development of AAP's Web-based database (Koo *et al.* 2013), and the development of a holistic plan for long-term, open-access, online data sharing and digital data stewardship (Kansa *et al.* 2007; Morgan and Eve 2012; Ashley 2015). As a project and team, we look forward to improving our workflows in reflexive ways that both intersect with innovative developments in digital archaeology and enhance the goals of our project.

Acknowledgments

We would like to thank the anonymous reviewer for their constructive and helpful comments on this chapter. These observations have added to the chapter's clarity and strengthened our argument. All errors remain our own.

https://mobilizingthepast.mukurtu.net/
collection/14-diy-digital-workflows-athienou-archae-
ological-project-cyprus

http://dc.uwm.edu/arthist_mobilizingthepast/6

REFERENCES

Ancona, M., G. Dodero, and V. Gianuzzi. 1999. "RAMSES: A Mobile Computing System for Field Archaeology," in H. W. Gellersen, ed., *Handheld and Ubiquitous Computing: First International Symposium, HUC '99, Karlsruhe, Germany, September 27–29, 1999. Proceedings. Lecture Notes in Computer Science* 1707. Berlin: Springer Verlag, 222–233.

Ashley, M. 2015. "Mukurtu CMS: Differential Access for the Ethical Stewardship of Cultural and Digital Heritage." Paper read at the Mobilizing the Past for a Digital Future: The Potential of Digital Archaeology Workshop, 28 February 2015, Boston.

Bevan, A. 2015. "The Data Deluge," *Antiquity* 89: 1473–1484.

Berggren, Å., N. Dell'Unto, M. Forte, S. Haddow, I. Hodder, J. Issavi, N. Lercari, C. Mazzucato, A. Mickel, and J. Taylor. 2015. "Revisiting Reflexive Archaeology at Çatalhöyük: Integrating Digital and 3D Technologies at the Trowel's Edge," *Antiquity* 89: 433–448.

Burdick, A., J. Drucker, P. Lunefeld, T. Presner, and J. Schnapp. 2012. *Digital Humanities.* Cambridge, MA: MIT Press.

Caraher, W. 2014a. "Digital Archaeology Practice Workshop: A Review." *Archaeology of the Mediterranean World,* https://mediterraneanworld.wordpress.com/2014/02/10/digital-archaeology-practice-workshop-a-review/

Caraher, W. 2014b. "Toward a Definition of Punk Archaeology," in W. Caraher, K. Kourelis, and A. Reinhard, eds., *Punk Archaeology.* Grand Forks: The Digital Press at the University of North Dakota, 99–103.

Caraher, W. 2015. "Understanding Digital Archaeology." *Archaeology of the Mediterranean World,* https://mediterraneanworld.wordpress.com/2015/07/17/understanding-digital-archaeology/

Counts, D. B., E. W. Averett, and K. Garstki. 2016. "A Fragmented Past: (Re)constructing Antiquity through 3D Artefact Modeling and Customised Structured Light Scanning at Athienou-*Malloura*, Cyprus," *Antiquity* 90: 206–218.

Daly, P., and T. Evans. 2006. "Introduction: Archaeological Theory and Digital Pasts," in T. L. Evans and P. Daly, eds., *Digital Archaeology: Bridging Method and Theory.* New York: Routledge, 3–9.

Dibble, H. L. and S. P. McPherron. 1988. "On the Computerization of Archaeological Projects," *Journal of Field Archaeology* 15: 431–440.

Ellis, S. J. R., and J. Wallrodt. 2011. "iPads at Pompeii." *Pompeii Archaeological Research Project: Porta Stabia*, http://classics.uc.edu/pompeii/index.php/news/1-latest/142-ipads2010.html

Faniel, I., E. Kansa, S. W. Kansa, J. Barrera-Gomez, and E. Yakel. 2013. "The Challenges of Digging Data: A Study of Context in Archaeological Data Reuse," in *JCDL'13: Proceedings of the 13th ACM/IEEE-CS Joint Conference on Digital Libraries*. New York: Association for Computing Machinery, 295–304. http://dx.doi.org/10.1145/2467696.2467712

Fee, S. B., D. K. Pettegrew, and W. R. Caraher. 2013. "Taking Mobile Computing to the Field," *Near Eastern Archaeology* 76: 50–55.

Greetham, D. 2012. "The Resistance to Digital Humanities," in M. T. Gold, ed., *Debates in the Digital Humanities*. Minneapolis: University of Minnesota Press, 438–451.

Kansa, E., and S. W. Kansa. 2011. "Towards a Do-It-Yourself Cyberinfrastructure: Open Data, Incentives, and Reducing Costs and Complexities of Data Sharing," in E. Kansa, S. W. Kansa, and E. Watrall, eds., *Archaeology 2.0: New Approaches to Communication and Collaboration. Cotsen Digital Archaeology* 1. Los Angeles: Cotsen Institute of Archaeology, 57–91.

Kansa, S. W., E. Kansa, and J. Schultz. 2007. "An Open Context for Near Eastern Archaeology," *Near Eastern Archaeology* 70: 188–194.

Koo, K., J. M. Gordon, and M. K. Toumazou. 2013. "Paperless Archaeology." Paper read at the *EDUCAUSE Learning Initiative Annual Meeting*, 6 February 2013, Denver, Colorado.

Levy, T. 2014. "From the Guest Editor," *Near Eastern Archaeology* 77(3): inside cover.

Morgan, C. 2015. "Punk, DIY, and Anarchy in Archaeological Thought," *AP: Online Journal in Public Archaeology* 5: 123–146.

Morgan, C., and S. Eve. 2012. "DIY and Digital Archaeology: What Are You Doing to Participate?" *World Archaeology* 44: 521–537.

Motz, C. F., and S. C. Carrier. 2013. "Paperless Recording at the Sangro Valley Project," in G. Earl, T. Sly, A. Chrysanthi, P. Murrieta-Flores, C. Papadopoulos, I. Romanowska, and D. Wheatley, eds., *Archaeology in the Digital Era: Papers from the 40th Annual Conference of Computer Applications and Quantitative Methods in Archaeology (CAA), Southampton, 26–29 March 2012*. Amsterdam: Amsterdam University Press, 25–30.

Nakassis, D. 2015. "Thinking Digital Archaeology." *Aegean Prehistory*, https://englianos.wordpress.com/2015/08/10/ thinking-digital-archaeology/

Olson, B., and R. Placchetti. 2015. "A Discussion of the Analytical Benefits of Image-Based Modelling in Archaeology," in B. Olson and W. Caraher, eds., *Visions of Substance: 3D Imaging in Mediterranean Archaeology*. Grand Forks: The Digital Press at the University of North Dakota, 17–26.

Opitz, R. 2015. "Teaching Practice while Developing Practice: Mobile Computing at the Gabii Project Field School." Paper read at the Mobilizing the Past for a Digital Future: The Potential of Digital Archaeology Workshop, 28 February 2015, Boston.

Prins, A. B., M. J. Adams, R. S. Homsher, and M. Ashley. 2014. "Digital Archaeological Fieldwork and the Jezreel Valley Regional Project, Israel," *Near Eastern Archaeology* 77: 192–197.

Roosevelt, C., P. Cobb, E. Moss, B. Olson, and S. Ünlüsoy. 2015. "Excavation is ~~Destruction~~ Digitization: Advances in Archaeological Practice," *Journal of Field Archaeology* 40: 325–346.

Serrano Araque, M., and A. L. Martínez Carillo. 2014. "El sistema TooWaste, ver. 0: Tecnologías para la traslación arqueológica de las historias en la tierra," *Siete Esquinas* (Centro de Estudios Linarenses) 5: 15–16.

Toumazou, M. K., P. N. Kardulias, and D. B. Counts, eds., 2011. *Crossroads and Boundaries: The Archaeology of Past and Present in the Malloura Valley, Cyprus. Annual of the American Schools of Oriental Research* 65. Boston: American Schools of Oriental Research.

Toumazou, M. K., and D. B. Counts. 2011. "Excavations at Malloura (1990–2010): Context, Methods, and Results," in M. K. Toumazou, P. N. Kardulias, and D. B. Counts, eds., *Crossroads and Boundaries: The Archaeology of Past and Present in the Malloura Valley, Cyprus.*

Annual of the American Schools of Oriental Research 65. Boston: American Schools of Oriental Research, 67–86.

Toumazou, M. K., D. B. Counts, E. W. Averett, J. M. Gordon, and P. N. Kardulias. 2015a. "Mobile Computing in the Malloura Valley," *Journal of Field Archaeology* 40(2) *Online Supplement*, http://dx.doi.org/10.1179/0093469015Z.000000000112

Toumazou, M. K., D. B. Counts, E. W. Averett, J. M. Gordon, and P. N. Kardulias. 2015b. "Shedding Light on the Cypriot Rural Countryside: Investigations of the Athienou Archaeological Project in the Malloura Valley, Cyprus, 2011–2013." *Journal of Field Archaeology* 40(2): 204–220.

Wallrodt, J., K. Dicus, L. Lieberman, and G. Tucker. 2013. "Beyond Tablet Computers as a Tool for Data Collection: Three Seasons of Processing and Curating Digital Data in a Paperless World." *Paperless Archaeology*, http://paperlessarchaeology.com/2013/03/25/beyond-tablet-computers-as-a-tool-for-data-collection-three-seasons-of-processing-and-curating-digital-data-in-a-paperless-world/

Watrall, E. 2011. "iAKS: A Web 2.0 Archaeological Knowledge Management System," in E. Kansa, S. W. Kansa, and E. Watrall, eds., *Archaeology 2.0: New Approaches to Communication and Collaboration. Cotsen Digital Archaeology* 1. Los Angeles: Cotsen Institute of Archaeology, 171–183.

Zubrow, E. B. W. 2006. "Digital Archaeology: A Historical Context," in T. L. Evans, ed., *Digital Archaeology: Bridging Method and Theory.* New York: Routledge, 10–32.

1.5.
Enhancing Archaeological Data Collection and Student Learning with a Mobile Relational Database

Rebecca Bria and Kathryn E. DeTore

This chapter reviews the benefits and challenges of using a digital data collection protocol to teach archaeological methods to university students. In particular, it reflects on the three seasons during which the Proyecto de Investigación Arqueológico Regional Ancash (PIARA) taught an archaeological field school in rural Peru using a mobile relational database and tablet system designed to document, manage, and analyze excavated data. This contribution provides a brief introduction to the PIARA research project and field school at the archaeological site of Hualcayán (highland Ancash, Peru; FIG. 1) and reviews the project's mobile digital database system, emphasizing how it was developed and used during the field school. Through this review we offer evidence suggesting that students who use a digital and relational database can develop analytical skills that enhance the way they perceive the multiple dimensions of the archaeological record. In particular, it is suggested that students who used the database were better able to contextualize their empirical observations and more quickly visualize chronological and spatial relationships between the materials and features at Hualcayán.

THE PIARA ARCHAEOLOGICAL PROJECT AND FIELD SCHOOL

The Proyecto de Investigación Arqueológico Regional Ancash began in 2009 as the primary author's doctoral dissertation research project at the archaeological site of Hualcayán, and it has since grown into a collaborative project and field school involving dozens of archaeologists and students. Hualcayán has an exceptionally long history,

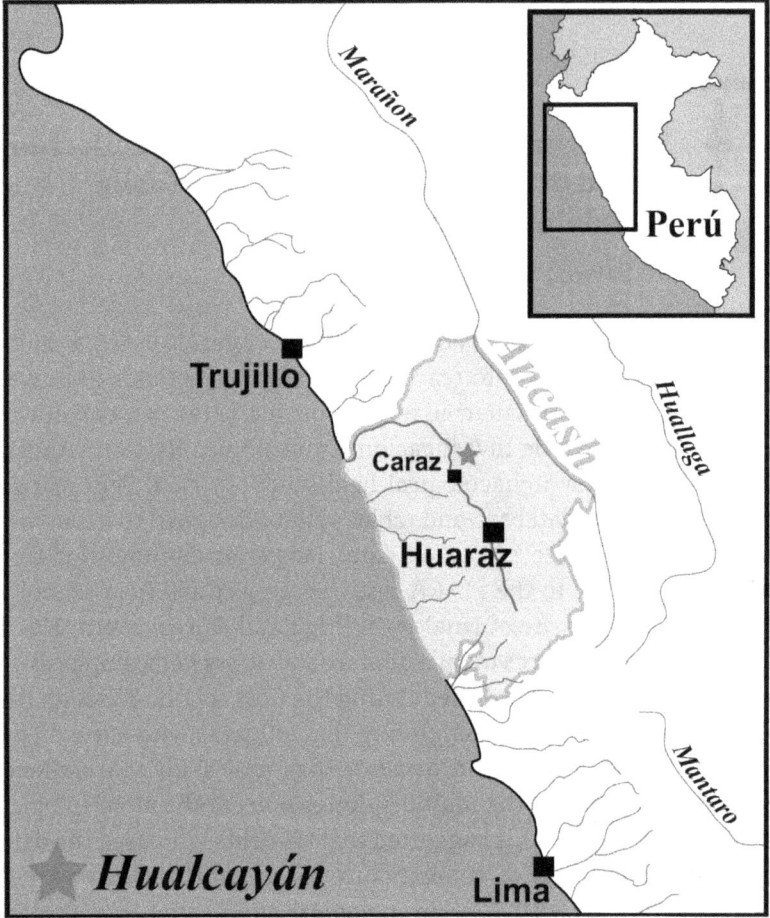

Figure 1: Map of northern Peru indicating the location of Hualcayán.
Map by Rebecca E. Bria.

with nearly 4,000 years of continuous prehistoric occupation from approximately 2300 B.C. to at least A.D. 1450. The majority of the research at Hualcayán has focused on changes in ritual practice that occurred with the rise and decline of a regional religion and political network called Chavín, and the emergence of a subsequent culture called Recuay (900 B.C.–A.D. 700). In particular, fieldwork has been centered on the excavation and material analysis of a central platform mound and its surrounding structures to examine how local people ritually constituted and transformed their community after Chavín. Complementary field research has been conducted at the site in pre-Chavín–era temples in the mound, in domestic areas, and in Recuay and post-Recuay tombs called *chullpa* and *machay*. As such, a major focus of PIARA's collaborating student and professional scholars has been the bioarchaeological study of Hualcayán's human remains, addressing questions related to diet, health, violence, body modification, and migration.

In 2011 the PIARA project expanded into an archaeological field school in collaboration with the National University of Ancash (UNASAM) in Huaraz, Peru. Between 2011 and 2013, PIARA taught eight field school sessions that were four to six weeks long. Managed by a team of six to 10 staff members, each session had from 13 to 22 students, who came mostly from the United States and the United Kingdom, totaling 138 international students over three years. We also taught archaeological methods to 45 Peruvian students, most of whom were from UNASAM or the Universidad Nacional Mayor de San Marcos in Peru's capital city of Lima. The field school focused its student training on excavation methods, total station mapping, bioarchaeology, ceramic analysis and illustration, and basic geographic information system (GIS) skills. Each field school session concluded with a series of student-led research projects that were conducted and presented in groups of three to five students. These projects were designed around the students' analytical interests and were shaped by a set of themes—such as ritual practice and religious authority, sacred landscapes, community organization and politics, and social memory—that the students explored during the field school through readings, lectures, and discussions.

In an effort to both support the project's research objectives and benefit student learning, PIARA designed a relational database that used touchscreen tablet computers to manage field and laboratory

Figure 2: Kathryn DeTore uses the PIARA mobile database to discuss and record excavated features with a field school student at Hualcayán, Peru.

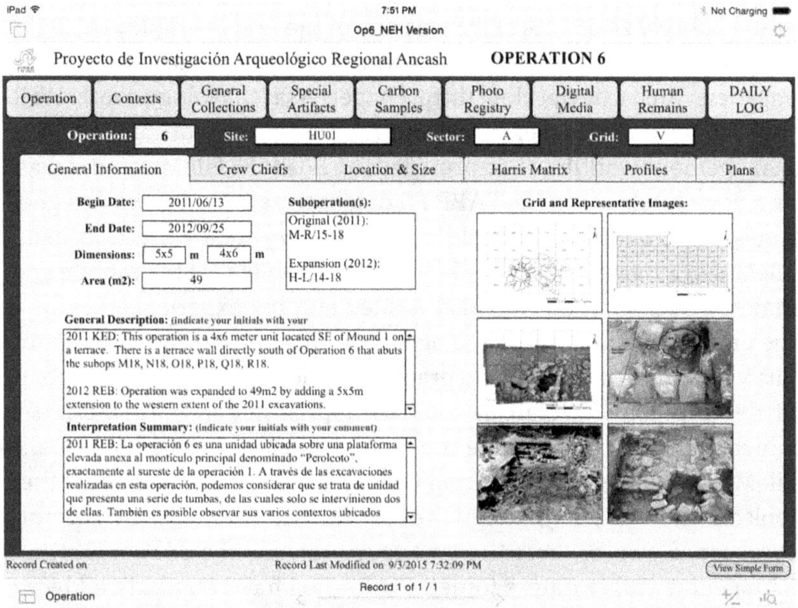

Figure 3: Screenshot showing the "General Information" tab of the "Operation" form. The subsequent tabs provide places for additional details about the unit, including the names of all crew chiefs, the location of the unit in space, the unit's complete Harris matrix (uploaded from OmniGraffle once complete), and fields to enter plan maps, profile drawings, and final photographs.

data (FIG. 2). The decision to develop a mobile relational database for PIARA was directly inspired by the pioneering and publicized work of John Wallrodt and Steven Ellis of the Pompeii Archaeological Research Project: Porta Stabia (PARP:PS; see: Ellis, Ch. 1.2; Wallrodt, Ch. 1.1). Although it was not the first project to incorporate mobile computing or relational databases in the field (see, e.g., Spinuzzi 2003; Zubrow 2006), PARP:PS was one of the first to employ the light-weight and portable iPad tablets to collect their data. Through his *Paperless Archaeology* blog (http://paperlessarchaeology.com), Wall-rodt provided detailed explanations for his digital data collection and management workflow and provided the PARP:PS FileMaker database as a download. Using the PARP:PS database as a model, we designed a relational database for field and laboratory data collection using FileMaker Pro, which was loaded onto iPad tablets via the mobile File-Maker Go application. Michael Ashley and his experienced team at the Center for Digital Archaeology (codifi.org) supported us by gener-ously providing technical and practical advice during the initial phase of development. Overall, it took us approximately four months—which included considerable trial and error as we learned how to use FileMaker—to design a working version of the field database. It then took another month to design the core functionality of the laboratory database. However, over the past four years, as the project matured and as new collaborators joined PIARA, we have regularly added to and streamlined the database. Therefore, several additional cumula-tive months of work have produced the version presented here.

THE PIARA MOBILE DATABASE

Objectives

After exploring both established and experimental digital workflows for excavation and artifact analysis, as well as reviewing approaches to digital archaeology more broadly (e.g., CoDA 2011; Cross *et al.* 2003; Evans and Daly 2006; Ellis and Wallrodt 2011; Kansa *et al.* 2011; Wall-rodt 2011), we recognized three principle advantages to developing a customized mobile database system for the PIARA project and field school.

The first reason we developed the mobile database was to stream-line and systematize the data entry process to improve speed and accuracy (cf. Motz, Ch. 1.3). On the most basic level, using a digital format to record data would speed our data collection by eliminating the need to type paper records into a computer at the end of the day or season. A digital format would also consolidate all related information about a specific record onto a single digital "page," meaning we could dynamically add unlimited information to existing records without the physical limitations of paper (cf. Ellis, Ch. 1.2). Furthermore, by digitizing data as it was collected, we could address, as part of our research design, the growing need and responsibility to archive archaeological data digitally (McManamon and Kintigh 2010; Ashley *et al.* 2011). Beyond these more straightforward benefits of a digital format, a FileMaker database in particular could standardize our form responses by presenting value lists as pop-up menu choices (FIG. 3). These standardized responses would minimize student (and crew chief) confusion as they learned the terminology needed to record archaeological data correctly and according to the PIARA protocol. This would eliminate the need to memorize or look up the possible responses for a particular field and instead focus attention on performing the analysis of the archaeological context or attribute being examined (cf. Motz, Ch. 1.3). More precisely, students could make comparisons between a pop-up menu's available responses, and have the proper terminology available to discuss the archaeological remains with their crew chief. Because FileMaker allows users to edit these pop-up menus, crew chiefs would also have the flexibility to add values to the menus in the field as needed—for example, if an unexpected category of data is discovered. Finally, with FileMaker's adaptable interface, we could also add images next to pop-up menus to help users choose an appropriate response (FIG. 3). Overall, we recognized that these standardized value lists and visual guides would increase data accuracy and minimize the "data cleaning" activities that are typically needed when analyzing data that are produced by a variety of archaeologists and students.

Second, we developed a mobile digital database to relationally link data as they were collected (cf. Wallrodt, Ch. 1.1). A relational database eliminates redundancy because an infinite number of fields (i.e., attributes) can be linked to a single context or artifact record by designating relationships between the tables that contain these data (Keller 2009). These relationships also make it possible to easily search and sort the range of visual and textual information associated with excavated contexts and artifacts. Most importantly, we wanted this searchability and the visibility of relationships in the data to be available during everyday fieldwork so that the excavation crew could make more informed decisions and more robust interpretations. More specifically, by cross-referencing and linking data in a mobile relational database, we could provide the excavation team with a comprehensive understanding of the archaeological record that is not possible by flipping through paper forms attached to a clipboard. As the field school progressed, we increasingly realized how this functionality enhanced student research skills, which will be reviewed in greater detail below.

Third, we developed a digital database to directly associate the more objectively collected data, such as photographs, with the more interpretive and subjective data that is the principal work of archaeologists—that is, context descriptions, artifact attributes, drawings, and notes. These different types of data and media that pertain to an excavated context or artifact are traditionally kept in separate locations: forms and drawings on a clipboard, photographs in a camera, notes in a notebook, and attributes in a spreadsheet. By combining the capabilities of a mobile tablet—a device capable of creating, manipulating, and viewing these diverse data and media types—with the relational nature and clear interface of a FileMaker database, we would be able to consolidate and integrate these data in ways that would be impossible with paper methods. More precisely, we sought to design a tool for crew chiefs and students to easily document and review their findings quickly and with a high level of visual detail (e.g., by allowing image and text data to be created, sorted, searched, and viewed in multiple formats) and also help them better understand and recognize relationships between excavated contexts and their artifacts (e.g., by linking all photographs, drawings, and descriptive attributes of excavated contexts in a relational manner). By integrating these diverse visual and textual data in a relational database, we also sought to break down the interpretive boundaries between these diverse media and their archaeological discourses (Shanks 1997: 99).

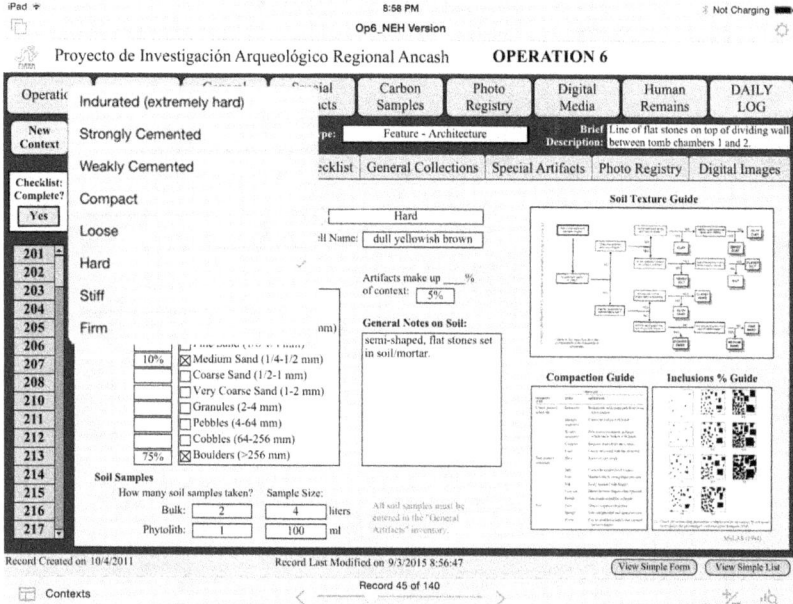

Op6_NEH Version

Proyecto de Investigación Arqueológico Regional Ancash   **OPERATION 6**

| Operatic | Indurated (extremely hard) | | ial | Carbon Samples | Photo Registry | Digital Media | Human Remains | DAILY LOG |

New Context

Strongly Cemented   pe: Feature - Architecture   **Brief** Line of flat stones on top of dividing wall **Description:** between tomb chambers 1 and 2.

Checklist: Complete?

Weakly Cemented   cklist | General Collections | Special Artifacts | Photo Registry | Digital Images

Yes

Compact   **Soil Texture Guide**

Loose   Hard

201
202   Hard   ll Name: dull yellowish brown
203
204   Stiff   Artifacts make up ____ % of context: 5%
205   Firm   nm)   **General Notes on Soil:**
206   semi-shaped, flat stones set
207   10%   ☒ Medium Sand (1/4-1/2 mm)   in soil/mortar.
208   ☐ Coarse Sand (1/2-1 mm)
210   ☐ Very Coarse Sand (1-2 mm)   **Compaction Guide**   **Inclusions % Guide**
211   ☐ Granules (2-4 mm)
212   ☐ Pebbles (4-64 mm)
213   ☐ Cobbles (64-256 mm)
214   75%   ☒ Boulders (>256 mm)
215   **Soil Samples**
216   How many soil samples taken?   Sample Size:
217   Bulk: 2   4   liters   All soil samples must be entered in the "General
                Phytolith: 1   100   ml   Artifacts" inventory.

Record Created on 10/4/2011   Record Last Modified on 9/3/2015 8:56:47   (View Simple Form) (View Simple List)

Record 45 of 140

⊞ Contexts   < ———————— >

Figure 4: Pop-up menu choices (left) and visual analysis guides (right) in the FileMaker database systematize the data entry process and also aid instructors when teaching core terminology and soil analysis protocols to students in the field. Users can zoom into the visual analysis guides by "pinching out" on the iPad screen.

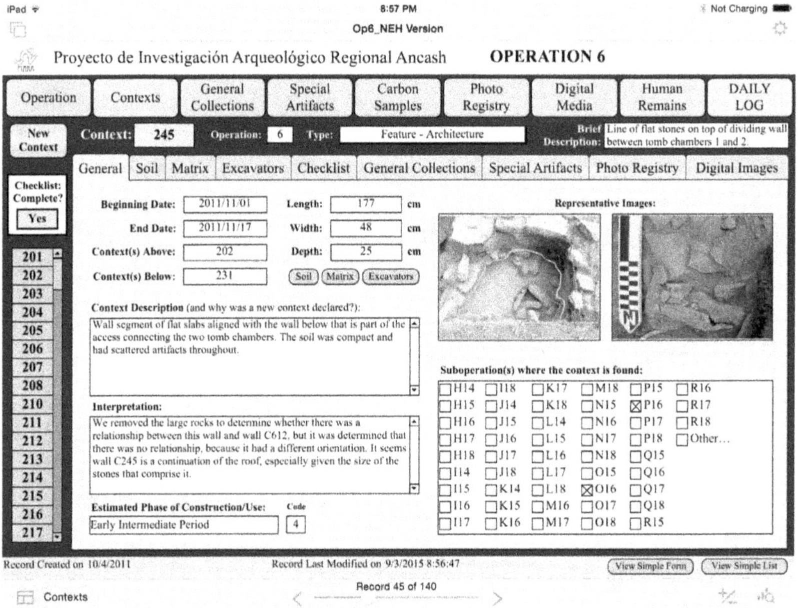

Figure 5: Screenshot showing the primary, or "General," tab of the "Context" form, where excavators enter the basic information for each context. Areas to enter and view additional details about the context are accessible by clicking on the following tabs: "Soil," Matrix," "Excavators," and so on.

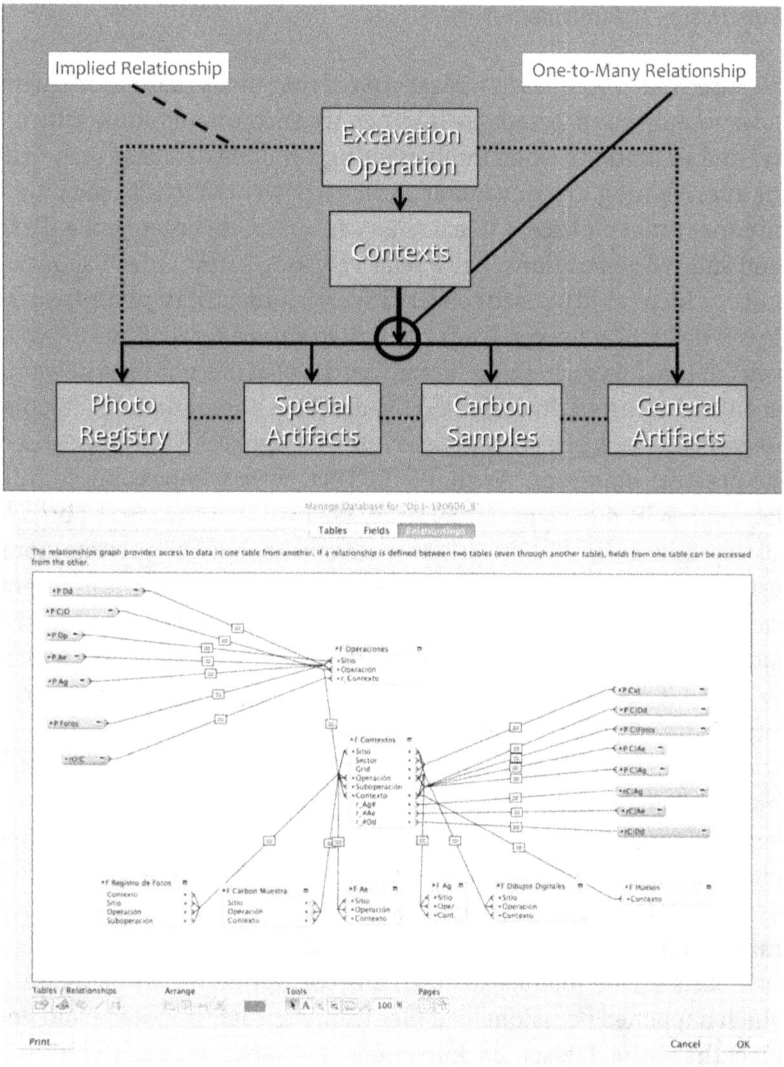

Figure 6: Schematic flowchart (above) and FileMaker relationships graph (below) show the one-to-many relationship between the "Contexts" field and other data and attribute fields in the database. Note: the database was first created in Spanish to make it possible for Peruvian project members to collaborate on its design.

From Design to Implementation

Because Hualcayán lies in a rural area of the Andes that has frequent power outages and unreliable Internet, we encountered some difficulties and limitations when implementing a mobile database system at the site. Although inconvenient at times, power outages posed only a minimal problem except in extreme cases, mainly because the iPads (2nd and 3rd generations) had a relatively long battery life of about 10 hours, which could be used conservatively in order to last two full workdays if needed. All seven iPads (increased from a total of five in 2012) were charged daily, making it rare that an iPad did not have power if an outage occurred. In designing the database's operational protocols, however, the lack of a 3G or greater Internet signal at Hualcayán posed the greatest limitation. Without Internet, it was impossible to link data across iPad devices in real time. We explored the idea of broadcasting a local Wi-Fi network as a substitute, but the mountainous terrain and the vast distance between the field house and the different excavation units (called "operations" by the PIARA team and in the database) made such a system impractical for our budget. Therefore, we found it necessary to create separate database files for each excavation unit, which were loaded onto individual iPads and managed by each unit's crew chief, who worked with a team of approximately four students at a time (see also Motz, Ch. 1.3). This system worked very well for us, with the only additional limitation being that artifact analyses had to be conducted on separate database files in the laboratory and then linked to the excavation databases at a later date. An unforeseen benefit to keeping these database files separate was that their sizes stayed manageable and any corruption in one database—which happened occasionally if files were improperly closed—did not affect the entire dataset. Backups were made approximately twice per week with little data loss over three years. A designated staff member throughout the season managed these backups, and a single charging station ensured that iPads would be both backed up and charged each night. The authors conducted introductory workshops with students and crew chiefs at the beginning of the field school, and then the crew chiefs worked closely with the students on a daily basis to record their finding in the field and laboratory, rotating the various data entry responsibilities throughout the week.

Proyecto de Investigación Arqueológico Regional Ancash   **OPERATION 6**

Daily Log for 7/27/2012

| Return to Contexts | New Day |

Operation: 6   **Date:** 7/27/2012   **Crew Chief:** Emily Sharp

Diary:

ES: Defined new contexts: 640, 641, 642, 643, 645, 646, 647, 648, and 649. 640 is the semi circle of stones which enclose subops K15, some of K16, J15, some of J16, and a portion of I15. 641 is it he interior of the semi circle. 624 includes the Formative wall that extends from M17. 643 is the north-south wall that extends approximately from subop L18 to approx. L16. 644 is the rock wall surrounding the aforementioned "pit" and north-south running rock fall on the west side of the pit. 645 includes the large "capstones" and the small area of soil in subop I15. 646 includes the soil between the late formative wall and the now standing rock wall. 647 is the soil in the pit. 648 is the soil surrounding the semi circle rock wall (context 640) in an "L" shape, also is the remaining soil in the operation. 649 includes the soil next to the large capstones approx subop I17. After defining the new contexts, me, Dina, and Fatima took munsell samples of the new contexts.

Photo/Video Diary:

Photo at top left should show the entire operation and be taken from the same perspective and position at the end of each day

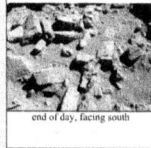
end of day, facing south

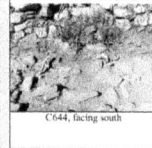
C644, facing south

Today's Excavators:

Dina Kostrow
Fatima Gavrish
Kevin Haley

Other Excavators?

N/A

C645, facing south

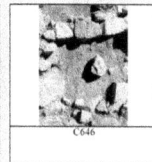
C646

Contexts Excavated Today:

☐201 ☐219 ☐236 ☐603 ☐620 ☐637 ☐1004 ☐1021 ☐1038
☐202 ☐220 ☐237 ☐604 ☐621 ☐638 ☐1005 ☐1022 ☐1039
☐203 ☐221 ☐238 ☐605 ☐622 ☐639 ☐1006 ☐1023 ☐1040
☐204 ☐222 ☐239 ☐606 ☐623 ☒640 ☐1007 ☐1024 ☐Other…
☐205 ☐223 ☐240 ☐607 ☐624 ☒641 ☐1008 ☐1025
☐206 ☐224 ☐241 ☐608 ☐625 ☒642 ☐1009 ☐1026
☐207 ☐225 ☐242 ☐609 ☐626 ☒643 ☐1010 ☐1027
☐208 ☐226 ☐243 ☐610 ☐627 ☒644 ☐1011 ☐1028
☐210 ☐227 ☐244 ☐611 ☐628 ☒645 ☐1012 ☐1029
☐211 ☐228 ☐245 ☐612 ☐629 ☒646 ☐1013 ☐1030
☐212 ☐229 ☐246 ☐613 ☐630 ☒647 ☐1014 ☐1031
☐213 ☐230 ☐247 ☐614 ☐631 ☒648 ☐1015 ☐1032
☐214 ☐231 ☐248 ☐615 ☐632 ☒649 ☐1016 ☐1033
☐215 ☐232 ☐249 ☐616 ☐633 ☐650 ☐1017 ☐1034
☐216 ☐233 ☐250 ☐617 ☐634 ☐1001 ☐1018 ☐1035
☐217 ☐234 ☐601 ☐618 ☐635 ☐1002 ☐1019 ☐1036
☐218 ☐235 ☐602 ☐619 ☐636 ☐1003 ☐1020 ☐1037

Suboperations Excavated Today:

☐H14 ☒K16 ☐O17
☐H15 ☒K17 ☐O18
☐H16 ☒K18 ☐P15
☐H17 ☒L14 ☐P16
☐H18 ☒L15 ☐P17
☒I14 ☒L16 ☐P18
☒I15 ☒L17 ☐Q15
☒I16 ☒L18 ☐Q16
☒I17 ☒M16 ☐Q17
☒I18 ☒M17 ☐Q18
☒J14 ☒M18 ☐R15
☒J15 ☐N15 ☐R16
☒J16 ☐N16 ☐R17
☒J17 ☐N17 ☐R18
☒J18 ☐N18 ☐Other…
☒K14 ☐O15
☒K15 ☐O16

Figure 7: Screenshot of the "Daily Log" form, which serves as a diary of each day's activities. The list of contexts available for selection at the bottom left of the form are populated as new contexts are added to the database.

Several linked forms constitute the PIARA field database, which are accessed primarily via a series of blue buttons at the top of the main layout and turn green when selected. First, all the general information for each excavation unit, such as its location, size, grid layout, dates of excavation, general photographs, Harris matrix, crew chiefs, drawings, and overall interpretations, is entered into the "Operation" (i.e., unit) form (FIG. 4). The "Contexts" form, however, is the central hub for recording and viewing excavation data (FIG. 5). Contexts were our central unit of analysis: a context number was assigned to any soil or architectural feature, such as a fill, floor, ash lens, or wall section. Thus, all excavated materials (e.g., artifacts, carbon samples, and human remains) were linked to unique context numbers in a one-to-many relationship—that is, context records were entered only once, and all excavated data was associated with one of these context records through linked tables (FIG. 6). The remaining buttons to the right of "Contexts" navigate to forms where these linked data can be entered and viewed. In particular, these forms provide space to inventory and describe the different types of artifacts and materials recovered during excavation, including our "General Collections" (i.e., all materials collected in bulk), "Special Artifacts" (i.e., highly diagnostic or unique materials collected individually and point provenienced), Carbon Samples (carbon for C^{14} dating), and "Human Remains." Two additional buttons, "Photo Registry" and "Digital Media," provide areas to respectively record the photographs and drawings or videos of the unit's contexts.

Finally, the database provides areas for excavators to monitor and visualize their progress. First, a "Daily Log" button navigates to a field diary where excavators can add general notes about each day's activities along with photos and videos that visually document the excavation's progress (FIG. 7). In the daily log and in context descriptions, students and crew chiefs would precede their notes with their initials in order to preserve their authorship and to capture multiple perspectives in the trench. In addition, a context completion checklist ensures that all required activities, such as inventorying artifact bags or taking photographs, elevations, and soil samples, are complete before beginning a new context. Conditional formatting changes from red to green on the Contexts form when this checklist is completed, which provides an easy way for crews to check the status of their work (FIG. 8; cf. Motz, Ch. 1.3). Also, a simplified matrix form provides

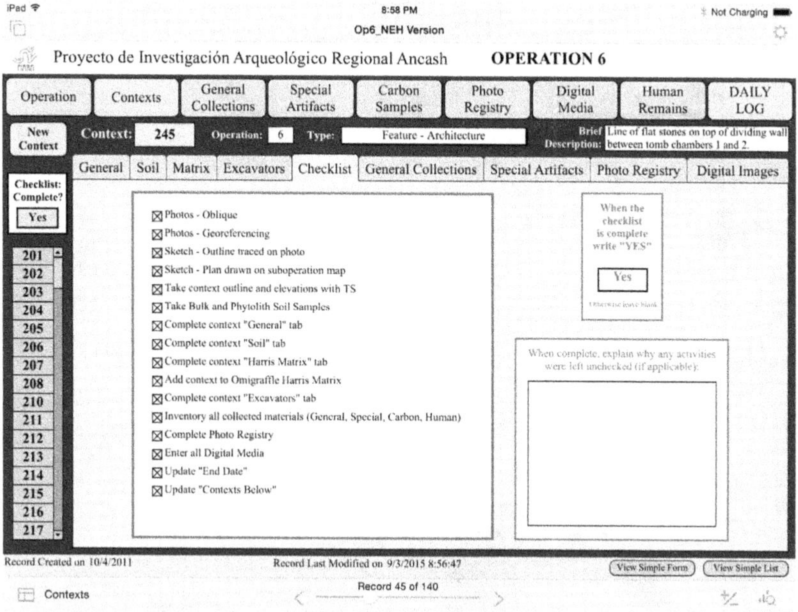

Proyecto de Investigación Arqueológico Regional Ancash   **OPERATION 6**

Operation	Contexts	General Collections	Special Artifacts	Carbon Samples	Photo Registry	Digital Media	Human Remains	DAILY LOG

New Context	**Context:** 245	**Operation:** 6	**Type:** Feature - Architecture	**Brief Description:** Line of flat stones on top of dividing wall between tomb chambers 1 and 2.

General	Soil	Matrix	Excavators	Checklist	General Collections	Special Artifacts	Photo Registry	Digital Images

Checklist: Complete?

Yes

| 201 |
| 202 |
| 203 |
| 204 |
| 205 |
| 206 |
| 207 |
| 208 |
| 210 |
| 211 |
| 212 |
| 213 |
| 214 |
| 215 |
| 216 |
| 217 |

☒ Photos - Oblique
☒ Photos - Georeferencing
☒ Sketch - Outline traced on photo
☒ Sketch - Plan drawn on suboperation map
☒ Take context outline and elevations with TS
☒ Take Bulk and Phytolith Soil Samples
☒ Complete context "General" tab
☒ Complete context "Soil" tab
☒ Complete context "Harris Matrix" tab
☒ Add context to Omnigraffle Harris Matrix
☒ Complete context "Excavators" tab
☒ Inventory all collected materials (General, Special, Carbon, Human)
☒ Complete Photo Registry
☒ Enter all Digital Media
☒ Update "End Date"
☒ Update "Contexts Below"

When the checklist is complete write "YES"

Yes

Otherwise leave blank

When complete, explain why any activities were left unchecked (if applicable):

Record Created on 10/4/2011   Record Last Modified on 9/3/2015 8:56:47   (View Simple Form) (View Simple List)

🔲 Contexts   < ————————————— >   ✕ ⟲

Figure 8: Screenshot of the Context "Checklist" tab.

Proyecto de Investigación Arqueológico Regional Ancash **OPERATION 6**

Operation	Contexts	General Collections	Special Artifacts	Carbon Samples	Photo Registry	Digital Media	Human Remains	DAILY LOG

New Context	Context: **245**	Operation: **6**	Type: Feature - Architecture	Brief Description: Line of flat stones on top of dividing wall between tomb chambers 1 and 2.

General	Soil	Matrix	Excavators	Checklist	General Collections	Special Artifacts	Photo Registry	Digital Images

Checklist: Complete?

Yes

| 201 |
| 202 |
| 203 |
| 204 |
| 205 |
| 206 |
| 207 |
| 208 |
| 210 |
| 211 |
| 212 |
| 213 |
| 214 |
| 215 |
| 216 |
| 217 |

Stratigraphic Matrix

202 — post occupation depositional soil disturbance layer from plowing

Later

If context is from another Operation, indicate which.

245 =

231 — area of lighter, sandier soil below the architecture of the tombs in O15 and P15
641 — soil and mortar of the roof of tomb chamber 1

Earlier

Instructions:
(1) Enter the associated contexts that are earlier, later, or equal to the context.
(2) Hit the Return key after each context number to enter a new number in the list.
(3) Enter all numbers in sequential order, regardless of their chronological position.

For example
21   38
31   not   23
38   31

Describe the spatial and chronological relationships between these contexts (use descriptive verbs such as overlies, underlies, contains, cuts):

Wall segment C245 is found beneath the post depositional/disturbed soil of C202, and partially overlies the sandier soil C231 found immediately beneath the wall. C245 was constructed immediately on top of C231, and C231 appears to be a Formative Period layer that was cut into and then covered to construct the tomb. It is still unclear in what sequence the different tomb wall elements were constructed, but C245 seems to be late in the construction sequence, and was laid in order to stabilize the tomb's large roof slabs, directly atop of C641 mortar stones.

Then, draw these relationships in the master Harris Matrix in **Omnigraffle.**

Record Created on 10/4/2011   Record Last Modified on 9/5/2015 2:15:15

Record 45 of 140

View Simple Form   View Simple List

Contexts   <   >

Figure 9: Screenshot of the "Matrix" tab of the "Contexts" form, which provides a space for adding and describing the contexts that are abutting and immediately earlier and later to the context being described. Multiple earlier and later contexts can be entered. This flexibility is particularly useful when it is not yet clear how different abutting contexts are related in the matrix. The brief description of each abutting context is immediately pulled from those context records and displayed to the right of the context numbers. The relationships between all contexts listed on the form can be described in the text box to the right, and can include a description of any unclear associations that need to be followed up.

Proyecto de Investigación Arqueológico Regional Ancash   **OPERATION 6**   Enter or View a Special Artifact

Operation	Contexts	General Collections	Special Artifacts	Carbon Samples	Photo Registry	Digital Media	Human Remains	DAILY LOG

AE #	Site - Sector	Operation	Sub Op.	Context	Material	Description	TS Point	Date	Person
212	HU01-A	6	M16	210	Ceramic	ceramic with possible molded	10741	2011/08/10	Kathryn DeTore
213	HU01-A	6	O15	211	green mineral	clump/collection of green stone/	10751	2011/08/11	Kathryn DeTore
214	HU01-A	6	M16	210	Ceramic	ceramic animal head	10802	2011/08/12	Kathryn DeTore
215	HU01-A	6	O16	211	Ceramic	giant olla, in two bags	10804	2011/08/15	Kathryn DeTore
216	HU01-A	6	O16	211	Ceramic	ceramic rim top with white paint	10817	2011/08/15	Kathryn DeTore
217	HU01-A	6	N15	212	Ceramic	circle and dot motif, possible	10936	2011/09/05	Kathryn DeTore
218	HU01-A	6	Q15	212	Lithic	gorgeous point found in northern	N/A	2011/09/05	Kathryn DeTore
219	HU01-A	6	R15	212	Ceramic	curving piece of ceramic with	10946	2011/09/06	Kathryn DeTore
220	HU01-A	6	P17	218	Ceramic	several large sherds (approx 7)	10947	2011/09/07	Kathryn DeTore
221	HU01-A	6	P17	221	Ceramic	small (5-10cm) vessel with a	11124	2011/09/07	Kathryn DeTore
222	HU01-A	6	P17	221	Lithic	part of a broken grinding stone	11123	2011/09/07	Kathryn DeTore
223	HU01-A	6	O17	224	Bone	Bone flute found on surface of	11143	2011/09/09	EAD
226	HU01-A	6	O17	224	Ceramic	circle and dot rim inside T2 that	N/A	2011/09/09	Kathryn DeTore
224	HU01-A	6	P17	227	Ceramic	rim sherd with a handle that	11209	2011/09/09	Kathryn DeTore
225	HU01-A	6	O17	224	Human Bone	Toe bone with drill hole -->	N/A	2011/09/09	EAD
227	HU01-A	6	P15	212	Ceramic	finely polished blackware-esque	N/A	2011/09/12	Kathryn DeTore
228	HU01-A	6	O17	223	Metal - Copper	pedazo de cobre, posiblemente	NA	2011/09/09	EAD
229	HU01-A	6	Q16	204	Ceramic	rim sherd with circle and dot	N/A	2011/09/18	Kathryn DeTore

Special Artifacts   <   **Record 16 of 608**   >

Special Artifact Registry   Return to Special Artifact List   Return to Contexts

AE Artifact #:	214	Material:	Ceramic	Date:	2011/08/12
Context:	210	Operation:	6	TS Point:	10802
Site:	HU01	Suboperation:	M16		
Sector:	A	Person:	Kathryn DeTore		
# of Fragments:	1				

Description: ceramic animal head fragment

Photo:

Laboratory Only   Weight (g): 49

Duplicate Record

Delete Record

New Record

Figure 10: Screenshots of the "Special Artifacts" form in two views. The top image shows the default form view, which is a scrollable and sortable table of all Special Artifact entries in the excavation unit. The bottom image shows the detailed form view, which is accessed from the green button at the top right of the default view, named "Enter or View a Special Artifact." This second form view provides a space for more detailed data entry and viewing of photographs. The example here shows Special Artifact number 214, which was recovered from Context 210.

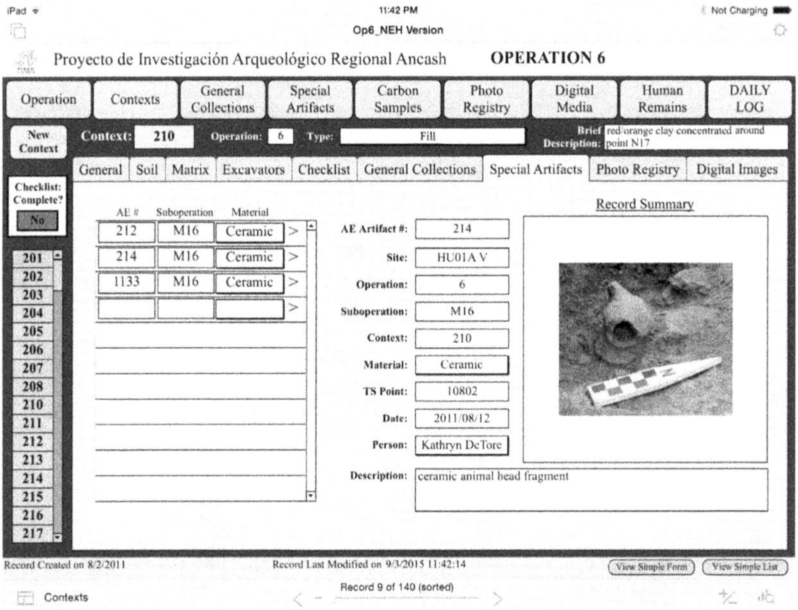

Figure 11: Screenshot of the "Special Artifacts" tab in Context 210. This tab isolates and displays the Special Artifacts collected in the currently viewed context record. In this example, the tab reveals that three Special Artifacts were recovered from Context 210, and that all were ceramics collected from Suboperation M16. By clicking the ">" arrow, the entry for each special artifact can be individually displayed to the right for more information.

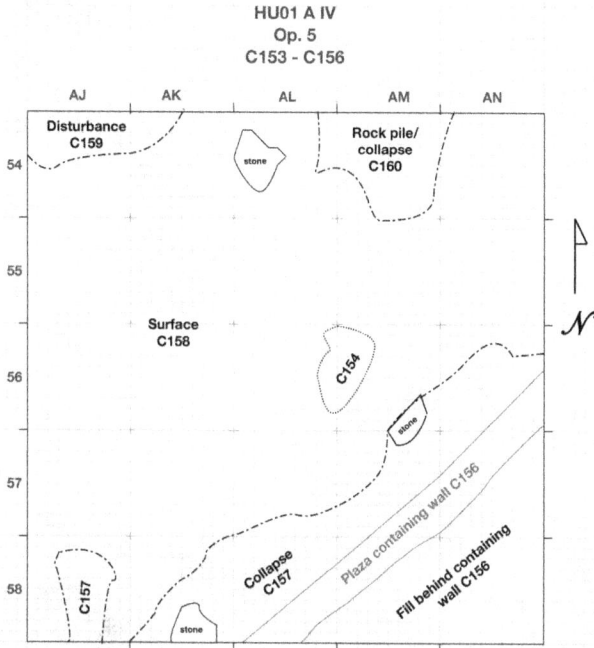

Figure 12: An example of a simple "scaled sketch" produced with iDraw. While total station points and georeferenced photographs were taken to record the precise extent of each context, scaled sketches provided a more immediate way to visualize spatial relationships in the field—without having to measure the features a second time via tape measures. To produce scaled sketches, context outlines were drawn over a pre-made layer of the unit's 1 x 1 m suboperation grid. The size, shape, and overall position of each context was estimated and drawn based on its placement within the unit's grid, using the suboperation corners, marked by nails in the ground, as visual guides.

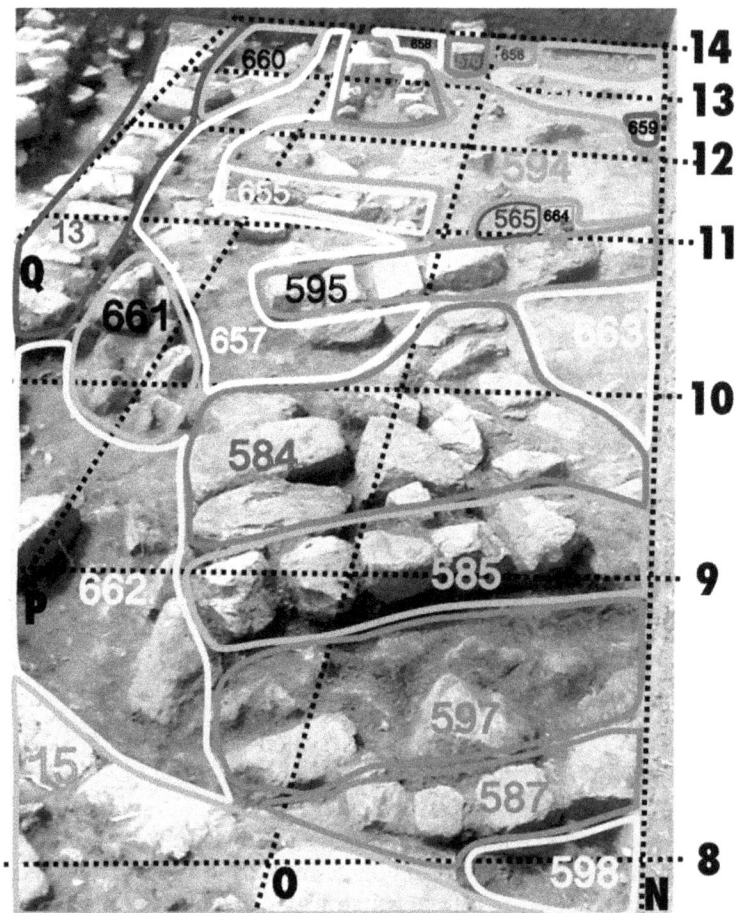

Figure 13: Example of an iDraw annotated photograph with lines and colors indicating the location and division of distinct fills and features within a platform building episode. Crew chiefs and students referenced these annotated images to keep proper provenience of materials as they excavated. This somewhat grainy image was taken with the iPad 2 in 2011; future generation iPads produced more refined results. We also used Apple SD card readers to upload high quality images to the iPad when greater precision was desired.

space where archaeologists can enter the associated contexts that are earlier, later, and equal to (i.e., the same as) a particular context being recorded (FIG. 9). Upon entry, the database will display the linked brief descriptions of those associated contexts, which helps excavators remember what features the contexts numbers represent. In so doing, excavators can better visualize, at a glance, how different contexts are associated in the matrix. Excavators then use these simplified matrix guides to construct a master Harris matrix for the unit as they excavate, using the flowchart application OmniGraffle.

The database is designed such that the excavation data can be entered and viewed in several layouts and locations (FIG. 10). Sorting the data in multiple ways allows users to examine vertical and horizontal relationships between artifacts of a particular type. For example, an approximation of the stylistic changes and time periods present in an excavation unit can be quickly revealed by viewing the "Special Artifacts" table, isolating all ceramic artifacts recovered from one or several Suboperations (i.e., their 1 m² location in the excavation grid), and sorting them in the order they were excavated. In addition to viewing these data in aggregate as tables, records can be viewed individually, which is the preferred layout when users first add the artifact to the database or if they wish to view photographs of artifacts already entered. To make it easier to isolate the materials of a particular context, we also displayed artifact registries as tables on the "Contexts" form, linking individual artifacts to the specific context records in which they were recovered. These linked artifact registries are accessed in a series of tabs visible on the "Contexts" form, where they can be edited as well as viewed (FIG. 11). This built-in redundancy adds a high level of flexibility to how data are entered, viewed, and sorted, and it also makes it possible to quickly view relationships between a variety of data types and with just a few clicks on the digital touchscreen.

We used a variety of applications on the tablets to create digital plan and profile drawings, sketches, and annotated photographs that were then imported into the FileMaker database. We primarily used iDraw (and later, TouchDraw) to create scaled drawings on the iPad, which has precision drawing capabilities and can manipulate textual, photographic, and vector data in distinct layers. Scaled digital drawings were often time-consuming to complete, however, especially for students unfamiliar with both archaeological mapping and vector drawing (see: Ellis, Ch. 1.2; Gordon *et al.*, Ch. 1.4). To speed the process of making plan maps, we simply created "scaled sketches"—or sketches drawn on a premade grid that corresponded to the 1 x 1 m suboperation nails placed in the excavation unit—to locate contexts in space. Because each context was precisely recorded with a total station and photographed for georeferencing in GIS, these scaled sketches provided enough accuracy to visualize spatial relationships in the field (FIG. 12).

We also used iDraw to produce annotated photographs for in-field visualization. Each context was photographed at an oblique angle, outlined, and labeled, and then imported into the context's record in the database. This technique, while simple, proved critical for interpreting contexts that were difficult to visualize using two-dimensional drawings, such as juxtaposed construction events in the ceremonial mound. For example, "singular" construction events, such as the placement of fill, were rarely executed by placing a uniform layer of soil and stone. Instead, the ancient builders laid distinct soils and stones in different areas to fill the platform. To carefully understand this process of construction, and to avoid mixing artifacts from discrete activities, we assigned each distinct soil its own context (FIG. 13). These annotated photographs became essential to how teams maintained clarity and control over provenience and stratigraphy as they excavated. They also helped the author decode the sometimes awkward context descriptions made by students and staff long after the season ended (cf. Gordon *et al.*, Ch. 1.4).

We also used the text annotation features of iDraw and the application Photogene to swiftly apply labels to individual artifacts and human remains on photographs. These text labels were particularly useful for recording small and commingled remains where a measured drawing at each stage of recovery would have been impractical (FIG. 14). In these situations, we only created scaled drawings of the top and bottom of the context and used annotated photographs to document the location of the small remains as we collected them. By recording finds in this way—at each level and stage of recovery—we could then reconstruct their depositional sequences by simply sequencing the images. Moreover, these annotated photographs were often visually clearer than abstract two-dimensional drawings. They were also far easier to produce, which minimized differences in students' drawing abilities. While all students learned to create scale drawings, only

Figure 14: Annotated images produced to document the relative position of commingled or clustered materials before and during their excavation. Images A and B, which were created in the application iDraw, show the position of in situ smashed ceramic bowls and guinea pig remains before they were excavated (A), and after the first layer of remains were removed (B). Image C, created in the application Photogene, shows the numbers assigned to individual bone elements of commingled human remains before they were collected. Image D, created in iDraw, shows how excavators often represented artifacts and contexts in a single photo to highlight their relationships. All of these annotated photographs took relatively little time to produce yet provide ample details of the depositional sequences of small remains.

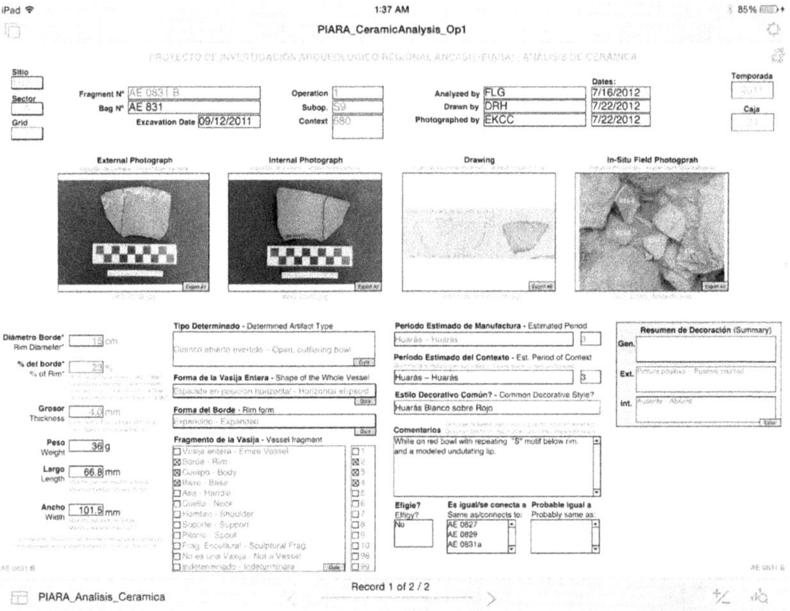

Figure 15: Screenshot showing the top of the ceramic analysis form. This area provides a quick view of the various size, form, and decorative attributes recorded for an artifact. Additional attribute fields and analysis guides for recording temper, color, surface treatment, and other attributes are accessed by scrolling down on the form. Side-by-side comparisons of the artifact's in situ photograph, lab photograph(s), and scaled drawing provide a convenient way for instructors to check the accuracy and consistency of basic attributes that were recorded by students and other collaborators.

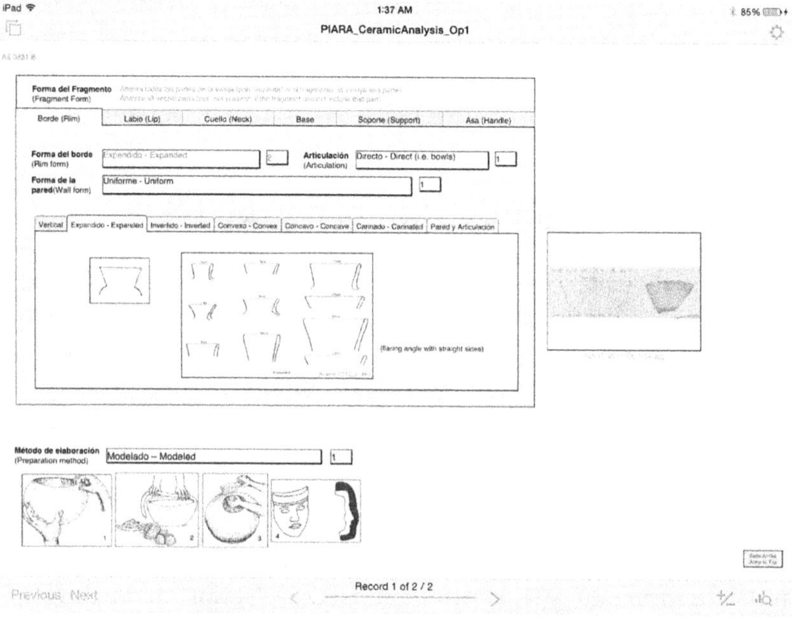

Figure 16: Screenshot of a section of the ceramic analysis form, showing several attribute fields and the visual guides to aid in their analysis.

some were particularly adept drawers; virtually all students could quickly and accurately create text annotations, however, which maintained the data's precision yet ensured that everyone received regular practice recording their observations visually. Moreover, these acts of photographing and annotating were instructional moments in which students could reflect upon their role in representing and constructing a narrative of the past (Shanks 1997; Shanks and Svabo 2013).

The PIARA field database is complemented by a laboratory database for artifact attribute analysis. Without an Internet or Wi-Fi connection at Hualcayán, this laboratory database remained separate from the field database so that both field and laboratory work could be advanced simultaneously. Nonetheless, FileMaker's capabilities make it fairly simple to link these databases by cross-referencing unique context and artifact bag numbers at the end of the field season. The artifact analysis database uses similar elements as the field database, including fields for photographs and drawings, analysis guides, and pop-up menus to aid both students and professionals in completing the analysis with precision. We also found that by accompanying an artifact's attributes with a variety of visual fields for its photograph in situ, its photograph after cleaning, and its illustration, instructors can not only monitor any inventory issues that arise during the artifact's processing (e.g., the mixing of bag tags after washing), but they also can check a student's analysis for errors or consistency in attributes such as form, decoration, and estimated period (FIGS. 15, 16).

In sum, the mobile tablet and the relational database enhanced how the PIARA team recorded and interpreted the archaeological record because it: (1) linked all data to excavated contexts in a one-to-many relationship, (2) provided multiple ways to view, sort, and enter the data, and (3) incorporated a high quantity of digital drawings and annotated photographs. The systematic, visual, and relational nature of the database also made it possible for new crew chiefs and students to quickly familiarize themselves with previously excavated data by simply scrolling through the existing context records while examining the unit in the field—something that is near impossible to do in a short amount of time while flipping through paper forms. In fact, the high level of visual content and relational links of the PIARA database proved essential to how we maintained consistency in our excavations, particularly in the units that were excavated by different teams over the course of two or three years.

ENHANCING STUDENT LEARNING IN ARCHAEOLOGY WITH A
MOBILE DATABASE

Archaeologists have widely recognized that the digital recording of data on mobile tablets improves productivity and precision. Yet beyond these virtues, PIARA's experience using visually rich relational databases on mobile tablets suggests that these technologies are much more than a means for efficient and precise data collection in archaeology. Rather, they also increase critical thinking and analytical skills, particularly for students who are first learning archaeological research methods (Stewart and Johnson 2011; see also Gordon *et al.*, Ch. 1.4). These dual benefits—efficiency and analytical thinking—reflect the debate over whether digital technologies simply aid in productivity or whether they alter the way we think. For example, there are debates over whether GIS is a tool or a "science" that gives researchers a new spatial awareness and analytical sensitivity (Wright *et al.* 1997; Reitsma 2013; Hall 2014). More broadly, scholars have debated the degree to which digital technologies are changing human analytical abilities (Bennett *et al.* 2008; Prensky 2009; see also: Caraher, Ch. 4.1; Ellis, Ch. 1.2; Motz, Ch. 1.3). Regardless, most scholars agree that digital technologies, such as relational databases, are more than simply tools for efficiency—they are tools for thought (Shaffer and Clinton 2006)—and therefore we should consider the ways that digital technologies might bolster (or hinder) the process of learning and doing research (Zubrow 2006).

In our experience, the mobile database enhanced our students' understanding of the material and spatial relationships in the archaeological record because it allowed for "computational thinking" throughout all phases of data collection and analysis. Broadly defined, computational thinking is the process by which relationships between complex, abstract, or large sets of data can be analyzed and visualized using the analytical concepts, software, and/or hardware of computers (Wing 2008). Since personal computers became commonplace in university settings decades ago, archaeologists have regularly employed relational databases and other computational tools to organize, analyze, and visualize their data (e.g, Reilly 1989). Yet only recently have they used mobile tablets as part of an in-field data collection strategy for excavations (e.g., Tripcevich and Wernke 2010; DeTore and Bria 2012; Ellis and Wallrodt 2011; Houk 2012; Pettegrew

2012; Fee *et al.* 2013; Vincent *et al.* 2013; Austin 2014; Sharp and Litschi 2014; Berggren *et al.* 2015; Roosevelt *et al.* 2015). Still, although scholars have explored the effectiveness of using digital archives and 3D simulations in university classrooms (e.g., Agbe-Davies *et al.* 2014), few have discussed how mobile databases can be used to enhance student learning and research skills in the field (e.g., Stewart and Johnson 2011).

A detailed account of the field school's final student projects illustrates how the PIARA relational database and mobile tablet system enhanced student learning. During the field school, a student's abilities to conduct research and think critically were most clearly revealed as they completed their final research projects. For this final project, the students collected, analyzed, researched, and presented the analysis of excavated remains. All of these stages of the final project were conducted on the PIARA iPads: relevant databases were loaded in File-Maker Go for students to edit and reference, PDF resources were made available in iBooks for students to perform literature reviews, and the students prepared their presentations in Keynote. At the end of the project, groups presented their findings by plugging their iPad into a projector. Students were required to contextualize their findings within the culture history of the region and site, and then interpret the results within a theoretical framework to draw out the broader impacts of their original research. For example, students could have chosen to examine changes in the social dynamics of feasting by looking at trends in the forms, designs, and distributions of ceramic vessels through time, either in a particular excavation area or between discrete structures. Or they could have tested whether periods of known community reorganization were associated with changes in labor-related stress by analyzing patterns of degeneration on human vertebra from tombs at Hualcayán.

Students were encouraged, but not required, to use the database as an analysis tool as they conducted their final research projects. With each year of fieldwork, the database's usefulness as an analytical tool increased as the project's data expanded. Therefore, by examining and comparing students' use of the database in their final research projects between 2011 and 2013, and also by comparing the student projects that incorporated the database to projects by students who only examined and discussed the data they had themselves recorded in the laboratory (e.g., ceramic attribute analysis from a particular context), we could gauge how well the students could research, understand, and contextualize their data. We assessed the students by evaluating whether they were making first, second, and third order relations in the data. First, were the students linking the different associated materials of a particular context? Second, were they making connections between the materials or conditions in different contexts of the same unit? And third, were they recognizing similar patterning across the site (between units)? We also evaluated whether and how the students forged links between the data they had collected and the data collected before they arrived to the project.

We consistently found that the students who used the PIARA database excelled in all these dimensions of comprehension. In particular, students who used the database were more able to identify links between discrete contexts and data types than the groups who relied on less formal observations of unit and site-wide patterns, such as those gained through everyday excavation experience, discussions with instructors, and lectures. Similarly, students who used the database produced more substantive and empirically supported conclusions than those who simply analyzed a discrete dataset without contextualizing these data. Finally, comparisons between the final projects revealed how students who used the database began to think in a relational manner about the data they were analyzing and presenting.

A few examples illustrate how the relational database enhanced students' research skills during their final projects. In the first example, two groups, one in the 2012 field season and another in 2013, performed attribute analysis on a sample of ceramics from excavation unit Operation 7. Broadly, the research objective for each group was to identify and examine the activities of Recuay feasting within a particular structure. While both groups used the database to enter and organize their ceramic attribute data, the 2013 group also used the database to select an appropriate sample for their project, and then to compare their ceramic data to other excavated materials. Although both groups produced valid results, there were marked differences in how the students both approached and summarized their data.

In particular, the 2012 group became interested in their final project—Recuay feasting in Operation 7—after their excavations in the unit revealed a context with extensive burning, ceramics, and animal bones. To examine the hypothesis that feasting occurred in this space, they performed an attribute analysis of approximately 40 decorated diagnostic ceramics from the context, primarily to identify ratios of serving and cooking vessels and the prevalence of decorative styles. They grouped the ceramics by vessel form and also compared the decorative styles from the context to documented types. Given the high percentages of finely decorated serving wares in this context, they concluded that their analysis indicated feasting, and to further contextualize their findings, the group discussed their own observations, which were made during their excavations of burned areas and refuse scatters in Operation 7.

In contrast, the 2013 student group *began* their research by identifying an appropriate sample within the database to analyze. Choosing to begin the research by exploring the database was in part because the excavation of several units, including Operation 7, was not continued in 2013 (instead, the 2013 students gained excavation experience in mortuary contexts). Thus, starting with a broad interest in examining Recuay feasting, the students first explored the database by performing simple sorts and queries to reveal differences between contexts, particularly in the quantities and distributions of decorated vessels. These functions not only identified which contexts had a high probability of ritualized consumption activity, but the sorting of ceramic styles also provided an estimated terminus post quem or terminus ante quem—that is, the latest and earliest possible period to which a context can date—for particular structures and layers. In addition to exploring the distributions of ceramic styles and forms, the functions were used to explore the relative quantities of faunal and lithic remains from these contexts. Even though formal analyses had yet to be conducted on these materials, inventories and preliminary counts and weights provided a general indicator for potential food preparation and consumption activities associated with these materials. The students used these data to choose an appropriate sample that had a high quantity of decorated ceramics, as well as high quantities of faunal and lithic remains. Once an appropriate sample of ceramics was chosen, the students completed their attribute analysis. By combining their results with the estimated quantities and types of associated faunal and lithic artifacts from the analyzed context, the students were able to push their analysis beyond a descriptive presentation of form types and styles in their final presentations. That is, in addition to presenting their findings from ceramic attribute analysis,

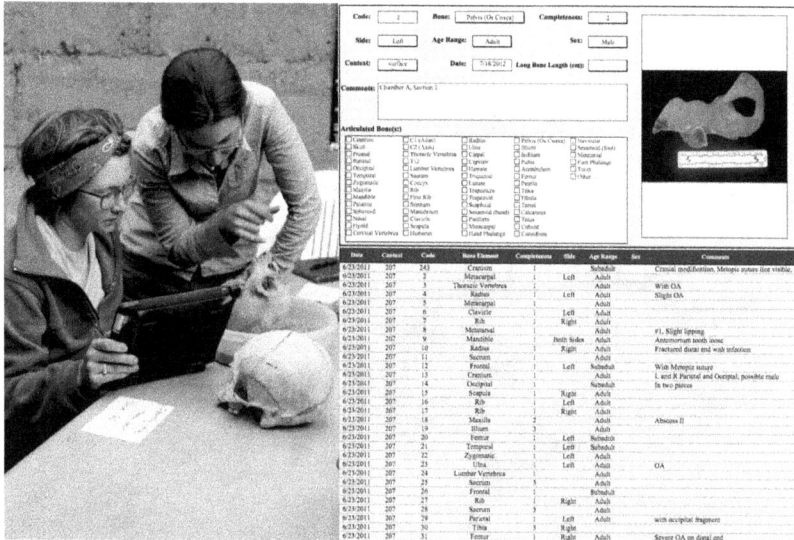

Figure 17: In their final projects, students first examined preliminary patterns in the data and developed viable research questions by sorting and querying existing records in the database. Then, in a second phase of their project, students completed a more formal analysis to test their hypotheses.

Figure 18: 3D photogrammetric model of excavated architecture at Hualcayán, shown in perspective. Model produced by Rebecca E. Bria.

they were able to explore how the ceramics formed part of a feasting assemblage. In particular, they postulated that serving vessels, such as decorated bowls, were highly associated with carbonized cultigens. They also associated these finds with the presence of lithics, such as cores, flakes, and hammerstones, which suggested that food was likely prepared in the same space as consumption activities. Finally, by comparing the soil descriptions (i.e., the presence/absence of ash and burned earth) in different areas of the structure, and by reviewing which suboperations in Operation 7 contained the identified artifact assemblage, they also proposed that the feast's food preparation and consumption activities extended across most of the structure's interior.

Although the students were aware that their results were preliminary, the members of the 2013 group expressed how the database gave them insight into how archaeologists draw together multiple lines of evidence to contextualize and substantiate their findings. Furthermore, the 2013 example shows how the database made it easier for the students to visualize and understand contexts that they themselves did not excavate and to explore the project data on their own. Although the students used the field inventories and special artifact registries that were created during excavations, rather than data from formal analysis (which had yet to be completed by specialists), they were able to gain key insights into how various materials constituted an assemblage. The students demonstrated how using a relational database allowed them to identify preliminary yet valid associations between discrete datasets that archaeologists traditionally take weeks (or even months) to identify, particularly when having to read through notebooks, review sketches, and wait for specialists to complete their material analyses before these preliminary associations can be made. Moreover, by adding to and analyzing data from the project's database, as opposed to completing a fabricated workshop exercise, both groups recognized that they were producing results that, even in a small way, contributed to the advancement of the research project overall. Several students returned to Hualcayán to complete undergraduate and graduate theses to expand upon their field school projects. For example, one student from the 2013 group used her group's findings to prepare a grant proposal to return to Hualcayán and conduct undergraduate thesis research on Recuay feasting (McAllister 2015).

Students training in bioarchaeological field methods employed the database in other ways to enhance their final projects. First, because we photographed, identified, and sided human skeletal remains in the field as they were recovered from comingled burials, analyses such as minimum number of individuals could be immediately estimated by sorting and counting how many specimens existed for a particular bone element and side. Other rapid preliminary analyses included determining sex and age ratios or evidence for trauma. Student groups would use the sorting results to narrow the topic of their final research project according to what datasets might produce both interesting and relevant results. For example, if a group of students was interested in examining questions related to violent trauma, and the preliminary sorting of the data suggested there were no juveniles or females present in a sample, then a study of how trauma rates differed by age group or sex was eliminated as a productive focus of the research project. Though similar preliminary analyses could be performed in an Excel spreadsheet, the database made it possible to easily relate their bioarchaeological findings to other data such as tomb location, associated artifacts, and stratigraphic levels. They were also able to compare human skeletal assemblages between different tombs at the site. This made the database a superior tool for accessing and processing large sets of data in short amounts of time (FIG. 17). Furthermore, the execution of sorting and querying tasks was made less tedious with a database that could be explored by students on their own, via a single application, and on a tablet that can be passed around. In several cases, field school students were encouraged to present their exceptional bioarchaeological work from these final projects at professional conferences, which they co-authored with PIARA supervisors (e.g., Calabria *et al.* 2014).

These examples reveal how the relational database provided a powerful and immediate analysis tool for students. They reveal how, by creating relational connections between discrete datasets such as excavation forms, inventories, and previously analyzed data, the database helped students not only collect, but also contextualize their data in the laboratory. Moreover, the examples reveal how the database allowed students to quickly explore patterns in the data as a *preliminary step*, rather than *end product*, of their research project. Without the relational database, the exploration of initial patterns in the data may have constituted the entire final project's analysis rather than form the foundation of more complex research questions.

CONCLUSIONS

In sum, PIARA's use of digital technology not only aided the archaeological project's in-field and laboratory data collection procedures, analyses, and interpretations, but it also advanced the analytical abilities of our student archaeologists. The PIARA example illustrates how using a mobile tablet equipped with relational databases, readings, and a variety of programs to collect and illustrate findings—in our case, an iPad with FileMaker Go, iBooks, iDraw/Photogene, and Keynote—can provide students with an all-in-one powerful and collaborative tool to collect, prepare, and present research. PIARA's experience also suggests that when students use a mobile relational database, their ability to recognize and interpret complex relationships between archaeological materials, contexts, and features is enhanced because the database allows them to examine broad patterns in the data with relative ease.

Future expansions of our mobile data collection and student instruction protocols will focus on incorporating mobile GIS and photogrammetry into our workflow (cf. Tripcevich and Wernke 2010; Berggren *et al.* 2015; Roosevelt *et al.* 2015). Recently, we began to create 3D photogrammetric models of excavated architecture at Hualcayán (e.g., FIG. 18). In the future, these models—which are more expedient, precise, and less abstract than polygons produced with a total station or outlines drawn on photographs—will be produced for each excavation context. Furthermore, because photogrammetry is becoming a common and essential tool for archaeological research, students will learn how to process and use these models. As part of our workflow, the photogrammetric models will be loaded onto the iPads once they are created, and they will then be used as analytical guides for students and crew members as they excavate, contextualize their analyses in the laboratory, and tour the archaeological site for the first time. We will also use these 3D models to bring Hualcayán's ancient past to life for local schoolchildren during educational workshops. To this end, and in an effort to involve local children in the preservation and representation of their community's heritage (cf. Bria and Cruzado Carranza 2015), we have begun to teach high-school students how to photograph and produce photogrammetry models of reconstructed artifacts from Hualcayán (see also Sayre, Ch. 1.6). Finally, other future directions will seek to incorporate data from multiple sites in highland Ancash into a regional database (cf. Gero 2006), with a focus on creating a pedagogical tool for Peruvian and international students.

As technology continues to change and students become researchers, the computational tools currently available will change in directions that are difficult to fully anticipate. Tools such as relational databases make it notably easier to explore and interpret larger data sets. The way PIARA students were able to explore the project database may be, in part, tied to their generation's collective immersion in digital technologies (Palfrey and Gasser 2013). For the current generation of college students, the mining of digital data has always been a common exercise, for example, when surfing the Internet or searching a library database. Nonetheless, while skills in the manipulation of "big data" may be more intuitive for the current generation of students, there is an increased need for students to understand how relational databases are constructed in order for them to be data producers rather than mere data consumers. Although relational databases have long been essential to archaeology, it may be increasingly important for archaeological instruction, in field schools and graduate-level coursework, to incorporate a database design component.

Still, approaches to data recording and analysis are highly varied between researchers across the globe, and instructors cannot predict the kinds of projects students will assist on or lead in the future. Therefore, instructors may consider teaching students how to be resourceful in low-tech (and low-budget) environments by ensuring competency in "traditional" as well as digital methods. After all, archaeology can be done with a few rudimentary tools. Yet as technology continues to change and expand, there is a growing need for archaeological field schools to teach the foundations of digital data collection, management, and analysis. By intentionally incorporating digital approaches into student training, instructors can prepare students to participate in the current and coming digital era of social science and humanities research.

ACKNOWLEDGMENTS

We sincerely thank the "Mobilizing the Past" workshop organizers for their invitation to participate, and to all workshop participants for their insights and feedback on the PIARA database project. Michael Ashley and the Center for Digital Archaeology selflessly and enthusiastically gave us their time and advice throughout the project. Beth Grávalos and Elizabeth Cruzado Carranza also contributed considerable time to the development of the laboratory databases, and Emily Sharp assisted in the design of the human remains database form. Thanks are also due Anna Guengerich, Steve Kosiba, this volume's editors, and the anonymous reviewers for their helpful feedback during the preparation of this paper. Final thanks go to the many PIARA students, crew chiefs, and other collaborators who patiently worked with us as we improved the database each year. Final appreciation goes to the community of Hualcayán, who have warmly hosted the PIARA project in recent years.

https://mobilizingthepast.mukurtu.net/collection/15-enhancing-archaeological-data-collection-and-student-learning-mobile-relational

http://dc.uwm.edu/arthist_mobilizingthepast/7

REFERENCES

Agbe-Davies, A. S., J. E. Galle, M. W. Hauser, and F. D. Neiman. 2014. "Teaching with Digital Archaeological Data: A Research Archive in the University Classroom," *Journal of Archaeological Method and Theory* 21: 837–861.

Ashley, M., R. Tringham, and C. Perlingieri. 2011. "Last House on the Hill: Digitally Remediating Data and Media for Preservation and Access," *Journal on Computing and Cultural Heritage (JOCCH)* 4(4): 13.

Austin, A. 2014. "Mobilizing Archaeologists: Increasing the Quantity and Quality of Data Collected in the Field with Mobile Technology," *Advances in Archaeological Practice* 2: 13–23.

Bennett, S., K. Maton, and L. Kervin. 2008. "The 'Digital Natives' Debate: A Critical Review of the Evidence," *British Journal of Educational Technology* 39: 775–786.

Berggren, Å., N. Dell'Unto, M. Forte, S. Haddow, I. Hodder, J. Issavi, N. Lercari, C. Mazzucato, A. Mickel, and J. S. Taylor. 2015. "Revisiting Reflexive Archaeology at Çatalhöyük: Integrating Digital and 3D Technologies at the Trowel's Edge," *Antiquity* 89:433–448.

Bria, R. E., and E. K. Cruzado Carranza. 2015. "Making the Past Relevant: Co-creative Approaches to Heritage Preservation and Community Development at Hualcayán, Ancash, Peru," *Advances in Archaeological Practice* 3: 208–222.

Calabria, L. M., S. K. Becker, J. J. Lesnik, and R. E. Bria. 2014. "Mapping Activity Patterns through Musculoskeletal Stress Markers: Vertebral Anomalies of a Middle Horizon Population in the North-Central Highlands of Peru." Poster presented at the 83rd Annual Meeting of the American Association of Physical Anthropologists, 10 April 2014, Calgary, Canada.

CoDA. 2011. *Center for Digital Archaeology*, electronic blog, http://www.codifi.info/blog/

Cross, J., Baber, C., Woolley, S.I., 2003. "Layered annotations of digital images for data collection in the field", in *Digest of Papers of the Seventh International Symposium on Wearable Computing*. IEEE Computer Society, Los Alamitos, CA, pp. 154–159.

DeTore, K., and R. Bria. 2012. "iArchaeology: Explorations in In-Field Digital Data Collection." Paper presented at the Archaeological Sciences of the Americas Symposium, 19 April 2012, Nashville, Tennessee.

Ellis, S. J. R., and J. Wallrodt. 2011. "iPads at Pompeii." *Pompeii Archaeological Research Project: Porta Stabia*, http://classics.uc.edu/pompeii/index.php/news/1-latest/142-ipads2010.html

Evans, T. L., and P. Daly. 2006. *Digital Archaeology: Bridging Method and Theory.* London: Routledge.

Fee, S. B., D. K. Pettegrew, and W. R. Caraher. 2013. "Taking Mobile Computing to the Field," *Near Eastern Archaeology* 76: 50–55.

Gero, J. M. 2006. "Cooperative? Or Coordinated? Investigations in the Sierra de Ancash," in A. Herrera, C. Orsini, and K. Lane, eds., *La complejidad social en la Sierra de Ancash: Ensayos sobre paisaje, economía y continuidades culturales.* Milan: Comune di Milano-Raccolte Extra Europee del Castello Sforzesco, 193–195.

Hall, A. C. 2014. "GI Science, not GIScience," *Journal of Spatial Information Science* 9: 129–131.

Houk, B. A. 2012. "The Chan Chich Archaeological Project's Digital Data Collection System," in B. A. Houk, ed., *The 2012 Season of the Chan Chich Archaeological Project. Papers of the Chan Chich Archaeological Project* 6. Lubbock: Texas Tech University, 73–82.

Kansa, E., S. W. Kansa, and E. Watrall, eds. *Archaeology 2.0: New Approaches to Communication and Collaboration. Cotsen Digital Archaeology* 1. Los Angeles: Cotsen Institute of Archaeology.

Keller, A. H. 2009. "In Defense of the Database," *SAA Archaeological record* 9(5): 26.

McAllister, H. 2015. *Reconstructing a Recuay Feasting Event at Hualcayán, Peru through Ceramic Analysis.* B.A. thesis, University of Wisconsin–La Crosse.

McManamon, F., and K. Kintigh. 2010. "Digital Antiquity: Transforming Archaeological Data into Knowledge," *The SAA Archaeological Record* 10(2): 37–40.

Palfrey, J., and U. Gasser. 2013. *Born Digital: Understanding the First Generation of Digital Natives.* New York: Basic Books.

Pettegrew, D. 2012. "iPads in Cyprus: Practical Matters in Fieldwork. The Pyla-Koutsopetria Archaeological Project," http://pylakoutsopetria.wordpress.com/2012/07/05/ipads-in-cyprus-part-4-practical-matters/

Prensky, M. 2009. "*H. sapiens* Digital: From Digital Immigrants and Digital Natives to Digital Wisdom," *Innovate:Journal of Online Education* 5(3): 1.

Reilly, P. 1989. "Data Visualization in Archaeology," *IBM Systems Journal* 28: 569–579.

Reitsma, F. 2013. "Revisiting the 'Is GIScience a Science?' Debate (or Quite Possibly Scientific Gerrymandering)," *International Journal of Geographical Information Science* 27: 211–221.

Roosevelt, C. H., P. Cobb, E. Moss, B. R. Olson, and S. Ünlüsoy. 2015. "Excavation is ~~Destruction~~ Digitization: Advances in Archaeological Practice," *Journal of Field Archaeology* 40: 325–346.

Shaffer, D. W., and K. A. Clinton. 2006. "Tool for Thoughts: Reexamining Thinking in the Digital age," *Mind, Culture, and Activity* 13: 283–300.

Shanks, M. 1997. "Photography and archaeology," in B.L. Molyneaux, ed., *The Cultural Life of Images: Visual Representation in Archaeology*. New York: Routledge, 73–107.

Shanks, M., and C. Svabo. 2013. "Archaeology and Photography: A Pragmatology," in A. González Ruibal, ed., *Reclaiming Archaeology: Beyond the Tropes of Modernity*. New York: Routledge, 89–102.

Sharp, K., and M. Litschi. 2014. "Maximizing E-Data Collection," *Advances in Archaeological Practice* 2: 104–122.

Spinuzzi, C. 2003. "Using a Handheld PC to Collect and Analyze Observational Data," in D. G. Novick and S. B. Jones, eds., *SIGDOC 2003: Proceedings of the 21st Annual International Conference on Documentation*. New York: Association for Computing Machinery, 73–79.

Stewart, M. E., and L. L. Johnson. 2011. "The Excavation is the Classroom," *SAA Archaeological Record* 11(3): 22–27.

Tripcevich, N., and S. A. Wernke. 2010. "On-Site Recording of Excavation Data Using Mobile GIS," *Journal of Field Archaeology* 35: 380–397.

Vincent, M. L., F. Kuester, and T. E. Levy. 2013. "OpenDig: In-Field Data Recording for Archaeology and Cultural Heritage," in C. Jianping, Z. Ying, and W. Juan, eds., *Proceedings of the Digital Heritage International Congress (DigitalHeritage) 2: Federating the 19th International VSMM, 10th Eurographics GCH, and 2nd UNESCO Memory of the World Conferences, 28 Oct–1 Nov 2013, Marseille, France*. Piscataway: Institute of Electrical and Electronics Engineers, 539–542.

Wallrodt, J. 2011. *Paperless Archaeology*, http://paperlessarchaeology.com/

Wing, J. M. 2008. "Computational Thinking and Thinking about Computing," *Philosophical Transactions of the Royal Society of London A: Mathematical, Physical and Engineering Sciences* 366: 3717–3725.

Wright, D. J., M. F. Goodchild, and J. D. Proctor. 1997. "Demystifying the Persistent Ambiguity of GIS as 'Tool' versus 'Science,'" *Annals of the Association of American Geographers* 87: 346–362.

Zubrow, E. B. W. 2006. "Digital Archaeology: A Historical Context," in T. L. Evans, ed., *Digital Archaeology: Bridging Method and Theory*. New York: Routledge, 10–32.

1.6.
Digital Archaeology in the Rural Andes: Problems and Prospects

Matthew Sayre

The prospects for digital archaeology are exciting and they can broaden our sense of community archaeology. The opportunity to expose new generations of students and community members to the stirring analytical possibilities that digital archaeology can provide opens up new areas for dialogue. As technology changes rapidly, and we train new generations of students who have never had the experience of using a film camera, we must be aware that this can lead them to assume that "Slow Archaeology" (Caraher 2013; Ch. 4.1) or paper recording are antiquated. Archaeologists, of all people, however, should realize that older technologies often continue to be useful. In this chapter I attempt to present and investigate these issues in an accessible manner. The two major issues addressed are (1) the process of implementing digital recording methods, and (2) our project's effort to engage in a community-focused effort to decolonize digital archaeology.

I describe here the attempts of the archaeological project at Chavín de Huántar, in Peru, to move fully into digital recording of archaeological data (for similar topics, see Ellis, Ch. 1.2; Motz, Ch. 1.3; Wernke *et al.*, Ch. 2.3). There were both pragmatic and theoretical difficulties in our attempts to transition into a digital program, and while the pragmatic and theoretical concerns did overlap, some of the theoretical difficulties could also be regarded as ethical issues.

Many of the problems that our project experienced in converting to digital recording methods were related to the particulars of the site. As will be described below, there are distinct concerns that arise working in a rural setting in the developing world, and many of these

Figure 1: Map of Chavín de Huántar in Peru.

issues would not emerge in the same way if our project were situated near an urban center in the "First World." While many of these issues arise due to economic inequality, there are also issues about who gets to use advanced technology and how archaeologists can decolonize the acquisition and processing of data.

THE PROJECT AT CHAVÍN DE HUÁNTAR, PERU

Chavín de Huántar is a UNESCO World Heritage Site that was inscribed in the UNESCO list in 1985 (FIG. 1). Its early inclusion on the list was in recognition of its tremendous importance in the history of the Andean region as well as in the history of Peruvian archaeology. The site and similarly named culture principally developed between 1200–500 B.C. (Rick *et al.* 2011). It is recognized that the site functioned as a ceremonial and pilgrimage center that attracted people from across the region. This site is composed of an elaborate stone temple, constructed plazas, and surrounding ritual facilities. The ceremonial and monumental nature of the site is visible in its fine stonework with elaborate iconography that depicts anthropomorphic as well as zoomorphic imagery from across the region, as well as in its internal gallery system and extensive canal network that runs across the site, connecting it to other water movement features at the boundaries of the temple (Burger 1995; Rick 2008). Sites of this complexity often have formally separated ritual space along with evidence of inter-regional interaction (Rowe 1963; Moore 2005).

The Stanford Project began work at the site in 1994, and although the early years of the project were devoted to the then-novel technology of theodolite mapping (Kembel 2008), the group has since moved beyond mapping and now encompasses many different aspects of anthropological and archaeological research. Initial work at the site focused on the monumental center, but later projects have expanded to include encompassing areas (Mesia 2012; Contreras 2014; Sayre *et al.* 2015). Over the years the project has expanded, and there has been a consistent emphasis on including new technologies that permit more accurate recording of spatial and archaeological data (Ristevski 2006; Kembel 2008; Contreras 2009; Rick *et al.* 2011).

The project has included archaeologists from around the world, but the majority of the professional team is Peruvian and there are many local workers on the project who have developed expertise over decades of fieldwork. This on-the-job training shares similarities with the archaeological field school experience, but the local excavators often come from farming families. As such, these workers come to the project with extensive expertise in working with local soils and sediments.

In the rural Andean region of Peru there are many areas with high levels of poverty (Matos Mar 1984). Since colonial times, much of the wealth of the country has been concentrated on the coast and in the capital of Lima. This has left the highlands as a region that has suffered both economic and racial injustice. Up until the 1960s, inhabitants of the highlands were commonly referred to as indians (*indios*), which was considered a pejorative term (Matos Mar 1984). Currently, people in the region commonly refer to themselves as peasants (*campesinos*), a term that was preferred by government officials. Many aspects of the project at Chavín are impacted by this history of working in an under-resourced region with a history of mistreatment by coastal elites.

Our Experience with Digital Recording

The Chavín archaeological project was an early adopter of digital recording techniques, beginning with its use of laser theodolites in the 1990s. Many of the problems that arose with the early adoption of digital technologies were inherent to the process of applying recently developed software to a new region. The software that our team, in particular John Rick of Stanford University, was trained in in 2011 was the PC-based REVEAL platform (Reconstruction and Exploratory Visualization: Engineering meets ArchaeoLogy). The platform was deployed significantly in the 2011 field season.

REVEAL's developers state that it is "a system for streamlined powerful sensing, archiving, extracting information from, visualizing and communicating, archaeological site-excavation data" (https://vision.lems.brown.edu/project_desc/Reveal), and the platform is available to the archaeology community as an open-source project. It provides core computer-vision/pattern-recognition/machine-learning research with applications to archaeology and the humanities. The website describes this process, stating ". . . REVEAL Analyzer provides the excavator, researcher, or student with integrated multi-format access to the tables, photographs, and 3D models in the database. Exploring and filtering the data in plan view, 3D view, photo view, or tabular view generates automatic back-end queries to extract, format, and display relevant information from the database." While this program is admirable in its ambition and scope, we encountered some difficulties applying this program to fieldwork in the rural Andes.

Many of the complications that arose were due to differences in archaeological practice around the world. Much of the REVEAL program appears to have been developed with the terminology and techniques of Mediterranean archaeology in mind, but different standards and methodologies around the world lead to different definitions of artifacts, site types, and soil counts. For example, trenches and spits are typical spatial excavation areas in the Mediterranean, whereas many projects in the Americas rely on spatial units of varying sizes. The denotation of units is also an issue as more and more projects in the Andes are moving away from using standardized unit sizes (such as 2 x 2 m units) and moving toward using the locus system of excavation that permits users to easily construct Harris matrices (Harris 1979). This is further complicated by the issue in Peru that some governmental authorities prefer to see standard unit areas when they inspect excavations, while others require the use of the locus excavation system and the completion of a Harris matrix at the end of the season. Another difference in technique is that in the Andes, archaeologists routinely use bucket counts in order to document the density of finds, and in this case the REVEAL program allowed for baskets of dirt, which did not seem to connect immediately with density computational outputs (e.g., the Chavín project typically uses 10-liter buckets to measure soil volume). These examples highlight the tension that exists between standardized group software and bespoke systems designed by individuals for use by a small and specialized excavation team (for more specialized discussions of this issue, see Castro López et al., Ch. 3.1; Dufton, Ch. 3.3).

There were issues with the REVEAL software that arose at our field site that would likely not be major issues in regions of the world that have reliable Internet access. The lack of reliable access led to syncing problems, including the inability to synchronize data files easily with Dropbox accounts. In general, a significant advantage to digital recording of archaeological field data is the capacity to export data files into online databases. If this is possible, it enables specialists to access field data immediately as well as help all members of the field team avoid the double duty of entering paper field forms into databases that are generally stored online. The project was unfortunately unable to avoid this double recording of forms.

Some of the strengths of the REVEAL software were compelling enough to make our team excited about future possibilities. The software had great compatibility with PC-based tablets and the software synchronized well across desktops and laptop computers (this is always an issue in areas with limited access to wireless Internet). Many of the problems of synchronization were resolved once a local intranet was established. Additionally, the tablets were compatible with Windows, and access to other operating systems in Peru can be difficult to manage.

One final issue we faced was how to create documents for government review agencies. This matter arose as many forms are recorded in both Spanish and English. While the original forms are all in Spanish, some of the team members (primarily North American undergraduate students) are monolingual English speakers, and we have to consistently translate content into Spanish. This problem continues to exist and will likely not be eliminated by technology. This double work of translation may eventually be solved by translation software, but for now the manual entering and translating of paper field forms into databases is still more clearly managed by having only one typed, final form.

EARLY ADOPTERS, STUDENTS, AND THE VALUE OF DIGITAL METHODOLOGIES

The varied backgrounds of excavators on projects are something that all larger excavation teams will encounter. This is a particular issue on field schools where participants are just beginning to learn archaeological terminology. As directors train students in new terminology and skills, such as recording differences in micro-stratigraphy, the means by which they record those notes may be less of hindrance to the students than the challenge of fieldwork itself (see Ellis, Ch. 1.2, for a critical discussion of this issue).

The collection and correction of written forms is a standardized practice on most projects and this is an area where the online management of group files facilitates work. If supervisors have access at all times to students' field forms, they can correct and add notes at any point in time. As we train students in field note taking and digital methodology it is possible to show them that these skills are applicable outside of archaeological excavations. The ability to synthesize, store, and process large amounts of digital data is a skillset that is transferable to many other fields. This is part of the advantage of being early adapters of new technologies; the skills learned in a class setting can then be taken outside of the classroom and integrated into private and public sector occupations (cf., Bria and DeTore, Ch. 1.5; Kansa, Ch. 4.2)

As I have previously discussed, field schools are an example of the flipped classroom (Sayre 2014). In these settings, students are taking material from lectures and books and applying it to a real world context. Their supervisors are responsible for answering questions and guiding them through the learning process so that they can begin to identify stratigraphic changes and significant finds on their own. The goal of developing independent and self-guided learners is one that melds well with the digital domain. As information is recorded and uploaded to digital databases, it enables new learners to pose questions of their peers and supervisors, thus creating a more open and questioning community of archaeologists than would be possible if field excavators were simply recording their notes in field notebooks that would solely be reviewed by their immediate supervisor.

One area of laboratory work where we have rapidly implemented digital methodologies is in the recording and processing of architectural and ceramic data. These two types of cultural material traditionally required specialists to spend tremendous amounts of time drawing in the field and in the laboratory. As digital photography and photogrammetry have become increasingly more advanced over time, we have been able to spend less time drawing these objects and more time creating accurate three-dimensional models of artifacts, ceramics, and walls (FIG. 2). The team members who specialize in creating these models can take these digital skills and apply them to many domains. This was a central topic of the documentary that I helped to produce (www.intothefieldfilm.com), which seeks to present the importance of archaeology to a broad public audience.

Figure 2: Creating a photogrammetry model of architecture at Chavín. Figure courtesy of J. Rick.

Technical Advantages of Digital Archaeology

There are many advantages to switching toward digital archaeology. While this chapter has emphasized some of the difficulties of this work, in particular those that arise while working in a rural setting in a developing nation, one of the reasons why this transition is occurring is because there are significant benefits to changing practices.

The real-time processing of data, both visual and textual, is important. As three-dimensional visual data becomes more nuanced and detailed, it will permit researchers to ask new questions of the spaces that have been excavated and how those spaces relate to the broader world around them. The syncing of written records with online databases will provide access for remote researchers, particularly specialists who are not always present on-site, to provide insights and ask question of field researchers. It will also permit fluid exportation of visual and textual data for final reports and later academic research. The relative ease with which researchers can share their data with the public could lessen the tendency of contract and academic archaeology to produce grey literature that is not easily accessible to interested parties.

Digital archaeology also provides the possibility of creating a more environmentally sustainable archaeology. The lower reliability on paper will lessen the impact on the environment, and the increased emphasis on digital tools could lead more projects to invest in solar digital chargers and other sources providing clean energy for archaeological field and laboratory projects. While this transition has not yet occurred, a fully digital project may feel greater need to make this change. This does not mean, however, that there are still not social issues involved in the transition to digital recording.

"No One Steals Paper," or Digital Archaeology within a Developing World Context

Digital archaeology does not solely exist in the ethereal "series of tubes" that is the Internet; rather, its application and practice occurs in real world settings. For example, there were less than five telephones in town when I first came to Chavín de Huántar in Peru in 2002. Soon the number of fixed lines expanded and people began to construct Internet cafés. Over the years these cafés converted into gaming and chat centers as the Internet connections were too slow to engage in any serious work. This change was soon followed by the introduction of cellular phones, which soon became the dominant means of communication in town. In fact, they remain the primary means of communication with the outside world as there is still verypoor reliable Internet access. While our project has established a good intranet system, there is still little access to outside connections.

The local population continues to have little connection to email or cloud services. This lack of availability prevents our project from being able to reliably store terabytes of archaeological/visual data online. Limited connections also prevent us from engaging in some of the more compelling aspects of digital archaeology, such as the immediate uploading of visual data onto cloud platforms that are accessible by outside researchers working offsite. While we currently maintain databases that are accessible after the field season, there is a positive impact resulting from the lack of cloud access at the site as it makes it necessary for project members to come to the site and interact with their fellow archaeologists. These in-person moments can lead to conversations and correlations that may not have happened if people were not physically present on the project site.

There are a number of cost requirements that have also impeded the project's transition to a fully digital program (see Castro López *et al.*, Ch. 3.1; Ellis, Ch. 1.2). Some of the hardware costs will be clear to all researchers, but some of the costs vary based upon the location and local realities of the project site. For example, a major international project working at pre-ceramic sites in coastal Peru has stated that they anticipate having a three-year replacement timeline for all hardware (J. Rick, personal communication 2015). This rapid replacement timeline is partially a result of working in a desert environment where dust and wind negatively impact the preservation of equipment. Field archaeology, however, is always hard on equipment and dirt is omnipresent at archaeological field sites, and a three-year timeline for replacing all tablets, desktops, and field computers is a high cost for most academic or contract archaeology projects.

One particular concern that arises in many places in the developing world is that class difference becomes apparent when archaeologists are seen carrying tablets and digital equipment around town in local communities. The value of this equipment, which routinely is above a thousand dollars per instrument, is beyond the purchasing power of nearly all people in the developing world. For example, the daily wage in many areas of rural Peru is routinely less than US$10 per day (Zambrano *et al.* 2014), and many people do not have access to paid labor positions. Thus, there are many members of these communities who get by on less than US$5 per day (Matos Mar 1984; Zambrano *et al.* 2014). This wealth discrepancy can lead to tensions within the local populace, who can begin to view the archaeological project as a wealthy influx of outsiders with little knowledge of how difficult life can be for common people in their communities. It could also attract the unwanted attention of criminal elements that exist in all communities around the world.

One particular concern in recent years in Peru has been payroll robberies, and one Peruvian project on the coast of Peru experienced such an event in recent years (J. Rick, personal communication 2015). Local community members learned the payday of local field workers and realized that the cash payments were being delivered once every two weeks by truck. This truck was stopped at gunpoint on the road and robbed. Quite clearly, no member of an archaeology project wishes to put any member of the project in the face of deadly harm. While some payments can now be made directly into bank accounts, it is also clear that there is not too much of a distinction between cash robberies and robberies focused on hardware and equipment. This is why some members of the archaeological community (J. Rick, personal communication 2015) say, "no one steals paper." The recording of excavation data on paper limits the amount of visible valuable equipment in the field and also adds to the sense that the work is academic in nature and not engaged in ostentatious displays of wealth.

DECOLONIZING ARCHAEOLOGICAL PRACTICE

There are inherent social tensions in almost all realms of archaeological practice. These tensions are often magnified when archaeologists work abroad, and they can be further compounded when a group of archaeologists from the global north works in the global south. This is the case with our project, where the directors of the project are Peruvian and North American. While the permitting process for all fieldwork in Peru is managed and granted by the cabinet-level office of the Ministry of Culture, there are also non-bureaucratic concerns that

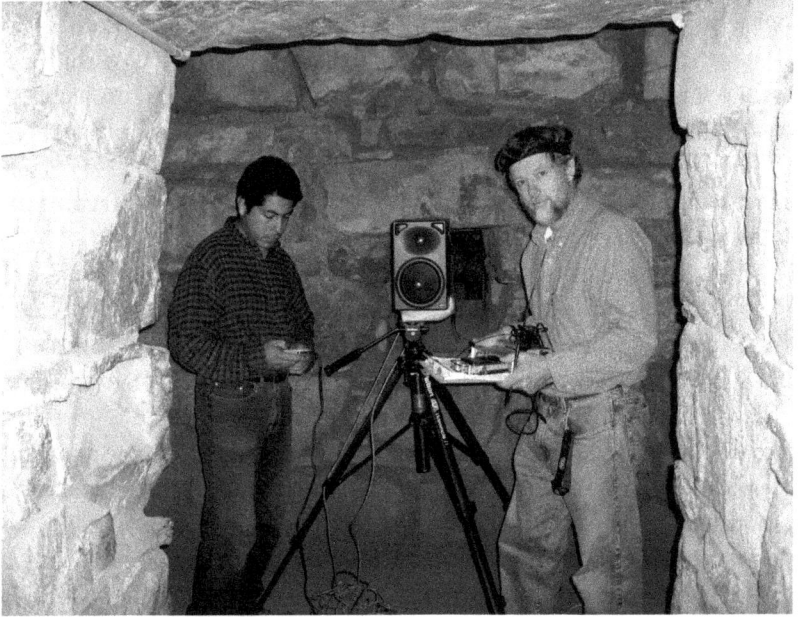

Figure 3: Dr. John Rick and local expert José Luis Cruzado Coronel working on the digital archeoacoustics project.

have to be addressed. Some of these concerns center around economic inequality and access to technology.

The Chavín project works in a rural Andean town where many of the local inhabitants lack formal employment. When formal work does exist, it routinely pays less than the official minimum wage of 750 soles (roughly US$230) per month. This leaves a community composed of workers who generally earn less than US$5 per day. While many members of the local community grow and raise most of their food, they also seek to own technology and material goods that connect them to the broader world.

The Chavín archaeological project uses standard technology for its research. These include personal computers, desktops, digital cameras, tablet computers, theodolites, and scanning machines. Each of these pieces of equipment generally costs over US$1,000. This represents almost half a year's salary for many members of the local community and undoubtedly causes tension. Many members of the archaeological project find it awkward when a local community member asks them how much their camera, phone, or shoes cost, but it must be acknowledged that these are natural questions that provide useful information to people who need to negotiate their salaries and other forms of compensation with people who are coming from other areas of the country or from abroad. The differences in income and access to material goods can lead to problems and adversely affect community relations.

One of the means by which our project director has attempted to enhance community relations is by making sure that members of the local community are trained in the use of advanced technology. Beginning in 2003, Rick began to hire local high-school students to learn how to use digital cameras and to process the images they took on project computers using sophisticated software. The removal of expensive equipment from the archaeologists' hands and its place-ment in the hands of local community members visually displayed how technology can be democratizing (FIG. 3). In this case, trust and openness with local community members led to increased recipro-cated trust. In addition, many of these local students took the digital skills that they learned and applied them in other careers.

If we are to decolonize archaeology, we must go beyond simply handing the camera over to a different set of hands. The local *camp-esino* has more to offer than day labor. As workers collaborate together on the excavation process, many local insights should be added into the interpretation process. Some of those insights involve training outside archaeologists to view the landscape and environment through local eyes. An additional means of decolonizing the discipline, and turning to more community-based research has been simply to ask what the local community would like from the archaeological project. In our case, the answers have varied tremendously—everything from language lessons to enhanced business contacts with the tourism industry have been requested. As the project responds to the needs and requests of the community, they expand the scope and importance of the project.

In the end, much of the research at the site has been guided by the words of previous Chavín project director, Luis Lumbreras (1981: 6, with translation by the author):

La arqueología no es, como no lo es ninguna ciencia, una etérea actividad académica aislada de los problemas de la sociedad donde se desarrolla; es, y siempre ha sido, un instrumento activo de la lucha social que [. . .] sirve para cohesionar y dar sustento a la clase social que la utiliza. La Arqueología es arma de opresión cuando sirve para justificar la explotación de los campesinos indígenas de nuestros países, desarrollando teorías que muestran su inferioridad histórica frente a los invasores europeos y su proclividad a la decadencia. Es arma de opresión cuando saluda y engrandece el pasado para denostar el presente, creando la retrógrada convicción de que 'todo tiempo pasado fue mejor' [. . .] Es arma de opresión cuando convierte en objeto al sujeto histórico. La arqueología, en cambio, es arma de liberación cuando descubre las raíces históricas de los pueblos, enseñando el origen y carácter de su condición de explotados; es arma de liberación, cuando muestra y descubre la transitoriedad de los estados y las clases sociales, la transitoriedad de las instituciones y las pautas de conducta. Es arma de liberación cuando se articula con las demás ciencias sociales, las que se ocupan de los problemas de hoy, y muestra la unidad procesal de la historia en sus términos generales y en sus particularidades regionales o locales.

Archaeology is not, as it is not any other science, an esoteric academic activity isolated from the problems of the society in which it develops; it is and it has always been, an active instrument of social struggle that [. . .] serves to unite and support the social class that uses it. Archaeology is a weapon of oppression when it justifies the exploitation of indigenous peasants in our countries, while developing theories that show their historical inferiority to the European invaders and their proclivity toward decadence and decline. It is a weapon of oppression when it enhances the past to insult the present, creating the retrograde conviction that 'all the past was better' [. . .] it is a weapon of oppression when it converts an historical subject into an object. Archaeology, however, is a weapon of liberation when it discovers the historical roots of the people, teaching them the origins and character of their current exploited status; it is a weapon of liberation, when it reveals the transience of states and social classes, the transience of institutions and patterns of behavior. It is a weapon of liberation when it joins with the other social sciences, those dealing with the problems of today, and shows the procedural/processual unity of history in general terms along with its regional and local particularities.

Much of this chapter has focused on the real world problems and benefits of switching to digital platforms. As the quote from Lumbreras makes clear, we must always be cognizant of the fact that the knowledge we produce has real world implications and the tools that we use in developing that knowledge can also serve similar ends.

Conclusion

As Sonya Atalay (2012: 2) stated: "If we problematize archaeology's future, three important considerations come to the forefront: the issue of *relevance*, the question of *audience*, and concerns about *benefits*." Digital archaeology must also confront these same three issues. One might argue that the relevance, audience, and benefits of digital archaeology are primarily designed for and associated with wealthy universities. But this chapter has attempted to demonstrate that digital archaeology is relevant to a broader public and community audience than only academics in the global north. There are many in the public who find digital methods to be both relevant and beneficial to their communities. However, these communities are not always naturally included stakeholders in these conversations, and this remains an issue that must always be acknowledged and addressed.

The chapters in this volume come from a workshop that brought together a broad array of researchers in an attempt to formulate future best practices in digitizing archaeology. While many of the chapters directly engage with some of the technical tools involved in the transition to digital archaeology, this contribution has hopefully added more of the human element into the picture. We must remain committed to working in communities and creating scholarly work that engages with, and is influenced by, the people and communities that surround us.

https://mobilizingthepast.mukurtu.net/
collection/16-digital-archaeology-rural-andes-prob-
lems-and-prospects

http://dc.uwm.edu/arthist_mobilizingthepast/8

REFERENCES

Atalay, S. 2012 *Community-Based Archaeology: Research with, by, and for Indigenous and Local Communities.* Berkeley: University of California Press.

Burger, R. 1995. *Chavin and the Origins of Andean Civilization.* London: Thames and Hudson.

Caraher, W. 2013. "Slow Archaeology," *North Dakota Quarterly* 80: 43–52

Contreras, D. 2009. "Reconstructing Landscape at Chavín de Huántar, Perú : A GIS-Based Approach," *Journal of Archaeological Science* 36: 1006–1017.

Contreras, D. 2014. "(Re)constructing the Sacred: Landscape Geoarchaeology at Chavín de Huántar, Peru." *Archaeological and Anthropological Sciences*, doi 10.1007/s12520-014-0207-2

Harris, E. C. 1979. *Principles of Archaeological Stratigraphy.* London: Academic Press.

Kembel, S. R. 2008. "The Architecture of the Monumental Center of Chavín de Huántar: Sequence, Transformation, and Chronology," in W. J. Conklin and J. Quilter, eds., *Chavín: Art, Architecture, and Culture. Monograph Cotsen Institute of Archaeology at UCLA 61.* Los Angeles: Cotsen Institute of Archaeology, 35–81.

Lumbreras, L. 1981. *La arqueología como ciencia social.* 2nd edn. Lima: Ediciones Peisa.

Matos Mar, L. 1984. *Desborde Popular y crisis del Estado: El nuevo rostro del Perú en la década de 1980. Perú problema 21.* Lima: Instituto de Estudios Peruanos.

Mesia, C. 2012 "Uso de Estimados de Densidad Kernel en la investigación de grupos cerámicos del periodo Formativo provenientes de Chavín de Huántar," *Arqueología y Sociedad* 24: 161–190.

Moore, J. D. 2005. *Cultural Landscapes in the Ancient Andes: Archaeologies of Place.* Gainesville: University Press of Florida.

Rick, J. W. 2008. "Context, Construction, and Ritual in the Development of Authority at Chavín de Huántar," in W. J. Conklin and J. Quilter, eds., *Chavín: Art, Architecture, and Culture. Monograph Cotsen Institute of Archaeology at UCLA 61.* Los Angeles: Cotsen Institute of Archaeology, 3–34.

Rick, J., R. Rick, S. Kembel, D. Contreras, M. Sayre, and J. Wolf. 2011. "La cronología de Chavín de Huántar y sus implicancias para el Periodo Formativo," *Boletin de Arqueologia PUCP* 13: 87–132.

Ristevski, J. 2006 "Feature: Laser Scanning for Cultural Heritage Applications," *Professional Surveyor* 26.3: 6.

Rowe, J. H. 1963. "Urban Settlements in Ancient Peru," *Ñawpa Pacha: Journal of Andean Archaeology* 1: 1–27.

Sayre, M. 2014. "Student-Initiated Projects, the Flipped Classroom, and Crowdfunding," *SAA Archaeological Record* 14(1): 14–17.

Sayre, M., M. Miller, and S. Rosenfeld. 2015. "Isotopic Evidence for the Trade and Production of Exotic Marine Mammal Bone Artifacts at Chavín de Huántar, Peru." *Archaeological and Anthropological Sciences,* doi 10.1007/s12520-015-0230-y

Zambrano, O., M. Rosales, and D. Laos. 2014. *Global Boom, Local Impacts: Mining Revenues and Subnational Outcomes in Peru 2007–2011. International Development Banking Working Paper Series* no. IDB-WP-509, https://publications.iadb.org/handle/11319/6487

1.7.
Digital Pompeii: Dissolving the Fieldwork-Library Research Divide

Eric E. Poehler

Sometime before October 31, 1766, excavation began inside a porticoed building in the south of an area that would soon become the archaeological site of Pompeii (FIG. 1). The pace of work to clear the building was swift but episodic as crews were frequently reassigned to more exciting discoveries in the early years of Pompeii's rediscovery. Moving in bursts along the southern colonnade, the excavators seemed to be able to move at least 140 m³ of material in a week before halting for nearly two months. Another burst of activity pushed to reveal the southeast corner, and the first half of 1768 was spent clearing the eastern colonnade (Pagano and Prisciandaro 2006: 58–64). Excavation of the northern and western colonnades is not specifically dated in the archival records, but images show that into the 1780s a great mound of volcanic debris at least 4 m high still covered much of these areas and persisted into the first decade of the 19th century (FIG. 2). In the course of those excavations, stunning images and artifacts were revealed, including real and painted armaments that would give the Quadriporticus its colloquial name: the Barracks of the Gladiators (FIG. 3).

The precise date when excavation in the Quadriporticus was completed is not terribly important as the volume of material removed was astounding: over 15,000 cubic meters of earth, ash, and lapilli were removed, as well the trees that grew atop the buried city. On average, 18th-century excavators (and we should hesitate to call them archaeologists) removed at least 300 m³ of material each year from the Quadriporticus, but that average dramatically underestimates the pace of work. We know that at times they could shift

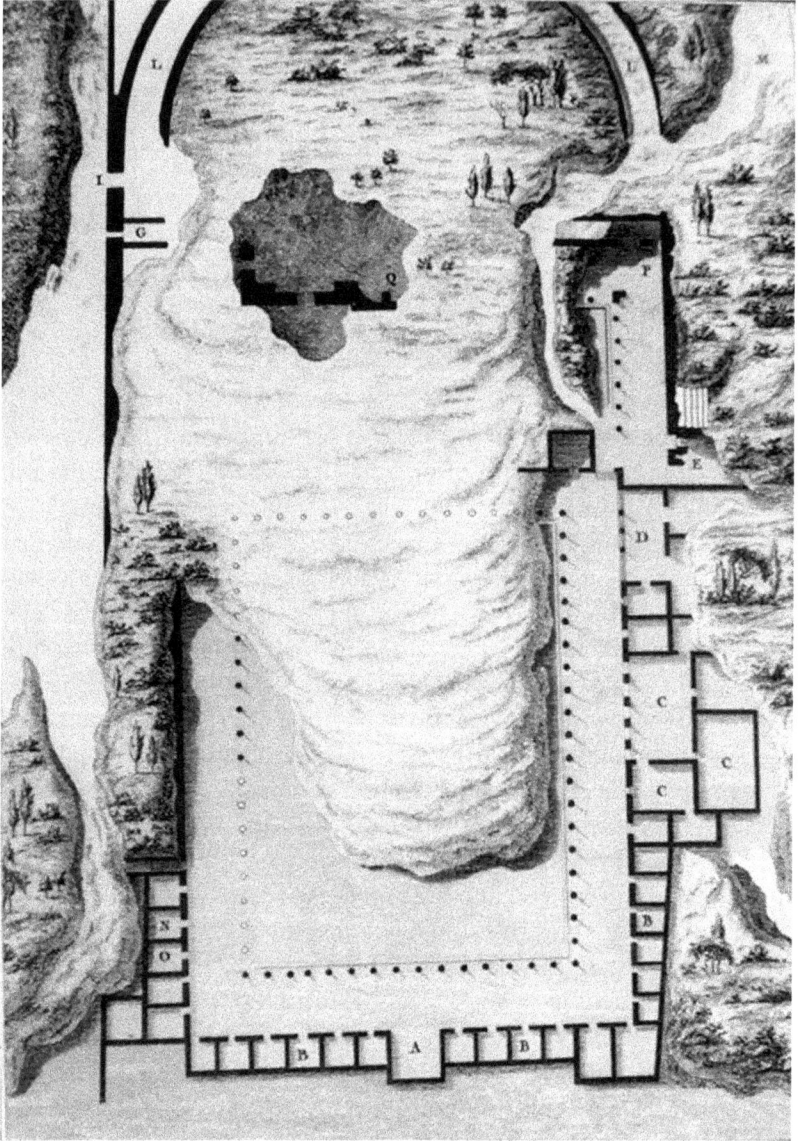

Figure 1: Plan *Géométral de l'Etat actuel de la fouille du Quartier des Soldats à Pompeii*. Reproduced from de Saint-Non 1781–1786, vol. 2, pl. 84.

Figure 2: *Vue Perspective de la Colonnade du Quartier des Soldats à Pompeii.* Reproduced from de Saint-Non 1781–1786, vol. 2, pl. 86.

Figure 3: Detail of a gladiator's helmet in a fresco depicting armaments from the Quadriporticus. (MANN n. 9702). Photo by Bettina Bergmann.

Figure 4: Insulae VIII 7, 1-15 and I.1: plan of trenches, 2005–2012. Pompeii Archaeological Research Project: Porta Stabia. Map courtesy of Steven Ellis.

two-thirds of that in a single week; for example, from February 14th to February 21st, 1767, an estimated 212 cubic meters of material from the southern exedra and its adjacent colonnade was cleared (Pagano and Prisciandaro 2006: 60). By contrast, modern excavation at Pompeii is excruciatingly slow. In eight years of research on the pre-79 A.D. development of insulae VIII 7, 1-15 and I.1 (FIG. 4), the Pompeii Archaeological Research Project: Porta Stabia (hereafter, PARP:PS; http://classics.uc.edu/pompeii), directed by Steven Ellis, excavated 40 trenches below the final Roman levels, exploring 770 m² of the 2,660 m² of these humble city blocks, and removed about 1,150 m³ of material (see Devore and Ellis 2005, 2008; Ellis and Devore 2006, 2009, 2010; Ellis *et al.* 2011, 2012, 2015).

The PARP:PS excavation seasons are only five weeks long, so the average pace of excavation is 29 m³ per week, or 10% of the average rate of the previous (Bourbon-era) excavators. While only 80 objects were recorded in the Quadriporticus (concentrated almost entirely in the first three years; Pagano and Prisciandaro 2006, vol. II, 259–60), PARP:PS recovered more than 280,000 objects during their eight years of investigation. Moreover, Ellis and his team identified and documented over 4,500 individual stratigraphic units (SUs) to which these finds belong and relate, providing, on average, an archaeologically meaningful distinction to every 0.25 m³ of soil at a rate of 114 times a week (S. Ellis, personal communication). By contrast, the archival records of the Quadriporticus make no useful mention of any distinction in what they were digging through.

Between 2010 and 2013 I directed a non-invasive, born-digital, architectural analysis project in the Quadriporticus with Ellis that sought to decode the construction and life history of this remarkable structure that had existed for over two hundred years in both the ancient (ca. 130 B.C.–A.D. 79) and modern (1766–present) eras. In addition to understanding the building, part of our research design was to test how far one could extend and how much one could gain from non-invasive techniques and technologies. Our plan included the use of excavation data from PARP:PS, but permitted no new trenches. In the four, three-week campaigns of the Pompeii Quadriporticus Project (hereafter, PQP; https://www.umass.edu/classics/pqp) we recorded over 2,500 stratigraphic units reflecting changes to the masonry, decor, and function of the Quadriporticus and documented another 1,700 SUs within the 77 columns of its colonnades. On average, we identified and documented more than 350 stratigraphic units per week.

WORKFLOW IS DATAFLOW

The point of this unequal and perhaps even unfair comparison is to draw a stark, unmistakable line around an obvious statement: as the priorities of archaeological research have changed, so too have our methods, techniques, and results. The dominant trend, at Pompeii and elsewhere, has been an ever-widening gulf between the decreasing volume excavated and the density of material recovery and documentation. Indeed, PQP recorded as much stratigraphic information as any other research project without conducting any excavation. While modern research projects have fewer infrastructural and logistical challenges compared to early modern excavations in managing smaller labor forces for shorter periods, our ethos of information maximization has replaced these with an enormous data management load. Today, every project has a database and most have an organizational chart of personnel that represents a map of dataflow through that project: from excavators to trench supervisors to object specialists to directors (e.g., see: Motz, Ch. 1.3; Wallrodt, Ch. 1.1). On the front line of excavation are spatial people, the taphonomic specialists (i.e., excavators) who interpret and faithfully record every aspect of a trench, but who also give up much of their object analysis to the next layer in the flow of evidence. It is the object specialists who provide the final identifying, functional, and chronological information for the artifacts recovered. In some cases it is first up to the trench supervisor to minimally reintegrate the specialist's spot reports back into excavation practice. Ultimately, it is the project director's responsibility to reunite the space of a trench and the objects ripped out of it and place it within a historical narrative that explains the social forces in the past that brought these material realities into being. There are still more processes and personnel on a modern research project. Many projects have an artifact registrar, spatial specialists (who work with survey instruments, computer-aided design (CAD), geographic information systems (GIS), or the like), and now dedicated information technologists to deal with the constant flow of data and metadata that results from archaeological research.

In addition to and in place of these information specialists, some projects have looked longingly toward the revolution in portable computing and information technologies. These devices and software (particularly tablets and drafting apps) have allowed archaeologists to take the work of data management back to the trench edge and make it the point of origin for precise and accurate digital recording. As many contributions to this volume demonstrate, we have already witnessed the first part of the revolution of our discipline: the transformation of archaeological methods of data collection and, to a lesser extent, how such data are accessed and deployed in the field. Today iPads are everywhere, and though they are the flavor of the moment and eventually will be superseded, they are not going away.

Such is the formulation of modern archaeological practice: dense networks of technology and personnel enmeshed within an ethos to collect more evidence from smaller trenches using less invasive methods. It is within this context that I want to explore what I believe will be a second act in our revolution in digital archaeological practice. Put simply, in the very near future, an entirely new set of tools and an enormous dataset for archaeological inquiry will also arrive at the trench edge: the library. It is a good thing in theory to bring all information to bear on a given inquiry, but in practice we know that it is not only impossible, but often counterproductive to try to employ every method or apply every dataset to a given problem. Breaking down the geographical wall between fieldwork and library research— the hundreds to thousands of miles separating the field site and the university—is well underway, but its impact on how archaeologists do research is yet unknown (or rather, yet undecided by us).

TECHNOLOGY > METHOD > INTERPRETATION

In what remains of this article I want to outline very briefly two projects I direct that scratch the surface of this second act in digital archaeological practice in order to explore very briefly what the future might look like. These examples demonstrate the value of doing archival research in the field and that soon a visit to Pompeii can mean a tour through its bibliography as well. The mechanisms by which we deliver secondary materials to the field are already being built, and now we must begin to question how to incorporate books and articles (at least) into our actual fieldwork practices. To do this we need to begin to imagine not only the possibilities, but also the impediments: when do we dig and when do we read? Most importantly, if we are going to integrate a significant component of secondary source material, we must also ask: where in the process will we find the time to do so?

Figure 5: Watercolor of fountain and interior of the Quadriporticus. W.J. Hüber, lithograph by L. T. Müller, 1818–1819. Columns of tholos are circled in light blue. Reproduced from Pagano and Prisciandaro 2006: 176; copyright by N. Longobardi.

The first project, the Pompeii Quadriporticus Project, has already been introduced as part of the opening discussion on the increasing elision between fieldwork practices and information management. In this context, PQP's use of more than 186 archival images in the field to identify and document changes to the building that occurred in the two and one half centuries since its initial excavation are also relevant to the fieldwork-library question. These images were loaded into both an offline database and an online (and now defunct) platform called DM, which provided a set of basic markup tools for drafting and annotating the images themselves as well as creating links between images (Poehler and Ellis 2014: 3–4). It was during the process of examining these archival images, and creating an absolute (by the dates of the images) sequence of modern architectural changes to the Quadriporticus, that we first noticed that a few important components of the building's architecture had been removed. The most obvious removal was the large fountain that several artists and cartographers had depicted in the northeast corner of the portico prior to 1837 (FIG. 5).

Less obvious was the circular, colonnaded structure that had once existed—or was still under construction—in the center of the Quadriporticus. Hints of this tholos-like structure were first noticed as curious stray column drums along the edge of the unexcavated central mound and in the column standing in the tunnel excavated through it (FIG. 2). It was only when looking for images of the lost fountain that we noticed a circle of column drums surrounding a cylindrical altar or cistern head (Poehler and Ellis 2014: 4–6). That some circular structure inhabited the middle of the Quadriporticus was not surprising to us: our ground-penetrating radar (GPR) results had already proven its existence (FIG. 6). A cursory examination of early maps of Pompeii (and an over-abundance of caution), however, had convinced us that these subsurface structures were related to the center of a modern cruciform garden design imposed on the interior of the colonnade (Poehler and Ellis 2012: 3–4). The combined weight of imagery from both the 19th and 21st centuries, however, could not be ignored and caused us to change our interpretation. Interestingly, another image with evidence for the circular structure was identified by Ellis while in the audience at the "Mobilizing the Past" workshop (FIG. 7). The drawing by Gudeson, made from his balloon flight over Pompeii in the

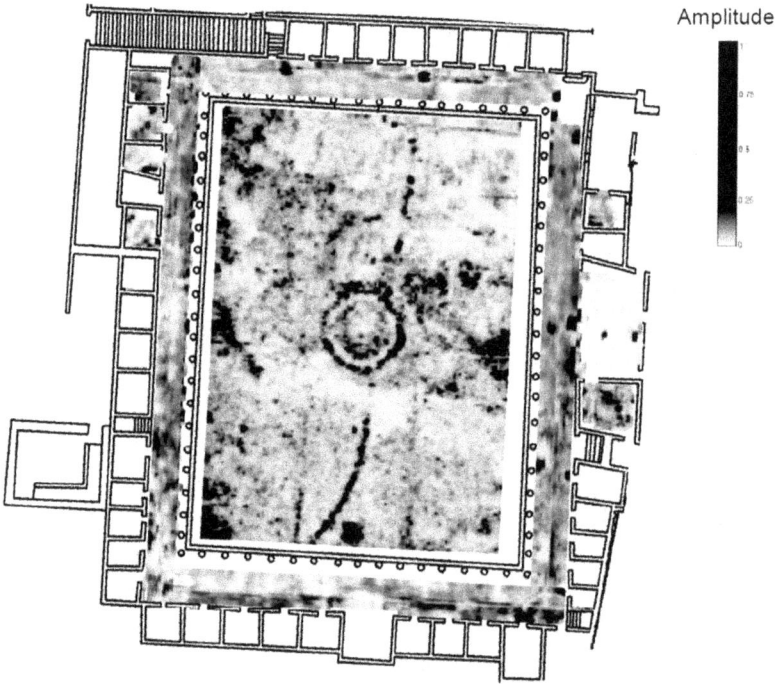

Figure 6: Ground-penetrating radar image of the Quadriporticus, slice 4 (depth ca. 66–92 cm).

Figure 7: *Vue prise au dessus de l'Odéon de du Téàtre tragique.*
Drawing by A. Gudeson, reproduced from Etiennez 1849–1852, pl. 15.

1840s, shows—when highly magnified or when projected onto a 30 foot screen—a circular projection in the center of the Quadriporticus.

For PQP, the impact of having and interrogating archival materials in the field—in databases on our iPads and in online markup environments (DM)—was both immediate and enormous. Suddenly, our building possessed a structure not seen in nearly 180 years, which changed that building's basic appearance from a Hellenistic gymnasium to a 2nd-century A.D. Macellum. It is the aspiration of the second project I direct to make this kind of discovery from in-field archival and secondary-source research possible for every building at Pompeii. The Pompeii Bibliography and Mapping Project (PBMP; http://digitalhumanities.umass.edu/pbmp/) is the attempt to graft a bibliographic catalog of more than 20,000 references onto an online GIS map (or maps) with thousands of spatial objects. On their own, each component creates a new tool for researching the city that has never before been available in digital form. Together these datasets offer an unique opportunity to explore at once the physical, cultural, and narrative landscapes of the most important site in the world of Roman archaeology. By collocating spatial and bibliographic information within a single representation, users can find information about the ancient city in a particularly intuitive manner—by simply clicking on the space of one's interest.

The true value of the PBMP, however, will come as a querying tool. Attaching the bibliographic data to the GIS permits one to use spatial categories to sort through thousands of citations that might be related only by the locations referenced in those texts. Moreover, because one can sort the bibliography first by the size or variety of a building type (e.g., a house or its area in m^2), its locations in the city (e.g., insula 1 of Region I), and their relationships to other kinds of structures (e.g., workshops), unique and powerful questions that once took weeks to generate the data for will now only take minutes. It is in such experimentation that I hold the greatest hope for the PBMP and where I expect that its use in the field will be the most novel (see Poehler 2014 for an example). Certainly, the ability to quickly find materials on topics related to one's fieldwork will be valuable, but greater still will be the ability to create maps and bibliographies of comparanda for the features and finds discovered in the course of archaeological research.

While the PBMP will have an important impact, it is important to recognize that we already choose from among many possible aspects of research moment by moment while in the field: from excavation, to primary and secondary analyses, to phasing and contextualization, and finally to report and publication writing. To put this more simply:

> we collect data,
> we analyze them,
> we interpret them,
> we synthesize them, and
> we narrate them.

These activities are natural allies in a process of understanding the past, and there are many reasons why doing all these aspects in the field makes sense. But the purpose of this reductive adumbration is to make easier the task of considering the times when we currently introduce information from secondary sources and where we might add still more in the future.

So when do we think we would want to have access to and read secondary sources? Situations include:

1. *Excavation*: when discovering an unusual feature (e.g., a kiln or soil layer).
2. *Artifact analysis*: when discovering an unusual object (e.g., rare material or form).
3. *Synthesis*: when the combined data lead to a surprising result (e.g., when discovering your building is another building).
4. *Writing*: when making an argument supported by facts (i.e., all the time).

Currently, at the moment of excavation, there are relatively few opportunities to incorporate library resources. Excavation, or equally pedestrian survey or masonry analysis, is primarily a manual process of sampling, collection, and recording that tends to limit the subjects relevant to read about. Background information on the geology or later ancient and modern histories of a location seems an appropriate topic to investigate while digging (or equally, in preparation for digging). The discovery of an important feature, such as the kiln found near the Porta Stabia in 2012, might also drive an excavator toward secondary source materials in order to help understand the function, distributions, and known forms of other excavated kilns (Dicus 2014:66–67;

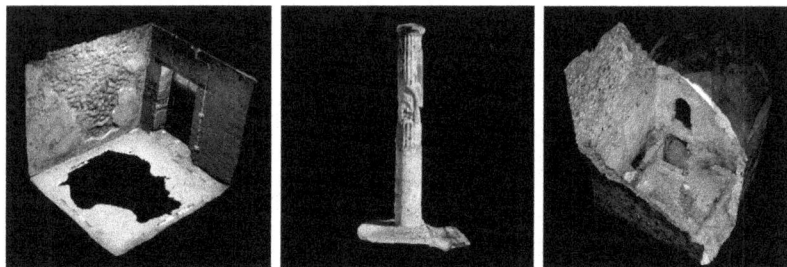

Figure 8: Photogrammetrical models of (from left to right) Room 35, Column 59, and Room 61 from the Quadriporticus.

Figure 9: View inside the Altstadt sewer, facing north toward the Large Theater and farther to Stabian Baths.

Ellis *et al.* 2015: 2–5). The study of unusual objects at the level of artifact analysis would also benefit from a direct connection to sources of comparanda for identification, dating, and the determination of function. Looking toward the future, we should imagine consulting not only standard reference materials of canonical types, but also multiple examples from previously excavated sites in the form of narrative, detailed imagery, and three-dimensional models (FIG 8; see also Kansa, Ch. 4.2).

In the future, the point of synthesis seems a natural place to expand our use of library resources in the field. Synthesis is an all too neat word for the sloshing back and forth between individual interpretations of data and the arguments they are meant to support. Such messiness, however, makes room for other peoples' interpretations, for comparanda, and for unexpected parallels. I suspect that this will be one activity expanded by access to a library in the field. At the same time, it seems equally likely that the some of the research burden for making initial identifications and interpretations of objects, features, or soils will fall to the trench supervisor during the workday. Those excavators who can generate not only an interpretation of the trench's stratigraphy, but also equally timely and synoptic bibliographies on the fish vats, bar counters, drains, or beaten earth streets will make a valued contribution to the stage of synthesis and writing.

PAY IT FORWARD: DOING MORE WITH MORE

How, then, will we "pay" for the extra time needed to do secondary source research in the trench or at the specialist's desk or at the dig house dinner table? That is, how will we replace the lost time for digging, analysis, interpretation, or, more likely, for sleep or relaxation? Excavating fewer trenches certainly is a possibility, but studying them with less intensive methods is not. Another answer will be to find efficiency elsewhere in the process. For example, for PQP, it was in part the speed at which we could document (not make) our interpretations of each wall in a drawing that bought the time to do both the archival research and the detailed examination of the columns in the Quadriporticus. What once took an hour to an entire day for two people to accomplish—stringing a baseline, setting up a drafting board and Mylar sheets, taking scores of individual measurements by hand and shouting them to a draftsperson who transposed them into a scale drawing—now could be done by a single person in 30 minutes using the camera and a drafting app on the iPad. Additionally, because PQP closely and intentionally paralleled the processes of archaeological workflow (organization of fieldwork practices) and the dataflow (organization of data derived from fieldwork practices) we made thousands of archaeological observations instantly ready to be combined not only with the observations from other walls but also from rooms and even whole sections of the building. For us, an explicit goal was to reach a stage of interpretation and synthesis beyond an individual wall while still in the field. To do this, we utilized the expertise created within our staff – those individuals who had just analyzed those walls – as well as our digital infrastructure that had contained explicit linkages between evidence and its interpretation. We "paid" for the time to synthesize our interpretations with the increased speed in graphically recording those interpretations.

If the Pompeii Quadriporticus Project were to be started 10 years from now, I imagine we would put greater emphasis on reading about the implications of our initial observations and interpretations, such as understanding the rest of the great Altstadt sewer (FIG. 9) that passes through the Quadriporticus or the use of specific construction techniques and materials in the rest of Pompeii. Certainly, in this imagined future I might have tackled the archival and bibliographic research in search of the tholos structure the very week the GPR results were received, rather than two years later. Finally, I imagine that we would build time to accommodate the most important analog tool we will still be using: the human brain and all its psychological conditioning and quirks (for more on this topic of "Slow Archaeology," see Caraher, Ch. 4.1). Though I have no doubt the future will be "slower" than it is today, I am equally sure that the time for such reflection will come, ironically, on the back of efficiency somewhere else in the fieldwork system.

In sum, the library is coming to a future trench near you. With it are possibilities and pitfalls yet unimagined. This paper has tried to illustrate a few ways the introduction of published scholarship (but only hinted at published, open-data archives) might impact archaeological fieldwork and further imagine its place in the digital archaeological practice of the future. But these few hundred speculative words cannot compare with the value of our collective endeavors— and failures—in the coming decade. Our experiments to dissolve the library-fieldwork divide will not only find the best and worst places to insert this new dataset into our practices, but they also will bargain with other activities to find the time for such insertions. New efficiencies will be found to implement the library resources and they likely will come at the trench edge, squeezing excavation supervisors—the middle management of archaeological fieldwork—between a confrontation with the physical world and an increasingly complex digital representation of it.

https://mobilizingthepast.mukurtu.net/
collection/17-digital-pompeii-dissolving-fieldwork-library-research-divide

http://dc.uwm.edu/arthist_mobilizingthepast/9

References

de Saint-Non, J.-C. R. 1781–1786. *Illustrations de Voyages pittoresques de Naples et de Sicile*. Paris: Clousier.

Devore, G., and S. J. R. Ellis. 2005. "New Excavations at VIII.7.1-15, Pompeii: A Brief Synthesis of Results from the 2005 Season." *The Journal of Fasti Online* 48, http://www.fastionline.org/docs/FOLDER-it-2005-48.pdf

Devore, G., and S. J. R. Ellis. 2008. "The Third Season of Excavations at VIII.7.1-15 and the Porta Stabia at Pompeii: Preliminary Report." *The Journal of Fasti Online* 112, http://www.fastionline.org/docs/FOLDER-it-2008-112.pdf

Dicus, K. 2014. "Resurrecting refuse at Pompeii: The Use-Value of Urban Refuse and Its Implications for Interpreting Archaeological Assemblages," in H. Platts, J. Pearce, C. Barron, J. Lundock, and J. Yoo, eds., *TRAC 2013: Proceedings of the Twenty Third Annual Theoretical Roman Archaeology Conference, King's College, London 2013*. Oxford: Oxbow, 56–69.

Ellis, S. J. R., and G. Devore. 2006. "Towards an Understanding of the Shape of Space at VIII.7.1-15, Pompeii: Preliminary Results from the 2006 Season." *The Journal of Fasti Online* 71, http://www.fastionline.org/docs/FOLDER-it-2006-71.pdf

Ellis, S. J. R., and G. Devore. 2009. "The Fourth Season of Excavations at VIII.7.1-15 and the Porta Stabia at Pompeii: Preliminary Report." *The Journal of Fasti Online* 146, http://www.fastionline.org/docs/FOLDER-it-2009-146.pdf

Ellis, S. J. R., and G. Devore. 2010. "The Fifth Season of Excavations at VIII.7.1-15 and the Porta Stabia at Pompeii: Preliminary Report." *The Journal of Fasti Online* 202, http://www.fastionline.org/docs/FOLDER-it-2010-202.pdf

Ellis, S. J. R., A. C. L. Emmerson, K. Dicus, G. Tibbott, and A. K. Pavlick. 2015. "The 2012 Field Season at I.1.1-10, Pompeii: Preliminary Report on the Excavations." *The Journal of Fasti Online* 328, http://www.fastionline.org/docs/FOLDER-it-2015-328.pdf

Ellis, S. J. R., A. L. C. Emmerson, A. K. Pavlick, and K. Dicus. 2011. "The 2010 Field Season at I.1.1-10, Pompeii: Preliminary Report on the Excavations." *The Journal of Fasti Online* 220, http://www.fastionline.org/docs/FOLDER-it-2011-220.pdf

Ellis, S. J. R., A. L. C. Emmerson, A. K. Pavlick, K. Dicus, and G. Tibbott. 2012. "The 2011 Field Season at I.1.1-10, Pompeii: Preliminary Report on the Excavations." *The Journal of Fasti Online* 262, http://www.fastionline.org/docs/FOLDER-it-2012-262.pdf

Etiennez, H. 1849–1852. *L'Italie à vol d'oiseau, ou histoire et description sommaires des principales villes de cette contrée . . . accompagnées de quarante grandes vues générales dessinées d'après nature par A. Guesdon*. Paris: A. Hauser.

Pagano, M., and R. Prisciandaro. 2006. *Studio sulle provenienze degli oggetti rinvenuti negli scavi borbonici del Regno di Napoli: Una lettura integrata, coordinata e commentata della documentazione*, 2 vols. Castellamare di Stabia: N. Longobardi.Poehler, E. E. 2014. "The Pompeii Bibliography and Mapping Resource." *ISAW Papers* 7.21, http://dlib.nyu.edu/awdl/isaw/isaw-papers/7/poehler/

Poehler, E. E., and S. J. R. Ellis. 2012. "The 2011 Season of the Pompeii *Quadriporticus* Project: The Southern and Northern Sides." *The Journal of Fasti Online* 249, http://www.fastionline.org/docs/FOLDER-it-2012-249.pdf

Poehler, E. E., and S. J. R. Ellis. 2014. "The 2013 Season of the Pompeii *Quadriporticus* Project: Final Fieldwork and Preliminary Results." *The Journal of Fasti Online* 321, http://www.fastionline.org/docs/FOLDER-it-2014-321.pdf

Part 2: From Dirt to Drones

2.1.
Reflections on Custom Mobile App Development for Archaeological Data Collection

Samuel B. Fee

PKapp is a mobile application that facilitates the electronic collection and recording of archaeological field data. Initially implemented during the 2012 season of the Pyla-Koutsopetria Archaeological Project (PKAP), PKapp weds archaeological methodology with technological innovation (see Bria and DeTore, Ch. 1.5; Ellis, Ch. 1.2; Motz, Ch. 1.3; Poehler, Ch. 1.7). Building on the widespread adoption of tablet computers in 2010, the app turns traditional paper-and-pencil data collection into an electronic process with improved efficiency and speed, which, ultimately, frees up time for researchers to devote to analysis and education.

PKapp was designed as a Web app, rather than a native application. Native apps are written for specific operating systems, whereas Web apps are based on the HTML5 specification. The timing was ripe for developing such an electronic data collection form—HTML5 had become a relatively stable standard in 2011, and mobile computing devices were widespread and inexpensive. From a development standpoint, coding in HTML5 was easier and more reliable than working with earlier, separate versions of HTML and JavaScript (Stark 2010; Stark *et al.* 2012). Also, this approach made it easy to install, test, and operate the software on tablet computers across vast geographic distances—a particularly important point as the developers were in the United States and the archaeologists were in Cyprus.

Tablet computing had quickly been adopted in 2010 for archaeological work (Apple Inc. 2010). The details of that work were already available, making it possible to shape our vision for PKapp from the descriptions of the experience of others (Ellis and Wallrodt 2011). Those early efforts employed apps created by other developers. The

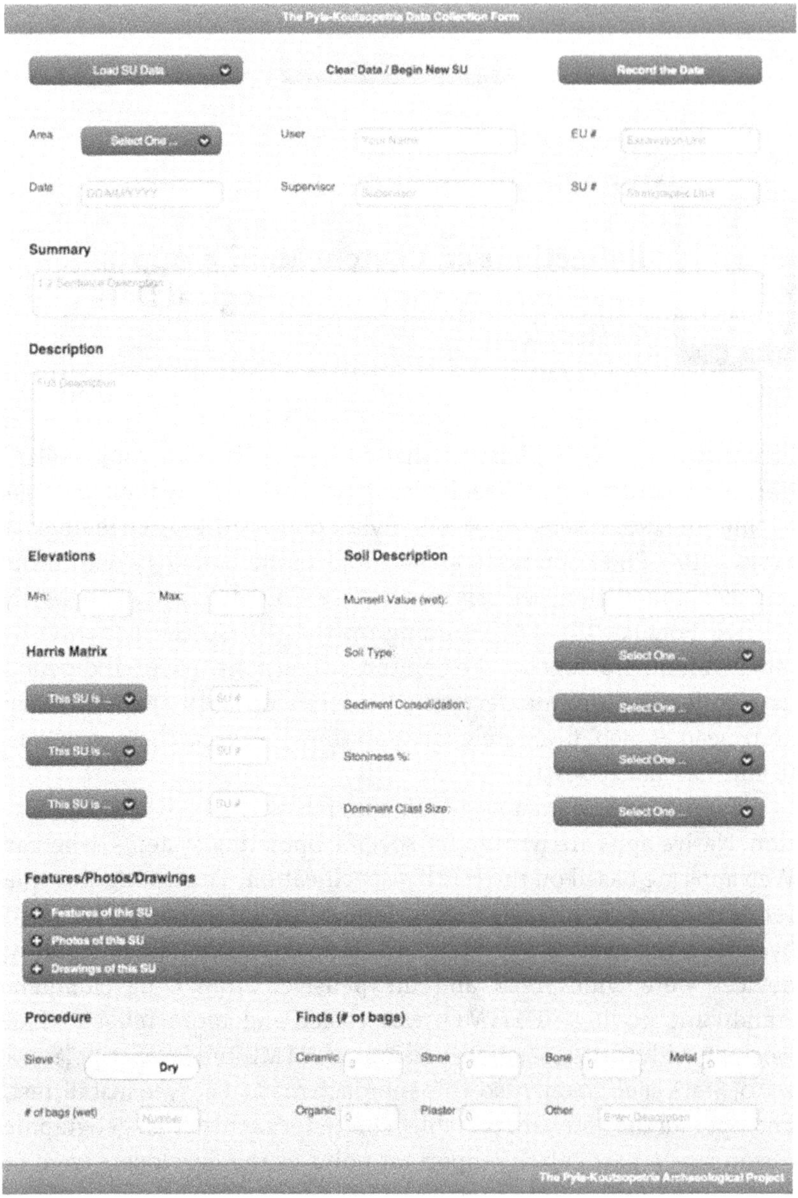

Figure 1: The PKapp mobile app.

development of PKapp was an effort to explore the possibilities of custom software development. In the end, and most importantly, PKapp taught us how to write software for mobile devices while also illuminating numerous possibilities for digital workflow in field research.

The uses for the app have been detailed in a brief article that William Caraher, David Pettegrew, and I composed for *Near Eastern Archeology* (Fee *et al.* 2013). During the 2012 field season, Caraher and Pettegrew were co-directors for the project along with R. Scott Moore. Caraher served also as database administrator, Pettegrew served as Field Director, and I was in charge of software development. The purpose of this chapter is to describe the technical planning and development behind the app, identify some of the most challenging programming problems we encountered, and suggest current directions for app development given the rapid advance of programing libraries and frameworks (tools that make it easier and faster to develop an application like PKapp today than it was in 2012) for custom mobile app development.

DESCRIPTION OF THE APP

PKapp represents a natural progression from traditional paper collection forms, replacing a two-page paper document with a single electronic form for recording basic, required information and unstructured descriptions (FIG. 1). The basic unit of excavation at PKAP is the stratigraphic unit (SU), and thus the entire electronic form is constructed around recording or recalling data for each SU.

As we began planning the project in 2012, we identified a number of parameters that needed to be addressed carefully during the development process:

1. There could be no data loss.
2. Data entry should follow a simple process.
3. Data validation was imperative.
4. The software must run locally on the device (without Internet access).
5. A simple data export mechanism was required.
6. Updates should be accessible remotely.
7. The software must be platform-agnostic, and must run on any mobile device.

We returned frequently to this list in our planning of both design and programming elements (such as the export of data). Several of the criteria, which resulted from the needs of researchers working in remote locations with unreliable internet access, had some technical implications for our work. We worked with the form validation abilities built into HTML5 to ensure that any data entered was of the right type before it ever got to the primary database. We also ensured that the app would write data directly to the device without wireless access, and that it would upload data from the device to the primary database easily—a task easier to theorize than to implement.

Finally, our desire to access updates remotely meant we needed to develop a Web app for use outside of the app-store environment. With such an approach, we could continue to test and revise while working in the field. We could post new versions of the software overnight and have them in use in the field the next day, which would not have been possible with the current app-store distribution model that requires a lengthy approval process. Because we were avoiding app-store distribution and developing a stand-alone Web app, we could embrace fully the open-source standards of HTML5 and ensure that PKapp would run on any device with a stable and current Web browser.

App Design

As mentioned previously, the paper form for recording the field data at PKAP was composed of two pages. The first page asked the recorder to write down information about the context, including name and identifiers (date, supervisor, recorder), location (area, excavation unit, elevation, stratigraphic relationships, universal transverse mercator (UTM) coordinates), soil descriptors (soil type, clast size, Munsell color), associated data (features and photographs), method, and relative quantity of finds by bag. The second page contained identifying fields in case that page became separated from the first, with blank lines for narrative description and interpretation of the area.

With multiple excavators working on site, a major advantage of the digital form is that it forces the recorder to enter data in standardized ways (see Bria and DeTore, Ch. 1.5; Ellis, Ch. 1.2). Some fields require the user to choose from selectable menus, ensuring more normalized data, while in most other data entry locations the user can only enter specific type of information that actually fits the way the data is tracked in the database. For instance, since the excavation unit (EU) numbers are only two digits—the user cannot enter any more than two into that field. The same holds true for SU numbers, elevations, or any text entry area within the form. The app thus guarantees that the data is formatted in a way that will import directly and correctly into the primary database.

Another PKapp feature that helps with data validation is the ability to bring up the correct numeric or alphabetic keyboard for specific entry fields, thereby reducing the number of button clicks and saving time overall (Clark 2010). This can be done through the use of regular expressions. Regular expression attributes in HTML5, which were most commonly used in the past to evoke pattern matching for searches, allow the software to check the value of the pattern attribute against a regular expression to see if it is valid or not. For instance, this expression:

pattern="[0–9]*

included as an attribute to the input element would limit the input to numeric values. If it is valid, the form submits; if it is not, the user is asked to correct the format of the entry. Thus, in addition to bringing up the right keyboard in the app, regular expressions give us another means to ensure data validation.

In addition to the above features, there are buttons that facilitate interaction. These buttons enable the primary functions for interacting with the app, and they are also used to access data export functions, which enable the app's data to be exported and later incorporated into the primary database.

Interacting with PKapp

The buttons at the top of the application allow the user not only to enter data correctly, but also to interact with the data that is already stored locally on the device (FIG. 2). For data collection purposes, the stratigraphic unit, which is the primary method of identification for records for fieldwork at PKAP, was used as the unique identifier for the local database.

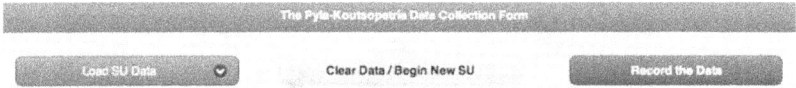

Figure 2: Interacting with the data on the device.

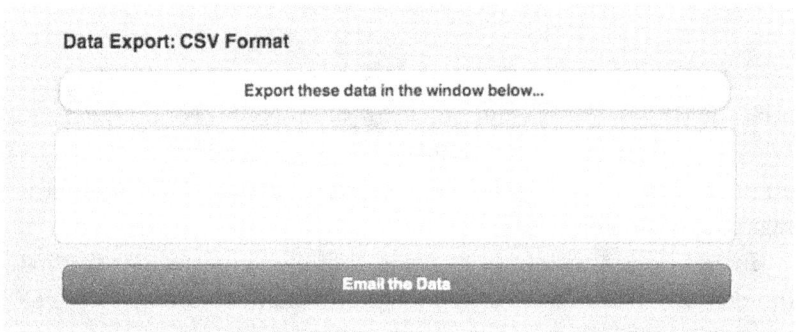

Figure 3: Exporting the data.

From the top left, the "Load SU Data" button loads any previously entered SU data. Because PKapp takes advantage of the local storage on the device, a user may view and edit the previously collected data. In essence this function is similar to auto-completion on Web forms through PHP, except that it is loaded from the local database rather than a remote server.

Located in the center, the "Clear Data/Begin New SU" button removes data from the form so the user can enter new data, though previous data can always be re-loaded using the "Load SU Data" button.

The "Record the Data" button writes the data to the local SQL database. This feature is similar to a "Submit" button, but it is modified with specific scripts that execute additional functions, which are discussed below in the "technical difficulties" section.

The remaining interface elements within PKapp allow for the export of data. The "Data Export" section at the bottom of the form contains two buttons and a text field that serve as a window for viewing the data (FIG. 3). The upper button exports the data on the device into CSV (comma-separated version) format and displays those data in the associated window (CSV is a simple, tab-delimited plain-text format that is easily imported into almost any database). This enables users of the app the opportunity to review and validate the data once again before sending it to the database administrator for incorporation into the primary database. The lower button, "Email the Data," simply emails the data directly to a unique address that has been established for receiving these data for PKAP.

Technical Difficulties

Creating PKapp was especially challenging because we were implementing an innovative but immature toolset—specifically, HTML5 on newer versions of mobile browsers. The HTML5 specification is a collection of HTML, CSS, and JavaScript along with a much more robust support for Web forms. In many ways, this makes it perfect for what we intended with PKapp: a Web app that could be easily and remotely updated even while being deployed in the field. The app therefore consisted of highly customized HTML5, along with the jQuery Mobile library, and specifically the jQuery Mobile JavaScript libraries that handled a lot of the look-and-feel of the app. The customizations made to the library included the additions of form mark-up and a number of attributes to help validate the data and eliminate a number of potential user errors in the input of data. For the most part, this was all straight-forward, and creating this type of app was relatively easy. There were, however, three significant problems with the software that needed to be addressed during our development process.

1. *Features we wanted but could not provide.* We would have liked the app to have the ability to capture photos and attach them to the exact data record for the SU being recorded and to record GPS coordinates for the areas under observation. We simply could not implement these features in 2012 because the application program-ming interface (API)—code instructions that link into preexisting programs or hardware controls—for the internal camera and GPS were not reliable. Today such APIs, which enable us to make use of certain hardware features we could not otherwise access without developing a native app, are widely available, and these capabili-ties could be incorporated within PKapp.

2. *The database.* Our local storage on the device consisted of a WebSQL database implemented through JavaScript. It was a chal-lenge to decide which database model to implement since WebSQL had already been deprecated from the HTML5 specification despite the fact that the HTML5 spec had only been published the previous year. (Deprecated elements are removed from the specification and no longer considered "valid"). The alternatives were localStorage, which was being used to save data for the current form so it could not be lost before being saved, and IndexedDB, which unfortunately still was not fully implemented in WebKit browsers such as Google Chrome or Apple Safari. Since WebSQL was deprecated, support and documentation were very limited. This made the implementa-tion of a stable database harder to accomplish. The actual saving of the data simply required a basic understanding of SQL—that itself was not very difficult—but getting the data out of the database in CSV format or back into PKapp for viewing was more challenging.

3. *Exporting the data.* Given that the app was designed with HTML5, we faced an additional problem in that WebKit browsers had not implemented the fileSystem API at the time of development. This meant that the app could not simply write data files and access them later. This then created hurdles in exporting the data, which were circumvented by sending the data to the screen, then using

a separate function to access a remote PHP script to send the data via email. Obviously, this last function only operates when Internet connectivity is present. But this functionality enabled users to review the data locally even if they did not have access to the remote database server.

By far the biggest problem of the three articulated above concerned the transfer of data. Had a reliable form of wireless communication been available, the simpler solution would have been to send the data directly to a PHP script and import it into any SQL server on the Internet. Yet our software solution had to run locally as there was no wireless connectivity at the site at Pyla-Koutsopetria. Thus PKapp needed to be able to view the data locally and send it out when the Internet was accessible. To the best of my knowledge, the process of taking data from localStorage, placing it into the app, exporting it into an email, and sending it onward is an approach that had not been tried before.

Another development option would have been to write the app natively as an iOS and/or Android application. Such an approach would have avoided the challenge with data export, and it would have enabled our implementation of local files. But this would have conflicted with our desire to remain platform agnostic and accessible on any mobile device. A native app approach could have also allowed us to work with the Dropbox API, making storage easier and allowing for replication of data when connection was restored. But in order for us to update the app overnight, a native app could not be used without numerous complications for the researchers collecting data in the field.

REFLECTIONS ON AND FUTURE POSSIBILITIES FOR CUSTOM MOBILE APP DEVELOPMENT

There were different approaches to writing the software for the application development process, each with their own pluses and minuses (Koch 2014). This underscores the importance of developing a vision for the project at the outset, before sitting down to write any code. Had we not collectively held that vision, we could have easily gone astray at several development stages and ended up with an app that did not address all of the issues that we felt were important to the project.

Because the technological toolset itself was changing even as we were developing PKapp, it would have been easy to change direction at several points—but implementing any of those new tools might have brought innovation in one regard at the expense of another, or even the entire project. And such technological change has only accelerated since 2012.

In 2012 we wrote PKapp with a text editor, various browser software, and the jQuery Mobile framework. An alternative approach could have incorporated so-called off-the-shelf software; indeed, several other projects described in this volume very successfully took that approach (see Gordon *et al.*, Ch. 1.4; Bria and DeTore, Ch. 1.5; Ellis, Ch. 1.2; Motz, Ch. 1.3). But we wanted the control afforded by creating our own custom app. At that time, writing the code manually was the only viable way to accomplish our end by developing a Web form that would operate effectively on a mobile device (Wroblewski 2011). Today there are many tools available for making that process both simpler and more direct, and many of the technical difficulties we faced in 2012 have subsequently been addressed through the release of more formalized JavaScript APIs that now provide access to additional hardware in mobile devices. Finally, the simple maturation of HTML5 has brought about increased stability for the local storage of data within the browser that provides additional reliability for the app itself and confidence in the data integrity of the content that we receive from the device.

One of the core features of HTML5 is the improved handling of forms. Prior to HTML5, expanding form functionality (particularly with data validation) required extensive and often problematic JavaScript programing. With the incorporation of regular expressions into the HTML5 specification, this is now a feature provided through the simple addition of attributes to the form elements. Because PKapp is essentially a data collection form, this aided our development immensely. In addition, the development of JavaScript frameworks and libraries in recent years has made more of the development work we undertook in the past easier today.

JavaScript Frameworks

While libraries, or collections of code available for integration into new programs, typically perform a specific but limited function, frameworks refer to a larger structure—a collection of existing libraries, or scripts, or code that can be utilized to create custom programs. While there are many new JavaScript libraries and frameworks today, we found the jQuery Mobile framework was the best option at the time of development. It was particularly well suited for handling Web forms and all of the components we would likely want for a custom field-data collection tool (items such as selection menus, toggle switches, text entry areas, checkboxes, and the like). New tools for prototyping or further developing jQuery Mobile based apps mean that not everything must be coded manually, nor must all the hooks into the framework be created through a text editor. Software now enables anyone with minimal coding experience to build, at the very least, the front-end of a Web app. This places the design of any custom data collection app firmly within the hands of the archaeologist, and not necessarily a programmer.

These tools come with different approaches and business models. Some are drag-and-drop, others are WYSIWYG ("what you see is what you get"); some are free, yet others are provided at considerable cost. Codiqa is a preferred option. It is available in online and desktop versions, and is free for academic use; however, a $79 desktop version enables you to keep local control of your files, which is something that is important for any developer. Codiqa exports the HTML, CSS, and JavaScript that is needed to build an app.

Once these files are created, building the front end of the app involves simply modifying and customizing the appearance (via CSS). To create a custom field-data collection tool, one need only to add in the regular expressions to reinforce data validity, set up the local database, and develop an export feature. Some newer JavaScript APIs can further enhance the feature set of the app as described in the next section.

JavaScript APIs

Since we wrote PKapp, two APIs were released that are of particular interest to archaeologists: the camera API and the geolocation API, two features we wanted but could not provide (as noted above). The camera API allows you to take a picture with your device's camera and load it to the current page. The geolocation API provides the location of the device to the app. These APIs enable the building of a more robust app than we could manage in 2012 with PKapp, though current support for various browsers is still mixed. Nonetheless, these represent the future capabilities for custom data collection apps, so exploring their potential is worth the effort.

There are two caveats to keep in mind with both of these APIs. First, the camera API places an image into the app, then saves it to the database (assuming the database can accept image files). Image files will be large, so the time required for uploading the data to the primary database will become correspondingly significant and the overall size of the database will swell. In fact, most databases contain a data type known as a BLOB (Binary Large OBject) just for such use, but this slows the process of data transfer. Second, the geolocation API defaults to a very imprecise setting. When a mobile device cannot quickly acquire a GPS signal, the default settings of the API try to specify location based on Wi-Fi signal or IP address instead. Obtaining good coordinates will require some programming work as well as a recognition that the implementation of this feature will slow down the app, and acquiring good data for location will also likely require connection to a cellular network. In the end, incorporating these APIs will likely require more than a basic knowledge of HTML, but a non-programmer with some considerable skill in HTML5 could complete such a project.

Database Advances

When the HTML5 specification was released in 2010 (although not "officially" released until 2014), there were three approaches to handling client-side databases: localStorage, IndexedDB, and WebSQL. The first, localStorage, was problematic in that it does not always indicate when the stage of insufficient storage is reached, which raises the potential for data loss. The second, IndexedDB, was not yet recognized by browsers and could not be implemented at the time. Therefore, we chose the third option, WebSQL—the most broadly used implementation for databases in most browsers—in spite of the fact that it had already been terminated in 2011. At the same time, because it was still fully functional in programs like Apple Safari and Google Chrome, we decided it was our best option and chose to move forward.

Today, the choices are largely the same, but browser support is greatly improved. IndexedDB is now supported in Google Chrome and iOS 8, which means that programs using this technology will continue to be supported on browsers in the future. Fortunately, there are even JavaScript libraries that will provide WebSQL translation for older browsers (iOS before version 8). This means that you can count on the work you do today to be relevant in the future.

The primary benefit of the changes over the past few years is that the future direction for development is clear, and those creating apps now do not need to be concerned with issues of obsolescence. Also, more developers are approaching their projects through the use of IndexedDB, and as a result, online resources and information can assist with the development of apps that incorporate IndexedDB storage. Nonetheless, the entire database backend of any custom data collection app is fraught with technical problems. This could very well be the most technically complex aspect of the development project. These difficulties revolve around the challenges of selecting the right database approach and the lack of documentation available for such work.

For those seeking to develop a similar app today, the recommended approach is to utilize IndexedDB while also including a JavaScript library to provide backward compatibility for browsers with WebSQL support. This would give the app a much broader reach in terms of supported devices, and it would also ensure the relevancy of the approach to the local database into the future.

Export Problems

Despite the advances of the past few years, data export remains a difficult conundrum for anyone developing a custom app designed to run without connectivity. Apple has not implemented the fileSystem API to help address this issue, but there are other good approaches that simply require some work. For PKapp we exported the data and emailed it so that we could provide another check on the data before incorporating it into the primary database. Today, many other "to-do list" and note-taking apps provide such functionality through Dropbox or other similar cloud-based services. Use of a Dropbox account and the Dropbox API may be a particularly attractive option for any apps currently being developed.

Of course, should a project enjoy reliable connectivity—even occasionally—an app could be created that simply sends the data to a primary database on a server when connected to the Internet. Since each entry could be given a unique timestamp, entries could be searched daily to verify data integrity. In such a circumstance, data transfer becomes a very smooth operation that risks few technical problems.

In the end both of these solutions are simpler than the one we implemented for PKapp in 2012. With reliable connectivity, an app could possess a richer feature set in this regard than an app designed to work exclusively offline.

Conclusions

The development of PKapp taught us a number of important lessons about implementing mobile apps for data collection in archaeological fieldwork. In their simplest forms, mobile apps are not difficult to create—a simple one can be built based upon an RSS feed in minutes. But when considering the collection, storage, and access of data specific to the PKAP project, there were no pre-existing commercial tools that could accomplish our goals. In the end we implemented an app written with HTML5 and some custom JavaScript coding.

Native apps are written for specific operating systems. Web apps are based on the HTML5 specification. We decided on a Web app approach so that we could update the app at any time and post it online for the team to install in Cyprus almost instantaneously. We could fix bugs as they appeared, or modify features based upon actual field use. We thus could actively address our design parameters, which called for easy and quick updating of the software. We also avoided having to write the app for multiple platforms and getting each app and each update approved for delivery through its respective app store.

The Web app development process is even easier today as a host of new tools exist to facilitate such projects. In addition to a number of JavaScript libraries, frameworks, and APIs, there are a plethora of tools such as Codiqa to aid the actual development of the front-end of an app built with HTML5. The ease-of-use present in these tools means that the archaeologist can be actively engaged in the development of the app, and the software development process becomes truly participatory. With these tools technical support is needed primarily for the development of the local database and the eventual communication with the primary database, wherever it may reside.

In the end, collecting data via PKapp was easy and the app worked remarkably well, matching our design parameters and meeting all of our fieldwork goals. As a result of our experience using the app successfully, we see benefits in the incorporation of mobile technologies for collecting data in the field. There are significant improvements in efficiency and overall time saved, because entire steps in the older process—particularly the manual process of completing paper forms, converting that data into electronic format, and reviewing the resulting electronic data—can be streamlined. The ability to incorporate automatic data validation into the entry process also makes this approach an improvement over traditional methods, which required additional manual validation. This is not to say that such technical efficiencies do not come without a cost (Caraher 2013). Indeed, any field team should weigh the benefits of efficiency as they reflect upon *where* and *when* the analysis and interpretation occurs in the archaeological process for the project.

But a season of testing provided us with enough observation for our data integrity concerns that we have great confidence in the quality of data collected via PKapp. With the advancements and implementation of the HTML5 specification, as well as broader implementation of JavaScript APIs, we could today even more easily produce Web apps for field data collection that run without connectivity. Consequently, this process is increasingly accessible to most researchers, and it seems worthy of consideration for most projects.

https://mobilizingthepast.mukurtu.net/collection/21-reflections-custom-mobile-app-development-archaeological-data-collection

http://dc.uwm.edu/arthist_mobilizingthepast/10

REFERENCES

Apple Inc. 2010. "Discovering Ancient Pompeii with iPad." http://www.apple.com/ipad/pompeii

Caraher, W. R. 2013. "Slow Archaeology," *North Dakota Quarterly* 80: 43–52.

Clark, J. 2010. *Tapworthy: Designing Great iPhone Apps*. Sebastopol, CA: O'Reilly Media.

Ellis, S. J. R., and J. Wallrodt. 2011. "iPads at Pompeii." *Pompeii Archaeological Research Project: Porta Stabia*, http://classics.uc.edu/pompeii/index.php/news/1-latest/142-ipads2010.html

Fee, S. B., D. K. Pettegrew, and W. R. Caraher. 2013. "Taking Mobile Computing to the Field," *Near Eastern Archaeology* 76: 50–55.

Koch, P. 2014. *The Mobile Web Handbook*. Freiburg: Smashing Magazine GmbH.

Stark, J. 2010. *Building iPhone Apps with HTML, CSS, and JavaScript*. Sebastopol, CA: O'Reilly Media.

Stark, J., B. Jepson, and B. MacDonald. 2012. *Building Android Apps with HTML, CSS, and JavaScript*. 2nd edn. Sebastopol, CA: O'Reilly Media.

Wroblewski, L. 2011. *Mobile First*. New York: A Book Apart.

2.2.
The Things We Can Do with Pictures: Image-Based Modeling and Archaeology

Brandon R. Olson

It has been five years—a near eternity in technology years—since Agisoft publically launched PhotoScan, the first cost efficient and intuitive image-based modeling software, and two years have passed since the first wave of peer-reviewed studies implementing and testing the applicability of such software for archaeological purposes (i.e., Verhoeven 2011; Verhoeven *et al.* 2012a, 2012b; de Reu *et al.* 2013; Olson *et al.* 2013). The combination of these and many other publications, along with numerous colloquia, conference panels, and workshops, solidify the place of image-based modeling as an integral tool for digital archaeology. The intention here is to present a critical analysis of the technology by drawing on a set of field applications that highlight how this technology continues to transform the discipline through a diverse set of methodological and interpretive frameworks.

IMAGE-BASED MODELING: A SHORT INTRODUCTION

Three-dimensional modeling is not a new addition to the archaeological toolkit, as laser scanners and other 3D modeling techniques, though expensive and requiring highly trained personnel, have been available for years (Barceló *et al.* 2003; Pollefeys *et al.* 2003). The creation of digital 3D models from photographs using photogrammetric methods and various algorithms such as structure-from-motion, however, is a newer innovation. The technology, referred to here and elsewhere as image-based modeling (Olson and Caraher 2015; Roosevelt *et al.* 2015), is available through a handful of commercial (Olson *et al.* 2013: 248) and open-source software options (Green *et al.* 2014), but Agisoft

Figure 1: Image of a secondary apse from a Late Roman basilica at Polis-Chrysochous, Cyprus, depicting the five stages of creating a 3D model using an image-based modeling technique: A) Capturing strategy with automatic photo alignment; B) Aligning photographs and generating a sparse point cloud; C) Generation of a dense point cloud; D) Building a monochromatic 3D model; and E) Texturing the 3D model.

PhotoScan (www.agisoft.com) has solidified itself as the software of choice due to its ease of operation and quality outputs. The 3D model creation process is pretty straightforward, and it can be used to model 3D environments from archaeological objects to trenches and architecture (FIG. 1) to entire sites (Olson *et al.* 2014a; Roosevelt 2014; see also Wernke *et al.*, Ch. 2.3). After capturing a set of digital photographs that provides total coverage of the target, these photographs are automatically located within a locally or geolocated rectified environment (FIG. 1A). The location of the images serves to reconstruct complex spatial information from 2D data, common points are tracked across images, and their relative positions are mathematically determined. Following the creation of the sparse point cloud (FIG. 1B), the program returns to the photographic dataset to generate a dense point cloud (FIG. 1C). The dense point cloud is in fact just that, dense. Note the visual similarities in points C (the dense point cloud) and E (the 3D model with photorealistic texture) on Figure 1. The sparse and dense point clouds are essentially the skeleton of the final model, representing known points in the structure of the scene around which the computer can calculate the geometry of a monochromatic 3D model (FIG. 1D). Finally, remembering the relationship between the points in the photographs and the spatial information in the geometric model, a photorealistic texture is conformed to the 3D geometry (FIG. 1E).

From the processed 3D model, several outputs are possible, the most useful for archaeological purposes are 3D PDF, GeoTIFF, and Wavefront OBJ. The accuracy of the outputs depends on numerous factors (e.g., resolution of the photographs, software settings, spatial extent), but studies have shown spatial accuracy levels of 1–3 cm for areas up to 700 m² and sub-centimeter for areas less than 25 m² in area (de Reu *et al.* 2013: 1111; Olson *et al.* 2013: 257; Prins *et al.* 2014: 193; Quartermaine *et al.* 2014: 116, 124; Roosevelt *et al.* 2015: 340). Processing times vary from less than an hour to days depending on scene size, the number of images captured, software settings, and the performance of the computer processing the model.

Object Level Analyses

Archaeology, as the study of the past via material culture, is a discipline centered on objects (Hodder 2012; Olsen 2012). The ability to photorealistically generate a 3D model of an object has opened up new avenues of artifactual analysis. Several scholars have commented on the visual merits of high-fidelity photorealistic 3D models, which have recently been followed up by studies offering critical assessments of their interpretive value (Roussou *et al.* 2015; Caraher, Ch. 4.1). For example, Olson and colleagues used image-based modeling software to create 3D models of prehistoric handaxes (Olson *et al.* 2014b). These models were then converted into a printer friendly format (PLY) and three-dimensionally printed (see also McKnight *et al.* 2015). Using both qualitative and quantitative methods, the authors demonstrated that a handaxe printed in both ABS (acrylonitrile butadiene styrene) plastic and resin retained the features a lithics specialist would need to read and study the object (Olson *et al.* 2014b: 171). The authors proved that 3D models, printed from digital models produced with an image-based approach, as opposed to laser scanning, can in theory stand in for the original.

Rabinowitz, however, cogently points out that digital renderings, and by extension their printed outputs, are not true "surrogates" of the original because their creation, unlike line drawings and sketches, lacks an interpretive framework (Rabinowitz 2015: 34). Manual illustration and recording strategies force a level of archaeological engagement and interpretation (e.g., stratigraphic relationships, architectural associations), while digital recording does not necessarily require such a level of preliminary interpretation (Rabinowitz 2015; Caraher, Ch. 4.1). On the other hand, the handaxe modeling experiment also indicates that whether the interpretive process occurs before, during, or after the crafting of a 3D model of an object, the resulting digital and tangible 3D models clearly have intrinsic scholarly value.

Bevan and colleagues adopted an image-based approach to model various features of the terracotta warriors found at Qin Shihuang-di's mausoleum in China (Bevan *et al.* 2014). The 3rd-century B.C. site contains life-sized replicas of an estimated 8,000 soldiers, 520 chariot horses, and 150 cavalry horses, all of which were constructed from terracotta using sets of standardized molds (Portal 2007). Artists would also add clay to the face and ears to add a level of individuality to each warrior. Bevan and colleagues modeled certain features to undertake a 3D morphometric analysis of the warriors, focusing primarily on ears, but also hands and faces. In adopting a comparative taxonomic approach, the authors are able to identify a series of micro-styles achieved through subtle variations in construction techniques (Bevan *et al.* 2014: 251–254). Beyond mere visual inspection, the authors devised a method for examining a distance matrix expressing dissimilarity of certain ear features to others within the assemblage by using the model's dense point cloud. The method is based on the real-world assumption that ear morphology exhibits variation among humans to such a degree that it can be used as a forensic identifier akin to dentition and finger prints (Pflug and Busch 2012; Abaza *et al.* 2013). Bevan and colleagues conclude that although there are a series of core shapes, there is also abundant subtle variation and no two ears are exactly the same (Bevan *et al.* 2014: 254). Their work shows that significant resources were spent by Qin Shihuangdi and his court to individualize the terracotta army in an attempt to mimic a real military force. This study, as well as others like it (Clarkson *et al.* 2014; Shipton and Clarkson 2015 on Hawaiian adzes; Grosman *et al.* 2014; Spring and Peters 2014 on ancient lithics), demonstrate the potential of image-based modeling and 3D modeling in general for morphological and taxonomic analyses of objects.

Landscape/Field Recording and Volumetrics

Arguably, image-based modeling has had the largest impact in the field, with numerous projects adopting the technology in various iterations at the sub-site level (Miller *et al.* 2014), site level (Quartermaine *et al.* 2013, 2014; Forte 2014a; Roosevelt *et al.* 2015; Toumazou *et al.* 2015), in underwater contexts (Demesticha *et al.* 2014; Jaklic *et al.* 2015; Buxton *et al.*, Ch. 2.4), and across landscapes (Opitz and Cowley 2013; Roosevelt 2014; Smith *et al.* 2014; Opitz and Limp 2015; Wernke *et al.*, Ch. 2.3). Of these studies, three merit special consideration here as they, in this author's humble opinion, will serve as benchmarks for future digital recording strategies.

The 3D Digging Project, which began at Çatalhöyük (Turkey) and was spearheaded by Maurizio Forte in 2009, endeavors to record in 3D complete stratigraphic profiles from a selection of excavation units in an attempt to reconstruct digitally the deposits as well as interact with them in a virtual environment (Forte 2014a: 4). Under the larger umbrellas of cyberarchaeology and teleimersive archaeology (Gordon *et al.*, Introduction; Forte 2010, 2014b; see also Levy *et al.* 2012), Forte uses the orthorectified georeferenced TIFF image (henceforth, an orthophoto—a photorealistic image with spatial distortion corrected that is embedded with a real-world coordinate system) to digitize and annotate features. For Forte, the scholarly value of image-based modeling is in its ability to generate accurate and photorealistic reproductions that aid in spatial recording and for its use with other technologies, such as laser scanning and infrared photography, within virtual reality for education, public outreach, and as a means to interact with archaeology in a new way (Forte 2014a: 26–28).

Underwater archaeology presents certain obstacles that terrestrial archaeology simply does not have to overcome (see Buxton *et al.*, Ch. 2.4). Issues such as short underwater study windows, limited visibility, the mobility of the ocean/river/lake bed, and the significant financial investment necessitate a dynamic recording system. In investigating the Mazotos Shipwreck site in Cyprus, Demesticha, Skarlatos, and Neophytou offer an image-based modeling approach that harnesses the dense point cloud and orthophoto, as opposed to the photorealistic model, as the primary basis of their recording framework (Demesticha *et al.* 2014). The authors utilize the orthophoto as the main method for basic recording, labeling, and digitizing features. Yet their innovative use of the dense point cloud as a collection of reference points to model and thereby record the remains comprising the site in three dimensions is a pioneering use of image-based modeling (Demesticha *et al.* 2014: 146–147; see also Grøn *et al.* 2015). The dense point cloud provides the outlines of individual ceramic forms, and the authors' familiarity with Hellenistic and Roman transport shapes are combined to create an accurate, true-to-scale 3D reconstruction of the underwater site. This method also allows them to approximate a ship's overall volume and inventory, and to trace the taphonomic processes following the initial wreck, simply on the basis of a systematic photography session with good ground visibility.

Any image-based modeling practitioner who has deployed this technology in the field is aware of certain limitations, especially from a mobility standpoint. The current author experienced two recurring problems at a number of Eastern Mediterranean sites. First, depending on the number of photographs taken, image-based modeling software tests the limits of even better-equipped computers and laptops. This will likely be a nonissue in the near future, but at present it is difficult to process a 3D model in the field owing to both environmental (e.g., heat, dust, and precipitation) and practical (e.g., interruption of work-flow, on-site distractions, access to electricity) considerations. Second, the transfer of data from the individual processing the images to the field team and the manipulation of the 3D model and its 2D derivatives on-site can be problematic on account of large files sizes and issues related to versioning and storage location. Roosevelt and colleagues, however, have made great progress in solving these issues with the Kaymakçı Archaeological Project in Turkey (Roosevelt *et al.* 2015). Their "born digital" (Roosevelt *et al.* 2015: 326; for the term, see also Austin 2014) recording system is multi-faceted and uses the following outputs for its image-based models: orthophotos (as a reference for digitization, measuring, and the like), georeferenced digital elevation models (for spot elevation checks and vertical control), and dense point clouds (to calculate volume; for volumetrics, see Miller *et al.* 2014; Jaklic *et al.* 2015; see also Castro López *et al.*, Ch. 3.1). To alleviate the issues raised above, the authors devised a wireless communication system to exchange photographic datasets and processed models between team members on-site and those at an off-site computer lab. The wireless network was also connected to a relational database stored on a server, which permitted secure data storage and a means to reliably access previously saved data anywhere with an Internet connection. From an image-based modeling standpoint, the project's infrastructure helped alleviate issues related to the mobility of the software, while the use of the software served as an integral component to their 3D and, more importantly, volumetric approach to recording.

Both the Kaymakçı Archaeological Project and the excavations at Cástulo (Spain) are using dense point clouds to create watertight volu-metric renderings of stratigraphic units (Roosevelt *et al.* 2015: 337–339; Castro López *et al.*, Ch. 3.1). Having processed dense point clouds with PhotoScan, the projects use separate 3D modeling programs (Cloud-Compare for Kaymakçı and Blender for Cástulo) to develop a closed volumetric entity representing the 3D area of the unit modeled. Both projects acknowledged the potential of volumetric recording for ongoing excavation. On-site manual drafting is mostly replaced with image-based modeling, whereby the software is tasked to record the tops and bottoms of all units. The records are then combined and modeled using PhotoScan and either CloudCompare or Blender to generate volumetric records. This process is revolutionary for on-site recording as it provides a truly accurate digital 3D record of excavations and can take the human element out of stratigraphic recording, which, as noted above, has both positive and negative implications.

CONCLUSIONS AND MUSINGS ON FUTURE DIRECTIONS

As the number of presentations at the "Mobilizing the Past for a Digital Future: The Potential of Digital Archaeology" workshop made abundantly clear, image-based modeling in archaeology has evolved from a simple means of visual display to a legitimate analytical tool by means of its combination with other technologies, recording strategies, and interpretive frameworks at site and object scales. Its deployment in the field has led to faster and more accurate data recording with comparatively small financial investment. Yet, the technology's scholarly value as more than a tool for simple visualization is contingent upon its interaction with, and ultimately assimilation into, existing modes of artifactual analysis (e.g., seriation, taxonomy, taphonomy) and systems of recording. Its adoption as a component to larger digital recording systems is underway, and one would expect to see development in the future along the lines of Forte (2014a), Roosevelt and colleagues (Roosevelt *et al.* 2015), Opitz and Limp with high-density survey and measurement (HDSM; Opitz and Limp 2015), Castro and colleagues (Castro López *et al.*, Ch. 3.1), and the most recent iterations of Reconstruction and Exploratory Visualization: Engineering meets ArchaeoLogy (REVEAL; for an introduction, see Fabbri and Kimia 2010; Galor *et al.* 2010; Gay *et al.* 2010; Kimia 2010). Granted, these reports vary intellectually and practically, but they have a shared view in that image-based modeling can and should be utilized in the same way as a total station, differential GPS unit, geographical information system (GIS) software, or digital camera. Given its many benefits image-based archaeological recording is here to stay, and in the immediate future, the question of how to integrate it into existing or redeveloped methods and practices will likely be a subject of scholarly discussion and debate. Ideally, such pluralist discourse will inform best practices.

On the technological side, faster processors, larger memory capacity, and more robust graphics cards will speed up processing times in the future. Since its initial public offering in December 2010 with version 0.7.0, Agisoft has released 45 updates to PhotoScan. Some updates are simple bug fixes, while others are significant revamps that introduce new tools. With an average of a new version every five weeks, companies like Agisoft make a concerted effort to keep the technology current, which will likely continue given the demand. It is also possible that the process itself, which consists of five steps (not including exporting outputs), will be streamlined either within the software or with the development of hardware capable of processing models immediately after photo capture. Needless to say, the pace of change in technology is rapid, and there is nothing to suggest that image-based modeling has reached its floruit in technological or archaeological terms.

https://mobilizingthepast.mukurtu.net/
collection/22-things-we-can-do-pictures-image-
based-modeling-and-archaeology

http://dc.uwm.edu/arthist_mobilizingthepast/11

References

Abaza, A., A. Ross, C. Hebert, M. A. F. Harrison, and M. S. Nixon. 2013. "A Survey on Ear Biometrics," *ACM Computing Surveys* 45: 22–35.

Austin, A. 2014. "Mobilizing Archaeologists: Increasing the Quantity and Quality of Data Collected in the Field with Mobile Technology," *Advances in Archaeological Practice* 2: 13–23.

Barceló, J. A., O. De Castro, D. Travet, and O. Vicente. 2003. "A 3D Model of an Archaeological Excavation," in M. Doerr and A. Sarris, eds., *The Digital Heritage of Archaeology: Computer Applications and Quantitative Methods in Archaeology. Proceedings of the 30th Conference, Heraklion, Crete, April 2002*. Heraklion: Hellenic Ministry of Culture, 85–90.

Bevan, A., L. Xiuzhen, M. Martinón-Torres, S. Green, Y. Xia, K. Zhao, Z. Zhao, S. Ma, W. Cao, and T. Rehren. 2014. "Computer Vision,

Archaeological Classification and China's Terracotta Warriors," *Journal of Archaeological Science* 49: 249–254.

Clarkson, C., C. Shipton, M. Weisler. 2014. "Determining the Reduction Sequence of Hawaiian Quadrangular Adzes Using 3D Approaches: A Case Study from Moloka'i," *Journal of Archaeological Science* 49: 361–371.

Demesticha, S., D. Skarlatos, and A. Neophytou. 2014. "The 4th-century B.C. Shipwreck at Mazotos, Cyprus: New Techniques and Methodologies in the 3D Mapping of Shipwreck Excavations," *Journal of Field Archaeology* 39: 134–150.

de Reu, J., G. Plets, G. Verhoeven, P. De Smedt, M. Bats, B. Cherretté, W. De Maeyer, J. Deconynck, D. Herremans, P. Laloo, M. Van Meirvenne, and W. De Clercq. 2013. "Towards a Three-Dimensional Cost-Effective Registration of the Archaeological Heritage," *Journal of Archaeological Science* 40: 1108–1121.

Fabbri, R., and B. B. Kimia. 2010. "3D Curve Sketch: Flexible Curve-Based Stereo Reconstruction and Calibration," in *Proceedings of the IEEE Conference on Computer Vision and Pattern Recognition*. San Francisco: IEEE Computer Society Press, 1538–1545.

Forte, M., ed. 2010. *Cyber-Archaeology. BAR International Series* 2177. Oxford: BAR.

Forte, M. 2014a. "3D Archaeology: New Perspectives and Challenges—The Example of Çatalhöyük," *Journal of Eastern Mediterranean Archaeology and Heritage Studies* 2: 1–29.

Forte, M. 2014b. "Virtual Reality, Cyberarchaeology, Teleimmersive Archaeology," in F. Remondino and S. Campana, eds., *3D Recording and Modelling in Archaeology and Cultural Heritage: Theory and Best Practices. BAR International Series* 2598. Oxford: Archaeopress, 113–127.

Galor, K., D. Sanders, and A. Willis. 2010. "Semi-Automated Data Capture and Image Processing: New Routes to Interactive 3D Models," in S. Campana, ed., *Space, Time, Place: Third International Conference on Remote Sensing in Archaeology, 17th–21st August 2009, Tiruchirappalli, Tamil Nadu, India. BAR International Series* 2118. Oxford: Archaeopress, 179–188.

Gay, E., K. Galor, D. B. Cooper, A. Willis, B. B. Kimia, S. Karumuri, G. Taubin, W. Doutre, D. Sanders, and S. Liu. 2010. "REVEAL Intermediate Report," in *Proceedings of CVPR Workshop on Applications of Computer Vision in Archaeology (ACVA '10), June 2010.* San Francisco: IEEE Computer Society Press, 1–6.

Green, S., A. Bevan, and M. Shapland. 2014. "A Comparative Assessment of Structure from Motion Methods for Archaeological Research," *Journal of Archaeological Science* 46: 173–181.

Grøn, O., L. O. Boldreel, D. Cvikel, Y. Kahanov, E. Galili, J.-P. Hermand, D. Naevestad, and M. Reitan. 2015. "Detection and Mapping of Shipwrecks Embedded in Sea-Floor Sediments," *Journal of Archaeological Science: Reports* 4: 242–251.

Grosman, L., A. Karasik, O. Harush, and U. Smilansky. 2014. "Archaeology in Three Dimensions: Computer-Based Methods in Archaeological Research," *Journal of Eastern Mediterranean Archaeology and Heritage Studies* 2: 48–64.

Hodder, I. 2012. *Entangled: An Archaeology of the Relationships between Humans and Things.* Oxford: Wiley-Blackwell.

Jaklic, A., M. Eric, I. Mihajlovic, Z. Stopinsek, and F. Solina. 2015. "Volumetric Models from 3D Point Clouds: The Case Study of Sarcophagi Cargo from a 2nd/3rd Century A.D. Roman Shipwreck near Sutivan on Island Brac, Croatia," *Journal of Archaeological Science* 62: 143–152.

Kimia, B. B. 2010. "HINDSITE: A User-Interactive Framework for Fragment Assembly," in *Proceedings of CVPR Workshop on Applications of Computer Vision in Archaeology (ACVA '10), June 2010.* San Francisco: IEEE Computer Society Press, 62–69.

Levy, T. E., N. G. Smith, M. Najjar, T. A. DeFanti, F. Kuester, and A. Yu-Min Lin. 2012. *Cyber-Archaeology in the Holy Land.* San Diego: Biblical Archaeology Society, California Institute for Telecommunications and Information Technology.

McKnight, L. M., J. E. Adams, A. Chamberlain, S. D. Atherton-Woolham, and R. Bibb. 2015. "Application of Clinical Imaging and 3D Printing to the Identification of Anomalies in an Ancient Egyptian Animal Mummy," *Journal of Archaeological Science Reports* 3: 328–332.

Miller, V., S. Filin, D. Rosenberg, and D. Nadel. 2014. "3D Characterization of Bedrock Features: A Natufian Case Study," *Near Eastern Archaeology* 77: 214–218.

Olsen, B., M. Shanks, T. Webmoore, and C. Whitmore. 2014a. *Archaeology: The Discipline of Things.* Berkeley: University of California Press.

Olson, B. R., and W. R. Caraher., eds. 2015. *3D Imaging in Mediterranean Archaeology*. Grand Forks: The Digital Press at The University of North Dakota.

Olson, B. R., J. M. Gordon, C. Runnels, S. Chomyszak. 2014b. "Experimental Three-Dimensional Printing of a Lower Palaeolithic Handaxe: An Assessment of the Technology and Analytical Value," *Lithic Technology* 39: 162–172.

Olson, B. R., R. A. Placchetti, J. Quartermaine, and A. E. Killebrew. 2013. "The Tel Akko Total Archaeology Project (Akko, Israel): Assessing the Suitability of Multi-Scale 3D Field Recording in Archaeology," *Journal of Field Archaeology* 38: 244–262.

Opitz, R., and D. C. Cowley, eds. 2013. *Interpreting Archaeological Topography: 3D Data, Visualisation and Observation*. Oxford: Oxbow Books.

Opitz, R., and W. F. Limp. 2015. "Recent Developments in High-Density Survey and Measurement (HDSM) for Archaeology: Implications for Practice and Theory," *Annual Review of Anthropology* 44: 347–364.

Pflug, A., and C. Busch. 2012. "Ear Biometrics: A Survey of Detection, Feature Extraction, and Recognition Methods," *IET Biometrics* 1: 114–129.

Pollefeys,M., L. Van Gool, M. Vergauwen, K. Cornelis, F. Verbiest, and J. Tops. 2003. "3D Recording for Archaeological Fieldwork," *IEEE Computer Graphics and Applications* 23: 20–27.

Portal, J., ed. 2007. *The First Emperor: China's Terracotta Army*. Harvard: Harvard University Press.

Prins, A. B., M. J. Adams, R. S. Homsher, and M. Ashley. 2014. "Digital Archaeological Fieldwork and the Jezreel Valley Regional Project, Isreal," *Near Eastern Archaeology* 77: 192–197.

Quartermaine, J., B. R. Olson, and A. E. Killebrew. 2014. "Image-Based Modeling Approaches to 2D and 3D Digital Drafting in Archaeology at Tel Akko and Qasrin, Two Case Studies," *Journal of Eastern Mediterranean Archaeology and Heritage Studies* 2.2: 110–127.

Quartermaine, J., B. R. Olson, and M. Howland. 2013. "Using Photogrammetry and Geographic Information Systems (GIS) to Draft Accurate Plans of Qazion," *Journal of Eastern Mediterranean Archaeology and Heritage Studies* 1: 169–174.

Rabinowitz, A. 2015. "The Work of Archaeology in the Age of Digital Surrogacy," in B. R. Olson and W. R. Caraher, eds., *Visions of*

Substance: 3D Imaging in Mediterranean Archaeology. Grand Forks: The Digital Press at the University of North Dakota, 27–42.

Roosevelt, C. H. 2014. "Mapping Site-Level Microtopography with Real-Time Kinematic Global Navigation Satellite Systems (RTK GNSS) and Unmanned Aerial Vehicle Photogrammetry (UAVP)," *Open Archaeology* 1: 29–53.

Roosevelt, C. H., P. Cobb, E. Moss, B. R. Olson, S. Ünlüsoy. 2015. "Excavation is ~~Destruction~~ Digitization: Advances in Archaeological Practice," *Journal of Field Archaeology* 40: 325–346.

Roussou, M., L. Pujol, A. Katifori, A. Chrysanthi, S. Perry, and M. Vayanou. 2015. "The Museum as Digital Storyteller: Collaborative Participatory Creation of Interactive Digital Experiences." *MW2015: Museums and the Web 2015*, http://mw2015.museumsandtheweb.com/paper/ the-museum-as-digital-storyteller-collaborative-participatory-creation-of-interactive-digital-experiences/

Shipton, C., and C. Clarkson. 2015. "Flake Scar Density and Handaxe Reduction Intensity," *Journal of Archaeological Science: Reports* 2: 169–175.

Smith, N. G., L. Passone, S. al-Said, M. al-Farhan, and T. E. Levy. 2014. "Integrated Data Capture, Processing, and Dissemination in the al-Ula Valley, Saudi Arabia," *Near Eastern Archaeology* 77: 176–181.

Spring, A. P., and C. Peters. 2014. "Developing a Low Cost 3D Imaging Solution for Inscribed Stone Surface Analysis," *Journal of Archaeological Science* 52: 97–107.

Toumazou, M. K., D. B. Counts, E. W. Averett, J. M. Gordon, P. N. Kardulias. 2015. "Shedding Light on the Cypriot Rural Landscape: Investigations of the Athienou Archaeological Project in the Malloura Valley, Cyprus, 2011–2013," *Journal of Field Archaeology* 40: 204–220.

Verhoeven, G. J. J. 2011. "Taking Computer Vision Aloft—Archaeological Three-Dimensional Reconstructions from Aerial Photographs with Photo-Scan," *Archaeological Prospection* 18: 67–73.

Verhoeven, G. J. J., M. Doneus, and C. Briese. 2012a. "Computer Vision Techniques: Towards Automated Orthophoto Production," *AARGnews* 44: 8–11.

Verhoeven, G. J. J., M. Doneus, C. Briese, and F. Vermeulen. 2012b. "Mapping by Matching: A Computer Vision-Based Approach to Fast and Accurate Georeferencing of Archaeological Aerial Photographs," *Journal of Archaeological Science* 39: 2060–2070.

2.3.
Beyond the Basemap: Multiscalar Survey through Aerial Photogrammetry in the Andes

Steven A. Wernke, Carla Hernández, Giancarlo Marcone, Gabriela Ore, Aurelio Rodriguez, and Abel Traslaviña

Unmanned aerial vehicles (UAVs, popularly known as "drones") have revolutionized archaeological mapping. More broadly, computational photography has transformed our capabilities to capture high-resolution spatial representations of archaeological phenomena in the field, from the scale of small features within excavations (Opitz 2015; Poehler 2015; Roosevelt *et al.* 2015) to large sites and encompassing landscapes (Chiabrando *et al.* 2011; Mozas-Calvache *et al.* 2012; Falla-vollita *et al.* 2013; Olson *et al.* 2013; Wernke *et al.* 2014). A quiver of generally inexpensive and efficient photogrammetric field tools are now within the reach of most practitioners across these scales (FIG. 1). High-resolution and high-fidelity orthomosaics, digital elevation models, and textured 3D models can now be captured using consumer-grade digital cameras through photogrammetric software. In just the last few years, technical and cost barriers have lowered and the use of these technologies has spread from innovators to early adopters to what is now the early majority of the bell curve of the archaeological research and conservation communities. The benefits are readily evident: richer and more granular datasets through fast, simple, and inexpensive techniques (see also Olson, Ch. 2.2). In addition to these developments, digital 3D and 3D-printed distribution also have greatly broadened the accessibility and impact of the results to researchers, educators, descendent communities, and global publics.

Here we present a multiscalar perspective on the progress and prospects of digital aerial photogrammetry in archaeology: at the scale of

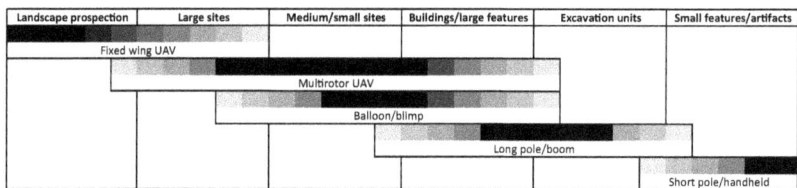

Landscape prospection	Large sites	Medium/small sites	Buildings/large features	Excavation units	Small features/artifacts

Fixed wing UAV

Multirotor UAV

Balloon/blimp

Long pole/boom

Short pole/handheld

Figure 1: Schematic of photogrammetric tools for different scales of subject matter.

landscape prospection using a fixed wing UAV, at the scale of large site survey using a meteorological balloon, and at the scale of individual domestic architectural complexes using pole aerial photography. We illustrate how these aerial photo systems equipped with inexpensive digital cameras can be used to rapidly acquire mass imagery for processing into a variety of 2D and 3D digital images and models. We contend that the efficiency, fidelity, and cost-effectiveness of these methods are of such a qualitatively different character compared to traditional methods that they are transformative for the practice of both research-oriented field archaeology and cultural heritage management. That is, rather than acting as an add-on to traditional survey or excavation projects, these methods enable new kinds of field methodologies, in large part because conventional compromises between scale and granularity of spatial representation are greatly mitigated. This emerging field of "spatial archaeometry" (Casana 2014) promises to more fully and quickly capture the complexity of ancient settlements and landscapes (Wernke *et al.* 2014).

These advances are of equal importance for cultural heritage management. With the alarming loss of archaeological heritage around the world—including the recent specific targeting of monumental archaeological sites for violent destruction (Danti 2015; Harmansah 2015)—the importance of capturing whole-site "digital surrogates" (sensu Rabinowitz 2015) through aerial photogrammetry transcends academic interests (see, e.g., Ioannides *et al.* 2012; Hesse 2013). Archaeological patrimony in general is inexorably degrading and disappearing. It is a one-way, entropic process mitigated only by expensive conservation projects, usually at monumental sites. Given the expense and technical barriers to 3D scanning technologies, scanning efforts have also been largely limited to projects at monumental sites by specialized consultancy firms such as CyArk (see http://www.cyark.org/about/). Aerial photogrammetry has now dramatically lowered those barriers to enable the production of whole-site digital surrogates of the many "lesser" (i.e., the great majority) threatened sites and landscapes.

With these concerns in mind, this chapter addresses both heritage management and research-oriented problems. The first part presents a case study in rapid aerial photogrammetry documentation of sites and landscapes along the road network of the Inka Empire in Peru. This project was a collaborative effort between Giancarlo Marcone, director of the Proyecto Qhapaq Ñan (Inka Royal Highway Project), and Steven Wernke (Vanderbilt University). Together with the other co-authors of this paper, we set out to document sections of the Qhapaq Ñan associated with major Inka imperial installations from locations near sea level to 3,900 m found along one of the main transverse highways that connects the primary imperial highway along the Pacific coast to its counterpart in the highlands.

While the Qhapaq Ñan case study illustrates the speed and utility of UAV-based photogrammetry for heritage management, the second part of the paper explores its richness and potential for integration with tablet-based architectural survey using high-resolution (sub-decimeter to centimeter) balloon- and pole-based aerial orthomosaics and 3D models. This research project, the Proyecto Arqueológico Tuti Antiguo (PATA, Ancient Tuti Archaeological Project) was designed from the ground up to use high-resolution aerial photogrammetry as central spatial reference data for mobile GIS-based mapping (see Wernke and Siveroni Salinas 2013; Wernke et al. 2014; Wernke 2015). While PATA is directed by Wernke, Gabriela Oré, Carla Hernández, and Abel Traslaviña all played instrumental roles in the execution of its methodology. The projeect investigates the transition from late prehispanic to Spanish colonial times, focusing on an Inka administrative center that was converted into a planned colonial town in the high Andes (4,100 m) and built as part of the *Reducción General de Indios* (General Resettlement of Indians), a mass resettlement program executed throughout the Viceroyalty of Peru in the 1570s. This large town—originally named Santa Cruz de Tuti—encompasses nearly 40 ha at an elevation of 4,100 m, with about 500 remarkably well-preserved buildings in a gridded street plan. With its excellent architectural preservation, Santa Cruz de Tuti provides an ideal context to investigate little-understood aspects of the General Resettlement, but it also poses significant challenges given its scale, complexity, and remoteness. Traditional mapping techniques would require major outlays in time and labor, and would result in a relatively impoverished cartographical representations. We present a methodological approach for mapping extensive and complex architectural remains using orthomosaics as base imagery for tablet-based, in-field digitization, with a much richer attribute data registry than possible through traditional mapping methods.

Digital Heritage Management:
The Inka Royal Highway Project

The Proyecto Qhapaq Ñan (Inka Royal Highway Project), a special project of the Ministry of Culture, Peru, faces the monumental challenge
of documenting and conserving the many thousands of kilometers
of ancient roads of the Inka Empire in Peru (see http://www.cultura.
gob.pe/en/tags/proyecto-qhapaq-nan). From a heritage management
perspective, the Proyecto Qhapaq Ñan faces major challenges of
scale and representation as it encompasses much of the territory of
the modern republic of Peru, with over 3,000 km of the ancient road
system documented in the field and many hundreds of associated
Inka sites (FIG. 2). Mapping the entirety of the ancient road network
in detail would be impractical, and non-commercial satellite imagery
is not of sufficient resolution to detect important elements of the road
system or preserved architecture in archaeological settlements. Thus,
UAV-based mapping is especially attractive for the Proyecto Qhapaq
Ñan due to its speed and low cost, its ability to render a variety of
vector- and raster-based 2D and 3D formats, and the possibility of
recording sites and landscapes many times, which enables seasonal or
inter-annual, and long-term monitoring (longitudinal or time series
analysis). Our collaboration is part of a broader effort by the Peruvian
Ministry of Culture to seek methods for using UAV photogrammetry
to document its thousands of archaeological sites (see, e.g., Neuman
and Blumenthal 2014).

The Proyecto Qhapaq Ñan is also developing a new approach to
managing this vast cultural patrimony, moving away from a previous
site-based framework toward one centering on cultural landscapes
and corridors around the Inka roads. This is more appropriate to the
ancient practices associated with the Inka imperial road network
itself, and in terms of patrimonial stewardship. Inka aesthetics and
engineering worked at the scale of entire landscapes rather than settlements, neighborhoods, or buildings (Protzen 1993; Niles 1999; Kosiba
and Bauer 2012; Nair 2015). From a stewardship perspective, the scale
of the Qhapaq Ñan far exceeds the resources of the state and descendent communities are often literally dislocated from their cultural
patrimony through the declaration of sites as "intangible zones."
Through a cultural landscape concept, the Proyecto Qhapaq Ñan seeks
the participation of local stakeholders, placing sites within a living,

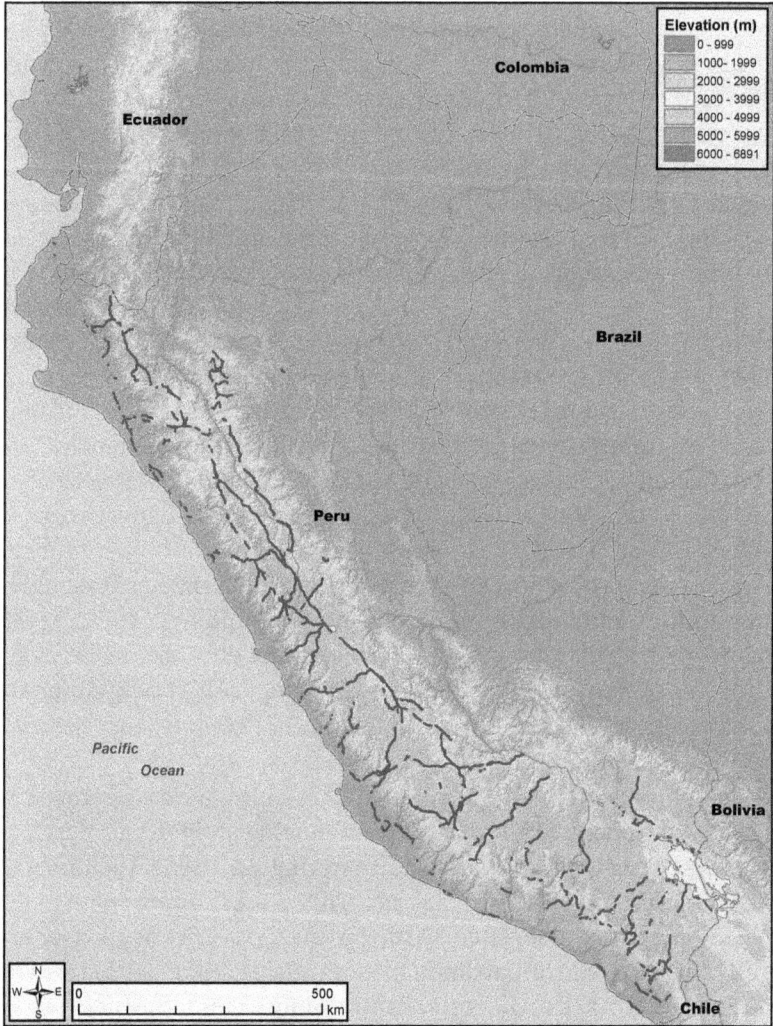

Figure 2: Overview of the sections of the Inka road system documented in the field by the Proyecto Qhapaq Ñan.

working contemporary landscape. As part of this new approach, the Proyecto Qhapaq Ñan is organized by *tramos* (tracts) between major Inka imperial centers. Our collaborative project focused on one of the major transverse Inka highways connecting the coast and highlands: the tramo between the monumental center of Tambo Colorado, located in the upper reaches of the coastal Pisco valley, and Vilcashuamán in the highlands of the department of Ayacucho.

The collaboration also enabled performance testing of a fixed-wing UAV at different elevations. Compared to multirotor designs, fixed-wing UAVs fly faster, with longer flight times, and a broader altitudinal range of operation, making them optimal for this kind of large site and landscape prospection. The UAV used for the project was based on the TechPod (http://hobbyuav.com/), a large fixed-wing airframe. This design was chosen for its large wingspan (2.67 m) and wing area (3903 cm²), facilitating large payload (1 kg of battery/payload), long flight times (capable of flights in excess of 1 hour), and slow cruising speed (59 km/hr). The large wingspan and wing surface are also crucial for achieving adequate lift for takeoff and stable flight in high elevation contexts. The TechPod is an open-source and low-cost UAV. For imagery capture, we equiped the TechPod with a small consumer point-and-shoot camera (Canon w/Canon Elph 300 HS camera, along with a 12.1 megapixel CMOS (complementary metal-oxide semiconductor) sensor) with CHDK (Canon Hack Development Kit) installed to enable the use of an intervalometer script and capture of images in raw format (uncompressed values from the CMOS sensor). Photos were taken every four seconds—an interval chosen based on the relatively high flight paths we planned for large-scale landscape aerial survey (a short video of a flight at Tambo Colorado can be downloaded at http://www.vanderbilt.edu/sarl/Images2/Tambo_Colorado_flight03.mp4).

Case Study: Tambo Colorado

Tambo Colorado is an elaborate Inka imperial center of painted adobe palaces, plazas, and ceremonial structures located in the Pisco valley. It is sited on the main Inka highway that connects to the highland imperial center of Vilcashuamán and eventually leads onward to the imperial capital of Cuzco. Just to the northwest of Tambo Colorado, the

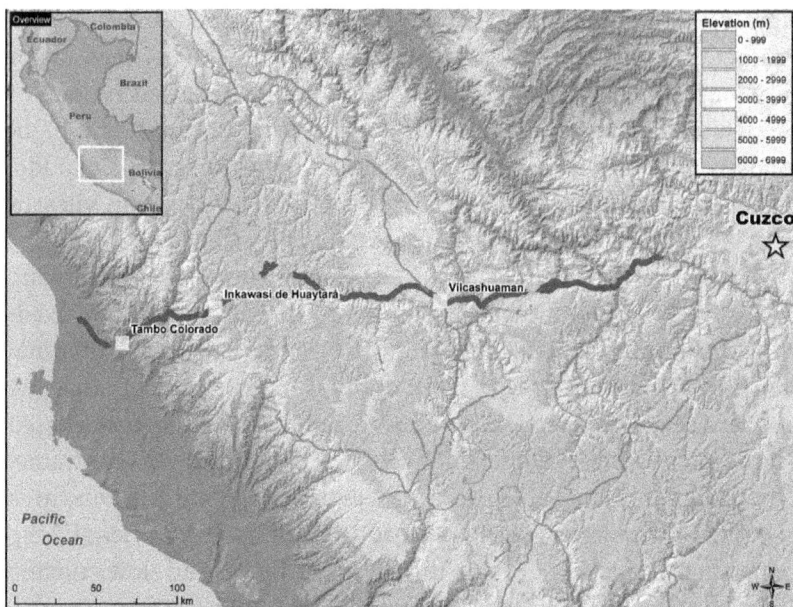

Figure 3: Overview of the Pisco–Vilcashuamán tramo (thick, dark red).

Figure 4: Tambo Colorado: overview of the area mapped by UAV, showing areas of prior mapping efforts.

Qhapaq Ñan turns northwest toward the Chincha valley and joins the main coastal highway (FIG. 3).

With its spectacular layout and architectural preservation, Tambo Colorado has a long history of research and archaeological mapping. German archaeologist Max Uhle mapped and excavated there in 1901. His remarkably accurate maps remain a vital reference for researchers. Later, in 2001, Jean Pierre Protzen and Craig Morris began a long-term investigation of the site. This project included extensive 3D laser scanning by CyArk during four field seasons (2001, 2003, 2004, 2005) in several areas of the site core, providing unprecedented renderings of palace complexes and many features, including details such as the many trapezoidal niches, windows, and doorways (see http://www.cyark.org/projects/tambo-colorado/overview). The logistical complexities of terrestrial laser scanning, however, ultimately limited the coverage of these operations. Our objective was to complement these previous efforts by contextualizing the site of Tambo Colorado in its broader landscape—mapping at mid-scale—while also providing adequate resolution to discern architectural detail.

Our fieldwork at Tambo Colorado took only two days: one day to set ground control points (GCPs) using a RTK GNSS (real-time kinetic global navigation satellite system (Topcon GR5)) with sub-centimeter accuracy (0.5 cm horizontal, 0.9 cm vertical), and one day to obtain the UAV-based imagery (GCPs were recorded in UTM coordinates (zone 18S), WGS 1984 datum, using Geoid EGM Peru 2008 for elevations). Two flights—one approximately 10 minutes, the other approximately 20 minutes—were flown over the site and surrounding landscape, following the course of the Qhapaq Ñan into and out of the site.

From the flight imagery, 467 images were selected for photogrammetric processing in Agisoft PhotoScan (v.1.1.5), performed in the Spatial Analysis Research Laboratory at Vanderbilt University (http://www.vanderbilt.edu/sarl). Of these, 465 images were automatically aligned in about two hours of processing time on an advanced workstation (workstation specifications include Intel Xeon E5-1650 v3 CPU, 128 GB RAM, and dual NVIDIA K4200 GPUs). In-field processing on a laptop would also be possible by dividing processing into two or three "chunks" (groups of photos covering contiguous areas). The resulting orthomosaic encompasses an area of 70 ha at a pixel resolution of 6.8 cm (FIGS. 4, 5). The DEM (digital elevation model) resolved to a 13.6 cm raster grid cell size (FIG. 6). The shape of the area prioritizes

Figure 5: Tambo Colorado: UAV orthoimage detail: north palace.

Figure 6: Tambo Colorado: DEM generated from UAV imagery.

documentation of the ancient road in relation to the site, which runs roughly parallel to the river and modern highway.

Compared to previous mapping efforts at the site, our UAV-based orthoimagery, DEM, and 3D model document a much larger area, placing Tambo Colorado in its fuller landscape context, while still at sufficient resolution to observe most architectonic details. It thus complements the work of Uhle, Protzen, and Morris, which focused on the monumental core. The scale and resolution of this project enable new observations and heritage management capabilities. For instance, the orthoimagery and 3D models enable the project to evaluate risks not only to the monumental core but also to the sections of the Inka road the run through the site. In the core of the site, the primary threats are tourist foot traffic and damage from alluvial and colluvial flows. The photographic source data for the orthomosaics facilitates monitoring of foot traffic, since patterns of movement through the site can be inferred from the imagery itself. To the east of the site core, a remarkable section of the ancient road is preserved upslope of the modern highway. There, the ancient road traverses a number of *quebradas* (ravines) as the road directed traffic to and from the highlands. In these crossing points between the quebradas and the road, the highway was reinforced with large stone-faced revetments. These revetments are variably preserved and threatened. The orthoimagery enables monitoring of ongoing and active alluvial and colluvial flows through these quebradas and across the ancient road, thus facilitating prioritization of conservation efforts. Because of the low cost and time investment in this method, site monitoring could be completed on a regular (e.g., annual) basis to monitor site changes and erosion. The area documented can also be observed in 3D by exporting a COLLADA (COLLAborative Design Activity) 3D solid model. This model has been uploaded to Sketchfab.com, a 3D model-sharing site, for viewing and downloading (https://skfb.ly/HwDP).

Finally, the orthoimagery provided a guide for fast vector-based representation of the architectural core, which was done using a computer-aided design (CAD) program in compliance with Ministry of Culture reporting requirements (FIG. 7). Though CAD editing was done on a desktop computer, such digitization work could also be accomplished on a mobile GIS platform on a tablet (or laptop) in the field (using, e.g., the FAIMS mobile platform (Federated Archaeological Information Management System; see Sobotkova *et al.*, Ch. 3.2),

Figure 7: Tambo Colorado: site core vector mapping.

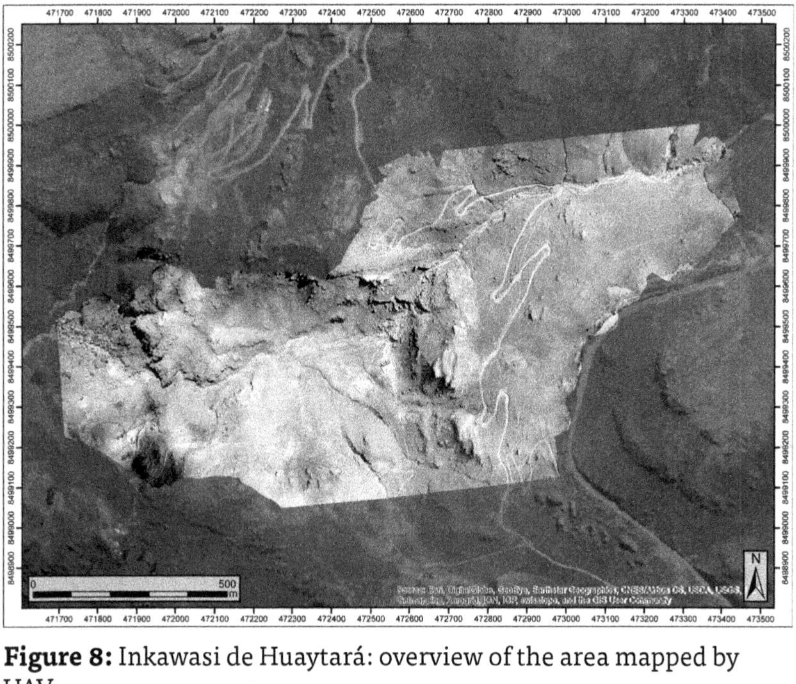

Figure 8: Inkawasi de Huaytará: overview of the area mapped by UAV.

GIS Pro, or QGIS for Android). As discussed below, this methodology offers considerable advantages in speed and richness of attribute data registry compared to traditional total station–based approaches to producing site architectural plans.

Case Study: Inkawasi de Huaytará

Inkawasi de Huaytará is the next major Inka imperial site inland from Tambo Colorado on the Pisco–Vilcashuamán tramo of the Qhapaq Ñan. Located high in the western range of the central cordillera, Inkawasi is situated at 3,850 m, at the lower edge of the *puna* (high elevation grassland). Inkawasi is a curious site, and its basic functions remain in question. It is small and isolated from local settlements, but other attributes point to highly exclusive elite-only access to certain sectors of the site. Unlike Tambo Colorado, Inkawasi has been the subject of very little systematic study. During the same 1901 expedition that produced the architectural map of Tambo Colorado discussed above, Uhle briefly visited the site and speculated that it may have served as a *tambo* (waystation) for the Inka to rest after one day's journey inland on the Qhapaq Ñan from Tambo Colorado (Protzen and Harris 2005: 87–88). John Hyslop reconnoitered Inkawasi de Huaytará as part of his survey of the Inka road system (Hyslop 1984: 105–106) and drafted a sketch map. Given that the road climbs another 1,200 vertical meters in just the 14 km between Inkawasi and Huaytará, the next Inka site to the east (Hyslop 1984: 104), facilities for lodging, water, and food might be expected there.

Inkawasi was certainly more than a waystation, however, since its architectural complexes include features such as double-jamb trapezoidal doorways (which marked thresholds to exclusive elite spaces) and buildings made of fine precision-fitted Inka stone masonry— clearly the work of specialized imperial stonemasons and features found only at elite Inka imperial sites (Gasparini and Margolies 1980; Protzen 1993; Niles 1999). It may have functioned as a provincial estate for traveling Inka nobility and the emperor himself (S. Chacaltana, pers. comm. 2015). Typical of Inka "aesthetics of alterity" (van de Guchte 1999), the site also appears to have been emplaced in the local landscape with an eye toward fitting its highly exclusive spaces in relation to a prominent cliff band and rock outcrop in the gorge

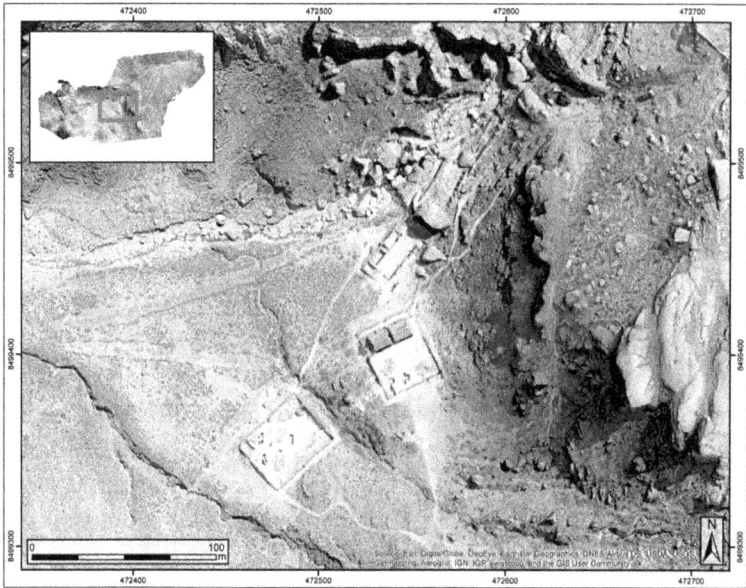

Figure 9: Inkawasi: UAV orthoimage detail: site core.

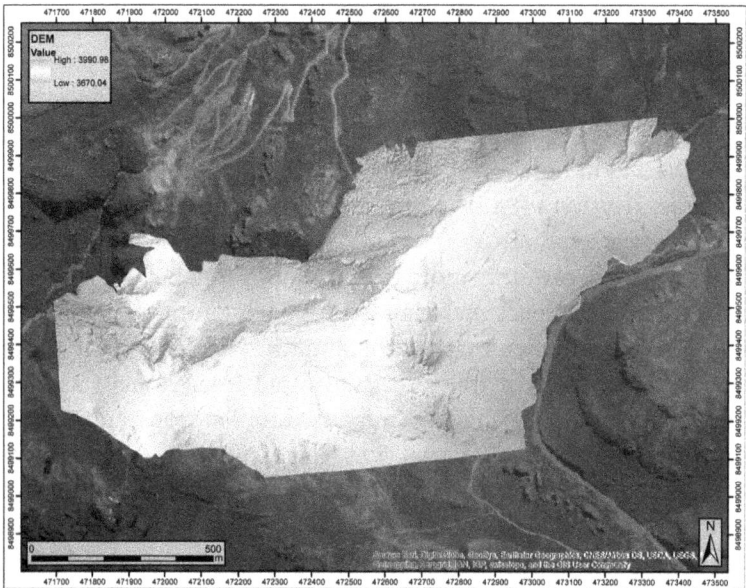

Figure 10: Inkawasi: DEM generated from UAV imagery.

of the Inkawasi River. The royal highway itself passes through a cleft in this outcrop, producing a dramatic framing of the site as travelers descend from the highlands. Rituals connecting humans to the chthonic beings in the landscape were almost certainly central to its placement and design. Understanding or conveying these aesthetic and functional possibilities requires something beyond a basemap: spatial representations at finer resolution than off-the-shelf satellite-based DEMs or imagery, and richer than traditional topographic and architectural survey. UAV-based high-resolution 3D mapping meets these requirements.

Most recently, the Proyecto Qhapaq Ñan completed follow-up conservation work at Injawasi to check and repair earlier site conservation by the Ministry of Culture, Peru, and it is working with the local community to develop an integrated conservation, tourism, and community development plan, which includes the site and its surrounding landscape (Antezana Ruiz 2015). Our collaboration to produce UAV-based mapping was designed as an integral part of the information that the Proyecto Qhapaq Ñan and local community authorities will use in formulating this plan. Thus, both research and heritage management goals are addressed by the project.

Our UAV work at Inkawasi was completed in one afternoon, following a day of work placing the ground control points with a RTK GNSS. We used the same flight parameters, motor, and propeller as at Tambo Colorado, and the TechPod performed well. Achieving takeoff required throwing the UAV from a steeply sloping hilltop (download short video online at http://www.vanderbilt.edu/sarl/Images2/Inkawasi_first_flight.mp4), permitting an initial drop in altitude to gain speed and sufficient lift. The imagery was captured over three brief flights (all lasting about 10 minutes). The intervalometer was again set to four seconds, and the imagery used in photogrammetric processing was captured in about 25 minutes over the course of three flights. Of the selected photos, 343 were aligned to produce an orthomosaic and DEM covering an area of 99.8 ha. Within this large area, the orthomosaic resolved to a pixel size of 8.6 cm (FIGS. 8, 9), while the DEM provides 17.3 cm resolution—resolution very close to that achieved at Tambo Colorado (FIG. 10).

The orthoimagery, DEM, and 3D models will be integral to this project's subsequent operations, obviating the need for costly and slow traditional topographic survey, with much higher resolution topographic results, combined with precise color orthoimagery of the site in its fuller landscape context (see the 3D model online at https://skfb.ly/HwEo).

ARCHITECTURAL SURVEY AT A PLANNED COLONIAL TOWN: MAWCHU LLACTA

The speed and resolution of UAV-based photogrammetry are of obvious utility, especially in this era of accelerating loss of archaeological patrimony. But the technological advances in both the UAV and photogrammetry fields have been so fast that methodological frameworks have generally not yet adapted to the new capabilities and challenges they present. Building on previous work in integrated photomapping and mobile GIS excavation workflow (Tripcevich and Wernke 2010), Wernke recently began a new archaeological project focused on a planned colonial town with extensive well-preserved architecture in the high reaches of the Colca valley of southern Peru. This settlement, Santa Cruz de Tuti, is known today as Mawchu Llacta ("Old Town") by its descendent population in the modern community of Tuti, who reside just a few kilometers downslope from their ancestral town.

Mawchu Llacta was built as a *reducción* (literally, "reduction") town as part of the mass forced resettlement program known as the Reducción General de Indios ("General Resettlement of Indians") in the Viceroyalty of Peru. This was one of the largest forced resettlement programs enacted by a colonial power, affecting some 1.4 million native Andeans (Mumford 2012). The Viceroy Francisco de Toledo, charged with establishing a new colonial order after a generation of Spanish plunder, indirect rule, and Inka insurrection, ordered the forcible resettlement of indigenous communities as part of a general survey of the Viceroyalty of Peru between 1570 and 1575. This massive social experiment was premised on the notion that by rebuilding indigenous communities literally from the ground up, they would become more like model subjects and Christians and a new social order (*policia*) would emerge.

A theory of built environment was at the core of the Reducción. But archaeological research on the topic is just beginning, and surprisingly little archival research has focused on it to date. Basic questions remain about how the actual resettlement and construction of these towns was enacted, how decisions were made about where and how many to build in a given area, and how domestic and public life within them was organized. Mawchu Llacta is both exceptionally well-preserved and exceptionally documented in written texts, providing a virtually unparalleled opportunity to elucidate these dimensions of the resettlement. As an archaeological microhistory, the archaeological research at Mawchu Llacta would have to begin with detailed mapping and architectural survey and surface collections. Wernke's project has just completed this first phase, with the subsequent phase of excavations beginning in 2016 (see Wernke 2015).

Mawchu Llacta site is situated at 4,100 m in the high puna grasslands, and it is quite extensive, comprising a regular checkerboard grid of urban blocks extending about half a kilometer on a side, with a total site area of about 40 ha. Within this gridded street plan are over 500 standing fieldstone buildings in varying states of preservation. The site is also situated in the location of a major Inka site, which was likely the administrative center for the upper section of the Colca valley. The site core centers on two plazas—one of which is trapezoidal and was likely the center of the Inka settlement, and the other rectangular with six chapels. The church, facing the trapezoidal plaza, is very large with a 50 m long nave. The arched entry to the church and one of its bell towers remain intact as well.

The site thus presented both major opportunities and major challenges: an accurate "base map" was clearly required to address the core research questions, but producing one through traditional methods (via total station survey) would be a daunting, slow, and ultimately expensive undertaking with relatively data-impoverished results. Ideas for producing something "beyond a basemap" during the first phase of the project developed at a time when a number of the technologies (widely discussed in this volume) were only nascent (but quickly ramping up): iPads and early Android tablet devices were introduced to the market in 2010; a relatively small number of manufacturers and "do-it-yourself" hobbyists and professionals were coalescing in a burgeoning UAV market and maker culture. It seemed opportune to design a project building on these tools from the outset.

Technical details of the project design have been presented elsewhere (Wernke *et al.* 2014), but in outline, the concept for mapping and architectural survey was to conduct UAV-based low-altitude photogrammetry combined with tablet-based mobile GIS. The orthoimagery from the UAV would serve as the primary spatial reference for digitizing buildings, walls, and other features directly on screen in the field using a mobile GIS app. Mapping and architectural survey could thus be conducted simultaneously, producing rich datasets that combined color orthoimagery with vector based plans of building and other architectural elements, with attribute data associated with each feature.

The project eventually succeeded in executing this methodology, but not in sequence and not without initial setbacks, most of which were a consequence of the immature nature of the technologies at the time of the first phase of fieldwork (during July and August of 2012 and 2013), and the difficult conditions of the site setting—especially the challenges of high-altitude atmospheric conditions for UAV flight. Experimentation with two different UAV platforms in 2012 and 2013 failed to produce reliable flight in these extreme conditions. These difficulties were the initial impetus for moving to the TechPod and developing the collaboration with the Qhapaq Ñan Project discussed above. Though we did capture over 2,000 images with the UAVs at the site, image quality and coverage were uneven and photogrammetric results did not meet the project requirements. Thus, during the 2013 season, we opted to use a tethered meteorological balloon as the photographic platform (a widely used and proven method; see Bitelli *et al.* 2004; Olson *et al.* 2013; Poehler 2015). This technique was not without its difficulties and was much slower, but it did produce virtually full-coverage orthoimagery of the site.

The architectural survey with tablet-based mobile GIS proceeded apace despite the challenges the project faced with the UAVs. The project was experimental in this aspect as well, since we initially acted as alpha testers for an early version of the Android-based mobile application for the FAIMS (see Sobotkova *et al.*, Ch. 3.2) project. The FAIMS project is now several generations beyond this early version and is a field-proven product, but at the time, we were just starting to work out issues of user interaction, data structure, and data synchronization, so it was not yet ready to be used as a primary data collection system. After these FAIMS field experiments, we switched to a commercial mobile GIS for iOS—GISPro by Garafa Inc. Fortuitously, GISPro met most requirements of the project: the user can create point, line, and polygon themes (exported as shapefiles) that can be generated by activating the tablet GPS (with options for using an external antenna) or by plotting on screen. It is designed as a single-user/team system, however, and it has no central database. Therefore, data synchronization to a central geodatabase was manual, requiring considerable data-management effort.

In the field, however, GISPro worked quite well, especially in terms of user interaction, requiring minimal training (most students could learn the interface and data entry aspects in a single day). We drew features on-screen for nearly all aspects of the project since we were digitizing architectural features using a georeferenced airphoto as reference data. It was critical for our teams to be able to draft in the field while directly observing the feature in question to ensure proper registry of wall joins and seams and many other architectonic details (e.g., niches, doorways with lintels intact, which are not evident in plan view). GISPro also allows user specification of attributes using an intuitive form-based interface (including options for controlled vocabularies in the form of drop down menus). For buildings, we produced an extensive form with up to 65 attributes on building style, form, dimensions, and a range of architectural details (e.g., niches, doorways, and other features). We also made polygon themes for miscellaneous features and for collection areas within structures, line themes for walls that define unroofed areas (domestic compounds, corrals, blocks, and streets) and for canals, and point themes for lichenometric specimens (we measured specimens of the Rhizocarpon lichen to date architecture at the site), piece plotted surface collections, and dogleash surface collections. Using this system, four survey crews moved through the site and collected all data, generally covering 1–2 blocks (depending on architectural complexity and density) per team per day. In approximately three months of fieldwork, a draft GIS of the site was completed, with all attributes recorded in the field.

Our balloon-based imagery capture was completed over the course of three days. The low atmospheric pressure at this altitude requires a larger volume of helium, and thus a much larger balloon than would be needed nearer to sea level. We used a 3 m³ latex meterological balloon to ensure adequate lift for our camera (the same Canon Elph 300 HS). We used two tethers to help control the balloon and to minimize the visibility of the string in the frame (by spreading the two walkers widely). Also, the camera was strung between the tethers on a picavet to aid in maintaining a nadir camera orientation. The balloon was generally flown 25–40 m in altitude, with the camera

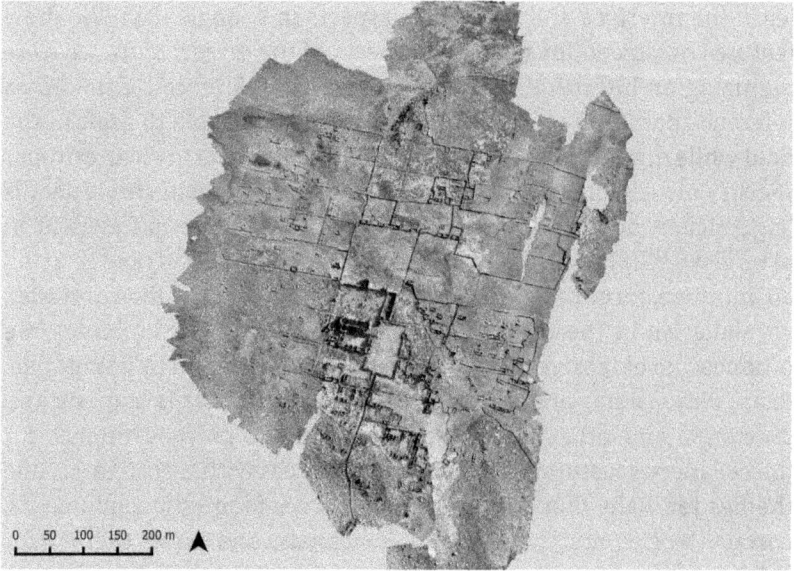

0 50 100 150 200 m

Figure 11: Mawchu Llacta: overview of the area mapped by meteorological balloon.

Figure 12: Orthomosaic details: Mawchu Llacta: site core (top); domestic compound (bottom).

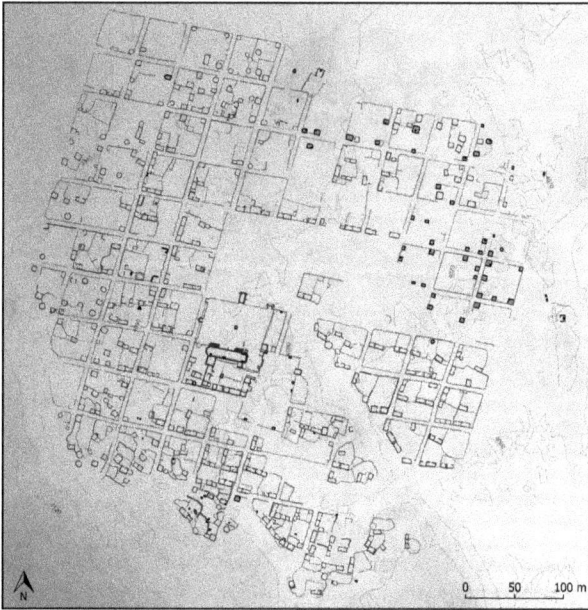

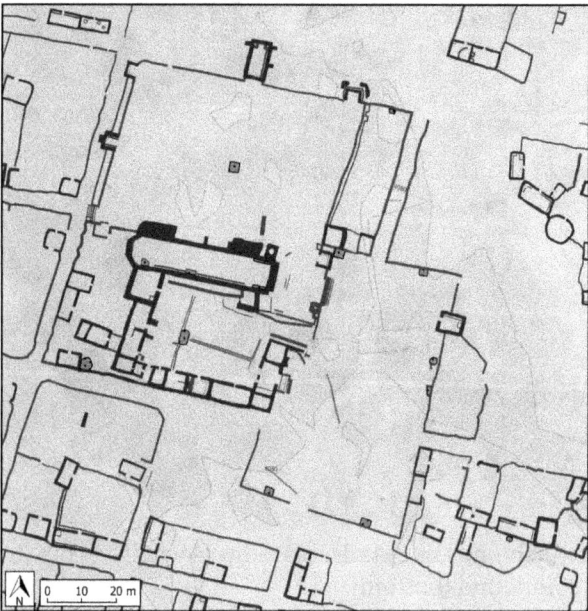

Figure 13: GIS architectural map: Mawchu Llacta: overview (top); detail of site core (bottom).

intervalometer set at 10 seconds, as operators walked in a lawnmower pattern through the site.

Over 3,000 usable photos resulted from the balloon flights. Photo sequences were divided into eight chunks for photogrammetric processing. These chunks provide virtually full coverage of the site (with a few small voids). The resulting orthomosaics are quite detailed, with 5 cm resolution in most cases. At this resolution, individual stones that make up the tops of walls are generally clearly visible (FIGS. 11, 12).

With the processed orthomosaic finished in 2014, we then revised the draft geometry of the architecture digitized in the field from the coarser airphotos. The key to maintaining fidelity in this process is that the original field data, though geometrically imprecise, was topologically correct—that is to say, wall joins and the like were drafted as observed. These are the key data for relationships of horizontal stratigraphy, and they were preserved through the editing process. Of course, this step would be obviated had the original workflow gone according to plan. But our situation can be considered something of a special case given the extreme conditions of the site compared to most archaeological projects. In any case, now, with our larger UAV and experiences from the Qhapaq Ñan collaboration, we expect that the UAV-orthoimagery-feature digitization/attribute registry workflow will work in future projects. Also, consumer multirotor UAVs have emerged in just the last year that far outperform anything that was available when we started the project: the DJI Phantom 3, DJI Inspire, and 3DR Solo are all rated to fly at least to 4,500 m (the Solo and Phantom 3 can go considerably higher). As a measure of the rapid evolution of these technologies, during July, 2016 (just prior to the time this paper goes to press), we successfully flew several photogrammetry missions over the site with a DJI Phantom 4 quadcopter, producing sub-5 cm orthomosaics. In short, the technical barriers that impeded the UAV aspect of our project have been overcome.

The resulting GIS for Mawchu Llacta is composed of 495 structures (themselves composed of 597 structural elements), 1,258 walls, and a number of other features with all field-collected attribute data integrated in a PostGreSQL/POSTGIS database with remote access (FIG. 13). This is now the central database for the project, which we are accessing and editing both locally and remotely via QGIS.

Pole Aerial Photography for Detailed Architectural Rendering

Lastly, in preparation for the excavation phase of the project, we selected areas of interest for excavation for more detailed photogrammetric survey using pole aerial photography (PAP). Pole-based photography is inexpensive, simple in execution, and enables closer and more precise camera placement with respect to the subject matter than UAVs. We used an 11 m carbon fiber fishing pole modified for PAP through the Public Lab (http://store.publiclab.org/collections/mapping-kits/products/pole-mapping-kit). We set ground control points with RTK GNSS (ca. 1 cm horizontal accuracy) and photomapped domestic compounds and other areas of interest, using a Canon S110 and GoPro Hero4, set at an interval of 5–6 seconds. We inserted the base of the pole in a flag pole holster to distribute the weight of the pole/camera rig and improve maneuverability.

Three days of fieldwork produced photos of four areas of interest: three compounds we identified as likely households of ethnic lords (*kurakas*) and an area adjacent to the trapezoidal plaza that we hypothesize was a ceremonial platform or other important shrine (*huaca*) in the original Inka center. A chapel is oriented in one corner of this area, its entry facing the opposite direction, oriented toward the primary entry and facade of the main church. The (nominal) resolution of the resulting orthomosaics is remarkable, with subcentimeter to submillimeter pixel resolution. The 3D models are sufficiently detailed to view and explore architectural details on-screen. These "digital surrogates" are important for both analytical purposes and use as virtual archives of these areas before archaeological interventions. Examples of the resulting models can be viewed and downloaded from Sketchfab (for the chapel and shrine area, see https://skfb.ly/HwOn; for the elite domestic compound, see https://skfb.ly/JN6X).

CLOSING THOUGHTS

The projects discussed here took place through different phases of the UAV and photogrammetric revolution in archaeology—from an era of early adopters to the current era in which it is approaching standard fieldwork practice among an increasing number of practitioners. As a piece on computational archaeology, this chapter plays a similarly transitional role. It is likely that essays like this arguing for the benefits of UAVs and photogrammetry in archaeology will become less common in the near future, as technical barriers are lowered to the point that they are part of standard practice. But we have also argued that "standard practice" will need to change to capitalize on the extended observational capabilities that these technologies allow. We share the concern that the growing dominance of digital recording can, if used in traditional research designs, impede observation and interaction with the actual stuff of archaeological research: the tactile and sensory—observational—experience of primary archaeological data collection (see Caraher, Ch. 4.1). We have spent many hours both in the field and with archaeological digital surrogates in the days, weeks, and years following fieldwork (Rabinowitz 2015). Designing new workflows which minimize the extent to which digital surrogates interfere with primary field observation presents perhaps the central epistemological challenge going foward. It is likely, for example, that excavation project designs will be best served to move to a more specialized mapping/photogrammetry team model so that crew chiefs and excavators can focus on the primary instruments of observations rather than manipulating various digital-sensing instruments at a remove (seeCastro López *et al.*, Ch. 3.1; Wallrodt, Ch. 1.1).

But from a heritage management perspective, the world will not wait. The inexorable loss of patrimony to deliberate destruction, urban sprawl, development, and a host of other threats compels us to find new ways to rapidly document global archaeological patrimony. In this case, however, usual compromises between speed, granularity, and accuracy do not apply. There is no downside that we can see as long as the digital surrogates we can produce quickly, cheaply, and easily do not displace our continued advocacy for the importance of conserving and experiencing ancient places.

https://mobilizingthepast.mukurtu.net/collection/23-beyond-basemap-multiscalar-survey-through-aerial-photogrammetry-andes

http://dc.uwm.edu/arthist_mobilizingthepast/12

REFERENCES

Antezana Ruiz, D. 2015. *Proyecto de Investigación Arqueológica Inkawasi de Huaytará con fines de diagnóstico para la puesta en uso social.* Technical Report to the Ministry of Culture, Peru.

Bitelli, G., V. Girelli, M. Tini, and L. Vittuari. 2004. Low-Height Aerial Imagery and Digital Photogrammetrical Processing for Archaeological Mapping. *Proceedings of the XXXV Congress of the International Society for Photogrammetry and Remote Sensing.* http://www.isprs.org/proceedings/XXXV/congress/comm5/papers/605.pdf

Cassana, J. 2014. "New Approaches to Spatial Archaeometry: Applications from the Near East," *Near Eastern Archaeology* 77: 171–175.

Chiabrando, F., F. Nex, D. Piatti, and F. Rinaudo. 2011. "UAV and RPV Systems for Photogrammetric Surveys in Archaeological Areas: Two Tests in the Piedmont Region (Italy)," *Journal of Archaeological Science* 38: 697–710.

Danti, M. D. 2015. "Ground-Based Observations of Cultural Heritage Incidents in Syria and Iraq," *Near Eastern Archaeology* 78: 132–141.

Fallavollita, P., M. Balsi, S. Esposito, M. G. Melis, M. Milanese, and L. Zappino. 2013. "UAS for Archaeology: New Perspectives on Aerial Documentation," *International Archives of Photogrammetry and Remote Sensing* 61 (1/W2): 131–135.

Gasparini, G., and L. Margolies. 1980. *Inca Architecture.* Bloomington: Indiana University Press.

Harmansah, Ö. 2015. "Isis, Heritage, and the Spectacles of Destruction in the Global Media," *Near Eastern Archaeology* 78: 170–177.

Hesse, R. 2013. Using Structure-from-Motion to Document Threats to Archaeological Heritage in Coastal Peru. https://www.academia.edu/4610499/Using_structure-from-motion_to_document_threats_to_archaeological_heritage_in_coastal_Peru

Hyslop, J. 1984. *The Inka Road System. Studies in Archaeology.* Orlando: Academic Press.

Ioannides, M., D. Fritsch, J. Leissner, R. Davies, F. Remondino, and R. Caffo, eds. 2012. *Progress in Cultural Heritage Preservation: 4th International Conference, EuroMed 2012. Limassol, Cyprus, October 29–November 3, 2012: Proceedings. Lecture Notes in Computer Science* 7616. New York: Springer.

Kosiba, S., and A. M. Bauer. 2012. "Mapping the Political Landscape: Toward a GIS Analysis of Environmental and Social Difference," *Journal of Archaeological Method and Theory* 14: 61–101.

Mozas-Calvache, A. T., J. L. Pérez-García, F. J. Cardenal-Escarcena, E. Mata-Castro, and J. Delgado-García. 2012. "Method for Photogrammetric Surveying of Archaeological Sites with Light Aerial Platforms," *Journal of Archaeological Science* 39: 521–530.

Mumford, J. R. 2012. *Vertical Empire: The General Resettlement of Indians in the Colonial Andes*. Durham, NC: Duke University Press.

Nair, S. 2015. *At Home with the Sapa Inca: Architecture, Space, and Legacy at Chinchero*. Austin: University of Texas Press.

Neuman, W., and R. Blumenthal. 2014. "New to the Archaeologist's Tool Kit: The Drone." *New York Times*, 13 August 2014, http://www.nytimes.com/2014/08/14/arts/design/drones-are-used-to-patrol-endangered-archaeological-sites.html

Niles, S. A. 1999. *The Shape of Inca History: Narrative and Architecture in an Andean Empire*. Iowa City: University of Iowa Press.

Olson, B. R., R. A. Placchetti, J. Quartermaine, and A. E. Killebrew. 2013. "The Tel Akko Total Archaeology Project (Akko, Israel): Assessing the Suitability of Multi-Scale 3D Field Recording in Archaeology," *Journal of Field Archaeology* 38: 244–262.

Opitz, R. 2015. "Three Dimensional Field Recording in Archaeology: An Example from Gabii," in B. R. Olson and W. R. Caraher, eds., *Visions of Substance: 3D Imaging in Mediterranean Archaeology*. Grand Forks: The Digital Press at The University of North Dakota, 73–86.

Poehler, E. 2015. "Photogrammetry on the Pompeii Quadriporticus Project," in B. R. Olson and W. R. Caraher, eds., *Visions of Substance: 3D Imaging in Mediterranean Archaeology*. Grand Forks: The Digital Press at The University of North Dakota, 87–100.

Protzen, J.-P. 1993. *Inca Architecture and Construction at Ollantaytambo*. New York: Oxford University Press.

Protzen, J.-P., and D. Harris, eds. 2005. *Explorations in the Pisco Valley: Max Uhle's Reports to Phoebe Apperson Hearst, August 1901 to January 1902. Contributions of the University of California Archaeological Research Facility* 63. Berkeley: Archaeological Research Facility.

Rabinowitz, A. 2015. "The Work of Archaeology in the Age of Digital Surrogacy," in B. R. Olson and W. R. Caraher, eds., *Visions of Substance: 3D Imaging in Mediterranean Archaeology*. Grand Forks: The Digital Press at The University of North Dakota, 27–42.

Roosevelt, C. H., P. Cobb, E. Moss, B. R. Olson, and S. Ünlüsoy. 2015. "Excavation Is ~~Destruction~~ Digitization: Advances in Archaeological Practice," *Journal of Field Archaeology* 40: 325–346.

Tripcevich, N., and S. A. Wernke. 2010. "On-Site Recording of Excavation Data Using Mobile GIS," *Journal of Field Archaeology* 35: 380–397.

van de Guchte, M. 1999. "The Inca Cognition of Landscape: Archaeology, Ethnohistory, and the Aesthetic of Alterity," in W. Ashmore and A. B. Knapp, eds., *Archaeologies of Landscape: Contemporary Perspectives. Social Archaeology.* Oxford: Blackwell Publishers, 149-168.

Wernke, S. A. 2015. "Building Tension: Dilemmas of the Built Environment through Inca and Spanish Rule," in M. Barnes, I. de Castro, J. Flores Espinoza, D. Kurella, and K. Noack, *Perspectives on the Inca: International Symposium from March 3rd to March 5th, 2014. Tribus,* special ed. Stuttgart: Linden-Museum,165–189.

Wernke, S. A., J. A. Adams, and E. R. Hooten. 2014. "Capturing Complexity: Toward an Integrated Low-Altitude Photogrammetry and Mobile Geographic Information System Archaeological Registry System," *Advances in Archaeological Practice* August 2014: 147–163.

Wernke, S. A., and V. Siveroni Salinas. 2013. *Proyecto Arqueológico Tuti Antiguo, Valle del Colca. Fase III: Levantamiento y prospección de los sitios de Mawchu Llacta y Laiqa Laiqa.* Technical report submitted to the Ministry of Culture, Peru.

2.4.
An ASV (Autonomous Surface Vehicle) for Archaeology: The Pladypos at Caesarea Maritima, Israel

Bridget Buxton, Jacob Sharvit, Dror Planer, Nikola Mišković, and John Hale

This chapter seeks to inform the archaeological community about a robotic autonomous surface vehicle (ASV) currently being developed for shallow-water applications in marine sciences and archaeology (Mišković *et al.* 2011, Mišković *et al.* 2013; Vasilijević *et al.* 2015). The ASV Pladypos (a PLAtform for DYnamic POSitioning; FIG. 1) was developed at the University of Zagreb Faculty of Electrical Engineering and Computing, in the Laboratory for Underwater Systems and Technologies (LABUST). Its main characteristic, from which it obtained its name, is dynamic positioning at sea. The Pladypos uses GPS to keep a steady position at a requested location or along transects while actively compensating for external disturbances such as wind, waves, and currents (FIG. 2). The Pladypos can deploy with a variety of cameras and sensors to survey submerged ancient harbors and coastal settlements, or any underwater landscape where current digital recording strategies do not scale well beyond the size of individual shipwreck sites.

The Pladypos was originally developed to answer research needs identified by underwater archaeologists and other marine scientists, and collaboration between the engineers and archaeologists on real field missions was planned from the outset as a means to increase interdisciplinary understanding and identify areas for improvement. Here we present some preliminary results and describe the experience of an interdisciplinary team using the Pladypos to create a georeferenced bathymetric map and integrated photomosaic of the submerged ruins at Caesarea Maritima in Israel (FIG. 3).

Figure 1: The Pladypos ASV at Caesarea Maritima, Israel, in 2014.

Figure 2: The Pladypos following a preprogrammed survey pattern in the intermediate Herodian harbor at Caesarea in 2014; the vehicle's ability to stay on course is not significantly affected by the 0.5 m swell.

Figure 3: Aerial view of Caesarea Maritima.
Image courtesy of the Israel Antiquities Authority.

In 2014, a three-day expedition focused on the task of mapping the submerged breakwaters and interior of King Herod's ancient harbor of Sebastos in Caesarea Maritima (henceforth, we refer to the entire underwater site as "Caesarea"). In 2015, the Pladypos spent two full days in the ancient harbor recording the area of a new ship-wreck discovery. It will return in 2016 to complete its task of mapping approximately 3 km² of Caesarea's underwater archaeological area. The Pladypos can potentially map 10 km² at maximum resolution in an eight-hour work day, and larger areas can be done in the same time span at lower resolution. The three-year duration of our project reflects the fact that our research goals and funding are primarily for technical development and experimental field trials rather than to answer any specific archaeological research questions. The field trials tested the Pladypos' capabilities in a variety of scenarios and sea conditions for shallow-water mapping, and an unexpected opportunity to utilize the robot on an Israel Antiquities Authority (IAA) shipwreck excavation at Caesarea in 2015 further demonstrated the robot's versatility.

The Pladypos began the first experimental merged acoustic and photographic imaging of Caesarea's sunken port structures in May 2014. One archaeological goal of this ongoing mission is to create the first fully georeferenced underwater site map of King Herod's famous harbor with a level of accuracy and detail normally only seen in under-water archaeology in the excavations of single ancient shipwrecks. Achieving centimeter levels of accuracy in recording the architectural features of large Mediterranean terrestrial sites has been the standard for more than a century, so this was the goal we set for the Pladypos in mapping Herod's harbor.

Our longer-term expectation is that by collaborating on real research missions, the archaeologists and engineers will be able to improve the Pladypos' utility for underwater archaeology, with a view to developing the system into an affordable, commercially viable off-the-shelf technology. Based on the Pladypos' performance to date, we eagerly anticipate a not-too-distant future in which highly portable and versatile autonomous robotic vehicles like the Pladypos are fully integrated into the underwater archaeologist's toolkit, and the recording of large and complex underwater inshore sites does not fall short of the established standards in terrestrial archaeology.

DIGITAL ARCHAEOLOGY UNDERWATER

Digital site-recording strategies in underwater archaeology have developed along a different trajectory from parallel advances in terrestrial archaeology. An appreciation of the Pladypos' strengths and limitations requires that we begin with an overview of the current state of underwater site mapping, and understand some of the unique challenges of vehicle localization and accurate site recording in marine environments.

While underwater excavation techniques using dredges and airlifts have changed little in the last 50 years, at least on sites lying within the range of scuba divers, advances in digital photogrammetry for site recording and acoustic sensors for landscape survey have revolution-ized the discipline. Many underwater archaeologists in the field today began excavating at a time when digital photo-modeling was not yet considered trustworthy enough to forego slate and tape measure. Early computer-aided design (CAD) programs came into widespread use in the late 20th century, generating digital reconstructions as an alternative to 2D site maps, but not initially removing the need for tape measures and manual triangulation. Today, massive quantities of spatial data can now be stored and visualized in digital formats, making the printed page increasingly obsolete as a medium for storing and disseminating excavation and survey results. Arguably, only a lingering resistance to digital publication continues to prevent the full potential of the new media from being realized.

Photogrammetry, photo-modeling, simultaneous localization and mapping (SLAM), structured light imaging, multibeam and various other acoustic sensing technologies have all been utilized on Medi-terranean underwater sites in the last decade (Brandon *et al.* 2004; Brandon 2008; Demesticha 2011; Buxton 2012; Skarlatos *et al.* 2012; Drap *et al.* 2013; Scaradozzi *et al.* 2013). It is increasingly common, though not universal, to find underwater archaeologists well versed in the use of CAD and GIS (geographic information systems), and who are able to conduct their own underwater surveys with off-the-shelf oceanographic sensors and imaging software. The digital revolu-tion has had a dramatic impact on underwater recording strategies, enabling archaeologists to think far more ambitiously about seafloor survey. What Mediterranean underwater archaeology currently lacks is any kind of single, widely adopted digital recording standard and toolkit for high-resolution imaging of large sites—that is, those larger than a typical ancient shipwreck, but smaller than a landscape survey area where sidescan sonar alone might provide adequate coverage. For shallow sites on the scale of harbors and submerged settlements, there are as yet no standard tools and conventions equivalent to the total stations and FileMaker databases now in widespread use in terrestrial classical archaeology.

There are many reasons for the divergence between terrestrial and underwater archaeological site recording technologies and strategies. Because of the unique exigencies of the underwater environment, underwater archaeology is the only major academic specialization within archaeology that is defined by an environmental variable rather than a cultural division or category of evidence. This rift is exacerbated by the technological divide between the oceanographic sciences and their terrestrial counterparts, extending even into different protocols for basic data collection. For example, on an oceanographic expedition, the most important organizational baseline for incoming data is often units of time, whereas recording in archaeology is organized by spatial units (though time is increasingly seen as a relevant variable for archaeological recording when site formation processes are considered; Demesticha 2011).

The incompatibility of standard scientific recording technologies and conventions on land and sea is not problematic for most scientists, whose research questions typically exist only in one sphere or the other. For archaeologists, on the other hand, the research questions do not necessarily change whether we are investigating the terrestrial or submerged sections of an ancient settlement, but the resources needed to answer those questions differ in each case. The archaeological investigation of large, shallow coastal sites presents unique challenges that require customized solutions adapted from oceanographic technology.

Unlike on land sites where the tradition of Wheeler squares and the locus system have created linear frameworks for organizing spatial data, the basic measure of detail, if not accuracy, in digital underwater site mapping is the point cloud. A point cloud is the number of data points recorded within a given three-dimensional space defined by x, y, and z coordinates, which represents the external surface of an area being recorded. Underwater, a point cloud is typically created using acoustic sensors, which may simultaneously be collecting data to aid a

Figure 4: Caesarea shore operations base in 2014 (top) and 2015 (bottom).

Figure 5: The Pladypos surveying the intermediate Herodian harbor in 2015.

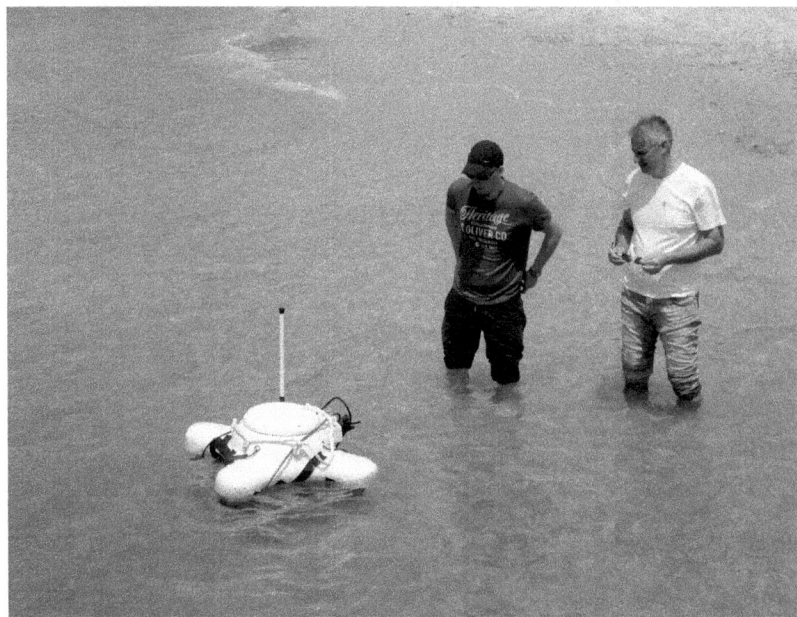

Figure 6: Launching the Pladypos from Sdot Yam beach, south of Caesarea, in 2014.

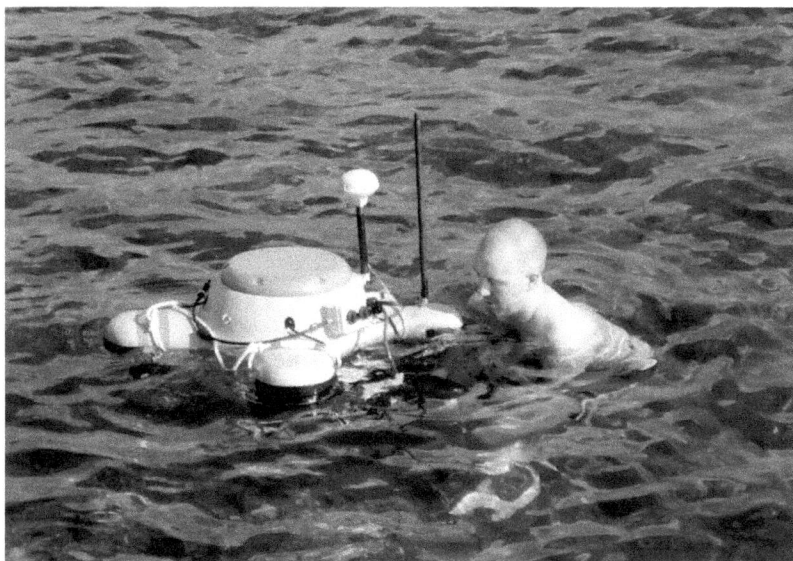

Figure 7: LABUST engineer Nikola Stilinović with the Pladypos in the intermediate harbor, Caesarea (2015).

robotic vehicle's localization. Although the term 3D is often used casually to describe the product of this type of recording, when the point cloud is produced solely from bathymetric data (the relative depth of each point), it is more accurate; as a result, it is gradually becoming conventional to describe the resulting digital models as 2.5D.

The technology required to integrate point clouds and photomosaics to produce archaeologically useful diagrams and publication-quality georeferenced 2.5D maps of underwater sites is exclusive to underwater environments. Because archaeologists typically lack the training or resources to own and operate oceanographic remote-sensing technology or to process the data themselves, producing state-of-the-art underwater site maps can be a costly undertaking. Oceanographic mapping tools are often developed with the budgets and requirements of industry and deep water environments in mind. The shallow coastal regions where archaeological material is concentrated demand different, low-cost solutions.

In these coastal underwater archaeological scenarios, marine robots are not faced with the technical difficulty or high cost of operations found in deep water exploration, but they arguably face a far greater challenge in that they are entering direct competition with highly efficient human divers who are often "free" volunteers. These human advantages start to disappear, however, as the area to be mapped gets larger or deeper and the datasets and high-definition image libraries become so massive as to be unmanageable outside a purely digital recording system. The advantage of deploying robotic drones whenever the mapping task gets too big is also illustrated in Steven Wernke and colleagues' chapter in this volume (Ch. 2.3). The ancient port of Caesarea and its surrounding coastal and submerged features is the perfect example of a site that is simply too big to be recorded to centimeter accuracy by human divers working alone, even with the aid of powerful imaging tools (Brandon *et al.* 2004; Brandon 2008). At the same time, shallow water and good visibility make Caesarea an ideal site to record the seafloor from a surface vehicle.

THE PLADYPOS: TECHNICAL SPECIFICATIONS

The ASV Pladypos surface vehicle was designed for inshore underwater mapping and visualization as one of its primary scientific functions. The Pladypos utilizes a differential GPS to adhere to

Figure 8a: Google Earth image of Caesarea's intermediate harbor with superimposed survey transects (2014).

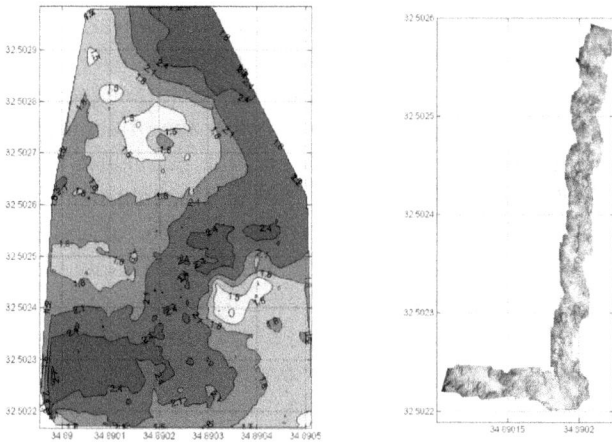

Figure 8b: Sample draft photomosaic produced from the survey area delineated in FIG. 8a.

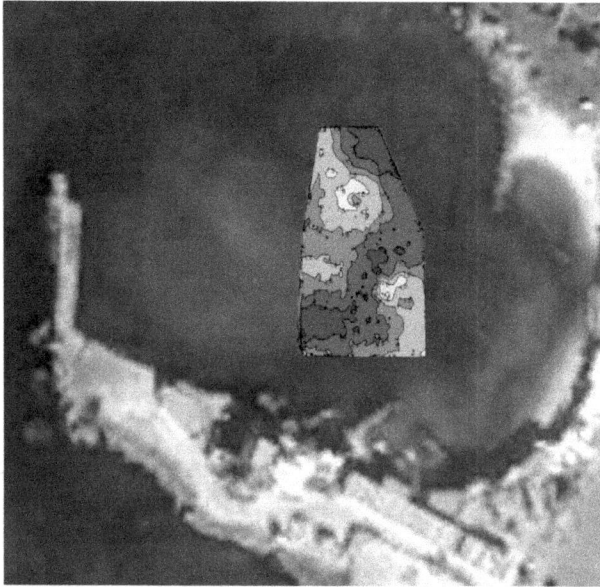

Figure 8c: Bathymetric data collected from the survey area delineated in FIG. 8a.

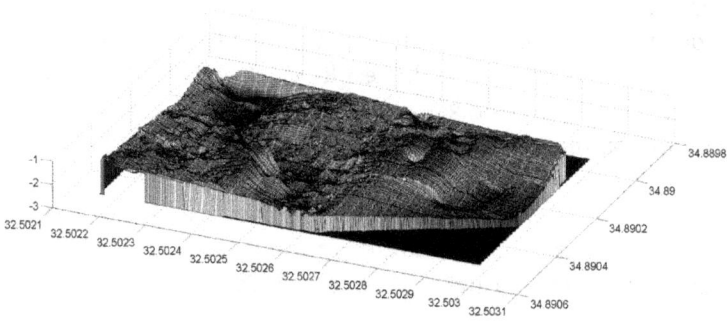

Figure 8d: 2.5D visualization of ancient tower foundations from the survey area delineated in FIG. 8a.

systematic survey patterns with far greater precision than is possible for a human swimmer or even a submersible robotic vehicle (satellite navigation and localization using GPS is not possible underwater). By staying on the surface, the Pladypos can maintain a wireless link for instant communication between the robotic vehicle and the operator on shore (FIGS. 4, 5), unlike the slow acoustic communication channel required to link with an autonomous underwater vehicle.

Also appropriately called an unmanned surface vehicle (USV), the Pladypos can operate either autonomously, following a pre-programmed mission such as a typical "mowing the lawn" survey pattern, or maneuvering under the remote control of a human operator with a laptop (FIGS. 4a, b). The vehicle can switch between the pre-programmed task and direct control on command, and the mission can even be changed once the vehicle is deployed and working on the water. This degree of flexibility and responsiveness is a necessity for an ASV built to operate in dynamic coastal environments where there is more likely to be marine traffic and other hazards.

The Pladypos maneuvers using four thrusters arranged in an X configuration, vaguely though not deliberately resembling its namesake aquatic mammal, and it can move easily in any horizontal direction. The symmetrical design makes efficient use of an onboard battery power source. A simple lead-acid battery may be used, which also provides more options for air-shipping the vehicle. Once it arrives at its destination, another advantage of the Pladypos when compared to many remotely operated vehicles (ROVs) or AUVs is its portability. The Pladypos measures 0.35 m high, 0.707 m wide and long, and it weighs approximately 25 kg without payload. This lightweight design allows the Pladypos to be manually launched and recovered by two people from a beach or jetty, with no need for a winch or a support boat (FIG. 6). In good sea conditions the Pladypos' operations were limited only by battery time and the schedules of the humans waiting on shore.

The basic tool set of the Pladypos includes a number of data-gathering sensors such as mono cameras, stereo cameras, and, in 2015, a high-resolution ARIS multibeam sonar (adaptive resolution imaging sonar) was added to provide higher-resolution point clouds than those produced by the DVL (Doppler velocity log) used in 2014. The Pladypos has a ROS-based architecture (robot operating system; http://www.ros.org) for control, communication, telemetry, and acoustic and optical data logging. The navigation sensors provide a level of localization accuracy within tens of centimeters and consist of 9-axis INS (inertial motion sensor), high-precision GPS, and DVL. The 4-beam DVL (LinkQuest 600) is capable of 5 Hz depth sampling in shallow water, and it generates a point cloud at the rate of 20 points per second. At a cruising speed of 1 knot, the DVL produces a non-homogeneous point cloud density of 40 points per square meter. The DVL is used to measure speed over ground but also to provide depth measurements. For documenting an underwater archaeological landscape extending over several square kilometers, this represents extremely detailed coverage, though improving the point cloud resolution and the efficiency of post-processing software continues to be a goal for the future development of the system.

The control computer (isolated from environmental disturbances inside the Pladypos hull) is in charge of performing control and guidance tasks (dynamic positioning, path following, diver following) and all the data processing. Apart from the compass, GPS, DVL batteries, and CPUs, the Pladypos is equipped with a mono camera for seafloor mapping, an ultra-short baseline (USBL) system used to determine the position of a scuba diver relative to the robot (the anticipated role of scuba divers in Pladypos operations is discussed further below). The USBL is used simultaneously for localization and two-way data transmission via an acoustic link with the scuba diver; a second modem is mounted on a scuba diver when the vehicle is operating as a surface dive buddy. Support for Pladypos operations from the shore station, which may also be set up on a small boat, includes the controller's laptop and laptops for monitoring the vehicle's sensors, along with WiFi antennae and a wireless modem used to transmit data between the Pladypos and the base of operations (FIG. 7).

During the initial sea trials in Israel in 2014, the Pladypos was equipped to collect two types of data: a georeferenced point cloud of the seabed and sunken archaeological features using the DVL, and visual imaging using the Bosch FLEXIDOME IP starlight 7000 VR mono camera, in a custom-made waterproof housing. A GoPro Hero3 camera in a waterproof housing was also taped onto the vehicle to gather additional high-definition color video. The georeferenced point cloud was acquired by following pre-programmed transects across the survey area with a certain amount of overlap to facilitate the fusion of the data.

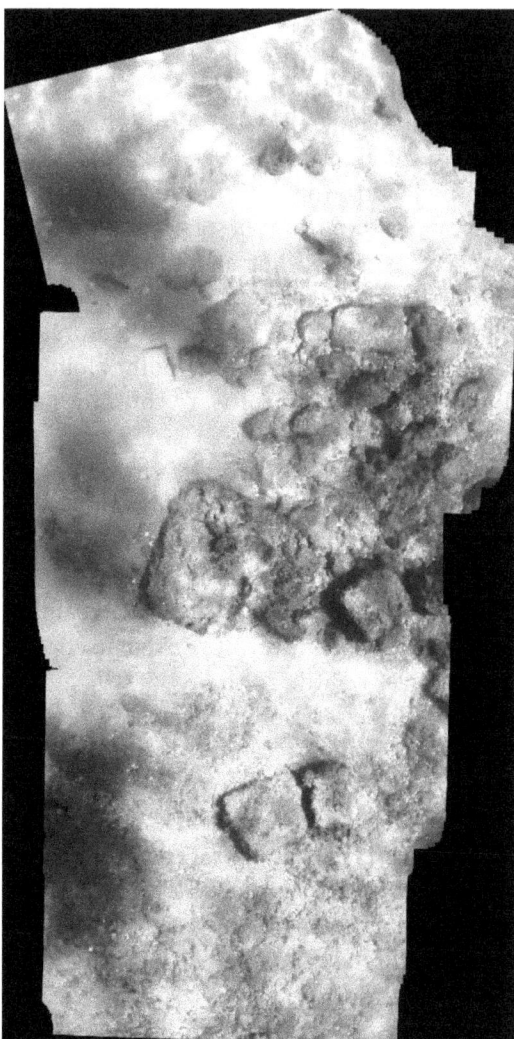

Figure 9: Pladypos photomosaic of ruins from Caesarea's intermediate harbor created with Microsoft ICE freeware (2014).

One of the first requirements of a robotic survey vehicle designed for shallow coastal and underwater archaeology is that it can be ready to launch on a new mission ideally within hours, and it can respond swiftly to changing weather or chance discoveries. Assuming the presence of a trained operator, Pladypos missions can be plotted out relatively quickly using Google Earth (FIGS. 8a, b). Since the Pladypos can be operated either manually (teleoperation mode) or autonomously, the ability to adapt missions that are already in progress when circumstances demand is a very convenient feature. Directing the vehicle manually is as simple as manipulating a joystick or pointing to a GPS destination on Google Earth, and does not require specialist training.

After the issue of cost, which we will return to, the key to integrating the Pladypos into a digital recording system for underwater archaeology that will have widespread appeal is the efficiency and user-friendliness of the software, especially the user interface. In 2014, the Pladypos relied on a custom set of scripts produced by LABUST for the georeferenced bathymetry presentation. Scripts written in MatLab were used to unpack the logged data, to fuse navigation and depth measurements, and to generate 2.5D bathymetry images. For the photomosaic, Microsoft Image Composite Editor (ICE) software was used to stitch together the images, while LABUST MatLab script was used to fuse navigation data with large-scale images (FIG. 9). This data was processed off-line to create a microbathymetry map, and a 2.5D digital model of the survey area was also extracted and created from the same data set. The optical data was then merged with the telemetry data to build a photorealistic model of the seafloor along the survey transects. The main limitation on the amount of data gathered along each transect was the width of the visual field on the downward-facing camera, which naturally varied with the depth of the water.

The most technical part of the operation followed the completion of fieldwork, when the LABUST team set to work stitching together the optical data with Microsoft ICE for the final georeferenced photomosaics. The completed images were then aligned with the telemetry data in subsequent processing. In fact, LABUST has developed software to fuse optical and telemetry data for both image stitching and georeferencing. On the final large-scale, high-resolution site map produced from this process, information such as the absolute

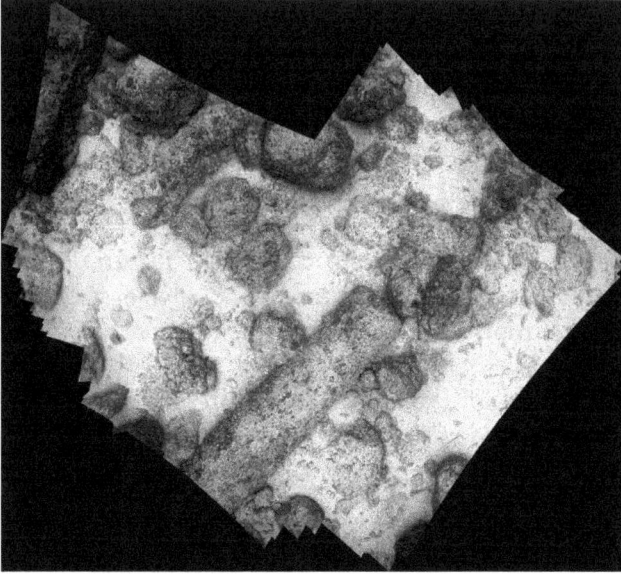

Figure 10a: Pladypos photomosaic of architectural debris in Herod's intermediate harbor, Caesarea (2015).

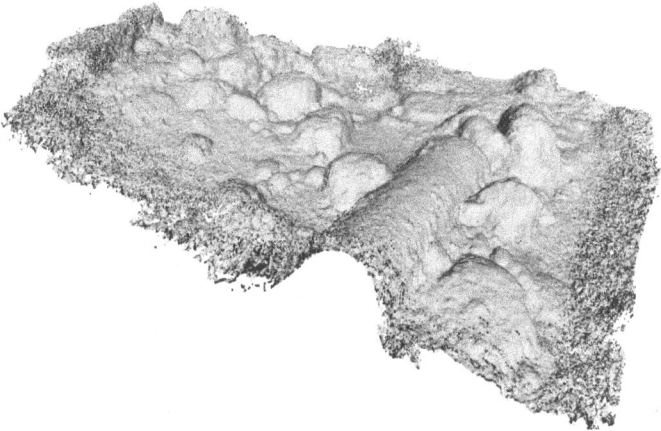

Figure 10b: Point cloud of the architectural debris from FIG 10a.

Figure 10c: Map of architectural debris in Figure 10a from merged video and georeferenced bathymetric data.

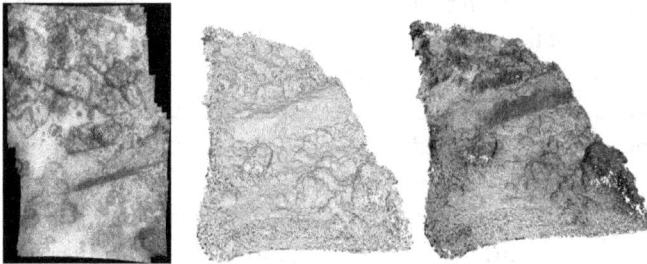

Figure 11: Another example of merged Pladypos photomosaic and point cloud images of submerged architectural debris from Caesarea (2015).

positions of underwater objects and features and their dimensions can be determined within a range of centimeters. In this way, the Pladypos achieves a centimeter-level of precision in small area maps, but it can reproduce this performance on a scale of many square kilometers given time and appropriate conditions.

The choice of Google Earth for the GIS overlay was simple given its universality and ease of use, and also because Google Earth does not treat the land-sea interface as a barrier (FIG. 8c). On dynamic coastal archaeological sites where the visible remains are often changing, being able to visualize the relationship between submerged and semi-submerged coastal features is very important. Observing change over time around the interface of the land and underwater landscapes can help local authorities to monitor erosion and other long-term changes that threaten coastal archaeological sites.

The evolving site map that archaeologists work from in the field is necessarily rougher than the site map produced for a final publication, and the Pladypos preserves this convention by producing "rough and ready" SLAM-generated photomosaics while collecting the data that will eventually be transformed during post-processing into a high-resolution 2.5D map (FIG 8d). Preliminary mosaics were produced on-site at land stations set up on Caesarea's modern breakwater, providing real-time information to the archaeologists. At present, there is scope for improvement in the speed of the high-level post-processing, which required many hours of work by the engineers in the weeks following the conclusion of the fieldwork (see FIGS. 10a, b, and c, and FIG. 11 for examples of the generated results). It is not unusual to wait for weeks or months to obtain processed bathymetric data and photomosaics on oceanographic expeditions, but as a future goal, it is obviously preferable for the required processing from raw data to publication-ready 2.5D maps to be automatic, or nearly so.

Caesarea Maritima

An important goal of the collaboration between the archaeologists and Pladypos engineers was to give the latter a greater understanding of the kinds of research the robot was intended to support. The IAA's important ongoing archaeological work at Caesarea provided this opportunity, giving the engineers first-hand experience of a typical coastal fieldwork environment, and an appreciation of how the archaeologists hoped to use the Pladypos' data.

The first-century A.D. Jewish writer Josephus described King Herod's gigantic artificial harbor at the Judean city of Caesarea Maritima as "a triumph over nature" (*Bellum Judaicum* 1.410–412). The name Caesarea came from the family name of Rome's first ruling dynasty, the Caesars. The actual harbor was technically called Sebastos, after the Greek rendering of Augustus, the first of Rome's emperors and an important political patron of King Herod (d. 4 B.C.). The maritime gateway to King Herod's new city was the largest completely artificial harbor in the Mediterranean world, with breakwaters encompassing over 20 hectares (FIG. 3). Upon its completion in the last decade of the first-century B.C., Caesarea Maritima's port provided one of the Levantine coast's only deep water anchorages (Raban *et al.* 2009).

One of the reasons that archaeologists are eager to have more accurate maps of the ruins of Caesarea's Roman harbor is because it was the most ambitious port construction of its day (Hohlfelder 2007). Caesarea's engineers used hydraulic cement in the creation of the breakwaters, employing a special mortar composed of lime and pozzolana, a volcanic ash imported from central Italy. The scale of the project was beyond even Herod's abundant resources, reflecting the power and wishes of the new imperial government in Rome. The new port helped Caesarea to prosper, and the city soon grew to be five times the size of Jerusalem; it remained one of the most important towns on the Levantine coast until the Muslim conquest. During this time, Caesarea appears to have been damaged by several major earthquakes and tsunamis, though the impact of these ancient disasters on the Herodian port structures is still being investigated (Reinhardt *et al.* 2006). The damage caused by natural disasters has to be set against evidence of the port's decline through simple lack of maintenance and flaws in the original construction (Hohlfelder 2007). Exactly what caused the outer breakwaters of one the ancient world's most magnificent ancient harbors to fall into disrepair even before the end of the first century A.D. is one of the questions that a comprehensive underwater map of the entire port area could help us to answer.

Unlike the archaeologists of the previous century, we can now integrate a vast amount of georeferenced bathymetric and photographic data into a GIS, meaning we are no longer forced to choose between coverage and accuracy in the underwater recording of exceptionally

Figure 12: Before (top) and after (bottom) the storm season at Caesarea Maritima.

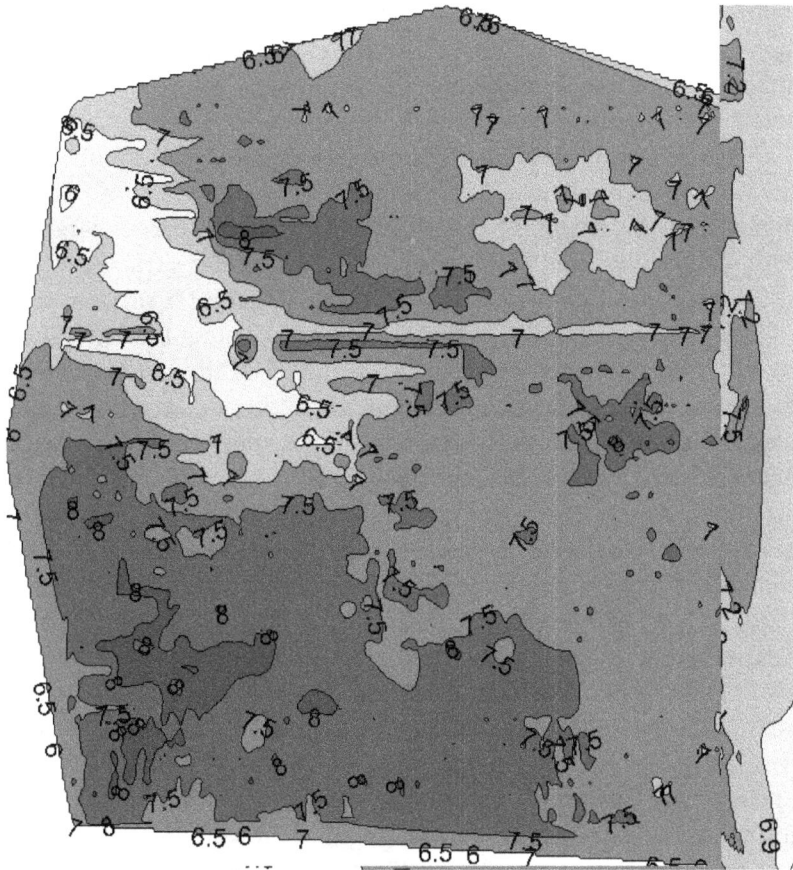

Figure 13: Bathymetric data collected at the site of a medieval shipwreck containing Fatimid coins, near Herod's southern outer breakwater, Caesarea (2015).

large sites. Until recently, however, there has not been an appropriate vehicle for conducting such a large-scale systematic underwater survey at Caesarea that offered a cost-effective improvement over simply integrating local results into a regional plan derived from aerial photographs.

We are certainly not the first team to seek a solution to the problem of how to map the ancient harbor in its entirety. Experiments with earlier digital mapping systems based on PhotoModeler were hampered by variable visibility and the heavily eroded, irregular surfaces of the sunken ruins at Caesarea (Brandon 2008). Underwater site mapping techniques based purely on visual data and photogrammetry, such as that used at the Mazotos shipwreck site off of the southern coast of Cyprus, also require the placement of calibration targets, such as plastic disks or distinctively marked ceramic tiles (Demesticha 2011; Santagati *et al.* 2013). Even on small sites, these targets get moved around in dynamic sea conditions, and the technique is simply not practical for large port structures. Once again, Caesarea is a good example of a well-known and historically important underwater site that has been extensively excavated and studied but never comprehensively mapped because of these challenges.

Today, Caesarea's sunken ruins are the centerpiece of a national park, and the innermost of the three Herodian harbor basins is covered by lawns and restaurants. The scattered remains of the intermediate and outer harbors present an ever-changing puzzle for archaeologists as the open sea regularly uncovers new features and moves or reburies others (FIGS. 12a, b). Israel's winter storms in 2010 were powerful enough to tear down Caesarea's modern rein-forced-concrete breakwaters, and at this point the need for a new conservation assessment of the ancient harbor became clear. Figures 12a and 12b show how environmental changes over the past few years have transformed the appearance of the underwater ruins, in some areas revealing new features that were missed in earlier archaeolog-ical studies. Completing the first georeferenced digital imaging of the entire underwater site of Caesarea will not only help us to integrate the results of previous excavations into a unified up-to-date GIS, but it will also aid the IAA in future planning and conservation efforts.

The 2014 Mission

In 2014, the ASV Pladypos was deployed at Caesarea in a collaboration between the Israel Antiquities Authority and researchers from the University of Zagreb, the University of Rhode Island, and the University of Louisville. Over a period of three days, the Pladypos was manually launched from the shore and travelled under its own battery power to a series of small survey areas, where it mapped the seabed using a combination of downward cameras and a DVL to create a merged georeferenced photomosaic and digital point cloud. The 2014 surveys took place both within and beyond the modern breakwaters in the Herodian harbor, and the foundations of a Roman pier were also mapped at nearby Sdot Yam to the south. When sea conditions allowed, the Pladypos operated out in the open sea, where the water depth and acceptable seafloor visibility extends to approximately 10 m depth in normal conditions. When the sea became too rough, the Pladypos surveyed the ruined foundations of Roman towers in the intermediate basin protected by the modern seawall, an area that ranges in depth from 1–3 m (FIGS. 8a, b, c, d).

Like many of Caesarea's submerged structures, these semi-buried tower foundations are not immediately obvious or comprehensible to a swimmer on the surface. The sand and rubble, however, transform into recognizable architecture when reconstructed as a 2.5D digital image (FIG. 8d). The Pladypos generated a georeferenced microbathymetric map of this area using LABUST's customized MatLab-based software. The data that the Pladypos produces is less like a traditional site-map and more like a scale digital reconstruction of an archaeological landscape. The results are suitable for GIS presentation, for example using Google Earth as shown in Figure 8c. Unlike a traditional paper map, moreover, the Pladypos reconstruction has the same "zoom" functions as the Google Earth GIS framework in which it is imbedded.

The exercise of surveying the tower foundations in the sheltered intermediate harbor, which took little more than an hour, provided a preview of what we could expect from a high-resolution 2.5D map of the entire port. Herod's outer harbor is more exposed and deeper (up to 10 m in places), with a depth range of 3–8 m in most of the area surveyed in 2014. This exposed area out in the open sea posed a greater challenge for the small Pladypos to stay on target while buffeted by wind, waves, and a moderate 1–1.5 knot longshore current. Despite these conditions and Caesarea's infamous surge, the Pladypos held position and continued to collect good data. Three missions were performed along a 250 m stretch of the submerged southern break-water, and the results were merged to create a 2.5D reconstruction and a microbathymetry map. When the open sea became too rough, work in the intermediate harbor continued (FIG. 5).

THE 2015 MISSION

An important lesson of the 2014 Caesarea expedition was that having the archaeologists and robotics scientists working collaboratively in the field resulted in a far greater mutual understanding than if the archaeologists had simply viewed the engineers as technicians providing a service, or the engineers viewed the archaeological mission purely as a field trial. In this volume, the Federated Archaeo-logical Information Management System (FAIMS) team likewise found that ongoing dialogue between the software developers and archaeol-ogists was extremely helpful (see Sobotkova *et al.*, Ch. 3.2). Concepts such as mapping and measuring can have surprisingly different mean-ings across different disciplines, and it was valuable for all involved to have their assumptions highlighted and questioned. An ambitious "to-do" list to enhance the Pladypos' performance and utility from an archaeological perspective was another important result of the 2014 season. One conclusion was that more precise measurement of the depth below the Pladypos would significantly enhance the quality of the photomosaics. For that reason the LABUST group integrated the high-resolution ARIS multibeam sonar onto the vehicle when it returned to Caesarea in 2015.

The Caesarea mapping project resumed in July 2015, though the vagaries of international shipping meant that the Pladypos itself was delayed for a week in Madrid and was only available for two full days of fieldwork on its second visit. During this brief time, however, the Pladypos surveyed or re-surveyed an estimated 60–70% of the inter-mediate Herodian harbor and over 25% of the outer harbor. The ARIS multibeam system generated a high-resolution 3D point cloud of the seabed, in addition to the image mosaic produced by the survey (some results are illustrated in FIGS. 10a-c, 11, and 13). In 2015, the Pladypos' mapping mission took on an unexpected urgency, as Caesarea became the scene of an Israel Antiquities Authority rescue excavation of a recently exposed medieval shipwreck site.

In February 2015, winter storms exposed a scatter of gold coins lying among the rocks in King Herod's outer harbor, where they were discovered by local scuba divers. IAA underwater archaeologists Jacob Sharvit and Dror Planer led the subsequent recovery operation, and over 2,500 coins were retrieved from the surface of the seafloor during the following days. The coins dated from the 10th to 11th centuries A.D. and were minted by the Fatimid Caliphs of Egypt (the Fatimids were an Ishmaili Shia dynasty that ruled the Levantine coast during the early Medieval period). IAA numismatist Robert Kool identified the name of Abu 'Ali Mansur al-Hakim bi-Amr-Allah (A.D. 996–1021) on many of the coins. Al Hakim was the sixth Caliph to rule the Fatimid Empire, and he is a controversial figure revered in the traditions of Israel's Druze community. The presence of medieval anchors near the hoard suggested the coins came from a shipwreck that probably occurred in the period of the 1020s to 1030s.

The likelihood of further storms and wave action destroying the archaeological context of the discovery posed the greatest immediate threat to the site. The accessibility of the shallow site in an area frequented by scuba divers was also a concern. The IAA immediately provided resources for a rescue excavation. The site presented unusual challenges, however, as it had no obvious center or limits, and it consisted primarily of scattered rubble and sand. Such amorphous and complex shapes provide few "hard edges" as spatial reference points and are notoriously difficult to map.

In Israel and other regions of the world where the preservation of a rich inshore archaeological heritage is complicated by a highly dynamic coastal environment, the scenario described above is not unusual. During Israel's winter storms, historic shipwrecks and submerged structures can appear in the coastal surf zone and then be reburied or destroyed within the space of a few days. An unknown number of sub-seafloor sites must experience this fate every winter without archaeologists ever being aware of their existence. Even in the case of the Caesarea Fatimid coin hoard discovery, which, fortuitously, was immediately reported and investigated by archaeologists, the limitations of current technology for underwater site recording and rescue excavations were highlighted. The discovery nevertheless provided an unexpected opportunity for the Pladypos to demonstrate

Figure 14: After the top layer of rocks was removed from the Fatimid shipwreck site in July 2015, a second pocket of gold coins was located using a JW Fisher Pulse 8x metal detector.

Figure 15: Medieval coins recovered from the Caesarea Fatimid gold hoard site, July 2015.

Figure 16: The Pladypos provides real-time diver localization to a GIS on an underwater tablet and relays the diver's typed messages to shore operations (underwater archaeologist Krunoslav Zubcić testing the system on a submerged Roman villa site at Colentum in Croatia).

its ability to create a large high-resolution seafloor map in a rescue excavation scenario (FIG. 13).

After the initial recovery effort removed the most easily accessible coins, the excavation of the Fatimid shipwreck site did not begin until July 2015 (FIG. 14). This delay was deliberate and planned to coincide with the return of the LABUST University of Zagreb engineering team (FIG. 4b). The Pladypos now focused on mapping the area of the coin hoard discovery. The clear, relatively shallow water enabled the Pladypos to obtain approximately half a million high-resolution photographs of the site and the surrounding seafloor in a matter of hours. These fully georeferenced images preserve important information that may not be immediately obvious to human divers searching the rock-strewn seafloor. Confident that no critical information would be lost, the archaeologists were now able to remove rocks along a transect in the area of the discovery, revealing a second substantial pocket of gold dinars in the sand underneath and bringing the total hoard to over 3,000 coins (FIG. 15). It was during this work that a 10 cm-long iron spike was discovered with gold coins concreted to it, providing the strongest evidence yet that the hoard came from a shipwreck. A preliminary photomosaic of the area produced in the field was also available for immediate use by the archaeologists as the work of excavation proceeded.

The Caesarea Fatimid coin hoard discovery provided the perfect illustration of the utility of a robot that can produce a high-resolution georeferenced 2.5D site map of an area larger than a football field in a matter of hours, enabling a rescue excavation to proceed without fear of losing critical data in the rush to recover fragile evidence. However, the experience also highlighted the importance of having the Pladypos on-site and ready to deploy at a moment's notice, not standing by in an engineering lab on another continent. The Pladypos also has a long way to go before it can be an affordable, "ownable" piece of technology that is ready to deploy off the back of a pickup truck without needing a team of four LABUST engineers to operate it. We conclude with some considerations and plans for the future of the Pladypos, with a view to developing a commercially-viable product that end users can own and operate without specialist training.

Conclusions and Future Directions

The recent development of DVL and multibeam systems compact enough for deployment on small USV/ASV platforms such as the Pladypos creates important new opportunities for the recording and monitoring of large shallow-water coastal archaeological landscapes. Using these capabilities of the Pladypos, we are able to meet and even surpass the high standards of accuracy in manual site mapping established by scuba divers in the late 20th century—and this achievement can now be replicated on a much larger scale in a very short time. The rescue excavation of the Caesarea Fatimid coin hoard site in July 2015 demonstrated that the Pladypos could be just as useful for the intensive recording demands of a small-scale rescue excavation as it has been for high-resolution landscape survey at Caesarea, and in other experiments conducted on shallow archaeological sites at Colentum in Croatia (FIG. 16) and Lake Valgjärv in Estonia.

To be as effective and useful as a human diver for the management and excavation of coastal archaeological sites, the Pladypos needs to be able to arrive on the site and be ready to go to work with the same speed as the archaeologists. In 2015, the Pladypos was able to start work overseen from a makeshift operations center within hours of arriving on-site, and it completed its recording tasks efficiently. A minimum of two people were needed to operate the vehicle: one to monitor the robot itself, and the other to monitor and begin processing the incoming data.

It follows that the most obvious area of improvement for future iterations of the Pladypos is not in technical capability, or even the general compatibility of its data products with archaeological conventions, but in "ownability." A function of durability, ease-of-use, and cost, ownability will determine which robotic vehicles and their dependent digital recording systems will ultimately become an everyday part of an underwater archaeologist's toolkit, and which will merely hold a place in the evolutionary process. The first affordable and user-friendly off-the-shelf robotic technology to pass this threshold and come into widespread use within the realm of scientific diving will reshape archaeological methodology underwater in the same way that the evolution of iOS-based paperless systems is currently transforming terrestrial archaeology. From the archaeologist's perspective, the Pladypos will not achieve "ownability" until the entire system

Figure 17: Diver using the underwater tablets (image supplied courtesy of LABUST).

can be purchased for under $20,000, and the graphic user interface (GUI) is intelligible to even the most non-technical user. In addition, the data products (geo-referenced data, videos, still images, and the DVL/sonar point cloud) must be able to be integrated into a GIS by a non-expert user with readily available commercial software, or, ideally, freeware. At this stage, it is difficult to predict when this might happen: we are still in the first phase of establishing proof-of-concept with the Pladypos itself.

To this point we have been discussing operations in very shallow water, which may be defined as the depth at which the seafloor is still visible from the surface for the purpose of creating photomosaics. However, the utility of the Pladypos does not end there, and future missions will develop and demonstrate the vehicle's applications in deeper water. While in some respects the Pladypos' sphere of operations puts the vehicle into competition with human divers, it is more appropriate to say that the vehicle is designed to complement human capabilities. When deployed as a surface dive buddy, the Pladypos integrates human functionality to accomplish tasks in deeper water that would be expensive, difficult, or even impossible for the current generation of underwater robotic vehicles.

As mentioned earlier, the Pladypos is equipped with an integrated ultra-short baseline (USBL) localization system, which it can use to hover above and track a scuba diver with a tank-mounted transponder and battery pack. An acoustic modem maintains a low bandwidth link with the surface, allowing the two-way transfer of email messages, photos, and GIS data between the diver and the land base via an ordinary Android tablet in a waterproof housing designed by LABUST (FIG. 17). Currently the 2014 Samsung Galaxy Note 10.1 is the tablet best adapted for use with the waterproof housing, but its main drawback is that the FileMaker-based applications popular in terrestrial archaeology are not available for Android devices at the time of writing. The popularity of iPads in terrestrial archaeology illustrated by other projects discussed in this volume, and the appearance of a new commercially available underwater casing for iPads, the iDive (http://idivehousing.com/), provide compelling incentives to make the next iteration of the Pladypos compatible with iOS-based technologies.

Using the Pladypos' current system, a diver can access most of the tablet's applications using a modified touch-screen pen (FIG. 17). While the archaeologist gathers data and images from the seafloor using the tablet, the Pladypos collects multibeam data from the surface and relays information to the diver about his or her location on the map, including transect lines and GPS coordinates. In this way, the robot does not lose the ability to produce georeferenced photomosaics at greater depth or in poor visibility: it simply delegates the visual part of the task to a human diver with a tablet computer—or, in another project currently under development, a second autonomous robotic vehicle.

The Pladypos is also intended to enhance diver safety. It can serve as a mobile surface marker for the diver's position (very useful when manually checking sonar targets in offshore live-boating situations), but in future it will also be able to monitor the diver's physical state, duplicating the role of a dive buddy as well as a scientific assistant.

In addition to conducting archaeological research and completing the mission at Caesarea, the over-arching goal of the Pladypos project in Israel is to develop through interdisciplinary collaboration the first universal standard ASV customized to support digital underwater archaeology, and to make it as versatile, robust, and affordable as possible. The brief 2014 and 2015 missions helped the engineering team to identify and address technical issues, and to experience first-hand a real archaeological project environment. The mission itself helped to build mutual understanding of the needs of specialists in two very different fields, as well as improving their ability to communicate productively and work together toward common goals. Importantly, the engineering team were able to leverage their resources and grants for technological development to keep the cost to the archaeologists of the 2014 and 2015 Pladypos deployments under U.S. $10,000 per week.

We view the ongoing Caesarea expeditions as early steps along a path to the full integration of robotic vehicles into all aspects of the underwater archaeologist's work, making underwater research faster, safer, better—and ultimately much more cost-effective. Such a major transformation will require further improvements in the technology, and the culture and methodologies of underwater archaeologists will also need to adapt to the new, fully digital environment. Collaborative field trials, such as the ones described here, help to achieve both goals.

Acknowledgments

The research presented in this paper was performed in the framework of the U.S. ONRG (Office of Naval Research Global) funded project "DINARO" and the E.U. FP7 (Framework Programme for Research and Technological Development) funded project "EUROFLEETS" (grant agreement no. 312762). The authors express their gratitude to the Israel Antiquities Authority (IAA), the Oceangate Foundation, Mr. Steve Phelps, Anonymous Donors, project Diving Safety Officer Eran Rosen, and IAA numismatist Dr. Robert Kool. Many divers helped with the excavation of the Fatimid shipwreck site, and we thank Uzi Dahari, Eyal Israeli, Rami Tzadok, Beverly Goodman-Tchernov, and Yigael Ben Ari from the Israel Nature & Parks Authority, and underwater photographer Hagai Native. Special thanks are due to Israel Hason, Director of the IAA, for providing the budget and support for the excavation and subsequent laboratory processing, documentation, and research. ONRG Visiting Scientist Program grants helped bring the Pladypos and the LABUST team to Israel in 2014 and 2015. All photos and images belong to the authors unless otherwise noted.

https://mobilizingthepast.mukurtu.net/collection/24-asv-autonomous-surface-vehicle-archaeology-pladypos-caesarea-maritima-israel

http://dc.uwm.edu/arthist_mobilizingthepast/13

References

Brandon, C. J. 2008. "Roman Structures in the Sea: Sebastos, the Herodian Harbor of Caesarea," in R. L. Hohlfelder, *The Maritime World of Ancient Rome: Proceedings of "The Maritime World of Ancient Rome" Conference Held at the American Academy in Rome, 27–29 March 2003. Memoirs of the American Academy in Rome Supplementary Volume 6.* Ann Arbor: The University of Michigan Press, 245–254.

Brandon, C., J. Boyce, E. Reinhardt, A. Raban, and M. Pozza. 2004. "Marine Magnetic Survey of a Submerged Roman Harbour,

Caesarea Maritima, Israel," *International Journal of Nautical Archaeology* 33: 122–136.

Buxton, B. 2012. "Underwater Archaeology," s.v., in N. A. Silberman and N. Ashe, eds., *The Oxford Companion to Archaeology*, 3 vols. Oxford: Oxford University Press.

Demesticha, S. 2011. "The 4th-Century B.C. Mazotos Shipwreck, Cyprus: A Preliminary Report," *International Journal of Nautical Archaeology* 40: 39–59.

Drap, P., D. Merad, J. Seinturier, A. Mahiddine, D. Peloso, J.-M. Bo, B. Chemisky, L. Long, and J. Garrabou. 2013. "Underwater Photogrammetry for Archaeology and Marine Biology: 40 Years of Experience in Marseille, France," in *Proceedings of the 2013 Digital Heritage International Congress (DigitalHeritage)*, vol. 1. Piscataway: Institute of Electrical and Electronics Engineers, 97–104.

Hohlfelder, R. 2007. "Constructing the Harbour of Caesarea Palaestina, Israel: New Evidence from ROMACONS Field Campaign of October 2005," *International Journal of Nautical Archaeology* 36: 409–415.

Mišković, N., Z. Triska, Đ. Nađ, and Z. Vukić. 2011. "Guidance of a Small-Scale Overactuated Marine Platform: Experimental Results," in P. Biljanović, ed., *MIPRO 2011: 34th International Convention on Information and Communication Technology, Electronics and Microelectronics. May 23–27, 2011, Opatija, Croatia: Proceedings.* Piscataway: Institute of Electrical and Electronics Engineers, 684–689.

Mišković, N., E. Nađ, N. Stilinović, and Z. Vukić. 2013. "Guidance and Control of an Overactuated Autonomous Surface Platform for Diver Tracking," in *2013 21st Mediterranean Conference on Control & Automation (MED): Conference Proceedings. June 25–28, 2013, Platanias-Chania, Crete, Greece.* Piscataway: Institute of Electrical and Electronics Engineers, 1280–1285.

Raban, A., M. Artzy, B. Goodman, and Z. Gal, eds. 2009. *The Harbour of Sebastos (Caesarea Maritima) in Its Roman Mediterranean Context.* BAR International Series 1930. Oxford: Archeopress.

Reinhardt, E., B. Goodman, J. Boyce, G. Lopez, P. Hengstum, W. Rink, Y. Mart, A. Raban. 2006. "The Tsunami of 13 December A.D. 115 and the Destruction of Herod the Great's Harbor at Caesarea Maritima, Israel," *Geology* 34: 1061–1064.

Santagati, C., L. Inzerillo, and F. Di Paola. 2013. "Image-Based Modeling Techniques for Architectural Heritage 3D Digitalization: Limits and Potentialities," *International Archives of Photogrammetry, Remote Sensing and Spatial Information Sciences* 40(5W2): 550–560.

Scaradozzi, D., L. Sorbi, F. Zoppini, and P. Gambogi. 2013. "Tools and Techniques for Underwater Archaeological Sites Documentation," in *OCEANS: San Diego, 23–27 Sept. 2013*. Piscataway: Institute of Electrical and Electronics Engineers, 1–6.

Skarlatos, D., S. Demesticha, S. Kiparissi. 2012. "An 'Open' Method for 3D Modelling and Mapping in Underwater Archaeological Sites," *International Journal of Heritage in the Digital Era* 1: 1–24.

Vasilijević, A., B. Buxton, J. Sharvit, N. Stilinović, Đ. Nađ, N. Mišković, D. Planer, J. Hale, Z. Vukić. 2015. "An ASV for Coastal Underwater Archaeology: The Pladypos Survey of Caesarea Maritima, Israel," in *OCEANS 2015: Genova, 18–21 May 2015*. Piscataway: Institute of Electrical and Electronics Engineers, 1–6.

Part 3: From Stratigraphy to Systems

3.1.
Cástulo in the 21st Century: A Test Site for a New Digital Information System

Marcelo Castro López, Francisco Arias de Haro, Libertad Serrano Lara, Ana L. Martínez Carrillo, Manuel Serrano Araque, and Justin St. P. Walsh

The Ibero-Roman city of Cástulo, located on the right bank of the Guadalimar River in Spain, was one of the major centers in the south of the Iberian Peninsula during antiquity, as is evident from the extent of its walled enclosure (50 ha) and from its strategic position at the head of the Guadalquivir valley, which leads 250 km to the Atlantic Ocean. The city stood out as a major hub in the road network of its time, and throughout its history it maintained privileged access to the mineral resources of the Sierra Morena. The *oppidum*, or fortified settlement, of Cástulo was initially the most important population center of the Iberian region of Oretania; later it became a Roman *municipium* before finally serving as an episcopal see during the late Roman imperial era (FIG. 1).

Classical authors gave special recognition to the city of Cástulo. Pliny the Elder (*HN* 3.25) described its role during the Second Punic War, and Livy (*Ab urbe condita* 27), Polybius (10.38.40), and Appian (*Iberia* 34) each chronicled the events surrounding the battle of Baecula (208 B.C.), located in the vicinity of Cástulo, which took place between the Roman commander Cornelius Scipio (Africanus) and the Carthaginians under Hasdrubal. Polybius (3.3.37) and Silius Italicus also described the strategic importance of this region for mastering a hold on the Iberian Peninsula and its mineral resources. Hannibal was aware of the importance of this location, and he sought to make a pact for control of Cástulo's territory by arranging his own marriage with the Oretan princess, Imilké. The Romans arrived in the peninsula under the command of the brothers Publius and Gnaeus Cornelius Scipio

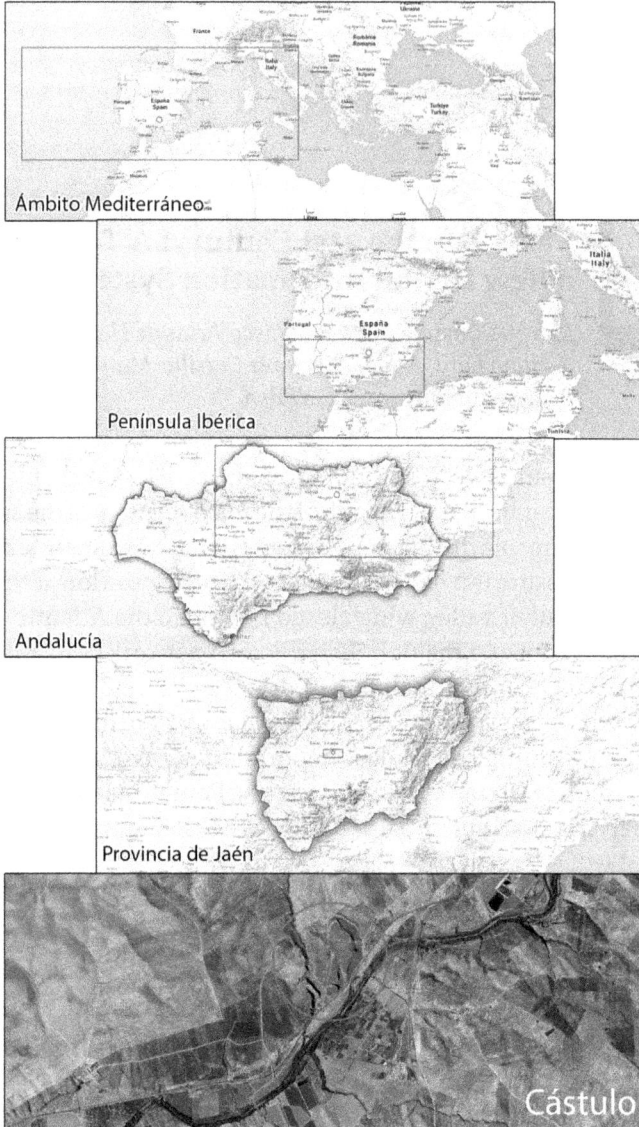

Figure 1: Map of the Iberian Peninsula with increasing level of detail showing the location of Cástulo.

in 218 B.C., and by 214 B.C. they were already showing interest in the mining area of Cástulo. Publius and Gnaeus were ultimately defeated, but Cornelius Scipio Africanus (Publius' son and Gnaeus' nephew) won a victory for the Romans at Baecula, inflicting a bloody revenge on Cástulo's neighbor Iliturgi, and finally earning the surrender of Cástulo. From this point on, the city remained under Roman rule. Strabo (*Geographia* 3.4.2) described how, during the Roman imperial period, when Hispania Baetica (now modern Andalusia) was constituted as a senatorial province, the border of neighboring Hispania Tarraconensis (an imperial province) was purposely arranged so that the emperor maintained direct control of Cástulo. Despite the city's initial faithfulness to the Carthaginian cause, the negotiation of its surrender and its alliance with Rome allowed Cástulo to maintain an unusual political independence, including the right to coin money (Cabrero 1993: 183–196).

In April 2011, the geographic definition of the archaeological site of Cástulo was published in the *Official Journal of the Government of Andalusia* (*Boletín Oficial de la Junta de Andalucía*), and in July of that year a decree formally creating the archaeological site was passed by the Andalusian regional government (http://www.juntadeandalucia.es/boja/2011/155/26). At that time, the excavation project Forvm MMX materialized with a workplan titled, *Location and first characterization of the forum of the Roman city of Cástulo*, intiating the archaeological fieldwork. Forvm MMX is a project of the Institute for Iberian Archaeological Research (University of Jaén), and it is promoted by the City of Linares and funded by the Ministry of Economy, Innovation, Science and Employment of Andalusian regional government. Excavation began in 2011, and permission was granted to continue from 2012 to 2014, with further activity aimed at conservation and upgrading the excavated areas for presentation to the public. These seasons of excavation have revealed two important public buildings from the monumental center of the Roman city (the city's forum has not yet been located in the areas under investigation).

Overall, the data collected indicates that the city built major public works between the first and second centuries A.D., including a bath complex and latrines, which were already known from previous excavations in the 1970s and 1980s. Levels for much of the second and third centuries are scarce, indicating a collapse in political and economic activity during which institutions were located in the earlier public

Figure 2: Orthophoto of the area covered by the archaeological site, representing more than 3,230 ha within the territories of three city councils: Linares, Torreblascopedro, and Lupión. To the northeast (just right of center in this image), next to the river, is the oppidum, or fortified settlement.

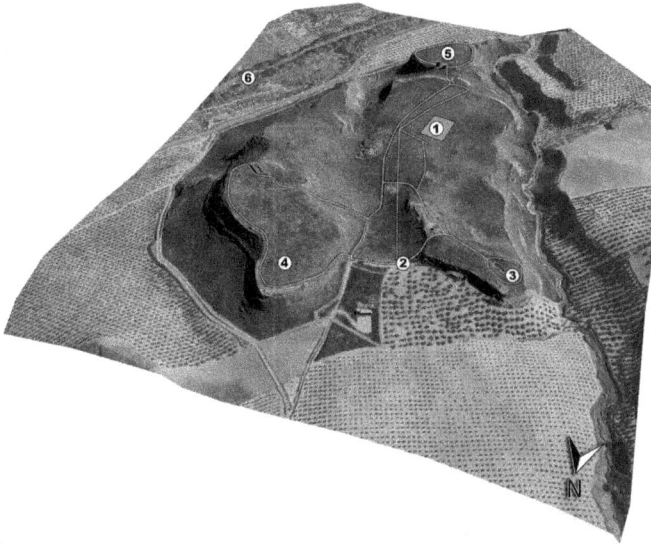

Figure 3: Cástulo oppidum, with the areas of Forvm MMX's major archaeological interventions marked with numbers.

Figure 4: Technology used in the field with Imilké recorder system: digital smartpen, paper form, and smartphone.

architecture. Additionally, an increase of activity in the two areas explored indicates that the city seems to have risen from the ashes once more during the fourth and fifth centuries (Blázquez 1975).

Cástulo's designation only recently as an "Andalusian Archaeological Ensemble" (*Conjunto Arqueológico de Andalucía*) means that the remains recovered so far are somewhat fewer relative to other sites with longer excavation histories; nevertheless our efforts clearly demonstrate the high heritage value of Cástulo and provide a better idea of the work that remains to be done (for further information about the Andalusian Archaeological Ensembles, see http://www.museosdeandalucia.es/cultura/museos/).

STRATIGRAPHY: REGISTRATION AND VIRTUAL DOCUMENTATION

Forvm MMX is an interdisciplinary team whose members come from a variety of backgrounds (e.g., conservation, topography, biology, computer science, public dissemination, education), and whose work will offer open-access results in a digital format to other researchers and educators interested in a holistic global analysis of the documentation generated by an archaeological excavation. Since 2011, Forvm MMX received a total of €1.1 million in funding from the Regional Ministry of Education, Culture, and Sport of Andalusia to hire these specialists and to develop digital techniques. Our project has developed since its initial seasons. Upon reflection on the inner workings of how archaeological information is recorded at all phases of research, we felt it was necessary to develop a unique recording system. This system, named "Imilké" (for the princess of Cástulo), has been designed so that information derived from archaeological excavation is simplified and rationalized (Castro López 2014: 16).

The Imilké system starts from a series of paper forms relating to different kinds of archaeological information, including stratigraphy, objects, and locations. Working in two computer applications, one for the real-time scanning of the paper forms to the centralized database in the laboratory, and a second application that allows further editing of the data from the intranet, the system was designed in collaboration with the private technology company Ayco as a bespoke archaeological register system for Cástulo. The computerization of the data collected on the paper forms is carried out as follows: data is recorded by hand on the forms, which are completed with a smartpen. The pen scans the data from the paper form as it is written and interprets it by OCR (optical character recognition), before sending it to a smartphone. The phone forwards the data via cellular connection and stores it in the database. So, once the pen translates the text into digital form and the smart phone has translated the data, all of the information is instantly available from the database for the consultation, editing, and export for use in other applications (FIG. 4).

The first item of note is our project's emphasis on the documentation and preservation of data while information is being recorded in the field. This is essential because of the destructive nature of archaeological excavation and ephemeral quality of the information. As a result of these problems, the permanence and accuracy required for documentation is clear. This priority forms the basis for all of the assumptions, approaches, and interpretations that define a particular excavation, and the recording system should therefore be designed to be as rational and homogeneous as possible, and modified as often as is necessary (Kimball 2014: 24). Using Imilké, we obtain a highly accurate visual description of the components that form the archaeological context (volumes, surfaces, layers of materials, and object records). This detailed recording also enables further 3D virtual reconstruction.

Of course, our system also allows the digital capture and recording of textual and related graphical information in the field. For this task, several special forms have been designed for recording data such as the type of deposit, the materials recovered, and the excavation process. The first type of unit defined is the "volume." A volume is a three-dimensional unit defined by horizontal coordinates (x, y), with levels associated with the vertical (z). The form distinguishes between four different types of volumes: (1) surface level, (2) division by a complete construction of the space, (3) division of space by a wall, or, finally, (4) a conventional and arbitrary excavated area of space. The second type of unit defined on a form is the "stratum," a unit into which volumes are divided, and which itself can contain different subunits, referred to as "levels." For each of the registered levels it is possible to add an image and to record its universal transverse mercator (UTM) coordinates, which are taken using a total station. Later, through GIS, those UTM coordinates allow us to recompose the puzzle in Imilké's virtual model, using the parts we have measured to create a three-dimensional model of a volume.

Recording Visual Information

In our project, we use the following photogrammetric process for data capture and information processing. The data capture method is fast and simple; for every area excavated it is sufficient simply to take several photographs of the area. The photographer moves around the perimeter of the trench, taking photos in sequence. The same procedure is repeated each time the excavation level is changed (i.e., when a new stratum or volume is identified). The greater the number of pictures taken, the more information the 3D model will have, but we must also bear in mind that this will generate a larger file. Following the data capture, the pictures are then processed with Agisoft Photo-Scan software (http://www.agisoft.com). During this process, the images are sent to the server where a 3D model is then generated. The process can take minutes or hours depending on the size of the photographs taken and sent to the server. This software also allows for previewing the generated 3D model.

The visual documentation that has been generated in the field (such as photographs taken in a determined area and turned into a 3D model) can also produce 2D visual documentation (such as accurate scale drawings of trench plans and stratigraphic profiles) from a 3D model of the volume selected. This represents a quantum leap in the quality of visual information preparation, as the usual method is the reverse (creation of 3D reconstructions from time-consuming excavation profile or plan drawings).

Using photogrammetry, we are thus able to create 3D models of every excavated stratigraphic unit. These are integrated into the database using GIS, which gives universal access to them in a virtual form and allows users to understand stratigraphic relationships and their interpretation directly on a geographical virtual model of the archaeological site. The UTM coordinates associated with every stratigraphic unit (inside every volume) facilitate the use of a site map in the Imliké's GIS database (Supplemental Material 1).

ARCHAEOLOGICAL ARTIFACTS:
REGISTRATION AND VIRTUAL DOCUMENTATION

Archaeological artifact records are divided into either three-dimensional records or individual records. Using a form designed specifically for them, three-dimensional records are spatially linked to the volume that contains them; this kind of form also determines the type of content and treatment of materials and it is possible to add pictures of the process, details, and/or results at any time during the excavation process.

Individual records, by contrast, are reserved for objects that are thought to be particularly significant, such as complete vases found in situ. The form for individual records for artifacts contains the same information as the three-dimensional records, but with the difference that in these tables the object's exact position has been marked in order to be able to reproduce it later; hence, we assign $x/y/z$ coordinates.

The artifacts are processed in various stages as they make their way through the project: conservation, cataloging, drawing and photography, publication, and didactic use. We have multiple goals that are achieved through the use of 3D recreations. These models obviously enable greater study and public dissemination of cultural heritage, but they also help us improve our conservation activities. For example, they reveal the state in which the artifact appeared during excavation and initial treatment. A model can therefore be used as a point of comparison with the conserved object at a later date, during or after treatment, and if, by some chance, damage to or loss of the object occurs, the model can even serve as a record of it.

Our 3D models form part of the database's "catalog card" as an interactive PDF document and, like all of the system's data, the models will be available for study and research by future archaeologists (the models will be made available at http://www.europeana.eu/portal/ and http://3dicons-project.eu/eng/About). Our analysis collects all possible data about the item, starting logically from an archaeometric and morphological definition, along with a topological analysis. Both analyses are essential for the development of a particular and general chronology, indicating the object's relationship with other nearby materials and its archaeological context. We thereby enable an exhaustive archaeological analysis of the object, including all the data needed for interpretation. Nonetheless, we are aware of some complications related to certain kinds of data, such as texture, weight, and measurements that are to be specified in the interactive "catalog card." We have therefore not yet made our prototype catalog cards public in the 3D PDF format and are instead waiting until we can develop them to an appropriate degree (Supplemental Material 2).

On 27 October 2011, the European Commission made a recommendation to all European Union member states in which some objectives and deployment advice for digitization and preservation of cultural heritage were included. The digitization of more than 30 million objects, including great European masterpieces that are no longer restricted by copyright, is promoted by this policy and by a project called CARARE (http://www.carare.eu/) (D'Andrea *et al.* 2013: 163). In related policy documents known as the "Principles of Seville" and the "London Charter," cautionary recommendations regarding the creation and use of virtualized cultural heritage were put forward (see http://www.londoncharter.org/introduction.html). These documents noted that the possibilities offered by visualizations for public outreach activities might yield "spectacular" results, however, they can also become obstacles to the sense of research and scientific rigor required from a digital record of archaeological items. Following principles laid out by the London Chapter, therefore, we never edit the artifact mesh obtained by photogrammetry in order to produce "nicer" (but ultimately inaccurate) results.

Our working practice focuses on interdisciplinary approaches to the 3D models. The modeling team consults with the restoration and cataloging teams to reach their conclusions regarding the artifact before we start developing and editing the model in Blender or SketchUp open-source 3D modeling suites (http://www.blender.org/manual; http://www.sketchup.com). We decide whether it is possible to reconstruct the artifact (and if, e.g., it is an interesting architectural component, whether it could be worthwhile to restore it as part of a virtual building). We also consider whether the 3D artifact could form part of a study of how to deploy virtual light and shading, and whether we might be able to create a presentation in which a hypothesis for the function or use of artifacts could be tested (Escriba Esteban and Madrid García 2010: 14). Our public dissemination efforts are not intended to replace an exhibition of the real artifacts in our museum in the city of Linares, but they are rather intended to create a virtual experience that forms part of the museography designed for presentation in the interpretative center at the archaeological site itself, or online as part of a website.

The ability to link literary and planimetric data, the infinite possibility of modifying hypotheses, and the proximity and force a virtual model can exert on the public are some advantages of virtual archaeology. But as a synthesis we share Rabinowitz's sentiment that "a good surrogate is not merely a copy: it is supposed to provide, in some sense, access to the original, now made ubiquitous and opened for inspection on a level of detail that the original itself might not allow" (Rabinowitz 2015: 29).

That the virtual model can serve as a surrogate for an artifact is particularly advantageous when it comes to matters of restoration. The digital visualization of archaeological artifacts can show the possible results of restoration of a piece prior to actual intervention on it and allow for different approaches for future treatment at a higher level of detail than traditional restoration methodologies that work directly with the physical object. Virtual models and reconstructions are indeed beneficial, as we note here, but they can never replace the ultimate goal: the preservation and exhibition of the artifact (Roof Sebastian 2005: 135). Our ideas about virtual restoration work are clearly articulated by Aparicio Resco (2015) when he states: " . . . las reconstrucciones virtuales nos permiten planear con mayor cuidado las reconstrucciones reales y nos dan la posibilidad, posteriormente, de imprimir en 3D los fragmentos perdidos para incorporarlos a nuestra pieza durante la restauración real, otorgando a este proceso una precisión mucho mayor que si fuera realizado con un modelado manual" ("virtual reconstructions allow us to plan actual restorations more carefully, and give us the possibility, later, to print the missing parts in three dimensions so that we can incorporate them during the actual reconstruction, giving the process a much greater precision than if it were done with manual modeling") (Supplemental Material 3).

With regard to the public dissemination of applications of "virtual archaeology," our process offers similar advantages of speed and accuracy as those found in our documentary archaeological study. Data and visualizations can be publicized using different social networks, meeting scientific expectations, and entertaining at the same time, and they can thereby awaken the interest of the public, who, in general, enjoy and value cultural heritage (Tejado Sebastián 2005:

Figure 5: The application of augmented reality to display an artifact: a 3D view of the paten from Cástulo created using a smartphone app, as demonstrated at the 20th Congress of the International Association for the History of Glass. 2015, Switzerland.

Figure 6: Oculus Rift experience displayed during the International Feria of Tourism, Madrid, 2015.

Figure 7: Detail of the "Mosaico de los Amores" from the second-century A.D. public building discovered in 2012.

147). For example, we use the Sketchfab platform for opening and displaying 3D models (see https://sketchfab.com/forvm_mmx), and we use YouTube to document the virtual reconstruction process (see https://www.youtube.com/user/forvm2010).

Finally, we are particularly interested in the possibilities represented by this format as a powerful motivational tool for art history and archaeology students since it allows us to customize our emphasis on the scientific content of the virtualized artifact, depending on the educational level of those students (Chysanthi and Caridakis 2014: 169-175) (Supplemental Material 4).

Augmented Reality and Virtual Reality Experiences

Overall, the virtual documentation of archaeological remains and artifacts obtained through photogrammetric techniques has facilitated the processing of information for scientific interpretation while allowing the creation of a basis for public dissemination of documented archaeological remains. Modeling 3D documentation of the archaeological remains with Blender or SketchUp software has allowed the development of different hypotheses about the areas of the site under investigation, thus facilitating interpretation and allowing the general public to interact with them through virtual reality experiences and augmented reality (FIGS. 5, 6). Virtual reconstructions of archaeological remains have been exported to the FBX format for use in Unity 3D, where reconstructed virtual environments can be developed for augmented-reality applications, such as using the Vuforia plugin to display different scenarios on the archaeological remains themselves through mobile devices like tablets or smartphones.

We offer an immersive approach to the history of the city of Cástulo using Oculus Rift, a virtual-reality headset. For example, users can take a tour of the major public building where the second-century "Mosaico de los Amores" was discovered in 2012 (FIG. 7). Through this format, visitors are brought in direct contact with the mosaic's extraordinary technical work and iconographic complexity (the "Mosaico de los Amores" is now available for further studies with millimeter-resolution through the GigaPan web platform at http://gigapan.com/gigapans/129300). The other major artwork recovered by the project, a glass paten showing Christ in Majesty, can be observed in Oculus Rift, allowing an approach to its findspot with a virtual flight through the 3D model of its "volume," as well as a virtual recreation of the paten, one of the earliest and best-preserved examples of Christian art yet known from the Iberian peninsula.

POTTERY STUDIES: PRE-INVENTORY

The Imilké system is also useful for collections management. It generates a unique QR code for every single artifact in the database, including all pottery (an example of a QR code to document a pottery sherd and the virtual recreation of the whole form of the pottery sherd is accessible at https://sketchfab.com/models/8bb762e5c0054f-3ba0af4b6eb1090b20; see also Martínez Carrillo *et al.* 2010: 117). The code is attached to the fragment (and a context QR code is placed in and on each set of pottery or other artifacts, in case the object code becomes detached from individual sherds), allowing for instant iden-tification of any object and its relationship to the site. The typology of each ceramic fragment is documented and we calculate the total weight of the pottery set (classified by type), giving us a comprehen-sive picture of it.

CONCLUSIONS

Our system has a variety of benefits. In addition to its technical capa-bilities for research, it is also inexpensive in economic terms. Once the system is implemented, the only requirements are a cellular-data connection and the maintenance of computer equipment, so it can be extended to the vast majority of archaeological operations. In short, the development and consolidation of this system aims at creating a tool for use in the future work in the archaeological zone of Cástulo, with the longer-term goal of achieving consistency of documentation recording in excavations more generally.

High technical skill is clearly a highlight of the Forvm MMX project, but we also have a desire to continue to experiment and focus on public outreach. Therefore, our approach in the work of public dissemina-tion is to create a new (virtual) experience that allow a closer approach to the ancient city of Cástulo through the archaeological objects found in it. We hope to create a more active, participatory encounter with the past through the use of online platforms such as Sketchfab, YouTube, and others. The virtual recreation of housing spaces and 3D models of artifacts and transects have almost become sensory elements for visitors through the experience of site reconstructions using an Oculus Rift viewer. As with the rest of the methodology outlined in this chapter, the objectives of public dissemination have been improved by new technologies, which, at the same time, "improve" our ability to create a final documentation of the archaeological process. It is our goal that the results obtained have a sufficient level of standardization to permit the use of the same archaeological recording system by other future teams.

https://mobilizingthepast.mukurtu.net/collection/31-cástulo-21st-century-test-site-new-digital-information-system

http://dc.uwm.edu/arthist_mobilizingthepast/14

References

Aparico, P. 2015. "Restauración virtual de escultura: fotogrametría y diseño 3D al servicio del Patrimonio." *PAR Patrimonio y tecnologia*, 20 January. https://parpatrimonioytecnologia.wordpress.com/2015/01/20/restauracion-virtual-de-escultura-fotogrametria-y-diseno-3d-al-servicio-del-patrimonio/#/h

Blázquez, J. M. . 1979. *Cástulo II: Excavaciones arqueológicas en España.* Madrid: Ministerio de Cultura.

Cabrero, J. 1993. "Relaciones entre una ciudad provincial y el poder romano: el caso de Castulo," *Universidad de Valladolid Hispania Antiqua* 17: 183–196.

CARARE: http://www.carare.eu/

Castro López, M. 2014. "FORVM MMX nos ha convocado," *Cástulo en Movimiento, 7 esquinas: Revista del Centro de Estudios Linarenses* 6: 7-9.

CATA PROJECT: http://cata.cica.es

Chysanthi, A. and G. Caridakis. 2014. "The Archaeological space via visitor movement and interaction. A hybrid computational approach," in C. Papadopoulos, E. Paliou, A. Chrysanthi, E. Kotoula, and A. Sarris, eds., *Archaeological Research in the Digital Age. Proceedings of the 1st Conference on Computer Applications and Quantitative Methods in Archaeology*, Greek Chapter (CAA-GR), Rethymno, Crete, 6–8 March 2014. Institute for Mediterranean Studies – Foundation of Research and Technology, 169-175.

D'Andrea, A., F. Niccolucci, and K. Fernie. 2013. "3D-ICONS Metadata Schema for 3D Objects," *Newsletter di Archeologia CISA* 4: 159–181.

Escriba Esteban, F., and J. A. Madrid García. 2010. "El mundo virtual en la restauración: Aplicaciones virtuales para la Conservación Restauración del Patrimonio," *Arché: Publicación del Instituto universitario de Restauración de Patrimonio de la UPV* 4 and 5: 11–20.

Kimball, J. L. 2014. *3D Delineation: A Modernisation of Drawing Methodology for Field Archaeology*. M.A. thesis, Lund University. Lund: Lund University Libararies.

Martínez Carrillo, A. A. Ruiz Rodríguez, and M. Á. Rubio Paramio. 2010. "Digitalización y visualización 3D de cerámica arqueológica," *Virtual Archeology Review* 1.2: 117–120.

Rabinowitz, A. 2015. "The Work of Archaeology in the Age of Digital Surrogacy," in B. Olson and W. R. Caraher, eds., *Visions of Substance: 3D Imaging in Mediterranean Archaeology*. Grand Forks: The Digital Press at the University of North Dakota, 27–42.

Roof Sebastian, J. M. 2005. "The 3D Scanning and Archaeological Prototype: New Technologies in the Registry, Preservation and Dissemination of Archaeological Heritage," *Iberia* 8: 135–158.

Tejado Sebastián, J. M. 2005. "Escaneado en 3D y prototipado de piezas arqueológicas: Las nuevas tecnologías en el registro, conservación y difusión del patrimonio arqueológico," *Iberia* 8: 135–158.

3.2.
Measure Twice, Cut Once:
Cooperative Deployment of a Generalized, Archaeology-Specific Field Data Collection System

Adela Sobotkova, Shawn A. Ross, Brian Ballsun-Stanton, Andrew Fairbairn, Jessica Thompson, and Parker VanValkenburgh

[W]hen people use [mobile devices] they end up just using technology to consume things instead of making things. With a computer you can make things. You can code, you can make things and create things that have never before existed and do things that have never been done before.

That's the problem with a lot of people . . . they don't try to do stuff that's never been done before, so they never do anything, but if they try to do it, they find out there's lots of things they can do that have never been done before.

Russell Kirsch, 20th-century computing pioneer (Runyon 2012)

Archaeologists face an immediate, fundamental decision once they decide to digitize field data collection: put together a solution from several pieces of general-purpose, usually proprietary, software aimed at the commercial market (often supplemented by continuing use of paper); commission a bespoke mobile application tailored to their specific project; or use one of the growing number of "generalized," often open-source, platforms designed specifically for archaeological fieldwork. Generalized software allows deep customization, adapting to the user's approach and procedures rather than requiring than the user adapt to the software, while still being designed specifically for archaeology. Examples of open-source, generalized (or at least highly customizable) software developed with archaeological data in mind include the Archaeological Recording Kit (ARK; http://ark.lparchaeology.com/; see also Dufton, Ch. 3.3), Heurist (http://heuristnetwork.org/), and the subject of this paper, the Federated Archaeological Information Management Systems (FAIMS; http://faims.edu.au/) mobile platform. Bespoke applications can meet the particular requirements of archaeological fieldwork, but producing and maintaining them exceeds the resources of almost all projects or institutions. Commercial data-entry applications offer lower barriers to entry (although it remains resource-intensive in the long run), but they adapt poorly to the exigencies of the field and require archaeologists to make many compromises. Generalized, open-source tools designed for field research bring the advantages of bespoke software within reach of "typical" projects.

Perhaps more importantly, generalized tools also allow archaeologists to *participate* in software development, not merely consume software. Such co-development involves a partnership between field archaeologists and a software development team. This partnership can ease the transitions from paper to digital fieldwork, illuminate the advantages digital approaches offer, and ensure that software is fit-to-purpose. Its benefits and rationale are analogous to those of Open Context's model of "data sharing as publication," where data editors collaborate with data creators (Kansa, Ch. 4.2). In this paper, three project directors who co-developed and deployed a FAIMS recording system in collaboration with the FAIMS team report their experiences. Having first-hand experience of co-development, they reflect on the challenges and benefits of working with the FAIMS project team to produce a customized implementation of a generalized field recording system.

THE FAIMS PROJECT

The FAIMS project is a university-based, e-research initiative that was launched in 2012 to develop national, domain-wide information management infrastructure for archaeology and related disciplines (Ross 2013, 2015; Sobotkova *et al.* 2015). It was initially based at the University of New South Wales, Sydney, and funded by a grant from the Australian National eResearch Collaboration Tools and Resources (NeCTAR) eResearch Tools program (RT043; AUD $949,500). In consultation with Australian and international archaeological communities, the FAIMS project developed a generalized, mobile, offline, multi-user collection platform for structured, free-text, geospatial, and multimedia data (the "FAIMS mobile platform," discussed below), which entered public beta release in November 2013. The project also supported enhancements to the Heurist online data refinement and analysis service developed at the University of Sydney, and established an Australian implementation of the Digital Archaeological Record (tDAR; https://www.tdar.org/), an online data archive developed by Digital Antiquity. In 2014, the FAIMS project received an Australian Research Council (ARC) Linkage Infrastructure Equipment and Facilities (LIEF) award (LE140100151; AUD $945,000 total ARC funding and university co-investment), allowing a second phase of development that emphasized field deployments of the mobile platform at partner universities, three of which are presented in this paper. Experience from these deployments informed ongoing development of FAIMS software, resulting in the release of FAIMS 2.0, the current production version, in November 2014 (FIGS. 1, 2). The project moved to Macquarie University, Sydney, in January 2015.

The sustainability plan of the FAIMS project involves iterative applications for research infrastructure funding, primarily through the ARC LIEF program. LIEFs are matching grants that require partner organizations (primarily universities) to contribute approximately one-third to one-half of the total budget. Universities that commit cash to a LIEF receive a commensurate amount of support from the FAIMS project; the two Australian projects discussed in this paper fall into this category. This infrastructure grant income is supplemented by fees charged for customization, field support, server hosting, and other services (a typical open-source business model; cf. Raymond 2001: 136; Popp 2015); the United States–based project discussed here paid for services directly. To that end, we encourage research projects that plan to use FAIMS to include an appropriate budget line in their grant applications. To date, fees have accounted for about 5% of the FAIMS budget, with infrastructure grants constituting the other 95%—although these figures exclude in-kind contributions of time by academic staff and other participants, which, for example, total approximately $100,000 per year at Macquarie University alone. We envision that within five years, service fees will constitute perhaps 25% of our budget, but the project will likely remain largely

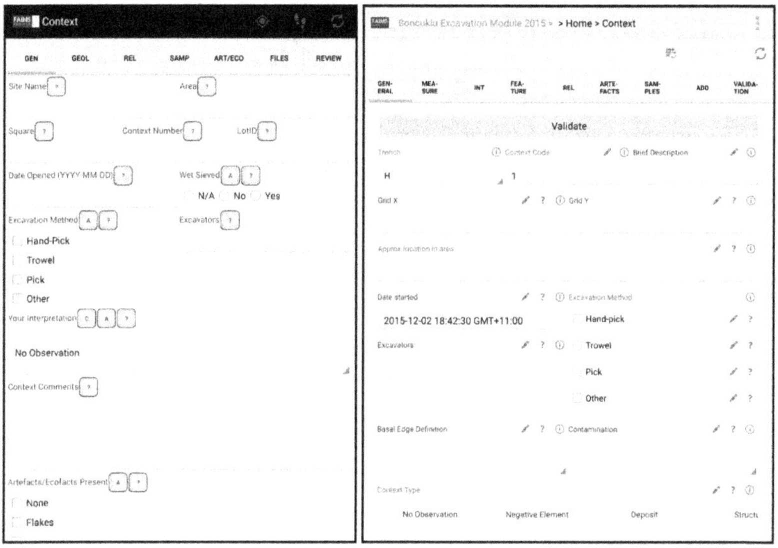

Boncuklu 2014 Module: Context Tab   Boncuklu 2015 Module: Context Tab

Figure 1: The "Context" tab in the Boncuklu excavation module in 1.3 and 2.0 version of FAIMS on Nexus 7 and Nexus 9, respectively, showing improvements in interface design.

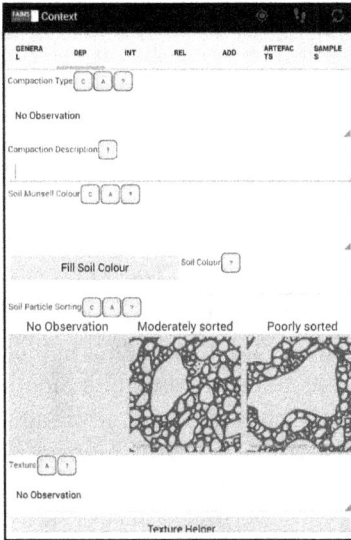

Boncuklu 2014 Module: Deposit Tab   Boncuklu 2015 Module: Deposit Tab

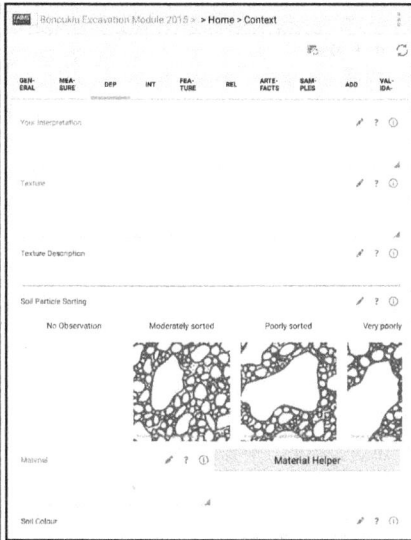

Figure 2: The "Deposit" tab in the Boncuklu excavation module in 1.3 and 2.0 version of FAIMS on Nexus 7 and Nexus 9 respectively, showing differences in the rendering of picture dictionaries, annotation and certainty icons, module path and indicator bar.

dependent upon infrastructure grants and in-kind contributions. This funding allows the FAIMS project to employ a professional software engineering team (as well as student programmers) to ensure that our software meets high standards and avoids some of the shortcomings often associated with academic software (which often remains a prototype, built to run on specific infrastructure at a particular time, making it fragile and difficult to reuse in new contexts; cf. Sun 2012; Might 2015).

The FAIMS Mobile Platform

The "core" software of the FAIMS mobile platform does a lot of the "heavy lifting" required of archaeological software: automatic synchronization of data among multiple users, maintaining record histories for review and reversion of changes, backup, data export, internal and external sensor management, and provision of a mobile GIS. Since FAIMS is generalized, however, it has to be customized for each project. Such a "deployment" involves tailoring the core software by creating or modifying "definition documents," primarily Extensible Markup Language (XML) files, which produce customized data collection "modules" (Ross *et al.* 2015). Each module accommodates specific data and workflow requirements, as required by different approaches to archaeological survey, excavation, and artifact processing. So, for example, the "Boncuklu excavation module" is an implementation of FAIMS customized for single-context recording method as it is practiced at the excavation of a Neolithic tell in Turkey (see below).

The FAIMS project uses GitHub, an online version control tool for collaborative software development, to publish and manage individual modules (https://github.com/FAIMS; cf. Ross *et al.* 2015). Software or other text documents stored on GitHub can be downloaded, edited, copied, and adapted at will. As an example, in 2013, the FAIMS team developed a "deluxe excavation" module, which provided the foundation for the three deployments discussed here (Boncuklu Höyük in central Turkey, the Malawi Earlier-Middle Stone Age Project (MEMSAP), and Proyecto Arqueológico Zaña Colonial (PAZC) in Peru). This module was duplicated ("forked") and modified to meet the needs of each project. Using GitHub not only made the definition documents for all four modules (the original plus the three adaptations) publicly available, but it also allowed for the most useful changes to each of the derivative modules to be incorporated ("pulled") back into the original "deluxe excavation" module. Users can now choose whichever of these four modules best fits the requirements of their own fieldwork (the three customized modules can be found in the Supplementary Material folder). It has been a guiding principle of FAIMS to build a growing library of modules that accommodate as many archaeological activities, and variations of them, as possible.

Customizing and Deploying the FAIMS Mobile Platform

The Mobile Platform consists of an Android mobile application (available on Google Play) and a Linux server (available on GitHub). All FAIMS project software is free and open source (GPLv.3 license). The mobile software will run on most recent Android devices (current specifications are available from http://www.faims.edu.au/). The server either can be a local, physical computer or can reside online. Users with the time and expertise can implement FAIMS themselves, or they can purchase that service from the FAIMS team. Two small projects, both undertaken by doctoral students, have successfully customized and deployed their own systems. Most users, however, have chosen to purchase customization and support services from the FAIMS team; to date, we have created 19 workflows for 17 projects and supported 11 of them in the field since the public release of our software in November 2013. That number is likely to double by the end of 2017.

Users can establish a local or online server themselves by installing Linux (specifically, the most recent Long Term Service release of Ubuntu) and executing a few commands to download and install the FAIMS server software. Once in the field, the server is essentially an appliance that synchronizes devices and performs automatic backups, requiring little attention. Users only access the server (via a Web interface from any other device on the network) to adjust controlled vocabularies, manage users, view record histories and revert changes, export data, and perform other administrative tasks. For those new to the system, the FAIMS project offers temporary, pre-configured, online servers for trials at no cost.

For users who want to purchase a pre-configured server, the FAIMS project has established relationships with vendors in Australia and the United States who can provide and support local or online servers. Purchasing a pre-configured local server with all necessary hardware

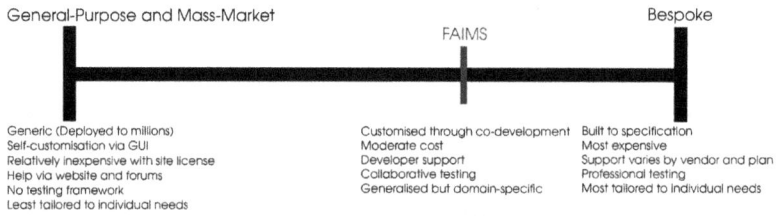

General-Purpose and Mass-Market   FAIMS   Bespoke

Generic (Deployed to millions)   Customised through co-development   Built to specification
Self-customisation via GUI   Moderate cost   Most expensive
Relatively inexpensive with site license   Developer support   Support varies by vendor and plan
Help via website and forums   Collaborative testing   Professional testing
No testing framework   Generalised but domain-specific   Most tailored to individual needs
Least tailored to individual needs

Figure 3: The spectrum of customization options.

costs AUD $1,700–$3,500 from one of these vendors (excluding tablets). Alternatively, an online or local server can be leased for approximately AUD $150–$200 per month. In the case studies presented below, Boncuklu and MEMSAP purchased preconfigured local servers, while PAZC used an online server (but later switched to a local server in a subsequent season).

After the establishment of a server, do-it-yourself users can customize the mobile application for their own work in four ways, which require progressively more effort and technical expertise, but also allow more nuanced control over the resulting module:

1. Reuse an existing module as-is, which requires only downloading the application from Google Play and selecting the desired module from a list;
2. Use Heurist (an online data service), which provides a graphic user interface for the generation of definition documents (suitable for relatively simple modules);
3. Use a simplified module generator, which requires writing a single XML file that generates definition documents (suitable for modules of moderate complexity);
4. Modify an existing module, or create a new one, by editing the definition documents directly, which requires proficiency with XML and BeanShell (a scripting language).

The FAIMS project has developed extensive documentation to assist users who want to establish their own server and customize their modules using any of these approaches (https://www.fedarch.org/support/#2), which was improved recently through a 2015 NeCTAR grant specifically targeted at user support. The project team provides free support on a time-available basis.

Thus far, however, most users have approached the FAIMS team for customization services, including those in the case studies presented here. In such cases, we employ a combination of the third and fourth methods described above, automating whatever code generation we can to reduce development costs, while maintaining fine-grained control over data structures, user interfaces, and automation where necessary. When a project hires the FAIMS team to adapt an existing module or develop a new one, this service generally costs approximately AUD $1,500–$15,000 per season for the mobile platform, depending on the complexity and novelty of the recording system required. Deployments of a module for subsequent seasons are usually less expensive because users only pay for changes and support. Customization and support work for the Boncuklu and MEMSAP projects presented here, for example, was valued about $15,000 each for their first year of deployment (but only $3,250 for a subsequent deployment for Boncuklu). Because the PAZC project was willing to reuse an existing module, their first year cost only $900 (a subsequent deployment cost $2,400, after they identified some additional modifications), illustrating the savings that redeployment can offer. These costs include support for the duration of fieldwork and assistance with data export (we fix bugs and other errors at no additional charge, but users pay for significant in-field changes and priority support). As will be seen below, customization and support costs of this magnitude can be largely recouped from later savings in data digitization and reconciliation, aside from any other benefits of digital recording (cf. Spigelman *et al.*, Ch. 3.4). Finally, the FAIMS team also offers development-in-trade for in-kind help with testing, documentation, and other activities to students, another common practice in open-source communities.

It is our hope that by building free and open-source software to high standards using research infrastructure funding, by providing extensive documentation and as much support as possible for do-it-yourselfers, by building a library of modules for various activities, and by offering customization, deployment, and support services at a reasonable cost, we can deliver purpose-built field-recording software to projects and organizations who otherwise could not afford it.

BETWEEN OFF-THE-SHELF AND BESPOKE SOFTWARE

Software development strategies fall along a spectrum (FIG. 3). On one end are consumer-grade, "general purpose," desktop database management systems (DBMS) with graphical user interfaces, which put "simple" customization into archaeologists' hands. At the other end sits bespoke software development, where archaeologists (for example) request features they want, as they would select cloth from a high-end tailor making a custom suit, and software developers produce a tailored mobile application from scratch.

FAIMS lies near the middle of this spectrum. Compared to a general-purpose DBMS, FAIMS is "generalized" in the sense it has no predetermined data schemas or user interface, instead offering a degree of control over data structures and forms similar to DBMSes like Microsoft Access or FileMaker Pro. It is not general-purpose, however, in that it has been purpose built to perform well under difficult field conditions and includes functionality specifically requested by archaeologists (through stocktaking activities, cf. Ross *et al.* 2013). As a result, for a customization effort similar to that required by a general-purpose DBMS, researchers get software optimized for archaeological fieldwork.

For illustration, one example of a fieldwork-specific feature is the capacity of FAIMS to synchronize across many devices in a degraded-network environment. Most DBMSes store data on a single server that can be accessed by many clients. Mobile applications also typically use this architecture, which is simpler and has performance advantages. These applications, however, expect a regular—if not continuous—connection to a server. Archaeological fieldwork frequently suffers from intermittent or disrupted network communications. To accommodate these conditions, devices running FAIMS have no need for a continuous connection to maintain data integrity; they happily operate offline and synchronize whenever a Wi-Fi network is available (according to configurable rules). The FileMaker application and DBMS, conversely, have been designed for more "normal" deployment situations, and they operate grudgingly in a network-degraded field environment, requiring work-arounds when asked to collect data simultaneously on multiple offline devices. An example of such work-arounds regarding synchronization and offline use is seen with FileMaker:

> For real-time access to the most up-to-date information, host solutions with FileMaker Server. For this option, purchase of concurrent connections is required along with access to a local wireless or cellular network. Or to share your solutions offline, copy files to FileMaker Go using iTunes File Sharing, email or AirDrop (FileMaker 2015).

Keeping a change history and managing geospatial data are even more difficult. It does not make sense for FileMaker to optimize for these unusual conditions, as they require significant trade-offs in complexity and performance, and return benefits only in specific and limited situations. FileMaker was designed for everyone; FAIMS was developed around the expressed requirements of archaeologists to manage the high-friction environment of fieldwork.

FAIMS offers similar optimization for other issues specific to fieldwork, such as the need to collect a variety of data, work in multilingual settings, and promote the production of compatible datasets for large-scale, synthetic research. FAIMS tightly binds the diverse data fieldwork generates (e.g., structured, free text, geospatial, and multimedia), connects to internal and external sensors, allows tracking and reverting changes to the data, supports customizable data export in a variety of common formats, translates the interface between languages or conceptual vocabularies, and maps local concepts to open, linked-data vocabularies (thus promoting both syntactic and semantic data compatibility; cf. Limp 2011: 277–279; Wallrodt, Ch. 1.1). These fieldwork-specific capabilities get inherited by each module; they need not be newly programmed upon user request. They are all there waiting on users to take advantage of them (or not). This combination of flexibility and domain-specific features is what makes FAIMS "generalized."

A bespoke Android or iOS app, *if properly resourced and designed*, may outperform FAIMS for any *single* data collection task, but at considerable cost. The requirements gathering, planning, development, and testing required to produce software reliable enough for field archaeology are expensive and demanding. Even after development is "complete," software has significant maintenance costs such as bug-fixing and keeping up with the biennial mobile OS update cycle (not to mention updates to other components of the software "stack" that underlies every application). These development and maintenance costs are beyond the resources of all but the best-funded projects and organizations, such as is iDig, created by the Athenian Agora Excavations of the American School of Classical Studies (http://idig.tips/; cf. Fee, Ch. 2.1). Because the core FAIMS software is common to all deployments, however, the fixed costs of development and maintenance can be shared across many users, projects, and institutions. Improvements that benefit all users can be made incrementally as resources come available. This shared core library also allows customization and deployment to be accomplished more quickly than bespoke development. A generalized, but fieldwork-specific, application has the potential to attract a large enough user base to sustain it (cf. Kansa, Ch. 4.2).

THE NATURE OF CO-DEVELOPMENT

Participating in open-source development is different from buying software from a vendor. There are responsibilities, trade-offs, and significant benefits. Instead of purchasing a finished product, which can either be accepted or rejected, open-source tools can be re-invented and co-developed to fit specific needs. As a generalized platform, FAIMS must be customized by the researchers who use it. This co-development increases the likelihood that individual projects will achieve their goals, but it also requires archaeologists' active participation and willingness to reconsider information management during fieldwork.

Developing a data capture and management system for an archaeological project using FAIMS constitutes a miniature software deployment project. To an extent, the same is true of development using desktop DBMSes like Microsoft Access or FileMaker, but FAIMS is perhaps more transparent about it, in that development is accomplished through editing text files rather than manipulating a graphic user interface. The apparent ease of development provided by mass-market DBMSes seduces users into thinking that information systems can be built and maintained with minimal investment or technical expertise. Eventually, however, even desktop DBMSes require considerable scripting to accommodate archaeological workflows. As a result, the landscape is littered with half-finished or abandoned databases created using desktop systems (including, admittedly, several built by some of this paper's co-authors). Because the software development looks easy, projects under-resource it.

FAIMS treats complex archaeological work with the seriousness it deserves. The FAIMS approach, partly dictated by the nature of the software and partly by our experience, has us treat each deployment as an authentic, miniature software development project that requires proper "scoping" (requirements gathering, software design, and development planning), coding, and "quality assurance" (testing at each step of development to ensure that software works and is fit-to-purpose). As such, the authors believe that our experience also offers lessons to those who choose to customize commercial DBMS software.

THREE CASE STUDIES AND THREE THEMES OF OBSERVATION

The three FAIMS implementation case studies presented here include: (1) a Neolithic tell excavation in central Turkey, (2) a Middle Stone Age excavation and surface survey in Malawi, and (3) a late Prehispanic/ early Colonial excavation in coastal Peru. Three researchers, one from each case-study site, generously offered to share and discuss their experiences deploying FAIMS during 2014 fieldwork. They took the time to complete post-project questionnaires, and also exchanged many emails and chat messages with the FAIMS team before, during, and after their fieldwork. These sources provide the quotations below; their complete, unedited communications with the FAIMS project are available via the digital supplement to this volume (see the files contained in Supplementary Material 1: "Fairbairn: Boncuklu Case Study"; "Fairbairn: Chat Log.pdf"; "Thompson: Malawi Case Study"; "VanValkenburgh: PAZC Case Study"). Their observations can be woven into three themes, demonstrating common challenges, concerns, and benefits shared across all three projects.

Andrew Fairbairn, an Australian Research Council (ARC) Future Fellow and Associate Professor at University of Queensland (UQ), co-directs excavations at the Neolithic tell of Boncuklu Höyük (Boncuklu) in central Turkey (Baird *et al.* 2012; http://boncuklu.org/). About his site, he wrote:

> One peculiarity of the site is its extremely fine layering and the complex intercutting of archaeological features, caused by rebuilding of houses on the same site time and time again. . . . [a single context in] Boncuklu may be resolved within <5 cm of deposit. . . . As a result, excavation has necessarily been fine-grained, utilising a single context recording method better to understand the subtle interrelationships of the site's building sequences and extra-mural areas. Single context recording describes each deposit, cut and feature in detail, including spatial coordinates and contexts (artefacts, samples) as well as basic descriptives (form, size, etc).

Jessica Thompson, then an ARC Postdoctoral Research Fellow also at UQ (now an Assistant Professor at Emory University), directed the

Malawi Earlier-Middle Stone Age Project (MEMSAP), which included excavation and pedestrian survey (Thomson *et. al.* 2015; http://memsap.org/). Of their project, she wrote:

> MEMSAP based its excavation recording system on a single-context form-based system modified from Marean *et al.* (2010). Given the range of backgrounds represented on the project, it was desirable that the recording protocols contain as many checks and constraints as possible, but also that there was ample opportunity to freehand any observations that may not fit into one of the pre-designated categories.

Parker VanValkenburgh, then an Assistant Professor at the University of Vermont (now an Assistant Professor at Brown University), directed the Proyecto Arqueológico Zaña Colonial (PAZC), a multidisciplinary project focusing on late Preshipanic and early colonial Peru that includes excavation (VanValkenburgh 2012). He wrote:

> In our 2012 field season at Carrizales, PAZC team members recorded data using a single-context recording system on paper forms. We also drew orthographic illustrations on large-format millimetric graph paper and captured digital photographs of the tops and bottoms of each excavated context.

THEME 1: UPFRONT COSTS, BACKEND PAYOUTS

One of the themes that emerged from these case studies involves the shift in time and energy from digitization and cleansing of data at the end of the project, to scoping, development, and testing of recording systems at the beginning of the project. Even considering the up-front time requirement, however, time savings at the end of the project were substantial—even revolutionary; an entire season's data could be retrieved immediately, without tedious digitization and the errors it inevitably introduces (cf. Spigelman *et al.*, Ch. 3.4).

Scoping and Development

Requirements gathering, planning, and development is a lengthy, iterative process that requires frequent communication, consultation, and feedback. Established projects with stable procedures have an advantage during software customization, since they can articulate requirements and priorities quickly and coherently. Even so, field projects with complex workflows still require several months for development to ensure that the end product satisfies their needs. Thompson commented on the numerous discussions and feedback loops she engaged in during module scoping and prototype testing:

> Prior to the field season, the FAIMS leadership team met with several of its partners at UQ, including those involved in MEMSAP. . . . Several hours were spent in discussions with all senior project personnel to ensure that all data types they wanted recorded were represented in the modules, and then after the workshop detailed plans for the tab layout and controls were developed mainly by the project leader but in consultation with other project personnel. . . . Ultimately only three iterations of the excavation module and two iterations of the survey module were needed before a functional system could be deployed in the field. However, this was likely because all of the data categories and relationships had been worked out—in paper version—over the course of previous field seasons.

Converting from paper to digital workflows is an involved and time-consuming process. It requires making the implicit knowledge embedded in paper forms explicit. Digital forms are also more formalized and restrictive than paper forms; relationships between entities, controlled vocabularies, and other aspects of the data model must be defined and encoded (cf. Gordon *et al.*, Ch. 1.4; Motz, Ch. 1.3, who had to write full protocol manuals to ensure users understood their data model). Paper forms can approximate the desired data collection strategy, with exceptions, omissions, and edge cases written in the margins or on the back of the form. Despite some FAIMS features like the "annotations" field embedded in all attributes where users can make contextual notes, which reproduce the freedom of the paper page (cf. Ellis, Ch. 1.2), digital forms must be more precise and complete, or their primary advantage—the production of clean, consistent data—is lost. The conversion from fuzzy paper forms to sharp digital recording often instigates a thorough review and revision of existing recording procedures and workflows. Fairbairn noted the benefit of this revision process:

> In the process of defining the parameters of the future FAIMS module I also got the opportunity to thoroughly review and refine the Boncuklu recording system to the last field and attribute, which identified some redundancies and allowed better definition of the attributes expected in the system.

The critical resource during software development is time, which may be allocated to scoping, to developing new features, to improving performance, or to testing, bug fixing, and ensuring fitness for purpose. Since time is a finite resource, these activities must be balanced against one another. At some point, the archaeologist must finalize their data model—their list of entities, attributes, and vocabularies—so that development can end and testing may begin, with enough time to fix and finalize the module before fieldwork starts. The "perfect" module may be a moving target, and the perfect can become the enemy of the good. Sometimes we should settle for good, but imperfect, software to do fieldwork. In order to collect useful data while controlling the time spent on scoping and development, Fairbairn recommends:

> Consider your recording needs in depth well before deployment of your module and learn to articulate those needs explicitly. Time is money and imprecise, poorly articulated demands increased the developers' time on this module. Provide precise instructions and well-articulated aims to your developers.

VanValkenburgh followed this advice, and his module was produced quickly:

> The total time that elapsed between first contact with FAIMS leadership and deployment of the finished PAZC module was approximately three and a half weeks.

The PAZC module also benefited from reusing the Boncuklu module with some modifications (emphasizing the advantages of an open source, document-based customization strategy: modules can be rapidly modified and redeployed, while each new module or modification improves the whole system). The FAIMS team translated the Boncuklu module into Spanish and customized it where required by editing the Boncuklu definition documents, a process that required less than one week after the requirements were fully specified. The speed of production was possible because of VanValkenburgh's pragmatism and willingness to adapt an existing module. As this example illustrates, a system with a generalized core can spawn new deployments rapidly in a way that neither bespoke nor general-purpose systems can.

Testing and Training

> To test, or not to test—that is the question: Whether 'tis nobler in the mind to suffer the slings and arrows of crashes and incorrectly implemented features or to allocate development time against a sea of trouble tickets and by opposing end them. To ship, to commit no more—and by shipping we end normal development and the thousand emails that development is heir to.
>
> Brian Ballsun-Stanton (after a late night of bug-fixing)

Software development requires that scoping, programming, and testing be finite, limited, and in balance with one another. In the FAIMS experience, archaeologists tended to prioritize the development of new features at the expense of testing. This is hardly surprising, as feature development is exciting and novel, as opposed to the rote, but essential, work of testing. While feature planning is rewarding and creative, it must be kept in check, and it cannot outrun the resources available for ensuring performance, quality, and fitness to purpose: "Testing the module prior to fieldwork ensured it was technically functional, and allowed for communication of changes that would be hard done remotely" (Thompson).

All project directors tested their modules ahead of fieldwork, but eventually they all regretted not doing so more thoroughly, with more participants, and in more authentic situations.

Thompson realized the shortfalls of her own testing only when she was in the field:

> Once in the field the use of modules revealed other usability issues that varied across the team. Simulation of fieldwork is highly advised here. Or better yet, training a project novice in the use of the module is where potential misunderstandings (of the workflow) become apparent.

Fairbairn, too, found a problem of fitness-to-purpose on the first day of fieldwork that had slipped through his earlier testing: "A significant problem with the app design has arisen. It is one that I flagged earlier but somehow it got through my later checks . . .". Fairbairn's module had to be updated while live in the field. Live updates, designed for situations like this one (where a problem is identified after deployment) can be useful (cf. Fee, Ch. 2.1), but they pose risks of failure due to the lack of testing and should be avoided.

Hardware can cause its own problems, such as device-specific bugs. Software that worked during internal testing by the FAIMS team (or even by archaeologists prior to fieldwork) did not always work on different tablets, even if they were made by the same manufacturer. These compatibility problems are the price paid for the wide range of devices offered within the Android ecosystem. It therefore proved necessary to test the FAIMS mobile platform on each device. Fairbairn explained the importance of specific and realistic testing:

> Test your module and, if you are using multiple tablets, the server and its system extensively before you depart for the field with real data including every field and recording type you may use; bugs may be hard to find and you need to be sure the system works for your needs.

Several months may sound like a long time for complex module development, but for a typical software development project it is a very short timeframe. While the FAIMS approach of customizing generalized software can produce recording systems faster than bespoke software development (Kitchenham *et al.* 2002), the modules still require extensive testing. The amount of testing necessary is a product of the complexity of the module, the degree of automation and flow logic it incorporates, and other features like GIS integration, translation, or multimedia file management. The rigor of testing determines the quality of the fieldwork experience and resultant data, which from the perspective of the FAIMS team, make it worth a significant investment of everyone's time.

The Payoff: Clean, Granular, Digital Data

After fieldwork, the FAIMS team asked each of the project directors to reflect on the design, development, and deployment of their module, and tell us what they found the most worthwhile payoff for their efforts.

Fairbairn appreciated having his data available to him shortly after the end of fieldwork, especially the ease of export into the desktop software he normally uses (Microsoft Access). He received his comma separated value (CSV; a standard spreadsheet-type format) data files and created an Access database from them, all in the time before the paper forms (used as a backup to FAIMS as part of the transition to digital recording) arrived at Australia:

> [I have received the CSV file and] the data are present and useable. I am now waiting for [the other project director] to send me the forms . . . (excerpted from Google Hangouts between Brian and Andrew Fairbairn, 18 September 2014)

VanValkenburgh enjoyed the "richness and integrity" of digitally-born data:

> [. . .] our final review of data collected by the PAZC in 2014 suggests that using FAIMS improved both the richness and integrity of our data. Context descriptions are generally more detailed, and the range of fields in the FAIMS default module meant that project members recorded types of data (such

as parameters of soil matrices and inclusions) that we had formerly treated in an inconsistent fashion.

Thompson agreed, noting the benefits would accrue over multiple field seasons:

> The FAIMS data outputs [. . .] required [. . .] much less cleaning, organization, and streamlining for consistency than transcribed data. [. . .] However, it was clear that once this initial hurdle was overcome it would be far faster and error-free to append FAIMS data from subsequent seasons onto these merged databases than to return to a paper form recording system.

The data management benefits were especially clear in the MEMSAP survey team's change of opinion over the quality of survey data when collected with tablets. Thompson emphasized the improved consistency of data and the value of having various types of data (structured, geospatial, and image) automatically linked, something that is difficult to implement with general-purpose database software:

> When the survey data were examined and analysed during post-season work, it became very clear to the survey team that the tablets presented a huge advantage. During post-processing all the data were tied together already and did not require the manual integration of paper forms with separate photo logs and GPS records—nor did they suffer from the inevitable transcription error that in this case cost at least six person-hours to investigate and rectify. There were fewer errors made in data recording with the tablets, and the pre-defined categories made the data far easier to sort, search, and analyse. When the scope of data entry, cleaning, analysis, and archiving is considered, the tablets saved at least eight person-days of work, although this may have been an extreme case because one of the main post-season challenges [during previous seasons] was the integration of both paper and tablet data into a single database.

Fairbairn also quantified the time-savings and cost-benefit of clean, born-digital data to his project:

The greatest gains in the FAIMS system were found after the excavation season was finished with post-processing of the data and checking taking 2–3 hours in comparison to several hundred hours for entry of the >300 context records generated in a typical season. This saving in paid RA time equates to c. AU$5,000–10,000 per annum. Post-processing required specialist input by FAIMS to extract CSV files from the data tarball [.tar, a common Linux file archive similar to .zip], but the outcome was easily accessible and useable data which can be uploaded to a database. In the Boncuklu case the CSV tables did not match the legacy database, however, some relatively quick (0.5–1 day) [edits] ... allowed the data to be uploaded. The benefits to the excavation project in financial/labour terms are hugely significant, equating to a total of 1–1.5 days of handling time using FAIMS against 25–30 days when not in use per annum, in other words a 95% labour saving.

Finally, Fairbairn discovered an unexpected benefit of having his digital data available immediately: the timely discovery of errors. "I also can see all the inconsistent entries that were made by people who should know better." His data was digital and ready for review promptly at the end of the season, which revealed problems that would otherwise have gone undetected until the paper forms were digitized—perhaps months later—when the errors would have been far more difficult to correct. Even when digital data creation does not prevent errors, it exposes them.

While many projects prefer to collect data first and spend effort cleaning it later, our partners chose to invest effort before fieldwork, in order to have cleaner, richer data for immediate analysis. Learning the capabilities of FAIMS software and engaging in the scoping and testing required by co-development all took more time before fieldwork than producing paper forms would have. After fieldwork, however, they got rich, well-structured data at the push of a button, while errors and inconsistencies in the data could be detected immediately rather than during later digitization or processing. Fairbairn and Thompson could readily quantify the savings in time and resources this trade-off produced; based on their experience, most projects would likely come out ahead.

The Importance of High-Quality Support

Exceptional support is necessary when deploying new technology in the field, especially software that is purpose-built for the research community (Fisher *et al.* 2010). Only the availability of high-quality and timely support can provide the peace of mind necessary for archaeologists to risk moving from commercial software to new systems designed specifically for our domain. The FAIMS team's provision of such support proved crucial to the success of field deployments. To date, the FAIMS project has provided support as part of the module development package.

Thompson makes the importance of support very clear:

> The app has been such an incredible advantage in terms of workload, data quality, and a number of other data management issues with which archaeologists regularly have to deal. It readily links disparate data types that are otherwise stored separately—such as photographs, tabular logs, and context relationships. I can see this user-friendly app being easily transferrable to other projects, and the support team has been brilliant. The hardware system was also quite remarkable in the way that it collected data, then synced and backed it up daily. Even projects like ours where we have no electricity on site can use the setup as long as there is power back at the home base. There were the usual start-up bugs, but the FAIMS team has already done an immeasurable amount of work to remedy all of them. From this already very exciting start, I can only see the FAIMS initiative becoming even more of a boon to archaeologists everywhere.

From the perspective of the FAIMS team, the biggest challenges were (1) communicating with archaeologists in remote locations, and (2) reproducing software errors back at our office. The stochastic nature of communication across time zones, often using unreliable channels, hampered technical support. Instruction in the effective reporting of bugs and other problems was also necessary, especially from remote locations under the stress of fieldwork. Once identified and reproduced by the FAIMS team, bugs were quickly fixed, unclear workflows were explained, and alternative paths around design shortcomings were developed—but accurately reporting problems so that they can be reproduced is an acquired skill.

Over time and with use, software becomes more mature, and fewer bugs and problems arise. Developers and users can also cooperate to produce documentation that gradually replaces live support. For the innovators and early adopters introducing new technologies to complex projects, however, there is no substitute for patient, timely, and comprehensive support from developers.

THEME 2: TRADE-OFFS AND SHARED LESSONS

The shared responsibilities of developers and researchers are perhaps clearest in the context of the trade-offs between features and performance that must be made during the production of a field recording system. Each of these choices can have serious consequences when the final system is put under the stress of a full deployment. Two seemingly minor decisions, the use of complicated autonumbering, and the choice between local and online servers, offer examples of such trade-offs.

Legacy Features vs Performance:
How to Auto-Generate Smart Context Numbers

One of the major deployment challenges the FAIMS team experienced was archaeologists' requirement that FAIMS reproduce complicated context numbering schemes. These numbers did more than identify a context, they also encoded multiple pieces of information about it. Archaeologists wanted these numbers to be generated automatically and validated against all other records in the database to ensure they were properly ordered and unique.

Some of the project directors asked for auto-generated context "numbers" (actually alphanumeric identifiers) that would conform to legacy systems inherited from paper forms; for example, "Context name|HHAB" (Fairbairn) or "2228|SS|11|I|F5" (Thompson). These identifiers had to be generated according to specific rules to avoid duplication, ensure sequential numbering, and eliminate gaps (i.e., reuse identifiers that had been deleted). While FAIMS did automatically generate such identifiers, doing so slowed performance. Each time a new context was opened and an identifier generated, the software had to read every record in the database, parse related records to determine the next appropriate identifier, and write the new number according to specific rules, all the while checking it against a growing list of existing identifiers for duplication, omission, and sequential order. The FAIMS team anticipated that this process would slow the software down, but it was difficult to communicate the seriousness of the threat. Performance degradation was barely perceptible during testing, which involved only a few records, but it worsened exponentially as the database grew (more precisely, as a square function of the number of records). Fairbairn commented: "More serious was the slowdown of the system halfway through its period of use. A record which initially took 20 minutes to input took over an hour due to slow syncing and updating." VanValkenburgh agreed: "These improvements (digital data) have come at a cost—namely, less efficient data collection in the field. While we have yet to keep time-on-task records for either paper-based recording or FAIMS, project members universally reported that data entry using FAIMS took longer than using our previous analog system."

Thompson's "2228|SS|11|I|F5" identifier, for example, encapsulates the distinct attributes of LotID, Site Code, Context ID, AreaCode, and Grid Location Reference. Five variables combined into one code may be easy for humans to read (although they can become obscure to future users of the data if coding sheets are not included with the data), but it is resource-intensive for machines to parse, especially when each variable is subject to a different set of rules. The implementation of this five-variables-in-one-field feature was possible, but it reduced performance and cost significant development time, which could have been better spent on other features or on testing.

This slowdown was avoidable because the actual information encoded in the context identifier can be captured in ways that do not compromise performance. Those five pieces of information did not have to be forced into the context identifier. Instead, they can be stored normally in five separate fields. The critical part of the identifier (the context number) can be automatically incremented from a manually assigned starting number (a "seed"). Assignment of seeds to individual devices, combined with server-side validation after all devices synchronize, ensures uniqueness of the critical portion of the overall identifier without performance degradation. The five separate fields can be concatenated on export into a combined identifier to maintain the expected output.

Context numbering illustrates a larger issue. The question of "how closely do we duplicate our paper forms" is common to archaeological projects that are going digital. It is worthwhile to step back and consider the purpose behind legacy recording approaches, and weigh the problems and benefits of replicating them. Sometimes automation of a faithful replica is desirable and worth the cost in development time and performance, but at other times, a more robust digital approach will capture the purpose of legacy system, save time, improve performance, and offer additional benefits (in this case, verbose, human-readable context information that does not require decoding a complex identifier). In 2015, both continuing projects (Fairbairn's and VanValkenburgh's) chose simpler context numbering approaches.

Local vs Online Servers

Like most databases, the FAIMS mobile platform is a server-centered system, although client devices are coupled more loosely than usual to the server. The FAIMS server can take different forms. A virtualized instance of the server can run online (e.g., in the Australian NeCTAR Research Cloud) or on client laptops, or clients can commission a customized and preconfigured hardware package ("FAIMS-in-a-box") with a dedicated server, network equipment, and certified tablets. Each hardware option has its trade-offs, which project directors will need to consider. Purchasing a FAIMS-in-a-box is more expensive than renting an online server and a suite of tablets for short-term deployments, but it offers greater reliability and faster synchronization, completely avoiding Internet connectivity and bandwidth problems that plague remote (and sometimes not-so-remote) locations. An online server required less attention from archaeologists than a hardware server, and was not subject to the wear-and-tear, intermittent electricity, and other hazards of deployment in the field. Different options are available because each project has different needs. Fairbairn had the best experience using FAIMS-shipped hardware:

> Also, it is worth noting that the equipment—FAIMS-in-a-box—worked very well and with the exception of 1 tablet

screen—cracked when an item fell on it from the edge of the trench—came through the season in great condition. This was in spite of very dusty conditions and a somewhat unreliable electricity supply. The server worked throughout and the [wifi] provided excellent coverage (75–80% signal strength at 80m, the furthest excavation trench. The server hung only once, when the UPS plug was knocked out during a power outage, but was simply re-booted using an external keyboard.

Fairbairn's experience highlights the advantages of a local server. Thompson encountered a few more problems, but still used a FAIMS-in-the-box effectively. Debugging her setup under field conditions proved challenging, reinforcing the need for more authentic testing and comprehensive support for new technologies going into the field:

Setting up the network was also much more of a challenge when in the field than during a trial run in an office. There were several technical difficulties with the boot-up of the server, leading to many instances when data would not sync or when the server required an external keyboard and monitor to troubleshoot. The technical support provided by FAIMS was exceptional, and through a combination of their support and the fortuitous possession by project personnel of the needed hardware, all issues were overcome and have now been addressed by subsequent iterations of FAIMS hardware supply. This scenario would be much more difficult to negotiate in a field situation where internet is not readily available, and so in spite of the improvements that have been made, the necessity to fully set up and field test the entire system from start to finish before going to the field cannot be over-emphasized.

Instead of using a dedicated hardware server, VanValkenburgh attempted to install a virtual server on his laptop. Unfortunately, the installation failed, and an online server was deployed instead. His subsequent problems demonstrate the unreliability of the Internet in fieldwork settings:

We began with futile attempts to set up our own FAIMS server in the field house, in an Ubuntu virtual machine run off of a Windows laptop. Because we did not possess the resources to dedicate an entire machine to serving FAIMS, the development team provided us with access to their cloud server, and we set up a wireless access point in our dig house by running a 100-meter network cable from a nearby internet café and connecting it to a wireless router. Using this system, our upload speeds consistently averaged 25 Kbps—too slow for syncing, even when tablets were left to do so overnight. [I] then attempted to sync tablets on weekend trips to a city located one hour's drive away from Zaña. However, the large numbers of photographs we were attaching to our data records made complete syncs impossible. In the end, the FAIMS development team adjusted the PAZC module to allow syncing of our textual data alone, and we manually backed up all photographs onto external hard drives.

The lesson from these experiences echoes other aspects of co-development: reliability and performance require an investment from archaeologists as well as the development team. Local, dedicated hardware servers are more expensive than online servers, and they require that users test and maintain them, but they are faster and more robust than online servers.

THEME 3: DIGITAL RECORDING AND ARCHAEOLOGICAL INTERPRETATION—WHERE IS THE BENEFIT?

When asked to assess the direct impact of the digital recording on their research, project directors first emphasized improvements in the quantity, quality, and availability of data. Thompson reported: "Because FAIMS enabled data to be collected and processed so efficiently, we were able to collect more data, and this expanded the interpretations we could make from a field season of the same duration as when we used paper forms." Likewise, VanValkenburgh remarked that "the richness and integrity of our field data have both increased," an assessment echoed by Fairbairn "the conversion [to digital recording] increases quality of information available and makes post-excavation reconstruction of the site (the aim of the record) much easier . . . [it also] sped up exchange of information on site between excavators and specialists." Although "efficiency" should not be the only, or perhaps the overriding, goal of digital research (cf. Caraher, Ch. 4.1; Kansa, Ch. 4.2), project directors nonetheless reiterated that enhanced speed, accuracy, consistency, and granularity represent important contributions of digital recording to archaeological interpretation.

The process of building data models and accommodating the precision of digital systems also compels archaeologists to review their recording practices more generally. Fairbairn observed:

> [I]mportantly, the technology has opened up a broader dialogue about the recording process, increased awareness in the excavation group of the challenges and requirements of recording and opened a quite fixed system to change.

As part of that review, Fairbairn also noted how digital recording preserved previously undocumented interim steps of fieldwork:

> [W]e have had a very archaic use of "official site photos" which are of the cleaned up contexts. Well, now everyone can take images as they go, including as contexts are under excavation (rather than tidy-for-archive shots) and this improves the chances of understanding the features and contexts we see.

More continuous recordkeeping, including of "messy" work-in-progress, not only helps researchers at a later time better understand what they have excavated, but may contribute toward both making workflows more transparent and "openly exposing the process of research" (Kansa, Ch. 4.2), thus improving the reproducibility and professionalism of field research.

Digital data collection may not immediately alter researchers' aims or interpretive agendas. Fairbairn began his response to questions about impact by observing that "so far conversion [to digital recording] has not changed our substantive research goals." VanValkenburgh concurred, admitting that "I'm not sure I feel comfortable at this point asserting that digital field recording methods led us, in linear fashion, to a series of different conclusions about the past." It can, nevertheless, allow researchers to follow hunches as the project progresses, and to prove or disprove these intuitions later. VanValkenburgh also expects digital approaches to help separate real relationships among his data from accidents of preservation:

> The richer, more organized field notes that FAIMS has provided us will allow me to efficiently move between scales of data during post-field analysis, comparing trends between sites and closely examining contexts with distinct patterns to evaluate whether they are the products of differences in past human behavior, post-depositional processes, or recording errors.

Similarly, Thompson thought that the standardization of digital data "clarified the analyses that were needed in order to address questions about the spatial relationships of artifacts, landforms, and other objects of interest." The ability to make this sort of data-driven, quantitative argument improves the explanatory power and reproducibility of archaeological research, especially when it is combined with dissemination of the underlying data itself.

Finally, some of the benefits of digital recording may not be realized immediately. VanValkenburgh noted that the full impact of digital recording would not be clear until after post-fieldwork analysis and integration were complete. Looking even further ahead, digitally born data makes the timely publication of datasets more likely: "the ready availability . . . of our digital data is going to greatly facilitate making it publicly accessible in approximately two years." It is perhaps at the comparative or synthetic level, beyond individual projects, that we should seek the greatest interpretive impact. Only after digital datasets are published and researchers start reusing and combining them will the full potential and impact of digital methods be realized.

Conclusions

As field researchers transition to digital archaeology, they face a number of choices. They must decide the extent to which they want to go digital, whether to pursue mass-market, generalized, or bespoke solutions, and how involved they want to be in software development—bearing in mind that archaeological recording is complex, heterogeneous, and idiosyncratic enough to require significant development, regardless of the particular approach (cf. Kansa and Bissel 2010). On one hand, giving developers sufficiently specific instructions, and making implicit knowledge explicit, is time-consuming, tedious, and prone to failure (Segal 2005). On the other, sticking with paper minimizes upfront time investments, at the cost of extensive digitization, data cleansing, and error correction later (Roberts 2011: 147, cited in Huggett 2012: 542). "Just doing it yourself" with commercial software has a certain attraction, but it requires significant compromises because no mass-market software package was built with field archaeology in mind. It also hides, but does not eliminate, much of the effort of scoping, development, and testing, an obfuscation that may lead to significant technical debt and expensive maintenance later (Kruchten *et al.* 2012). Bespoke applications, while capable of producing good outcomes, are expensive to build and difficult to sustain.

The authors of this paper believe that FAIMS strikes a good balance between the re-deployability of general-purpose database software and the domain- and project-specific capability of bespoke applications. Software co-development in a generalized framework like FAIMS, involving a genuine partnership between archaeologists and technologists, is a difficult but productive process that can yield systems that are effective and fit-to-purpose. Archaeologists know their particular projects and where they are likely to be improved by technological intervention, but not always what can be achieved within a reasonable time and cost. Technologists know the capabilities of their software, and, in cases like the FAIMS project, they have accumulated experience across many deployments, including both successes and mistakes. FAIMS 2.0, released in November 2014 is itself an example of co-development as it benefited enormously from the three projects discussed in this paper.

In this context, our case studies revealed a number of consistent themes: (1) moving to digital recording requires an up-front investment of time and resources balanced by a payoff of clean digital data later in the project lifecycle, (2) co-development helps archaeologists and technologists make appropriate decisions to balance features, reliability, and performance, and (3) higher quantity, quality, and availability of digitally-born data is a welcome immediate benefit to the (oft-painful) transition to digital workflow, ahead of potential long-term benefits, like more rigorous analyses and dissemination of comprehensive digital datasets, which may eventually revolutionize interpretations.

The case studies presented here offer lessons applicable to any field software development project, including customisaton of commercial software or development of bespoke applications. Time invested up-front during development pays off with time saved digitizing and cleansing data. Define your requirements and plan carefully, but expect some miscommunications that will only be resolved through iterative testing and development. Leave time for iterating. Leave time for testing. Test early and often. Do not overemphasize features at the expense of performance, testing, and bug fixing. Test *all* hardware and software again under authentic conditions. Ensure field researchers have excellent in-field support. Developing software that is fit-for-purpose is hard, but the benefits of doing it right are worth it.

ACKNOWLEDGMENTS

We would like to thank the organizers of the National Endowment for the Humanities funded "Mobilizing the Past" workshop and everyone involved in the production of this volume, particularly the reviewers and editors who provided such valuable feedback. The FAIMS project was funded during 2012–2013 by the National eResearch Collaboration Tools and Resources (NeCTAR) eResearch Tools program (RT043), and from 2014 to 2016 by the Australian Research Council (ARC) Linkage Equipment, Infrastructure, and Facilities (LIEF) program (LE140100151). The University of New South Wales (2012–2014) and Macquarie University (2015–present) have offered the project a home and made significant cash and in-kind contributions to the LIEF (which is a matching grant). Other organizations providing cash and in-kind contributions to the LIEF-funded phase of the project include: the University of Queensland, the University of Sydney, La Trobe University, Flinders University, Southern Cross University, the University of California, Berkeley (Open Context), the University of Chicago (OCHRE), Digital Antiquity (tDAR), and the University of York (the Archaeology Data Service). For more project information, see http://www.faims.edu.au/.

https://mobilizingthepast.mukurtu.net/collec-
tion/32-measure-twice-cut-once-cooperative-deploy-
ment-generalized-archaeology-specific-field

http://dc.uwm.edu/arthist_mobilizingthepast/15

References

Baird, D., A. Fairbairn, L. Martin, and C. Middleton. 2012. "The Boncuklu Project: The Origins of Sedentism, Cultivation and Herding in Central Anatolia," in M. Özdogan, N. Basgelen, and P. Kuniholm, eds., *The Neolithic in Turkey: New Excavations and New Research*. Istanbul: Archaeology & Art Publications, 219–244.

FileMaker Inc. 2015. "FileMaker Go for iPad & iPhone." https://www.filemaker.com/au/products/filemaker-go/

Fisher, C., M. Terras, and C. Warwick. 2010. "Integrating New Technologies into Established Systems: A Case Study from Roman Silchester," in B. Frischer, J. W. Crawford, D. Koller, eds., *Making History Interactive: Computer Applications and Quantitative Methods in Archaeology (CAA). Proceedings of the 37th International Conference, Williamsburg, Virginia, United States of America, March 22–26, 2009*, http://discovery.ucl.ac.uk/1324501/1/1324501.pdf

Huggett, J. 2012. "Lost in Information? Ways of Knowing and Modes of Representation in e-Archaeology," *World Archaeology* 44: 538–552.

Kansa, E. C., and A. Bissell. 2010. "Web Syndication Approaches for Sharing Primary Data in 'Small Science' Domains," *Data Science Journal* 9: 42–53.

Kitchenham, B., S. L. Pfleeger, B. Mccoll, and S. Eagan. 2002. "An Empirical Study of Maintenance and Development Estimation Accuracy," *Journal of Systems and Software* 64.1: 57–77.

Kruchten, P., R. L. Nord, and I. Ozkaya. 2012. "Technical Debt: From Metaphor to Theory and Practice." *IEEE software* 29 (6): 18-21, doi:10.1109/MS.2012.167.

Limp, W. F. 2011. "Web 2.0 and beyond, or on the Web, Nobody Knows You're an Archaeologist," in E. C. Kansa, S. W. Kansa, E. Watrall, eds., *Archaeology 2.0: New Tools for Communication and*

Collaboration. Los Angeles: Cotsen Institute of Archaeology Press, 265–280.

Marean, C. W. 2010. "Introduction to the Special Issue: The Middle Stone Age at Pinnacle Point Site 13B, a Coastal Cave near Mossel Bay (Western Cape Province, South Africa)," *Journal of Human Evolution* 59: 231–233.

Might, M. 2015. "The CRAPL: An Academic-Strength Open Source License." http://matt.might.net/articles/crapl/

Popp, K. M., ed. 2015. *Best Practices for Commercial Use of Open Source Software*. Norderstedt: Norderstedt Books on Demand.

Raymond, E. S. 2001. *The Cathedral and the Bazaar: Musings on Linux and Open Source by an Accidental Revolutionary*. Rev. ed. Beijing: O'Reilly.

Roberts, J. 2011. *An Anthropological Study of War Crimes against Children in Kosovo and Bosnia-Herzegovina in the 1990s*. Ph.D. dissertation, Glasgow University, http://theses.gla.ac.uk/2562/

Ross, S., B. Ballsun-Stanton, A. Sobotkova, and P. Crook. 2015. "Building the Bazaar: Enhancing Archaeological Field Recording through an Open-Source Approach," in A. T. Wilson and B. Edwards, eds., *Open Source Archaeology: Ethics and Practice*. Warsaw: De Gruyter Open, 111–129.

Ross, S., A. Sobotkova, B. Ballsun-Stanton, and P. Crook. 2013. "Creating eResearch Tools for Archaeologists: The Federated Archaeological Information Management Systems Project," *Australian Archaeology* 77: 107–119.

Runyon, J. 2012. "An Unexpected Ass Kicking." *Impossible*, http://impossiblehq.com/an-unexpected-ass-kicking/

Segal, J. 2005. "When Software Engineers Met Research Scientists: A Case Study," *Empirical Software Engineering* 10: 517–536.

Sobotkova, A., B. Ballsun-Stanton, S. Ross, and P. Crook. 2015. "Arbitrary Offline Data Capture on All of Your Androids: The FAIMS Mobile Platform," in A. Traviglia, ed., *Across Space and Time: Papers from the 41st Conference on Computer Applications and Quantitative Methods in Archaeology, Perth, 25–28 March 2013*. Amsterdam: Amsterdam University Press, 80–88.

Sun, Q. 2012. "The Scientific Software Developer in Academia." *Software Sustainability Institute*, http://www.software.ac.uk/blog/2012–05–01-scientific-software-developer-academia

Thompson, J. C., A. Mackay, D. K. Wright, M. Welling, A. Greaves, E. Gomani-Chindebvu, and D. Simengwa. 2015. "Renewed Investigations into the Middle Stone Age of Northern Malawi," *Quaternary International* 270: 129–39.

VanValkenburgh, P. 2012. *Building Subjects: Landscapes of Forced Resettlement in the Zaña and Chamán Valleys, Peru, 16th–17th Centuries* c.e. Ph.D. dissertation, Harvard University.

3.3.
CSS for Success? Some Thoughts on Adapting the Browser-Based Archaeological Recording Kit (ARK) for Mobile Recording

J. Andrew Dufton

The Archaeological Recording Kit (ARK) is an open-source system for flexible, Web-based archaeological data management. Designed in 2005 to facilitate simultaneous data creation and dissemination through a customizable Web interface, ARK faces new challenges with the growing use of tablets for on-site, paperless recording. At least two pressing questions have emerged: how do mobile devices interact with ARK's current codebase, which relies on a single Web server? And is now the time for the ARK team to develop a stand-alone, offline tablet application?

This chapter looks at the first 10 years of ARK's history to situate these questions within the wider trajectory of its development, and within broader trends of mobile computing. Understanding the initial goals of the project, and the background of the project team, helps to identify the underlying ideologies structuring ARK data and functionality, the projects that have historically shaped its growth, and the likely paths for future expansion. Detailed attention will then be given to different examples of projects—from the commercial sector, in academic research, and in community-based archaeological practice—that have chosen to employ ARK with tablets; these case studies demonstrate some strengths and weaknesses of such an approach for both paperless and paper/digital hybrid recording. In each example, the customization of the Cascading Style Sheet (CSS) controlling the HTML interface for ARK emerges as a cost-effective means of facilitating concurrent data recording and viewing on tablet-, phone-, laptop-, and desktop-based systems without a need for changes to the

Figure 1: Paper illustration of ARK's EAV data structure, using Post-It Notes to represent individual data fragments.

existing data framework or core functionality. Further work toward a fully responsive design, rather than a focus on an offline application, is presented as one possible future for an ARK that respects the push toward sharing data online—a commitment that remains at its ideological core.

What is ARK?

The Archaeological Recording Kit, or ARK, is a Web-based toolkit for the collection, storage, and dissemination of archaeological data (Archaeological Recording Kit 2015; the ARK system can be downloaded at: http://ark.lparchaeology.com). Developed using the Apache, MySQL, and PHP stack commonly used for Web applications, the system relies solely on open-source software, and it is also released on an open-source license—meaning the code is freely available to download and customize by individual projects for non-commercial use. The ARK system was originally released and is still maintained by L-P: Archaeology, a commercial partnership of archaeologists working within the United Kingdom (http://www.lparchaeology.com).

The ARK data is structured using an entity-attribute-value (EAV) data model, in which fragments of data are linked to a primary key—in most cases, the context record or stratigraphic unit (Eve and Hunt 2008). The SQL table structure abstracts these different data fragments into a series of basic data types, such as text, attributes, dates, actions, temporal spans, or uploaded files. These individual fragments are then pulled by a collection of PHP subforms, to be displayed or edited within a Web browser according to a series of configurable settings files. A context record, for example, could be attached to a number of different data fragments: text entries for color, compaction, or composition; various uploaded photographs; metadata surrounding the record author or its date of creation; or its stratigraphic relationship with other context records (FIG. 1). The user interface for entering or viewing these data is controlled by CSS, a programming language dedicated to styling the HTML output of Web documents and controlling things such as the font, spacing, background, or layout of a given page.

The configuration of ARK is organized using a modular structure, where each module represents a different type of archaeological record. The details of an individual context record, for example, are

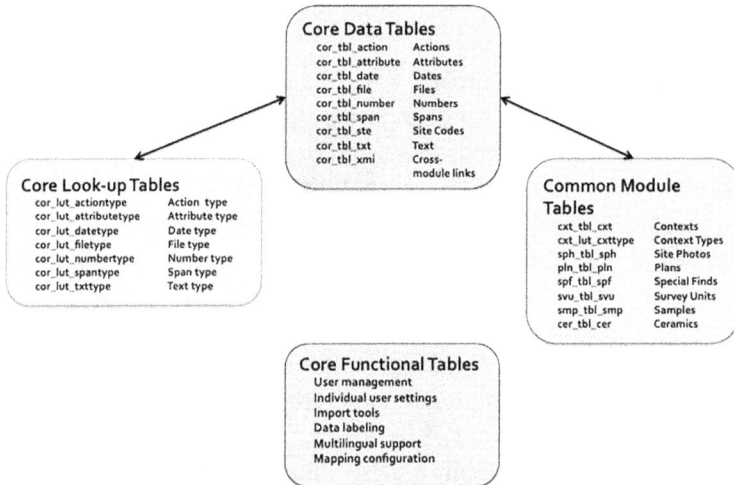

Figure 2: A simplified schematic representation of core and module-specific tables for ARK.

controlled by a dedicated PHP settings file with associated fields added to a series of MySQL tables. In the case of a pedestrian survey, contexts may be replaced by survey units. Some form of photographic module is usually included, as are modules for drawn plans, finds, and ceramic data. Although each module requires a single table to hold the primary record identifiers—the unique context number, photo number, or find number common in almost all recording systems— the core functionality and table structure is otherwise unchanged (FIG. 2). Thus ARK projects can install as many, or as few, modules as are needed simply by installing the relevant configuration files, and can also create new custom modules or edit existing ones according to the site conditions without additional programming (see Sobotkova *et al.*, Ch. 3.2, for a similar take on modular application development).

Entirely Web-based, ARK requires no external software beyond a Web browser to create, view, or share data—a use of Web tools for archaeological data management similar to other browser-based systems, such as the PKapp of the Pyla-Koutsopetria Archaeological Project (Fee *et al.* 2013; Fee, Ch. 2.1). This does not mean that ARK requires an active Internet connection to function, but rather that ARK relies on Web technologies to create and manipulate data. The basic Apache/MySQL/PHP package required for ARK can easily be installed in any Linux, Windows, or Apple operating system, essentially creating a local Web server on any computer. Users can then access this local Web server on laptops, phones, or tablets, either over a dedicated wireless network or connected directly to a wired local area network (LAN). Such a set-up is possible both in the lab or site museum for end-of-day data entry and also, in the case of many long-standing excavations, over a site-wide wireless network for on-site digital recording.

How Did We Get Here?

Much of the debate that emerged during the "Mobilizing the Past "workshop and throughout this volume focuses—quite rightly—on the ways in which archaeological practice is impacted by the technological choices we make in the field. Such a discussion is situated within a much wider dialogue about the relationships between new digital tools and the archaeologists who adopt them (Huggett 2000;

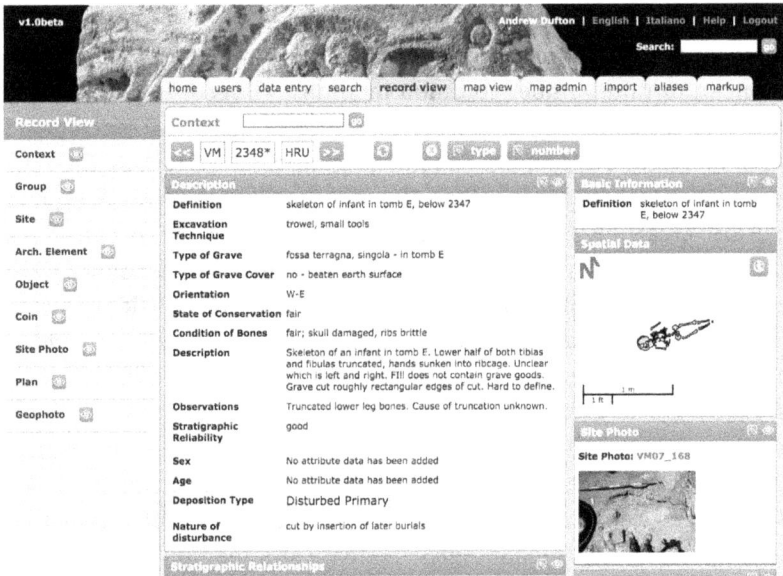

Figure 3: A screenshot of a basic context record from an early implementation of ARK at the Villa Magna Project, 2006–2010.

Zubrow 2006; Chrysanthi *et al.* 2012; Perry 2015). A shift from paper to tablet recording, like evolving digital data systems more generally, has great potential to increase fieldwork efficiency and introduce new ways of thinking about and with data "at the trowel's edge" (Chadwick 2003; Dufton and Fenwick 2012; Berggren *et al.* 2015). Yet without critical and ongoing reflection, these technologies risk the kind of techno-logical determinism and unquestioned positivism that are described by Caraher (Ch. 4.1), and that also characterized adoption of similar "new" technologies within the past 25 years, such as geographic infor-mation systems, commonly referred to as GIS (Llobera 1996; Wheatley 2000; Huggett 2004; Hacıgüzeller 2012; Llobera 2012).

An acknowledgement that the tools archaeologists use, digital or otherwise, structure our relationships with resulting archaeological data—its creation, storage, and use in generating wider narratives about the past—has lead Jeremy Huggett to propose a new manifesto for an "Introspective Digital Archaeology" (Huggett 2015). Huggett suggests moving beyond solely the details or justification of the appli-cation of digital methods, to a "third wave" of digital archaeology (2015: 88): "which seeks to examine the ways in which digital technol-ogies may have changed what we do, how we do it, how we represent what we do, how we communicate what we do, how we understand what we do, and how others understand what we do."

This introspection requires, in particular, a look at the choices made during the conception and application of various technolo-gies. What research problem was the technology created or adapted to address? What were the goals of the original application? Who were the developers? These questions—and the underlying tensions between the sometimes conflicting needs of effective data collection, use, and dissemination—are best answered with an ethnographic examination of the development process (Huggett 2012: 546; 2015).

Any manner of deep ethnographic study of the origins and trajec-tories of the ARK system are well beyond the scope of this discussion. Nevertheless, a few details surrounding the early conception of ARK, and the backgrounds and theoretical leanings of the development team, will suffice as an introduction to subsequent consideration of the strengths and weaknesses of the system for tablet recording.

The initial creation of ARK, as well as the bulk of its ongoing evolu-tion, was undertaken by a team of archaeologists with a strong digital focus, as opposed to programmers with specialized technical training but little archaeological experience. The ARK codebase was compiled in 2005, drawing from existing data systems originally designed by L-P: Archaeology for various projects: the *FastiOnline* database of Mediterranean excavations produced by the International Association of Classical Archaeology (Rome); the excavations of the Institute of Classical Archaeology (University of Texas at Austin) at the National Preserve of Tauric Chersonesos (Rabinowitz *et al.* 2007); and private, developer-funded archaeology at various sites within the United Kingdom, such as the Prescot Street Project (Hunt *et al.* 2008; Morgan and Eve 2012). Continuing with bespoke solutions for these unrelated projects was proving increasingly ineffective given limited resources and manpower. A single, heavily customizable system that could be adapted to archaeological recording in research and commercial contexts, to site gazetteers and beyond, was thus created to streamline code development (FIG. 3).

The initial goals of the ARK system were fivefold: multivocality, reflexivity, data integration, openness, and flexibility (Eve and Hunt 2008). The first two goals, in particular, were heavily inspired by a sense of teamwork and camaraderie between excavators, supervisors, and digital specialists, which was fostered during months of excavation throughout a rainy, gray London winter. Rather than relying solely on the supervisor during the process of synthesis, we asked how a database system could facilitate contributions from all members of the team. How might the ongoing process of excavation and data recording feed more directly into emerging interpretations and site narratives? These questions from 2005 are still directly relevant to discussions of tablet recording in 2015. In the case of ARK, the frustrations of archaeologists working within the British commercial sector with the top-down, post-excavation analysis of fieldwork results led to a functionality allowing multiple interpretations—each attributed to individual team members, each informed by the latest site and laboratory findings, and each noting the date of interpretation to keep track of how these may change throughout the course of a project.

The other three goals for ARK revolved, at least to an extent, around more practical concerns. The integration of drawn, photographic, spatial, and textual materials into a single digital system mirroring the paper record saved time and resources on commercial projects. Research projects also benefitted from a digital archive incorporating spatial data and photographs, yet requiring no specialist software.

A need by early ARK projects to synchronically create and freely disseminate data, and to access these data from across the globe, was best met by a Web-enabled solution. Finally, developing a flexible data structure that could easily be adapted by international projects without restricting those projects to a specific (usually national) recording standard, and releasing the code for the system on an open-source license, encouraged contributions to the functionality of ARK. This flexibility and openness helped spread the costs of new features between a larger body of stakeholders than would have been possible with a more bespoke solution relying on proprietary software (see Sobotkova *et al.*, Ch. 3.2).

WHERE DO WE GO NEXT?

The result of the early aspirations of the ARK project—to make an open, Web-based system for data entry and dissemination—is a platform that continues to evolve, even now over a decade after its initial creation. Yet ARK is also a system conceived before born-digital data recording became increasingly common practice with the widespread accessibility of tablets. The modification of the existing code for handheld devices, therefore, is an ongoing challenge for the core ARK development team. In a nutshell, the team must assess how ARK can—using limited resources and development time and causing minimal upgrade disruption for existing projects—be adapted to allow for tablet recording.

To understand the most likely trajectory of future advances requires a consideration of three characteristics common to those projects most invested in ARK, and therefore most willing to contribute time or funding to its further expansion. First, the majority of projects relying on ARK as part of their on-site practices are not making an active push toward a paperless archaeology. Most projects instead implement a hybrid recording practice of traditional paper records and hand-drawn plans, later digitized on laptops in the site hut or laboratory, with digital photography and born-digital registers of basic record metadata entered on tablets. It is important to remember in any discussion of tablet recording that many national or state guidelines still recommend paper archives for written, photographic, or drawn records for both research- and commercially-driven archaeological work (see Spigelman *et al.*, Ch. 3.4). Furthermore, local organizations accepting digital-only data for archiving purposes may lack the robust infrastructure provided by centralized groups dedicated to creating stable digital resources—such as the Digital Archaeological Record (tDAR) in the United States, or the United Kingdom's Archaeology Data Service (ADS). Projects should thus consider not only whether to export their data into plaintext, Rich Site Summary (RSS), or comma separated values (CSV) formats, but also whether any of these digital formats can be sustainably archived.

Second, any changes to the ARK code to enable tablet use should respect existing and legacy projects, maintaining the data structure that has always been central to the success of the ARK system. The need for all new functionality to be abstract enough to work in many different contexts can make changes to the codebase more time consuming than would be the case in a bespoke, single-site system. New features also require a degree of backward compatibility with older releases, or a suite of upgrade tools for existing projects—expansive and expensive developments that are difficult to fund within individual project budgets. A solution to adapt ARK for mobile recording that does not require extensive changes to the existing system is preferred.

Finally, many ARK projects currently in the field take advantage of either an established, site-wide local wireless network, or reliable 3G access, to simultaneously enter data both on laptops in the laboratory and on tablets in the trenches using only a standard Web browser. As such, there has been no real impetus for development of a standalone ARK application for tablets to facilitate data collection in offline environments, nor a need to integrate existing (largely proprietary) systems with data storage and syncing functionality into ARK's open-source workflow. A desire to make data available as soon as possible from the field—to specialists, and to the general public—has often been the reason behind many projects' choice to use ARK. These projects already have the infrastructure needed to run "online," and they are unlikely to return to a model where data publishing and dissemination occurs only when fieldwork has been completed, or requires an additional step to convert from proprietary data formats used during field collection to open online systems for final archiving.

SOME LESSONS FROM THE TRENCHES

So where, then, does this leave the potential exportation of ARK's browser-based recording to mobile devices? It is ARK's primary use for paper/digital hybrid recording, desire for flexibility with minimal PHP coding, and goals of concurrent data entry and dissemination, that have thus far suppressed any great desire by the ARK user community for the development of a new, stand-alone mobile application. The easiest and most cost-effective solution to-date has, rather, been the modification of the HTML styling of ARK's interface, using custom CSS, to allow for concurrent tablet-, phone-, laptop-, or desktop-based data entry and viewing.

In a Web-based system such as ARK, a combination of changes to CSS and project-specific configuration files can display the same data in highly different ways while also requiring less intensive programming knowledge than modifying the existing codebase or creating new functionality. Creating a new theme or skin to change the display of data for various devices on-the-fly can in fact meet the needs of many fieldwork sites, does not require any additional software downloads beyond the Web browser already included on mobile equipment, and respects the existing data structure and stated development goals of the ARK system more generally.

This discussion will now turn to three types of project relying on custom CSS for ARK, representing the different project needs of commercial archaeology, academic research, and community archaeology.

Commercial Archaeology

A first example of the use of ARK for on-site tablet recording comes from the United Kingdom's commercial sector, at the site of 100 Minories in London's East End (http://100minories.lparchaeology. com). Excavations undertaken by L-P: Archaeology over the course of a year at the site—which is located less than 500 m from the Tower of London and the Thames River—recorded deposits up to 8 m in depth, and materials ranging in period from the defensive circuit of the Roman city, to medieval and Tudor housing, to a large 18th-century Georgian development (100 Minories 2014). Fieldwork at the

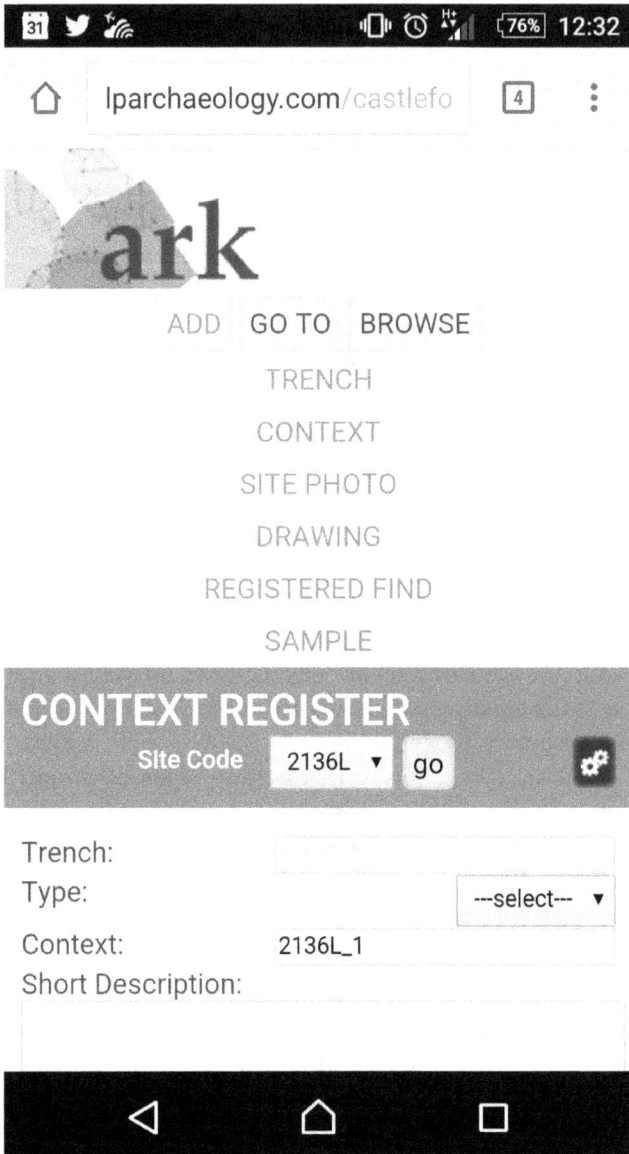

Figure 4: A simplified tablet stylesheet customized for data entry at the 100 Minories project.

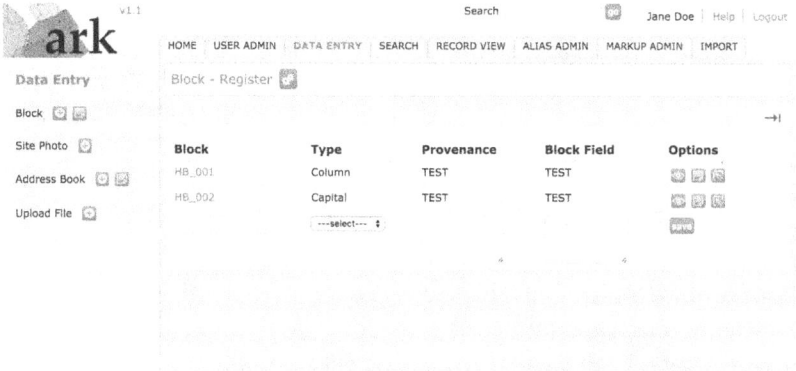

Figure 5: The default stylesheet of ARK when accessed through a desktop or laptop Web browser.

site was completed in advance of the construction of a new luxury hotel and funded by the developer, Grange Hotels. In addition to the full excavation of existing deposits, the site team completed a series of associated outreach activities, including a symposium of research talks by members of the project team, a number of pop-up museums displaying the latest recorded finds, and the online dissemination of live excavation data using ARK (100 Minories 2015a, 2015b).

The use of the ARK system for such a commercial enterprise within London comes as no great surprise, considering the British origins of ARK and its London-based development team. L-P: Archaeology had previously used ARK for a similar combination of developer-funded archaeology and public engagement at another East London site on nearby Prescot Street (Hunt *et al.* 2008; Morgan and Eve 2012; Prescot Street 2014). Fieldwork at Prescot Street was completed before the release of an affordable tablet robust enough to survive the archaeological trenches, and so mobile recording was not part of that project's digital strategy. However, Prescot Street's combination of a strong Web presence linking contributions from individual field staff to live archaeological data—facilitated by ARK's Web-based functionality—served as a template informing the work at 100 Minories.

Excavations at 100 Minories were completed under the guidance of the Greater London Archaeological Advisory Service at Historic England, and were thus subject to the archival requirements of all British archaeological practice (for an example of similar legal restrictions in a North American context, see Spigelman *et al.*, Ch. 3.4). These requirements dictate the need for a written paper record on standardized recording sheets, as well as bracketed photographs of individual contexts and drawn plans of the same on archival-quality gridded drafting film; all must be in accordance with the standards outlined in the site-recording manual of the Museum of London (Spence 1993). Tablet data entry was still possible for those items not restricted by Museum of London standards, such as the registering of new context, photo, or small find numbers at the trench. The 100 Minories site's central London location meant no local network or server was needed. Tablets on site were able to upload and access ARK data held in a remote location over a 3G wireless network—even at depths over 2 m below modern street level—using standard mobile broadband data provisions. The system's data entry functionality was simplified and streamlined using a custom mobile CSS, the new "skin" limiting the more complex data entry or spatial tools but allowing for quick and easy creation of new context, find, or photo records (cf. FIGS. 4, 5).

The ARK system was also used to view context records and finds data from an earlier 2012 archaeological evaluation of the site. These older data, accessed on tablets in the field by excavators, assisted the ongoing processes of excavation and interpretation, and introduced an aspect of reflexive practice not often attempted within a commercial context (Howard 2013). Specialists working on the cleaning and consolidation of finds, a process handled off-site by Museum of London Archaeology, were able to view the latest excavated materials as they came out of the ground, connecting traditionally segregated excavation and post-excavation workflows.

The work at 100 Minories is but one example of a hybrid paper/digital system within the context of developer-funded work (see also Gordon *et al.*, Ch. 1.4, for a research-driven example). This hybrid approach increases the efficiency of site-recording practices—taking advantage of some of the basic benefits of a paperless system (see Wallrodt, Ch. 1.1)—while maintaining the archival standards required of sound commercial practice in a British context.

Academic Research

Research projects have been, in many ways, the early drivers of ARK development. The flexible parameters found in ARK were designed to suit its implementation in the highly varied circumstances of international research. Much of the current codebase was developed to meet the needs of disparate early adopters such as the Institute of Classical Archaeology at the National Preserve of Tauric Chersonesos (Rabinowitz *et al.* 2007; http://www.utexas.edu/cola/ica/projects/chersonesos/introduction.php), and the joint excavations of the University of Pennsylvania and the British School at Rome at the imperial Roman site of Villa Magna (Dufton and Fenwick 2012; http://villa-manga.org). The freedom often afforded to academic researchers to experiment with new methodologies or techniques is well suited to exploring novel ways to think about data creation, use, and dissemination. It is somewhat surprising, then, that such projects have been less instrumental in adapting ARK's existing functionality for use with mobile technologies (for a notable exception, see Opitz *et al.* in

Figure 6: Map of some of the sites featuring key research projects contributing to the ARK codebase.

press). Why are research projects already using the system not making a greater push for a paperless ARK?

There are a few reasons for this seeming discrepancy. Academic fieldwork is often planned and initiated with a specific time period or funding cycle in mind; the two projects listed above, for example, have moved on to a publication phase where tablet/ARK interoperability is less of a concern than tracking the evolution and use of project data (Esteva *et al.* 2010; Trelogan *et al.* 2013). Other projects currently in the field are content with a workflow of on-site paper recording and daily data-entry off-site, either due to a methodological loyalty to the perceived benefits of the paper record, or because experimenting with new digital data techniques is—quite understandably—not part of the research agenda.

A more significant barrier, however, is the absence of a stand-alone, offline, data-syncing alternative for ARK. The system's open-source codebase makes it difficult to track all projects currently using the system—at the time of writing, the latest version had been downloaded over 2,300 times in the one year since its release—but a look at the distribution of some of the higher-profile research projects using ARK shows a decidedly Mediterranean focus (FIG. 6). Unlike commercial excavations in the heart of London, rural sites in Sardinia, Tunisia, Turkey, or Jordan still lack the reliable network connectivity needed for tablet-based data entry over mobile broadband. Mediterranean fieldwork projects are content with data entry from paper records into the ARK system, but demonstrate an unsurprising reluctance to rely solely on on-site, born-digital recording when the possibility of establishing a site-wide wireless network, or the reliability of 3G coverage, is so hard to guarantee (see, e.g., the experiences of the Athienou Archaeological Project in Cyprus, Gordon *et al.*, Ch. 1.4). This is particularly the case for landscape survey projects covering a much wider study area—such as Brown University's Petra Archaeological Project—where regular 3G access to a remote server would be the only viable option but network coverage is not yet sufficient for such an approach (http://brown.edu/go/bupap).

Although individual devices can be configured to run a stand-alone system, there is at present no method for syncing a series of disparate ARK data tables into a single database at the end of a day's fieldwork—a function not as important to commercial excavations at a single, well-defined site, but essential for the use of tablets across multiple excavation areas or between simultaneously active field survey teams, situations that characterize much academic research. Attempts to integrate ARK with stand-alone, offline data-capture systems such as FileMaker Pro have so far resulted in unwieldy workflows lacking the efficiency benefits that draw projects to paperless recording in the first place. Thus far, the combination of network concerns and other priorities for existing research using ARK has resulted in a slow uptake of born-digital data recording on many academic projects.

Public Outreach

A final example from the realm of public or community archaeology provides further insight into the use of ARK for mobile recording: the DigVentures social enterprise promoting crowdfunded archaeological fieldwork (http://digventures.com). The DigVentures team started in 2012 with a summer excavation season at the Bronze Age site of Flag Fen near Peterborough (United Kingdom). The project relied on existing public interest in this well-known monument—and in archaeology more generally—to fund the excavations, ultimately establishing a community of over 250 funders, many of whom also participated directly in work on-site (DigVentures 2015b).

In 2013, DigVentures fieldwork moved to the medieval site of Leiston Abbey, Suffolk, for a second season of crowdfunded and crowdsourced excavations. The Leiston Abbey project also established the *Digital Dig Team*, an online website/ARK hybrid to provide live data from the excavations at the moment of discovery. As with the 100 Minories example, a custom CSS was created for ARK to streamline data entry using tablets on-site, relying on existing 3G network access to connect to a remote Web server. These largely stylistic changes to the ARK system connected the archaeological data with broader Web content, such as daily blog entries by project participants, video updates, or news items.

Claims that this initiative should be seen as "the world's first entirely paperless recording system" are problematic (DigVentures 2015a; see Wallrodt 2011; Ch. 1.1, for earlier examples). Yet it does embody a very early attempt at combining paperless systems with online dissemination tools to make, in effect, all data public data from the moment of initial collection through analysis and interpretation. Although designed primarily as an incentive to encourage donations to project funding, this approach also takes a valuable step toward a greater integration between digital data and other aspects of the archaeological process, such as documenting fieldwork practices, interpretation, and dissemination (Rabinowitz and Sedikova 2011).

The need to find effective, long-distance means of communicating archaeology has recently been highlighted, not least since geographic, financial, or physical restrictions can prohibit in-person involvement with archaeological sites or museums (Alcock *et al.* 2015). This is particularly relevant for a project such as DigVentures that is designed for, and funded by, the public. Web-based recording systems such as ARK provide an opportunity to connect field practices and the excitement of discovery more directly to a population eager to participate, either directly or virtually, in the archaeological process.

Mobilizing ARK for a Digital Future

Advances in mobile technology within the last decade have drastically changed the way archaeologists think about data collection. As a result, fieldwork projects now face a number of choices with far-ranging implications: to embrace paperless recording, or maintain some degree of traditional documentation; to develop a bespoke system, or adopt an existing archaeological database; to use an open-source platform, or licensed proprietary software; to prioritize data dissemination and reuse, or efficiency of on-site workflows.

The examples outlined above, when understood within the context of ARK development, provide some insight into the role of mobile recording using Web-based systems, such as ARK, in these wider debates. On the one hand, ARK's ability to eliminate the gaps between data collection and online dissemination has always been a major strength, and it is no surprise that those projects best deploying the system with mobile technologies include a substantial public-facing component. On the other hand, research projects are proving more hesitant to rely on a tablet system that can only function with local wireless or mobile broadband access, especially given the lack of such connectivity in many fieldwork settings. Yet research projects are not providing the funding for the majority of ARK development and, for better or worse, it seems unlikely that a syncing, offline version of ARK will be produced in the coming years. A stand-alone, paperless system is not a priority for the projects actively developing the ARK platform at present, and existing software, such as FileMaker Pro, offers a less time-consuming alternative for bespoke, offline mobile recording.

More generally, a shift to Web-based site recording—on tablets or otherwise—also requires a broader paradigm shift within academic practice, encouraging open data not only as an afterthought to publication but as an active part of the fieldwork process. Advocates for the current trend toward open data stress the potential strengths of such an approach: reduced research costs, increased research quality, and better communication of archaeological findings (Kansa and Kansa 2011; Kansa 2012). Open data initiatives have traditionally worked with published or archival data sets, demonstrating the benefits of online publication for system interoperability or linked open data (LOD), text-mining, and data reuse (Isaksen *et al.* 2010; Atici *et al.* 2013; Kansa *et al.* 2014). Projects have been slower to adopt these principles for ongoing fieldwork, showing less willingness to sacrifice on-site efficiency for more unwieldy interfaces offering future data interoperability, nor to provide open access to data prior to its re-examination, possible correction, and traditional publication—a process that often takes years. Academic systems of appointment and promotion further contribute to an unwillingness to go digital by often placing a higher value on traditional print publications rather than on collaborative, open, and online initiatives (see Kansa, Ch. 4.2). An uptake in Web-based data creation on-site is unlikely unless it is accompanied by a change in the distinction we make between live and archived data, and a continued effort to make open-data systems more accessible to users with all degrees of technical competence.

This negative outlook does not mean that there is no potential for mobile, born-digital data collection using ARK. Longstanding excavation projects often have the resources necessary to establish local wireless infrastructure, and in some cases they have begun using ARK for paperless data capture (Opitz *et al.* in press). Furthermore, the latest figures provided by the International Telecommunication Union—the United Nations' specialized agency for information and communication technologies—show global access to 3G networks increased from 45% to 69% coverage in the period from 2007 to 2015 (International Telecommunications Union 2015). Industry projections suggest up to 85% 3G-network coverage worldwide by 2017 (Ericsson

2012). High-speed Long-term Evolution (LTE), often referred to as 4G LTE, has shown a similar expansion in coverage over the last five years; a 2015 survey of 68 countries demonstrated that in 53 (or 78%), users had access to LTE signals for over 50% of their total time connected to mobile networks (Open Signal 2015). Of course not all projects will be able to count on this coverage, particularly those working in highland or rural remote locations. It is reasonable to suggest, however, that reliable 3G/LTE coverage on archaeological sites will only become a more realistic expectation in the coming years. Future ARK development to streamline data entry on mobile devices is possible, and much can be accomplished with simple changes to ARK's CSS to create a responsive interface tailored to effectively display and enter data both on computers in the lab, and on tablets or smartphones in the trenches.

A significant strength of open-source software is that there is no single answer to the question of "where next?" Individual ARK projects will continue to follow their own trajectories based on individual project needs and research aims. This discussion presents only one perspective on the future of ARK and mobile technologies, a future where simple CSS customization takes advantage of the benefits of mobile, Web-based data collection while maintaining the goals of openness and flexibility that lie at the heart of ARK's development history.

https://mobilizingthepast.mukurtu.net/collection/33-css-success-some-thoughts-adapting-browser-based-archaeological-recording-kit-ark

http://dc.uwm.edu/arthist_mobilizingthepast/16

References

100 Minories. 2014. "The 100 Minories Site." http://100minories. lparchaeology.com/about/

100 Minories. 2015a. "100 Minories Pop Up Museum." http://100minories.lparchaeology.com/ research/100-minories-pop-up-museum/

100 Minories. 2015b. "The 100 Symposium." http://100minories. lparchaeology.com/about/symposium/

Archaeological Recording Kit. 2015. "About ARK." http://ark.lparchaeology.com/about

Alcock, S. E., J. A. Dufton, and M. Durusu-Tanrıöver. 2015. "Who Are the People," in J. F. Cherry and F. Rojas, eds., *Archaeology for the People: Perspectives from the Joukowsky Institute. Joukowsky Institute Publication* 7. Oxford: Oxbow Books, 129-143.

Atici, L., S. W. Kansa, J. Lev-Tov, and E. C. Kansa. 2013. "Other People's Data: A Demonstration of the Imperative of Publishing Primary Data," *Journal of Archaeological Method and Theory* 20: 663–681. doi:10.1007/s10816-012-9132-9

Berggren, Å., N. Dell'Unto, M. Forte, S. Haddow, I. Hodder, J. Issavi, N. Lercari, C. Mazzucato, A. Mickel, and J. S. Taylor. 2015. "Revisiting Reflexive Archaeology at Çatalhöyük: Integrating Digital and 3D Technologies at the Trowel's Edge," *Antiquity* 89: 433–448. doi:10.15184/aqy.2014.43

Chadwick, A. 2003. "Post-Processualism, Professionalization and Archaeological Methodologies: Towards Reflective and Radical Practice," *Archaeological Dialogues* 10: 97–117. doi:10.1017/S1380203803001107

Chrysanthi, A., P. Murietta-Flores, and C. Papadopoulos, eds. 2012. *Thinking beyond the Tool: Archaeological Computing and the Interpretive Process. British Archaeological Reports International Studies* 2344. Oxford: British Archaeological Reports.

DigVentures. 2015a. "Digital Dig Team." http://digventures.com/ digital-dig-team/

DigVentures. 2015b. "Our Story." http://digventures.com/about-us/

Dufton, A., and C. Fenwick. 2012. "Beyond the Grave : Developing New Tools for Medieval Cemetery Analysis at Villamagna , Italy," in A. Chrysanthi, P. Murrieta-Flores, and C. Papadopoulos, eds., *Thinking beyond the Tool: Archaeological Computing and the*

Interpretive Process. British Archaeological Reports International Series 2344. Oxford: Archaeopress, 155–167.

Ericsson. 2012. "Ericsson Mobility Report." http://www.ericsson.com/res/docs/2012/ericsson-mobility-report-november-2012.pdf

Esteva, M., J. Trelogan, A. Rabinowitz, D. Walling, and S. Pipkin. 2010. "From the Site to Long-Term Preservation : A Reflexive System to Manage and Archive Digital Archaeological Data," *Archiving* 7: 1–6.

Eve, S., and G. Hunt. 2008. "ARK: A Developmental Framework for Archaeological Recording," in A. Posluschnya, K. Lambers, and I. Herzog, eds., *Layers of Perception: Proceedings of the 35th International Conference on Computer Applications and Quantitative Methods in Archaeology (CAA), Berlin.* Kolloquien zur Vor- und Frühgeschichte 10. Bonn: Halbelt.

Fee, S. B., D. K. Pettegrew, and W. R. Caraher. 2013. "Taking Mobile Computing to the Field," *Near Eastern Archaeology* 76: 50–55.

Hacıgüzeller, P. 2012. "GIS, Critique, Representation and Beyond," *Journal of Social Archaeology* 12: 245–263. doi:10.1177/1469605312439139.

Howard, C. 2013. "Integrating Excavation and Analysis on Urban Excavations." http://urban-archaeology.blogspot.com/2013/02/integrating-excavation-and-analysis-on.html

Huggett, J. 2000. "Computers and Archaeological Culture Change," in G. Lock and K. Brown, eds., *On the Theory and Practice of Archaeological Computing.* Oxford: Oxford University Committee for Archaeology, 5–22.

———. 2004. "Archaeology and the New Technological Fetishism," *Archeologia e Calcolatori* 15: 81–92.

———. 2012. "Lost in Information? Ways of Knowing and Modes of Representation in E-Archaeology," *World Archaeology* 44: 538–552.

———. 2015. "A Manifesto for an Introspective Digital Archaeology," *Open Archaeology* 1: 86–95. doi:10.1515/opar-2015-0002

Hunt, G., C. Morse, and L. Richardson. 2008. "Watching the Past Unfold before Your Eyes," *London Archaeologist* 12: 41–45.

International Telecommunication Union. 2015. "ICT Facts and Figures: The World in 2015." http://www.itu.int/en/ITU-D/Statistics/Pages/facts/default.aspx

Isaksen, L., K. Martinez, N. Gibbins, G. Earl, and S. Keay. 2010. "Linking Archaeological Data," in B. Frischer J. Webb Crawford, and D. Koller, eds., *Making History Interactive. Computer Applications and Quantitative Methods in Archaeology (CAA). Proceedings of the 37th International Conference, Williamsburg, Virginia, United States of America, March 22–26, 2009*. British Archaeological Reports International Series 2079. Oxford: Archaeopress, 1–8.

Kansa, E. C. 2012. "Openness and Archaeology's Information Ecosystem," *World Archaeology* 44: 498–520.

Kansa, E. C., and S. W. Kansa. 2011. "Toward a Do-It-Yourself Cyberinfrastructure: Open Data, Incentives, and Reducing Costs and Complexities of Data Sharing," in E. C. Kansa, S. W. Kansa, E. Watrall, eds., *Archaeology 2.0: New Tools for Communication and Collaboration*. Los Angeles: Cotsen Institute of Archaeology Press, 57–92.

Kansa, S. W., E. C. Kansa, and B. Arbuckle. 2014. "Publishing and Pushing : Mixing Models for Communicating Research Data in Archaeology," *International Journal for Digital Curation* 9: 1–15. doi:10.2218/ijdc.v9i1.301

Llobera, M. 1996. "Exploring the Topography of Mind: GIS, Social Space and Archaeology," *Antiquity* 70: 612–622.

———. 2012. "Life on a Pixel: Challenges in the Development of Digital Methods within an 'Interpretive' Landscape Archaeology Framework," *Journal of Archaeological Method and Theory* 19: 495–509. doi:10.1007/s10816-012-9139-2

Morgan, C., and S. Eve. 2012. "DIY and Digital Archaeology: What Are You Doing to Participate?" *World Archaeology* 44: 521–537.

Open Signal. 2015. "The State of LTE (September 2015)." *Open Signal*, http://opensignal.com/reports/2015/09/state-of-lte-q3-2015/

Opitz, R., M. Mogetta, and N. Terrenato, eds. in press. *A Mid-Republican House from Gabii*. Ann Arbor: University of Michigan Press.

Perry, S. 2015. "Changing the Way Archaeologists Work: Blogging and the Development of Expertise." *Internet Archaeology* 39, doi:http://dx.doi.org/10.11141/ia.39.9

Prescot Street. 2014. "The 2008 Excavations." http://www.lparchaeology.com/prescot/about

Rabinowitz, A., S. Eve, and J. Trelogan. 2007. "Precision, Accuracy, and the Fate of the Data: Experiments in Site Recording at Chersonesos, Ukraine," in J. T. Clark and E. M. Hagemeister, eds., *Digital Discovery: Exploring New Frontiers in Human Heritage. CAA 2006: Computer Applications and Quantitative Methods in*

Archaeology. Proceedings of the 34th Conference, Fargo, United States,
April 2006. Budapest: Archaeolingua, 243–255.

Rabinowitz, A., and L. Sedikova. 2011. "On Whose Authority? Interpretation, Narrative, and Fragmentation in Digital Publishing,"
in E. Jerem, F. Redo, and V. Szevérenyi, eds., *On the Road to Recon-*
structing the Past: Computer Applications and Quantitative Methods
in Archaeolgy (CAA). Proceedings of the 36th International Confer-
ence, Budapest, April 2–6, 2008. Budapest: Archaeolingua, 134–140.

Spence, C., ed. 1993. *Archaeological Site Manual.* 3rd ed. London:
Museum of London.

Trelogan, J., A. Rabinowitz, M. Esteva, and S. Pipkin. 2013. "What Do
We Do with the Mess? Managing and Preserving Process History
in Evolving Digital Archaeological Archives," in F. Contreras, M.
Farjas, and F. J. Melero, eds., *CAA2010: Fusion of Cultures. Proceed-*
ings of the 38th Annual Conference on Computer Applications and
Quantitative Methods in Archaeology, Granada, Spain, April 2010.
British Archaeological Reports International Series 2494. Oxford:
Archaeopress, 597–600.

Wallrodt, J. 2011. "Why Paperless?" *Paperless Archaeology,* http://pa-
perlessarchaeology.com/2011/01/03/why-paperless/

Wheatley, D. 2000. "Spatial Technology and Archaeological Theory
Revisited," in K. Lockyear, T. J. T. Sly, and V. Mihailescu-Birliba,
eds., *CAA 96 Computer Applications and Quantitative Methods in*
Archaeology. British Archaeological Reports International Series 845.
Oxford: Archaeopress, 123–132.

Zubrow, E. B. W. 2006. "Digital Archaeology: A Historical Context," in
T. L. Evans and P. Daly, eds., *Digital Archaeology: Bridging Method*
and Theory. London: Routledge, 10–31.

3.4.
The Development of the *PaleoWay*: Digital Workflows in the Context of Archaeological Consulting

Matthew Spigelman, Ted Roberts, and Shawn Fehrenbach

In this chapter we present the development of our *PaleoWay* digital workflows, designed in-house by PaleoWest Archaeology, and offer insight into the development of digital archaeology within the private sector in the hope that our solutions may serve as an exemplar and model for academic and non-academic projects alike. PaleoWest Archaeology is a full-service cultural resources consulting firm, with offices across the United States. PaleoWest's archaeological services include archaeological resource assessments (ARAs); literature and site file searches (Phase 1A); reconnaissance and intensive archaeological surveys (Phase 1B); preservation and treatment plans; programmatic agreements (PAs); memoranda of agreements (MOAs); historic architectural documentation, site testing, and evaluations (Phase 2); full-scale excavation for data recovery and mitigation (Phase 3); and construction monitoring. We offer surveys using the full suite of geophysical instruments commonly used in archaeological surveys: ground-penetrating radar (GPR), gradiometry, electromagnetic induction (both magnetic susceptibility and conductivity), and resistivity. PaleoWest leverages the latest positioning technologies such as real-time kinetic (RTK) geographic positioning system (GPS) and robotic survey stations to collect subsurface imaging surveys quickly with precise spatial positioning. We also employ low altitude aerial photography for the creation of high-resolution orthomosaics, as well as digital elevation models (DEM). In fact, PaleoWest is the only archaeological firm nationwide to commercially hold a FAA 333 exemption permit to collect unmanned aereal vehicle (UAV), or drone, data. Our goal is, more broadly, to create an approach to archaeology focused on born-digital data and built-in quality assurance and quality control that provides clear and logical paths for turning field observations into client-ready deliverables.

Our needs in developing the *PaleoWay* digital workflows demanded they be scalable, customizable, and able to operate both with and without cellular connectivity. Scalability, which for our purposes was the ability to field multiple crews working simultaneously, was important because the size of our projects vary widely. A typical survey could be as small as a single plot being developed for residential or commercial use, a few miles of pipeline being added to a natural gas-collection network, or as large as a hundred-thousand-acre military base or a several-hundred-mile long water distribution system. Customizability was important because our work is variable and occurs across the 50 states and beyond. The goals for projects differ widely based on client needs, and the project deliverables vary across states and between government agencies. We therefore stress that *PaleoWay* is a system of digital workflows (plural) because the variety of our projects, geographic locations, and regulatory requirements make the development of a single, one-size-fits-all, system impractical.

The great benefit of being a successful archaeology-only consulting firm is that we have had a large number of projects through which to develop and refine the *PaleoWay* digital workflows. Since our founding in 2006, we have successfully completed over 1,100 cultural resource investigations. In this paper we present an overview of the process of developing the *PaleoWay* digital workflows, provide several projects as case studies to highlight the strengths of a digital data system, and reflect on how the position of the data and mapping specialist has become a key position in the firm. First, however, since we are the only contributors to the volume speaking from a cultural resource management (CRM) perspective, we provide a brief overview of the environment in which archaeological consulting is practiced within the United States. This context informs all of the decisions we have made, and continue to make, in developing and implementing the *PaleoWay* digital workflows.

ARCHAEOLOGICAL CONSULTING

As archaeological consultants our job is to help local, state, federal, and private entities manage the cultural resources under their care. The largest of these entities are federal organizations and agencies, such as the Bureau of Reclamation (BOR), the U.S. Forest Service (USFS), the National Park Service (NPS), Department of Defense (DoD), Army Corps of Engineers (USACE), and the Bureau of Land Management (BLM), each responsible for millions of acres of land and the management of millions of archaeological sites and other historic properties located on public land. The smallest entities are developers or other landowners embarking on a project that requires a federal, state, or municipal permit and therefore triggers historic review. The cultural resources we are hired to record and evaluate include, but are not limited to, archaeological sites. We are also charged with identifying other historic features on the landscape, such as petroglyphs, irrigation canals, roads, fences, and historic buildings. Also falling within the category are less tangible cultural resources, such as ethnographic knowledge, natural resources of cultural significance, and traditional cultural properties (TCPs) where important activities continue to take place.

Much of this work is federally mandated by section 106 of the National Historic Preservation Act (NHPA), but also other parallel pieces of legislation (King 2013: fig. 1.1). This work is mandated at the federal level but regulated at the state level. Each state maintains a State Historic Preservation Office (SHPO), which is responsible, among other things, for reviewing work done to satisfy the section 106 legislation, for maintaining a statewide inventory of historic properties, and for nominating historic properties to the National Register of Historic Places (NRHP). Historic properties are typically defined as anything greater than 50 years of age and are considered significant for what they can tell us about our collective history, both before and after the founding of the Unites States of America (for an overview of the relevant legislation, see King 2013: 1–54).

This work typically proceeds along a three-step process of (1) identifying cultural resources, (2) an evaluation of their eligibility for inclusion on the NRHP, and (3) determining if construction or other events will have a negative impact on those resources and proposing mechanisms to avoid or mitigate those impacts (King 2013: 55–82).

In practical terms, this process results in our being hired to survey archaeologically the proposed project areas (hundreds or thousands of acres), identify archaeological sites, and assess the impacts of any proposed activities on those sites and other identified historic properties. When negative impacts to a significant cultural resource are unavoidable, one method of mitigating those impacts is to research and record the cultural resource in order to gather information of importance to human and American history. Again, in practical terms, mitigation often results in extensive site excavation, the purpose of which is to gather data from an archaeological site or other cultural resource before it will be destroyed or made inaccessible by construction, mining, or other activities. For this reason, these projects are typically referred to as "data recovery" excavations.

As archaeological consultants, each project we complete results in a set of deliverables that are reviewed by the SHPO. For surface (pedestrian) surveys, these deliverables will typically include a report on the work conducted and an inventory form for each archaeological site or other historic property identified. The report allows the SHPO to evaluate if the appropriate federal requirements have been met, while the inventory forms contain all of the information necessary for the SHPO to update their statewide inventory of historic places. For data recovery excavations, the deliverables also include the thousands or millions of artifacts and other material recovered during the work, all of which must be cataloged and processed for long-term storage. Our job is, therefore, to conduct archaeological research in the service of managing the historic resources of our nation. Effective and efficient work is central to this process, to meet both the management needs of the resource and our own needs as a private company working on competitively priced projects with low profit margins and little tolerance of inefficiencies.

THE PALEOWAY DIGITAL WORKFLOWS

The goals for the *PaleoWay* digital workflows are twofold: to produce higher quality data and to do so in a more efficient and cost effective manner. The creation of all digital workflows requires the reimagining of how we prepare for fieldwork, conduct fieldwork, collect data, analyze data, and produce deliverables for our clients. We developed the *PaleoWay* as a suite of tools that removes paper maps, paper records, and paper forms, replacing them with digital devices and digital data.

The first phase of developing the *PaleoWay* digital workflows was one of research and experimentation, as new hardware (most notably the first and second generation iPads) and a host of new applications became available. The challenge in this phase was to create a culture shift within our organization and industry similar to paradigm shifts occurring in academic archaeology (Dufton, Ch. 3.3; Gordon *et al.*, Ch. 1.4; Wallrodt, Ch. 1.1). This culture shift included encouraging and empowering project managers, crew chiefs, and field technicians to find new way to conduct fieldwork and produce deliverables. In doing so, we were forced to confront deeply engrained practices, many of which dated back to the early years of CRM in the 1970s and 1980s. These paper-based workflows were well honed, but they were also increasingly inefficient due to the need to digitize eventually all data for final computerized report production, map drawing, and production of client-specified deliverables (see Caraher, Ch. 4.1).

The second phase of development was product development. In conjunction with a period of rapid growth in the company, many of the workflows that had been established in the first phase using a host of standalone applications were consolidated into a single, centralized database. While many options were explored, the solution chosen was to build a customized database within the FileMaker Pro program. This choice of an established software package has proven successful, allowing us to focus on the development and improvement of the database itself (and to do more archaeology), without having to worry about the fundamental software reengineering associated with each and every hardware and operating system release (for perspectives on proprietary vs off-the-shelf solutions, see: Fee, Ch 2.1; Motz, Ch. 1.3; Sobotkova *et al.*, Ch. 3.2; Wallrodt, Ch. 1.1). The resulting software is now utilized in all of our projects, ranging from survey, through testing, to large-scale excavation.

THE OLD WAY

The old way of conducting archaeological consulting was developed as a paper-based workflow, with computers and other digital devices uncomfortably inserted after the fact (Eiteljorg 2007). Field data was recorded on paper, in a manner that has changed little since the devel-

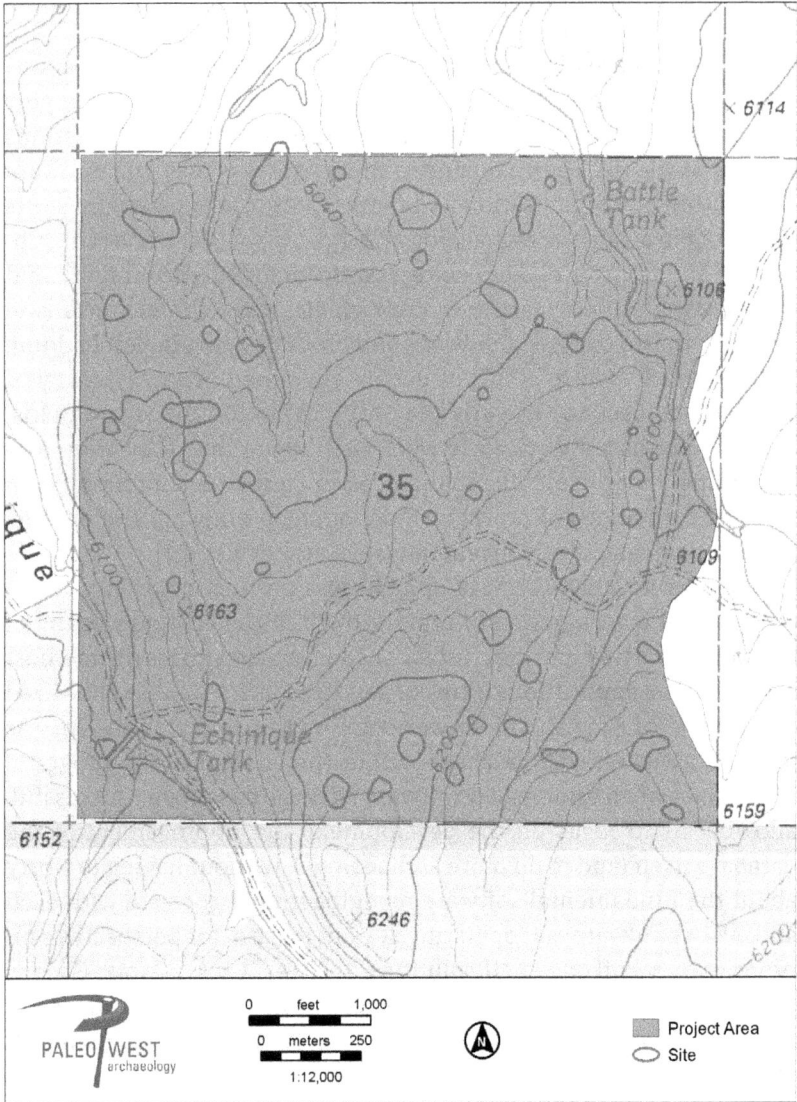

Figure 1: Map of typical site density (does not depict actual site locations).

opment of CRM in the 1970s. Deliverables were also paper-based, with printed reports and site forms filled out by hand or using a type-writer. Archaeological consulting companies introduced computers into this workflow as a means to organize data as it returned from the field and produce better looking maps, but as of 2010, computers had not meaningfully changed how fieldwork was conducted. Similarly, multi-thousand-dollar GPS units (most made by Trimble™) and high-quality digital cameras had been introduced into fieldwork, but both were inserted into the traditional methodology (see Ellis, Ch. 1.2). The crew chief, who previously recorded site and isolated artifact locations by hand on a paper map, now recorded those locations using the GPS unit. This initial insertion of technology only served to reinforce the hierarchical nature of field crews, creating greater distance (and at times animosity) between field crews and their crew chiefs and project managers.

As of 2010, computers were allowing archaeological consultants to organize better data, render high-quality maps, and record more accurate spatial data. These benefits, however, came at a cost. Field-work now required several pieces of expensive equipment, while still producing only paper records and hand-drawn maps as a result. Upon leaving the field, paper records now needed to be typed into the computer before data could be tabulated and included in reports. Hand-drawn maps needed to be scanned and loaded into Adobe Illustrator or AutoCAD, where they were then re-drawn again. High-er-quality data was being collected and higher-quality deliverables were being produced, but there were, as of yet, only efficiency losses and no efficiency gains.

The Development of Digital Workflows for Pedestrian Survey and Site Recording (2010–2011)

The development of the *PaleoWay* digital workflows took place in 2010 and 2011, a period of tough economic times. Commercial property development had ground to a halt, taking away a formerly lucrative source of archaeological contracts. The work that remained was largely generated by government agencies, such as the USFS, BLM, BOR, and various branches of the military. These projects were publicly advertised and highly competitive, susceptible to low bids by those willing to cut corners. The goal of PaleoWest was therefore to leverage technology not just in an attempt to maintain and improve the quality of the data coming out of the field, but also to increase efficiency and lower costs in this competitive environment.

PaleoWest bid aggressively on contracts during this time and won work throughout the American Southwest and West on large projects in Arizona, New Mexico, Utah, Wyoming, and Colorado. These projects were largely extensive surveys in archaeologically rich landscapes (FIG. 1). Projects were usually non-collect surveys, meaning that all artifact analysis was conducted in the field, and that only photographs, records, and maps returned to the lab. The deliverables for these projects were a final report and the completion of Agency-specific inventory forms, typically accompanied by appropriate pictures and maps. While core staff members (project manager, field director, and some crew chiefs) remained fairly consistent from project to project, field crews were typically hired on a per-project basis. Most projects covered 500 to 1,000 acres, had crews of 4 to 12 people, and lasted anywhere from 10 days to a month. This was an ideal environment to test and innovate new solutions, allowing for near continuous iterative development.

The economic downturn of 2010 and 2011 simultaneously ushered in a period of rapid technological development and lowering costs of hardware and software (see Ellis, Ch. 1.2; Motz, Ch. 1.3; Poehler, Ch. 1.7; Wallrodt, Ch. 1.1). While the launch of the iPad was an important piece of this process, so too were the appearance of lower-cost and higher-quality GPS units and digital cameras. During this beta testing period, a concerted effort was made to engage all members of the field crew to adopt the technologies and embrace the changes in the personnel dynamic associated with going digital in all stages of the archaeological process. The goal was to give everyone access to the technology and to empower everyone to identify problems, find solutions, and spread these results throughout the field crews and the greater company. This was an exciting time: new technology was being adopted in real time while under constant pressure to bring projects in under budget and on schedule.

The main task in going digital was to convince everyone from the top down, and the bottom up, to buy into the process. Previously, when new technology had been introduced, it had been jealously guarded by the crew chief (see Sayre, Ch. 1.6), with the unfortunate consequence of creating both hierarchy and resentment, but also of introducing inefficiency, as able crew members sat idle while the crew chief recorded coordinates, drew maps, filled out paperwork, or took pictures. Our goal, instead, was to put technology in each crew member's hands, giving everyone a job to do in parallel to one another, thereby increasing efficiency in the process. This approach was directed at all stages of the archaeological process, replacing the traditional archaeological toolkit with a digital one.

The system that developed to further this approach was a suite of technology and software (see Motz, Ch. 1.3; Wallrodt, Ch. 1.1). A crew of four now went to the field with four Garmin handheld GPS units, three iPads, and one Trimble high-precision GPS unit. Each crew member had their own GPS, which was pre-programed with their designated survey lines. That all crew members had a GPS made field walking more efficient, and it also streamlined the process of recording isolated artifact occurrences. Crew members, upon spotting an isolated artifact, could now quickly and efficiently make their identification, note the coordinates, and call out the information to be recorded. Paper site-recording forms were now digitized into fillable PDFs that were pre-loaded with applicable information and ready for digital data collection. Because these were the same forms that would later be printed and submitted to the client, fieldwork was directly producing the project deliverables, thereby removing all of the digitization and typing that used to be required. Similarly, site plan maps were produced directly on the iPad, using off-the-shelf vector mapping programs. By pre-loading a template with an appropriate symbology, field vector mapping increased efficiency by removing the need for the post-field digitization of paper maps, and it also produced higher-quality data by standardizing symbology, layout, and other aspects of the map between team members and across field crews (see Bria and DeTore, Ch. 1.5; Motz, Ch. 1.3; Ellis, Ch. 1.2).

With the introduction of the second generation iPad, it became possible to bring site and artifact photography fully into the digital realm as well. Whereas previously it was necessary to juggle a camera, a GPS unit, and a paper photo log, now these three lines of data were brought together within a single device (see Ellis, Ch. 1.2; Fee, Ch. 2.1; Gordon et al., Ch. 1.4). In this first phase of development the solution was an off-the-shelf application that digitally marked photographs with all of the necessary information: location, direction, time, and space for a note, thereby removing the need for a separate photo log.

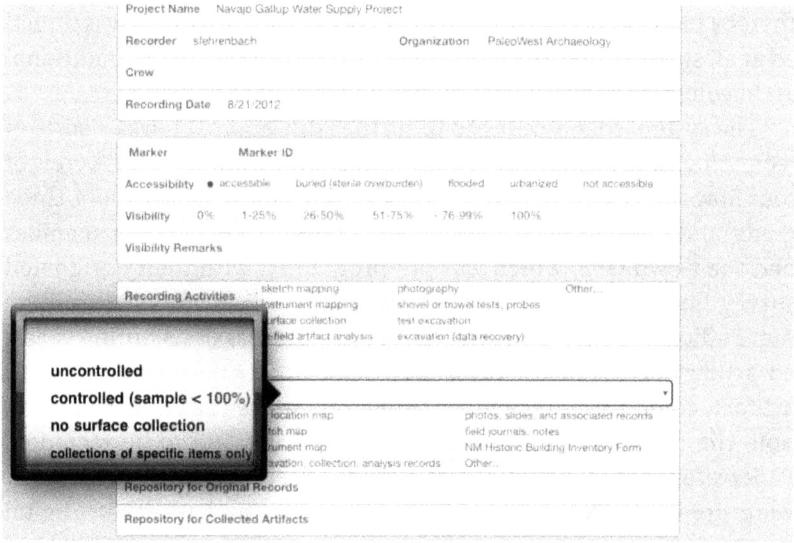

Figure 2: Screen shot of the NGWSP database.

The Development of an
Integrated Database Solution (2011–2012)

We transitioned from a phase of research and development during 2010 and 2011 to the creation of an integrated database solution in 2011 and 2012. This transition occurred when PaleoWest was awarded the cultural resource management component of the Navajo-Gallup Water Supply Project (NGWSP). The NGWSP is a $1.3 billion undertaking, consisting of a 280-mile-long system of pipelines and pumping stations that will bring water to parts of the Navajo Nation that are currently without a clean and sustainable water supply. This cultural resource management contract was, at the time, the largest federally funded CRM contract ever awarded in the United States. The NGWSP is a complex and demanding project, requiring a digital data solution that could accommodate archaeological survey, testing, and excavation, as well as ethnographic research (Potter *et al.* 2013). The cultural resource portion of the project is also slated to take at least a decade to complete, and construction is estimated to extend through 2024. This complex project with an extended timeline required the creation of a robust system that could handle all of the diverse project needs, but it also necessitated a flexible system that can be adapted and altered over time. This solution was developed in the context of the NGWSP (cf. Chuipka 2015), and in the years since, it has been implemented by PaleoWest on that project and other survey and excavations projects, both large and small.

The *PaleoWay* digital workflows designed and implemented for the NGWSP are based around a collection of nested modules in a FileMaker Pro database (FIG. 2; see also Gordon *et al.*, Ch. 1.4; Motz, Ch. 1.3; Wallrodt, Ch. 1.1). These modules create guided pathways for collecting data for survey, excavation, and other regularized tasks. While we explored many different software options, including customized app development and other solutions, the decision to utilize commercial database software was made to avoid the time and expense of re-engineering software for each hardware or operating system upgrade. We also needed the ability to work without cellular connectivity, as much of the NGWSP runs through rural areas, and it was also necessary to have the ability to integrate and coordinate data in real time, such as on large and complex excavation sites.

This too resulted in higher-quality data because it eliminated the all-too-common occurrence of the photo log and the camera falling out of sync, thus ensuring that the location, direction, and subject of every photo was always recorded.

Lastly, going digital allowed crews to take whole libraries of information with them to the field, and to organize that information in a usable manner. Having digital libraries in the field pays dividends both in recording newly discovered artifacts and sites and in re-visiting and re-recording previously identified cultural resources. Having identification libraries at hand is key for maximizing productivity among field crews, members of which might be working one week in Utah and the next week in Arizona; they might find a prehistoric lithic scatter in the morning and an early 20th-century campsite in the afternoon. When revisiting sites, the digital library for that site could be easily consulted, forms could be pre-filled with known information, and the old site map consulted to see if subsequent changes required the drawing of a new one.

This research and development phase continued through 2010 and 2011 and reached a mature state with the capabilities of the second generation iPads with their onboard cameras. Using off-the-shelf hardware and applications we achieved notable productivity gains, both in the field and in the time it took to go from field to deliverables. Utilizing all team members, each with their own role in the process and each inputting data to their own device, the recording of a lithic scatter went from over an hour in the paper era to under 15 minutes using the *PaleoWay* digital workflow. The time spent recording an isolated artifact went from 10 minutes to less than a minute. Major productivity gains and quality control was gained by removing digitization entirely from the process. The move from field records to deliverables went from two weeks to two days. This period of research and development required overcoming technological changes, but, more importantly, it required a cultural shift as people learned to trust the technology and see the benefits of collecting digital data directly in the field (see Ellis, Ch. 1.2; Poehler, Ch. 1.7).

National Registrer of Historical Places Eligibility
Evaluations at Fort Irwin, California

A major opportunity for testing the *PaleoWay* as implemented in the FileMaker Pro database was a large survey project carried out at Fort Irwin, California. We were hired to evaluate 731 previously identified archaeological sites, located within a 642,000 acre active military facility (Roberts *et al.* 2012, 2013). This project was ideally suited to a digital approach: the archaeological sites were previously identified, so the task was to re-locate, re-record, and evaluate their eligibility for the NRHP in the most efficient manner possible. A digital workflow utilizing a four-person team, with three iPads and Trimble GPS unit, was devised. One team member surveyed the site, tallied artifacts, marked artifact positions and the site boundaries with survey flags, and recorded coordinates with the Trimble GPS. The remaining team members all used iPads. One member took photos and completed the integrated photo log, a second filled out the site form, and the third used a vector mapping application to draw a site map. The vector map template was populated with current project information, thus eliminating the need for redundant and repetitive efforts. This workflow engaged all team members in the site-recording process, with data integrated after the fact through the centralized database. This digital approach also allowed for unprecedented flexibility at Fort Irwin, as necessitated by the demands of working in an active military facility. Field crews were empowered to shift to new sites or new areas of the base seamlessly, as all of their background research and all necessary field forms and maps were carried with them digitally at all times.

Large-Scale Excavation at the
Ironwood Village Site, Arizona

The *PaleoWay* digital workflows have proven particularly successful at managing the large volumes of physical and digital data produced by large-scale excavation projects. In 2013 and 2014, PaleoWest was hired to excavate the Ironwood Village site, a ca. seven acre (2.8 ha) Hohokam settlement, located midway between Phoenix and Tucson, Arizona (Bostwick *et al.* 2015). The project represents the first all-digital large-scale excavation in the nation. Excavation was conducted on an extremely tight schedule, with the goal of gaining clearance for

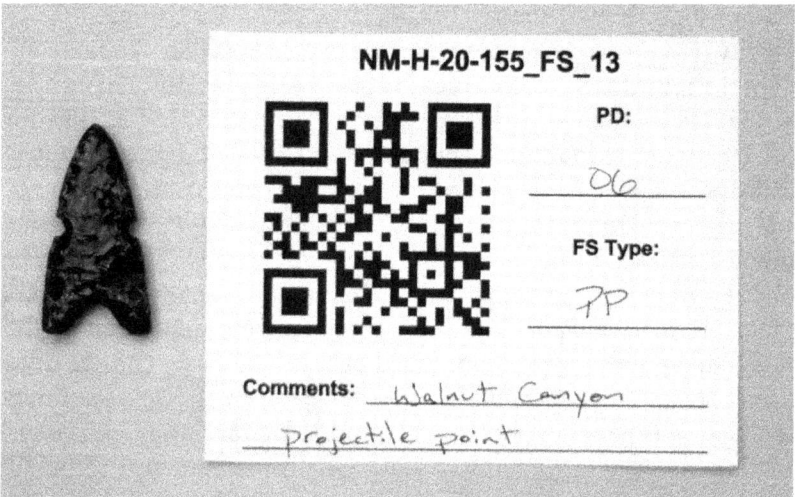

Figure 3: QR code for artifact and sample tracking.

the construction of the Marana Center commercial development in advance of the 2015 holiday shopping season. The goals of the project were therefore efficient and high-quality excavation, followed quickly thereafter by reporting and clearance for the project to proceed. These demands required that the excavation, data analysis, and initial technical report assembly phases be conducted coincident with one another. The project was successful, with the technical report submitted the day after fieldwork was complete, due to the capabilities of the *PaleoWay* digital data workflows. Two aspects were particularly important: access to a centralized database from both the field and the lab, and the use of artifact and sample tracking using quick response (QR) codes.

The excavation of the Ironwood Village site utilized a centralized database hosted in the company's Phoenix headquarters and was accessed in the field over cellular networks in real time. This allowed full access to all field records, photographs, and other information by all members of the project team as soon as they were created. Most importantly, records were being continuously checked and cleaned by a full-time data manager. The data manager was responsible for maintaining standardization and identifying potential issues that could be addressed while features, contexts, and artifacts were still fresh in excavators' memories and crews were still in the field. Over 500 distinct archaeological features were excavated at the site, including a ball court and numerous houses, roasting pits, and burials. Each feature was digitally mapped in the field using a vector drawing app and coordinates taken from the site grid. These maps were revised in the lab using control points taken with a total station.

A large and diverse artifact assemblage was recovered from the Ironwood Village site, and samples for flotation, pollen, botanical, and C^{14} analysis were also collected. In total, nearly 4,000 bags of artifacts were recovered in the field and transferred to the lab for analysis. Each artifact bag was tracked throughout this journey using a unique QR code (FIG. 3; see also Castro López et al., Ch. 3.1). Representing a distinct advancement over traditional barcode systems (see, e.g., McPherron and Dibble 2002), QR codes require no special equipment to produce or read them—they simply are printed on regular paper (or waterproof Tyvek) and then attached or included in sample bags in the field. The codes can be read quickly and accurately using the camera on any smartphone or tablet. The use of QR codes within a centralized database also allows for efficient custody tracking.

The tracking of artifacts and other samples as they leave the site, enter the lab, and move from conservation, through analysis, to storage is critical to the success of a large project. Custody tracking is, however, mandatory and essential when dealing with human remains. Human remains and associated funerary objects were discovered as both distinct cemeteries and isolated occurrences at the Ironwood Village site. The methods for excavating, housing, and repatriation of these remains were determined in consultation with the Tohono O'odham Nation and described in the project's Burial Agreement. A member of the Tohono O'odham Nation was on-site during fieldwork and participated in the excavation of many burial features. A core part of the burial agreement is an establishment of trust between PaleoWest and the Tohono O'odham Nation that the material recovered from burial features will be handled and housed respectfully at all times. The use of a centralized custody tracking system was an essential part of this process. Within the framework of appropriate treatment and transport of these highly significant and sensitive items (as outlined in the Burial Agreement), the chain of custody could be demonstrated immediately wherever and whenever the need for access to this information arose.

The *PaleoWay* digital workflows proved particularly useful in the context of large-scale data recovery excavations, such as the Ironwood Village site. The use of a centralized system allowed for the real-time coordination and control over the digital data and physical artifacts that was impossible using paper records alone. Key to these efforts is not just the construction of a functional and efficient database system, it is also the assignment of personnel to the maintenance and use of such a system, thereby establishing the role of the data manager within the archaeological consulting firm.

The Data Manager

The development, implementation, and maintenance of the *PaleoWay* digital data workflows positions the data manager (and mapping specialist) as a core member of any project team. In the paper era, data collection was the responsibility of the field director, data processing the responsibility of the lab director, and the production of the project deliverables was the responsibility of the principal investigator. The data manager and mapping specialist now play key roles at each stage of a project's lifecycle. In preparation for fieldwork they conduct site file searches of already identified sites within the project area, compile these data in ArcGIS, and output geoPDFs for use in the field. They are also responsible for preparing a blank database for fieldwork by customizing fields, dropdown menus, and other aspects as necessary for the specific project. During large and complex projects they are responsible for database integration and quality control, often allowing problems to be identified and corrected while the team is still in the field. After fieldwork is complete they are responsible for moving data out of the database in which it was collected and into the various formats of the project deliverables. These typically include the project report, site forms, and associated maps and photographs. It is becoming increasingly common for SHPOs to require that spatial data be delivered as shapefiles, which necessitates site coordinates and other information to be brought back into ArcGIS for export. All of this is to say that while we have created digital data workflows and removed paper from the system, we have not removed people from the system.

Conclusions

Our goal in developing the *PaleoWay* digital data workflows was to produce higher-quality data and to do so in a more efficient and cost effective manner. We have found that collecting digital data in the field produces higher-quality data due to the quality assurance and quality control (QA/QC) mechanisms built into the process. As a result, this QA/QC process improves archaeological interpretation by eliminating redundant or bad data. For database input we can limit choices to a predefined set of values, thereby standardizing recording across personnel and field crews, and we can also create required fields, thereby ensuring that all data is collected before leaving a given archaeological site. Vector mapping in the field also produces a higher-quality work product because map symbology, scale, and conventions are all built directly into the pre-loaded template. Perhaps the greatest efficiency gains, however, have been achieved by removing the need to digitize large volumes of field forms, decipher the handwriting of multiple field crew members, and reconstruct missing data after the fact. We now move directly from fieldwork to the production of deliverables. This closer linking of fieldwork and reporting allows the synthesis of results to occur much closer to when the work actually took place, again resulting in a high-quality product and efficiency gains.

The irony of our current efforts is that while our data workflows are entirely digital, our project deliverables remain largely paper-based. State and federal laws are built around the archival stability and permanence of paper records. The SHPOs are just beginning to bring site databases online and integrated with spatial data. We expect, therefore, that the shift from paper to digital deliverables is at hand, and we will soon be accompanying our digital spatial data deliverables with digital databases of our results as well. Our *PaleoWay* digital workflows position us well to adapt to these changes.

The development of the *PaleoWay* digital workflows benefited in its early phases from our high project throughput, allowing many new technologies to be employed. The successful technologies were developed and refined, while the onerous or inefficient were culled. The development of a more effective and efficient paperless system was particularly advantageous as we operate in many areas of the country that are densely populated with a rich diversity of archaeological sites, thereby compounding even small efficiency gains into sizeable benefits. And more recently it has benefited from our participation in large and complex projects, which provided the time and budget to build more integrated and robust systems and capabilities. We have found, however, that it is not possible or desirable to produce a single application or database that contains all the necessary functionality our system requires. Vector mapping remains most efficiently done in an external application, and we continue to utilize handheld GPS units and total stations running their own proprietary software. Recreation-grade GPS units remain the most rugged and economical option for providing surveyors with their routes through the project area, while we turn to professional-grade GPS units for recording tasks requiring greater accuracy.

In this paper we have reviewed the development *PaleoWay* digital workflows and highlighted several projects in which they have proven particularly effective. The NGWSP highlights the ability of the *PaleoWay* digital workflows to utilize a centralized database to integrate a highly varied set of project tasks, which are simultaneously taking place over hundreds of miles of archaeologically rich land, and which will extend over more than a decade of work. The re-recording and evaluation of previously identified archaeological sites at Fort Irwin highlights the ability of digital data workflows to efficiently collect data while maintaining high quality over time. Efficiency was produced by designing a workflow in which all team members were actively engaged in site recording for the duration of the time spent at each site. Lastly, the Marana Data Recovery Project (the Ironwood Village Site) was a large-scale excavation of a Hohokam Village site conducted in advance of commercial development. This project was executed on an extremely tight timeline, and its successful deployment highlights the ability of the *PaleoWay* digital workflows to create an active flow of information between the field and the lab.

https://mobilizingthepast.mukurtu.net/ collection/34-development-paleoway-digital-work-flows-context-archaeological-consulting

http://dc.uwm.edu/arthist_mobilizingthepast/17

REFERENCES

Bostwick, T. W., D. R. Mitchell, and C. North, eds. 2015. "Life and Death at a Hohokam Ballcourt Site: Archaeological Excavation of Ironwood Village in Marana, Arizona," *PaleoWest Technical Report*: 15–36.

Chuipka, J. P. 2015. "The Navajo-Gallup Water Supply Project, Archaeological and Ethnographic Investigations along Reach 12A, Navajo Nation and McKinley County, New Mexico," *PaleoWest Technical Report*: 15–26.

Eiteljorg, H. 2007. *Archaeological Computing*. Bryn Mawr: Center for the Study of Architecture.

King, T. F. 2013. *Cultural Resource Laws & Practice*. Lanham, MD: AltaMira Press.

McPherron, S. P., and H. L. Dibble. 2002. *Using Computers in Archaeology: A Practical Guide*. New York: McGraw Hill.

Potter, J. M., D. Gilpin, and J. P. Chuipka. 2013. "Navajo-Gallup Water Supply Project Archaeological Research and Sampling Design," *PaleoWest Technical Report*: 12–06.

Roberts, T., D. Gilpin, D. Mitchell, J. Potter, L. Clark, and K. Miller. 2012. "National Register of Historic Places Eligibility Evaluations of 581 Archaeological Sites at Fort Irwin and National Training Center, San Bernardino County, California," *PaleoWest Technical Report*: 12–35.

Roberts, T., D. Gilpin, L. Clark, and K. Miller. 2013. "National Register of Historic Places Eligibility Evaluations of 150 Archaeological Sites at Fort Irwin and National Training Center, San Bernardino County, California," *PaleoWest Technical Report*: 13–11.

Part 4: From a Paper-based Past to a Paperless Future?

4.1.
Slow Archaeology: Technology, Efficiency, and Archaeological Work

William Caraher

Slow archaeology is a concept that I developed to offer a counterweight to recent trends in archaeology that emphasizing digital tools as a way to improve efficiency in fieldwork. Drawing on recent academic and popular criticism of the increasing speed of capital, technology, and daily life, slow archaeology similarly calls attention to the negative impacts of the accelerated pace of archaeological work made possible by digital tools. Awareness of efficiency and speed in fieldwork, of course, is not new, but has roots both in the long-term development of industrial practices within archaeology as a discipline and in scientific practices that alternately disclose and occlude elements of knowledge production. Bruno Latour's concept of the "black box" is useful to understand how certain efficiencies achieved by digital tools create, reinforce, or obscure archaeological practice and methodology (Latour 1987: 1-21). For Latour, black boxes hide certain processes or maneuvers either owing to their complexity, their routine character, or their location outside of the expertise of disciplinary work (Latour 1987: 2-3). The contribution explores certain aspects of digital innovation in archaeological field practices and methodology and argues that the discipline would benefit from considering some of the critiques offered by proponents of the slow movement.

My idea for a slow archaeology draws upon the scholarly criticism of speed that is most frequently associated with larger critiques of modern capitalism. For David Harvey, for example, the speed of capital in contemporary society has outstripped human conceptions of time and space and has led to "the annihilation of space by time" through "time-space compression" (1990: 260–307). Marc Augé (1995) recognized the speed of the contemporary world as a significant contributor to the serialized production of non-places that exchange the distinguishing characteristic of place for the efficiency of legibility. Paul Virilio, in his concept of dromology, has stressed the transformative aspects of speed and, perhaps more importantly, acceleration in modern society. Beginning with the industrial revolution, the drive to make things and processes faster, more efficient, and more connected has become an end unto itself. For Virilio, speed produces a distinct realm of experience and knowledge (Virilio 1986; see also James 2007: 31–32). A traveler in a car both experiences and produces the landscape in a way that is distinct from the experience of the landscape on foot (Virilio 2005). Hartmut Rosa (2013: 1–32), following Virilio and Augé, argues that the rapidly shrinking present has created a kind of fluid, unstable, and unfamiliar world.

Popular media has explored the critique of speed through concepts like "slow food," which celebrates the deliberate preparation of locally sourced food as a challenge to the homogenized and generic fast food experience. Initially championed by the Italian activist Carlo Petrini (2003), the idea of slow food offered another way to critique the speed of contemporary life. Carl Honoré (2004) and others have extended Petrini's idea of slow food to a wide-ranging critique of the cult of speed in the modern world. These writers, however, have endured criticism especially from those who see the opportunities to slow down as only possible because of prosperity only available to the privileged and provided by the inhuman efficiency of the industrial world (see, for example, Sassatelli and Davolio 2010 and Andrews 2008: 165–182). Despite these critiques, these authors have offered practical advice on how to slow down individual engagements with the world. Petrini, for example, celebrates local food ways, while Honoré advises that we set aside time to unplug and savor the pleasures of experience without interruption or mediation. Absent the distractions of technology, the local environment takes on greater significance and vividness.

Slow archaeology calls upon archaeologists to recognize the influence of speed on archaeological practice. This chapter will not ask archaeologists to discard their digital tools or reject the remarkable benefits of technology in the name of a romanticized past. Rather, I will offer a critique of certain digital practices and, perhaps more importantly, the way in which these tools are described and promoted in the scholarly discourse. I remain skeptical that archaeology will benefit from tools that offer greater efficiency, consistency, and accuracy alone, and my hope is that this skepticism has particular significance at a time when a new generation of digital tools are entering the field.

Unpacking the implications of our use of digital tools and the adoption of streamlined practices require some attention to the intersection of scientific and industrial practices in archaeology. The recent growth of contract, salvage, and rescue archaeology has made the influence of speed and capital on archaeological work particularly visible. The pressures of development and the efficient management of heritage as a resource have provided ample reason for the enthusiastic adoption of digital tools and practices. Among academic archaeologists, shrinking resources, the pressure to "publish or perish," increasingly intensive field methods, and the expectations of host countries have likewise put pressure on the pace of fieldwork. The goal of slow archaeology is to recognize the particular emphasis on efficiency, economy, and standardization in digital practices within the larger history of scientific and industrial knowledge production in archaeology. This contribution also seeks to carve out space within the proliferating conversation about digital archaeology to identify practices and tools that embrace the complexity of archaeological landscapes, trenches, and objects. In this way, slow archaeology recognizes that archaeological presentation and publication tends to simplify the impact of technologies and the often-messy relationship between evidence and argument. The concern for data as both publication and evidence finds common cause with Eric Kansa's recent interest in "slow data," which embraces the dynamic and profoundly human character of archaeological datasets as an element of added value rather than distracting complexity (see Kansa, Ch. 4.2).

My position as a tenured, academic archaeologist provides a distinct professional context for slow archaeology. My efforts to develop slow archaeology come from a position of privilege. As an academic archaeologist, I rely on his research for professional advancement, but not professional survival. Tenure provides opportunities for a more deliberate pace toward publication. Academic projects also tend to align research goals closely with the personnel, time, and funding. These luxuries have allowed us to consider a wide range of archaeological documentation processes without particular concern for efficiency. We have deployed a range of digital tools and practices from the use of iPads (Caraher *et al.* 2013) and structure-from-motion (SfM) 3D imaging (see Olson, Ch. 2.2) to now standard reliance on differential GPS units, relational databases, and geographic information systems (GIS). This article then is not the frustrated expressions of a Luddite outsider, but an argument grounded in a familiarity with digital field practices.

THE INDUSTRY OF DISCIPLINARY KNOWLEDGE PRODUCTION

Latour has argued that in the history of science, there arose a division between nature, which was the object of scientific inquiry, and culture, which provided the tools and language for understanding the relationship between these observations (Latour 1993). This division between nature and culture encouraged the development of processes that emphasized data collection (from nature) as distinct from interpretation and analysis (as culture). Moreover, it also influenced how scholars present the production of knowledge and how they separated the process of collecting observations from the analyzing and organizing these observations (Latour 1993; Martin 2013: 69–70). Latour studied practice as a way to critique the division between nature and culture, and he argued that science produces knowledge not through simple observation, but as a result of a dense network of entities and actions that range from funding agencies, governments, fellow scientists, institutional priorities, and innumerable small decisions made on the basis of assumptions about how nature works. For Latour, the inseparability of nature and culture at the level of scientific practice is distinct from the representation of research in publications. The former embodies a network of relationships between human and nonhuman, animate and inanimate, institutional and individual, whereas the latter represents the data as independent realities that support scientific arguments. In archaeology, this distinction manifests itself in a division between "raw data" in archaeology (Gitelman and Jackson 2013)—often presented in scientifically structured catalogues—and the narrative or expository historical arguments. Awareness of this division has provoked recent discussions of digital data collection strategies that stop short of demonstrating how these changes produce new arguments or understandings of the past.

The use of technology in archaeology is not new, and, in fact, it has deep roots in the complicated intersection of the discipline, science, and industrial practice from the field's 19th-century origins. Heinrich

Schliemann, for example, funded his work at Troy and Mycenae through his former life as an industrialist and brought industrial organization to his excavations. Mortimer Wheeler and August Pitt-Rivers both drew upon both their military backgrounds and industrial practice by employing relatively unskilled workmen to excavate while leaving the interpretative responsibilities to their more discerning eye (Lucas 2001: 8). As Berggren and Hodder (2003: 422) have noted, the workers were "replaceable tools in the machinery." Such hierarchical organization of the archaeological workforce persists today. In cultural resource management (CRM) practice, "field technicians" represent a subordinate group to the archaeologists who supervise and interpret the results of excavation for official reports (Lucas 2001: 11–12). Many academic excavations have clear divisions between the inexperienced excavators, who are often students, and the more experienced trench supervisors. This coincides with the practice of separating the manual work of excavating from the "more intellectual" work of recording and documenting, although it is worth noting that many excavations recognize the tremendous value of local workers who are deeply familiar with local conditions. In general, the organization of archaeological projects reinforces a division between data collection and interpretation and analysis.

The division between data collection and its interpretation located practices separated the work of removing earth, counting objects, and describing contexts from the work of analyzing and, ultimately, publishing, archaeological conclusions. This made data collection susceptible to efforts that would both increase efficiency and improve the quality of data collected. Nowhere are these practices more visible than in CRM (see Spigelman *et al.*, Ch. 3.4), where streamlined data collection methods certify that the recording of archaeological information keeps pace with development and are efficient enough to ensure that the firms involved remain solvent. Various contributors to the British CRM industry, in particular, have developed streamlined recording sheets (and attendant practices) that ensure that data is recorded in a standardized way according to best practices (Pavel 2010: 16–17). As Catalan Pavel has pointed out, the practice of documenting archaeological sites carefully is closely tied to the official "preservation by record" policies of the British government—policies that rest on the assumption that an archaeologist might be able to reconstruct the site after its destruction from the record collected during the rescue excavation process.

The rise in CRM archaeology has made the links between archaeological practice and the pressures and pace of capitalism more explicit, and it has amplified a tendency toward industrial practices present in academic contexts as well. Academic archaeology developed as a professional discipline alongside the emergence of industrialized academic disciplines in the modern university (Menand 2010) as well as emerging museums (Dyson 2006: 133–171). This shared trajectory reinforced the industrial organization of archaeological knowledge production. In a disciplinary context, industrial practice and professional archaeology are inseparable both chronologically and institutionally. The university developed systematic ways to educate young adults with courses arranged across disciplines to build key skills, provide professional credentials, and produce productive contributors to American society (Novick 1988; Menand 2010). While variation existed across universities, over the course of the late 19th and early 20th century, many oriented their curriculum toward the challenge of providing credentials for the growing body of professionals required by industry and our increasingly specialized society. This desire for specialization found its most extreme manifestation in the logic of the assembly line, which assigned individuals to perform single, exceedingly limited tasks over and over. Through coordinating the hyper-specialized actions of dozens of individuals, the assembly line produced a single product as efficiently as possible. Higher education employed a similar approach to producing educated individuals by dividing up the process of education among various specialized experts in particular disciplines.

Historically, these industrial influences on higher education have incurred resistance, although much of resistance is not articulated as such. Disciplines like history, art history, literature, anthropology, and archaeology have periodically used the word "craft" to describe their undertakings (e.g., Bloch 1953; Frisch 1990), but this perspective was rarely positioned explicitly as a countercurrent to industrial models of education and knowledge production (Maguire and Shanks 1996; Taylor 1998). Recently there has emerged a more consistent resistance to the "audit culture" surrounding university education, and this has pushed cultural anthropologists to emphasize the holistic, embodied, and immersive experience of fieldwork (Herzfeld 2007). Scholars of art and literature historians have championed the open-ended and contemplative process of close reading, or the patient, unhurried examination of a work of art (Roberts 2013). All these approaches to disciplinary knowledge have a few elements in common. They resist the fragmentation of tasks common to industrial practices and ground disciplinary knowledge in the willingness to embrace the slow process of experience. As a result, these disciplines generally have ignored calls for efficiency and embraced practices and knowledge derived from careful examining, close reading, and contemplation.

Archaeologists have looked beyond contemporary practice to emphasize the foundation of their discipline's craft practices. Michael Shanks and Matthew Johnson, for example, have explored the origins of archaeology in 18th-century traditions of historical perambulations, landscape painting, and literature (Johnson 2006; Shanks 2012). The historical English countryside came alive not through the systematic treatments by specialist scholars, but through contemplative encounters mediated through art and literature. These pre-industrial approaches to the landscape cast a long shadow across the discipline and served as a counterweight to the influence grounded in industrial practices. While the 18th- and 19th-century rural wanderers were members of the economic and social elite seeking to inscribe their aristocratic vision on a landscape as a counterweight to industrialized wealth, craft continued to embody non-aristocratic approaches to knowledge as well. Despite the historical awareness of pre-professional practices in archaeology (and other disciplines), Shanks and Marxist archaeologist Randall Maguire considered the impact of craft to be "latent" in the field of archaeology and primarily manifest in the creativity of the archaeologist's work where "hand, heart, and mind are combined" (Maguire and Shanks 1996: 82).

As Mary Leighton's recent article (2015) has emphasized, the tension between craft elements in archaeological practice and the ordered routine of industrial production varies widely across the discipline. In her important study, she compares Andean archaeological practice to the CRM practices pioneered by the Winchester Research Unit in the United Kingdom (for the Winchester Research Unit model, see Pavel 2010: 27–28, 44–45). The Andean project had largely unskilled, local workmen supervised by graduate students who maintained paperwork and was overseen by project directors who coordinated the efforts of field teams, the orderly flow of artifacts, and the collection of completed forms. In the practices of the United Kingdom project, open-area, single-context excavations placed the excavator trench-side "with both a pen and a trowel" (Leighton 2015: 81) and focused on the production of single-context forms. Both projects concluded with the creation of Harris matrices to describe the archaeological contexts present in an area. Leighton observes that despite the similarities of the output of these projects, significant variation exists in archaeological practice. In the Mediterranean, for example, the hybrid system employed by Corinth Excavations demonstrates how highly skilled local workers can lead inexperienced graduate student "supervisors" through the complexities of single-context excavation (Pavel 2010: 90-92). In other words, the systematic organization of archaeological labor occludes a range of trench-side practices that preserve the "latent" impact of craft practices beneath layers of scientific management.

Process and Practice

The tension between practice, archaeological method and methodology, and publication is the space where slow archaeology and craft meet the industrial demand for efficiency and speed. For archaeology, stratigraphic excavation embodies certain aspects of industrial practice and modes of organization by parsing complex situations into more granular entities (McAnany and Hodder 2009; Leighton 2015). The identification and removal of discrete levels and the systematic arrangement of these strata in relation to one another structures the archaeological record in a way that allows for chronological and spatial descriptions of past depositional events. The work of dividing the excavated world into distinct strata paralleled the use of fragmentation as a tool of efficiency in industrial practice. Working from strata to strata across a trench, stratigraphic excavation defined the complexity of time and space through distinct slices. Each stratum received careful documentation in notebooks including textual descriptions, illustration, and photography (with the spread of affordable photographs, see Bohrer 2011).

Some scholars have recognized Latour's "blackboxing" in the process of stratigraphic excavation (Latour 1987; Mickel 2015). The widespread use of Harris matrices to reduce stratigraphic levels into uniform boxes further supports this observation since these matrices create uniform divisions or contexts for artifacts later studied by specialists (Harris 1979). The artifacts and relationships often help to assign either relative or, in a best-case scenario, absolute dates to each level, to associate a function with the space, or to define particular archaeological events. As the discipline of archaeology and methods of excavation have become more complex, a larger number of specialists are relied upon to assist in identifying and analyzing the material present. The largest projects now rely on dozens of specialists who work in parallel with excavators, wheel-barrow drivers, trench supervisors, area supervisors, field directors to produce archaeological knowledge. Both the assumptions surrounding archaeological practice and the specialists who contribute to it encourage the maintenance of industrial discipline to ensure that the fragmented data sets might be re-integrated at a later point. As Leighton points out, however, the implementation of this kind of industrial order comes at the level of practice. For her, blackboxing defines both the processes of archaeology and the way that the product of these processes hides variations in practice (Leighton 2015).

The New Archaeology of the second half of the 20th century contributed to the interest in processes that fragmented archaeological information recovered during fieldwork. The interest in quantitative analysis and studies that relied upon the precise plotting of sites across a region or artifacts within a site required the identification and sometimes isolation of discrete objects (Lucas 2001: 126–127; Thomas 2004: 76–77). New Archaeologists were confident that collecting data from the field systematically was the central concern for fieldwork, and the understanding of this data through hypothesis testing and theory building was a secondary process that often occurred in a separate place (Witmore 2004). Regional, intensive pedestrian survey adopted the techniques of New Archaeology to construct palimpsests of overlapping maps produced by a range of specialists and, ultimately, computer-generated algorithms (e.g., Gillings *et al.* 2000; Alcock and Cherry 2004). The maps derived from rigorous fieldwork and laboratory analysis allowed archaeologists to visualize artifact scatters, sites, and settlements across richly detailed regional scales. Over the past decade, methodological debates in Mediterranean archaeology and a growing interest in behavioral archaeology and formation processes have increased the intensity of artifact collection and the complexity of the resulting maps, but the basic structure of field practices and analysis remain unchanged (e.g., Bevan and Conolly 2013; Caraher *et al.* 2014).

The development of systematic practices in intensive survey paralleled the spread of Harris matrices in excavations. This practice reflected the growing interest in documenting vertical spatial relationships and depositional contexts in a way that regularized the units of archaeological interpretation. The tidy character of the Harris matrices presents stratigraphic deposits in a formal and generalized way that allowed them to be compared over open-area, single-context excavations while preserving the autonomy of individual excavators (Leighton 2015). In other words, Harris matrices represent the product of trench-side interpretation that forms the basis for understanding the archaeological structure of the site.

DIGITAL TOOLS AND PRACTICES

The intersection of science and industrial practices in archaeology resulted in archaeological methods based on standardized procedures linked directly to the production of consistent and regular results. As Leighton notes, however, formal descriptions of archaeological processes obscure messy archaeological practices and complex data sets to facilitate analysis. It is important to recognize that some normalization of archaeological results is necessary to communicate complex situations, idiosyncratic environments, and dynamic social and political relationships present in any archaeological process. Christopher Witmore and others have identified mediation as a key element in archaeological work (González-Ruibal 2008; Witmore 2009). At the same time, these processes that archaeologists use to produce consistent data are under pressure both from within the academy and from the cultural resource management industry. A new crop of digital tools has entered into this situation with promises to reinforce and accelerate longstanding tendencies in archaeological knowledge making. Slow archaeology challenges archaeologists to consider how this acceleration has led to the transformation of the discipline.

Archaeologists have largely seen the adoption of digital tools as a way to improve efficiency (Olson *et al.* 2014; Roosevelt *et al.* 2015; Wilhelmson and Dell'Unto 2015; see also Spigelman *et al.*, Ch. 3.4; Wallrodt, Ch. 1.1). By doing things faster without losing accuracy or precision, archaeological projects can collect more information, which is typically encoded as bits of data that allows them to reconstruct archaeological contexts more completely in less time. Digital tools have reinforced tactics used by archaeologists to standardize their practices and continued trends in producing discrete bits of data useful for the kinds of studies developed in New Archaeology. As Pavel has argued, these archaeological methodologies manifest themselves in the slow replacement of trench diaries or notebooks with detailed forms that became widely used in the last decades of the 20th century (Pavel 2010). While most forms preserve space for interpretation and analysis at trench-side, the dominant trend has been toward more atomized recording designed to improve accuracy in the field, to normalize description for comparison or seriation across a site, and to facilitate quantitative analysis.

Today's use of iPads or other tablet computers at trench-side or in the field reproduce many aspects of paper forms while enforcing additional regularity in recording. The use of iPads by Steven Ellis's Pompeii Archaeological Research Project Porta Stabia crystalized the potential of tablet computers to streamline trench-side data collection (Pettegrew *et al.* 2013; see also Ellis, Ch. 1.2; Fee, Ch. 2.1; Poehler, Ch. 1.7; Wallrodt, Ch. 1.1). The best-designed applications, like those used by Ellis's and Poehler's teams at Pompeii and similar databases described by other authors in this volume, include a combination of dropdown menus and open text fields to encourage trench supervisors to be both consistent and detailed (Dufton, Ch. 3.3; Motz, Ch. 1.3; Spigelman *et al.*, Ch. 3.4). Moreover, these databases make it possible to track changes to entries through time, thus allowing project directors to observe how trench supervisors adjusted their data throughout the excavation process. The data recorded at trench-side eventually becomes part of the larger project database and is made available on devices throughout the project. In short, the data collection process becomes more straightforward, consistent, transparent, and efficient.

In addition to neatly delineated recording forms and the digital versions replacing the more free-form notebooks, 3D "structure-from-motion" photography offers a method to further streamline trench and artifact illustration (Olson *et al.* 2014; Roosevelt *et al.* 2015; Olson, Ch. 2.2). By documenting a trench as a series of individual photographs, software like AgiSoft PhotoScan can produce an accurate 3D model of the trench. On a day-to-day basis, it is possible to use these methods to document individual strata in a trench, or at least to capture the spatial arrangement of various important contexts at a much greater speed than traditional trench illustration. At the end of an excavation season, when time always seems at a premium, my project on Cyprus—the Pyla-Koutsopetria Archaeological Project—was able to use structure-from-motion images that reproduce overhead trench photographs without the inconvenience of erecting a scaffolding or hiring a lift to provide accurate overhead images of the entire trench. The time-saving possibilities and increases in efficiency are notable and real. At the same time, by working to automate a key component of archaeological documentation, archaeologists continue to marginalize practices that involve craft modes of production like illustration or the skilled work of the excavator (Perry 2015). Moreover, the emphasis on the efficiency of these practices runs the risk of undermining the specialized awareness that these practices have the potential to encourage (Morgan 2009, 2012; Perry 2015).

To achieve these efficiencies, standardized recording sheets, whether in paper or digital form, and structure-from-motion photography transform the archaeologist and archaeological information in similar ways. First, both techniques involve the archaeologist breaking the site into fragments. For recording sheets, this involves dutifully filling in a series of predetermined descriptive fields ranging from soil Munsell color to dimensions, elevations, and features. It is hardly surprising that survey projects that developed directly from the ideas expressed in New Archaeology relied on forms and digital recording from the start of the famed "second wave" surveys in Greece (Bintliff *et al.* 1999; Cherry 2003). Structure-from-motion photographs are likewise fragmented views of the trench that rely on computer algorithms to reconstruct their proper relationships.

The fragmented, if more comprehensive, records created by digital practices in archaeology almost always require reassembly after the archaeologist leaves the field. The longstanding focus on the systematic collection of data in the field has produced a body of information that requires reassembly according to traditional archaeological practice (Lucas 2001). As the information collected in the field has become more granular and more digital in character, the tools and techniques required to reassemble it have become more complex. The archaeologist is at the top of a system of excavators, surveyors, and specialists but also interacting with complex hardware and software applications that range from "basic" Microsoft Access and FileMaker databases, to more complex applications like ArcGIS maps and 3D imaging suites, as well as other intermediary programs that allow for data to move between applications and devices. This software, as well as the hardware used to collect data at the trench-side or in the survey unit, function as parts of a larger digital ecosystem (for the use of the term "ecosystem" in the context of digital archaeology, see Forte *et al.* 2010; Kansa 2012). This ecosystem requires qualified personnel and additional levels of vigilance to maintain the system in which these bits of data make sense. Compared to the relative simplicity of an excavation notebook, which requires almost no particular technology to read and understand, the modern excavation or survey dataset is a virtually meaningless mass of encoded data.

Our dependence on technology to reconstruct archaeological contexts becomes even more acute when dealing with data produced by 3D-imaging technologies which rely on either bespoke or proprietary software to produce legible results. Even if we accept that the basic data behind 3D images, such as point clouds, are actually quite simple to decode and understand, and that it is possible to archive the photographs, point clouds, and even polygons from which a 3D model derives, the process of producing a 3D model and the 3D models itself are often the distinct product of proprietary software. Moreover, as the contributors to this volume demonstrate, our ability to produce 3D models has existed for quite some time, but these models remain difficult to publish outside a few academic publishers, and they remain challenging to preserve in a reproducible way (Opitz 2015; Reinhard 2015). These limitations do not diminish their potential utility, but they do reveal one side-effect of fragmenting our archaeological data in an effort to manipulate it in more efficient (and also more dynamic) ways. Without attention to the larger digital and social ecosystem in which they function, however, we run the risk of decontextualizing our archaeological processes.

Just as data collection strategies that privilege a more efficient, but fragmented, workflow have separated the work of excavating or field walking from the work of analysis, so too have an increasing reliance on digital tools—some of which are proprietary and many require specialized skill to manipulate—complicated the social organization of the interpretative process. Archaeologists must now approach critically the digital tools that we use and recognize our limited access to the structure of these tools and the technologies and code that makes them work. While archaeologists have always relied to some extent on tools that they did not entirely control (after all, who knows how a Marshalltown trowel is really made), digital tools are particularly fraught because the interplay between proprietary software and hardware across a digital ecosystem produces a network of subordinate assumptions, but nevertheless shape the basic structure of our research.

Toward a Slow Archaeology

Slow archaeology calls for a critical appreciation of the accelerated pace that digital tools have brought to industrial practices in archaeology. New Archaeology fortified the longstanding industrial influences in archaeology through its emphasis on methodology and adoption of neatly organized forms that serve to standardize archaeological observation at the point of recording. While reflexive and ethnographic treatments of archaeological practices have demonstrated that standardized forms occlude variation in the execution of the well-defined methods (Mickel 2015), most recent publications focusing on digital tools and practices have done little to rectify this disjuncture (e.g., Roosevelt *et al.* 2015), outside a few high profile examples (Berggren *et al.* 2015). As a result, the adoption of digital tools is particularly fraught because they tend to reinforce a methodological discourse that itself already represents a Latourian "black box." If methodology risks obscuring the range of actual practice, many digital tools actually celebrate their reliance on obscured complexity by presenting technology "that just works."

Slow archaeology also contends that the change in pace promised by digital practices is not simply the continuation of a trend toward greater efficiency in the field, but represents a substantive change in how archaeologists realize this efficiency and speed. The tendency of these new tools to produce "black box" solutions to problems of efficiency reflects the growing pressures on both academic archaeologists and those in the field of cultural resource management to produce results at the pace of development and capital. In other words, as digital tools accelerate the pace of archaeological work, more aspects of archaeological practice become obscured by technology.

In practice, slow archaeology encourages a more deliberate approach to archaeological fieldwork and to the adoption of digital technologies. To be clear, this does not require a rejection of digital tools or new techniques, but rather an adjustment in how we document the implementation of these tools in archaeological work. Allison Mickel's work on notebooks as a place for unstructured and reflexive recording demonstrates how preserving traditional recording alongside more standardized forms reproduces much of the same information in synthetic and narrative forms (Mickel 2015). While Mickel's study does not distinguish between digital and analogue practices—a field diary could be in paper or digital form and integrated into a larger digital ecosystem—the narrative diary nevertheless stands out as distinctly separate from field-recording practices associated exclusively with digital tools (Gordon *et al.*, Ch. 1.4). In the digital era, form-based recording of the kind documented by Pavel (2010) operates at the intersection of New Archaeology and digital practices geared toward efficiency. On the Western Argolid Regional Project, we asked team leaders to stop recording their detailed forms periodically throughout the day and to look across the landscape to understand the larger context for their work. Conversely, David Pettegrew (a team leader on the Eastern Korinthia Archaeological Survey) discovered that he had to return to the Corinthian landscape for several field seasons after he reassembled the data collected from the intensive survey in order to understand the neatly arranged maps from within the physical landscape of the isthmus. A narrative notebook or diary provides the opportunity for synthetic documentation of the fragmented data collected on a form, and it captures both the integrative experience of the landscape and recursive decision-making that shapes our encounter with excavated contexts.

The emphasis on digital tools for making archaeological work more efficient also transforms the character of archaeological practice. In earlier drafts of this paper and elsewhere, I used the term "de-skilling" to characterize the change in practices brought about by "black box" technologies in the field (Caraher 2013). For example, the basic skill of illustrating a trench is a proficiency that some archaeologists have suggested can be replaced by more efficient 3D-imaging technology. In place of the craft of illustrating, these technologies offer the digital skill of preparing a 3D image (Roosevelt *et al.* 2015). The main difference, however, is that in traditional practice, illustrating the trench involves interpreting the representation of relationships between objects and resolving the myriad of small relational conflicts between the features visible in the trench. The goal of producing a dynamic 3D image, in contrast, is to gather as much information as accurately as possible. While the final illustration almost certainly obscures the decision-making process, it does capture the data points and features that the archaeologist considers crucial for their conclusions. In other words, illustration is the product of an explicitly interpretive process, and it reinforces careful observation and decision-making while excavating. The removal of the time-consuming illustration process from excavation work does not necessarily guarantee the de-skilling of the excavator, but it certainly transforms a crucial step in the documentation process from one requiring detailed and careful knowledge of the features in a trench and of the conventions of illustration to one requiring the understanding of a digital camera and relevant software. The former is vital to the archaeological process whereas the latter is not.

Finally, slow archaeology, like the slow food movement, emphasize on the local and argues that the distributive tendencies of digital practices transform the place of archaeological knowledge production as well as the methods. To return to the example of 3D imaging, traditional trench illustrations locate archaeological argument-making at the edge of the trowel. In contrast, the use of a digital camera and software to produce a representation of the trench involves the passive collection of images at trench-side for later processing and study. The digital process shifts the illustration of the trench to the lab, computer room, or office. The illustration is based not on a physical encounter with the relationships visible in the trench, but on the series of photographs. Intensive pedestrian survey has likewise featured the almost mechanical collection of highly granular data from the field. This data relies upon remote processing to produce meaningful artifactual landscapes. There is no question that these remotely-created landscapes have added significantly to our understanding of the premodern countryside, but, at the same time, these digital maps risk being divorced from the physical encounter with the countryside. As fieldwork becomes increasingly associated with data collection and analysis, the space of interpretation shifts from the field to the office. The emphasis on place in archaeology contrats with the placelessness of digital efficiency.

Slow archaeology challenges any claim that gains in efficiency through the use of digital tools is sufficient reason alone to incorporate them into the archaeological workflow. It also recognizes that even though technological changes in archaeology occur in tandem with changes in method, practices, and the social organization of archaeological work, technology nevertheless has independent consequences. As Harvey (1990), Rosa (2013), Virilio (2005), and even Petrini (2003) have observed, the accelerating pace of a world saturated with technology has created new categories of experience, economic structures, and social relationships. The Latourian black boxes that have proliferated in archaeological research and have appeared regularly in archaeological methodology reflect a tendency toward uncritical occluding of technological processes in archaeological practice. Slow archaeology argues that the rapid pace of technological change and a critical, reflexive archaeology requires renewed attention to the place of digital tools in both field practices and methodology.

https://mobilizingthepast.mukurtu.net/
collection/41-slow-archaeology-technology-efficiency-and-archaeological-work

http://dc.uwm.edu/arthist_mobilizingthepast/18

References

Alcock, S., and J. Cherry, eds. 2004. *Side-by-Side Survey: Comparative Regional Studies in the Mediterranean World*. Oxford: Oxbow.

Andrews, G. 2008. *The Slow Food Story: Politics and Pleasure*. London: Pluto Press.

Augé, M. 1995. *Non-Places: Introduction to an Anthropology of Supermodernity*. London: Verso.

Berggrenn, Å., and I. Hodder. 2003. "Social Practice, Method, and Some Problems of Field," *American Antiquity* 68: 421–434.

Berggren, Å., N. Dell'Unto, M. Forte, S. Haddow, I. Hodder, J. Issavi, N. Lercari, C. Mazzucato, A. Mickel, and J. S. Taylor. 2015. "Revisiting

Reflexive Archaeology at Çatalhöyük: Integrating Digital and 3D Technologies at the Trowel's Edge," Antiquity 89: 433–448.

Bevan, A., and J. Conolly. 2013. *Mediterranean Islands, Fragile Communities, and Persistent Landscapes: Antikythera in Long-Term Perspective.* Cambridge: Cambridge University Press.

Bintliff, J., P. Howard, and A. Snodgrass. 1999. "The Hidden Landscapes of Prehistoric Greece," *Journal of Mediterranean Archaeology* 12: 139–168.

Bloch, M. 1953. *The Historian's Craft.* Trans., P. Putnam. New York: Vintage Book

Bohrer, N. 2011. *Photography and Archaeology.* London: Reaktion Books.

Caraher, W. 2013. "Slow Archaeology," *North Dakota Quarterly* 80(2) [2015]: 43–52.

Caraher, W., S. B. Fee, and D. K. Pettegrew. 2013. "Taking Mobile Computing to the Field," *Near Eastern Archaeology* 76: 50–55.

Caraher, W., D. K. Pettegrew, and R. S. Moore. 2014. *Pyla-Koutsopetria I: An Archaeological Survey of an Ancient Coastal Town.* American Schools of Oriental Research Archaeological Reports 21. Boston: American Schools of Oriental Research.

Cherry, J. 2003. "Archaeology beyond the Site: Regional Survey and Its Future," in J. K. Papadopoulos and R. M. Leventhal, eds., *Theory and Practice in Mediterranean Archaeology: Old World and New World Perspectives. Cotsen Advanced Seminars* 1. Los Angeles: Cotsen Institute of Archaeology, 137–59.

Dyson, S. 2006. *In Pursuit of Ancient Pasts: A History of Classical Archaeology in the Nineteenth and Twentieth Centuries.* New Haven: Yale University Press.

Forte, M., S. Pescarin, E. Pietroni, and N. Dell'Unto. 2010. "An Integrated Approach to Archaeology: From the Fieldwork to Virtual Reality Systems," in F. Nicolucci and S. Hermon, eds., *Beyond the Artifact: Digital Interpretation of the Past. Proceedings of CAA2004, Prato, 13–17 April 2004.* Budapest: Archaeolingua, 325–334.

Frisch, M. H. 1990. *A Shared Authority: Essays on the Craft and Meaning of Oral and Public History.* Albany: State University of New York Press.

Gillings, M., D. J. Mattingly, and J. van Dalen. 2000. *Geographical Information Systems and Landscape Archaeology. Populus Monograph* 3. Oxford: Oxbow.

Gitelman L., and V. Jackson. 2013. "Introduction," in L. Gitelman, ed., *"Raw Data" Is an Oxymoron*. Cambridge, MA: MIT Press, 1–14.

González-Ruibal, A. 2008. "Time to Destroy: An Archaeology of Supermodernity," *Current Anthropology* 49: 247–279.

Harris, E. C. 1979. *Principles of Archaeological Stratigraphy*. London: Academic Press.

Harvey, D. 1990. *The Condition of Postmodernity: An Enquiry into the Origins of Cultural Change*. Oxford: Blackwell.

Herzfeld, M. 2007. "Deskilling, 'Dumbing Down,' and the Auditing of Knowledge in the Practical Mastery of Artisans and Academics: An Ethnographer's Response to a Global Problem," in M. Harris, ed., *Ways of Knowing: New Approaches in the Anthropology of Experience and Learning. Methodology and History in Anthropology* 18. Oxford: Berghahn Books, 91–110.

Honoré, C. 2004. *In Praise of Slowness: How a Worldwide Movement Is Challenging the Cult of Speed*. San Francisco: HarperSanFrancisco.

James, I. 2007. *Paul Virilio*. New York: Routledge.

Johnson, M. 2006. *The Idea of Landscape*. Oxford: Blackwell.

Kansa, E. 2012. "Openness and Archaeology's Information Ecosystem," *World Archaeology* 44: 498–520.

Latour, B. 1987. *Science in Action: How to Follow Scientists and Engineers through Society*. Cambridge: Harvard University Press.

Latour, B. 1993. *We Have Never Been Modern*. Trans. C. Porter. Cambridge, MA: Harvard University Press.

Leighton, M. 2015. "Excavation Methodologies and Labour as Epistemic Concerns in the Practice of Archaeology: Comparing Examples from British and Andean Archaeology," *Archaeological Dialogues* 22: 65–88.

Lucas, G. 2001. *Critical Approaches to Fieldwork: Contemporary and Historical Archaeological Practice*. New York: Routledge.

Maguire, R., and M. Shanks. 1996. "The Craft of Archaeology," *American Antiquity* 61: 75–88.

Martin, A. M. 2013. *Archaeology beyond Postmodernity: A Science of the Social*. Lanham, MD: Altavista Press.

McAnany, P. A., and I. Hodder. 2009. "Thinking about Stratigraphic Sequence in Social Terms," *Archaeological Dialogues* 16: 1–22.

Menand, L. 2010. *The Marketplace of Ideas*. New York: W. W. Norton.

Mickel, A. 2015. "Reasons for Redundancy in Reflexivity: The Role of Diaries in Archaeological Epistemology," *Journal of Field Archaeology* 40: 300–309.

Morgan, C. L. 2009. "(Re)Building Çatalhöyük: Changing Virtual Reality in Archaeology," *Archaeologies: Journal of the World Archaeological Congress* 5: 468–487.

Morgan, C. 2012. *Emancipatory Digital Archaeology*. Ph.D. dissertation, University of California, Berkeley.

Novick, P. 1988. *That Noble Dream: The "Objectivity Question" and the American Historical Profession*. Cambridge: Cambridge University Press.

Olson, B. R., J. Gordon, C. Runnels, and S. Chomyszak. 2014. "Experimental Three-Dimensional Printing of a Lower Palaeolithic Handaxe: An Assessment of the Technology and Analytical Value," *Lithic Technology* 39: 162–172.

Opitz, R. 2015. "Three Dimensional Field Recording in Archaeology: An Example from Gabii," in B. R. Olson and W. R. Caraher, eds., *Visions of Substance: 3D Imaging in Mediterranean Archaeology*. Grand Forks: The Digital Press at The University of North Dakota, 73–86.

Pavel, C. 2010. *Describing and Interpreting the Past: European and American Approaches to the Written Record of the Excavation*. Bucharest: University of Bucharest Press.

Perry, S. 2015 "Crafting Knowledge with (Digital) Visual Media in Archaeology," in R. Chapman and A. Wylie, eds., *Material Evidence: Learning from Archaeological Practice*. London: Routledge, 189–210.

Petrini, C. 2003. *Slow Food: The Case for Taste*. New York: Columbia University Press.

Pettegrew, D. K, S. Fee, and W. R. Caraher. 2013. "Taking Mobile Computing into the Field," *Near Eastern Archaeology* 76: 50–55.

Reinhard, A. 2015. "Three- and Four-Dimensional Archaeological Publication," in B. R. Olson and W. R. Caraher, eds., *Visions of Substance: 3D Imaging in Mediterranean Archaeology*. Grand Forks: The Digital Press at The University of North Dakota, 43–50.

Roberts, J. L. 2013. "The Power of Patience: Teaching Students the Value of Deceleration and Immersive Attention." *Harvard Magazine*, http://harvardmagazine.com/2013/11/the-power-of-patience

Roosevelt, C. H., P. Cobb, E. Moss, B. R. Olson, and S. Ünlüsoy. 2015. "Excavation is ~~Destruction~~ Digitization: Advances in Archaeological Practice," *Journal of Field Archaeology* 40: 325–346.

Rosa, H. 2013. *Social Acceleration: A New Theory of Modernity*. New York: Columbia University Press.

Sassatelli, R. and F. Davolio. 2010. "Consumption, Pleasure and Politics: Slow Food and the Politico-Aesthetic Problematization of Food," *Journal of Consumer Culture* 10: 202-232.

Shanks, M. 2012. *The Archaeological Imagination*. Walnut Creek: Left Coast Press.

Taylor, K. S. 1998. "Higher Education: From Craft Production to Capitalist Enterprise?" *First Monday* 3, http://firstmonday.org/ojs/index.php/fm/article/viewArticle/618/539

Thomas, J. 2004. *Archaeology and Modernity*. London: Routledge.

Virilio, P. 1986. *Speed and Politics: An Essay on Dromology*. Trans. M. Polizzotti. New York: Columbia University Press.

Virilio, P. 2005. *Negative Horizon: An Essay in Dromoscopy*. Trans. M. Degener. New York: Continuum.

Wilhelmson, H., and N. Dell'Unto. 2015. "Virtual Taphonomy: A New Method Integrating Excavation and Postprocessing in an Archaeological Context," *American Journal of Physical Anthropology* 157: 305–321.

Witmore, C. 2004. "On Multiple Fields: Between the Material World and Media. Two Cases from the Peloponnesus, Greece," *Archaeological Dialogues* 11: 133–164.

Witmore, C. 2009. "Prolegomena to Open Pasts: On Archaeological Memory Practices," *Archaeologies* 5: 511–545.

4.2.
Click Here to Save the Past

Eric C. Kansa

This paper takes a critical look at how the branding, promotion and financing of digital solutions and services impacts archaeology. Digital data obviously has much promise: it can help us engage with wider communities, explore new research questions, and create and preserve a vastly enriched body of archaeological documentation. Digital data also has a certain glamour, gained in large part through its associations with the burgeoning tech industry. At conferences, digital initiatives are often marketed like tech startups as solutions to make archaeology faster, more efficient, and cutting-edge. The look and feel of archaeological websites owes a great deal to styles and user interface designs coming from the commercial Web. Overall, the quickly growing field of "digital archaeology" brings freshness and excitement to archaeology.

While I welcome the increasing limelight cast in areas that align with my particular research interests, I worry about the institutional context that currently surrounds digital data's growing prominence. In Kathleen Fitzpatrick's study of the dysfunctions of scholarly monographs as the sole route to tenure and promotion in many areas of the humanities (2011: esp. 47–49), she notes how scholars rarely focus critical reflection on the institutions and tacit rules that govern their own professions. Just as we need critical focus on why scholars fail to engage with new media, we also need critical reflection on how new media become part of our profession. If digital archaeology is to really fulfill its promise and widen participation and opportunities for exploring the past, we urgently need more reflection on the forces that shape the branding, management, and financing of digital data in archaeology.

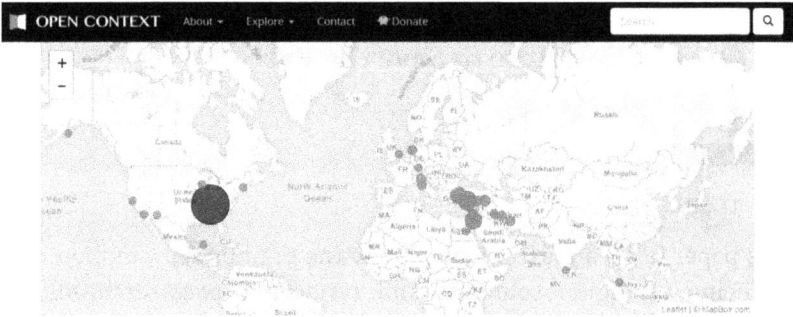

Figure 1: Open Context home page.

BACKGROUND

Since reflection in digital archaeology is in short supply, rather than focus specifically on my work with Open Context (http://opencontext.org), a data publishing service for archaeology, this essay will explore some of the institutional challenges faced by Open Context in particular and digital archaeology more generally. The perspectives offered here stem from my experience over 12 years as a dedicated "digital archaeologist," founding and running a nonprofit endeavor to promote the dissemination and preservation of archaeological field data. Open Context is now referenced by the National Science Foundation (NSF) and the National Endowment for the Humanities (NEH) for data management for archaeology and the digital humanities. Its approach of "data sharing as publishing" emphasizes collaboration with dedicated editorial and information specialists to make data more intelligible and usable. Open Context publishes a wide variety of archaeological data, ranging from survey data to excavation documentation, artifact descriptions, chemical analyses, and detailed descriptions of bones and other biological remains found in archaeological contexts.

The range, scale, and diversity of these data require expertise in data modeling and a commitment to continual development and iterative problem solving. Open Context (FIG. 1) has undergone several upgrades, the most recent in the spring of 2015, in order to keep pace with technology changes and to leverage best practices in data stewardship. With data preservation through the University of California's California Digital Library (CDL), Open Context now publishes more than 1.2 million archaeological records from projects worldwide.[1] This is on a scale comparable to that of a major museum (for instance, the online collection of the Metropolitan Museum of New York makes some 407,000 records available). Open Context has made this remarkable achievement on a much more limited budget than the online collections of major museums. Grant funding from the William and Flora Hewlett Foundation, the NEH, the Alfred P. Sloan Foundation, NSF, and others has gone a long way largely because of the Alexandria

---

[1] Open Context now also benefits from mirror hosting and backups offered by the German Archaeological Institute (DAI; see: http://opencontext.dainst.org). We are now beginning to do software development in collaboration with the DAI.

Archive Institute's (AAI, the legally recognized corporation behind the Open Context publishing service) status as an independent non-profit organization with an overhead much, much lower than large research institutions. The AAI and Open Context have also benefited from the growth of the Web and the "ecosystem" of projects and individuals in similar roles who are undertaking innovative work outside of traditional academic roles. At the same time, our vantage point outside of the tenure track offers us a different perspective on the academy and its evolution. Those perspectives inform this essay.

Branding and Sustainability in Digital Archaeology

As a relatively new area of specialization, digital archaeology has emerged during a time of tremendous change in the academy. While we see technological transformations unfolding that make digital archaeology possible, we also see profound and often disturbing restructuring of wider economic and political institutions that impact university funding and governance. Simply put, "neoliberalism"—a loosely associated bag of ideologies that emphasize fiscal austerity and relentless competition, market transactions, and certain management techniques centered on metrics and surveillance—now permeates academic institutions (Feller 2008; Kansa 2014a, 2014b).

With the notable exception of Wikipedia, commercial players dominate much of our interaction with World Wide Web. Most, if not all, digital archaeology projects must interface with the commercial Web, commercial software, and other commercial platforms. Search engine optimization, marketing of digital archaeology projects on social media, and the embrace of GitHub for software (and sometimes data) version control all illustrate cross-cutting ties with the commercial tech sector. Much of the interface design, look and feel, and other aspects interactivity take their cue from the commercial tech sector. Many digital archaeology websites have familiar commercial social media icons to facilitate tweets and links to social-media sites platforms such as Facebook. Similarly, many of the "best practices" of digital archaeology, including project management methodologies (agile, iterative), user-centered design, and systems architectures (e.g., cloud computing, RESTful web service design) come directly from approaches developed in commercial settings. And at the same time, many digital archaeology projects are actually built by people working on short-term academic computing contracts that may cycle between the academic and commercial sector (these individuals are often called "Alt-Acs" or Alternative Academics; see Posner 2013; Kansa and Kansa 2015). As such, Alt-Acs, typically working on short-term "soft money," would be prudent to look toward the commercial sector if the grant money does not continue to flow; fluency in methodologies and skills demanded in the tech sector can offer Alt-Acs more employment options outside academia. All of these factors come together to make the practice and outcomes of digital archaeology seem similar to those of (low budget) commercial start-ups.

These factors make the character of digital-centered outputs very different from conventional academic outputs. Branding for conventional research, be they books or articles, works very differently than digital scholarship. The dominant branding factor for conventional research outputs centers on the publisher: certain publishers carry cachet and prestige, and that branding confers prestige to their authors. While branding matters, the connection between a conventional scholarly work and an individual scholar is more personal and direct. Books and articles are largely "marketed" on a researcher's curriculum vitae, clearly identified as a researcher's individual accomplishments.

The myopic focus of academic reward systems to reward individual accomplishments over collaborative endeavors has seen wide critique among digital humanists (Fitzpatrick 2011). Despite these critiques, digital projects usually still fall outside of normal academic recognition and reward systems. They mainly count for tenure in promotion only indirectly, either as a success in competitive granting, or as the subject of a conventional publication that sees recognition and reward. For Alt-Acs that fall outside of the tenure track, recognition comes from involvement with the project itself. As an alternative to conventional paths toward recognition, many digital archaeological projects establish their own unique brands. As is the case with commercial startups, digital humanities brands are expressed with domain names, logos, color palettes, font choices, and the like.

The issue of branding goes far beyond the mere fact that domain names and hosting are inexpensive. Rather, the ubiquity of branding in digital archaeology reflects its peculiar role in the larger discipline. Although some digital projects aim to disseminate results of a specific project, many attempt to develop and market tools or services. Thus, many digital projects, though requiring their own research and development, aim to facilitate the research or outreach of others. Unlike conventional archaeological scholarship, where impact is usually measured through citation, digital projects tend compete for adoption by wider communities. Branding recognition works toward that goal.

The need to brand digital projects in large measure reflects an institutional context shaped by neoliberalism. Digital projects largely have short-term grant financing. Generating positive buzz and recognition can improve chances for future grants. Similarly, in order to sustain digital projects (see below), many projects have adopted some sort of fee-for-service model; for that of the Digital Archaeological Record (tDAR) see Kintigh and Altschul 2010, but this is applicable to Open Context also). Paying for useful services harkens back to both the market orientation and instrumentalism that help to define neoliberalism. Knowledge production has to be measurable, and ideally have practical outcomes that can be monetized. The project focus of digital archaeology similarly emphasizes instrumentalism. Most work aims to conceptualize, and if funded, build easily marketed "deliverables." Practitioners loudly trumpet accomplishments, collaborations, new features, and new funding via social media, in a way calculated to enhance recognition for a project's brand and eventually drive sales.

Making and marketing practical tools and services is not inherently bad or damaging to archaeology. After all, we absolutely should celebrate the creation of good tools and services that help archaeologists achieve research, public outreach, and other goals more effectively. However, I note the issue of branding to highlight a key concern—namely, is digital archaeology to be scholarship in its own right, or is it to be a niche area for (semi)commercial services? At what point do marketing and branding imperatives become self-serving goals unto themselves? How does marketing buzz impact the way we understand and evaluate the scholarship encoded in digital archeology?

The current framing of "sustainability" centers around organizational and project continuity made possible by clever business models that market some sort of service for fees. Ideas about what sustainability means and how we should attain it draws very heavily from neoliberalism. Grants can be seen as a type of no-interest venture capital loan. They get projects going, but then it is up to the project to maintain itself. Success means a project (and its associated institution) has enough continued income to grow via non-grant sources of support.

The clearest example of this vision of sustainability is the online journal repository, JSTOR. JSTOR started with grant funding from the Andrew W. Mellon Foundation in 1995 and first launched its online services in 1997. In subsequent years, JSTOR's developers founded Ithaka, a nonprofit corporation to sustain and manage JSTOR. In many ways, JSTOR represents a singular success. It offers invaluable services to the scholarly community (that can afford institutional subscriptions) and now does so without depending on grant-based financing. In 2004, Donald Waters, a Mellon Foundation program officer, discussed how JSTOR came to be such a dominant player in digital scholarship, stating that "designing resources to take advantage of the economies of scale inherent in the digital environment is critical to sustainability" (Waters 2004). He also lamented the jumbled fragmentation of scholarly resources developed by many small and one-off projects (Waters 2004).

Is this vision of sustainability always desirable? One danger may be the encouragement of monopolies or oligarchies where "sustainability" is not just a means to an end (some sort of public service), but an end unto itself. Dominating a market and crowding out rivals is surely sustainable. Effectively, because JSTOR is so dominant, commands so much scholarly attention, and has contractual agreements with so many publishers and libraries,[2] it would be very difficult for others to build alternative discovery services, indexes, and interfaces to the content now delivered by JSTOR. One can imagine feminist or African American scholars developing special discovery, presentation, and text analysis tools as alternative ways of understanding and exploring the content now in JSTOR. But I cannot see how such alternative JSTOR-like platforms could now be financed, launched, and sustained. Thus, while JSTOR offers excellent services, these services come with opportunity costs.

I need to be clear that JSTOR does not deserve to be considered a villain in the world of scholarly communications. The (near) monopoly power of some commercial actors, especially Elseveir and

---

[2] On this issue, see http://www.theawl.com/2011/08/
was-aaron-swartz-stealing.

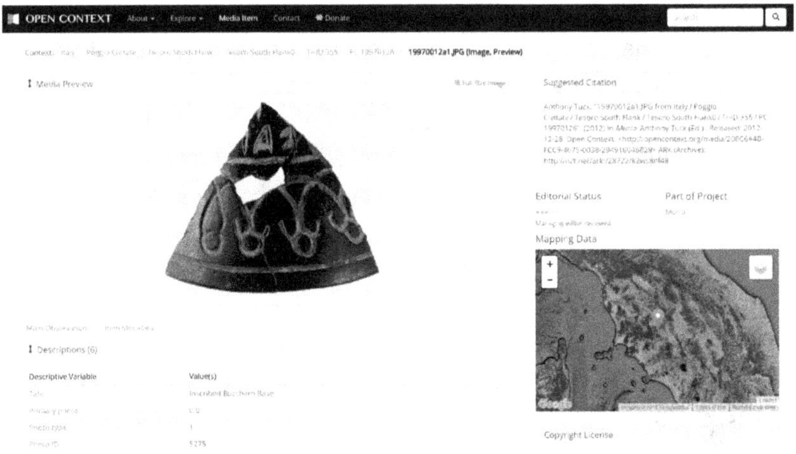

Figure 2: Example of an individual sherd, a URI-identified resource in Open Context.

Proquest, does far more to stifle new (and lower cost) alternatives.[3] Rather, I focus on JSTOR because it started as a grant-funded effort. It succeeded in dominating an important niche and pioneered a model for other grant funded projects to emulate, and that is the center of my concern. Another Mellon Foundation funded effort, Digital Antiquity, is working with its tDAR (the Digital Archaeological Record) repository to offer key and absolutely necessary digital preservation services for US-based archaeology. Like similar large-scale, long-term projects, Digital Antiquity must develop a sustainable business model for its services. In doing so, it has some parallels as well as some important differences with JSTOR. First, while JSTOR relies on institutional subscription-for-access income,[4] Digital Antiquity has largely adopted "open data" policies (see below) and charges for deposit (like Open Context). Although tDAR imposes some access restrictions because of the sensitive nature of some of its data, it is otherwise very open with the content it archives. Nevertheless, a proven method to gain sustainability would be to work toward the scale and institutional positioning achieved by JSTOR, a strategy outlined by Waters (2004):

> There is as yet on the horizon no real substitute for the vision, discipline, and commitment needed to build digital collections at a scale and level of generality that will attract a broad audience of users and have such an impact on scholarship that their disappearance is not an option.

JSTOR succeeded in amassing a collection so large and comprehensive that one cannot be an effective researcher in many fields without JSTOR access. Similarly, if Digital Antiquity succeeds in developing a comprehensive archive of American archaeology, it will be in a powerful position to become a similarly essential resource for the discipline.

---

[3] Thanks to Amanda French for highlighting the need to keep perspective with respect to JSTOR; see her comments: https://github.com/ekansa-pubs/ekansa-pubs.github.io/issues/23

[4] As pointed out by Ben Marwick (https://github.com/ekansa-pubs/ekansa-pubs.github.io/issues/25), JSTOR is an excellent source of open (or at least free-of-charge) data for text mining and other analyses. However, JSTOR has not embraced open-access distribution of articles and mainly maintains fee-for-access services.

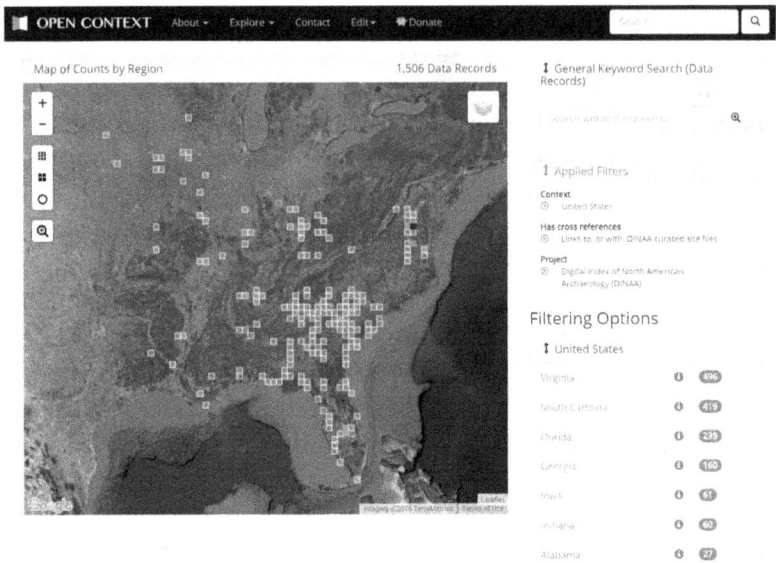

Figure 3: Map of Sites in the Digital Index of North American Archaeology (DINAA) that cross-reference with tDAR and other online collections.

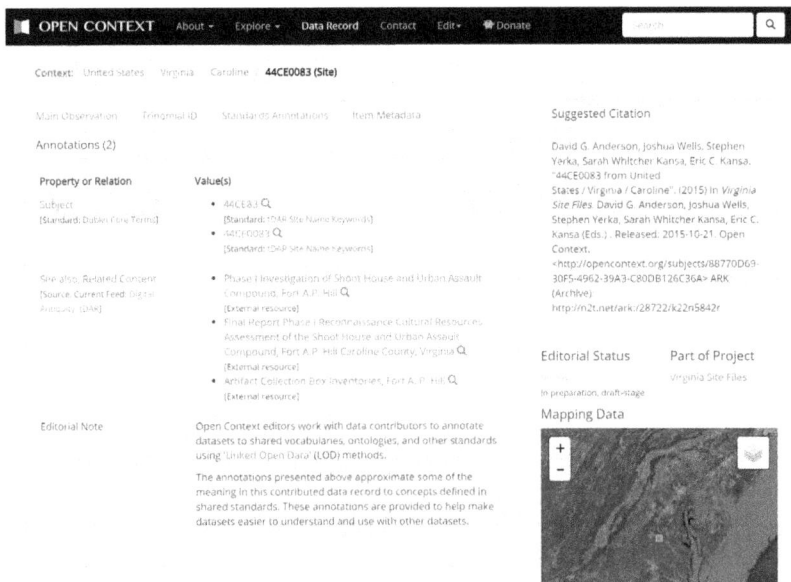

Figure 4: Example DINAA site-record cross-referencing tDAR and displaying tDAR archived reports via an API request.

Waters' emphasis on scale and centrality to explicitly achieve a JSTOR-like "lock-in" has potential drawbacks. Though it probably does lead to the long-term continuity of a given effort, it can also result in the crowding out of other programs, thereby inhibiting exploration of other paths toward innovation and other ways of organizing and representing digital scholarship. For example, Open Context has taken a very different (but complementary) route to managing and disseminating archaeological data than tDAR or other repositories. Open Context publishes digital data as granular Web resources ("one URL per potsherd;" see FIG. 2). This facilitates new opportunities to explore the approaches of Linked Open Data toward networking archaeological information. But it also represents something of a challenge to interface with a digital repository because most repositories (including tDAR) have different expectations about data organization and granularity. Nevertheless, we were able to collaborate with the California Digital Library (CDL) to arrange repository services that could accommodate the granularity of Open Context's resources. The fact that the CDL could tailor repository services to our specific needs allows us to explore different approaches to data curation while meeting preservation responsibilities.

Fortunately, recent collaborations between Digital Antiquity, Open Context, and the Digital Index of North American Archaeology (DINAA) project demonstrate that a JSTOR-like lock-in is not inevitable in digital archaeology. The DINAA project, led by Joshua Wells and David G. Anderson, uses Open Context to publish archaeological site file data curated by state officials with geospatial and other sensitive information redacted (Wells *et al.* 2014). In close collaboration with Adam Brin at Digital Antiquity, we recently cross-referenced the DINAA site file records with certain metadata records in tDAR using Linked Open Data approaches. Open data practice adopted by both Open Context and tDAR (FIGS. 3, 4), as well as technologies such as APIs (application program interfaces) and Linked Open Data that facilitate rich exchanges of data, can promote meaningful collaboration between distributed projects and collections. These same APIs and Linked Open Data methods would similarly allow completely new and independent projects to build upon tDAR and Open Context managed resources in novel ways.

A diversity of perspectives and approaches to digital data should be seen as a "feature" rather than a "bug." Archaeological data management issues involve significant theoretical, practical, and technological challenges. These intellectual challenges are as rich and deep as any other archaeological research question, necessitating a wide variety of perspectives and experiments. We should not sacrifice community-wide engagement and participation in digital archaeology in order to make one specific program "sustainable," however worthy it may be. Thus, part of our evaluation of digital archaeology projects should focus on how such projects promote and facilitate new and independent approaches. Developing institutional supports that promote the future work of others rather than our own parochial branded interests represents a key challenge for digital archaeology in the 21st century.

Branding Solutionism

Interestingly, branding dynamics in digital archaeology not only reflect the strategies of the creators and developers of digital projects, they also reflect performance strategies of people in wider communities. For example, the laptops of many "digital archaeologists" are often covered with stickers of different brands. One could have a GitHub "octocat" sticker to signal participation in current best practice of software version control (https://github.com), a Mukurtu logo to signal awareness and concern for indigenous rights issues in digital media (http://mukurtu.org), or a Creative Commons logo to signal participation in "open knowledge" (http://creativecommons.org). Though one need not seriously engage with indigenous rights or the political economy of intellectual property to use those logos, the logos can serve a serious purpose. That is, branding and logos in digital archaeology are beginning to play a role in performance, self-fashioning, and identity construction (see Deuze et al. 2012). The branding of our apps serves as a signal of our commitment to public engagement, reproducibility, and ethical practice.

This issue of branding and marketing identities within the profession raises a host of questions about how digital archaeology works as scholarship. As noted, the value of conventional scholarship is measured through citation impact. How does this impact work in digital archaeology given the complexities of how brands are marketed and worn in identity construction? The actual substance, development history, technical characteristics, or conceptual foundations of a specific platform or project can matter less than its importance as a signal of identity. After all, the specifics of any program are often opaque and difficult to discern, especially to a non-expert.

How does marketing-buzz and identity-signaling correlate with recognition of a project as an important element of archaeological practice? I argue that the issue of branding and identity construction relates to Evgeny Morozov's (2014: 5) critique of "solutionism," a technocratic tendency of:

> . . . recasting all complex social situations either as neat problems with definite, computable solutions or as transparent and self-evident processes that can be easily optimized—if only the right algorithms are in place!—this quest is likely to have unexpected consequences that could eventually cause more damage than the problems they seek to address.

Solutionism is appealing in a neoliberal academic institution because it suggests that complex and contested problems can be made tractable with the proper technologies and management practices. The initial (and now more tempered) enthusiasm for "Massive Open Online Courses" (MOOCs) to cheaply deliver "educational experiences" that can scale up is illustrative of solutionism in higher education. While it may seem obvious that education is an intensely social and complex process, MOOC proponents were highly effective at selling the idea that learning was a service ripe for cost-cutting disruption through digital media. It turns out that MOOCs are not simple turn-key solutions. MOOCs can, and occasionally do, broaden access to meaningful learning, but it takes more than simple delivery of course materials and interaction over the Web. Making MOOCs work requires institutional commitment and dedication to understand how to make technologies work within complex social contexts of learning (Earl 2014).

Temptations to celebrate simple branded solutions exist in digital archaeology. In the current context of cost-cutting and pressure for high-throughput and easily recognized research outputs, brands can unfortunately signal concern for larger research and engagement goals without necessarily investing meaningful effort. This is akin to "green-washing," a tactic where institutions adopt superficially "green" measures to promote ecological branding, but continue to follow environmentally destructive practices. A recent episode involving CyArk, a nonprofit organization that uses 3D laser scanning and other techniques to "preserve"[5] cultural heritage monuments, illustrates the challenge of discerning style from substance. CyArk has a beautifully designed web presence, and it branded itself under the banner of "open access."[6] However, in attempting to reuse CyArk data, Isenburg (2013) noted that he was blocked by severe legal restrictions. This prompted accusations of "open washing" (a play on the phrase "green washing"), where some claimed CyArk presented itself as an open-access data provider that highlighted Creative Commons licenses but actually maintained proprietary control over data in far less conspicuous fine-print. CyArk has since clarified what it means by "open access" and explained access and reuse restrictions on the basis of security issues and other sensitivities (see Barton 2014). While such restrictions may be justified, only a careful read and immersion in open-access licensing debates (see Hagedorn *et al.* 2011; Rocks-Macqueen 2013; Costa *et al.* 2014) would let one understand that CyArk is not open access in the sense of the Wikipedia, Public Library of Science (PLOS), tDAR, Open Context, or other efforts. Nevertheless, a Google Search of recent press coverage[7], shows that CyArk still clearly leverages "open access" branding in public promotion.

The fog of marketing and brand signaling to promote financial sustainability in digital heritage can complicate ethical practice, even for a project like Mukurtu, which is designed to empower communities to manage, share, and preserve their digital cultural heritage within their own ethical, cultural, and social parameters and protocols.[8] Mukurtu (http://mukurtu.net) plays a much needed and

---

[5] The rationale and efficacy of "scanning as preservation" are debatable but out of scope for this paper. In addition, it is not clear what measures CyArk takes to preserve data beyond file backups; it does not seem to use any recognized digital repository platforms or methods, nor does CyArk seem to partner with digital libraries or archives.

[6] See the Internet Archive preserved webpage from 2012: https://web.archive.org/web/20121011125856/http://archive.cyark.org/about. After the Isenburg 2013 blog post, CyArk clarified its policies on data restrictions, claiming such restrictions are passed on from site owners; see http://www.cyark.org/data-use-policy.

[7] See a Google News search for the keywords: CyArk and "open access": https://www.google.com/search?q=cyark+%22open+access%22&tbm=nws.

[8] See http://mukurtu.org/project/differential-access-for-the-ethical-stewardship-of-cultural-and-digital-heritage-april-28–2015/.

essential complimentary role in this space. Unfortunately, it faces the same pressures and dilemmas felt by other projects. Branding can collapse complex theoretical, policy, and ethical issues into simplistic and caricatured signaling. An extreme example could read, "Facing the complex negotiations and ethical challenges of working with a community subjected to 500 years of colonialism? There's a hosted solution and mobile app for that!"[9] We need avoid the tendency of branding that drifts toward glib solutionism and risks trivializing issues like cultural appropriation. Similarly, the sustainability imperative to monetize digital archaeology can further undermine the point of these efforts. For instance, because digital projects typically lack access to long-term funding, they need to bring in sales. Mukurtu, as a hosted solution, risks perverse incentives to achieve JSTOR-like market dominance over long-term management of sensitive traditional cultural expressions "as a service." While the Murkutu team launched this hosted service in response to the needs of their partners, this approach nevertheless raises difficult issues in governance and liability, especially since it brands itself as a long-term "safe keeping place."[10] The political economy of system architectures and associated business models, including the power and dependency issues arguably inherent with "software as a service," are rarely discussed in digital archives. But these issues are of key importance in the case of Mukurtu given its emphasis on working with communities struggling against colonialism.

Beyond Mukurtu.net, Kimberly Christen has taken steps to continually maintain the open-source code base for MukurtuCMS at the Center for Digital Scholarship at Washington State University. This long-term support can promote more ethically optimal approaches as the code can deployed, modified, and managed *independently* and thus more clearly help empower indigenous communities. But realizing these outcomes requires more generalized technical capabilities

---

[9] While drafting this paper, the exact phrase "there's an app for that," appeared in the press relating to a Mukurtu deployment; see https://www.adn.com/article/20151031/looking-preserve-native-culture-theres-app.

[10] The promise of safe-keeping forever comes from the Center for Digital Archaeology (CoDA) hosted service, Mukurtu.net. As is the case with CyArk, I cannot find any clear documentation that specifies digital preservation processes for Mukurtu.net, nor can I find reference to partnerships with digital libraries and repositories.

and skills, the cultivation of which requires larger and longer-term investments made directly to indigenous communities themselves, not necessarily the Mukurtu development team. In some cases, these communities may determine they need to sometimes prioritize systems other than Mukurtu. This is not to say the Mukurtu development team does not deserve financial support. Of course it does. But their livelihoods should be less dependent on pushing a particular suite of software or services. I raise this issue to highlight how scarce funding creates real pressures and tradeoffs. The fight for money carries marketing imperatives to push one's own branded solutions in order to win grants, generate buzz, collect service fees, and keep the servers running. We need to articulate and explore these pressures so as to better understand how to align the interests of Mukurtu and other digital humanities projects with the publics they serve.

Open Context, the (branded!) system I manage, faces similar dilemmas. It seeks to broaden participation to the research process but has to charge for its publishing services, and those charges can exclude less-advantaged researchers (such as independent scholars and graduate students) that lack institutional or grant support. I also face pressures to "oversell" Open Context as "the answer" to hugely challenging semantic, technical, and interoperability imperatives. Of course Open Context cannot solve all of archaeology's information challenges. Mukurtu is obviously a much better platform for community control and expression of their own materials, while tDAR is a good platform for general-purpose data preservation needs. Open Context serves different needs, and it only makes sense as a complimentary part of a much larger landscape. But who will finance the vast diversity of needs and niches in that landscape? Thus, digital archaeology—even when it promotes laudable goals like indigenous rights or responsible digital curation—faces strong commodification pressures. If digital platforms are to improve archaeological practice, they need to be parts of a much larger programs and commitments to quality and ethics. Reaching these more meaningful goals requires more understanding of the trade-offs and costs of grants with short budget cycles and institutions that seem concerned only with cutting costs, generating buzz, and maximizing quantified research efficiencies.

Moving beyond Solutionism

Most discussion of data management presumes and reinforces a normative institutional status quo for the organization and conduct of research. Research data management typically focuses on cost-cutting—"Doing More with Less" (Whyte and Tedds 2011)—by reducing waste (lost data) and increasing efficiencies (interoperability). However, institutionalizing data management only in terms of optimizing the business as usual *status quo* (but now with saving data!) side-steps important challenges. Research data management raises important questions about intellectual property, evaluation, reproducibility, and quality that go far beyond concerns over costs, efficiencies, and measurements of impact. Indeed, as discussed below, treating data as yet another research product needing to be managed and measured undermines both intellectual freedom and the ethical conduct of research.

As noted above, Open Context has adopted a model of "data sharing as publication." In recognition of the complexities of intellectual property, stakeholder engagement, and the semantic and quality challenges inherent in archaeology, we made the explicit choice to explore a model where data editors work in collaboration with data creators to share more meaningful and intelligible data. Open Context's approach has helped researchers share, integrate, and analyze datasets at a large scale, leading to significant research outcomes (Arbuckle *et al.* 2014; Kansa *et al.* 2014).

A key issue with Open Context, however, is that its approach requires human collaborative effort to drive editorial processes. Editing and integrating data require costly staffing and time commitments that do not readily scale, leading some to call it a "boutique data publisher" (see Kratz and Strasser 2014). Conventional publishing finances editorial and other productions costs through subscriptions and sales predicated on commoditizing the intellectual property of the copyright-protected content. But Open Context very deliberately employs open-access and open-data publishing models to avoid commoditizing content. In response to heavy lobbying by the media industry (including large scholarly publishers), Congress (and other legislative bodies outside the the United States) have enacted increasingly far reaching and draconian laws to protect business models that are based on commoditized intellectual property. These laws not only apply to entertainment, but also to scholarly communications. The recent tragic case of Aaron Swartz, an Internet activist who took his own life after the collapse of plea-bargain negotiations with federal prosecutors, illustrates the legal risks associated with commoditized intellectual property.[11]

The Swartz example shows how a complex thicket of contractual agreements and intellectual property laws enforced by surveillance and the threat of draconian punishment underpin normative academic publishing (Kansa *et al.* 2013). Reform efforts in scholarly communications have largely embraced the banner of "openness." The term "open" has assumed a special kind of valence in relation to digital technologies, especially in networking and communications (see the digital "commons" in Benkler 2006: 60-63). "Open" usually means legal and practical guarantees for inspection, reuse, and adaptation of a piece of content or a technology. Thus, the term "open" stands in opposition to "closed" or "proprietary," which imply legal and other restrictions that require negotiating specific permissions or licenses, usually for a fee, for even limited kinds of access and reuse. The varieties of "open" relevant to researchers include open standards, open formats, open-source software, open-access publications, and open data. Integrating all of these forms of openness together, especially in the context of "transparent" workflows, starts to approach ideals of "open" or "reproducible" science (Lake 2012; Marwick 2014). To some (Stodden 2009), openly exposing the process of research represents an intrinsic good, and an ideal of ethical practice and scientific professionalism.

Thus, while openness sometimes means access and permissive intellectual property frameworks, in the research context it increasingly means moving the knowledge creation process to more public forums that can, in principle, support wider engagement with more communities (Beale and Beale 2012). As I discuss below, emphasis on the research process, as opposed to neatly packaged outcomes (peer-reviewed papers or even archived datasets), has the potential to help digital archaeology move beyond solutionism.

---

[11] Swartz faced between 30 to 50 years of federal prison for alleged mass-downloads of papers from JSTOR. In contrast, he would have faced 20 years of prison for human-trafficking (slavery). See: http://www.propublica.org/article/hacktivism-civil-disobedience-or-cyber-crime

Fungible Data and Its Discontents

Placing more value on the process of knowledge creation can help turn back many of the worst dysfunctions of neoliberalism in today's research institutions. Unfortunately, the language we currently use to discuss digital data suggests that data is mainly a management or preservation problem. After all, two agencies of the United States government, the NSF and the NEH, require data management plans for grant-funded archaeological research. This language can lead some to consider data to be mainly a matter for bureaucratic compliance, not intellectual engagement.

Similarly, many discussions about data management frequently emphasize the central importance of standards. Common information standards help facilitate data discovery, interoperability, and integration. Standards make use of data at large scales efficient. With common standards data can open new research opportunities that require large-scale data analysis. But one may also see the imposition of standards as exactly that: an imposition. Common standards reflect a certain (and potentially contestable) set of perspectives, assumptions, and goals. Requiring the use of certain standards means requiring a certain agenda. Successfully imposing standards that prioritize certain kinds of questions and approaches may open new opportunities for easier, large-scale data analysis, while at the same time curtailing researcher autonomy to organize and describe materials in new ways. Interoperability standards may marginalize "artisanal" or "craft" (Shanks and McGuire 1996) research practices in favor of practices that lead to the "mass-production" of interchangeable, standardized, and fungible outputs (see also Limp 2011: 278). If interoperability and efficiency become our discipline's key concern with respect to data, we should expect pervasive and sometimes unwelcome impacts to the practice of archaeology.

One can make similar arguments about copyright licensing and interoperability. Open-science and open-data advocates note standardized liberal copyright licensing makes interoperability easier. Combining different datasets together represents a fundamental research need in using data. Ambiguous or incompatible licenses and access controls can complicate or preclude this form of reuse. Therefore, open-data advocates typically promote free access and attribution only licensing (i.e., the Creative Commons Attribution license) or "entanglement-free" public domain dedications (Creative Commons Zero; see Vollmer 2013; Costa *et al.* 2014).

While valuable in many circumstances, open-data licensing does not represent an ethical ideal for all cases. Ten years ago, several colleagues and I highlighted how Creative Commons licenses reflect ethical positions and norms that are not universally applicable, particularly in contexts of colonialism and cultural appropriation (Kansa *et al.* 2005; Kansa 2009). Similarly, Christen's critiques of open access motivated her to develop the Mukurtu platform. Christen considers open access as tending toward arbitrary technocratic colonialism, at least with respect to indigenous rights issues (Christen 2009, 2012). While I strongly agree with the vision of more ethical practice that Christen very articulately describes, I disagree with her characterization of "openness" as a root problem. In my experience,[12] open-data advocacy is not nearly so uniformly ideological and indifferent to social context as Christen suggests. Instead, theoretical and policy debates about "openness" can cross-fertilize debates about cultural appropriation. For instance, our 2005 paper discussed Creative Commons–inspired "some rights reserved" models to meet a wider range of needs for traditional cultural expressions. The paper had a large impact, and, as noted by Allison Fish (2014), Christen and colleagues implemented similar licensing and labeling ideas with their "Local Contexts" project (http://localcontexts.org; see also Anderson and Christen 2013; Christen 2015).[13] In addition, over the past several years, representatives from Open Context and other digital practitioners have debated cultural appropriation issues and policy concerns. We did so with iCommons (a former branch of Creative Commons),[14] the Intellectual Property in

---

[12] I obviously have a very different set of experiences and interactions that framed my perspectives here. There are many different issues, communities, and actors involved in this space, and my conversations about ethically situating openness seem to have taken a different tone than what Christen describes in her 2012 publication. So it maybe these different kinds of interactions led to very different conclusions about open advocacy.

[13] Fish recognized the similarities in these approaches; however (not to sound crabby), none of the scholarly papers about "Local Contexts" actually cite Kansa *et al.* 2005, a publication that led to my participation in fruitful meetings, panel discussions, and presentations about these topics with Christen and others.

[14] See, e.g., the blog post and discussion hosted by iCommons: http://web.archive.org/web/20071125100852/http://beta.icommons.org/articles/

Cultural Heritage (IPinCH) project,[15] scholarly debates about "open archaeology" (Kansa 2012; Lake 2012; Morgan and Eve 2012), ethics policies for the American Library Association (ALA, Christen herself participated in this),[16] and policy recommendations for government agencies.[17] Like the ALA, Michigan State University's MATRIX Institute similarly adopts different intellectual property frameworks into the practice of its digital cultural heritage collaborations. While some MATRIX projects adopt open models,[18] depending on context, others adopt stricter safeguards and protections for digital content.[19]

Public debate about mass-surveillance, online privacy, open access, open government, race and gender issues in social media, and more highlight the complexity of current information empowerment issues (Wells 2014: 28). Rather than blindly asserting that all "information must be free" ([sic] Christen 2009, 2012), even (non-anthropologically informed) advocates for openness often protest against ubiquitous data collecting and surveillance by government agencies and corporations. For instance, the Electronic Frontier Foundation seeks less severe copyright restrictions and penalties[20] and greater openness in science[21] and government,[22] while at the same time promoting civil

---

finding-common-ground-in-the-digital-commons

[15] See the IPinCH reserch team (http://www.sfu.ca/ipinch/about/ip-inch-people/research-team) and also the policy outcomes for Open Context (http://opencontext.org/about/intellectual-property).

[16] See the American Library Associations discussion of "traditional cultural expressions": http://wo.ala.org/tce/faq/.

[17] See Sarah Kansa's (Open Context's Editor) policy recommendations submitted to the White House Office of Science and Technology Policy on proposed frameworks for government-sponsored research data: http://sites.nationalacademies.org/cs/groups/dbassesite/documents/webpage/dbasse_083132.pdf#page=20.

[18] See the "Digital Archaeology Institute" ("ethic of openness") led by Ethan Watrall and Lynne Goldstein: http://digitalarchaeology.msu.edu/about/.

[19] See an example collection with "all rights reserved" copyright: http://aodl.org/islamicpluralism/.

[20] See, e.g., https://www.eff.org/wp/collateral-damages-why-congress-needs-fix-copyright-laws-civil-penalties, and especially: https://www.eff.org/issues/tpp.

[21] See, e.g., https://www.eff.org/document/student-activism-open-access.

[22] See, e.g., https://www.eff.org/deeplinks/2009/03/foia.

liberties protections through public use of strong cryptography[23] and communication networks free from corporate or government surveillance.[24] If one recognizes the central importance of power relations in information management, one can support both open data *and* privacy safeguards and other protections, depending on the context.

I agree with Christen (2012) that openness is not some sort of inevitable end-stage of technological progress (see also Kansa 2009). Rather, openness reflects choices motivated by ideologies, ethics, practicalities, and other factors, especially in how people navigate identity and power relations. If openness is to make meaningful positive contributions to the practice of archaeology, it needs to be situated within engaged research processes. Informed by anthropology and recent scholarship on privacy (e.g., Nissenbaum 2004), we should expect privacy, security, and cultural mores about information to vary across different historical and cultural contexts and social situations (Chander and Sunder 2004; Kansa *et al.* 2005; Hollowell and Nicholas 2008). Deep understanding of culture, history, and social context (not to mention a willingness to listen, learn, and take "no" for an answer) are required to negotiate issues about what information needs to be considered private, sensitive, sacred, or damaging if released, and even what information may need to be shared with urgency through certain channels.

Building these deep understandings necessarily requires the kinds of wider engagement and partnerships promoted by "community archaeology." This is the approach, explicitly advocated in Open Context's intellectual property policies.[25] These quiet and behind-the-scenes approaches also underlie the core value of Mukurtu's collaborative work. The same holds true for the decades-long partnerships developed between MATRIX and heritage institutions in West Africa, or the years invested in partnership between First Nation communities and museums with the Reciprocal Research Network (https://www.rrncommunity.org/). While exemplary, such deep and long-term investments in engagement are the exceptions and not the norms. Most researchers, including archaeologists, face tremendous pressures to "publish or perish" via venues that have business

---

[23] See, e.g., https://www.eff.org/encrypt-the-web

[24] See, e.g., https://www.eff.org/wp/
who-has-your-back-2014-protecting-your-data-government-requests.

[25] See http://opencontext.org/about/intellectual-property.

models explicitly centered on commercial appropriation. Open-data and open-science advocacy still lies at the margins of scientific practice and research norms. By far, most money and effort invested in scholarly communications flows into channels of commercial appropriation (conventional journals) rather than open-data systems or non-commercial archives with privacy safeguards.[26] In a context of cut-throat job competition, many archaeologists feel they cannot invest the great effort needed to make their research processes more open for wider engagement.

Thus, rather than seeing the main threats to ethical research practice in open-access or open-data advocacy (Christen 2012), I see pervasive academic Taylorism[27] as a far greater concern. The bureaucracies that govern research largely see value only in productivity and impact. Academic institutions ignore or even punish effort invested in more thoughtful and ethical practice when only a few types of research outcomes "count" in job performance metrics. Indeed, use of metrics to evaluate scholarship is simple and easy to administer, since it requires no deep insight in the context and process behind that scholarship. These neoliberal practices are corrosive to ethics, *regardless whether the outcomes are open or closed*. The thought and effort required for meaningful and ethical data curation is largely invisible and unrewarded by most research institutions. Thus, we should avoid caricatures where different digital humanities brands signal false dichotomies in prioritizing either open data or the self-determination rights of local and indigenous communities. Instead, we need institutions that encourage more thoughtful and ethical day-to-day practices

---

[26] The five largest University of California campuses spend together more than $90 million annually on commercial acquisitions and subscriptions in 2013–2014 (see http://arlstatistics.org/analytics). In contrast, during the same period the CDL allocated only about $3.5 million on digital repository services of the type supporting open access, open data, and protected research data; see http://www.cdlib.org/about/docs/CDLAnnualReport_2013_2014.pdf.

[27] "Taylorism" derives from Frederick Taylor, a pioneering business management theorist and developer of "Scientific Managment", a set of practices to improve worker and factory productivity through strict performance metrics and stream-lining of routine tasks. Many see digital technologies as a powerful means to implement Taylorist practices, see: http://www.economist.com/news/business/21664190-modern-version-scientific-management-threatens-dehumanise-workplace-digital

so that researchers have the time and intellectual freedom to navigate complex realities and trade-offs.[28]

Open data and reproducible research advocacy has raised important questions about relationships between commercial appropriation, academic reward systems, and research conduct (Kansa 2014a, 2014b). Rather than celebrating "big data" of a type and scale valued and (factory) farmed largely through corporate and government surveillance, we should highlight the value of small and properly contextualized data. Our community needs institutional supports that offer more space for thoughtful digital curation, or "slow data." The most important value of research data does not center on its scale, efficient collection, or even efficient interoperability. Rather, a slow data approach can highlight how data collection, management, and dissemination practices need to be considered integral to the larger ethical and professional conduct of research.

CONCLUSIONS

The idea of "slow data" introduced above owes much to Bill Caraher's notion of "slow archaeology" (Caraher 2013; Ch. 4.1). Slow archaeology captures the notion that we as a professional community should emphasize excellence in the research process, including taking time for thoughtful consideration, not simply high-throughput and efficient production of tangible research outcomes. Slow data is basically the digitized aspects of slow archaeology.

In the case of Open Context, we emphasize that making sense of aggregated data requires dedicated professionalism and thoughtful effort (Kansa *et al.* 2014). Minimal efforts to comply with grant data-management requirements by depositing messy and undocumented spreadsheets into a repository may not be sufficient to enable future reuse. Since such data curation is integral to the process of research, we need more policy emphasis on recognizing and rewarding the research process as a whole (see also Dallas 2015; Huggett 2015). The continued domination of fast-paced "publish or

---

[28] Christen (2012) argues for exactly such culturally aware mindfulness. Again, my main focus of disagreement centers not on her vision for better ethical practice (where I absolutely agree); instead, I have a different diagnosis of the root problems in that I think neoliberal institutions and reward systems cause far more harm than advocacy for research "openness."

perish" expectations will perpetuate perverse incentives to badly curate data and to ignore the ethical context of those data.

Slow archaeology can help us articulate more humane and insightful approaches to the "datafication" of archaeology. Simply adding digital technologies, platforms, and services to a disciplinary context of zero-sum competition and dwindling short-term finances will not promote ethical practice or more nuanced understandings of the past. Digital archaeology currently has a growing array of branded projects, many struggling with short-term financing, and all desperately competing for attention and market share. In the name of economies of scale and narrowly defined notions of sustainability, this could drive centralization and lock-in, making it much harder for new ideas and approaches to see experimentation.

It does not have to be like this. We can and should advocate for institutional and financial mechanisms that are more long term and offer more opportunity for reflection. Our memory institutions, namely libraries and museums, may offer some of the best organizational templates to sustain more reflective digital efforts. Though they too are now also struggling with fiscal austerity and neoliberalism, in many cases such organizations have provided invaluable public services for decades. Many of us participate in digital archaeology because we were dissatisfied with the *status quo* of conventional archaeology. Now that our area of practice has finally achieved some recognition, it is time to work toward a better institutional foundation to sustain our efforts in a manner that promotes and does not subvert our ethics and goals.

ACKNOWLEDGMENTS

While this paper benefited from the tremendous generosity and review of many colleagues, needless to say, I am solely responsible for any errors, omissions, or other problems with text. First of all, I want to thank Sarah Whitcher Kansa for her tireless edits, frank discussions, and her collaboration in crafting the programs and ideas presented in this paper. Also, in an experiment in "open peer-review," I posted a draft of this paper on GitHub and made revisions documented in its version control system. I am grateful for the thoughtful public reviews and comments made by Dagmar Riedel, Amanda French, Raymond Yee, and Ben Marwick. I also received private comments via the "back-channel" of email. While I'm keeping the identity of these people in confidence (because they chose to respond via a more private channel), I am also indebted for their helpful comments and suggestions. I am also grateful for the insightful comments and guidance from the anonymous peer reviewers organized by this volume's dedicated and highly effective editorial team. Through these various channels, I received thought-provoking and varied ideas about how to improve this paper, and I could only incorporate some of these suggestions into this current paper. Future publications will more fully address the feedback so generously offered by colleagues who responded to this contribution. And finally, I am grateful for the financial support of the German Archaeological Institute, the Harvard Center for Hellenic Studies, and the National Endowment for the Humanities (grants #HK-50037 and #PR-234235).

https://mobilizingthepast.mukurtu.net/collection/42-click-here-save-past

http://dc.uwm.edu/arthist_mobilizingthepast/19

References

Anderson, J., and K. Christen. 2013. "'Chuck a Copyright on It': Dilemmas of Digital Return and the Possibilities for Traditional Knowledge Licenses and Labels," *Museum Anthropology Review* 7: 105–126.

Arbuckle, B. S., S. W. Kansa, E. Kansa, D. Orton, C. Çakırlar, L. Gourichon, L. Atici, A. Galik, A. Marciniak, J. Mulville, H. Buitenhuis, D. Carruthers, B. De Cupere, A. Demirergi, S. Frame, D. Helmer, L. Martin, J. Peters, N. Pöllath, K. Pawłowska, N. Russell, K. Twiss and D. Würtenberger. 2014. "Data Sharing Reveals Complexity in the Westward Spread of Domestic Animals across Neolithic Turkey." *PLoS ONE* 9(6): e99845 http://dx.doi.org/10.1371/journal.pone.0099845

Barton, J. 2014. "Monumental Data, Monumental Data Access Challenges." *CyArk*, http://www.cyark.org/news/monumental-data-monumental-data-access-challenges

Beale, N., and G. Beale. 2012. "The Potential of Open Models for Public Archaeology." http://eprints.soton.ac.uk/355830/

Benkler, Y. 2006. *The Wealth of Networks: How Social Production Transforms Markets and Freedom*. New Haven: Yale University Press.

Caraher, W. 2013. "Slow Archaeology," *North Dakota Quarterly* 80(2): 43–52.

Chander, A., and M. Sunder. 2004. "The Romance of the Public Domain." http://papers.ssrn.com/sol3/papers.cfm?abstract_id=562301

Christen, K. A. 2009. "Access and Accountability: The Ecology of Information Sharing in the Digital Age. Visual Ethics, special issue," *Anthropology News* 50 (4): 4–5.

Christen, K. A. 2012. "Does Information Really Want to Be Free? Indigenous Knowledge Systems and the Question of Openness." *International Journal of Communication* 6, http://ijoc.org/index.php/ijoc/article/view/1618

Christen, K. A. 2015. "Tribal Archives, Traditional Knowledge, and Local Contexts: Why the 's' Matters." *Journal of Western Archives* 6, http://digitalcommons.usu.edu/westernarchives/vol6/iss1/3

Costa, S., A. Beck, A. H. Bevan, and J. Ogden. 2014. "Defining and Advocating Open Data in Archaeology," in G. Earl, T. Sly, P. Chrysanthi, P. Murrieta-Flores, C. Papadopoulos, I. Romanowska, and D. Wheatley, eds., *Archaeology in the Digital Era: Papers from the 40th Annual Conference of Computer Applications and Quantitative Methods in Archaeology (CAA), Southampton, 26–29 March 2012*. Amsterdam: Amsterdam University Press, 449–456.

Dallas, C. 2015. "Curating Archaeological Knowledge in the Digital Continuum: From Practice to Infrastructure." *Open Archaeology* 1, http://www.degruyter.com/view/j/opar.2014.1.issue-1/opar-2015-0011/opar-2015-0011.xml

Deuze, M., P. Blank, and L. Speers. 2012. "A Life Lived in Media." *Digital Humanities Quarterly* 6, http://digitalhumanities.org/dhq/vol/6/1/000110/000110.html

Earl, G. 2014. "First Thoughts from the Portus MOOC." *Hestia2 Seminar: Digital Pedagogy. How Are New Technologies Transforming* the *Interface between Research and Learning?*, https://www.youtube.com/watch?v=_LBArmT3XAY

Feller, I. 2008. "Neoliberalism, Performance Measurement, and the Governance of American Academic Science." http://cshe.berkeley.edu/neoliberalism-performance-measurement-and-governance-american-academic-science

Fish, A. 2014. "The Place of 'Culture' in the Access to Knowledge Movement: Comparing Creative Commons and Yogic Theories of Knowledge Transfer (Respond to This Article at http://www.therai.org. uk/at/debate)," *Anthropology Today* 30(5): 7–10.

Fitzpatrick, K. 2011. *Planned Obsolescence: Publishing, Technology, and the Future of the Academy.* New York: New York University Press.

Hagedorn, G., D. Mietchen, R. A. Morris, D. Agosti, L. Penev, W. G. Berendsohn, and D. Hobern. 2011. "Creative Commons Licenses and the Non-Commercial Condition: Implications for the Re-Use of Biodiversity Information," *ZooKeys* 150: 127–149. http://www.ncbi.nlm.nih.gov/pmc/articles/PMC3234435/.

Hollowell, J., and G. Nicholas. 2008. "Intellectual Property Issues in Archaeological Publication: Some Questions to Consider," *Archaeologies* 4(2): 208–217. http://www.springerlink.com/content/u48ht67q46012706/abstract/

Huggett, J. 2015. "A Manifesto for an Introspective Digital Archaeology." *Open Archaeology* 1, http://www.degruyter.com/view/j/opar.2014.1.issue-1/opar-2015-0002/opar-2015-0002.xml

Isenburg, M. 2013. "Can You Copyright LiDAR?" *rapidlasso GmbH*, http://rapidlasso.com/2013/04/14/can-you-copyright-lidar/

Kansa, E. C. 2009. "Indigenous Heritage and the Digital Commons," in C. Antons, ed., *Traditional Knowledge, Traditional Cultural Expressions and Intellectual Property Law in the Asia-Pacific Region. Max Planck Series on Asian Intellectual Property Law* 14. Frederick, MD: Kluwer Law International, 219–244.

Kansa, E. C. 2012. "Openness and Archaeology's Information Ecosystem," *World Archaeology* 44: 498–520. http://escholarship.org/uc/item/4bt04063/

Kansa, E. C. 2014a. "It's the Neoliberalism, Stupid: Why Instrumentalist Arguments for Open Access, Open Data, and Open Science Are Not Enough." *Impact of Social Sciences*, http://blogs.lse.ac.uk/impactofsocialsciences/2014/01/27/its-the-neoliberalism-stupid-kansa/

Kansa, E. C. 2014b. "The Need to Humanize Open Science," in S. Moore, ed., *Issues in Open Research Data*. London: Ubiquity Press. doi: http://dx.doi.org/10.5334/ban

Kansa, E. C., S. W. Kansa, and B. Arbuckle. 2014. "Publishing and Pushing: Mixing Models for Communicating Research Data in Archaeology," *International Journal of Digital Curation* 9: 57–70. http://www.ijdc.net/index.php/ijdc/article/view/9.1.57.

Kansa, E. C., S. W. Kansa, and L. Goldstein. 2013. "On Ethics, Sustainability, and Open Access in Archaeology," *The SAA Archaeological Record* 13(4): 15–22. http://www.saa.org/Portals/0/SAA/Publications/thesaaarchrec/September2013.pdf

Kansa, E. C., J. Schultz, and A. N. Bissell. 2005. "Protecting Traditional Knowledge and Expanding Access to Scientific Data: Juxtaposing Intellectual Property Agendas via a 'Some Rights Reserved' Model," *International Journal of Cultural Property* 12(3): 285–314. http://journals.cambridge.org/article_S0940739105050204; open access: http://citeseerx.ist.psu.edu/viewdoc/download?doi=10.1.1.107.3323&rep=rep1&type=pdf

Kansa, S. W., and E. C. Kansa. 2015. "Reflections on a Road Less Traveled: Alt-Ac Archaeology," *Journal of Eastern Mediterranean Archaeology & Heritage Studies* 3: 293–298.

Kintigh, K., and J. Altschul. 2010. "Sustaining the Digital Archaeological Record," *Heritage Management* 3: 264–274.

Kratz, J., and C. Strasser. 2014. "Data Publication Consensus and Controversies." *F1000Research* 3, http://www.ncbi.nlm.nih.gov/pmc/articles/PMC4097345/

Lake, M. 2012. "Open Archaeology," *World Archaeology* 44: 471–478. http://www.tandfonline.com/doi/abs/10.1080/00438243.2012.748521

Limp, F. 2011. "Web 2.0 and Beyond, or on the Web, Nobody Knows You're an Archaeologist," in E. C. Kansa, S. W. Kansa, and E. Watrall, eds., *Archaeology 2.0: New Tools For Communication and Collaboration. Cotsen Digital Archaeology 1*. Los Angeles: Cotsen Institute of Archaeology, 265–280.

Marwick, B. 2014. "Reproducible Research: A Primer for the Social Sciences." http://rpubs.com/benmarwick/csss-rr

Morgan, C., and S. Eve. 2012. "DIY and Digital Archaeology: What Are You Doing to Participate?" *World Archaeology* 44: 521–537.

Morozov, E. 2014. *To Save Everything, Click Here: The Folly of Technological Solutionism*. New York: PublicAffairs.

Nissenbaum, H. 2004. "Privacy as Contextual Integrity," *Washington Law Review* 79: 101–139. http://www.nyu.edu/projects/nissenbaum/papers/washingtonlawreview.pdf

Posner, M. 2013. "What Alt-Ac Can Do, and What It Can't." *Miriam Posner's Blog*, http://miriamposner.com/blog/what-alt-ac-can-do-and-what-it-cant/

Rocks-Macqueen, D. 2013. "Creative Commons Non-Commercial A Cruel Joke." *Doug's Archaeology*, https://dougsarchaeology.wordpress.com/2013/04/11/creative-commons-non-commercial-a-cruel-joke

Shanks, M., and R. H. McGuire. 1996. "The Craft of Archaeology," *American Antiquity* 61: 75–88. http://www.jstor.org/stable/282303

Stodden, V. 2009. "The Legal Framework for Reproducible Scientific Research: Licensing and Copyright," *Computing in Science & Engineering* 11(1): 35–40. http://scitation.aip.org/content/aip/journal/cise/11/1/10.1109/MCSE.2009.19.

Vollmer, T. 2013. "Deciphering Licensing in Project Open Data." *Creative Commons*, http://creativecommons.org/weblog/entry/38316

Waters, D. 2004. "Building on Success, Forging New Ground: The Question of Sustainability." *First Monday* 9(5), http://firstmonday.org/issues/issue9_5/waters/index.html

Wells, J. J. 2014. "Keep Calm and Remain Human: How We Have Always Been Cyborgs and Theories on the Technological Present," *Reviews in Anthropology* 43: 5–34. doi: 10.1080/00938157.2014.872460

Wells, J. J., E. C. Kansa, S. W. Kansa, S. J. Yerka, D. G. Anderson, T. G. Bissett, K. N. Myers, and R. C. DeMuth. 2014. "Web-Based Discovery and Integration of Archaeological Historic Properties Inventory Data: The Digital Index of North American Archaeology (DINAA)." *Literary and Linguistic Computing*, http://llc.oxfordjournals.org/content/early/2014/06/15/llc.fqu028

Whyte, A., and J. Tedds. 2011. "Making the Case for Research Data Management." *DCC Briefing Papers*, http://www.dcc.ac.uk/resources/briefing-papers/making-case-rdm#sthash.0hO3pxzV.dpuf

Part 5: From Critique to Manifesto

5.1.
Response: Living a Semi-digital Kinda Life

Morag M. Kersel

After I received the initial email inviting me to contribute to papers considering the ongoing digital revolution in archaeological field-work, the following exchange occurred. With respect to digital archaeology, I consider myself a "Luddite outsider," to quote Caraher (Ch. 4.1). My initial hesitation:

> "I am honored and intrigued by your invitation. I was impressed by the line-up for your conference (which I followed via Twitter); it appeared to be a great set of papers engendering a lot of inter-esting discussion. I hesitate, wondering if I am really the right person to respond to these papers. I am no "digital guru" – I do use and see the merits of various technologies and databases and advocate for Open Context etc. . . . but there are many folks better versed than I in the topics."

The editorial response to my anxiety:

> "For our second respondent we were looking for a field archae-ologist who would be able to comment on the usefulness, practicality, and value (or not) of these digital technologies in the field and analysis. Thus we were hoping you would be able to speak as an archaeologist that uses and implements digital technologies rather than as a creator of them."

I took this editorial charge to heart, and as such I will not comment directly on the sometimes very detailed technological aspects of the various contributions. I will admit that in examining the papers (I read the entire volume on an iPad, using GoodReader to annotate the PDF), I was often lost in the platforms, programs, and terminology used by the authors. Clearly there is a new language associated with digital technologies with which I am unfamiliar. In addition to the technical terms and programs I noted new "buzzwords" like granular, workflow, and born digital, which appear in almost every chapter. I was not "born digital," nor have I have been transformed into a completely digital being, but when the editors asked me to respond to the various papers from the National Endowment for the Humanities (NEH) funded workshop, I began to reflect on what it means to "live a digital life" vis-à-vis my own field projects.

I am an archaeologist working in the Eastern Mediterranean who has dabbled in the digital for a while. At the Galilee Prehistory Project of the Oriental Institute, the University of Chicago, we were early adopters of iPads in the field—in our 2012 season we used a single iPad as a test case, and in subsequent seasons each area supervisor had an iPad for all "in-field" recording. At the Early Bronze Age mortuary site of Fifa, situated along the Dead Sea Plain in Jordan, Austin (Chad) Hill and I were among the first teams to use drones, or unmanned aerial vehicles (UAVs) in the field. Equipped with cameras, the UAV flyovers at Fifa let us produce high-resolution digital elevation models, allowing us to use image-based modeling as a legitimate analytical tool for the monitoring of landscape change due to archaeological site looting (see also Olson, Ch. 2.2). I am—and have been since its inception—an avid supporter of the Alexandria Archive Institute and its web-based publication of research data, Open Context. When called upon, I attempt to provide intellectual insights on various ethical issues related to online publication and open access. But much of my work in and out of the field is still paper-based, either by design or by compliance (in both Israel and Jordan we currently are asked by the relevant antiquities departments to supply paper copies of our final reports on the field season). Spigelman, Roberts, and Fehrenbach (Ch. 3.4) point out the irony of having entirely digital in-field data workflows while the State Historic Preservation Office project compliance deliverables are required to be paper-based. Both Caraher (Ch. 4.1) and Kansa (Ch. 4.2) lament the failure of the academy to recognize digital publications as valid contributions to a portfolio of work in tenure cases, which may add to our anxieties about moving to a completely paperless life. In this particular moment, as a discipline, I believe we live a semi-digital kinda life (à la Third Eye Blind, the US rock band formed in the early 1990s) where we are part paper and part paperless.

In the following response I want to highlight a few of the recurrent themes and some general observations that struck me as I perused this intriguing collection of papers. What does it mean to live a (either semi- or fully) digital life? What are the ethical implications associated with living a digital life? In the spirit of full disclosure, I would not have read this volume cover to cover under normal academic circumstances, preferring instead to cherry-pick chapters directly related to my research. I thank the editors for this unexpected invitation to contribute my thoughts and observations on archaeological fieldwork in the digital age.

LIVING A DIGITAL LIFE

What does it mean to live a digital life? The chapters in this volume articulate the ways in which archaeologists can and do embrace the digital, and each provides a thoughtful and compelling analysis of the varied digital lives in places like Peru, Pompeii, coastal (underwater) Israel, Cyprus, and the American Southwest. These contributions demonstrate the global and temporal applicability of varied technologies to archaeological fieldwork. Many of the papers aver that going digital has resulted in a streamlined, systematized (Bria and DeTore, Ch. 1.5), efficient workflow, producing what Motz (Ch. 1.3) refers to as a data avalanche. Does this increase in productivity and capabilities improve our ability to interpret the archaeological record? Gordon and colleagues (Ch. 1.4) argue that data are now democratized, easily sharable and understandable, while Sobotkova and colleagues (Ch. 3.2) contend that real-time digital data allow for early detection of mistakes that previously may have gone unnoticed for an entire field season. Contributions to this workshop ably illustrate that digital methods are assisting not only in increased data recovery, but also in better data recovery (as there is less room for human error). I recognize that an impetus for many to lead a digital life is a "need for speed" as some archaeology is often carried out in advance of bulldozers, development, and situations of crisis and conflict.

In my "Introduction to Archaeology" classes, I start each academic quarter by showing the following standup skit by British comedian Eddie Izzard (2008):

> I love archaeology, it is like a detective thing—but it is very slow on telly: "We've been here 3 weeks on live television and we've dug a millimeter of topsoil so far" say men with brushes and beards. "We've found this and radiocarbon dated it to last Thursday, we are very excited." It's too slow for us, our attention spans are short, we need stuff, things, happening quick, quick—change the channel. We don't want slow archaeology, we want SPEED archaeology.

This amusing skit (which students love) encapsulates many of the tropes of archaeology culminating in a declaration of a need for speed archaeology—and many of the chapters in this volume assert that going digital results in just that: speed archaeology. "On the most basic level, using a digital format to record data would speed our data collection by eliminating the need to type paper records into a computer at the end of the day or season" state Bria and DeTore (Ch. 1.5) in a discussion of why speed matters. Technological advances make it easier and faster to record sites on a daily basis, to uncover features from the air (see Wernke *et al.*, Ch. 2.3) and from the sea bed (Buxton *et al.*, Ch. 2.4), and to replicate artifacts and sites (Dufton, Ch. 3.3; Olson, Ch. 2.2), thus freeing up time for greater reflection and discussion about the research goals and outcomes. Does this lead to more time for contemplation? Caraher (2015) suggests that with increased efficiency comes the increased temptation to dig more, which authors in this volume confirm. Dufton (Ch. 3.3) and Fee (Ch. 2.1) admit that the extra time garnered as a result of digital technologies did not always occasion further site/object contemplation but instead often brought about additional excavation and even larger amounts of amassed data. What are we doing with all of the data collected as a result of the digital revolution—are we publishing more? (I will return to this query below when discussing the ethical implications of living a dgital life.) I am also left wondering if the efficiency created by new technologies is really as liberating and progressive as practitioners proclaim. Nakassis (2015) and Caraher (2015) make an excellent case for the introduction of a different set of hierarchies as a result of digital

technologies. And indeed, do additional data result in better archaeology or just a different type of archaeology? Are we now freer as a
discipline, or is there a greater entanglement with data and site that
requires even more reflexive examination? Are we thinking more or
just inputting and gathering more data?

I am an archaeological surveyor, and until the time of the digital
revolution I was solely responsible for drawing the architectural plans,
sections, and features at the various Neolithic/Chalcolithic/and Early
Bronze Age sites where I work. In the last 10 years, my fieldwork life
has transformed dramatically. Overall, I embrace this transformation
as a good thing, although I do acknowledge that in the not-too-distant
future I may be out of a job. Howland and colleagues (2014) suggest
that less time-consuming and more accurate digitization from georeferenced orthophotographs has supplanted field drafting. The UAVs
and iPads used to record the daily changes in our excavations at the
Chalcolithic site of Marj Rabba in Israel (see Rowan and Kersel 2014)
rendered my hand-drawn daily top plans obsolete. As many of the
chapters (Ellis, Ch. 1.2; Gordon *et al.*, Ch. 1.4; Motz, Ch. 1.3; Poehler,
Ch. 1.7; Wallrodt, Ch. 1.1, among others) in this compilation demonstrate, this move to the digital for field recording resulted in greater
accuracy, consistency, and efficiency in the field (see also Roosevelt *et
al.* 2015). At the Galilee Prehistory Project, the use of TouchDraw to
annotate photographs taken with the iPad, which were then added to
existing records in FileMaker Go, enabled supervisors and students
alike the immediacy that going digital affords. No longer did area
supervisors have to wait for me to draw the architecture, which they
then transferred to the daily top plan for their area. Hampered only by
overheating and/or glare (see Gordon *et al.*, Ch. 1.4, for further discussion around the physical limitations of using technology in the heat
of the Eastern Mediterranean), the field seasons where we integrated a
digital life at Marj Rabba were more efficient; but I continue to worry
about what we are missing and how archaeology has changed through
the use of an iPad and UAVs in the field.

In 1993, as Gila Cook, the longtime archaeological architect for
the Tel Dan project in northern Israel, was dismantling her drawing
equipment, she noticed something out of the corner of her eye. On
the exposed tip of a basalt stone Gila observed some inscribed letters
and exclaimed: "I looked again and said to myself, Oh! This is a qof,
here's a mem Hebrew or Phoenician letters! It's an inscription . . . with

rows of characters" (for a full account of the discovery, see Cook 2003). An archaeological surveyor had discovered the Tel Dan inscription, a fragmentary Aramaic engraving referring to the "king of the House of David," one of the first archaeological finds supporting the existence of biblical figure of David. My point here is not to debate the veracity of the Bible vis-à-vis the Tel Dan inscription, but to wonder that if iPads and drones were in use at Tel Dan, would the inscription have been uncovered? As someone who draws thousands of stones each season, I often run my hands over features as I set up tapes—I am "up close and personal" with the site and its features. In addition to the excavators, supervisors, and directors, the surveyor can be another pair of eyes on the ground, but I acknowledge that so too can a drone be an "eye in the sky." At Marj Rabba we often identify features that we might/ would never have seen from the ground from the drone images. We are carrying out more comprehensive archaeology (or what Olson and colleagues (2013) labeled "total archaeology") and leading a digital life, but I worry that in our preoccupation with a paperless life we might overlook the legacy of paper and a closer connection to the site.

I am uneasy about an overreliance on the technological, what some have identified as a type of fetishism (Huggett 2016). Cameras mounted on drones take thousands of images for a variety of purposes, including photogrammetry and daily site record keeping. Digital processes provide another view of sites and artifacts at a different scale from hand-drawn paper records. If we turn exclusively to aerial photography as a comprehensive recording technique, what are we missing? It is a misconception to think that because we have thousands of images we have captured all of the data necessary both to reconstruct and to answer questions about the past. Whatever the method used for data collection, we are always missing things and we need to acknowledge this rather than promoting technology as the liberator of all of our past paper-based wrongs.

In our "semi-digital kinda life" at the Galilee Prehistory Project, we did not embrace fully the digital model as I and the field-school students continued to produce, by hand, on paper, the final architectural drawings, elevations, and sections at Marj Rabba. We are, however, convinced by the "born-digital" brigade (and I more so after reading the contributions to this volume), and in our future projects we will probably go forward in a fuller digital mode while remaining ever mindful of the lesson from Tel Dan and the words of Caraher (Ch. 4.1: 436):

> The removal of the time-consuming illustration process from excavation work does not necessarily guarantee the de-skilling of the excavator, but it certainly transforms a crucial step in the documentation process from one requiring detailed and careful knowledge both of the features in a trench and the conventions of illustration to one requiring the understanding of a digital camera and relevant software. The former is vital to the archaeological process whereas the latter is not.

The Ethics of Living a Digital Life

In April of 2015 I presented a keynote address at *The Future of the Past: From Amphipolis to Mosul* conference, held at the University of Pennsylvania Museum of Archaeology and Anthropology. My talk "Go Do Good! Responsibility and the Future of Cultural Heritage in the Eastern Mediterranean in the 21st Century" was both a call to arms for practitioners of cultural heritage management in the Eastern Mediterranean and an encapsulation of our ethical obligations as archaeological specialists. In my introduction I suggested "people need to come first, and while we rightly care about levels of science, of interpretation, and of knowledge acquisition, we should also be committed to the plight of humans as it relates to our practice as archaeologists" (Kersel 2016). Whether we are "born digital," semi-digital, or paper-based, our ethical obligations to the people, places, and objects with which we work remain the same.

Limited Access or Access for All?

The concept of "born digital" makes me anxious for the next generation of archaeologists. Gordon and colleagues (Ch. 1.4) assert that one of the logistical benefits of going digital is user-friendly technologies that allow for the recruitment of staff and students who have gown up with technology. In going digital, are we establishing an archaeology that excludes individuals who are not technologically inclined? Are we creating a digital divide between those with technological capabil-

Figure 1: An orthophotograph map of Fifa, Jordan, showing cumulative looting damage as of 2016. This map is constructed from several hundred aerial images of the site, recorded with a fixed wing drone, and combined with the coordinates for dozens of measured points on the ground. (Image by Austin "Chad" Hill, courtesy of the Follow the Pots Project)

ities and those who want to dig in the dirt and/or walk a transect? Will future field-school students consist only of those with digital proficiencies? In one of the more introspective chapters of this volume, Sayre (Ch. 1.6) pointedly asks: "Who gets to use advanced technology?" In pondering the question of whether data driven efficiency results in less engagement at the trowel's edge, Ellis (Ch. 1.2) asserts that digital recording methods actually have resulted in greater engagement through the use of tablets in the field—they are the great equalizer: everyone can and does participate. But does everyone? In their discussion of the field-school students at the Athienou Archaeological Project, Gordon and colleagues (Ch. 1.4) state that a supervisor on the project asked a salient question regarding the use of technology for technology's sake rather than for the betterment of archaeological praxis. In a reflective blogpost on detoxing from the digital, Jeremy Huggett (2016) asserts that "Digital Archaeology should be a means of rethinking archaeology, rather than simply a series of methodologies and techniques" – digital archaeology should be about more than the tools and techniques. This is to say nothing of the digital divide between those who can afford the technologies and those who cannot. In the underwater digital project outlined by Buxton and colleagues (Ch. 2.4), they acknowledge that only through the assistance of the engineering team were they able to keep the costs to under $10,000 USD per week. Going digital is not for the faint of budget (see additional examples: Castro López et al., Ch. 3.1; Ellis, Ch. 1.2).

Recently, Chad Hill and I submitted a paper to a notable academic journal on our "do-it-yourself" (DIY) drones and the monitoring of looting at an archaeological site in Jordan. The purpose of the paper was to highlight the use of low-cost drones to produce images (see FIG. 1) depicting change over time at a site with ongoing looting and to provide details on affordable UAV technologies. We outlined the methods, the gear (DIY drones), and some successes and some failures. Reviewer A asserted :

> "Although low-cost tools (better called toys) allow for the capture of some airborne imagery, they are very prone to failure—low-cost approaches should not be simulated. Despite this, archaeologists keep on publishing papers with these low-cost UAVs and these low-cost, unreliable machines are doing anything but revolutionizing efficient site recording."

In rejecting the paper, the editor offered this suggestion: "the issue of 'professional' vs. 'DIY' or low-cost drones could be discussed as a positive aspect of your research in a different paper." We were, of course, disappointed with the rejection of the submission but we were more disheartened by the dismissal of the DIY aspect of our research. How will the average archaeologist, graduate student, undergraduate, or local department of antiquities carry out research if they do not command the financial wherewithal for the more expensive technologies? And if they attempt to DIY, will peers with access to more expensive technologies always consider their research results inferior? Is the digital revolution creating inequality in the archaeological workplace? This inequality, I would argue, reinforces the colonial binary of the wealthy West versus the less-developed places in which many of us work. Do we have to go big or go home? And what if we are home but have no access to resources? Are we then forced to partner with wealthy institutions/individuals (in or out of country) in order to be digital archaeologists?

Boys with Toys?

As I read through this fascinating collection, I noticed that many of the voices were male. Of the 44 authors, 34 are men and 10 are women: women make up 23% of the contributors. Of the 17 chapters, 10 are single-authored, all by men. There is one chapter co-authored by two women and six chapters co-authored by both women and men. Males were lead authors in 82.3% of the chapters, women lead in 17.7% of the entries. These statistics mirror closely the trend in major archaeological journals as outlined in a 2014 study by Dana Bardolph of 4,500 peer-reviewed papers in 11 archaeology journals over a 23-year period. Among the articles surveyed in the major journals, Bardolph found 71.4% were lead-authored by men, and 28.6% by women. Bardolph argues that the low rates of publication perpetuate a marginalization of female researchers in academia and demonstrate what she called "a pernicious historical bias with regards to the visibility, recognition, presentation and circulation of women's writing" (Bardolph 2014: 534). In no way am I qualified to write a feminist critique (I will leave that to learned colleagues like Dana Bardolph, Meg Conkey, Joan Gero, Rosemary Joyce, and Ruth Tringham) on the allegation that the field of digital technology is filled with "boys and their toys," but

I did consult an active practitioner in digital media and a scholar of feminist theory for confirmation on the gender statistics in digital archaeology. Colleen Morgan of the University of York, a digital media and archaeology specialist, confirmed that women are a minority in the field of digital archaeology. Are digital technologies adding to the bifurcation of the discipline, meaning is it males, most often white, who do digital and females who do something else? Is digital archaeology man's work?

I am infamous for calling out projects, colleagues, and peers for not having enough (or any) women on projects, publications, or panels. In an exchange on Facebook I commented on a post by my colleagues Yorke Rowan [also my husband] and Chad Hill in which 5 males were pictured with a caption about going off to fly drones in the eastern desert of Jordan. I remarked: "I think you are missing some women on that adventure," which I suspect is often the case in digital/technological archaeology—women and minorities are missing. In no way am I suggesting that particular archaeologists are deliberately excluding women and/or minorities; I think the historical legacy of archaeology and science in general as a male-dominated field has resulted in the present situation, but I want those who embrace of the digital revolution to recognize that these historical precedents may be reinforced by current practices.

A discussion of public archaeology and digital technology (an element I found lacking in most of the chapters in this volume) is a topic for another paper (see Morgan 2012 for a detailed synthetic analysis of the topic), and only Chapter 1.6 (by Sayre) provides a comprehensive consideration of community archaeology and the digital divide created by new technologies, which makes archaeology beyond the reach of the local Andean *campesino* in terms of access and expense. In their recent blogpost on decolonizing anthropology, McGranahan and Rizvi (2016) propose, "Our history is full of taking information from communities without enough consideration of the impact." As a discipline we need to consider our relationships with communities—the broad ranging definition of community—because I would suggest that digital archaeology may have the potential to segregate rather than foster inclusion, as demonstrated in the discussion regarding overcoming local mistrust in the chapter (Ch. 1.6) by Sayre. One way to do this may be through a variety of publication platforms.

PUBLICATION AND DIGITAL ARCHAEOLOGY

While I found the gender imbalance (I fully acknowledge that I did not address the racial divide) disturbing, as a female in a male-dominated profession I was not surprised. I was however ~~surprised~~, no, shocked at the lack of engagement of what to do with the increasing amount of data produced as a result of these new technologies—most of the submissions stopped at the edge of the square or in the analysis stage of fieldwork; very few mentioned publication. In his excellent summation of the responsibilities of the Pompeii Bibliography and Mapping Project and the quest for an understanding of the past, Poehler (Ch. 1.7) states:

> we collect data,
> we analyze them,
> we interpret them,
> we synthesize them, and
> we narrate them.

Why does Poehler (Ch. 1.7) use *we narrate them* rather than the more direct *we publish them*? I concede fully that the focus of the workshop and subsequent volume was/is "Recent Approaches to Archaeological *Fieldwork* [emphasis mine] in the Digital Age," but I see fieldwork and publication as inextricably linked, and until we inculcate this position as a standard in the discipline, many are free to split the praxis of archaeology, thereby obscuring the need to publish. As Kansa (Ch. 4.2) eloquently states, traditionally varied funding mechanisms have cultivated this partition by continuing to sponsor fieldwork, new technologies, and analyses but by not providing much, if any, support for publication. This divide between fieldwork and publication has led to a discouraging predicament: the ongoing failure to publish the results of our research in a timely and accessible manner. If we are producing more data, faster, we should also be thinking about sharing our findings in a greater number of appropriate venues. After all, is not the raison d'être of archaeology knowledge production and its dissemination?

More than any other aspect of the discipline of archaeology, the production of digital data lends itself to SPEED publication (à la Eddie Izzard). Online digital repositories like Open Context concomitant with the recent requirements by both the NEH and National Science Foundation (NSF) for the inclusion of data management plans in grant applications should be the perfect storm for timely publication. At a very minimum, "data sharing as publication" (see Kansa, Ch. 4.2) should be the standard for all archaeological projects, and if an end result of digital technologies is immediately available data (as described by Ellis, Ch.1.2), each of the entries in this volume should have emphasized their data management plans and the publication of data through an online platform as part of any discussion of technology and fieldwork. I agree with Kansa (Ch. 4.2) when he reminds us that our commitment to the archaeological record does not stop with the bureaucratic NSF and NEH digital-management compliance. Requiring data management as part of funding is an excellent first step in meeting our ethical obligation to publish our findings. We still need to intellectually engage with, scrutinize, interrogate, inspect, synthesize, and *narrate* the data we deposit; but at the very least, web-based digital repositories should be a part of our digital (or semi-digital) lives.

I want to end with a recent case study in digital technology that I believe underscores some of the ongoing tensions between digital and semi-digital forms of archaeology and the need for a clearer articulation of why archaeology (digital and/or other forms) matters.

WHY DO DIGITAL? A CASE STUDY IN 3D

In April 2016, a two-thirds scale 3D model of the gate from the Temple of Bel at Palmyra was erected in London's Trafalgar Square. At the unveiling of the structure, then London Mayor Boris Johnson told spectators that they were gathered "in defiance of the barbarians [DAESH]" who destroyed the arch in the city located north-east of the Syrian capital of Damascus (Turner 2016). Vociferous discussion erupted in the digital "Twittersphere" surrounding the purpose, the utility, and the relevance of the 3D model.

> Tweet 1: "Palmyra arch 1/3 scale model surrounded by white men in suits congratulating each other #heritage" (@GabeMoshenka, April 19, 2016, 7:56am)

Tweet 2: "3D toy-archaeology in a wildly imperialist setting proves that WE are the civilized ones and THEY are the savages" (@GabeMoshenka, April 19, 2016, 8:06am)

Tweet 3: "HUGELY EXPENSIVE toy arch says exactly how much we value faux antiquity over helping living people :(" (@Eleanor_Robson, April 19, 2016, 8:09am)

Tweet 4: "Not even about archaeology, it's fun 3D print toys for boys." (@cwjones89, April 19, 2016, 8:10am)

Tweet 5: "It is technological fetishism at its worst" (@jobbew Apr 19, 2016, 8:49am)

Tweet 6: "LET'S TALK ABOUT DIGITAL COLONIALISM. #london #palmyraarch #palmyra #TrafalgarSquare." (@morehshin Apr 19, 2016, 3:57pm)

Tweet 7: "What's the Value of Recreating the #PalmyraArch with Digital Technology? #London" (@historylizer April 20, 2016, 8:20am)

Tweet 8: "Palmyra arch in Traf. Sq. without a shred of info for the visitor. Crowd of baffled tourists mostly asking what it is?" (@GabeMoshenka, April 20, 2016, 11:03am)

How is producing a 3D model of a destroyed architectural element from Syria archaeology? What does creating an isolated replica actually contribute to our understanding of the people of Syria, the history of Syria, and the archaeology of the Roman period, particularly if there were no accompanying signs to explain the meaning and/or purpose of the arch? As Christina Luke and I articulated in our 2013 volume on archaeology and cultural diplomacy, archaeologists and their work are used in various guises, in ways we least expect, which are often far removed from our original intent and goals (Luke and Kersel 2013). In this digital moment, the 3D model of the arch from Palmyra was used to demonstrate that the West cares about culture—a media moment timed to coincide with World Heritage Day. But the moment could have been so much more: the 3D arch could have served as proxy for future collaborations with the people of Syria on the protection and conservation of their cultural heritage.

Conclusions

At the Council for British Research in the Levant conference, *The Past in the Present of the Middle East* (April 2016), Eleanor Robson suggested that it was healthy to be self-conscious about what we do, and to ask ourselves "What are we doing locally and what are we doing with data we collect?" Her comments are particularly pertinent with respect to digital archaeology. After reading this volume, I am convinced that digital technologies have the propensity to create and/or reinforce divisions between males and females, developed and less-developed nations, and practice and theory. As a discipline we need to acknowledge these ruptures and work toward bridging the divides. Digital archaeology appears to be largely uncritical in execution, with a focus on equipment, platforms, and programs. Evaluation has been limited to debates over DIY versus professional, issues over standardization, and sometimes about output. This lack of self-assessment has left "archaeologists open to accusations of technological fetishism" (Huggett 2016, and see Tweet #5 above). While these same statements can be and have been leveled at paper-based archaeology, I was asked to provide my thoughts on the digital.

There is an absence of self-reflection in this volume's compilation, but there is still time, time to think about why we do what we do and how we could be doing it better. How will we use our innovations to "catalyse, support, develop, and enhance" (Huggett 2016) our production of knowledge about the past in order to make archaeology relevant in the 21st century?

With all due respect to the authors, editors, and participants in this volume and the amazing achievements in visualization, data storage, collection, documentation, and informatics demonstrated here (I am in awe of the body of knowledge and technological know-how displayed), I think now is the time to step back, to consider the "slow archaeology" of Caraher (Ch. 4.1) and contemplate our ethical obligations to publish (Kansa, Ch. 4.2); we must also take heed of the ethical responsibilities we have toward the communities with whom we work (Sayre, Ch. 1.6). We need to think through the additional layers that digital archaeology adds to our vocation.

I want to return to the question of what we might be missing when we are completely digital. In the influential paper by Roosevelt and colleagues (2015) on the "born-digital" Kaymakçı Archaeological

Project in western Turkey, the authors suggest that digital technologies assist in removing layers of abstraction. But in removing these layers without theoretical reflection, are we obfuscating the messiness of archaeology? Are we less creative in the field now that we can and do provide millimeter accuracy in our documentation? Does being one millimeter off in our calculations mean that the archaeology and the interpretations were poorly executed? Do we need room to be wrong?

The future is bright, very bright for digital archaeological field-work and data collection, but there is still work to be done. In many respects it is a good predicament that we are in a "semi-digital kinda life." There is time to improve and to expand and to include missing elements into digital archaeology.

ACKNOWLEDGMENTS

My many thanks to Erin Walcek Averett, Jody M. Gordon, and Derek B. Counts for the invitation to respond to such an interesting set of papers. I also thank each of the authors for their thoughtful and erudite contributions on digital archaeology. I am inspired by the breadth and depth of their commitment to archaeological fieldwork. I was challenged to think about archaeology and my own digital life, which is a good thing. In considering the volume, I sought feedback on some of my thoughts from Bill Caraher, Colleen Morgan, Gabe Moshenka, and Dimitri Nakassis; I thank them all for their wise insights, feedback, and reference recommendations. Any and all errors or omissions are my own.

https://mobilizingthepast.mukurtu.net/collection/51-response-living-semi-digital-kinda-life

http://dc.uwm.edu/arthist_mobilizingthepast/20

References

Bardolph, D. 2014. "A Critical Evaluation of Recent Gendered Publishing Trends in American Archaeology," *American Antiquity* 79: 522–540.

Caraher, W. 2015. "Understanding Digital Archaeology." *The Archaeology of the Mediterranean World*, https://mediterraneanworld. wordpress.com/2015/07/17/understanding-digital-archaeology/

Cook, G. 2003. "How I Discovered the 'House of David' Inscription," http://ngsba.org/en/excavations/tel-dan/ how-i-discovered-the-house-of-david-inscription

Howland, M., F. Kuester, and T. E. Levy. 2014. "Structure from Motion: Twenty-First Century Field Recording with 3D Technology," *Near Eastern Archaeology* 77(3): 187–191.

Huggett, J. 2016. "A Digital Detox for Digital Archaeology?" *Introspective Digital Archaeology*, https://introspectivedigitalarchaeology. wordpress.com/2016/04/

Kersel, M. M. 2016. "Go Do Good! Responsibility and the Future of Cultural Heritage in the Eastern Mediterranean in the 21st Century." The Future of the Past: From Amphipolis to Mosul. New Approaches to Cultural Heritage Preservation in the Eastern Mediterranean. *The AIA Site Preservation Publication Program.* https://www.archaeological.org/news/sitepreservationhcaspecialpubs/21700#sthash.723F2tJ9.dpuf

Izzard, E. 2008. "Eddie Izzard about Archaeology." *YouTube*, https:// www.youtube.com/watch?v=U6y-jn6jGbM

Luke, C., and M. M. Kersel. 2013. *U.S. Cultural Diplomacy and Archaeology. Soft Power, Hard Heritage. Routledge Studies in Archaeology 6.* London: Routledge.

McGranahan, C., and U. Rizvi 2016. "Decolonizing Anthropology." *Savage Minds*, http://savageminds.org/2016/04/19/ decolonizing-anthropology/

Morgan, C. L. 2012. *Emancipatory Digital Archaeology.* Ph.D. dissertation, University of California, Berkeley.

Nakassis, D. 2015. "Thinking Digital Archaeology." *Aegean Prehistory*, https://englianos.wordpress.com/2015/08/10/ thinking-digital-archaeology/

Olson, B. R., R. A. Placchetti, J. Quartermaine, and A. E. Killebrew. 2013. "The Tel Akko Total Archaeology Project (Akko, Israel):

Assessing the Suitability of Multi-Scale 3D Field Recording in Archaeology," *Journal of Field Archaeology* 38: 244–262.

Roosevelt, C. H., P. Cobb, E. Moss, B. R. Olson, S. Ünlüsoy. 2015. "Excavation is ~~Destruction~~ Digitization: Advances in Archaeological Practice," *Journal of Field Archaeology* 40: 325–346.

Rowan, Y. M. and M. M. Kersel. 2014. "New Perspectives on the Chalcolithic Period in the Galilee: Investigations at the Site of Marj Rabba," in J. Spencer, R. Mullins, and A. Brody eds., *Material Culture Matters. Essays on Archaeology in the Southern Levant in Honor of Seymour Gitin*. Winona Lake: Eisenbrauns, 221-238.

Turner, L. 2016. "Palmyra's Arch of Triumph Recreated in London." *BBC News*, http://www.bbc.com/news/uk-36070721

5.2.
Response: Mobilizing (Ourselves) for a Critical Digital Archaeology

Adam Rabinowitz

Nous déclarons que la splendeur du monde s'est enrichie d'une beauté nouvelle: la beauté de la vitesse. Une automobile de course avec son coffre orné de gros tuyaux, tels des serpents à l'haleine explosive . . . une automobile rugissante, qui a l'air de courir sur de la mitraille, est plus belle que la *Victoire de Samothrace*.

Filippo Tommaso Marinetti, *Le Figaro*, February 20, 1909[1]

A DISTANT DIGITAL APPROACH TO "MOBILIZING THE PAST"

Since the contributions in this volume revolve around the relationship between information and digital data in archaeology, it seems appropriate to begin by turning the volume itself into data to explore the results. The emerging discipline of Digital Humanities, when it is used in literary fields, treats words in a text as a series of data points, which when viewed in the aggregate ("distant reading": Moretti 2005: 1) can show patterns invisible to the close reader. Distant reading techniques such as topic modeling have been applied to archaeological discourses by Shawn Graham, and I follow Graham here in the notion that the words and syntax we use to talk about archaeology can illuminate our underlying interests or preoccupations.[2]

---

[1] "We declare that the splendor of the world has been enriched with a new beauty: the beauty of speed. A race-car with its hood adorned with huge exhaust pipes, like serpents with explosive breath... a roaring automobile, that seems to run on grapeshot, is more beautiful than the *Victory of Samothrace*."

[2] Graham's work in this area initially focused on archaeological databases (see his project statement on the Portable Antiquities Scheme (https://finds.org.uk/research/projects/project/id/375), but it has more recently turned to the analysis of site diaries, using material from Kenan Tepe stored in Open Context (e.g., https://rpubs.com/shawngraham/79365). For an overview of the tools, see Graham *et al.* 2012.

I am a novice in this area, so when reviewing the contributions in the present volume, I took advantage of two Web-based platforms that require very little specialized knowledge for basic text analysis and visualization: Voyant Tools and the collocation tool in the TAPoR toolkit.[3] I copied the text of the contributions from a PDF to a text file, deleted the figure references and bibliographies, and fed the results into those two platforms. Both platforms automatically remove the usual set of "stop-words"—commonly-occurring words like articles and prepositions that would otherwise dominate the results of frequency counts—and I added to this list a group of words that appeared with disproportionate frequency in this volume: predictably, "digital," "data," "archaeology," and "project", along with "et" and "al" from the parenthetical citations.

The result confirmed the impression I had while reading the manuscript. One of the words that remained at the top of the frequency list after all stop-words were removed was "time." Time, in fact, is a constant presence throughout the diverse chapters of this volume, from the efficiencies described by the contributions in Part 1, to the tools that now allow us to do in hours tasks that would have taken months a few years ago in Part 2, to the time needed for development, customization, and technical support in Part 3, to the final comments on the slowing of time in both archaeology and data management in Part 4. As I read the contributions, I felt, on an almost physical level, the attraction to the increased speed of our digital tools. The brakes applied to that momentum in the chapters by Caraher (Ch. 4.1) and Kansa (Ch. 4.2) only underline its power.[4] My simple distant reading of the text as a whole suggests a sense of time as a limited commodity: in the TAPoR platform, among the most frequent collocations of the 241 instances of the word "time" were variations of the word "save" (save, saving, savings, saved: 19 instances), "spend" and "spent" (11 instances), "-consuming" (eight instances), and, at the bottom end of the most frequent collocations, "cost" (five instances). The other top collocations were "data" (18 instances), "development" (15 instances), and "real" or "real-" (as in "real-time": 13 instances).

[3] Voyant Tools: http://voyant-tools.org/; TAPoR: http://taporware.ualberta.ca/~taporware/textTools/collocation.shtml?.

[4] Caraher's ongoing work continues to highlight this issue; see https://mediterraneanworld.wordpress.com/2016/04/25/6086/.

Time is, of course, both the object of fascination and the principal adversary of the archaeologist. Archaeology is by definition an attempt to recapture lost time—to recreate moments in the past through the analysis of traces time has failed to erase. And it is time, through the law of entropy, whose passage causes both our evidence and our documentation to decay; time that is always in too short supply when we are in the field; time that is consumed in alarmingly large chunks as we prepare the results of our research for publication. We are not alone in our preoccupation with time, however: the digital revolution brought about by the personal computer, the Internet, and the smartphone also revolves around time. The ever-increasing speed of computer processors allows our calculating machines to become smaller and faster; advances in fiber optics and wireless connectivity allow bits to be transferred at greater and greater rates of speed; in the world of work, efficiencies produced by digital platforms allow fewer people to do more work in less time. Our own sense of time has changed in response, as anyone who remembers dial-up Internet can attest. However much we embrace the need for slowness in theory, we still become frustrated when a streaming video stops to buffer or an operating system is slow to boot up. We have become addicted to digital speed.

The dialogue between archaeological and digital attitudes toward time provides one central theme of this response chapter. The intersection between time and money is another. Kansa's allusion to Frederick Taylor, the thinker behind the science of business management and the assembly line in the early 20th century (Ch. 4.2), is not simply a thought-provoking analogy: it reminds us that the work of archaeology in this century is deeply entangled with an economic system—capitalism—that is also responsible for the design and production of the digital tools we use. Although economies and tools have always been enmeshed, the paper, writing instruments, cameras and film of the analog era were not as closely coupled as our digital tools are to the agendas of corporate entities that prosper through constant innovation and change. There are only a few ways in which one can disrupt a pencil.

Two hundred and fifty years have passed since the excavations of the Quadriporticus at Pompeii (Poehler, Ch. 1.7). For 230 of those years, field documentation practices remained largely unchanged: archaeologists took notes using pen or pencil and paper, measured features with tapes and plumb-bobs, surveyed with transits and optical theodolites, and drew plans and sections by hand. Only one major technological advance took place during that time: the introduction of photography 60 years after the Quadriporticus excavations began, 190 years before the present. The dumpy level described in John Droop's 1915 excavation manual (Droop 1915, 11–12) was still in use when I dug at Cosa in 1995, 80 years later. But in the decade that followed, we moved from the adoption of basic digital databases to GIS-based, total-station-driven digital integration of relational and spatial data; and in the decade since, we have moved from digital photos, GIS, and the digitization of paper context sheets to the routine use of tablets and high-density survey and measurement techniques (HDSM; see Opitz and Limp 2015).

The combination of the rapid pace of technological change over the last two decades and the relative lack of theory in our consideration of our own documentation practices have left us poorly equipped to understand the effects our new digital tools are having on our ways of seeing and thinking.[5] We can immediately see how they help us do better what we have been trying to do, as archaeologists, for the last 200 years; we have a strong—but still somewhat inchoate—sense that they will help us go beyond those things we have traditionally attempted to do; but we seem to have very little sense at all of how they are shaping and constraining what we choose to look at, what we are able to see, and how we describe our observations. Yet the contributions to this volume make it abundantly clear that we are not just witnessing a change from one recording medium to another, like the transition from film to digital photography or from typewriters to word processors. What we are seeing is a more fundamental transformation of our knowledge-production practices—a paradigm shift

[5] This is not to say that there has been no consideration of archaeological documentation, but rather that theoretically informed analyses have appeared only fairly recently, and they are still catching up with the transformation of context-based paper systems after Harris's introduction of single-context recording and his eponymous matrix (Harris 1979). See, e.g., Lucas 2001; Pavel 2010 (cited several times in this volume); and Cobb *et al.* 2012. The theoretical consideration of photography took even longer: although it was integrated into archaeological practice by later 19th century, it was not until the 1990s that a serious inquiry into the highly constructed nature of archaeological photography began (Shanks 1997; Shanks and Svabo 2013; Carter 2015).

analogous to those caused by the introduction of the printing press or the ground-glass lens.

With that recognition we are faced with two paths. For the first, we can simply celebrate our advances—but in that case, a book like this will rapidly become a fossilized historical document like Droop's field manual, capturing a moment in the development of our discipline and inspiring the occasional reader to chuckle at the quaintness of our gadgets (A tablet you type into! A drone that stays aloft only for an hour!). The methods themselves, based as they are on ephemeral digital platforms and equipment, will quickly be outdated. I know this to be true from personal experience: within five years, the online publication of our stratigraphy from excavations at Cosa (Fentress and Rabinowitz 2003), retrofitted from a print model and novel at the time for an academic press, was being critiqued for its lack of data integration (Heinzelmann 2008), and within less than a decade, the publication of our "cutting-edge methods" at Chersonesos had been left far behind by PhotoScan-based 3D documentation workflows (Rabinowitz *et al.* 2007; cf De Reu *et al.* 2013; Olson *et al.* 2013; Roosevelt *et al.* 2015; see also: Castro López *et al.*, Ch. 3.1; Olson, Ch. 2.2; Wernke *et al.*, Ch. 2.3). If any theoretical framework can be associated with our wholehearted embrace of the potential of digital tools, I suspect it will eventually be called something like "New Archaeological Empiricism," and despite our protests, it will be a large and slow-moving target for the projectiles of the next generation of social theorists.[6]

The second path, I think, will give our current discussions a much longer use-life. Instead of treating our current practices as a triumphal step along the march of progress toward greater archaeological truth,

---

[6] Just as the technical aspects of Digital Humanities, despite its much richer body of reflexive critical thought, have recently been attacked in a controversial article in the *Los Angeles Review of Books* (Allington *et al.* 2016); see the response by Matthew Kirschenbaum on Medium [https://medium.com/@mkirschenbaum/am-i-a-digital-humanist-confessions-of-a-neoliberal-tool-1bc64caaa984#.46ty2dd2p] and the tidal wave of other reactions to this article summarized by Digital Humanities Now [http://digitalhumanitiesnow.org/2016/05/editors-choice-round-up-of-responses-to-the-la-neoliberal-tools-and-archives/] and dh+lib review [http://acrl.ala.org/dh/2016/05/05/neoliberal-tools-and-archives-a-political-history-of-digital-humanities/]. Of direct relevance to this volume is Caraher's own commentary on the piece (https://mediterraneanworld.wordpress.com/2016/05/03/digital-humanities-and-the-new-liberal-arts/).

we need a wake-up call that stirs us from our enraptured contemplation of speed, efficiency, accuracy, and three- or even four-dimensional digital surrogacy. We need to think, as many of the contributors to this volume do, about what we are sacrificing along with what we are gaining from digital methods. We need to think about who is included and who is excluded by this changing practice. We need to think about why we do archaeology, and how our dependence on tools that are not necessarily made for our benefit constrains, as well as expands, our ability to look at the past. We need to think about the role that money and power play in shaping our relationship with digital approaches. In short, we need a Critical Digital Archaeology.[7] We need a manifesto.

THREE MANIFESTOS

Luckily, we already have one, as a number of the contributors to this work have pointed out: Jeremy Huggett's "Manifesto for an Introspective Digital Archaeology" (Huggett 2015; see especially Dufton, Ch. 3.3). Huggett, who moves equally comfortably in the Digital Humanities, clearly understands the reasons that field has already produced a Critical Digital Humanities movement, and his manifesto raises many of the general issues that we should be addressing as we take advantage of tools that existed only in optimistic science fiction 20 years ago. I would like to push Huggett's manifesto a little further, however, and place it in the context of two other manifestos, one old and one new. Together, these three manifestos can help to frame the contributions to this volume and elucidate the ways in which its four parts work together. They offer three complementary perspectives from which we can view the current state of digital archaeology: celebratory, reflective, and cautionary.

The Celebratory Manifesto

This chapter began with an extract from the first of these manifestos: Filippo Marinetti's "Manifesto del Futurismo," the well-known

---

[7] I cannot imagine I have coined this term, despite its apparent absence from the published record, and in fact Google tells me that Lorna Richardson used it in a tweet during the CAA conference in Oslo in April 2016: https://twitter.com/lornarichardson/status/716120246545956864.

Futurist position statement that first received widespread attention when it was published in French in *Le Figaro* in the spring of 1909.[8] If we leave aside its explicit misogyny, its foreshadowing of Fascism, and its deplorable endorsement of violence, it is possible to see in Marinetti's manifesto a reflection of our own moment. The Futurist artists, like us, lived at a moment of rapid and disruptive technological change, a time when not only daily life but entire traditional systems were being transformed or torn apart by new ideas and new devices. They saw around them institutions and individuals who were slow to adapt, entrenched in traditional ways of doing and seeing, aesthetically and intellectually conservative, and resistant to the potential of new technologies, and they wanted to shake them from their slumber or run them over—as do the visionaries of Silicon Valley and their prophets of disruption, at the extreme end of the spectrum, but also, on a milder level, as do many of us who embrace digital technologies in our disciplinary practice. We have similar conversations about academic publishing, about tenure committees and university administrators, and about funding agencies.

Even the specific targeting of archaeology in the Futurist manifesto ("we want to deliver Italy," writes Marinetti, "from its gangrene of professors, archaeologists, tour-guides and antiquarians") finds certain parallels in the current discourse of digital archaeology. Roosevelt and colleagues have mounted a direct assault against the archaeological truism that "excavation is destruction" (Roosevelt *et al.* 2015: 325–326). A panel at the annual meeting of the Society for American Archaeology held in 2016 focused on the same topic, taking as its starting point a paper critiquing the reflexive habits that insist that all walls and floors at certain sites be preserved, no matter how unimportant they are or how much new information they prevent us from recovering.[9] And the Institute for Digital Archaeology can claim, in the face of damage wrought to the remains of Palmyra by ISIS—a group frequently described as "medieval" and opposed to

---

[8] A digital facsimile of the newspaper page bearing this manifesto is available at http://gallica.bnf.fr/ark:/12148/bpt6k2883730/f1.image.

[9] The panel was entitled "'Destruction' and the Rhetoric of Archaeological Excavation"; it was organized by Rachel Opitz, Nicola Terrenato, and Gregory Tucker, and the latter two provided the position paper, entitled "Architecture, Epistemic Conservation and Ideological Biases in Pluristratified Urban Sites: The Case of Roman cities in Italy."

modernity—that the digital documentation and reconstruction of archaeological monuments "can put these crucially important repositories of our cultural identity and shared history forever beyond the reach of those who would destroy them."[10] Futurism, in the minds of the artists who created it, would save Italy from the fetishists of the past. Similarly, digital archaeology, by releasing us from a single-minded Victorian focus on the authenticity of ruins frozen at a single moment in time, will save us from the current fetishization of the physical remains of the past as things to be utterly preserved or utterly destroyed. Rachel Opitz and Fred Limp have recently summarized this notion in pragmatic terms: the widespread adoption of new tools and techniques for HDSM will give us unprecedented access to the "thingness" of archaeological remains in an entirely digital form (Opitz and Limp 2015: 357).

And, of course, the Futurist Manifesto concerned itself with the speed, power, and potential of new machines. Through that focus, it truly did foster the development of new ways of thinking, seeing, and creating. It is thus an appropriate frame within which to celebrate the potential of our own new archaeological machines, whatever form of documentation—words, pictures, coordinates, point clouds—they are designed to capture. I mean this sincerely, as an enthusiastic user of digital tools in my own archaeological practice. While I share Caraher's concern with the "de-skilling" danger inherent in frictionless digital platforms for data collection (Ch. 4.1), I have also been responsible for several projects in the field, and I have rarely hesitated when offered a chance to do more with less. The paperless, tablet-based workflows described by Wallrodt (Ch. 1.1), Ellis (Ch. 1.2), Motz (Ch. 1.3), and Fee (Ch. 2.1) indisputably avoid the duplication of labor inherent in the transcription of paper records into a digital database. At Chersonesos, our trench supervisors spent many evenings typing their context sheets into first a Microsoft Access and later an

---

[10] See http://digitalarchaeology.org.uk/our-purpose/; see also http://www.theguardian.com/commentisfree/2016/mar/29/palmyra-message-isis-islamic-state-jihadis-orgy-destruction-heritage-restored. This is not an uncontroversial stance: a debate over the colonial implications of the reconstruction of the Triumphal Arch at Palmyra and its installation in Trafalgar Square is playing out as I write (e.g., http://theconversation.com/the-middle-east-heritage-debate-is-becoming-worryingly-colonial-57679), and it has been argued that ISIS is in fact much more like the Futurists in its embrace of new technologies in the service of an ideology of violence (Harmansah 2015).

Archaeological Recording Kit (ARK) database (see Dufton, Ch. 3.3), and when they inevitably fell behind on this work, we all had to spend additional time sorting out the mistakes that crept in as the backlog of paper documents mounted.

The advantages of a well-designed digital form with consistent vocabularies are also manifest: although we used digital data collectors with our total stations in the field at Chersonesos, we did not have preset vocabularies, with the result that we preserved an excellent record of human variability in the description of find types, but a rather less useful record for search and filtering (to map all the coins recovered from the excavation, e.g., one needs to filter the finds layer in the geodatabase for not only "COIN" but "3.COINS," "BRONZE.COIN," "BROKEN.COIN," and so on). Occasionally this resulted in labels that are likely to create future confusion, as with a small copper-alloy rod that was enigmatically categorized in the data collector (and thus the geodatabase) as a "PUKEN." The defined-value fields in a tablet-based system prevent this sort of user error from occurring, and even in situations where it is possible, the synchronization of different data streams makes it much easier to discover inconsistencies before they are propagated (see Sobotkova *et al.*, Ch. 3.2). Even more immediate are built-in validation tools like those described by Fee for PKapp (Ch. 2.1), which prevent users from making data entry mistakes in the first place.

"Real-time" validation and data integration are, in my opinion, among the most significant advantages offered by the paperless systems discussed in this volume. The frequency of the phrase "real time" in my basic textual analysis is indicative of the importance of this concept in paperless workflows. Here the beauty of digital speed shines brightest. For most of the 20th and well into the 21st century, information collected in the process of archaeological excavation jelled slowly and centrifugally. This remained true even after the adoption of digital technologies for documentation, as Wallrodt (Ch. 1.1) explains in his review of the history of digital fieldwork. By contrast, the syncing of visual, spatial, and textual records as they are collected by multiple users in the field and lab prevents data loss or corruption and, as Ellis demonstrates (Ch. 1.2), enables an interdisciplinary conversation between excavators, supervisors, and material specialists that can inform not only interpretation but excavation strategy in mid-stream. Here, the advantage of mobile devices lies in their form factor: even while acting as cameras, GIS platforms, and multi-user synchronized databases, these devices are still small and light enough to be carried around like notebooks. When one adds instant access to the sort of vast archives of previous records and publications that Digital Pompeii offers, Poehler (Ch. 1.7) is absolutely right to claim that a new dimension of "trowel's-edge" interpretation opens before us.

This new interpretive dimension is not just richer in information. It also offers greater opportunities for the democratization of archaeological interpretation in the field. This has long been a concern for Ian Hodder and other archaeologists who are interested in the internal hierarchies of archaeological research, in which the diggers—either local workmen or field-school students—are usually at the bottom, while those who weave together the various strands of evidence to create the story of the site are at the top (Berggren and Hodder 2003). The contributions of Gordon and colleagues (Ch. 1.4) and of Bria and DeTore (Ch. 1.5), as well as those of Ellis (Ch. 1.2) and Motz (Ch. 1.3), put the experiences of the students in the foreground, highlighting the way in which mobile devices provide integrated access to information not only to the director or supervisors, but also to the students themselves. Bria and DeTore's account of the way that their mobile database enhanced their students' ability to formulate sophisticated, self-directed, multidisciplinary projects is particularly compelling. Sayre's contribution (Ch. 1.6) goes even further in its description of the ways in which mobile platforms can help to mediate inequalities between foreign archaeological teams and local populations. The instructional potential of mobile recording systems increases dramatically when students and local collaborators are included as partners in the development and testing of these systems, and in the creation of the vocabularies and ontological frameworks that underlie the databases they use.

We should celebrate, too, the growing capacity of the sensors on our archaeological machines and the increasing computational power that makes it possible to apply ever more complex algorithms to the information they capture. The chapters by Olson (Ch. 2.2) and Wernke and colleagues (Ch. 2.3) neatly lay out the result: the transformation of a large number of high-definition digital photographs into a photorealistic 3D digital model of an entire site and its stratigraphy at millimeter-level accuracy. Processing power is still an issue, but requirements for time and human intervention have dropped precipitously (in 2007–2008, we employed a recent University of Texas graduate for months to manually match points to make fewer than a hundred 3D context models for Chersonesos using PhotoModeler; with PhotoScan, models of comparable quality can be created from the same sets of photographs in less than an hour apiece).

Nowhere are the possibilities of this new world of recording more apparent, however, than in the description of the Pladypos system offered by Buxton and her colleagues (Ch. 2.4). The mapping and recording systems involved are analogous to the drone-based sensors described by Wernke and his colleagues (Ch. 2.3). What is more apparent here, however, is the potential for autonomous action on the part of the recording machine. Drones can fly pre-programmed patterns, of course, but Buxton's article—and the ability of nautical ROVs (remotely operated vehicles) to function independently for longer periods of time than current UAVs (unmanned aerial vehicles)—made clearer the distinction between a machine controlled by a human operator and a machine carrying out recording essentially on its own, with the information it collects then being extracted and processed algorithmically. A few rounds of algorithm development down the road, and perhaps the machine could be trusted to make its own decisions about site identification and recording;[11] a few rounds after that, and perhaps it could be trusted to autonomously recognize, record, and extract certain types of objects. At that point, we have a robotic nautical archaeologist. A few more leaps forward in technology would probably be required for the emergence of a robotic terrestrial archaeologist, though watching a computer-driven router carve the architectural decoration of a copy of Palmyra's Triumphal Arch, one might be forgiven for imagining a machine that documents and removes stratigraphic layers by itself, using an array of sophisticated sensors coordinated with robotic excavation limbs. Olson (Ch. 2.2) notes that volumetric modeling of stratigraphy on the basis of 3D photogrammetry "can take the human element out of stratigraphic

---

[11] The sort of machine-learning/neural-network/artificial intelligence approach that this entails does not seem so far off: some projects are already combining adaptive pattern-recognition algorithms with crowdsourced information to extract data automatically from satellite imagery. See, e.g., the MicroMappers wildlife challenge: https://irevolutions.org/2015/02/09/aerial-imagery-analysis-combining-crowdsourcing-ai/).

recording." How long will it be before we are able to remove the human element altogether? And will we want to?

The Reflective Manifesto

Computers are better than humans at carrying out mathematical operations, a facility that extends to the organization and retrieval of digital data. Electronic and digital sensors are better than humans at perceiving and recording many of the qualities of the physical environment, especially when it comes to measurement. Since the measurement, recording, and organization of data are the primary goals of the process of archaeological documentation, why not turn this over to computers? What do humans have to offer to this process?

The answer to this question lies in the distinction between data, information, and interpretation. Machines can collect data, and they can begin to integrate them into the contextual systems that we think of as information, but they cannot perform the leap of informed imagination that enables the human archaeologist to propose explanations for why and how a stratigraphic deposit was formed, and they cannot (yet) tell the stories that archaeologists must create to explain the history of a site. Since, however, both the imaginative leap and the resulting story are a result of a close physical engagement with the material remains, and since they are both part of a process that involves a human being creating information at the trowel's edge and then filtering and transforming it for representation to other human beings, it is worth asking how the out-sourcing of some of the components of documentation to digital tools will affect the information we produce and the stories we tell. Here we arrive at the second manifesto: Huggett's 2015 essay.

Like Hodder's calls for a reflexive archaeology (Hodder 1997, 2003), Huggett's article asks us to think more critically about the interaction between our tools, our practices, and the knowledge that we seek to create: to develop "a form of introspective or more self-aware Digital Archaeology, one which consciously seeks to understand the underlying processes and behaviours that sit behind the tools, technologies, and methodologies applied" (Huggett 2015: 89). Hodder and his collaborators are currently concerned with some of the same issues, but their emphasis on the advantages of digital recording for the preservation of multivocality and the democratization of process takes a distinctly more celebratory tone (Berggren *et al.* 2015). Huggett, by contrast, argues that we should be aware not only of the doors digital technology can open, but of the other doors it closes.

Huggett's essay deserves to be read in its entirety, but I want to highlight here two recurrent themes: distance and categorization. As with the "distant reading" I performed on this volume at the beginning of this response, digital tools give us the ability to take an ever-more-distant vantage point from which to observe archaeological remains, from the perspective of a satellite to a 3D model of stratigraphic deposits viewed on a monitor in the lab. Huggett suggests that this perspective, while giving us greater access to information, also decreases the intimacy of our engagement with the object of our study. Moreover, "distant reading" approaches in literature reduce texts to pre-defined component parts, sense-units consisting usually of single words—but not all words, as some are excluded *a priori* as too frequent to be relevant. Database-driven digital recording systems, both spatial and textual, perform similar operations: they define in advance what sorts of data and information are relevant and how they should be described, limiting space to coordinates and vectors and attributes to defined values. Uncertainty, fuzzy boundaries, and uncategorizable features can be lost in the process (Huggett 2015: 90–93).

These are theoretical issues that one can explore in the field through systematic user-testing and comparative study, and indeed, many of the contributors to this volume have done so.[12] But there is a related area that might require less impressionistic investigation: the cognitive science of embodied human-computer interaction, specifically as it relates to touch and input devices. A growing body of scientific literature focuses on haptics, or the physical engagement of a human hand with a tool or device, and in particular on the different ways in which we process information when dealing with different writing tools (Mangen and Velay 2010, 2012). Most of this work has focused on the cognitive effects of handwriting, either as it is connected to the engagement of multiple centers of the brain in the process of learning to read and write (James and Atwood 2009; Long-camp *et al.* 2011; James and Engelhardt 2012; Kiefer *et al.* 2015), or as it is involved in the brain's ability to process and retain information

---

[12] It is also worth mentioning the long-term and farsighted program of testing at the Silchester Roman town site: e.g., Warwick *et al.* 2009.

through note-taking (Mueller and Oppenheimer 2014). The frame that researchers in this field have applied to the interaction between brain and hand(s) in writing is "embodied cognition" (Mangen and Velay 2012: 406), a theoretical concept that has already been used in the interpretation of past material culture (cf. Piquette and Whitehouse 2013), but which we have only just begun to apply to ourselves (Olsson 2016; Wright and Morgan, forthcoming). We should: not only do functional magnetic resonance imaging (fMRI) results from the studies mentioned above suggest that the input mechanism we use affects our processing of the information we input, but a few references in the recent medical literature on strokes suggest that engagement with text input on mobile devices uses a different part of the brain from that which otherwise processes language (Kaskar *et al.* 2013; Ravi *et al.* 2013; Hadidi *et al.* 2014). The time we gain through the use of touchscreen input devices may mask deeper sacrifices in our cognitive engagement with our objects of inquiry.

Huggett's idea of digital distancing and Caraher's connection of digital platforms with de-skilling reflect observable changes in practice. In our project at Chersonesos, this was most evident in the perception of scale and relevance: instead of ignoring tiny pebbles that cannot be represented in a 1:20 pencil-drawn plan, team members digitizing context plans from orthorectified photographs in ArcGIS tended to zoom in to vectorize all of them, without making a conscious decision about whether it was actually useful to preserve the position of those pebbles (Rabinowitz *et al.* 2007: 251). The effects (or lack of effects) of new input mechanisms on our cognitive processes, however, are invisible to us unless we look for them. Since we cannot discuss cognitive changes on a practical or theoretical level until we have actually investigated them, our reflective manifesto should spur us to do so. This is all the more true because we are the consumers, not the creators, of these new mechanisms, and thus we lack the benefit of insights acquired during the design and user-testing process that produced the digital tools we are adopting.

The Cautionary Manifesto

This brings us to the third and last of our manifestos. A recent post by @flyingzumwalt on medium.com charged, with polemical eloquence, that the Internet has been coopted by for-profit ventures that seek to control and contain the digital networks of human interaction that increasingly dominate it, and harvest the data that emerge from those interactions in order to turn them into money.[13] The author argues that the "cloud" is not a liberating development but the logical outgrowth of this theft, and that allowing corporations to preserve, manage, and monetize our social-media data is a fundamental act of alienation. As an alternative, a decentralized system based on peer-to-peer transactions between local databases is proposed, so that each user becomes the absolute owner of all of his or her social-media data. The organizing metaphor for this system is *swadeshi*, a Sanskrit term used to mean something like "self-sufficiency" and a fundamental tenet of the Indian independence movement and its resistance to British imperialism.

With a few substitutions—for example, swap "labor" for "data"—the parallels of @flyingzumwalt's essay with the Marxist critique of industrial capitalism become obvious. Those who control the digital means of production—that is, the software, the servers, the platforms, and the apps—are in a position to exploit the information generated by the online "work" of users and consumers. Kansa discusses similar trends in his chapter in this volume (Ch. 4.2), with a cautionary emphasis on the degree to which digital archaeology is dependent not only on commercial infrastructures (like the current version of the Internet), but also on commercial metaphors for value, in which branding becomes central and salesmanship can be more important than content. In addressing the tension between the open-data movement and what he sees as a "neoliberal" approach to digital archaeological information, he highlights the potential of more accessible data to change archaeological discourses. At the same time, however, he acknowledges the potential for exploitation that lies in the universal opening of data, and proposes, building on Caraher's "slow archaeology", a "slow data" approach that respects the human and ethical dimensions of the production of archaeological knowledge, rather than simply seeking to aggregate, homogenize, and centralize all archaeological data as efficiently as possible.

Kansa, as the director of a non-profit organization, knows all too well the feedback loop between grant funding and the perception

---

[13] "The internet has been stolen from you. Take it back, nonviolently": https://medium.com/@flyingzumwalt/the-internet-has-been-stolen-from-you-take-it-back-nonviolently-248f8d445b87#.nmjeolqvw.

of innovation, and his contribution pays explicit attention to the economic framework within which our digital work takes place—a framework that, like @flyingzumwalt's Internet, we do not own. His chapter is a fitting conclusion to the second half of this volume: if the first two sections are about the time we save in the field, the second two are an unmistakable reminder that time is money. All of the chapters in Parts 3 and 4 struggle, from a variety of perspectives, with the relationship between the intellectual quest for archaeological knowledge and the role of money in that quest. And while the goals of the projects represented in Part 3 are diverse, ranging from the development and application of customized data-collection tools (Castro López *et al.*, Ch. 3.1) to the profitable management of a large commercial cultural resource management (CRM) company (Spigelman *et al.*, Ch. 3.4), they all acknowledge the central role of capital in digital approaches to archaeology. Economic capital in the form of equipment, from cameras to servers; economic capital in the form of seed funding for the development of digital infrastructure from governmental or private sources; social and economic capital in the form of access to knowledge workers—all of these must be available for the sort of work described in this volume. And social and economic capital is unevenly distributed. How, then, can we keep digital archaeology from becoming an archaeology of privilege, an archaeology of exclusion, an archaeology of winners and losers?

Western archaeology has, of course, traditionally been all of those things. Colonialist states funded archaeologists (usually men of the upper classes) to uncover the past of lesser nations, and those privileged archaeologists embedded relations of class and power in their fieldwork, especially with respect to local workers, whose contribution was understood as purely mechanical. Leonard Woolley, for example, paid workmen by the find while digging at Ur between 1922 and 1934, translating to the excavation site the piecework logic of the industrialized West. And the archaeological community has always picked winners: nowhere is this more apparent than in the poignant image of Frank Calvert paddling out, in the winter of 1863, to the boat on which the director of the British Museum was traveling through the Dardanelles in order to solicit him for support to excavate at Troy, only to be sent away because the director was sleeping (Allen 1999: 98). Schliemann, the eventual winner, appeared on the scene to claim the glory seven years later. If we look at the economic framework within which

Schliemann and Woolley operated, however, there are some striking differences with our current situation. Schliemann was able to self-finance, having to pay only for workmen, tools, lodging, and his paper and pens while in the field. Woolley's field expenses, too, were largely associated with the payment of workmen and logistical costs for the staff.[14]

The extensive use of digital technology in archaeological projects, on the other hand, requires significant initial expenditures for equipment, software, and technical consultation, and then the ongoing costs related to the sustainability of both data and platforms. None of these come cheap unless the archaeologist directing the project or one of the senior staff is also a competent software developer and comfortable working with open-source code. A new Schliemann could fund all of this himself, but most of us have to compete for a dwindling pool of public money. As Kansa (Ch. 4.2) points out, this encourages winner-take-all efforts to brand our systems, to offer *the* solution, to emphasize our innovative approaches—and to continue to raise the bar in each round of grant-writing, promising newer and better and different tools and methods. In short, digital archaeological projects are encouraged to act as Silicon Valley start-ups in a Darwinian landscape in which the most innovative and disruptive players are the ones that deserve to survive. The market—in this case, which is composed not only of CRM clients but of sources of public funding—will decide. There is much less room for smaller players in this environment, especially as start-up costs rise and investors concentrate on proven performers.

The cautionary component of a manifesto for a critical digital archaeology must focus on this economic model. Left unchecked, it will push us toward an emphasis on form over function, on tools over knowledge, on the technological solutionism discussed by Kansa. Moreover, beyond our own funding struggles, we must recognize that the same factors are playing out in the broader field of digital technology, and that the way they play out will have a direct effect on the practice of archaeology. Away from bugs, humidity, and fire or flood, a notebook can sit on a shelf for a century and still be consulted. But computer hardware and software are intended to change constantly

---

[14] It is instructive to consult Woolley's account statements for 1926 to 1933 on the crowdsourcing website of the Ur Digitization project; e.g., http://urcrowdsource.org/omeka/files/original/4bc43d8e9ad6beb8973dfaba02ed2623.jpg.

to compel users to purchase new versions, and digital technology companies are rewarded for disruptive innovations that kill other platforms. For hardware, this means constant updates that make relatively recent iterations obsolete—and companies like Apple drop in valuation when they are not inducing everyone to buy new products quickly enough. At the same time, for software and digital content, a rental model is increasingly replacing ownership: where once one bought a personal copy of Adobe Creative Suite (and then could choose whether to buy updates), Adobe is now pushing users to rent the continuously updated Creative Cloud on a monthly or yearly basis. Libraries purchase access to e-books that can lapse or be revoked by the publisher, at which point the books simply disappear from the virtual shelves. Providers of software and hardware, like the providers of commercial social-media platforms decried by @flyingzumwalt, benefit by locking in customers and creating dependency.

This volume demonstrates the dependency of digital archaeology, and especially of mobile recording systems, on a constellation of hardware and software technologies that are owned by groups with different priorities. In the best cases—with projects like FAIMS (Federated Archaeological Information Management System) or ARK or Open Context—those owners, themselves archaeologists, share the disciplinary mission of archaeology. But they also have to pay their operating costs, even as the directors of field projects are focused on minimizing their own. In the more troubling cases, the owners of the technologies are corporations focused on maximizing shareholder profit, which may mean changing terms of service, discontinuing products, or creating entirely new platforms. The innovation cycle creates possibilities—10 years ago, before Apple's touch devices, this volume would have been inconceivable—but it also creates significant challenges for a discipline that is by nature concerned with the *longue durée*. We have to think carefully about the impact that changes in the tech industry can have on the systems we are developing, if only to explore the worst-case scenarios. How would we react if Apple, which now owns FileMaker, decides to discontinue it and build a new mobile operating system with which the old versions are incompatible? What effect would it have on archaeological workflows if AgiSoft were to end educational pricing for its PhotoScan photogrammetry software and switch to a yearly-fee licensing scheme at industry costs? Which changes to our hardware and software ecosystems would merely set us back, and which would cripple us? What impact would these changes have on our local collaborators, who in many cases lack the digital infrastructure and economic resources to benefit from these technologies in the first place?

I do not think it is possible, at this point, to embrace the radical self-sufficiency of a *swadeshi* movement in digital archaeology; even if we could all acquire cheap, programmable devices, programming skills are not equally distributed. But this cautionary manifesto should encourage us to keep in mind the socioeconomic factors that condition our use of digital tools, and the fundamental relationships of inequality and dependency that they create. This is all the more critical given the first two manifestos: the excitement of the celebratory manifesto can be blinding, while the reflective manifesto reminds us that we may not fully recognize the changes in ourselves that are being generated by our entanglement with digital technology.

Agency, Entanglement, and Transhuman Archaeology

Early in this response, I compared the transformations wrought by digital recording systems in archaeology to the invention of the ground-glass lens or the introduction of the printing press. Like the ground-glass lens, which expanded our perception to include very tiny and very distant things, digital tools allow us to change the scale of our observations from the human to the micro- or macroscopic, from submillimeter surface geometry to multispectral satellite images. And like the printing press, digital publication platforms and the Internet have made it possible to disseminate data widely and cheaply, democratizing access to information. Yet neither the printing press nor the microscope and telescope were meant to capture and reproduce reality in its entirety; the information they gathered or spread was always filtered by human agency, and according to individual agendas. We should remember that the same is true of digital documentation, despite claims about its objectivity, comprehensiveness, and capacity to act as a lossless surrogate for the physical world.

Furthermore, while ground-glass lenses led to new scientific discoveries, and while the products of the printing press transformed the reading habits of literate Europeans, neither microscopes and telescopes nor movable type and screw-presses became entangled in everyday life to the extent of digital tools. Here a better parallel may be Filippo Marinetti's roaring, smoke-belching, beautiful speeding automobile. Cars made it faster to get from an arbitrary point A to an arbitrary point B, improving on previous modes of transportation like the horse or the railroad. But when mass-produced on the assembly line, they also transformed culture and social life, changing our sense of speed, providing new modes of status display, and affecting our health, our foodways, and the spatial organization of our cities—not always for the better. Cars had agency even before they started to drive themselves, and we are only now, after a hundred years, realizing how durable and pervasive their influence is. Similarly, while the role of human agency in digital documentation should not be neglected, neither should the agency of the digital tools themselves. We usually ask only what new affordances digital tools offer, but a critical digital archaeology should also ask what affordances of the physical notebook are lost to the rise of the mobile device.

Not only do we need to actively theorize our tool use, we need to think carefully about the human dimensions of the management of the digital data we produce. If we seek to capture an exhaustive record of the reality of our object of inquiry, what are we going to do with that record? The digital revolution surpasses that of the printing press or the chemical photograph both in the quantity of information it is generating and in its inherent ability to create connections between different pieces of data. As Sobotkova and colleagues (Ch. 3.2) point out, "only after digital datasets are published and researchers start reusing and combining them will the full potential and impact of digital methods be realized." Why, then, have we been so slow to seek new knowledge through the reuse and combination of disparate datasets? There have been numerous steps in this direction, from the establishment of the "Recycle Award" at the Computer Applications and Quantitative Methods in Archaeology conference to the increasing application of Linked Open Data principles to archaeological datasets, but results have been slow to appear. A group of archaeozoologists have produced a scientific publication by aggregating data stored within Open Context (Arbuckle *et al.* 2014), but this seems rather the exception than the rule. Paperless recording systems and richer digital datasets have not yet spurred the sort of syntheses that this shift promised, and a critical digital archaeology would do well to investigate the possible explanations for this lag. The technical barriers to data sharing and integration are increasingly surmountable, which suggests that the absence of integrative work has more to do with culture than with technology.

One last area in which paperless recording systems in general, and the use of mobile devices in particular, can play an essential role in a critical digital archaeology involves "transhumanism," or the notion held by a new generation of Futurists that technology is being integrated with the human mind and body in ways that will enhance our abilities, perceptions, and lifespans beyond their biological limits (More and Vita-More 2013). In this context, it is not the idea of enhancement that I would like to emphasize, but the integration, into our bodies, lives, and work, of machines that document us. Database changelogs already record who made what emendation to a record, and even word-processing programs can track when, by whom, and for how long a document was opened. Mobile devices add the ability to record an individual's position in space, and personal fitness accessories can track heart-rate, caloric intake, or aerobic activity. Add computer-vision platforms that can identify visual trends in photographs taken by a particular photographer and natural-language-processing algorithms that can assess a writer's changing emotional state from a series of context descriptions, and we already have the means to create an independent, multidimensional picture of an individual's digital archaeological practice. Such rich documentation of the archaeologists themselves could bring us closer to more empirical measures of reliability and reproducibility in digital archaeological research.

In some ways, this is the realization of Hodder's vision: since he began work at Çatalhöyük in the 1990s, he and his team have experimented with documenting themselves documenting the excavation. This self-examination has taken forms ranging from personal observations in site diaries that were then published as part of the dataset, to the employment of videographers and cultural anthropologists to record the archaeologists at work.[15] Imagine, then, a similar project that could capture an independent digital record of every act of docu-

---

[15] For the former, see this 1999 entry by Ruth Tringham: http://www.catalhoyuk. com/database/catal/diaryrecord.asp?id=387. For a holistic presentation of the documentation of the archaeologists who worked on the University of California at Berkeley (BACH) team associated with Hodder's long-term project at Çatalhöyük, see Tringham and Stevanović 2012 and http://lasthouseonthe-hill.org/.

mentation—not only edits and emendations, but the state of mind of the writer, the confidence of her hand as she sketches on a photograph, and even her timestamped track through space for each day in the field.

This is also, of course, the realization of Frederick Taylor's vision, with its focus on the scientific management of human machines through quantification—and of Michel Foucault's nightmare of constant, ubiquitous surveillance (1979: 195-228.). The same tools that free us to collect more comprehensive documentation about both archaeological remains and the process of archaeological excavation also bring potential threats to the privacy, autonomy, and dignity of the researchers. As our devices collect more and more data about us, we will have to address a new set of questions about power and control that underline the need for a political sensibility in critical digital archaeology. Who decides what information about the archaeologists will be captured? What sort of mechanisms for consent should be set in place? Who has access to the information, and what role does it play in the project archive? Do participants who, in the future, decide they no longer want to appear in the documentation have a right to be forgotten?

The last question is very much of the moment, as right now Western culture is preoccupied with the idea that all of our past transgressions will remain on public display on the Internet forever. But this impression obscures the fundamental fragility of digital data, and the final word of our manifesto must touch on preservation. It is our moral imperative as archaeologists to ensure that the documentation of our research is not forgotten, and the more novel and proprietary the media we use to record and store that documentation become, the more obligated we are to develop strategies to ensure that our information is not dependent on a particular platform for its survival. We should work toward a paperless archive that will still be accessible, at least on a minimal level, a hundred years from now, just as the paper archives of our predecessors of a century ago can (in most cases) still be consulted. We must mobilize ourselves for a critical digital archaeology that will not seek only to save time or capture it, but that will place our work at this particular point in time's stream and send it— sealed, caulked, and labeled—downriver toward the future.

Acknowledgments

I would like to thank the organizers for the chance to contribute to this volume, and for their patience as I kept making last-minute adjustments; Joseph Carter, Director of the Institute of Classical Archaeology at The University of Texas at Austin, for the initial invitation to come to Chersonesos and for making possible the digital archaeological work we accomplished there; and the Packard Humanities Institute, to which I am grateful for the generous support that allowed us the luxury of experimentation. I must also thank Jessica Trelogan and Stuart Eve, with whom, over the course of many long, rambling, and occasionally frustrating conversations lubricated with Ukrainian beer at Chersonesos, I first began to think about many of the ideas presented here; Italo Giordano, who set his hand-drafting skills against the vectorization of georeferenced digital photographs in some of our early controlled experiments; and Jessica Nowlin, who implemented our digital recording strategies in the field and stayed on to hand-craft 3D models from our initial attempts at photogrammetry. And I would like to thank my co-director of excavations in the South Region of Chersonesos, Larissa Sedikova, now director of the "State-Museum Preserve 'Tauric Chersonesos,'" who always supported my experiments with digital documentation, sometimes against her better judgment; who had a keen sense of both the potential of digital approaches and the sustainability problems they create; and who is one of the finest field archaeologists I have had the pleasure to work with.

https://mobilizingthepast.mukurtu.net/collection/52-response-mobilizing-ourselves-critical-digital-archaeology

http://dc.uwm.edu/arthist_mobilizingthepast/20

REFERENCES

Allen, S. H. 1999. *Finding the Walls of Troy: Frank Calvert and Heinrich Schliemann at Hisarlik*. Berkeley: University of California Press.

Allington, D., S. Brouillette, and D. Golumbia. 2016. "Neoliberal Tools (and Archives): A Political History of Digital Humanities." *Los Angeles Review of Books*, https://lareviewofbooks.org/article/neoliberal-tools-archives-political-history-digital-humanities/

Arbuckle, B. S., S. W. Kansa, E. Kansa, D. Orton, C. Çakırlar, L. Gourichon, L. Atici, A. Galik, A. Marciniak, J. Mulville, H. Buitenhuis, D. Carruthers, B. De Cupere, A. Demirergi, S. Frame, D. Helmer, L. Martin, J. Peters, N. Pöllath, K. Pawłowska, N. Russell, K. Twiss, and D. Würtenberger. 2014. "Data Sharing Reveals Complexity in the Westward Spread of Domestic Animals across Neolithic Turkey." *PLoS ONE* 9(6): e99845. doi:10.1371/journal.pone.0099845

Berggren, Å., N. Dell'Unto, M. Forte, S. Haddow, I. Hodder, J. Issavi, N. Lercari, C. Mazzucato, A. Mickel, and J. S. Taylor. 2015. "Revisiting Reflexive Archaeology at Çatalhöyük: Integrating Digital and 3D Technologies at the Trowel's Edge," *Antiquity* 89: 433–448. doi:10.15184/aqy.2014.43

Berggren, Å., and I. Hodder. 2003. "Social Practice, Method, and Some Problems of Field Archaeology," *American Antiquity* 68: 421–434. doi:10.2307/3557102.

Carter, C. 2015. "The Development of the Scientific Aesthetic in Archaeological Site Photography?" *Bulletin of the History of Archaeology* 25(2), http://www.archaeologybulletin.org/articles/10.5334/bha.258/; doi:10.5334/bha.258

Cobb, H. L., O. J. T. Harris, C. Jones, and P. Richardson, eds. 2012. *Reconsidering Archaeological Fieldwork: Exploring On-Site Relationships between Theory and Practice*. New York: Springer.

De Reu, J., G. Plets, G. Verhoeven, P. De Smedt, M. Bats, B. Cherretté, W. De Maeyer, J. Deconynch, D. Herremans, P. Laloo, M. Van Meirvenne, and W. De Clercq. 2013. "Towards a Three-Dimensional Cost-Effective Registration of the Archaeological Heritage," *Journal of Archaeological Science* 40(2): 1108–1121. doi:10.1016/j.jas.2012.08.040

Droop, J. P. 1915. *Archaeological Excavation. Cambridge Archaeological and Ethnological Series*. Cambridge: University Press.

Fentress, E., and A. Rabinowitz. 2003. "Part 2: The Stratigraphy," In *An Intermittent Town: Excavations at Cosa, 1991–1997*. Ann Arbor: University of Michigan Press. http://www.press.umich.edu/webhome/cosa

Foucault, M. 1979. *Discipline and Punish: the Birth of Prison*. Translated by Alan Sheridan. New York: Vintage Books.

Graham, S., S. Weingart, and I. Milligan. 2012. "Getting Started with Topic Modeling and MALLET." *Programming Historian*, http://programminghistorian.org/lessons/topic-modeling-and-mallet

Hadidi, S. A., B. Towfiq, and G. Bachuwa. 2014. "Dystextia as a Presentation of Stroke." *BMJ Case Reports* 2014: bcr2014206987. doi:10.1136/bcr-2014-206987

Harmansah, Ö. 2015. "ISIS, Heritage, and the Spectacles of Destruction in the Global Media," *Near Eastern Archaeology* 78: 170–177. doi:10.5615/neareastarch.78.3.0170

Harris, E. 1979. *Principles of Archaeological Stratigraphy*. London and New York: Academic Press.

Heinzelmann, M. 2008. "Review of *Cosa V: An Intermittent Town, Excavations 1991–1997*, by Elizabeth Fentress, John Bodel, T. V. Buttrey, Stefano Camaiani, Fernanda Cavari, Laura Cerri, Enrico Cirelli, Sergio Fontana, Elisabetta Gliozzo, Katherine Gruspier, Elisa Gusberti, Michelle Hobart, Valentina Lolini, Francesca Lunghetti, Alex Moseley, Silvia Nerucci, Adam Rabinowitz, Alessia Rovelli, Rabun Taylor, C. J. Simpson, and Vera von Falkenhausen (Ann Arbor)," *Gnomon* 80: 34–39.

Hodder, I. 1997. "'Always Momentary, Fluid and Flexible': Towards a Reflexive Excavation Methodology," *Antiquity* 71: 691–700.

———. 2003. "Archaeological Reflexivity and the 'Local' Voice," *Anthropological Quarterly* 76: 55–69.

Huggett, J. 2015. "A Manifesto for an Introspective Digital Archaeology." *Open Archaeology* 1(1): 86–95. doi:10.1515/opar-2015-0002; http://www.degruyter.com.ezproxy.lib.utexas.edu/view/j/opar.2014.1.issue-1/opar-2015-0002/opar-2015-0002.xml

James, K. H., and T. P. Atwood. 2009. "The Role Of Sensorimotor Learning in the Perception of Letter-Like Forms: Tracking the Causes of Neural Specialization for Letters," *Cognitive Neuropsychology* 26(1): 91–110.

James, K. H., and L. Engelhardt. 2012. "the Effects of Handwriting Experience on Functional Brain Development in Pre-Literate Children," *Trends in Neuroscience and Education* 1(1): 32–42.

Kaskar, O., K. Patel, D. Miller, and E. Angus. 2013. "Case Report: 'Dystextia' as a Sole Manifestation of Expressive Aphasia in Acute Ischemic Stroke (P03.175)." *Neurology* 80 Meeting Abstracts 1: P03–175.

Kiefer, M., S. Schuler, C. Mayer, N. M. Trumpp, K. Hille, and S. Sachse. 2015. "Handwriting or Typewriting? The Influence of Pen- or Keyboard-Based Writing Training on Reading and Writing Performance in Preschool Children," *Advances in Cognitive Psychology / University of Finance and Management in Warsaw* 11(4): 136–146. doi:10.5709/acp-0178-7

Longcamp, M., Y. Hlushchuk, and R. Hari. 2011. "What Differs in Visual Recognition of Handwritten vs. Printed Letters? An fMRI Study," *Human Brain Mapping* 32(8): 1250–1259. doi:10.1002/hbm.21105

Lucas, G. 2001. *Critical Approaches to Fieldwork: Contemporary and Historical Archaeological Practice*. New York: Routledge.

Mangen, A., and J.-L. Velay. 2010. "Digitizing Literacy: Reflections on the Haptics of Writing," in M. H. Zadeh, ed., *Advances in Haptics*. Vukovar: INTECH Open Access Publisher, 385–402. http://www.intechopen.com/source/pdfs/9927/InTech-Digitizing_literacy_reflections_on_the_haptics_of_writing.pdf

Mangen, A., and J.-L. Velay. 2012. "The Haptics of Writing: Cross-Disciplinary Explorations of the Impact of Writing Technologies on the Cognitive-Sensorimotor Processes Involved in Writing," in M. Torrance, D. Alamargot, M. Castello, F. Ganier, O. Kruse, and A. Mangen, eds., *Learning to Write Effectively: Current Trends in European Research*. *Studies in Writing* 25. Bingley: Emerald Group Publishing Limited, 405–407. http://www.intechopen.com/books/advances-in-haptics/digitizing-literacy-reflections-on-the-haptics-of-writing

More, M., and N. Vita-More, eds. 2013. *The Transhumanist Reader: Classical and Contemporary Essays on the Science, Technology, and Philosophy of the Human Future*. Chichester: Wiley-Blackwell.

Moretti, F. 2005. *Graphs, Maps, Trees: Abstract Models for a Literary History*. London: Verso.

Mueller, P. A., and D. M. Oppenheimer. 2014. "The Pen Is Mightier than the Keyboard Advantages of Longhand over Laptop Note Taking," *Psychological Science* 25(6): 1159–1168. doi:10.1177/0956797614524581

Olson, B. R., R. A. Placchetti, J. Quartermaine, and A. E. Killebrew. 2013. "The Tel Akko Total Archaeology Project (Akko, Israel): Assessing The Suitability of Multi-Scale 3D Field Recording in Archaeology," *Journal of Field Archaeology* 38: 244–262.

Olsson, M. 2016. "Making Sense of the Past: The Embodied Information Practices of Field Archaeologists." *Journal of Information Science* 42(3): 410–419. doi:10.1177/0165551515621839.

Opitz, R., and W. F. Limp. 2015. "Recent Developments in High-Density Survey and Measurement (HDSM) for Archaeology: Implications for Practice and Theory," *Annual Review of Anthropology* 44: 347–364. doi:10.1146/annurev-anthro-102214-013845.

Pavel, C. 2010. *Describing and Interpreting the Past: European and American Approaches to the Written Record of the Excavation.* Bucharest: University of Bucharest Press.

Piquette, K. E., and R. D. Whitehouse, eds. 2013. *Writing as Material Practice: Substance, Surface and Medium.* London: Ubiquity Press. http://www.ubiquitypress.com/files/009-writingasmaterialpractice.pdf

Rabinowitz, A., S. Eve, and J. Trelogan. 2007. "Precision, Accuracy, and the Fate of the Data: Experiments in Site Recording at Chersonesos, Ukraine," in J. Clark, E. Clark, and E. Hagemeister, eds., *Digital Discovery: Exploring New Frontiers in Human Heritage CAA 2006: Computer Applications and Quantitative Methods in Archaeology. Proceedings of the 34th Conference, Fargo, United States, April 2006.* Budapest: Archeolingua, 243–256.

Ravi, A., V. R. Rao, and J. P. Klein. 2013. "Dystextia: Acute Stroke in the Modern Age," *JAMA Neurology* 70(3): 404–405. doi:10.1001/jamaneurol.2013.604

Roosevelt, C. H., P. Cobb, E. Moss, B. R. Olson, and S. Ünlüsoy. 2015. "Excavation is ~~Destruction~~ Digitization: Advances in Archaeological Practice," *Journal of Field Archaeology* 40: 325–346. doi:10.1179/2042458215Y.0000000004

Shanks, M. 1997. "Photography and Archaeology," in B. Molyneaux, ed., *The Cultural Life of Images: Visual Representation in Archaeology.* London: Routledge, 73–107.

Shanks, M., and C. Svabo. 2013. "Archaeology and Photography: A Pragmatology," in A. González-Ruibal, ed., *Reclaiming Archaeology: Beyond the Tropes of Modernity*. Milton Park: Routledge, 89–102.

Tringham, R., and M. Stevanović. 2012. *Last House on the Hill: BACH Area Reports from Çatalhöyük, Turkey. Monumenta archaeologica* 27. Los Angeles: Cotsen Institute of Archaeology Press.

Warwick, C., C. Fisher, M. Terras, M. Baker, A. Clarke, M. Fulford, M. Grove, E. O'Riordan, and M. Rains. 2009. "iTrench: A Study of User Reactions to the Use of Information Technology in Field Archaeology," *Literary and Linguistic Computing* 24: 211–223. doi:10.1093/llc/fqp006

Wright, H. and C. Morgan. Forthcoming. "Pencils and Pixels. The Entanglement of Drawing and Digital Media in Archaeological Field Recording." *Journal of Field Archaeology*.

Author Biographies

EDITORS

Erin Walcek Averett is Associate Professor of Archaeology in the Department of Fine and Performing Arts and Classical and Near Eastern Studies at Creighton University. She serves as the Assistant Director of the Athienou Archaeological Project (AAP) on Cyprus, where she has been excavating since 1997. She specializes in the art and archaeology of Greece and Cyprus, with special focus on terracotta figurines and Iron Age religion in the Eastern Mediterranean. Her research area additionally includes 3D imaging and digital tools in archaeology, with a specific interest in 3D artifact models for research and publication. She has recently published articles on Cypriot masks and the AAP 3D imaging project in the *American Journal of Archaeology* and *Antiquity*.

Derek B. Counts is Professor and Chair in the Department of Art History at the University of Wisconsin-Milwaukee. He has published extensively on the archaeology of Iron Age Cyprus, with a particular emphasis on Cypriot religion, as well as limestone votive sculpture and its associated iconography. His research interests also include 3D visualization in archaeology and its impact on interpretation and publication. He is Associate Director of the Athienou Archaeological Project (AAP), where he has been excavating for more than two decades. Recent books include *The Master of Animals in Old World Iconography* (2010, co-edited with Bettina Arnold) and *Crossroads and Boundaries: The Archaeology of Past and Present in the Malloura Valley* (2011, co-edited with AAP colleagues).

Jody Michael Gordon is an Assistant Professor of Humanities and Social Sciences at Wentworth Institute of Technology in Boston and an Assistant Director of the Athienou Archaeological Project (AAP). He received his Ph.D. in Classical Archaeology from the Department of Classics at the University of Cincinnati, where his dissertation involved an archaeological study of the effects of imperialism on local identities in Cyprus during the Hellenistic and Roman periods. In addition to working in Cyprus, Jody has excavated in Tunisia, Italy, and Greece, and his research interests include Roman archaeology, cultural identity, ancient imperialism, and computer applications in archaeology.

CONTRIBUTORS

Manuel Serrano Araque has a B.A. in Humanities, he has been a research assistant at Jaén's Institut Studies.

Brian Ballsun-Stanton received his Ph.D. from the University of New South Wales in 2012. He is currently a Research Associate at Macquarie University in Sydney, Australia. His research interests include exploring how people interact with and understand the nature of data and an investigation into the mechanics of ludic-narrative interactions in games. He is the Technical Director and Data Architect for the Federated Archaeological Information Management Systems (FAIMS) Project.

Rebecca Bria is an archaeologist with 15 years of field experience directing and collaborating on research projects in the Andes, Central America, the Mediterranean, the Middle East, and the United States. She has directed the Proyecto de Investigación Arqueológico Regional Ancash (PIARA) field school since 2011, and is currently writing her Ph.D. in Anthropology dissertation at Vanderbilt University.

Bridget Buxton is an Associate Professor in the History Department at the University of Rhode Island. She holds degrees from Victoria University in Wellington, New Zealand, and a Ph.D. from the Graduate Group in Ancient History and Mediterranean Archaeology at the University of California, Berkeley. Her areas of specialization are underwater archaeology, and Hellenistic and Roman archaeology and civilization, especially regarding the Augustus age. Bridget has conducted fieldwork and led expeditions all around the Mediterranean, most recently in Israel with the Israel Antiquities Authority Maritime Unit. She collaborates with European and American colleagues to apply new robotic technologies in underwater archaeology.

William Caraher is an Associate Professor in History at the University of North Dakota. His received his Ph.D. at Ohio State University in Ancient History. He has directed archaeological projects in Cyprus and worked extensively in Greece. He is the co-director of the North Dakota Man Camp Project with Bret Weber and the co-author of *Pyla-Koutsopetria I:Archaeological Survey of An Ancient Coastal Town* (2014) with R. Scott Moore and David K. Pettegrew.

Ana L. Martínez Carrillo holds a Ph.D. in Archaeology from the University of Jaén, and she has been a research assistant at the Institute for Iberian Archaeology.

Kathryn E. DeTore is a self-proclaimed "tech nerd," and an archaeologist with five years of experience working in the Andes, Ireland, and the United States. Her association with Proyecto de Investigación Arqueológico Regional Ancash (PIARA) started in 2009, which eventually lead to her helping to design and implement the digital data collection protocol used by the project starting in the 2011 field season. Currently, Kathryn considers herself a retired archaeologist and enjoys spending time with her family while she plans her next career adventure.

J. Andrew Dufton is a Ph.D. candidate at the Joukowsky Institute for Archaeology and the Ancient World, Brown University. His research considers urbanism and urban processes in Iron Age and Roman North Africa, as well as the methodological implications of the uses of digital technologies for the dissemination of archaeological data and narratives.

Steven J. R. Ellis is a Roman archaeologist whose research interests cover the social and structural formation of ancient cities. His publications have explored Roman retail spaces; urban waste management; superstition; Roman coins; site formation processes; urban and sacred infrastructure; movement; social structures and their hierarchies, especially of the urban sub-elites; archaeological fieldwork methodologies; and the Roman fish-salting industry. Steven has directed and published archaeological projects in Italy and Greece, including the Pompeii Archaeological Research Project: Porta Stabia (PARP:PS), a project of the University of Cincinnati, where he is Associate Professor of Classics, and the American Academy in Rome.

Andrew Fairbairn (Ph.D., University of London, 2001), is an Australian Research Council (ARC) Future Fellow at University of Queensland. He researches ancient agriculture, plant use and human environmental impact in Turkey, Italy (Pompeii), and Australasia via the analysis of archaeological plant remains (e.g., seeds, fruits, leaves), and he specializes in the study of plant macrofossil remains, such as seeds, fruits, leaves and wood, from archaeological sites to reconstruct past environments and economic practices. His research interests are currently focused on the origins of agriculture in Central Anatolia (Turkey) and the later development of the region's state economies. He also works in Australasia where he has been developing plant macrofossil techniques to disentangle ancient tree-fruit use and the development of food production in Papua New Guinea.

Samuel B. Fee is Professor and Chair of Computing and Information Studies at Washington & Jefferson College. His research interests extend into the realms of computing, archaeology, visual communication, and digital media production. His work pursues answers to questions such as: How do we best learn and conduct research with technology? How does technology change human interaction? He has co-edited a volume with Brian R. Belland on computing and education entitled *The Role of Criticism in Understanding Problem Solving: Honoring the Work of John C. Belland* (Springer, 2012), as well as a forthcoming volume with Amanda M. Holland-Minkley and Thomas E. Lombardi, *New Directions for Computing Education: Embedding Computing Across Disciplines* (Springer, 2017). More information is available via his website at http://samfee.net/.

Shawn Fehrenbach has served with PaleoWest since 2010 in many roles, including Archaeologist, Project Director, Director of Graphics and GIS, and Chief Information Officer. He was appointed PaleoWest's

COO in March of 2015. As head of operations, Shawn ensures Pale-oWest's methods are on the cutting edge to enhance the efficiency and quality of our work products. Shawn directs PaleoWest's IT systems, oversees the management and analysis of spatial and tabular datasets, and monitors training initiatives and project execution company-wide.

John R. Hale received his Ph.D. from Cambridge in Archaeology. His archaeological fieldwork and research projects include studies of Bronze Age Scandinavian watercraft; prehistoric sites in the Ohio River Valley; the Roman villa of Torre de Palma in Portugal; development of a dating method for ancient mortar and concrete using AMS radiocarbon analysis; investigations of Greek oracle sites in Greece, Turkey, and Albania; a search for Phoenician harbors on the Portuguese coast; and deep-submergence surveys in quest of ancient shipwrecks in the Aegean Sea and the Eastern Mediterranean. He has published in *Antiquity, Journal of Roman Archaeology, Scientific American*, and other journals; and his fieldwork has been featured in documentaries on the Discovery and History channels. He is currently Director of Liberal Studies at the University of Louisville.

Francisco Arias de Haro has been a member of the Andalusian Cultural Institution Agency of Archaeological Ensemble of Cástulo since 2009.

Carla Hernández is a graduate student at Vanderbilt University and formerly a graduate student and lecturer in the Pontifical Catholic University of Peru. Her dissertation research focuses on issues of imperial expansion, negotiation, ritual, ethnohistory, and spatial analysis in the Central Andes. She has conducted research in different regions in the Peruvian highlands and coast. Most recently, she has directed the archaeological project "Lurin Highlands," which addresses the interaction between the Inka Empire and the local polity in the province of Huarochirí in the central Peruvian highlands.

Eric Kansa (Ph.D., Harvard University) directs Open Context (http://opencontext.org), an open-access data publishing venue for archaeology referenced by both the National Science Foundation and the National Endowment for the Humanities for grant data management.

Eric's research explores research data management, data reuse, and scholarly communications within the changing institutional and professional context of the digital humanities and social sciences. He also researches policy issues relating to intellectual property, including text-mining and cultural property concerns. Eric is also on the board of the Shelby White and Leon Levy Program for Archaeological Publications, a granting program that funds archaeological publications. In June 2013, the White House recognized Eric's contributions to promoting open access and reforming scholarly communications with a "Champion of Change" award. In 2016, the Archaeological Institute of America selected Open Context as the winner of their 2016 Award for Outstanding Work in Digital Archaeology.

Kyosung Koo (Ph.D., University of Iowa) has served as an ITS specialist for the Athienou Archaeological Project (AAP) since 2011. In addition to providing advice on effective use of technology for digital data recording, he developed AAP's database and its web application. He is an academic technologist at Davidson College, where he promotes and supports best practices in the pedagogical uses of technology.

Libertad Serrano Lara is a Ph.D. student at the University of Jaén where she has previously earned a MA in Archaeology.

Marcelo Castro López holds a Ph.D. in Archaeology from the University of Jaén. Since 2010 he has been director of the Archaeological Ensemble of Cástulo.

Giancarlo Marcone is General Coordinator of the Qhapaq Ñan Project of the Ministry of Culture, Peru. His research interests focus on how local people relate to expansive states, and his heritage management work centers on the development of collaborative, and diversity-inclusive management models for world heritage monuments. Marcone also teaches classes in archaeology, anthropology, heritage management in several Peruvian universities. His recent publications include (with Enrique Lopez Hurtado, 2015) "Dual Strategies of the Rural Elites: Exploring the Intersection of Regional and Local Transformations in the Lurín Valley, Perú" *Latin American Antiquity* 26: 401–420.

Nikola Mišković (M.Sc. 2005, Ph.D. 2010) is an Associate Professor at the University of Zagreb where he teaches control engineering-related courses. He is a project coordinator of H2020 EXCELLABUST-Excelling LABUST in Marine Robotics, FP7 CADDY - Cognitive Autonomous Diving Buddy and ONR-G projects related to marine robotics. He was also involved in FP7 CURE, FP7 CART, NATO-NURC collaboration project and is currently involved in FP7 EUROFLEETS2 project and H2020 subCULTron project. He was a visiting researcher at Consiglio Nazionale delle Ricerche, ISSIA, Genova, Italy in 2008. He is a member of the IEEE Oceanic Engineering Society, the European Embedded Control Institute and the Association for Unmanned Vehicle Systems International. He is the author of two book chapters and more than sixty papers in journals and international conferences. His research interests include mathematical modeling, cooperative guidance, control and navigation of marine vessels (surface and underwater), nonlinear control theory and its applications in marine robotics.

Christopher F. Motz is a Ph.D. candidate specializing in Roman Archaeology at the University of Cincinnati. He received a M.A. in Classical Archaeology from Tufts University and a M.A. in Classics from the University of Cincinnati. His research interests include sub-elite material culture and spaces, the ancient economy, provinces and frontiers, material culture theory, archaeological methodology, and the application of technology in data acquisition, recording, and analysis. He has developed digital field recording systems for archaeological projects in Italy, Libya, and Belize, and he has consulted on systems for projects in Italy, Greece, Egypt, Ireland, and Jordan.

Brandon R. Olson (Ph.D., 2016, Boston University) is an affiliate faculty member in the History Department at Metropolitan State University in Denver, Colorado. His research interests include fluctuations in settlement and land use as a result of changing hegemonic powers and land use in the Eastern Mediterranean during the Hellenistic and Roman eras. He seeks to harness the analytical qualities of GIS and 3D modeling in every stage of the archaeological process to identify, assess, and disseminate diachronic and episodic change in human settlement.

Gabriela Oré is a graduate student in the Department of Anthropology, Vanderbilt University. Her interests include spatial analysis, remote sensing applications in archaeology, and archaeometry, with a topical specialization in the late prehispanic and early colonial Andes. She holds a Masters degree in archaeology from Pontificia Universidad Católica del Perú. Currently, her research focuses on a forced resettlement program in early colonial Peru and its regional-scale impacts on agricultural and pastoral production and landscape dynamics.

Dror Planer is an underwater archaeologist and technical diver with the Underwater Archaeology Unit of the Israel Antiquities Authority. Specializing in prehistory, he has participated in survey and excavation fieldwork and co-authored numerous publications on aspects of Israel's underwater archaeological heritage.

Eric E. Poehler is an Associate Professor at the University of Massachusetts, Amherst, specializing in Roman urbanism and digital archaeological practices, especially at Pompeii. He has published widely on aspects of Pompeii's urban infrastructure, including drainage, traffic, and pedestrian movement. Eric directs the Pompeii Bibliography and Mapping Project and co-directs the Pompeii Quadriporticus Project with Steven J. R. Ellis. Also with Ellis, Poehler works with the legacy data of the Panhellenic sanctuary at Isthmia, Greece, to reconstruct the site's history from previously excavated areas.

Adam Rabinowitz is Associate Professor in the Department of Classics and Assistant Director of the Institute of Classical Archaeology at The University of Texas at Austin. He is an active field archaeologist and is involved with various projects related to the collection, management, and publication of digital archaeological data. His interest in the use of digital platforms for archaeological documentation and publication began during his work at the Roman site of Cosa in the 1990s and intensified in the course of excavations in the South Region of the Greek, Roman, and Byzantine site of Chersonesos in Crimea in the mid-2000s. In the course of his preparation of the South Region excavations for publication, he has also become involved with long-term archival preservation and the digital dissemination of rich contextual datasets. He is an active participant in efforts to build infrastructure for the sharing and integration of digital archaeological data, as an associate editor of the Pleiades gazetteer, as a member of the editorial board of Open Context, and as co-PI of the NEH- and IMLS-funded PeriodO project, which seeks to build a gazetteer of historical period definitions (http://perio.do).

Ted Roberts has 16 years of experience performing numerous archaeological investigations and cultural resource roles while employed in the private sector, the government, and academic institutions. Ted serves as the Principal in PaleoWest's New York Office, and he earned a M.A. in Anthropology from Northern Arizona University.

Aurelio Rodriguez holds a Licenciate's degree in Archaeology from Pontificia Universidad Católica del Perú. His archaeological research and publications focus on the later prehispanic periods of the central coast of Peru. He is also a RC (Radio Crontrol) pilot with over 37 years of experience building and flying RC aircraft, combines his enthusiasm for UAVs with archaeological research. In his workshop in Lima, he designs and builds UAVs and RC aircraft, and teaches RC piloting. He also has extensive experience in aerial photogrammetry and video.

Shawn Ross (Ph.D., University of Washington, 2001) is currently an Associate Professor of History and Archaeology and Deputy Director of the Big History Institute at Macquarie University in Sydney, Australia. Shawn's research interests include the history and archaeology of pre-Classical Greece, oral tradition as history (especially Homer and Hesiod), the archaeology of the Balkans (especially Thrace), Greece in its wider Mediterranean and Balkan context, and the application of information technology to archaeology and the humanities more generally. He co-supervises the Tundzha Regional Archaeology Project (TRAP), a diachronic landscape archaeology project in Bulgaria, and directs the Federated Archaeological Information Management Systems (FAIMS) Project.

Matthew Sayre is an Assistant Professor of Anthropology at the University of South Dakota who has conducted his primary fieldwork at the UNESCO World Heritage site of Chavín de Huántar in the Peruvian Andes. His work focuses on the past and present ecological, agricultural, economic, and ritual practices of people in the Andes. He received his M.A. and Ph.D. in Anthropology from the University of California, Berkeley, his B.A. in Anthropology from the University of Chicago, and held a post-doctoral fellowship at Stanford University. His work has been funded by the National Science Foundation, the Global Heritage Fund, the Curtiss and Mary G. Brennan Foundation, and the Open Society Foundation.

Jacob Sharvit is the Director of the Underwater Archaeology Unit of the Israel Antiquities Authority. He has been working on land and underwater archaeology since 1988, including many excavations and surveys, and the management of the underwater and coastal archaeological heritage of Israel. His extensive publications include scientific articles, reports, and popular articles. He is member in the Israeli World Heritage Committee and was member of the Israeli delegation for the UNESCO convention on the protection of the underwater cultural heritage. He has participated in some European Union projects: Byzantium, STACHEM, etc. He has been a fully qualified commercial and technical diver for more than 30 years.

Adela Sobotkova (Ph.D., University of Michigan, 2012) is currently a Research Fellow at the School of Ancient History, Macquarie University in Sydney, Australia. Adela's research interests include the social complexity of Balkan and Black Sea indigenous communities during late prehistory, the methods of surface survey, and the application of spatial analysis and remote sensing to archaeology. She co-supervises the Tundzha Regional Archaeology Project (TRAP), a diachronic landscape archaeology project in Bulgaria, and serves as the Domain Expert for the Federated Archaeological Information Management Systems (FAIMS) Project.

Matthew Spigelman received his Ph.D. from New York University in 2015 while working as a consulting archaeologist in and around New York City. He has conducted fieldwork and museum research throughout the Eastern Mediterranean, with a focus on the island of Cyprus and ceramic technology and provenance. Matthew serves as a Project Manager in PaleoWest's New York Office, and in this capacity he has supervised projects throughout the northeastern United States.

Jessica Thompson (Ph.D., Arizona State University, 2008), is an Assistant Professor at Emory University. She is a paleoanthropologist with research interests that target two key periods in human behavioral evolution: the origins of modern behavioural complexity during the Middle-to-Late Pleistocene and the origins of meat-eating and dietary change during the late Pliocene. Her work emphasizes the systematic collection of stone tool and fossil data at the landscape scale.

Michael K. Toumazou is Professor of Classics at Davidson College, where he has taught since 1987. A field archaeologist with extensive experience in both Greece and Cyprus, he has directed the Athienou Archaeological Project (AAP) on his native island of Cyprus since 1990. His publications include articles in *Old World Archaeology Newsletter*; *Journal of Field Archaeology*; *Annual Report to the Department of Antiquities, Cyprus*; *Cahier du Centre d'Études Chypriotes*; and translations of several works from Greek to English. Michael's research, which has been funded by grants from Dumbarton Oaks, the National Endowment for the Humanities, and the National Science Foundation, centers on the history and prehistory of Cyprus, Greece, and the Levant, as well as on mortuary practices and ancient Greek art.

Abel Traslaviña is a graduate student in archaeology at Universidad Nacional Mayor de San Marcos (Peru), and serves a research associate of the Instituto Riva-Agüero. His interests center on issues of place, the built environment, and landscape in the late prehispanic and Spanish colonial eras in the Andean region, with a methodological focus on GIS, photogrammetry, and other spatial technologies. His Licenciate's thesis and recent publications (e.g., "Nuevas perspectivas sobre el diseño del espacio colonial rural: El caso de Nieve Nieve y Avillay en el valle de Lurín," in press) address the general resettlement of Indians in colonial Peru.

Parker VanValkenburgh (Ph.D., Harvard, 2012) is Assistant Professor of Anthropology at Brown University. His core research focuses on the political dimensions of landscapes, built environments, and human subjectivities. His primary current field project, the Proyecto Arqueológico Zaña Colonial (PAZC), has brought together settlement survey, spatial analysis, archival research, and household archaeology

532

to examine the impact of Spanish colonial–forced resettlement on the indigenous populations of Peru in the 16th and 17th centuries A.D.

John Wallrodt is a Senior Research Associate in the Department of Classics at the University of Cincinnati. He is a data architect for archaeological field projects in Turkey, Israel, Greece, and Italy sponsored by the department, and he has consulted on many archaeological projects in the Mediterranean. His research focuses on the interactive nature of disparate data sets created by divergent voices in large, multi-year, collaborative field projects. To this end, he is concerned with making archaeological data digital as soon as possible, a push that has lead him to remove paper entirely from the field. He publishes semi-regularly on this topic in his blog Paperless Archaeology at http://paperlessarchaeology.com.

Justin St. P. Walsh holds a Ph.D. from the University of Virginia and is an Associate Professor in the School of Art at Chapman University. He is the director of the Chapman Excavations at Cástulo project. Justin has worked for more than a decade at archaeological sites across the Mediterranean, including Italy and Spain; he is the recipient of a Rome Prize, Fulbright Grant, and numerous other awards. He is the author of several articles on Greek pottery, cross-cultural interactions, and the protection of cultural heritage; he recently published *Consumerism in the Ancient World: Imports and Identity Construction* (Routledge, 2014).

Steven A. Wernke is Associate Professor and Director of the Spatial Analysis Research Laboratory, Department of Anthropology, Vanderbilt University. His archaeological and ethnohistorical research focuses on themes of colonialism, community, landscape, and spatial analysis in the Andean region during late prehispanic and Spanish colonial times. His recent publications include *Negotiated Settlements: Andean Communities and Landscapes under Inka and Spanish Colonialism* (University Press of Florida, 2013), and "Capturing Complexity: Toward an Integrated Low-Altitude Photogrammetry and Mobile Geographic Information System Archaeological Registry System" (with Julie A. Adams and Eli R. Hooten), *Advances in Archaeological Practice* August 2014: 147–163.

www.ingramcontent.com/pod-product-compliance
Lightning Source LLC
Chambersburg PA
CBHW062147270326
41930CB00009B/1467